China 1949–2019

Paolo Urio

China 1949–2019

From Poverty to World Power

Paolo Urio
Department of Political Science
and International Relations
University of Geneva
Geneva, Switzerland

ISBN 978-981-13-8878-1   ISBN 978-981-13-8879-8   (eBook)
https://doi.org/10.1007/978-981-13-8879-8

© Springer Nature Singapore Pte Ltd. 2019, corrected publication 2019
This work is subject to copyright. All rights are reserved by the Publisher, whether the whole or part
of the material is concerned, specifically the rights of translation, reprinting, reuse of illustrations,
recitation, broadcasting, reproduction on microfilms or in any other physical way, and transmission
or information storage and retrieval, electronic adaptation, computer software, or by similar or dissimilar
methodology now known or hereafter developed.
The use of general descriptive names, registered names, trademarks, service marks, etc. in this
publication does not imply, even in the absence of a specific statement, that such names are exempt from
the relevant protective laws and regulations and therefore free for general use.
The publisher, the authors and the editors are safe to assume that the advice and information in this
book are believed to be true and accurate at the date of publication. Neither the publisher nor the
authors or the editors give a warranty, expressed or implied, with respect to the material contained
herein or for any errors or omissions that may have been made. The publisher remains neutral with regard
to jurisdictional claims in published maps and institutional affiliations.

This Springer imprint is published by the registered company Springer Nature Singapore Pte Ltd.
The registered company address is: 152 Beach Road, #21-01/04 Gateway East, Singapore 189721,
Singapore

Preface

This book analyses China's long march from poverty to world power. In 1949 China had just emerged from one century of foreign aggressions, a three-decade-long civil war, and a dramatic decline in economic, political, cultural and military resources. When in October 1949 Mao proudly declares to the world: 'Ours will no longer be a nation subject to insult and humiliation; we have stood up', the country is in no position to compete with foreign countries on any of the above-mentioned resources. But the Chinese leadership had the will to make the China dream, of becoming again a great power, come true. By building upon its plurisecular long history, its fundamental values, and by integrating into its thinking the Western values that were compatible with its culture, China has succeeded in realizing that dream, little by little, following its traditional way of conceiving and implementing the strategy.

In order to understand China's strategy, it is important to recognize that whereas its civilization developed outside our language, outside our history, independently from us, indifferently from us, China's strategy to escape from poverty and to reclaim world power status, needed to develop within the international world the West made, first by European powers in the nineteenth, then by the US in the twentieth century. In analyzing China's strategy to reclaim world power status in the twentieth century, it has been necessary to analyse the US's foreign policy in the Far East. By doing so in Chap. 6, I discuss and criticize the imperial foreign policy the US has implemented since the foundation of the First Republic (1912–1949). I believe my critique is well documented and has led me to findings that are shared by many critical American scholars, who will be duly quoted in the text. American mainstream scholars, journalists, and think tanks' researchers may be offended by such a strong criticism. To this reaction I can only reply by quoting Alexis de Tocqueville, who has praised American democracy more than any other European thinker: 'The American, used to participating in everything that takes place within this country [i.e. America], believes he has an interest in defending everything which is criticized, for it is not only the country that one is thus attacking, but himself: consequently one sees his national pride resorting to all the artifices and stooping to all the puerilities of individual vanity. There is nothing more annoying than this irritating habit of the Americans to feel obliged to exercise their patriotism at all times. The foreigner would agree willingly to praise a great deal in their country, but he would like to be allowed the right to criticize something, and that he is absolutely forbidden to do. America is a country of liberty where, however, in order not to hurt anyone's feelings, the foreigner must not speak freely either of private citizens, or of the governing powers, or of the governed, or of public enterprises, or of private enterprises, or anything, in fact, that one encounters there, except perhaps the climate and the soil; and you even find Americans ready to defend one or the other of those as though they had contributed to the making of them.' (Alexis de Tocqueville, *De la démocratie en Amérique*, Paris, Gallimard, pp. 353–56, my translation from the French).

In this book, I take stock of the research I have conducted on the rise of modern China, with emphasis on strategic public management. It is based upon the research I have conducted in China since 1997, the analysis of several important works of Western and Chinese scholars, official documents published by the Chinese and Western governments, discussions with Chinese senior civil servants and intellectuals, as well as more than 30 visits to mainland China, covering 16 provinces. Moreover, I have been invited to give conferences in China on public management topics by universities and party schools; thereby I have benefited from the questions and remarks put forward by the audience, professors and researchers, post-graduate students and senior civil servants.

I have published my findings in five books and four articles. They cover China's reforms and their positive and negative consequences, the comparison between the Western and the Chinese New Public Management, an evaluation of Private–Public Partnerships for in-transition countries (including China), the development of NGOs in China (both Chinese and Western), and China's strategy for reclaiming world power status. These books and articles constitute the basis for this new book, to which I have added several updates and new analyses and perspectives. Having covered several important aspects of the Chinese strategic public management, I felt the need to put some order into my 'Chinese construction site', to give some rational and documented meaning and coherence to the 'material' collected on various aspects of the Chinese modernization process. This is the originality of the book. Of course, I have taken many passages from my previous books and articles, often in summary or in another wording. But I have not hesitated to take several passages as they are in the original publications, whenever the original is exactly what I want to transmit today to the reader. In these cases, I considered that it would have been ludicrous to paraphrase the original for the sake of avoiding asking permission from the publishers concerned. Of course, I have asked permission whenever necessary.

Many contradictory analyses have been put forward, especially by Western scholars (but also by some scholars of Chinese origin living in the West) on the very nature of the Chinese political system, the market or non-market character of the Chinese economy, the role that the growing Chinese middle class may play in the political system (will it demand political freedom in addition to economic freedom?), the role that the so-called "Chinese red capitalists" may play (will they

Preface vii

favour a regime change?), the role of China's growing power in the international system dominated until recently by the West, and especially the US.

Based on these preliminary considerations, the book proposes an analysis of the contradictions that have developed within China since 1949, and the positive and the negative consequences of the public policies implemented to overcome these imbalances.

The starting point of the book is China's will to recover world power status. This fundamental objective, already put forward in my first book on China and further developed in my other books, has been the basis of the strategy of all Chinese governments since the late decades of the Qing Imperial Dynasty. It is of paramount importance for understanding the policies implemented since 1949, their rationale, content, implementation and consequences upon Chinese society and economy, as well as their sequence in time, i.e. the underlying grand strategy.

In writing this book, I have tried to avoid a too technical approach. While I address the results of my research to an academic audience, I present them in a form accessible to a wider public. The choice of this "intermediate" approach stems from the fact that too many unbalanced accounts on China are being published both in academic writings and in newspapers and magazines accessible to the general public. My aim is to present here a documented view of the Chinese situation, avoiding the catastrophic predictions of some people,[1] as well as the over-optimistic views of those who see China as a territory to be conquered, which is, in fact, the view of many Western businessmen.

In organizing the six chapters, I tried to present them according to a sequence that should make the reading as easy as possible: (1) in Chap. 1, I put the dynamics of China's development in the context of Xi Jinping's slogan about the 'China Dream', and explain under what conditions this dream may come true; (2) Chap. 2 presents an analysis of Chinese culture in order to understand the fundamental values of Chinese society that orient behaviour in the public domain, (3) in Chap. 3, I analyse the rationale of Deng's reforms and their positive and negative impact on Chinese society; (4) Chap. 4 analyses the policies adopted by the Chinese Government in order to correct the negative consequences of the reforms; (5) in Chap. 5, I analyze the innovations introduced in the management of the relation between State, society and economy, the opening of the decision-making process, the freedom given to NGOs and the resort to technologies and management techniques imported from the West; (6) in Chap. 6, I analyze China's strategy to reclaim world power status and the consequent restructuring of the international system that puts an end to the world America made. In the conclusion, I develop some considerations about the future of China and its position in the new international order.

As all the dimensions dealt with in the six chapters are linked to each other within a kind of structural interdependency, there will be many cross-references that have made repetitions necessary. The sinologist may find this way of presenting my

---

[1]See, for example: Gordon G. Chang, *The Coming Collapse of China*, New York, Randon House, 2001; Thierry Wolton, *Le grand bluff chinois. Comment Pékin nous vend sa « révolution » capitaliste*, Paris, Laffont, 2007.

argument rather tedious. My purpose in doing so was to facilitate the reading for laymen, so that each chapter may stand on its own. Each chapter can be read independently of the others, and should the reader wish to find more detailed explanations, he may refer to the other chapters as suggested in the text.

Geneva, Switzerland
April 2019

Paolo Urio

The original version of the book was revised: Missed out corrections in Chapters 2–6 have been incorporated. The correction to this book is available at https://doi.org/10.1007/978-981-13-8879-8_7

Acknowledgements

First of all, I should like to thank Prof. Hu Angang, Founder and Director of the Institute for Contemporary China Studies of Tsinghua University. Prof. Hu encouraged and helped me in my quest for understanding China's development strategy, by sharing his knowledge, providing his writings before they were published, appointing some of his assistants to help me collect data and documents, and introducing me to Chinese intellectuals.[2]

I also benefited from the profound knowledge of China from my other colleagues at Tsinghua University, Cui Zhiyuan, Wang Hui, Li Xiguang, and Liu Qiushi; as well as from Dong Keyong (Renmin University); Chen Dongqi, Sun Xuegong and Zuo Chuanchang (National Development and Reform Commissions —NDRC); Harry Liu Genfa (Party School of Shanghai Pudong); Su Wei (Chongqing Party School).

Wang Qizhen, of Tsinghua University, provided invaluable support already in 2016 when I stayed at Tsinghua to complete the information I needed for this book. Once I was back in Switzerland, she continued to help me, sending me the most recent data and relevant publications I needed for organizing and presenting in a meaningful way the material I had been collecting for over a decade. I am also indebted to He Shan, also at Tsinghua, who stepped in when Wang Qizhen was on leave. More particularly, Wang Qizhen and He Shan gave me invaluable support by updating the tables I used in my 2010 book, and by adding new data and tables kindly provided by Prof. Hu Angang. Chen Yali, a Ph.D. Chinese student at Geneva University, who has been working with me since 2012, also helped me with analysis of articles and papers from mainland China.

As usual, my British wife has helped me to put my English into a form acceptable to an international audience.

---

[2] A complete list of the persons (colleagues, assistants, civil servants, students) to whom I am indebted, without whom I could never have been able to write my books on China, can be found under 'Acknowledgements' of my books.

Last but not least, I should like to thank the publishers of my books for giving me permission to use parts of my previous publications. This book is based upon revised, updated and expanded versions of my writings on China published by

Routledge:

- *Reconciling State, Market, and Society in China. The Long March Towards Prosperity*, 2010;
- *China, the West, and the Myth of New Public Management. Neoliberalism and Its Discontents*, 2012; and
- *China reclaims World Power Status. Putting an End to the World America Made*, 2018.

University Press of America:

- *Public Private Partnerships. Success and Failure Factors in Transition Countries*, 2010 (editor), with a chapter on China.

Peter Lang:

- *L'émergence des ONG en Chine, Le changement du rôle de l'Etat-Parti*, 2014 (written with Yuan Ying).

Geneva, Switzerland   Paolo Urio
April 2019

Contents

1 Social Change and China's Dream: Will the China's Dream Come True? 1
  1.1 Preliminary Considerations 1
  1.2 Defining Social Change 2
  1.3 Defining Country Dreams 4
  1.4 How to Decide Whether Social Change Has Realized the Country Dream? 7
  1.5 The Western Experience: Between Dream and Nightmare 8
  1.6 The Chinese Experience: Will the Dream Come True? 9
  1.7 Towards the Country Dream: A Development Strategy that Is 'Society Friendly' and 'Environment Friendly'.......... 10
  References 16

2 Understanding China's Strategic Public Management 19
  2.1 Commonalities Between Chinese and Western Scholars for Analyzing Historical Processes: The Silent Transformations and the Long Time 19
  2.2 Market and Capitalism: Two Different Stories? 24
  2.3 Chinese Traditional Conception of Strategy 30
  2.4 China Political Culture: Stability and Change 33
    2.4.1 Deng Xiaoping: Changes and Continuity of Traditional Political Culture 36
    2.4.2 Interdependence Between Ideological and Practical Innovations of Deng's Strategy...................... 37
    2.4.3 Deng's Strategy and Mao's Succession 38
    2.4.4 Jiang Zemin's Contribution to CPC's Ideology: The Theory of the Three Represents 45

		2.4.5	Hu Jintao's Contribution to the CPC's Ideology: Equity, Justice, Innovation and Scientific Development ...	47
		2.4.6	The Contribution of Xi Jinping: Strengthening the Party and Assertive Global Foreign Policy	49
	2.5		The Cultural Difficulties on the Road to Market Economy	52
	2.6		Conclusion	55
	References			56
3	**The New Public Management Comes to China**			61
	3.1		Introduction: From Empire to the People's Republic of China....	61
		3.1.1	The Lessons from the Fall of the Empire	62
		3.1.2	China's Strategies for Recovering Wealth and Power	63
		3.1.3	Mao's Achievements	65
	3.2		Deng's New Public Management	66
		3.2.1	Deng's Strategy	67
		3.2.2	The Content of Deng's Strategy	69
		3.2.3	The Challenges of Deng's Strategy	72
	3.3		The Impact of Marketization on China's Modernization	77
		3.3.1	The Major Economic Indicators and the Changing Structure of Employment	77
		3.3.2	The Changing Structure of Chinese Society: Opportunities and Challenges	78
		3.3.3	The Impact of Economic Development upon the Environment	92
		3.3.4	The Impact of Economic Development: Achievements and Problems	94
	3.4		The Imbalances of Deng's New Public Management	102
		3.4.1	Disparities Between Provinces	103
		3.4.2	Disparities Between Rural and Urban Areas Within Provinces	106
		3.4.3	Disparities Between the Rural Areas Belonging to Different Provinces	106
		3.4.4	New Public Management, Income Distribution, and Inequality	109
		3.4.5	New Public Management and Poverty	111
		3.4.6	New Public Management and Health	113
	3.5		Conclusion	113
	References			115
4	**The Rebalancing of Chinese Society**			119
	4.1		The New Development Strategy: Putting 'People First'	119
	4.2		The Rebalancing Between Human and Physical Environments	123
	4.3		The Development of Social Security in Urban China	127

	4.3.1	Old Age Insurance	130
	4.3.2	Health Insurance	131
	4.3.3	Unemployment Insurance	132
	4.3.4	Other Insurances	133
4.4	The Development of Social Security in Rural China		134
	4.4.1	Old-Age Insurance	134
	4.4.2	The New Rural Cooperative Medical System	135
4.5	The Special Case of Migrant Workers		137
4.6	The Rebalancing Between Individuals		138
4.7	The Rebalancing Between Provinces		140
4.8	The Rebalancing Between Rural and Urban Areas		146
4.9	Conclusion		150
References			151

5 The Opening of China's Economy and the Changing Role of the Party-State 153

5.1	Analyzing Power in China and in the West		154
	5.1.1	Power in Western Countries	157
	5.1.2	Power in the People's Republic of China	160
5.2	The Opening up of the Political System		163
5.3	The Development of NGOs in China		169
	5.3.1	The Party's Strategy for Foreign NGOs	170
	5.3.2	The Strategy of Western NGOs in the International System	172
	5.3.3	Foreign NGOs and the New Generation of Mega Free Trade and Investment Treaties	174
5.4	The Import of Western Technologies		175
5.5	The Import of Management Tools: The Case of Public Private Partnerships		177
	5.5.1	Definition of PPPs	178
	5.5.2	PPPs, Contracting Out, New Public Management, and the 'Washington Consensus'	179
	5.5.3	Conditions for the Viability of PPPs	181
	5.5.4	The Distinction Between Hard and Soft Infrastructure	183
	5.5.5	PPPs and the Development Strategy	184
	5.5.6	The Special Case of PPPs in China	187
5.6	Conclusion		188
References			190

6 China and the New World Order. Why and How China's Foreign Policy Has Put an End to the World America Made 195

6.1 The Development of the Imperial US Foreign Policy 196

6.1.1 The Historical Origins of US Ideology: 'Chosenness', God, the 'Manifest Destiny' and the 'End of History' 199

6.1.2 The Actualization of American Ideology 206

6.1.3 The Implementation of the US Ideology to International Relations 218

6.1.4 The Development of the US Power Resources Since WW2 219

6.1.5 US Strategy Toward China in the XXI Century 224

6.1.6 US Foreign Policy of President Donald Trump 230

6.1.7 Conclusion 243

6.2 China's Strategy for Reclaiming World Power Status 245

6.2.1 The Improbable 'China Model' and the Origins of Contemporary China's Foreign Policy 246

6.2.2 The Construction of China's Strategy: Building Power Resources 249

6.2.3 The Belt and Road Strategy: Encircling the World 255

6.2.4 The Way Toward the Belt and Road Strategy 256

6.2.5 The Belt and Road Initiative, or China's Grand Strategy 288

6.2.6 The Belt and Road Initiative and the End to the 'World America Made' 293

6.2.7 Conclusion 298

References 305

Correction to: China 1949–2019 .... C1

Conclusion 321

References 331

Abbreviations

AI	Artificial Intelligence
AIIB	Asian Infrastructure Investment Bank
APEC	Asia-Pacific Economic Cooperation
bn	billion
BRI or OBOR	Belt and Road Initiative (also One Belt One Road—OBOR)
CPC	Communist Party of China
CSIS	Centre for Strategic and International Studies
EU	European Union
FBI	Federal Bureau of Investigation
FT	Financial Times
GDP	Gross Domestic Product
GNI	Gross National Income
HDI	Human Development Index
ILO	International Labour Organization
IMF	International Monetary Fund
IP	Intellectual Property
NDRC	National Development and Reforms Commission
OBOR or BRI	One Belt One Road (also BRI—Belt and Road Initiative)
PLA	People's Liberation Army
PPP	Purchasing Power Parity
PPPs	Public–Private Partnerships
PRC	People's Republic of China
R&D	Research and Development
RMB or YUAN	China's currency
SCMP	South China Morning Post
SCO	Shanghai Cooperation Organization
TPP	Trans-Pacific Partnership
TTIP	Transatlantic Trade and Investment Partnership
UNDP	United Nations Development Programme

USD	US Dollar, or $
WB	World Bank
WHO	World Health Organization

List of Figures

Fig. 3.1   Main challenges of China's reforms   73

Fig. 5.1   Public management from Mao to Xi Jinping   164

Fig. 5.2   The new structure of the decision-making process
"where do correct ideas come from?"   165

List of Tables

Table 3.1	China's main economic indicators	79
Table 3.2a	Changes in employment of the three economic sectors (1952–2016)	79
Table 3.2b	Changes in GDP of the three economic sectors (1952–2016)	79
Table 3.3	The Proportion of GDP (PPP) in the Total of the World (1820–2030)	96
Table 3.4	G20's GDP (PPP) proportion in the world (1990–2014)	97
Table 3.5	G20's imports and export volume proportion in the world (1990–2014)	98
Table 3.6	G20's economic strength proportion in the world (1990–2014)	99
Table 3.7	China's Urban Per Capita Annual Disposable Income and Rural Per Capita Net Income (1978–2017)	101
Table 3.8	Per Capita Annual Income of Urban and Rural Households in China's provinces (2006)	107
Table 3.9	Gini index and ratio of richest 10% to poorest 10% in 20 Western countries and China, ca. 2005	110
Table 4.1	People insured by the major social insurances in urban areas (millions) 2001–2016	128
Table 4.2	Fund Revenues of the old-age insurance, basic medical insurance, unemployment insurance, work-related injury insurance, maternity insurance in urban areas 2001–2016 (billion yuan)	129
Table 4.3	The minimum living standard line, 2005–2018	134
Table 4.4	Number of people covered by old age insurance in rural China 2010–2016	135
Table 4.5	The new rural cooperative medical system 2006–2014	136
Table 4.6	UNDP Gini index and Palma Ratio for 20 Western countries and China, ca. 2015	139

Table 4.7	HDI and ranking in 20 Western countries and China, ca. 2015	141
Table 4.8	Human Development Indexes of Various Regions in China (1982–2030)	142
Table 4.9	Per Capita Annual Income of Urban and Rural Households in China's provinces (2006–2017)	147
Table 4.10	Five groups of Provinces with different urban-rural personal income ratios (2006 and 2017)	149

Chapter 1
Social Change and China's Dream: Will the China's Dream Come True?

The goal of China's grand strategy to lift China from semi-colonial status to prosperity and world power status has been summarized, especially since the beginning of the Xi Jinping leadership, under the slogan of the 'China's Dream'. It is therefore necessary to first understand what are the underlying historical, political, and economic characteristics of China that should be changed in order to realize this dream (this chapter and Chap. 2), second to identify the dimensions of this comprehensive social change (Chaps. 2 and 5), and third to measure the improvements of the living conditions of the Chinese people and of the status of China in the international order (Chaps. 3, 4 and 6). Here I will focus more particularly on how to define a country dream and how to evaluate whether it has been realized or not.

1.1 Preliminary Considerations

Two preliminary remarks. The 'country's dream' has become a dominant theme in China during the last decade or so. It has gained new momentum since Xi Jinping, the new Party secretary general of the CPC, took office in 2013 and made it the central theme of his general approach to China's development for the next 10 years (Xi 2014, Part II, pp. 37–74). Of course, the theme of a 'country's dream' is not limited to China. The US has also developed this theme, probably right from the beginning of the construction of their federal State, going back to the War of Independence against England and to the expansion of the American settlements in the Western part of the country. This led to the Indian Wars and consequently to the confinement of the original inhabitants, the American Indians, to the Indian Reservations, and to the establishment of the new Member-States of the US located between the original

---

I develop here from an English non-published manuscript. A shorter version has been translated into Chinese by Ms Zhang Junling and published as: Paolo Urio "Shèhuì biàngé yǔ zhōngguó mèng" (Social change and China's Dream), Tànsuǒ (探索)—Probe), Chongqing, 15 October 2014, pp. 173–181.

© Springer Nature Singapore Pte Ltd. 2019
P. Urio, *China 1949–2019*, https://doi.org/10.1007/978-981-13-8879-8_1

Eastern 13 British colonies and the Pacific coast (Urio 2018, Chap. 4; Luttwak 1993). Moreover, the development of the US economy since the end of the XIXth century made it possible for a new middle class to have access to a comfortable way of living that has become the standard for the 'dream of individuals and families' not only in the US but also in other parts of the World. Europe has been more reluctant to develop the 'dream approach' to its future, maybe because of the realization, especially after the end of World War II, of the damage it has done not only to the rest of the World but also to its own population, through colonialism, imperialism and the related internal wars (in fact, European civil wars) between its major powers that led to the catastrophes of the First and Second World Wars. If there ever was a Europe's dream, this is probably the one developed by the people of my generation (born around 1940) shocked by the revelations of the horrors perpetrated by Nazi-fascism and by the Second World War, but convinced that the process of European integration initiated in 1950 would lead Europe towards peace (both internal and international) and to prosperity (Rifkin 2004). This was the beginning of a 30-year period of economic and social development called 'the Glorious 30-years' during which millions of Europeans recovered from the horrors of war, improved their standard of living and gained access to a set of social public policies (the Welfare State) that protected them during major dangers of life, namely illness, unemployment and old age. It is now to be seen if the dreams of these 3 parts of the world (China, the US, and Europe) have come true, or whether the policies implemented by their leaderships have developed into the contrary, i.e. a nightmare. In this chapter, based upon theoretical thinking and empirical evidence, I will develop a strategy (some would call it a model or, more modestly, a framework for analysis) to evaluate the impact of public policies on the population both for the past and the future, endeavouring to answer the question: dream or nightmare?

The 'country's dream' is of course linked to the second concept in this chapter's title, i.e. social change. We will see that social change is easier to define than 'country's dream'. Whereas a 'dream' depends to a large extent on the ideas (ideological, theoretical, and/or empirical) of individuals, groups of individuals, or countries' leaderships used for defining their dream, the definition of social change can be defined on the basis of empirical theory. Then, and only then can social change be evaluated on the basis of the dream. So, there is a link between social change and dream.

1.2 Defining Social Change

Let us start with the definition of social change. Social change can be defined as the set of changes that occurs within a society following the implementation of public policies that concerns one or several components of society, such as its different sub-structures (i.e. culture or ideology, economy, polity, legal structure, and communication structure); social, economic and political actors; and the physical environment (Urio 1984, 2010a, 2013). Changes may represent an improvement or a deterioration of the situation of individuals, groups of individuals (such as social

1.2 Defining Social Change

groups or categories, classes, political parties, interest groups, mass media, etc.), public institutions, or the country as a whole. Of course, the criteria for assessing whether the outcome of social change is positive or negative must be chosen either by the researcher or by the political leadership which has implemented the public policies that are at the origin of social change. Of course, we cannot exclude that other countries will also evaluate the consequences of social change occurring in the country concerned. And China is a good example in this context, as its public policies and their consequences are continuously being assessed and evaluated by other countries and by researchers, think tanks, political parties, interest groups, NGOs, mass media, multinational and national companies established in these countries, as well as by international organizations.

And this is where the difficulties begin. Just consider the following example taken from the actual situation of China between 1978 and 1997. The policies of China's opening up (both internally and externally) adopted under the leadership of Deng Xiaoping have produced a considerable increase of the country's GDP, as well as of the per capita GDP. This is simply an empirical assessment. As the goal of Deng was to improve the overall wealth of China (measured by GDP and GDP per capita), the empirical assessment will inevitably be associated with a positive evaluation of the social change induced by these policies. And this has been for a long time the official evaluation made by the Chinese leadership. Nevertheless, several researchers (both Chinese and foreign), since the end of the 1980s, have pointed out that along with the above-mentioned positive outcomes, there have also been some negative ones, such as the increase of social inequalities and environmental damages. This assessment has later been acknowledged by the Chinese leadership, and led to the implementation of policies that 'put people first', especially after 2002 (Urio 2010a, Chaps. 2 and 3; Urio 2012, Chap. 6). Moreover, during the first term of the Xi Jinping leadership, the results of those reform policies have been taken into account not only to continue and develop the policies that 'put people first', but also to project China abroad (the Belt and Road initiative) thus realizing the goal of reclaiming the world power status that was China's until the Opium Wars of the XIX Century (Urio 2018, Chaps. 5 and 6 below).

So, the empirical assessment and the evaluation of social change induced by public policies depend on the point of view of the researcher and/or of the political leadership of the country concerned. And they can also be evaluated by individuals and groups of citizens who have a stake in the policies concerned. Moreover, as similar public policies will tend to produce similar results, one can consider that if a country wants to evaluate ex-post or ex-ante the outcome of these policies, it would be well advised to analyse not only its own experience with these policies but also the experiences made by other countries. Therefore, in this chapter I will also provide a preliminary evaluation of the consequences of public policies in the West and not only in China as the title of the chapter may suggest. There is a good reason for this. Since the beginning of the 1980s China and the West have embarked upon a whole set of public policies that, in spite of some considerable differences, present nevertheless some remarkable similarities (for more detail Urio 2012, Chaps. 5 and 6). These policies can be put under the umbrella of one of the two armed wings of neoliberalism, i.e. the New Public Management, the other being the Washington Consensus.[1] These policies have in common the privatization of large sectors of State activities, the deregulation of markets (both nationally and internationally), and a focus on economic efficiency at the expense of social equity.

1.3 Defining Country Dreams

The dream that these policies are supposed to realize, depend, as I have already suggested, upon the point of view of the evaluator. As I am a university professor and researcher and therefore, inevitably, also an academic evaluator, it is for me necessary, before we go any further, to explain what my preliminary criteria are. Some would call them postulates, but I will more simply qualify them as reasonable starting points. First, it is reasonable to consider that 'country dreams' may be different from one country to another. And it can be demonstrated that they very often are different, as I have already suggested above by briefly comparing Europe and the US. This is due to their different, even if in part common, histories. As this is the case for the US and Europe, both belonging to the general category of liberal democracy with capitalist economies, this is very likely to be even more true when we compare China with the West.

Second, it is also reasonable to forecast that people and groups living in a country may conceive different dreams. Moreover, dreams of the same categories of people (e.g. the middle class) living in different countries may also be different. These differences depend upon the positions and roles individuals and groups play within their own country as a function of their social surface, i.e. their economic power, social status, access to political decision-making, prestige, and education. Just one example to illustrate this point: in the West the dominant opinion is that the developing Chinese middle class will inevitably assume the same values as the Western middle class. Consequently, it will evaluate the results of public policies in the same way and, more important, it will require the Chinese leadership to reform the political system so that it would benefit from the same kind of freedom enjoyed by the Western middle class. Although this hypothesis cannot be discarded in theory, it is by no means plausible, if we take into consideration the different histories, and therefore the different sets of fundamental values that emerged out of the very different paths along which the Western and the Chinese societies have developed through the centuries.[2]

Third, if we consider that 'country dreams' are most of the time constructed and diffused by the countries' leaderships, the question that immediately arises is: are the leaders able to understand, interpret and fulfil the needs of their people? It is

---

[1]On the similarities between these two-armed wings of neoliberalism see Urio (2012, pp. 47–50 and on the similarities between NPM and China's reforms see ibidem, Chaps. 3 and 4). The best definition of the Washington Consensus is the one given by John Williamson (1990) and (1993).

[2]I have developed this point in more detail in Chap. 1 of Urio 2010. For a good summary of the 'Chinese model' see the work of the Italian sociologist Domenico De Masi (2014), pp. 55–74.

here that the researcher has to unveil his preferences. If we take into consideration the formidable tragedies people of all countries have gone through in history (wars, famines, killings, torture, injustice, etc.) it seems reasonable to take as a starting point the Preamble of the Universal Declaration of Human Rights that has been undersigned by the great majority of the member-states of the United Nations.[3] On this basis, we should evaluate whether public policies implemented by the leadership of a country have effectively improved, and are reasonably apt to effectively improve in the future the living conditions of its citizens, so that they will 'enjoy freedom from fear and want', as stated in paragraph 2 of the Preamble of the Universal Declaration. Furthermore, the rights listed in the 30 articles of the Universal Declaration go well beyond the political and civil rights, generally mentioned by Western scholars and politicians. Indeed, they also deal with substantive rights such as 'the right to a standard of living adequate for the health and well-being of individuals and their families, including food, clothing, housing and medical care and necessary social services; and the right to security in the event of unemployment, sickness, disability, widowhood, old age or other hindrances to livelihood in circumstances beyond their control' (art. 25 of the Universal Declaration).

Furthermore, the rights enumerated by the Universal Declaration are so numerous and cover such an impressive range of different dimensions of the human condition that it seems reasonable to consider that they cannot be satisfied simultaneously, but will take a long period of time to be fulfilled. And the history of mankind, and in particular the history of Western countries, comfort this point of view. Consequently, it seems reasonable to accept that the leadership of a country may choose a strategy that gives priority to some rights over others. Furthermore, it seems reasonable to consider that there is not just one single historical path, the one experienced by the West, for a country to fulfil the rights of the Universal Declaration. Also, one has to admit that Western countries themselves are miles away from having satisfactorily satisfied a whole range of substantive rights. Consequently, I would accept as 'good' a strategy that leads to a society where nobody is poor, and everybody enjoys a sufficient protection in case of problems (unemployment, poverty, illness) sustained by an economy that is 'society friendly' and 'environment friendly'. I will come back to these two concepts. For the moment it suffices to mention that this type of society will reduce inequalities that, as Stiglitz has convincingly demonstrated, is good not only for assuring social justice but also for the improvement of economic efficiency (Stiglitz 2012; Piketty 2014; Urio 2012). Moreover, this type of society will prevent social unrest and contribute to social and political stability, a necessary condition for social and economic development. In short, a society in which the economy is at the service of the people and not the reverse.

Fourth, having said that, there is a controversy to which the researcher has to give a clear answer. Almost everybody agrees to a strategy aiming at increasing the

---

[3]The text can be found on United Nations website in English: http://www.un.org/en/documents/udhr/; and in Chinese: http://www.un.org/zh/documents/udhr/. The Universal Declaration is not an international treaty and, as such, is not legally binding for the countries who have signed it. Nevertheless, it may constitute a powerful moral incentive.

overall wealth basis (generally measured by GDP), starting from which a country may be able to satisfy its people's needs. The controversy arises over the following dilemma: is it better to first make the cake and then to divide it up, or is it better to distribute the cake while it is still in the process of being made? The first strategy is generally preferred by liberals, and even more by neoliberals, who claim to base this choice upon scientific considerations. And there are people in China who say exactly the same. Unfortunately for them, facts point in the opposite direction. In the real functioning of the economy the cake is divided up at the same time as it is being made. Just consider how the process of production of wealth is working in reality. An employee is remunerated generally at the end of the month as a reward for his contribution to the creation of wealth. But this is done so for practical reasons. In fact, he is contributing to the creation of wealth every week, every day, every hour, every minute while he is working. 'Normally' he should receive his salary in real time, as he is contributing to the creation of wealth in real time. But for practical reasons he is paid at the end of the month. Now, for him the problem is: do I receive a fair salary? Is it enough to place him above the poverty line? And for the people who are not needed by the economy, and therefore do not receive a salary, is there a public policy that allows them to obtain an allowance that permits them to be above the poverty line? The problem here is that for liberal and neoliberal the capitalist economy works on the basis of efficiency: people are given a job only if it is efficient for the economy to employ them. Moreover, when they are employed, their salary is determined by the overall efficiency of the company in which they work; which means that their salary may be fixed under the level of poverty if this level is compatible with the overall efficiency of the company.[4] People who are not needed by the capitalist economy (where the option 'you must first make the cake, and then you can distribute it' prevails) and who as a consequence do not participate in the creation of wealth, do not receive a salary. They can only survive if they can receive an allowance (in this case, some unemployment benefits) implemented by a public policy.[5] Of course, in practice, even in the most capitalist countries, some public policies are set up to help people who are not needed by the economy. But, empirical data show that the benefits of the social policies implemented in these countries are not enough to avoid rates of poverty that can go up to 15% and in some cases even above Urio 2012, Chap. 5).

So, the choice in favour of this way of considering the problem of the cake and of its distribution is not decided on the basis of scientific analysis, but on the ideological preference in favour of the efficiency of the economy over social equity. Scientific analysis cannot help us to choose between economic efficiency and social equity. Indeed, we are here in the domain of fundamental values that can only be chosen on the basis of ethical, moral or religious considerations and, in short, on an act of faith.[6] The economic efficiency principle dictates the choice in favour of organizing

---

[4]This strategy has given birth to a new category of employed people: the 'working poor', i.e. people who work full-time, but receive a salary that puts them under the poverty line.

[5]The same reasoning is valid for people who are not in a position of working due to illness, accidents, or old age.

[6]This position has been inspired by the works of the Nobel Prize winner Herbert A. Simon, *Administrative Behavior. Decision-Making Processes in Administrative Organizations*, New York, The

1.3 Defining Country Dreams

the economic processes so that it employs only the part of the workforce necessary for satisfying economic efficiency. Consequently, the economy creates wealth in a way that satisfies only one part of society and leaves the other part at best in a very modest situation (e.g. the lower middle class), at worst under the level of poverty (e.g. the working poor and the unemployed). In fact, the 'you must first make the cake' option is an intellectual fraud that, if implemented, can become a political, economical and social fraud. Only later, when the cake is big enough (but who makes this decision?), these people are given adequate means to run a decent life.[7] The history of capitalism (especially at the time of its neoliberal variant) shows that these people have been waiting for a very long time. Apart from the fact that this strategy ignores or, at least, gives inadequate attention to the principle of social equity, it ironically contradicts the very same principle that constitutes its ideological basis, i.e. economic efficiency. As I have already mentioned, Stiglitz has convincingly demonstrated that the decision of deliberately leaving outside of the economic process people who could on the contrary be employed to contribute to the creation of the common wealth constitutes an uneconomic waste of potentially productive means (Stiglitz 2012). As I have suggested above, I prefer the other solution ('making and dividing up the cake at the same time') and I would accept as 'good' a development strategy that leads to a society where nobody is poor, and everybody enjoys a sufficient protection in case of problems (unemployment, poverty, illness) sustained by an economy that is 'society friendly' and 'environment friendly'. More about this below.

1.4 How to Decide Whether Social Change Has Realized the Country Dream?

We must now turn to the difficult task of designing a strategy for measuring and evaluating social change induced by a development strategy. We have to look at facts. We have to look at public policies. But public policies are not the ultimate facts. They take the form of theories: if I implement policy A, I will obtain result B. But, after implementation, has B realized the aims of policy A? Or has it not realized them at all, or only in part; and is it possible that it has also realized some unwanted

---

Free Press, (1997) (4th ed.; 1st edition 1945), Chap. 3: "Facts and Values in Decision-Making", pp. 55–71. Simon summarizes the argument in this way: 'To determine whether a proposition is correct, it must be compared directly to experience—with facts—or it must lead by logical reasoning to other propositions that can be compared with experience. But factual propositions cannot be derived from ethical ones by any process of reasoning, nor can ethical propositions be compared directly with facts—since they assert 'oughts' rather than facts. Hence, there is no way in which the correctness of ethical propositions can be empirically or rationally tested', ibidem, p. 56.

[7]Of course, this is not the only problem with capitalism. Another important problem is that the capitalists tend to invest for the sake of making money; this goal can be achieved not only by investing in productive processes (that create real wealth) but also by investing in financial speculative products that increase the capital without creating real wealth (the so-called 'real economy'). The 2008 crisis shows very well that capitalists tend to invest more and more in these speculative financial products, thus subtracting investment from the real economy.

consequences C? If this is the case, what is the overall outcome for society and for its individuals and groups of citizens? To answer these questions, we have to look at the ultimate facts, that is at the impact that policies have on people and groups of people. As I have suggested elsewhere, we have to look at the following groups of indicators: (1) the quantity of employment, measured by its reverse, i.e. by the rate of unemployment; (2) the quality of employment, evaluated by the working conditions of employees in terms of salary, social benefits, working hours, paid leaves, protection against unjustified redundancy, work-related injuries, etc.; (3) income distribution; (4) poverty rates; (5) crime rates; (6) health of people; and (7) health of the physical environment.[8] I suggest to consider that the 'country dream' is realized if the results obtained on these 7 dimensions are overall good enough.

1.5 The Western Experience: Between Dream and Nightmare

Then, the question that arises is the following: what are the public policies to be implemented for obtaining good results on these seven dimensions? A first answer can be given by briefly looking at the results obtained in China and in the West between 1978 and 2008, i.e. before the explosion of the economic and financial crisis (for more detail Urio 2012, Chaps. 5 and 6). As I have suggested above, this is a legitimate strategy because during this period of time both China and the West have basically implemented the same types of policies (namely privatizations, deregulations, contracting-out and decentralization) in spite of remarkable differences in the organization of their societies. In the West this process has been implemented under the ideological umbrella of neoliberalism and one of its armed wings, New Public Management, and has given to the private financial sector the status of dominant layer within the capitalist economy. The results have been in short: less transparency, less competition, more economic efficiency (measured by GDP) and less social equity. Of course, there are differences amongst Western countries. Whereas in all countries income inequality, poverty rates, and crime rates have increased and public health has deteriorated, the countries which have implemented these reforms more deeply, such as the US, the United Kingdom and New Zealand are much worse off than continental European countries.[9] If we take for example income inequality, US, UK and NZ have the highest Gini index, and have also the highest poverty rate and crime rate (especially the US). True, these countries have had a lower unemployment rate compared to the continental European countries. But this was masked by a considerable deterioration of the quality of employment, attested by the increase of short term and part-time contracts, and low-paid jobs. As soon as the 2008 crisis explodes, these people are easily laid off, and the unemployment rate of these countries increases to levels comparable to those of continental Europe. After the outburst of the 2008

---

[8]I started to work on this approach in the 1990s; see Paolo Urio (1999), and (2012), pp. 55–63.

[9]I have no time or space to deal in this chapter with the special case of Southern European countries.

1.5 The Western Experience: Between Dream and Nightmare

crisis, people not needed or underemployed by the capitalist economy have not only increased in number but also saw their standard of living deteriorate in terms of per capita income and access to social services. This is particularly true for the southern European countries who were forced (and are still forced today) to implement a variant of the neoliberal agenda, the policy of austerity, imposed by the financial sector, under the leadership of the European Commission, the European Central Bank and the International Monetary Fund. The US experiences the same situation. So, for a great number of Western people the neoliberal reforms have resulted in a nightmare, whereas it has continued to be a 'dream come true' for the top 1%.

1.6 The Chinese Experience: Will the Dream Come True?

We will see in Chap. 3 that during the same period of time, China has embarked upon a programme of reforms that has given space to market mechanisms and, as a consequence, to privatizations, contracting-out and deregulations. This reform programme has considerably reduced the number of poor people, has increased the country's GDP by an annual rate of about 10% during three consecutive decades, and has improved the personal situation of large numbers of Chinese citizens. However, the per capita income places China far below in the world's hierarchy, far behind countries such as the US, Switzerland and the European Union. Moreover, at the same time, inequalities between people (for income and access to public services) have increased; and the disparities between regions, provinces and within provinces between rural and urban residents have increased as well. More worrying, the reduction of poverty came to a halt in 1997 and then poverty started to increase, as new forms of poverty arose both in the urban and in the rural areas, and huge numbers of migrant workers have been left without proper access to social services (especially health, education, and social insurances). Finally, environmental damages, already present during the imperial and the Mao eras, have further polluted soil, air and water with negative consequences for people's health (Hu and Ping 1991; Hu et al. 1992; Urio 2012). Of course, we must take into consideration that China is a big and very differentiated country. Several provinces have attained the same level of development as some Western countries, especially if we use the Human Development Index.

The Chinese government has recognized the seriousness of the situation from at least the end of the 1990s and has started to take measures to redirect the development strategy towards more social equity and less economic efficiency (Urio 2010a, pp. 103–155). Moreover, following the outburst of the 2008 crisis the Chinese government has heavily invested in infrastructure, structural adjustment, health and education, rural residents' well-being, energy savings and environmental protection, housing for low-income residents, and post-earth-quake reconstruction in Sichuan province. In other words, it has invested in the future of the country.

However, we must recognize that for the time being, the dream is far away for several millions of Chinese citizens, and for many, as is happening in the West, their actual situation looks more like a nightmare rather than a dream. It is for these reasons that Xi Jinping has perfected the policies implemented by his predecessors by projecting China's development strategy outside China's border. Further developing China would not have been possible without the internationalization of the development strategy, that is presented not only as a positive goal for China, but also for the rest of the world (the win-win slogan). It remains to be seen if this strategy will achieve these results.

However, there is a difference between China and the West: while China was investing for the future of its people after the outburst of the 2008 crisis, the West was investing heavily to save the upper layer of the capitalist economy, i.e. the financial system, which is responsible for the 2008 debacle, while imposing at the same time austerity programmes that hurt the Western lower middle class and especially poor people. As a consequence, the gap between the super-rich and the poor has further widened and protest movements have developed (and are still developing) in several Western countries. Even more worrying, several international moves made by Western governments give the impression that the Western leaders, incapable of solving their domestic problems, are turning, as often happens in such circumstances, to the international arena to find 'enemies' to fight against, thus trying to reclaim popular support by awakening the nationalist fibre of their citizenry. Military interventions in Libya and in other African countries, diplomatic and economic interventions in Georgia, Ukraine and Venezuela, policy of isolation toward Iran, direct and/or indirect intervention in Syria, development of aggressive policies of containment towards Russia and China, are clear signs of the fear the West (and especially the US) has of losing its dominant position acquired in the World since the Renaissance. A final example is the hysteria that has developed in the US, accusing Russia, without any clear proof of interfering in the 2016 Presidential election in order to sustain Donald Trump against the candidate of the establishment, Hillary Clinton (Sect. 6.1 below).

1.7 Towards the Country Dream: A Development Strategy that Is 'Society Friendly' and 'Environment Friendly'

I start from the premise that a development strategy should take into consideration four values: economic efficiency, social equity, developmental sustainability, and security.[10] The implementation of such a strategy cannot be confined to the domestic public policies but has also to take into consideration the international position of

---

[10]Efficiency, equity and sustainability are sufficiently known, whereas I need to define security as follows: 'Security' is taken here as one of the most important values contributing to sustainable development. The expression applies to all security considerations (community-level public safety, national security and international security) that are potentially influenced by, or can influence infrastructure and the preservation of vital assets for sustainable development. So defined, security is clearly also linked to equity and efficiency. Security requires a set of domestic policies aiming at establishing and maintaining a safe institutional, political, social, and physical environment favourable to social and economic development both nationally and internationally.

1.7 Towards the Country Dream: A Development Strategy … 11

China. For a very long time China has witnessed the interventions of Western powers all over the world, and in particular in its own territory. She has also witnessed Western interventions in Russia and in the former member-states of the Soviet bloc after the collapse of the Soviet Union; and in 2010 she was informed that the US had made the Pacific region the new pivot of its foreign policy. But whereas these events, although worrying, would not place China in an extremely difficult situation, two international treaties promoted by the US would have created serious problems for China both nationally and internationally: the Trans-Atlantic Trade and Investment Partnership (TTIP) negotiated between the US and the European Union and the Trans-Pacific Partnership (TPP) negotiated between the US and several far eastern countries (Lafer 2014; Wallach 2013; Bizzarri 2013).[11] The goal was to establish two free-trade and investment areas in which the multinational companies would be free to invest and sue the government which may implement laws contrary to the interests of the foreign investors. The TTIP would create a free-trade zone of approximately 800–900 million consumers in the most developed countries, and the TPP a free-trade zone dominated by the US in the Pacific region that would certainly become a strong competitor to China. The two treaties were a clear will of the US to integrate Europe into its own economic system, and to isolate Russia and China with the aim to force them to accept the rules of the international economic system the US made. Right at the beginning of his administration President Trump withdrew the US from the TTP and has put a halt to the negotiations on the TTIP. Nevertheless, it is not at all sure that he will not change his mind in the future, nor that his future successor will not restart negotiations on these two international agreements.

In addition to taking into consideration the international situation briefly referred to above, China's development strategy should implement a coordinate set of public policies aimed at building a society where each of the four values (efficiency, equity, sustainability and security) would be realized to a large extent, without damaging the others. Moreover, considering the characteristics of China's polity, economy and culture, the government should play the central role in coordinating the policies aimed at realizing those values. In particular, as I have suggested in 2012, the Chinese government (or, more precisely, the Party-State) should implement a development strategy that keeps under control and orientates the development of the private sector so that it contributes to the creation and distribution of the common wealth (the cake) for the benefit of all citizens and categories of citizens and not for just a minority (Urio 2012, pp. 208–209).

At the level of strategic management, here are the main components of such a strategy:

(1) further develop the policies that 'put people first' (especially social security, i.e. health, unemployment and old age insurance, housing, drinkable water and

---

[11] The TPP originated from an initiative taken by Singapore, New Zealand and Chile in 2003 under the name of *"Pacific Three Closer Economic Partnership"*. In 2008 the US joined the group and proposed to re-name it *"Trans-Pacific-Partnership—TPP"*. Since then the US pushed other countries in the region to join the TPP: Brunei, Australia, Canada, Peru, Mexico, Japan, Vietnam, Malaysia.

access to public services) that will help reduce disparities, especially income inequalities;

(2) for this purpose, it is also necessary to improve the well-being of the rural residents and migrant workers and this will help the smooth management of the process of urbanization;

(3) avoid all forms of market fundamentalism and continue on the road of Chinese pragmatism;

(4) keep politics in command over the economy and its actors;

(5) therefore, keep the new Chinese capitalists under control so that they do not develop behaviours similar to those of their Western colleagues that led to the dominance of the upper layer of capitalism (finance) and to the 2008 crisis;

(6) keep big banks, and the central bank, under control;

(7) promote the development of the 'real market': a market economy based upon competition and transparency, also considering that the market is not necessarily the best solution for public goods and services;

(8) for this purpose, it is necessary to regulate the market so that it produces efficiently what society needs;

(9) be ready to substitute the market when it fails to produce what society needs and maintain within the state sectors that may be considered as strategic for China's economy and/or necessary for providing affordable services to the citizens;

(10) further eradicate corruption and tax evasion and avoidance;

(11) further increase the fiscal capacity of the central government and its capacity to control the spending of local authorities by setting up an efficient debt-reporting system on local governments;

(12) further develop the policy of reducing pollution and the use of scarce resources (green economy);

(13) keep developing and improving the education system (which should be free of charge at the compulsory level and affordable at the upper levels), as well as science and technology;

(14) continue the policy of opening up to the global economy, but practice selective protectionism;

(15) for the time being, keep the capital account as closed as possible (as the 1997 and the 2008 crises strongly suggest).

At the level of public policies, the Party-State (central and/or local) should define and coordinate numerous public policies aimed at developing the economy, assuring security, safeguarding social equity as a guarantee of social cohesion, and protecting the environment. The central focus of these policies is the provision of hard and soft infrastructures (Urio 2010b). Before we go any further, it must be stressed that it is important to bear in mind the distinction between soft and hard infrastructure, the two vast domains where it is important to have clear ideas about the best means for providing the corresponding services. The first one, 'hard infrastructure', refers to physical resources and services (like roads, railways, energy, housing, etc.). Although hard infrastructure is not aimed at directly developing the human capital, it contributes nevertheless in a decisive manner to its improvement, provided people are in a position to have an equitable access to these resources. In order to enable people to take advantage of physical infrastructure it is necessary to develop the second type of infrastructure: 'soft infrastructure', whose aim is not to develop anything physical, but to directly improve human capital, namely attitudes, knowledge, skills, as well as physical and mental health. It is the domain of education, science and technology (including the dissemination of innovation and best practices) health, and more generally, the development of safety nets. This should allow people to have access to the labour market, where they can obtain the financial means to have access to goods and services, including those offered by hard infrastructures such as transportation.

The inter-dependence between soft and hard infrastructure is at the heart of the development strategy. Both are necessary for developing the country. A well-educated workforce, in good health and having the assurance to be able to count upon reasonable safety nets in case of problems, is a prerequisite for the development of all the economic sectors. It is also a powerful factor for promoting a more open and dynamic society, and to realize economic, social, and political stability, as well as a reasonable level of security, provided that wealth is distributed equitably amongst the different components of society. Education in advanced technologies (both technical and managerial) will help the country to develop those sectors that will free it from dependence upon outside countries, at least in the strategic sectors defined by the government. Fundamental research and R&D within both public and private institutions will further improve the innovation capacity of the country, necessary to compete in the local and global markets. So, the development of soft infrastructure will be a powerful driver for managing, maintaining, and improving hard infrastructure. But infrastructures (both soft and hard) must first be built. And it is possible that this may exceed the fiscal capacity of the central state or of the local governments. If this is the case, and if the development of infrastructures is considered urgent, then the resort to private capital may look like a good choice. But beware: private capital may not be suitable for assuring social equity, as I will explain below (Sect. 5.5).

Having clarified the contribution of soft and hard infrastructure, the main public policies needed to sustain economic development are enumerated hereafter: the development of an efficient and reliable banking and insurance system, and financial markets; and the related policy of sustaining and promoting the private sector (especially SMEs—Small and Medium Size Enterprises—as the major source of jobs creation). These policies should contribute to a 'society friendly job creation', i.e. a situation where the development of an efficient and competitive economy (source of jobs and revenues) is balanced by a set of policies aimed at the development and support of the human capital. This is done by developing education at all levels (including adult education) and providing a reasonable but efficient safety net, including health care and insurance, old age pensions schemes, and unemployment insurance that will result in equitable development, a balanced society, and social stability.

Moreover, the development strategy should also be 'environment friendly'. This is realized by implementing the following policies, and above all land use planning (including urbanisation and urban regeneration). This is a transversal policy aimed primarily at defining which types of economic activities can be developed on what part of the national territory. Not only it provides the economic actors with the legal security they need when planning their activities, but it also sustains several policies, namely economic development and the modernization of agriculture. This is interesting not only for improving the efficiency of this sector (for satisfying national strategic goals of assuring a relative autonomy in food production, and for favouring the exportation of some agricultural products), but also, in the general framework of the strategy of economic development favouring the transfer of manpower to the other sectors. The reform of SOEs is another important domain, not only for improving the efficiency of these enterprises on both the domestic and the global market, but also for environmental protection. Finally, the development of tourism (especially eco-tourism) and cultural activities that can contribute to both environmental protection and job creation. These policies will contribute to an 'environment friendly job creation' that will result in a sustainable economic development, a 'green economy', and a healthy society.

At the level of operational public management, the implementation of the development strategy described above must be evaluated by answering the following questions: what are the actual results of the development strategy? Towards what reality, towards what type of economy, of polity and society? Towards a dream or a nightmare? In order to answer these questions, we must answer the more practical questions that will enable us to discover the actual social and economic changes that have been realized. Here is a non-exhaustive list of such questions. Have the policies implemented been able to:

- improve the competencies of public officials (both administrative and political)
- improve the fiscal capacity of the State at all levels (central and local)
- improve education at all levels (from primary schools to university), as well as for continuous education
- improve social services, especially health, education, and housing
- improve access to social services,
- improve the social security system (health, unemployment, old age)
- improve the situation of poor families in rural and urban areas
- reduce the gap between rural and urban areas
- improve the conditions of transfer of migrant workers from the rural to the urban areas
- improve the quality of the physical environment (air, water, soil)
- improve the quality of, and access to, clean and drinkable water
- improve the security of individuals, groups and enterprises, in particular against crimes
- improve attractiveness for private investment (both from the country and from abroad)
- improve roads, railways, metro, and urban fast roads
- improve the general transportation network facilitating trade between the country (central and provincial) and the economic partners in China and abroad
- improve the telecommunication system (nationally and internationally)

1.7 Towards the Country Dream: A Development Strategy ...

- improve access to finance for private companies, especially for the Small and Medium Enterprises
- protect cultural and historical monuments.

However, in order to ascertain whether the policies implemented have realized the integrated goal of social and economic development, in other words that the China's dream has been realized, we have to come back to the basic indicators (Urio 2012, pp. 55–63, 145–197, and Chaps. 3 and 4 below). The dream is realized if the quality of employment has been improved, the rate of unemployment has diminished, the inequality of income distribution has decreased, the poverty rate and crime rates have also diminished, the health of the people and of the environment has improved. Of course, it will be difficult to do well on each of these indicators; most of the time the overall picture will be contrasted. As a consequence, it will be necessary to have a balanced approach to evaluation. And here we will find again, inevitably, the ideological biases of the evaluators: academic, politicians, public administrative high officials, head of state-owned enterprises, private entrepreneurs and investors. However, I am confident that these indicators constitute a simple and uncontroversial way of measuring the results obtained, and, consequently, also the quality of the management of the country at all levels of government. In short, it will allow to determine whether the country is developing in the right direction, i.e. if the China's dream is approaching for all the citizens and will be realized in a not too distant future.

Finally, the suggestions presented above at the strategic, public policies and operational levels should also result in the Chinese leadership dealing with what is very likely the major dilemma facing China's strategic management: fully integrate into the global economy that the West made while trying to limit the negative consequences of the implementation of market mechanisms, as Western countries have tried to do with the difficulties and failures we know, or develop China according to a mix of Western and Chinese values and policies, while safeguarding China's economy and polity major characteristics (i.e. harmony, stability and unity), thanks to an authoritarian regime that orients and controls the development of a sui generis market economy. The latter may necessitate the establishment of some limits to the integration of China into the global economy dominated by the West and the rules it has made, and, very likely, the rewriting of some of these rules, provided that Western powers are willing to take into consideration China's new role and its ambitions in the international system. I will come back to this point in the conclusion of this book.

For the moment, let me suggest a first approach for understanding China's strategy for dealing with the transition to modernity, by examining how China has managed, so far, the logical sequence of steps that lead to the implementation of strategies. We have, starting from the top: fundamental values, ideology, choice of institutions for realizing values and the associated goals, adoption and then implementation of policies within those institutions, evaluation of policies' outcomes, and feed-back. Of course, a real historical process is not that simple, i.e. linear. Moreover, steps can coexist at the same time. For example, at the moment of adopting a policy, decision-makers make reference to the fundamental values (e.g. freedom in the West, unity in

China), to the institutions chosen in the past that the policy is supposed to reinforce, and forecast that the measure taken within that policy will realize its objectives and thus confirm the validity of the fundamental values as well as the institutions (e.g. democracy for the West, the role of the Party for China). Moreover, at the end of the process, the evaluation leads generally to a feedback to the previous steps. This may be quite easy if the evaluation is positive. Similarly, returning to the previous steps is relatively easy if the evaluation points to the deficiencies of the implementation means (legal, administrative, financial, etc.). But if the evaluation suggests that a questioning of the policy is necessary, this will be more difficult, as the people responsible for the adoption of the policy will be reluctant to admit that they adopted a policy which was not apt to realize the stated goals. Even more difficult will be to question the validity of the institutions within which the policy has been adopted, and even more so if the validity of ideology and the fundamental values should be examined.

If we compare the West with China, we see that the West has made its choices for values, ideology and institutions between the end of the XVIII century and the first half of the XIX century. Which means that since then, feedback from successes and failures (and there have been many) concerned only policies and their implementation. Fundamental values, ideology and institutions (i.e. liberal democracy and capitalism) were not questioned. On the contrary, China has put into discussion all the levels, except part of the upper level (traditional values). It is true that after the collapse of the Empire, Confucianism was practically banned from Chinese political discourse by both Nationalists and Communists as they considered that Confucianism was at the origin (together with foreign aggression) of China's decline. But Confucian ideas were not eradicated from China's collective conscience and came back in the open after the tragedy of the Cultural Revolution. This is the clear manifestation of the Chinese capacity to take into consideration the 'real' situation and not to act on the basis of an ideal plan or model. Values, institutions, and policies are chosen, implemented, and eventually changed on the basis of their capacity to realize the fundamental goals of the Party-State. When we shall analyse, in Chaps. 3 and 4, China's strategy since the last decades of the XIX century, we will see that it looks like a quasi-perfect implementation of the Chinese traditional way of conceiving and implementing strategy.

References

Bizzarri, K. (2013). *A Brave New Transatlantic Partnership. The proposed EU-US Transatlantic Partnership (TTIP/TAFTA) and its socio-economic & environmental consequences,* Brussels, Published by the Seattle to Brussels Network, October.

De Masi, D. (2014). *Mappa Mundi. Modelli di vita per una società senza orientamento,* Milano, Rizzoli.

Hu, A., & Ping, Z. (1991). *China's population development.* Beijing: China's Science and Technology Press.

References

Hu, A., Yi, W., et al. (1992). *Survival and development: A study of China's long term development.* Beijing: Science Press.

Lafer, G. (2014). Partnership or Putsch? *Project Syndicate*, 14 January, www.project-syndicate.org.

Luttwak, Edward. (1993). *The endangered American dream.* New York: Touchstone Books.

Piketty, T. (2014). *Capital in the Twenty-First Century.* Cambridge (USA): Harvard University Press, (translation of *Le capital au XIXe siècle*, Paris, Seuil, 2013).

Rifkin, J. (2004). *The European dream. How Europe's vision of the future is quietly eclipsing the American dream.* New York: Penguin.

Simon, H. A. (1997). *Administrative behaviour. Decision-making processes in administrative organizations* (4th ed., 1st ed., 1945). New York: The Free Press.

Stiglitz, J. E. (2012). *The price of inequality. How today's divided society endangers our future.* New York: Norton.

Urio, P. (1984). *Le rôle politique de l'administration publique.* LEP: Lausanne.

Urio, P. (1999). La gestion publique au service du marché. In M. Hufty (Ed.) (sous la direction de), *La pensée comptable. Etat, néolibéralisme, nouvelle gestion publique* (pp. 91–124). Paris: Presses Universitaires de France, Collection Enjeux, Cahier de l'IUED, Genève.

Urio, P. (2010a). *Reconciling state, market and society in China, the long March towards prosperity.* London and New York: Routledge.

Urio, P. (Ed.). (2010b). *Private partnerships. Success and failure factors in transition countries.* Lanham (MD) and New York: UPA (University Press of America).

Urio, P. (2012). *China, the west, China, the west, and the myth of new public management. Neoliberalism and its discontents.* London and New York: Routledge.

Urio, P. (2013). Reinventing Chinese society, economy, and polity. A very short history and interpretation of China's reforms. *Politics and Society* (Vol 1, No. 2, pp. 1–37). Central China Normal University.

Urio, P. (2018). *China reclaims world power status. Putting an end to the world America made.* London and New York: Routledge.

John, Williamson. (1990). *Latin American adjustment: How much has happened.* Washington, DC: Institute for International Economics.

John, Williamson. (1993). Democracy and the Washington consensus. *World Development, 21*(8), 1331.

Wallach, L. (2013). Government by big business goes supranational. The corporation invasion. Paris: *Le Monde Diplomatique (English edition)*, December 2013.

Xi, J. (2014). *La gouvernance de la Chine.* Editions en Langues Etrangères: Beijing.

Chapter 2
Understanding China's Strategic Public Management

I have explained elsewhere through what intellectual journey I have come to avoid an ethnocentric perspective for approaching China (Urio 2010b, 2012, pp. 13–25). In this chapter I will first rely upon the commonalities existing between some well-known Chinese and Western scholars for building a set of theoretical and empirical tools in order to understand China's public management. Secondly, I will discuss the meaning of two inevitable concepts for analyzing China's strategy: market economy and capitalism. Thirdly, I will present an analysis of the traditional Chinese strategic thinking based upon the work of a French philosopher and sinologist, François Jullien. And finally, I will analyse China's political culture by showing the remarkable persistence of traditional values along with some important values imported from the West. The question will be: has China succeeded in integrating them within a robust political culture able to orient the policy process towards the intended objective as stated by President Xi Jinping at the 1917 Party Congress: 'Secure a Decisive Victory in Building a Moderately Prosperous Society in All Respects and Strive for the Great Success of Socialism with Chinese Characteristics for a New Era' (Xi 2017).[1]

2.1 Commonalities Between Chinese and Western Scholars for Analyzing Historical Processes: The Silent Transformations and the Long Time

Apart from François Jullien, who has introduced me to the traditional Chinese way of understanding and practicing strategy, and especially to the concept of the 'silent

---

[1] This is the official title of Xi Jinping speech at the 2017 Party congress (Xi 2017).

This chapter is based upon Urio (2010a, Chap. 1, in this chapter and Sect. 1.4 of Chap. 4), Urio (2012, Chap. 1), and Urio (2018, Chap. 1), with many updates and new comments.

The original version of this chapter was revised. The author given name is corrected in reference list. The correction to this chapter is available at 10.1007/978-981-13-8879-8_7

© Springer Nature Singapore Pte Ltd. 2019
P. Urio, *China 1949–2019*, https://doi.org/10.1007/978-981-13-8879-8_2

transformations', several other authors have helped me to construct the design of the research on which my books on China are based. And first of all, Fernand Braudel, who has developed two fundamental concepts. The first is an invaluable complement to the 'silent transformations', i.e. the idea that the time of history is not uniform or unique, but that there are several historical times, and one of them, the 'long time' (or the 'longue durée') very clearly complements François Jullien's 'silent transformations'. Moreover, Braudel is also, like Jullien, very careful in not attributing too much importance to 'events', and, as he says, to escape the 'dictatorship of events' (Braudel 1972).[2] Indeed, the latter are in fact the vociferous (i.e. audible), and evident (i.e. 'seeable') temporary manifestations of superficial phenomena, that do not explain in depth the evolution of history. Second, Braudel offers an in-depth historical analysis that allows us to make a clear distinction between market economy and capitalism. Complementary to these two authors, is the insight provided by Nicolas Zufferey who has compared Western philosophy to Chinese thought, by showing not only the remarkable differences that exist between them, but also the interesting similarities (Zufferey 2008).

Three Chinese authors, who have an in-depth knowledge of Western literature, present some commonality with Western thinking. Wang Hui (2003, 2009) develops a historical analysis of his country based upon long term changes, that correspond very well to Jullien's 'silent transformations' and shares with Braudel (whom he quotes on several occasions) the distinction between market economy and capitalism. In line with both Jullien and Braudel, Hu Angang (2007, 2011a, b) has developed an in-depth analysis of China's strategy to reclaim world power status based upon long term data series on the development of strategic resources that describe and explain China's growing power in the international system. Cui Zhiyuan considers, in line with Braudel's distinction between market and capitalism, that there is not necessarily a contradiction between public and private property, and therefore there is space for an economic system, different from both planned economy and capitalism, that associates these two dimensions of the economy into a 'socialist market economy' (Cui 2005, 2006).

The silent transformations, as they are commented upon by François Jullien, are based on an analysis of the traditional Chinese way of defining and implementing strategy. They are part of the traditional way Chinese have conceived the world in which they live. It is therefore interesting, before we go any further, to replace them in the general framework of Chinese philosophy. For this purpose, I will resort to a book written by the Swiss sinologist Nicolas Zufferey, significantly entitled: 'Chinese thought today. Better knowing ancient China for understanding XXI century China.' (Zufferey 2008; Cheng 1997). Right from the introduction, Zufferey draws our attention to the features of Chinese philosophy that may be of some interest to the West. First of all, its conception of the world where all its dimensions (nature, society and individuals) are interdependent, corresponding to our (very recent) interest in the respect of the environment, as well as our interest in Chinese medicine which considers human beings in their complex totality. Second, the idea that the process of becoming men or women is determined to a large extent by the process

---

[2]To my knowledge, Braudel is the only historian of the economy quoted by Jullien.

2.1 Commonalities Between Chinese and Western Scholars …

of socialization, corresponds to our interest (also relatively recent) in gender studies. Third, the fact that traditional Chinese thinkers do not consider theory and practice as two separate moments, is interesting for the revising of our definition of strategy and should lead us to question our obsession in 'first setting up a model and then orienting our action according to that model.' Finally, the fact that Chinese philosophy has not based morality upon the revelation of a transcendent God and the religion built upon it, should be interesting to us at a time when God and religion are losing their role as the reference for determining what is considered to be moral behaviour.

Moreover, for Zufferey, utility is an essential criterion for assessing the validity of philosophical postures in ancient China. Chinese philosophers do not like to be too abstract, but refer to circumstances or to examples drawn from the real world, both in the past and the present. Knowledge is always seen in view of action, to know how to act morally or politically. What is important is not 'what to know', but 'to know how to do it'. So, for them the question was: we already know what to do (the theory) and we have at the same time our way of how to do it (our practice); we just want to see how you do it (your practice), and if it is useful to us, we will introduce it into our 'what to do—how to do it.'[3] No wonder the Chinese participants were also very interested in 'action learning' as developed by some Western scholars and practitioners, that seemed to be in tune with the Chinese merging of theory and practice. For almost all the Chinese traditional thinkers the goal of action is to assure the stability of the political order. To this end, words are less important than training, i.e. of doing. Once again, we find here the opposition between model and action. (Zufferey 2008, pp. 22, 49–68).

It is not easy to summarize the works of François Jullien, who has published an astonishing number of books and articles (Jullien 1989, 2004, 2005, 2006, 2008, 2011).[4] Jullien's first suggestion is to distinguish between 'creation and process', the former corresponding to the Western way of thinking, the latter to the Chinese. Whereas the West (starting from Greek philosophy) has conceived the world as 'a creation', Chinese culture has developed a systematic conception of the world as a continuous, regular process, without a religious eschatology or a teleological interpretation. It is for this reason that Chinese culture is particularly apt for thinking the transformation, and it is from the reality of the transformation that it has given meaning to human life (Jullien 1989, pp. 11–17).

Moreover, the transformation is 'silent', i.e. it is not immediately audible, contrary to the events, such as reported in the news (especially on TV). The complete Chinese expression qualifying the transformation is 'qián yí mó huà', literally translated word for word as: 'invisible transformation silent transformation'. Jullien thinks that 'silent' is more appropriate than invisible because what is important is that one cannot hear the transformation that operates 'silently', independently from us. Wang Hui is also in favour of this interpretation and is even grateful to Jullien for having suggested to give more emphasis to the silent character of the transformation instead of the invisible. Moreover, this way of thinking sets some very strong limits on the freedom

---

[3] See the anecdote I report in Urio (2012), pp. 20–21.

[4] For a critique of Jullien see Billeter (2006).

of the individual (Jullien 2011, pp. 2–10, 16–17, 21–23, 65–69, 81–85, 100ss). Here Jullien has the same interpretation of the historical process as Fernand Braudel, who develops the concept of 'long time' or the '*longue durée*'. For Braudel too, the more important phenomena occur independently from the will of the historical subjects, whose freedom is thus considerably limited (Braudel 1958; Tomic 2008; Armitag 2014).

In the West, creation corresponds to action, which seems to be a good attitude when the strategist is confronted with a given situation where it is important to act in order to defeat the enemy. But action is local, limited in time and refers to a subject (the strategist), whereas the transformation is global, progressive, in the long time (or in the '*longue durée*'), silent, and therefore difficult to identify. In Jullien's words: 'The silent transformation, in contrast, does not use force or thwart anything; it does not fight; but, as the saying goes, makes its way, infiltrates, spreads, branches out and becomes pervasive—"spread like a stain". It integrates and disintegrates (…) This is also why it is silent; because it does not give rise to any resistance to it …' (Jullien 2011, p. 66).

Moreover, the Western way of thinking defines some clear opposite states, such as 'strong-weak', 'big-small', 'ugly-beautiful'. This leads inevitably to defining models. For example, the Venus of Milo, was the model for feminine beauty in ancient Greece. She was perfectly beautiful without the slightest trace of ugliness. When models are translated into strategies, they run the risk of losing touch with reality and its silent transformations. In Jullien's words, dealing with revolutions, 'it is the silent transformations, more than the force of the rebellious masses, the ultimate utopian representation of the Agent, which overturn and will overturn all the Ancient Regimes through progressive erosion of everything that supports them, in relation to which actions and revolutions are perhaps less catalysers than simply indicators' (Jullien 2011, p. 68). Similarly, based upon the 'Book of changes', Jullien suggests to analyse the transition from Growth to Decline, and vice versa. 'Growth, (…) does not give way at the approach of the Decline but, precisely as its development increases, it is itself already yielding towards decline. This is why, as the Growth comes to an end (…) a manifest decline is acknowledged. As I have been expending my strength with success during the time of the Growth, I have in fact already started to wear myself out, because the more I display my capabilities the more fragile they become, the more ground I occupy, the more I must toil to conserve it; the Roman Empire had pushed its *limes* too far not to collapse.' (Jullien 2011, pp. 82–83). Clearly, this will be useful when analysing China's rise and US decline in Chap. 6.

Finally, according to Jullien, the silent transformations are not only the opposite of action, but also of the events, as action inevitably becomes vociferous, as one can very well see looking at the news on TV, a patchwork of events to the detriment of in-depth analysis of the underlying forces, i.e. of the silent transformations (Jullien 2011, pp. 116–135: 'Mythology of Event'). It is here that one can see a strong similarity between Jullien's 'silent transformations' and Braudel's analysis of history. Indeed, Braudel considers that the time of history is a multiple time comprising the short, the medium and the long time (also defined as 'the longue durée'). The short time corresponds to events, that for a long time constituted the backbone of Western historical research.

Braudel's analysis of the development of economic activities is based upon an historical analysis that goes practically back to the 'beginning of history' (Wallerstein 1991; Goody 2006). In fact Braudel, whose approach contradicts many interpretations of the appearance and development of market economy and capitalism, complains about the lack of historical perspective of too many analyses: 'Journalists, economists, and sociologists [and I would add: political scientists] often fail to take historical dimensions and perspectives into account in their writings, and don't many historians do the same thing, as if the period they study existed in a vacuum, or was both a beginning and an end?' (Braudel 1979b, p. 113). In his historical analysis Braudel has chosen to deal with the long-term trends that led to the emergence of capitalism in different parts of the world: 'I chose to deal with long term equilibria and disequilibria. To my mind, the fundamental characteristic of the preindustrial economy is the coexistence of the inflexibility, inertia, and slow-motion characteristic of an economy that was still primitive, alongside trends—limited and in the minority, yet active and powerful—that were characteristic of modern growth. On the one hand, peasants lived (...) in autarchy; on the other hand, a market-oriented economy and an expanding capitalism (...) gradually creating the very world in which we live ...' (Braudel 1979b, p. 5).

For Braudel it is necessary to free oneself from the vociferous reality of the events as they are reported with much noise in the news, thus acquiring an importance that they do not necessarily possess. On the contrary, the skilful researcher (and for this book also the skilful strategist) should pay more attention to the long time, which may look motionless, but within which the silent underlying phenomena operate and shape all dimensions of society (social, political, economical), a clear reference to Jullien's 'silent transformations' (Braudel 1972, p. 4). The consequence is that 'the individual actor is imbedded into a history, which can be a very old one, i.e. the history of the language one speaks, of the religion one practises, in short into a civilization. So, one may have the illusion of having some kind of responsibilities, and therefore of freedoms, and to be able to choose among several possibilities. But in fact, one's freedom is much more limited, and one is not completely the master of one's destiny, because, in reality, he is submerged by the flow of history through the slow time ('*la marche lente*'). If the profound movements [Julien's silent transformations] are in your favour, you will be served, independently of your intelligence, your merits, your thoughts' (Braudel 1972, pp. 4–5). And Jullien adds this final comment: 'The danger would be to deal with the difference [between the West and China] in terms of nature or of mind-set ("he is Chinese", "the Chinese mind"). All my work has been devoted to show that there are [Chinese] coherences that we did not ignore in our experience, but to which we have devoted little attention.' (Jullien 2006, p. 312).

Two authors with very different profiles, confirm the analyses of Jullien and Braudel: the Chinese historian Wang Hui and the Sino-French economist André Chieng. Wang Hui confirms both Jullien's 'silent transformations' and Braudel's 'long time' (Wang 2003). André Chieng applies Jullien's analysis to a variety of contemporary situations in both business and public policy-making in China

24   2   Understanding China's Strategic Public Management

and in the West (Chieng 2006). It is interesting to note that in the 'Postface' to Chieng's book, Jullien considers that this book constitutes for him the empirical verification of his analysis of traditional Chinese strategy. He is particularly pleased that Chieng has used two of his major concepts: 'the situation potential' and 'the silent transformations'.

Finally, the analysis of the interactions of actors in the international domain necessitates the recourse to a clear theory of power, for which I have developed a framework for analysis starting from the seminal work of Max Weber and criticizing the concepts of 'soft power' and 'smart power' put forward by Joseph Nye (Urio 2018, Chap. 2), and relying on the framework defined by Hu Angang for the comparison between Chinese and American Comprehensive National Power (Hu Angang and Men Honghua 2004). This framework will be used in Chap. 6 below, that deals with the foreign policies of the US and China.

2.2   Market and Capitalism: Two Different Stories?

Among the many books published during the recent decades on capitalism, its origins and main features, the works of Fernand Braudel remain for me the most interesting and stimulating analysis. He has convincingly shown that there have been several stages in the historical process through which modern capitalism has emerged and, more disturbing, for Braudel, capitalism is not a form of market economy, but the upper layer of the hierarchical structure of human activities linked to production and consumption, that does not possess two of the major characteristics of a market: transparency and competition (Braudel 1969, 1979a, b; Wallerstein 1974, 1980, 2004).

For Braudel there are three worlds that he does not treat as three ideal-types (in the Weberian sense) but as real phenomena that have emerged through history: first, material life (where markets do not exist, yet); second, markets; and finally, capitalism. Moreover, the first world tends to persist after the appearance and the development of market economy and capitalism, and market economy tends to persist after the development of capitalism. Furthermore, these three worlds are organized within a hierarchy where, at the end of the process, capitalism becomes the upper and dominating layer. In fact, Braudel shows through his historical analysis that elements of market economy were already present at the time where material life was by far the most frequent way of organizing production and consumption (Braudel 1979a; Bergère 1986, 2007).[5] Similarly, elements of capitalism were already present

---

[5]Let us note that for Braudel 'material life' is sometimes defined as a 'no economy', sometimes as a 'very elementary economy', for example in the introductory remarks to the second volume of *Civilisation matérielle, économie et Capitalisme* (1979a, vol. 2, p. 7). For me what is important is that Braudel shows that, since the twelfth century, markets have emerged out of the "material life" well before capitalism (p. 15). Moreover, Braudel's shows that markets were already present in Africa, India, China, and in Islamic countries. For the emergence of market in China see especially pages 116, 120–125, 139–140, 146, and 255–256; on the emergence of capitalism pp. 268–287 for

2.2 Market and Capitalism: Two Different Stories?

when material life was in the process of being dominated, but not totally replaced by market economy; only during the process of the industrial revolution capitalism becomes the dominant layer, even if elements of material life and market economy persist. Braudel is persuaded that his findings show an opposition between a 'normal economic activity' on one hand and a 'sophisticated, superior economy' on the other. Moreover, economic agents, actions, and mindsets are not the same within the three layers, and, even more interesting, the laws of market economy, especially free competition as described by classical economics, are more rarely operating within the upper layer, which is one where calculations and speculation abound. Here there is a 'zone of shadow', and of insiders' activities; and this is what Braudel considers to be the root of the phenomena that can be put under the word of capitalism which is not the real, the true market economy, but so often its clear contradiction (Braudel 1979a vol. 2, pp. 8–9, 542–546). So, for Braudel what characterizes capitalism is the lack of transparency and of competition. How far we are here from the dominant discourse of liberals and neo-liberals in universities, mainstream media and political debates!

Let me end this short overview of Braudel's approach to market economy and capitalism by quoting his conclusion in his own words: "…capitalism has always been monopolistic, and merchandise and capital have always circulated simultaneously, for capital and credit have always been the surest way of capturing and controlling a foreign market. Long before the twentieth century the exportation of capital was a fact of daily life, for Florence as early as the thirteenth century (…) Need I observe that all methods, dealings, and tricks ["ruses" in the French edition, p. 118] of the financial world were not born in 1900 or in 1914? Capitalism was familiar with them all, and, yesterday as today, its uniqueness and its strength lie in its ability to move from one trick to another, from one way of doing things to another, to change its plans ten times as the economic conjunctures dictate—, and as a result, to remain relatively faithful, consistent with itself." (Braudel 1979b, pp. 113–114).

Even if we cannot interpret this assertion in the sense that capitalism is always totally monopolistic and that capitalist economic agents always behave in the absence of competition and transparency, it is evident that today transparency is limited, and competition concerns at best a small number of competitors, at worst totally absent either because competitors conclude cartel agreements or because only one economic agent dominates the sector. The functioning of the capitalist economy tends to exclude transparency and competition in the search of increasing market shares and profits to the point that, in Braudel's analysis, markets do not exist anymore in many important sectors.

But what is the interest of Braudel's analysis for understanding the nature of China's economy? According to Braudel, only when one of the three economic layers acquires a dominant role can we use its name to qualify the whole economic system: material economy before the advent of market economy, market economy before the advent of capitalism, capitalism when the upper layer succeeds in dominating the

---

the use of 'capital, capitalist, and capitalism'; and for the emergence of capitalism in China more especially pages 354–356, 708–723.

two subordinate layers. The difficulty arises when we have to decide at what point in time the characteristics of one layer have become so widespread and important that it has become the dominating layer. Many observers of China's economic development consider that the introduction of what I have called 'market mechanisms' is equivalent to the introduction of market economy. Moreover, as for them market economy is equivalent to capitalism, they come to the conclusion that China's economy has become capitalist, even if they are compelled to qualify this statement by using the expression of 'state-capitalism'. It seems to me that this conclusion is a bit too rash and indeed quite superficial. Here another passage of Braudel's *Civilization and Capitalism* is very useful: the partial character of market economy may be due to the importance of material life, or to the state that can take for its own use part of the production, or even more to the role of money that can artificially intervene in price formation, in thousands of different ways; market economy can therefore be limited from below by material life, as well as from above by capitalism (i.e. money) and/or by state intervention (Braudel 1979a, vol. 2, p. 262).[6] Following Braudel, we may say, that market (or at least market mechanisms) have been imposed in China from above (i.e. by the Party) whereas in the West capitalism, (and its more recent form under the neoliberal ideology) has been imposed also from above, but from the economic actors managing the use of capital in both economy and polity. This seems to be also the interpretation of Joseph E. Stiglitz.[7] When I evaluated the consequences of NPM on economy and society in China and in the West, I labelled the consequences on economy as 'a view from above', and the consequences on society as 'a view from below', thus following Braudel's approach as in the West NPM has been imposed 'from above' by neoliberals' capitalism, and in China by the Party-State with the result of determining 'below' a number of societal changes (Urio 2012, p. 159 ss).

Indeed, following Braudel's approach, it would be only partially correct to talk about the 'Chinese market economy'. It is true that China has introduced some market characteristics (i.e. competition and transparency) in parts of its economy. Nevertheless, market economy covers only part of China's economic system. Indeed, it is also true that markets do not exist in other parts of China's economy, as they are in fact the ownership, or are under the monopolistic control, of the Party-State. Moreover, it is also true that in some parts of China's economy some new capitalists are quite active and control to a certain extent the price formation by using monopolistic or quasi-monopolistic strategies (Dickson 2003, 2008). As mentioned before, some Western authors use this situation to qualify the Chinese economy as a "state-capitalism". This is not my opinion as I will explain hereafter.

Using 'market economy' to qualify the Chinese economy would run the risk of giving the impression of considering that China's economy is in fact already sim-

---

[6]The exact sentence in French: 'Le caractère partiel de l'économie de marché peut tenir, en effet, soit à l'importance du secteur d'autosuffisance, soit à l'autorité de l'état qui soustrait une partie de la production à la circulation marchande, soit tout autant, ou plus encore, au simple poids de l'argent qui peut, de mille façons, intervenir artificiellement dans la formation des prix.', *Civilisation et Capitalisme*, op. cit., p. 262.

[7]Joseph Stiglitz uses 'market mechanisms' when referring to the reform introduced in East Asian countries, including China, Stiglitz (2010), p. 245.

2.2 Market and Capitalism: Two Different Stories?

ilar to the Western one, or that it is at least moving in that direction. Indeed, it is the enlightening descriptions and analysis presented by Braudel that have suggested to me not to use 'market economy' when referring to the abandonment of planned economy by China and the concomitant opening up of economic activities to private entrepreneurships and capital (both domestic and foreign), but to design these innovations as the introduction of 'market mechanisms' instead of the adoption of 'market economy'. By this, I mean that the form of economic organization that has emerged in China after 1978 is by no means neither a market economy or a capitalist economy, but a socialist market economy with its own peculiar features, that the Chinese call 'Chinese characteristics.'

Many features of the new China system point in this direction. First, the freedom of the new Chinese capitalists mentioned above is limited by the Party-State: nothing can be done in the economic sphere without the explicit or implicit approval by the Party-State. One has also to remember that contrary to what happened in the former Soviet bloc, economic reforms introducing market mechanisms have been decided, implemented, developed and controlled by the Communist Party-state for a period of more than 40 years with the success we know. And there is evidence that the majority of Chinese capitalists have no reasons for opposing the Party, as it seems that the policies of the Party-State are the conditions of their economic and social success (Chen and Dickson 2008). Second, land is still collective property in China and this constitutes a powerful instrument in the hands of the Party-state for orienting and controlling the economic and social development. Third, as I shall further develop in Chaps. 3 and 4 and in the conclusion, the Party-State has re-oriented its public policies away from a strategy of 'economic development first' towards a strategy of 'putting people first', with a clear departure from the neo-liberal policies implemented during the 1990s in strategic domains such as health and education, alongside the replacement of the social functions of the state-owned enterprises of the Mao era with a modern safety net (Urio 2010a, pp. 119–155). Fourth, the banking system is still under the political control of the Party-state, in spite of several measures taken for improving its economic efficiency that have given to Western observers the impression that it was progressively reformed in order to make it compatible with capitalist criteria. Commenting China's reaction to the 2008–2010 crisis, Barry Naughton, writing for the influential *China Leadership Monitor* (of the influential think tank, the Hoover Institution, Stanford University) considers that: 'there are [in China] strong political forces that benefit from government patronage and extension of government power, and those interest groups do not show the slightest sign of being in retreat. (…) This continued failure to tackle some hard issues, trim back the power and resources controlled by the state (…) has made most economists increasingly frustrated. (…) it is very difficult to get change out of a political system that seems to be succeeding so brilliantly on its own terms.' Furthermore, commenting upon Premier Wen Jabao's report to the Chinese parliament, Naughton confirms his statement: 'This is probably the most unambiguous movement to reemphasize centralisation and administrative instruments to govern the economy since the term 'socialist market economy' was incorporated into the official Chinese rhetoric in September 1992.' (Naughton 2009, p. 7, also 2010).

28   2 Understanding China's Strategic Public Management

This predominance of the Party-State is a very clear indicator that the Chinese economy is by no means a capitalist economy. It is therefore in the presence of elements of material life (i.e. of large sectors of informal economy), of some important, but not dominating, capitalist economic agents, that market mechanisms have been introduced by a dominating Party-State that occupies a large sector of the economy and orients and controls the development of China's economic activities. There are clearly several differences from what happens in the West, where economic agents of capitalism dictate in fact the essential items of the political agenda and the essential content of public policies, as the way the West has managed the 2008 crisis has very well demonstrated.

The features of the present day Chinese economic and political system mentioned above are clear indicators of the progressive implementation of a 'socialist market economy', where the economic side stands for the development of market mechanisms under the control of the Party-State (and not of a neo-liberal elite), and the socialist side is represented by the policies that 'put people first'. Of course, this does not mean that there are no problems in the management and control of the interface between material life (i.e. informal economy), market mechanisms, and capitalist elements of the Chinese economic system (Urio 2010a, Chaps. 2 and 3). But so far, the capitalist elements are not yet sufficiently widespread and important enough for qualifying China's economic system as a capitalist economy, whatever the qualifying adjective. In conclusion, for the time being, the difference between China and the West is therefore one of nature and the two systems cannot be considered as simple variations within the type of 'capitalist economy'.[8] This does not mean either that the Chinese system may not evolve towards a capitalist economy in the future. But for the time being many indicators point to the opposite direction. Nevertheless, there are several new developments in China economy, that may lead either to a collapse of the Party (and very likely to the adoption of a more open political system) or towards a conversion of the Party to economic liberalism. In this case the Party will keep the control of the polity (as kept by the Western parties, in spite of the development of the power of capital) but will give more space to the economy and more freedom to the owners of capital in ways not basically different from what happens in the West. This will be the end of the 'socialist market economy with Chinese characteristics' and the birth of the 'capitalist market economy with Chinese characteristics' I will come back to this important question in the conclusion of this book. Needless to say, these policy options have given rise to a very intense debate among Chinese intellectuals (Urio 2012, pp. 35–47).

It is in this context that Cui, who refers to the works of Nobel Prize-winner J.E. Meade, envisages a strategy that will build 'wide public support by virtue of its efficiency as well as justice'; it 'aims to combine the best features of traditional capitalism and traditional socialism and has two main components: the labour-capital partnership and the social dividend.' (Cui 1997).[9] In short, labour and capital should

---

[8]For analyses of typologies of capitalism see Amable (2005), Hall (2001), Esping-Andersen (1990).

[9]This partnership is justified as follows: "because shareholders have only limited liability, they do not bear the full cost of a firm's actions and therefore cannot claim to be full risk-bearers. Moreover,

2.2 Market and Capitalism: Two Different Stories?

share, on an equal basis, the benefits and risks involved in the management of a business: investors will hold Capital shares, the workers Labour shares; the two parties will elect an equal number of members of the boards of directors, and these will elect a chairman with the power to cast a tie-breaking vote.

It is interesting to note that Cui has benefited from an opportunity to test his ideas in Chongqing. In fact, in 2007 Chongqing was designed by the Chinese government as an experimental zone for integrating rural and urban development. The local government has taken this opportunity to experimenting a whole range of policies that combine private and public investments with the aim to create a harmonious development that should benefit to all groups of citizens, especially the peasants and other groups that have not benefited, and in fact that have suffered from economic development so far.[10] Since the autumn of 2010 Cui has been detached from Tsinghua University to the Chongqing municipality as a special assistant to the director of the commission in charge of managing public assets. This experience has allowed him to conclude that the 'Chongqing experience shows that public ownership of assets and private entrepreneurship are not necessarily contradictory and that they are not substitutes for each other.' (Frenkiel 2011). This experiment apparently came to an end in 2012 following the destitution of the Chongqing Party Secretary, Bo Xilai, who was later sentenced to life-imprisonment on charges of corruption. Bo has also been accused of re-instituting some of the practices of the Cultural Revolution, as he widely encouraged the singing of Maoist patriotic songs. This accusation is hardly believable to those who know about the policies implemented in Chongqing during Bo Xilai's presidency. Apart from fighting against widespread crime (although with illegal measures), the building of new lodgings for migrant workers and poor urban citizens, the considerable improvement of the environment that transformed Chongqing from a dull and dirty town into a green city, and especially the development of the industrial basis thanks to the attraction of numerous foreign companies, all are contrary to the closed-door policy of the Mao era. Also, because the policies implemented by Bo Xilai have been further implemented in Chongqing after Bo's destitution, his disgrace is more likely due to a struggle inside the Chinese leadership in view of the changes that were to be made at the November 2012 Party Congress. If there is a dimension of Bo Xilai policy that should have worried his colleagues (and competitors) this would more likely be the open policy to private capital within the Chongqing economy that goes contrary to the will of the Party to strictly con-

---

while outside shareholders can diversify their stock and reduce risk through a portfolio of shares in different companies, one worker cannot work for several companies at the same time. (…) Hence (…) workers should be partners with outside shareholders in sharing control rights and cash flow rights over corporate assets." Finally, each citizen will receive a tax-free social dividend according to age and family status, meant to cover basic needs, especially in case of illness and unemployment.

[10]This has been recognized by the Chinese leadership. See for example Vice-premier Li Keqiang, reported by Reuter: '7oo million farmers couldn't benefit from the country's rapid growth and prosperity (…) This is about the accelerating change of the economy's development model—its development should be fast, but stable in the long run and allow all Chinese to participate in the fruits of reform (…) Restructuring income distribution, improving public service and establishing a social security system will help develop the untapped purchasing potential of more than one million Chinese.' Quoted by *Caijing,* 5 January 2011.

trol the economic development. Here again the real nature of China economy is at stake: market, socialism or capitalism, or a mixture of them all with some 'Chinese characteristics'?

2.3 Chinese Traditional Conception of Strategy

What should be the attitude of the skilful strategist? Let us first consider the conclusion arrived at by Jullien at the end of his comparison between the Western and the traditional Chinese way: the Chinese way looks like 'an unmodelled model of becoming' (Jullien 2011, p. 70; Urio 2012, pp. 209–210; Bell 2015, p. 180). In other words, the traditional Chinese strategy is not based upon the prior definition of a model that is subsequently used to orient action (as in the West) but on the analysis of the situation aimed at discovering the 'situation potential', i.e. the favourable and unfavourable elements that may have an impact upon the realization of the strategist's objectives. Starting from this analysis, the Chinese strategist adopts a mix of inaction and action. On the one hand, he does not act when the analysis of the situation shows that he does not have the means to intervene with success, and therefore he waits until the 'silent transformations' inevitably change ('transform') the situation, eventually in a way favourable to the realization of his objectives. But on the other hand, he acts when the situation shows that he has the possibility to intervene with success upon some elements so that, in the long run (Braudel's 'long time') the situation becomes overall favourable to the realization of his objectives. Thus, Jullien's understanding of the Chinese strategy contradicts the Western dominant opinion about the propensity of Chinese strategists toward inaction and slowness and to the idea of 'an eternal China' incapable of change, innovation and progress. On the contrary, the Chinese strategist acts very quickly when the situation is favourable, and when it is not he waits for the 'silent transformation' to materialize and, in the meantime, he acts upon the elements of the environment when he has a chance to change them to his advantage. I will develop this approach in Sect. 6.2 dealing with China's strategy to reclaim world power status.

Finally, the best Chinese strategist is the one who wins the war without fighting, its opponent being inevitably led to lose when the 'potential of the situation' has become helplessly negative for him, following the 'silent transformation' and the changes introduced by the actions of the Chinese strategist. This is very likely what is being revealed today by the new, partially isolationist, foreign policy by President Trump (see Sect. 6.1.6).

This is not to say that today China still uses its traditional ways of organizing strategy in all domains. Indeed, particularly in the natural sciences, China is using today the approach it learned from Western natural science, based upon Galileo's intuition that the universe is written in a model, based upon mathematical formulae. Today Chinese natural scientists have little to learn from their Western colleagues so far as methodology is concerned and have achieved remarkable results. Nevertheless, in the domain of public policy-making there is sufficient evidence that China is still

2.3 Chinese Traditional Conception of Strategy

today following the traditional way of organizing its strategy as presented by François Jullien. In fact, Jullien considers that today China walks on its two legs: the Chinese and the Western, and this would be its advantage, especially in international relations.

In his book André Chieng develops and confirms empirically some other dimensions of Jullien's analysis. More particularly, he insists on the importance of preparation instead of action, and on the capacity to adapt to the situation, without projecting a model on reality with the purpose (as we do in the West) to act by making reality correspond to the model. For Chieng, quoting François Jullien, the essence of strategy is on the one hand to gradually trap the competitor into a fixed position upon which the strategist can act, and on the other hand to constantly change its position in order to make its own strategy incomprehensible for the competitor (Chieng 2006, p. 210; Jullien 1995, Chap. 1).[11]

Moreover, as well as Jullien, Chieng insists on the importance of managing time, understood not in the Western sense of chance, or destiny, but as 'time-opportunity'. It is by leaving the course of 'things'—the occurrence of events—to develop, without interfering, that one can be most efficient, more precisely, by combining 'the acting' upon the elements one can change to its advantage, and 'the non-acting' when one has not a reasonable possibility to change the elements of the situation to one's advantage. 'In order to act efficiently, one must wait for the favorable occasion, the favorable moment; and it is here that it is possible and necessary to act. But this does not mean that the strategist must wait passively for the opportunity to occur. On the contrary, by manipulating reality 'upstream of the silent transformations', the Chinese strategist induces the opportunity, by a variety of covert actions. And this is the most efficient strategy. This is clearly linked to the concept of manipulation, in the sense of transforming the environment with the purpose of facilitating the advent of the favourable and intended outcome. The Chinese strategist does not wait for the 'chance' (in the Western sense) to appear; it induces it by working as far as possible 'upstream' (Chieng 2006, pp. 181–182, 196, 210, 214, 218–223, 225).

Contemporary China's strategy has been very strongly criticized by some western authors, for example by Michael Pillsbury, a defence policy adviser, former American government official (Pillsbury 2015).[12] Pillsbury, who is fluent in Chinese and

---

[11] Chieng was born in Marseille to Chinese parents. His family gave him a Chinese education and he attended the French school system up to the top, at the prestigious Ecole Polytechnique, the Ecole Nationale de la Statistique et de l'Adminstration economique and the Institut de Science Politique. He specialized in economics and taught the subject in China (1978–1980). On his return to France, he became director general of one of the oldest French commercial com-panies trading with China, Brambilla-AEC, and became its president in 1988. He is vice-president of the Comité France-Chine and Conseiller du Commerce Extérieur de la France en Chine.

[12] Michael Pillsbury is the director of the Center on Chinese Strategy at the Hudson Institute, is a former analyst at the RAND Corporation and is a member of the Council on Foreign Relations and the International Institute for Strategic Studies. During the Reagan administration, Pillsbury (...) was Assistant Under-Secretary of Defense for Policy Planning and responsible for implementation of the covert aid programme known as the Reagan Doctrine. In 1975–1976, while an analyst at the RAND Corporation, Pillsbury published articles on *Foreign Policy* and *International Security* recommending that the US establish intelligence and military ties with China. The proposal, publicly commended by Ronald Reagan, Henry Kissinger and James Schlesinger, later became US policy

knows the classical Chinese books on strategy as well as some of the major the works of François Jullien, starts by criticizing the Chinese language by stressing its essential ambiguity: 'There is no alphabet (…) The word for size combines the character for *large* with the character of *small*. (…) Adding to this complexity are the tones and pitches that delineate words. The effect of tones is to give a single word four possible meanings. (…) The language's very complexity is like a secret code. (…) What we [Americans] all must do better is to look not just at speeches [of Chinese leaders] but also at the context of those speeches, and we need to look for larger hidden meanings. For well over a half century, Americans have failed to do this. (…) We believed that America can aid fragile China whose leaders thought like us, would help China become a democratic and peaceful power without ambitions of regional or even global dominance. We underestimated the influence of China's hawks. (…) China has failed to meet nearly all of our rosy expectations' (Pillsbury 2015, pp. 5–7). Clearly, for Pillsbury, the US helped China with the hope that she would become like them. However, the Chinese leadership has 'misled and manipulated American policy makers to obtain intelligence and military, technological, and economic assistance. (…) The goal is to avenge or 'wipe clean' (*xi xue)* past foreign humiliations. Then China will set up a world order that will be fair to China, a world without American global supremacy, and revise the U.S.-dominated economic and political world order founded at Bretton Woods and San Francisco at the end of World War II. The [Chinese] hawks assess that China can only succeed in this project through deception, or at least by denial of any frightening plans.' (Pillsbury 2015, p. 12). So, it is clear for Pillsbury that China's deceptive and secret policies constitute a threat to the global supremacy of the United States. Nevertheless, he admits (evidently with some regrets and fears) that Chinese leaders are beginning to talk about the goal of their strategy 'more openly, perhaps because they realize it may already be too late for America to keep pace.' A clear acknowledgment of the efficacy of China's strategy, as explained by François Jullien and André Chieng (Pillsbury 2015, p. 16).

Pillsbury's analysis may be correct. It is true that, compared to China, US strategy is more open. But it forgets that this is possible given the extraordinary US advantage on almost every count, especially the military and the cultural resources, and for a long time also economic resources. Moreover, some of the US policies are not as open as one may think. The official number of military bases (around an astonishing total of about 650) very likely hides another 250 of which the public has no idea (Vine 2015). Also, the budget of the Pentagon is not an example of transparency and clarity, and the US has conducted several military or quasi-military covert operations all over the world. Finally, several operations aimed at inducing 'regime change' to establish governments more favourable to American interests, have been conducted

---

during the Carter and Reagan administrations. Pillsbury served on the staff of four US Senate Committees from 1978 to 1984 and 1986 to 1991. (…) He also assisted in drafting the legislation to create the National Endowment for Democracy and the annual requirement for a Department of Defense report on Chinese military power. In 1992, under President George H.W. Bush, Pillsbury was Special Assistant for Asian Affairs in the Office of the Secretary of Defense (…), https://en.wikipedia.org/wiki/Michael_Pillsbury (accessed 4 June 2016).

under the pretext of establishing democracy, human rights and free market economy, or more precisely capitalism.

2.4 China Political Culture: Stability and Change

I explained elsewhere the interest that there is in using the approach of political culture in order to understand the structuring of power in Western countries (Urio 1984, Chap. 4, pp. 139–216). But the interest in applying this approach to contemporary China is made even more obvious by the controversy which has long animated the discussions amongst Western sinologists as to the specificity of the Chinese culture compared to the Western culture (Billeter 2006; Jullien 1989, 1996, 2004).Taking culture as one of the keys for understanding China is not to say that culture can explain everything, but that it would be a mistake to leave aside this source of information and of understanding. I simply pose the hypothesis that culture may have a significant impact on individual and collective behaviours. As François Jullien has very well put it: we Westerners still today persist in believing that the West, which has dominated the world for such a long time, remains the reference for the way of thinking and doing. Moreover, we claim that we possess universal values that have become 'the law of reason'. Therefore, even when we claim that we have escaped this cultural ethnocentric posture, we still are submitted to it, without even being aware (Jullien 2006, p. 302, 2015, pp. 8–10). This has two consequences: first, we have difficulties in opening our mind to other coherences outside those with which we are familiar, those that are for us self-evident. Second, we have difficulties in articulating China's cultural dimension with its other dimensions, i.e. economy, polity and society, and this is for us an important point if we want to understand China's strategy for managing its development strategy and the strategy to reclaim world power status (Jullien 2006, pp. 202–206).

Moreover, it would be useless to seek to understand contemporary China only on the basis of what exists today. Just like it is necessary to go back to European antiquity (namely to Greek-Roman antiquity) to understand Western civilization and the forms of government which she adopted throughout her history, it is quite as essential to retrace in the history of China the origins of its current political culture, with an aim of discovering what remains today of the past, beside what has emerged these last years (Urio 2010a, Sect. 2.1: 'Chinese political culture: past and present).

Political culture can be defined as the whole set of the attitudes, beliefs and fundamental norms of behavior, which gives an order and a significance to the political process, and which orient the behaviour in the political system.[13] Moreover, following the work of Zhang Weiwei I use political culture as a concept similar to the concept of ideology that may have an impact on socio-economic changes (Zhang 1996, p. 5). But in return, socio-economic changes have also brought changes of mind

---

[13]The major references are: Pye (1968), p. 218, Almond and Verba (1963), Chap. 1, Almond and Powell (1966), Chaps. 1 and 2, and Pye (1968), pp. 218–224.

sets and ideologies. The relation between ideology and socio-economic changes is not a one-way but a two-way one. Moreover, political culture (or ideology) is also closely related to power, the leaders seeking to legitimize through ideological discourse the power they possess, and the policies they implement. Of course, as we shall see in Chaps. 3 and 4, it is not enough to 'preach', it is also necessary to provide people with what they need. In the case of Deng: economic development and access to goods and services. If the ideological discourse legitimates the existing power structure that places the CPC and its leaders at the apex of society, polity, and economy by promising to deliver what people need, it is plausible that ideology will accomplish its legitimating function. But one day or the other power will have to demonstrate that what it has promised has actually been delivered. Moreover, at the moment of taking stock, one will also have to take into consideration the unwanted consequences that often appear along with the intended results of the implemented policies.

Moreover, the distribution of political culture is not necessarily uniform in a given society. On the contrary, there can be inside a society social sub-groups each one bearing a specific political subculture (Almond and Powel 1966, p. 23). And, I add, there are historical cases, when the emergence of a new class or social group develops a political culture different from that of the traditional elites. The questions which one can then ask regarding contemporary China are primarily the following ones: first of all, through what intellectual means (in addition to material resources) has the new elite which seized power in 1949 succeeded in imposing its own values. Second, what is the difference between the political culture of this new elite and the political culture of the Imperial Era. Third, how does the political culture of the new economic elite that emerged at the time of reforms after 1978 fit into the ideology of the Party-State. Here, there are the problems of the harmonization of old and new values.

If one further develops the last questions, one can pose a few hypotheses. First, one can ask whether the new economic elite will develop a different political culture that may even be in opposition to that of the Party-State. Second, if this is the case, will the Party have to change its fundamental values in order to be in harmony with the values of the new economic elite, and thus being able to provide Chinese people with what they need and want? Third, it is the change of values of the Party-State's elite, converted to the benefits of capitalism in the process of managing the economic development, that allows the rise of the new economic elite, with whom it can make a kind of 'gentlemen's agreement'?[14] In both cases, there would be no fundamental opposition between these two elites, and one could even advance the hypothesis that China may evolve towards the same type of relationships which exist in Western countries between a liberal economic elite and democratic political parties, located on a left-right axis, each one of them being nevertheless converted to the benefits of capitalism.

---

[14]This last assumption corresponds to the attempt of Jiang Zemin to invite businessmen to join the Communist Party.

2.4 China Political Culture: Stability and Change

History shows that there will have to be a succession of phases: a political culture dominates at one historical moment and for a certain time, then declines gradually under the thrust of new values, but without losing its force completely, succeeding in imposing itself in certain cases, perhaps even integrating some of its features into the new system of values and eventually constituting a new hybrid culture; during a next phase the new values can possibly relegate the traditional ones to an unimportant marginal role.[15] Unfortunately, it is this that numerous Western sinologists propose in order to interpret the development of Chinese society after the collapse of the Empire: it was inevitable that China would undergo a radical and comprehensive change of the means and modes of transmissions of the political culture, as well as its contents. This opinion is generally founded by taking into consideration the changes introduced since 1978 into the economic system: from the moment China chose a market economy and opened its economy to the rest of the world, it would inevitably transform itself into a liberal democracy, based on the Rule of Law, the separation of powers, political competition, and thus a form of multi-party system and free elections; otherwise it would inevitably collapse (Chang 2001; Sorman 2008). If one cannot obviously exclude, at least in the long run, the realization of this hypothesis, it is as interesting to formulate the opposite hypothesis: certain features of the Imperial power and the political culture that has been its ideological support (set up and developed during two millennia), would persist still today and would tend to persist in the future, at least in the short and medium run; and the new political culture, integrating traditional and new values, could very well contribute to the stability of the regime.[16] Here it will be necessary to evaluate if China has succeeded in harmonizing some of the old Chinese values with new values imported from the West.

Let us see now what are the new cultural elements introduced by Deng Xiaoping, Jiang Zemin, Hu Jintao and Xi Jinping, and to what extent these novelties constitute a departure from traditional Chinese ideology, both Imperial and Marxists-Leninist, without leaving aside the hypothesis of a revival of certain traits of the Confucian tradition. For the moment it suffices to show that the structure and the formal organization of state power of the People's Republic of China are the first indicators of this persistence.

A first finding is evident: the traditional values of unity, harmony and stability are still at the core of the Chinese political culture after 1949 in spite of (or maybe because of) the adoption of Marxism-Leninism, although Mao has adapted this ideology to the Chinese situation. Although there are considerable differences between the traditional Imperial ideology and Marxism-Leninism, the implementation of the political ideals of the latter necessitates a centralized and unified political direction under the leadership of the Party. This is true first for the management of the revolution (1921–1949), and second for the implementation of the revolutionary ideals

---

[15]For an interpretation of a historical fundamental change that is generally qualified as 'the industrial revolution' as a process of continuous changes that lasted for several decades see Landes (1993).

[16]The major references are: Peerenboom (2002, 2006, 2007), Bell (1996, 2006, 2008), Zufferey (2008), Bell and Chaibong Hahm (2003).

after the victory over the Kuomintang (1 October 1949), in spite of the fact that the ideals based upon Marxism-Leninism constitute a radical change from the Imperial past.

2.4.1 Deng Xiaoping: Changes and Continuity of Traditional Political Culture

Deng Xiaoping is considered as the Chinese leader who led the country towards and on the road of reforms, by introducing several novelties into the PRC ideology, market mechanisms being the most important as it meant a departure from the implementation of a fully planned economy. Deng Xiaoping has further developed Mao's ideas by introducing the Four Cardinal Principles and the Four Modernizations, that in fact complete the Marxist-Leninist elements of the Party's ideology.[17] As these new elements will be confirmed by Deng's successors, they will acquire, in my opinion, the statute of fundamental elements of 'the traditional PRC ideology'. Moreover, the structure and formal organization of state power of the PRC, as well as the use of democratic centralism for managing the decision-making process within the CPC, are clear indications of the persistence of traditional cultural traits going back to the Imperial era.

Deng still adheres to some of the traditional elements of Chinese political culture, namely the principles of unity. Indeed, his definition of the Four Cardinal principles stresses the fundamental role of Marxism-Leninism and Mao thought as the ideological guidance of the PRC and the dominant role of the Communist Party as the leading organization capable to implement socialism in China. I will come back in more detail to Deng's role in forging both ideology and China's policies in Chap. 3.

---

[17]The Four Modernizations concern agriculture, industry, science and technology, and defence. I remind that the Four Cardinal Principles are: to keep to the socialist road and to uphold the people's democratic dictatorship, the leadership by the Communist Party, Marxism-Leninism and Mao Zedong Thought. 'The Four Modernizations were introduced as early as January 1963: at the Conference on Scientific and Technological Work held in Shanghai that month, Zhou Enlai called for professionals in the sciences to realize 'the Four Modernizations.' In February 1963, at the National Conference on Agricultural Science and Technology Work, Nie Rongzhen specifically referred to the Four Modernizations as comprising agriculture, industry, national defence, and science and technology. (…). In 1975, in one of his last public acts, Zhou Enlai made another pitch for the Four Modernizations at the 4th National People's Congress.' From Wikipedia, https://en.wikipedia.org/wiki/Four_Modernizations, accessed 20 September 2018.

2.4.2 Interdependence Between Ideological and Practical Innovations of Deng's Strategy

Let me simply summarize Deng's strategy. First, a fundamental remark: the ultimate goal of Deng's strategy is not different from that of the Empire at the end of the XIX century, that of Sun Yat Sen, of the Nationalists, or of Mao: to restore China as a world power and improve the standard of living of the Chinese population, the two objectives being strictly interdependent. Only the means differ. Bearing this in mind, I propose to subdivide Deng's strategy into two complementary components, i.e. the ideology and the economy-military levels. At the ideological level Deng reaffirms four of the main features of the Party's ideology by defining the four Cardinal Principles, i.e. to keep to the socialist road, to uphold the people's democratic dictatorship, to maintain the leadership by the Communist Party, Marxism-Leninism and Mao Zedong Thought. At the economic-military level, as mentioned above, Deng defines the target of China's modernization by identifying four domains necessary for restoring China's strength both internally and internationally, i.e. Agriculture, Industry, Science and Technology, and National Defence.

At the operational level the main goal is to improve economic performance and the standard of living of the Chinese people. The means for realizing this goal is the introduction of market mechanisms and opening up to global economy. The behaviours linking the strategic and the operational levels in the day-to-day implementation of this vast policy objective can be defined as follows: (1) maintain the leadership of the Party and restore (re-establish) its legitimacy; (2) introduce reforms on an experimental basis; (3) reform gradually (not like Russia); (4) privatize gradually and partially, by keeping the strategic economic sectors in the hands of the State, and reinforcing the macro-economic policies of the State; (5) maintain economic, social and political stability; (6) in case of difficulties, slow down or stop, then re-start.

Moreover, Deng's strategy is focused on two inter-related goals: on the one hand, the improvement of economic performances of China which will satisfy the Chinese population by putting at its disposal goods and services, and on the other hand the consolidation of the power of the CPC and of the personal power of Deng within the Party. These two related goals were a rational response to the damages of the Cultural Revolution both for the Party and the Chinese population. Posing the question of the 'real' or main purpose of Deng's policies (personal power, Party power, or the wealth of the people) is irrelevant in this context. What is at stake is the justification of the reforms and, as we will see in the next chapters, the introduction of market mechanisms (and thus competition amongst people and enterprises), as well as the actual results of the reforms in terms of benefits or damages to the Chinese people.

Reforms were not possible without changing at least part of the ideology of the Mao era. An ideological change was thus a condition necessary for orienting political, economic and societal change, i.e. the improvement of the standard of living of Chinese population, thanks to the introduction of market mechanisms and the consequent partial abandonment of the planned economy. If the ideological discourse legitimates the existing power structure that places the CPC and its leaders at the apex of society, polity, and economy by promising to deliver what people need, it is plausible that ideology will accomplish its legitimating function. But, as mentioned above, one day or the other power will have to demonstrate that what it has promised has actually been delivered.[18] Moreover, at the moment of taking stock, one will also have to take into consideration the unwanted consequences that often appear along with the intended results of the implemented policies (Chaps. 3 and 4). Let us examine Deng's strategy for realizing the ideological, political, economic and societal change that would satisfy the two above-mentioned objectives, i.e. economic development and legitimizing the restoration and the development of CPC power.

2.4.3 Deng's Strategy and Mao's Succession

In order to understand the importance of Deng Xiaoping as a leader, it is necessary to analyze Mao's succession. Mao had based his power more upon his own personality than upon the Communist Party as an institution, thus providing an outstanding historical example of one of Max Weber's types of legitimate power 'the charismatic power'. In fact, Mao's death in 1976 left a great vacuum in the Chinese power structure. It is clear that a delicate phase of transition was then opened, that could have sent China in different directions, none of which could have been void of negative consequences.

Weber's typology is very useful for understanding this moment of transition. Weber distinguishes three types of legitimate power: legal-rational power, resting on the belief in the legality of the adopted regulations, traditional power, resting on the belief in the holiness of traditions valid from time immemorial, and finally charismatic power resting on the submission to a person possessing a particular charisma (Weber 1978, pp. 215–216). For Weber, charismatic power is essentially exceptional, and thus it is brought to evolve irremediably: 'it traditionalizes or it rationalizes (i.e. legalizes itself)' (Weber 1978, p. 246). This evolution is particularly necessary when the charismatic leader disappears and succession difficulties arise.

Hua Guofeng, the immediate successor of Mao, was officially confirmed as chief of Party in July 1977 and introduced the famous slogan 'two whatevers': all that Mao decided must remain valid; none of the instructions of Mao must be violated (Schram 1984, p. 417). It is clear that Hua asserts a legitimacy of the traditional type. His leadership is legitimate because he is the successor of Mao, and its policies are legitimate because they are in line with Mao's policies. But Hua's economic programme soon proves to be unsuited to the Chinese situation; the second foundation of power, i.e. the delivery of goods and services the Chinese population needed to overcome the consequence of the Cultural Revolution, was not met. The socio-

---

[18]This is based upon the two Weberian foundations of power, i.e. the socio-psycho-sociological process of legitimation (be it traditional, legal-rational or charismatic) and the use of administrative and economic resources (Weber 1978).

2.4 China Political Culture: Stability and Change

economic conditions of the country made necessary a change of policy, and a rupture with the Cultural Revolution.

Although Hua Guofeng announces the end of the Cultural Revolution, thus marking a first break with Mao's era, he relies too heavily on the traditional legitimacy of Maoism, and this leads to a gradual crumbling of his power. Deng and his allies, who are more critical than Hu Guofeng of the policies pursued by Mao since 1958, launched an ideological attack against the slogan of the 'two whatevers'. In 1977 Deng declares that it was necessary to restore the traditions of the Party by 'seeking truth from facts' which was, according to him, the quintessence of the Maoist approach (Schram 1984, p. 419). Deng thus sought to assert his legitimacy in the same way as Hua: by appealing to the Maoist heritage, i.e. a legitimacy of the traditional type. Nevertheless, the reformists were not strong enough in 1977 to openly oppose Hua, without the risk of appearing to be against the Maoist heritage. Moreover, Deng has still to gain the support of the cadres of the Party, many of whom had remained faithful to Mao. In order to assess his power within the Party, Deng had to demonstrate being in line with Mao, and this continuity was against any kind of abrupt change. Nevertheless, the criterion of 'seeking truth from facts' is not simply an epistemological position; it is also an indicator of a break with the policy pursued by Mao. Such a departure from at least part of the Maoist legacy was necessary. Indeed, during the Cultural Revolution the Maoist ideology had lost a great part of its credibility within the Chinese population (Zhang 1996, p. 34). It is thus well and truly the legitimacy of the Party which is at stake here, and the reformists had very well understood that the Communist Party could not remain in power without a serious change of policy. Deng thus skillfully succeeded in presenting himself as Mao's successor, while defining the first steps of a radical policy change.

This new criterion of truth allows more flexibility, as it makes it possible to propose entirely innovative solutions to the difficulties as they arise, since one will not judge policies according to any dogma, but according to the results obtained. It is this same idea that one finds in the famous sentence: little matter that a cat is white or black, provided that it catches the mice. And this is in line with the traditional Chinese culture that prefers practical realizations to pure theoretical constructions (Zufferey 2008, pp. 22, 49–68, mentioned above). One can add that this change is not only a change in the process of legitimizing power, but also a change in behaviour. If we apply to this change Weber's typology about behaviours (which distinguishes emotional, traditional, value-rational ('wertrational') and instrumentally rational ('zweckrational') behaviours one can consider that with Deng's the way of making decisions passes from Hua's traditional behaviour (i.e. with actions 'dictated by practices, habits, and traditional beliefs'), to Deng's instrumentally rational behaviour (i.e. actions where 'the actor conceives the goal clearly, and implements the means in order to attain this goal', (Aron 1967, pp. 500–501). The goal set by the reformists, as I have already said, is conceived mainly in terms of economic performance (Zhang 1996, p. 24).

For realizing this objective, Deng understands that progress towards more democracy and the establishment of legality are the necessary conditions for economic development. This implies a democratization of political life within the Party and the state, enterprises, and society. More particularly, Deng is convinced that the

Party should leave more space to the initiative of the economic actors. For Deng, this was not possible in the past because Party leaders, especially Mao, enjoyed a too large personal power. Therefore, China must give up its traditional tendency towards authoritarian power, and opt for the 'Rule of Law', or at least for the 'Rule by Law', the latter being more in line with the task Deng attributed to the Party to be the guide on the road to reforms and economic development.[19] As has been stressed by Ronald Keith (Keith, p. 110) after the excesses of the Cultural Revolution, the law was seen as an institutional protection against the personal power of the leaders. This is the first important move towards the 'rule of law' and away from the 'rule of man'.

Obviously, the movement towards more democracy had its limits, and China could not become, from one day to the other, a democracy according to the Western model. However, the introduction of the concept of legality and Rule of Law (or the Rule by Law) can be interpreted as the beginning of an evolution towards a Weberian legal-rational state, in which the supremacy of rules over interpersonal relationships constitutes the core of this type of power. This shift from personal power to the Rule of Law, has led many Western scholars to consider, based upon the historical experience of the West, that the introduction of market mechanisms must inevitably be sustained by a more rational organization of all parts of society, especially by the rationalization of the state and of the behaviour of economic actors. According to Weber, the development of a rational economic system (be it a market economy or a planned economy) is based upon the capacity of economic actors to precisely calculate and foresee the results of their own actions as well as the behaviour of the other actors. As the state is also intervening in the economy, the behaviour of the state must also be taken into account, and must be foreseeable. The supremacy of law over interpersonal interactions is the condition for guaranteeing the predictability of an actor's behaviour, including the state. Therefore, predictability of economic actors' behaviour is the condition for the development of the economy when some kinds of market mechanisms are implemented. Nevertheless, it is not at all certain that China will adopt all the main features of the Western model as analyzed by Weber. We cannot exclude that China will eventually adopt either some 'functional equivalents' based upon some features of its traditional culture, or to implement at least some of the Western features. This could be done either by inventing new features or by using the characteristics of the traditional Chinese culture.

Moreover, Deng seeks to secure the support of the population by offering not only more freedom but also concrete results, namely the improvement of the standard of living, which corresponds to the Weberian conception of power, that must be supported by the two foundations of power: legitimacy assured by the rule of law and the provision of goods and services by using administrative and economic resources.

However, the movement towards democratization and the release of thought are not without limits. Deng is ready to accept democratization only if it does not put in danger the power of the Party. A strong tension appears for the first time during the

---

[19]It is interesting to note that this became the new title given to the old Planning commission set up in 1952 for the purpose of steering the planned economy. The new label is 'National Development and Reform Commission—NDRC, Reporting directly to the Prime Minister.

2.4 China Political Culture: Stability and Change

episode of 'the wall of democracy' in the autumn of 1978. Deng cannot accept this extreme challenge to the power of the Party, and he orders the closing of the wall, and the major activists are then arrested. He then poses the limits to the release of thought by defining the four Cardinal Principles, with which the reform policies must comply, i.e. to keep to the socialist road and the people's democratic dictatorship, the leadership by the Communist Party, and Marxism-Leninism and Mao Zedong Thought (Zhang 1996, p. 30).

One can see that the ideological discourse of Deng is somewhat changing direction: it is not only a question of marking a break with the Maoist era, of releasing the energies necessary to economic development, of democratizing the economic and political life of China, but above all of affirming that the power of the Party cannot be called into question. The Party appears as the only possible and plausible guarantor of the reform process. The reformers justify their authoritarian approach to power by the need for ensuring the stability of the country. Deng affirms that 'without stability and unity, we do not have anything, and things like democracy and economic growth are out of the question.' (quoted by Schram 1984, p. 424). Stability, including the continuous exercise of power by the Party, is considered as the necessary condition for the continuation of economic reforms.

It must be noted that Deng's strategy, trying to reconcile both reforms and faithfulness to part of Mao's heritage, would run the risk of being attacked from both the right and the left, the right trying to accelerate reforms, the left trying to go back to the 'two whatevers'. In order to avoid criticism from both the right and the left, Deng reinforces the rule of law as a legitimating socio-economic process by launching several campaigns against both the rightist and the leftist factions within the Party, and this would also convince the population to support the four Cardinal Principles by giving them a positive ideal. For this purpose, at the time of the 12th Congress of the Communist Party of 1982, two important topics are put forward by Deng (Zhang 1996, p. 45): first, Deng recommends the establishment of a spiritual civilization, i.e. not only the promotion of culture, science and education, but also of thought, of ideals, of communist discipline. Thus, whilst providing an ideal to the Chinese people, particularly to the young generation, spiritual civilization above all had the role of serving as a security, preventing democratization experiments from escaping the control of the leaders. It is feared that the opening up of China would end in an erosion of socialist ideals and their replacement by capitalist ones. Thus, the threat comes at the same time both from the right and the left.

Second, Deng feels that he has to justify the focus of his strategy on the other foundation of Weberian power, i.e. the development of the economy thanks to the introduction of market mechanisms, which may be interpreted as a contradiction to the socialist heritage of the Mao era. Socialism with Chinese characteristic means first of all that socialism cannot be applied everywhere in the same way. Each historical case requires an adaptation of the socialist ideas. Socialism is not a set of proposals to be applied as such; it is a question above all of adapting the means to the goals. Deng considers thus that in the first stage of socialism, all must be done to eliminate poverty and to improve the standard of living of the Chinese people, if not 'how could socialism be able to triumph over capitalism?' (quoted by Zhang 1996, p. 52).

These two innovations are essential for Deng because they reinforce the legitimacy of his power. Indeed, the reformists realize that economic development is not sufficient to ensure the legitimacy of the Party's leadership. The reforms launched by Deng (which, can be interpreted as a transition—even if partial—towards market economy, or at least towards some market mechanisms) run the risk of implementing the development and diffusion of rightist and bourgeois ideas, which would call into question the legitimacy of the Party. This is shown in the campaigns against bourgeois liberalization. The use of words is very important here. 'Socialism' is to some extent the fundamental axiom of the Party, its identity, its 'raison d'être'. It is what appears in the four Cardinal Principles: the socialist way and the Marxist-Leninist-Maoist thought are the principles upon which the actions of the Party are based. In the same way, the 'bourgeois' term, in the tradition of Marx, is at odds with socialism. To say that the way chosen by the Party is 'bourgeois' is to question the foundations of the Party.

This redefinition of socialism and the importance of the 'first stage of socialism' is further discussed at the time of the 13th Congress of the Party in 1987. That year, Deng affirms that China is not yet ready to engage into the socialist way (Zhang 1996, p. 162). This assertion was not made public, but provoked some very animated discussions within the Party. Its meaning is that the economic forces of China are still largely underdeveloped, and this prevents the country from fully engaging into the socialist way. Moreover, this redefinition constitutes in some ways a return to Marx, who affirms that capitalism is a preliminary stage necessary towards socialism. Capitalism, and the class that developed it (the bourgeoisie), is for Marx revolutionary, and he admired it very much (Aron 2002, p. 338). The bourgeoise has created more productive forces in 100 years (at the time when Marx writes the Manifesto) than have ever been produced before in history (Marx 2000, p. 12). The bourgeoise has destroyed feudalism, but by doing so it has created the class (the proletariat) that will defeat itself. As Marx says, '[the bourgeoisie] creates its own tombs' (Marx 2000, pp. 14–15, 25). In this conception of history, there is some kind of determinism: for Marx socialism cannot appear before the bourgeoisie has fulfilled its role. However, Mao had engaged directly in the socialist way. For Deng, China must initially find a functional equivalent to capitalism capable of creating a commodity economy before being ready for socialism (Pye 1968, p. 210).

This new ideological line makes it possible to reconcile, at least for a certain time, socialism and some market mechanisms. As comprehensive planning undermines the development of the productive forces, it is thus necessary to combine planning with some elements of a market economy (Zhang 1996, p. 116). To mark a clear distinction between socialism and capitalism, Deng affirms that the market economy is no more than a method for developing the economy, and is thus a neutral device in terms of values. He thus succeeded in integrating Western concepts into his discourse and his program of reforms by discharging them from any ideological connotation. The similarity with Braudel's distinction between market and capitalism is evident (above Sect. 2.2).

Despite the introduction of the changes in ideology and strategy mentioned above, Deng was not able to forecast the importance of the difficulties that could arise, and

2.4 China Political Culture: Stability and Change

that in fact arose, in managing the pace and scope of the reform process: i.e. the economic and social contradictions produced by the reform process, based upon the introduction of market mechanisms, that paved the road to the Tiananmen events.[20] How can we interpret these events? Were they a real challenge to the power and policies of the Communist Party, and therefore a clear demonstration of the failure of Deng to reconcile economic reforms and consolidation of power?

For Zhang Weiwei (1996, p. 177), the decision of Deng to employ force to subdue the revolt is clearly a rational decision of an actor who feels that his own power, as well as the power of the Communist Party, is called into question. Deng remains convinced of the paramount importance of political stability for the continuation of economic reforms, and is ready to use all the means necessary to arrive at his ends. Therefore, stability first (and by all means) if it is a condition for continuing the reform policies, that will improve the standard of living of the Chinese people and the power of China in the international arena.

But do these events mean a true erosion of Deng's and the Party's power? Michel Hammer clearly distinguishes the concept of revolt from that of revolution. Following Lenin, he proposes to define three conditions necessary to the outbreak of a revolution: first there should be a situation necessary for the outburst of the revolution, i.e. 'society should be already in the process of decomposition, undermined by chaos.' (Hammer 1998, pp. 97–98). Second, one also needs an organization, i.e. a network affording the revolutionists some solid support. Lastly, there should be a will, i.e. a strategy aiming at reversing the power. For Michel Hammer, none of these conditions were fulfilled at the time of the Tiananmen events.

Certainly, the demonstrators were revolting. But the true revolutionary would go beyond revolt, he would affirm the will to replace the existing order by a new order, he is moved by a political project, 'he sees beyond the riot.' The crisis of Tiananmen is the expression of a disappointment, of a discouragement, even of a rage against corruption, inflation, increasing disparities between the ordinary people and a cast of individuals who have found the means to profit for the relative (but real) liberalization of the economy. And there is also an anger against a power which refuses any freedom of expression (Kynge 2009). But there is no revolutionary situation. Moreover, the Chinese civil society is not organized politically; it has been dominated by a totalitarian political power for too long since the Empire. Lastly, there is no will, no true project aiming at reversing the existing power. The students of Tiananmen Square are revolted, but they are not revolutionaries.

According to this interpretation, we are led to think that this crisis, in spite of the difficulties which resulted for the Party, did not constitute a fundamental challenge to the power of the Party, and thus it does not constitute a failure of the strategy of Deng Xiaoping. Moreover, as Michel Hammer remarks, if the repression was bloody and

---

[20]I will not discuss here whether there has been a massacre in Tiananmen Square. Some witnesses stated that the killings took place in the nearby streets, where moreover several 'pacific' demonstrators were using weapons to attack police and soldiers, killing (i.e. massacring) several and setting on fire to some of the army's tanks. Nevertheless, it is admitted that demonstrators were killed, between a few hundreds and a few thousand depending on the sources. For a balanced analysis of the Tiananmen events see Kynge (2009); for a Marxist point of view see Losurdo (2009).

scandalous for many Western observers, it was relatively short in time, and not very wide, and in any case incomparable with what happened at the time of the Cultural Revolution. But what have been the consequences of the Tiananmen events on the course of reforms? (Hammer 1998, pp. 97–99).

As Wang Hui very rightly argued, far from undermining the efforts of reforms, the demonstrations on the Tiananmen Square and the repression which followed, gave a new dash to the reforms. For Wang Hui, Tiananmen has not caused a fundamental change of the way followed since 1978 (Wang 1998, p. 9). Reforms implemented since the beginning of the 1990s were even stronger than ever. Deng draws one conclusion from these events: it is necessary to speed up the reforms towards a market economy (Domenach 2002, p. 33). The defeat of the opponents leaves to some extent the Party free to pursue the reforms trend. Deng declares in 1989: 'Power must be very powerful or it must cease to exist. (…) It was our duty (…) to tear off the poisonous plants: we did it. China continues its long March.' (quoted by Hammer 1998, p. 99). Deng calls at the same time for several years of stability, showing his will not to tolerate expressions of opposition to the power of the Party, and his will to accelerate the reforms. It reaffirms in 1992 with force what he had already done in the discussions on 'socialism with Chinese characteristics', namely that 'the true nature of socialism is to release the productive forces.'

In a famous tour which he carries out in South China in 1992, Deng gives his interpretation of the fall of the Soviet bloc: it is above all the economic failure of the USSR which led to its fall. It is thus necessary to fight the leftist opponents to the reforms, who are likely to slow down the latter, with the risk of reviving the rightist opposition. At the end of 1992, at the time of the 14th Party Congress, Deng affirms that the central task of the Party is 'to develop a socialist market economy.'

In conclusion, we can consider that the contradictions within Chinese economy and society that lead to the Tiananmen events have never been important enough to fundamentally call into question the line followed by Deng. The two objectives laid down by Deng appear even sometimes perfectly compatible: the Party obtains its legitimacy thanks to the realization of economic performances. This is the profound meaning that it is necessary to give to the formulas 'socialism with Chinese characteristics', or 'socialist market economy'. Stability and unity remained two fundamental values of China's political culture. Socialism can be realized only with productive forces that are sufficiently developed, and to develop them one needs a market economy or at least some market mechanisms, that the leaders endeavour not to equate with capitalism. With that strategy, Deng Xiaoping has prepared the ground for a period of economic growth without precedent which China has known since the 1990s, in spite of the further development of contradictions I will explain in Chaps. 3 and 4.

2.4.4 Jiang Zemin's Contribution to CPC's Ideology: The Theory of the Three Represents

Jiang is totally in line with the ideology defined during the Deng era, and we can consider that to a large extent he has implemented policies in line with Deng's idea of reforms. It is interesting to note that some of these traditional cultural traits (both of the Imperial and the Mao eras) constitute the logic underpinning the speech President Jiang Zemin delivered at the XVI Congress of the CPC the 8 of November 2002.[21] While referring several times to Mao's and Deng's contributions (especially the Four Cardinal Principles), Jiang starts his speech by reaffirming some fundamental principles, above all the necessity of reinforcing the capacity of the Party to continue to exercise its leadership over Chinese society. And here again we have a clear reassessment of the concept of unity. Right from the beginning it is strongly reaffirmed that: 'Our Party must stand firm in the forefront of the times and unite with and lead the Chinese people of all ethnic groups …'.[22]

Even when dealing with his theory of the Three Represents (to be defined below), Jiang is very careful to affirm that the goal of this fundamental strategy is to reinforce the Party. The theory of the Three Represents, says Jiang, is a powerful theoretical weapon for strengthening and improving Party building and promoting self-improvement and development of socialism in China. By dealing then with the reform and the improvement of the role of the CPC, Jiang further defines the CPC role as follows:

> leadership by the Party mainly refers to its political, ideological and organizational leadership. The Party exercises leadership over the state and society by formulating major principles and policies, making suggestions on legislation, recommending cadres for important positions, conducting ideological publicity, giving play to the role of Party organizations and members and persisting in exercising state power according to law. Party committees, playing the role as the core of leadership among all other organizations at corresponding levels, should concentrate on handling important matters and support those organizations in assuming their responsibilities independently and making concerted efforts in their work.

In the final part of his speech Jang Zemin comes back to the necessity of strengthening the Party by showing the importance of the link between the reinforcement of the Party and the training of the Party's cadres (Lee 2015). He stresses the necessity 'to build a contingent of high-calibre leading cadres and form an energetic and promising leadership; (…) build the Party well at the primary level, reinforce its class foundation and expand its mass base'. Jiang further reaffirms that

---

[21] All the quotations are drawn from the official English translation published on the China Daily's website.

[22] He also says that: 'We should uphold and improve the system of multiparty cooperation and political consultation led by the Communist Party and the system of regional ethnic autonomy. We should promote political restructuring, develop democracy, improve the legal system, rule the country by law, build a socialist state under the rule of law and ensure that the people exercise their rights as the masters of the country.'.

> Party organizations in enterprises must carry out the Party's principles and policies, and provide guidance to and supervise the enterprises in observing the laws and regulations of the state. They should exercise leadership over trade unions, the Communist Youth League and other mass organizations, rally the workers around them, safeguard the legitimate rights and interests of all quarters and stimulate the healthy development of the enterprises. We should intensify our efforts to establish Party organizations in mass organizations and intermediaries. We should fully carry out Party building in Party and government organs, as well as schools, research institutions, cultural groups and other institutions.

Nevertheless, Jiang started to address some of the contradictions of the Deng era by implementing policies to re-balance the Chinese economy and society (which will be the goal clearly defined by Hu Jintao) especially investments in infrastructure in western Chinese provinces, and the setting up of the new fiscal policy giving more financial resources and power to the central government. Moreover, at the 2002 Party Congress Jiang developed his 'Three Represent' theory that has become, along with Marxism-Leninism, Mao's thought and Deng's thought, the recognized ideological basis of the Party. This theory affirms that the Party represents the advanced social productive forces, the advanced culture, and the interests of the overwhelming majority of the Chinese people. This is quite a radical change compared to the previous ideology that considered that the Party represented the interests of the proletariat.

The Impressive increase of GDP realized thanks to the implementation of Deng's and Jiang's development strategy, has been achieved at the expense of a fair distribution of the new wealth so created. The consequence is that, although the living conditions of the Chinese people have been improved, the old egalitarian social structure has been replaced by an increasing non-egalitarian one, with the emergence of new social strata, categories, or even social classes. In particular, in the light of what happened in the West after the industrial revolution and the development of market economy, an attentive observer of China reforms could have forecast the emergence of a new class of entrepreneurs whose values would not necessarily be in tune with the values of the leading political Party. In this framework, and considering that the values of unity and harmony are still at the core of the Party ideology, the 'Three Represents' can be appreciated as a rational decision whose goal is to reconstruct and reconcile within the Party the social fragmentation that has arisen within Chinese society, and to prevent the emergence of contradictions that may result from it which could jeopardize the trend of reforms under the leadership of the Party. It is well known that Jiang Zemin, at the moment of making his theory public, has at the same time addressed an appeal to the private Chinese entrepreneur (the new 'red capitalists') inviting them to join the Party. Informal evidence collected in China and interviews realized in China prove that many private entrepreneurs have in fact joined the Party, and some of them sit in several official bodies, like the national parliament (Chen and Dickson 2008).

2.4.5 Hu Jintao's Contribution to the CPC's Ideology: Equity, Justice, Innovation and Scientific Development

Jiang's successor, Hu Jintao, while introducing some important novelties which I will deal with hereafter, in his speech at the Party Congress of October 2007 remains nevertheless in line with some fundamental elements of the traditional Chinese political culture: the Four Cardinal Principles are confirmed as well as the necessity to further strengthen the Party.

For the purpose of appreciating Hu's contribution to the CPC's ideology it is interesting to compare Jiang Zemin's and Hu Jintao's strategies for legitimizing their policies. I will do this by comparing their speeches given at the National Party Congresses of 2002 (Jiang Zemin) and 2007 (Hu Jintao).[23] For doing so, I propose to take into consideration references to four legitimacies, and first of all to Marxism-Leninism. This seems quite an appropriate reference for leaders of a party that has introduced Marxism-Leninism as one of its "Cardinal Principles". Second, I will consider references to science. This, too, seems to be an understandable reference by Chinese leaders for legitimizing power, as Marxism is considered by its followers to be a scientific theory of history; moreover the 'Four Modernizations' defined by Deng clearly imply the use of a scientific approach to modernization (the 'seeking truth from facts' principle). Third, I will take references to the Chinese situation or, in Deng's terminology, to 'Chinese characteristics.' Finally, I will consider references to the new legitimizing values, i.e. the balance between economic efficiency and equity.

For identifying references to these four sets of values in the discourse of Jiang and Hu, I will use a number of indicators. For the traditional Marxist legitimacy I will consider references to Marxism, Marxism-Leninism, to Mao, Deng and to democratic centralism. For scientific legitimacy I will take the use of words like science, scientific, and scientific development. For the conformity to Chinese characteristics I propose to take: Chinese characteristics, stability, harmony and harmonious, and innovation. Using innovation as an indicator of the reference to Chinese characteristics may look a bit strange, but this corresponds quite clearly, especially in the discourse of Hu Jintao, to the assertion (or-reassertion) that China's fundamental goal is to become a major global player in the course of the XXI century. The consequence is that by considering this goal as the de facto China's fundamental policy goal, this goal becomes 'the new reality of Chinese characteristics.' And this will imply that if China wants to play a leading role in the international system it has to cease to imitate the West and start instead to invent its own ways of managing its society in all domains and of influencing the course of international affairs (Sect. 6.2 below). This last aspect of the third legitimacy constitutes the bridge towards the fourth one, i.e. the new legitimacy based upon the balance between economic efficiency and equity. For this new legitimacy I will use the following indicators: efficiency, market, equity,

---

[23]The length of the two speeches is almost the same; this means that we will not have to standardize the data. and we will simply use the frequencies, i.e. number of times Jiang and Hu refer to the indicators of different types of legitimacy I will define in the following paragraphs.

48   2   Understanding China's Strategic Public Management

justice, law and its derivatives, namely 'ruling by law' or 'according to law' and 'the rule of law.' Let us see what we discover by applying this methodology to Jiang's and Hu's speeches at the 2002 and 2007 Party Congresses.

Starting with the first type of legitimacy, i.e. the reference to the traditional legitimizing values of the Party (such as Marxism-Leninism, Mao, Deng and democratic centralism), I have found that they are present in the two speeches, although they are more numerous in Hu Jintao's speech. Nevertheless, it is interesting to remark that whereas Jiang mentions his predecessor, Deng Xiaoping, 62 times, Hu mentions Deng only 11 times, and only twice he mentions by name his predecessor (Jiang Zemin) and 8 times the "important thought of the Three Represents", but without mentioning the name of Jiang. It seems therefore that for Hu Jintao, referring to the values of Marxism-Leninism and to the leaders who have developed the Marxist ideology of the Party is less important for the purpose of legitimizing his policies. This does not mean that these values are of no importance to Hu Jintao, as they are nevertheless mentioned several times in his speech. What does this mean? Does it mean that Hu Jintao planned to refer to other legitimizing values, and that therefore he had to limit the time devoted to the traditional Marxist values in order to have sufficient time for developing and giving sufficient importance to the new values he had chosen? This is what I will discover by taking into consideration the other three legitimacies.

Taking now the second form of legitimacy, i.e. the reference to science, I found that both Jiang and Hu make many references to science as a legitimizing value, but a second difference appears: Hu is the only one to mention scientific development in relation to social harmony, and not just once, but 34 times.

This difference will become even more striking when we consider the following legitimizing values, i.e. based upon reference to the Chinese characteristics. Although both mention the necessity to take into consideration the Chinese characteristics in the process of implementing the development strategy, as well as the importance of safeguarding stability in the development process, the necessity to realize harmony and a harmonious society is mentioned only once by Jiang and 35 times by Hu. Even more striking, Jiang mentions only twice innovation, whereas in Hu's speech innovation is mentioned 47 times and appears to be one of the most central and important values. Hu develops a very complex discourse on innovation by first considering that it must be independent from other sources of inspiration. Very likely he refers here to the fact that in the past China has above all imitated foreign countries. For Hu, in the future innovation should be initiated by Chinese people. Moreover, Hu stresses that independent innovation should be implemented in a large number of important domains: re-balancing between regions, general management, banks, enterprises and their modernization, army, science and technology, Chinese investments abroad, and use of Foreign Direct Investments in China. This is clearly a sign that opens a new era in the development of Chinese society. This new trend is even more evident when we turn to the fourth and last source of legitimizing the role and policies of the Party.

The fourth type of legitimacy is based upon the reference to the necessity to establish a balance between economic efficiency and equity. I have found that both Jiang and Hu mention economic efficiency, market and law. Striking differences

2.4 China Political Culture: Stability and Change 49

appear when we look at the other indicators of the new legitimacy. Contrary to Hu, Jiang never mentions 'equity' and 'justice', and only links law with 'ruling by law' or 'according to law', but never with the 'rule of law'. Of course, this does not necessarily mean that Jiang is not sensitive to equity and justice. It simply shows that there has been a change in the importance that Hu is giving to the core values of the Chinese official ideology. This is a clear sign that the new Chinese leadership has taken very seriously the contradictions that have emerged in Chinese society in the process of modernization under Deng and Jiang. Moreover, at least at the ideological and political level, it also shows that the new Chinese leadership is ready to take several serious measures in order to re-balance Chinese society. Very clearly Hu says that it will be necessary to manage the relationship between efficiency and equity in the distribution of income by market mechanisms, and that the Party-State should pay an increasing attention to the redistribution of income. In Chap. 4 I will examine to what extent these measures have been effectively implemented.

The numerous references to harmony and stability (especially in Hu's speech within the second and third legitimacies mentioned above) seem to indicate a revival of traditional values inherited from the Imperial era. And there is certainly some truth in this statement. Whereas for a long time since the creation of the CPC Confucian values have been practically banned from the official ideology as they have been made responsible for the backwardness of China during the last century of Imperial power, this is no longer the case as is witnessed by the increasing interest of both Chinese intellectuals and political leaders in the values of Confucianism, especially for (re)affirming the originality of Chinese political culture and creating a barrier to the westernization of Chinese society (Zufferey 2008, pp. 221–250; Bell and Chaibong Hahn 2003; Bell 2008). For the Western scholar who is well acquainted with the influence that Greek philosophy and Roman law exert still today on Western societies, this revival of Confucian values comes with no surprise. But as is the case in the West for the Greek and Roman inheritance, the revival of Confucian values in China is to be placed and interpreted within the context of today's situation. Whereas during the Imperial era the values of stability and harmony were instrumental in maintaining the structure of Chinese society as it was, these same values are today used in the framework of a development strategy that aims at transforming China to an extent that maybe even the present Chinese leadership cannot fully predict.

2.4.6 The Contribution of Xi Jinping: Strengthening the Party and Assertive Global Foreign Policy

It is clear that Xi Jinping has defined his strategy by building on the strategies of his predecessors. Nevertheless, With Xi Jinping we cross an important limit to the construction of CPC's ideology as the vision of China presented by Xi Jinping is clearly projected outside China's borders and, to be precise, at the global level. As I will explain in Sect. 6.2, this was the inevitable development since the XIX century.

China was then confronted with the foreign policy of the major European countries, England and France, but also of the US that in 1844 signed its 'unequal treaty' (the Treaty of Wangxia) only two years after England signed the first such treaties following its victory in the First Opium War (1839–1842). Now, Western foreign policies have been designed at the global level since at least the XVI Century, which has resulted in the development of vast global Empires built upon their economic and military superiority. In order to confront these policies, the only way China could realize the goal of reclaiming world power status and to be respected again, was to build a global foreign policy. Or course, as we shall see in Sect. 6.2, this was not possible in the short run, the difference in power was too wide.

But by the time Xi Jinping becomes the Secretary General of the CPC, China has been able to develop a whole range of power resources that make it easy today to present China's idea of its role in the world in the open. And this of course is the Belt Road Initiative. Certainly, in his 2017 Party Congress speech Xi Jinping still refers to the traditional values of harmony (32 times), stability (19 times), and unity (16 times).[24] Moreover, he still refers, as do his predecessors, to Marxism and Marxism-Leninism (12 times). Even more interesting is that he only mentions by name, among his predecessors, Mao (twice) and not Jiang Zemin and Hu Jintao, who are referred to only through their 'Three Represent Theory" (Jiang) and the 'Scientific Outlook' (Hu). Finally, the clear sign that China will remain faithful to its culture is proved by the incredible number of times Xi Jinping mentions the "Chinese characteristics" (sometimes in relation to the 'China Dream'): 69, against 30 for Jiang Zemin and 57 for Hu Jintao.

Clearly, China is ready to assume an important role in the international system by offering to the world a whole set of international agreements and partnerships that will be beneficial to everybody, under the slogan of 'win-win'. In particular, Xi Jinping stated that:

> We have made all-round efforts in the pursuit of major country diplomacy with Chinese characteristics, thus advancing China's diplomatic agenda in a comprehensive, multilevel, multifaceted way and creating a favorable external environment for China's development. We have jointly pursued the Belt and Road Initiative, initiated the Asian Infrastructure Investment Bank, set up the Silk Road Fund, and hosted the First Belt and Road Forum for International Cooperation, the 22nd APEC Economic Leaders' Meeting, the G20 2016 Summit in Hangzhou, the BRICS Summit in Xiamen, and the Fourth Summit of the Conference on Interaction and Confidence Building Measures in Asia. China champions the development of a community with a shared future for mankind, and has encouraged the evolution of the global governance system. With this we have seen a further rise in China's international influence, ability to inspire, and power to shape; and China has made great new contributions to global peace and development.[25]

---

[24]For example, Xi Jinping says: 'There is greater unity in thinking both within the Party and throughout society'. All the quotations are drawn from the official English translation published on the China Daily's website.

[25]See also the following significant statements about China's will to pay an important international role: 'China's cultural soft power and the international influence of Chinese culture have increased significantly. (…) Taking a driving seat in international cooperation to respond to climate change, China has become an important participant, contributor, and torchbearer in the global endeavor

2.4 China Political Culture: Stability and Change

Moreover,

> t makes clear that major country diplomacy with Chinese characteristics aims to foster a new type of international relations and build a community with a shared future for mankind". Also: "The dream of the Chinese people is closely connected with the dreams of the peoples of other countries; the Chinese Dream can be realized only in a peaceful international environment and under a stable international order.

Finally, after having enumerated the results so far achieved (first phase), Xi Jinping project his country into the future (second phase):

> In the second stage from 2035 to the middle of the 21st century, we will, building on having basically achieved modernization, work hard for a further 15 years and develop China into a great modern socialist country that is prosperous, strong, democratic, culturally advanced, harmonious, and beautiful. By the end of this stage, the following goals will have been met: new heights are reached in every dimension of material, political, cultural and ethical, social, and ecological advancement; modernization of China's system and capacity for governance is achieved; China has become a global leader in terms of composite national strength and international influence; common prosperity for everyone is basically achieved; the Chinese people enjoy happier, safer, and healthier lives; the Chinese nation will become a proud and active member of the community of nations.

We may now conclude that during the post-Deng era the adoption of some remarkable novelties, like the market mechanisms promoted by Deng, has not weakened many of the traditional features of China's political culture inherited from the Imperial era, namely the values of unity and harmony. On the contrary, by integrating these novelties into Marxism-Leninism (as it was interpreted and adapted by Mao to the Chinese situation) the Chinese leadership has not weakened these traditional values, but has even strengthened them. In fact, Marxism-Leninism is quite in line with the idea of attributing the leading political role to the Party, considered as the sole and exclusive organization capable of guiding the country on the road towards socialism. In this perspective, the traditional values of harmony, unity and stability inherited from the Empire are the values the Party must promote and abide by, if it wants to build the ideological basis giving it the necessary legitimacy for accomplishing its historical mission. Moreover, by introducing market mechanisms within this ideological framework, the Party can justify its leading role as it is in charge not only of introducing elements of market economy while safeguarding stability, but also of being in the position, thanks to its leading role, of limiting the negative consequences of market economy.

The result of this mix of old and new cultural elements has been the emergence in the post-Mao era of a new traditional political culture (or ideology) combining traditional values inherited from the Empire, new values based upon Marxism-Leninism and, since the Deng era, market economy. The structure of this new ideology may

---

for ecological civilization. (...) We have strengthened military training and war preparedness, and undertaken major missions related to the protection of maritime rights, countering terrorism, maintaining stability, disaster rescue and relief, international peacekeeping, escort services in the Gulf of Aden, and humanitarian assistance. We have stepped up weapons and equipment development, and made major progress in enhancing military preparedness. The people's armed forces have taken solid strides on the path of building a powerful military with Chinese characteristics. (...)'.

look rather strange to Western scholars, used as they are to analyzing social phenomena through the lenses of their rational categories that do not allow the coexistence of such 'contradictory' values as unity, harmony and free market economy. For a Western mind, a 'socialist market economy with Chinese characteristics' is a flagrant contradiction in terms. Nevertheless, after 40 years of reforms based upon this 'strange marriage', we must concede that China is showing to the world that, at least so far, it can manage this 'contradiction' in a relatively satisfactory manner. Nevertheless, it is today widely recognized by both Western and Chinese scholars that the implementation of this ideology and political programme has produced several remarkable factual contradictions. But the present Chinese leadership seems to be seriously ready to address these contradictions in the near future, as has been confirmed at the National Party Congresses of 2007, 2012 and 2017. I will come back to these important trends in the following chapters of this book and try to evaluate to what extent they can indeed eliminate these contradictions.

2.5   The Cultural Difficulties on the Road to Market Economy

In Chaps. 3 and 4 I will analyse the difficulties facing the Chinese leadership resulting from the implementation of Deng's development strategy. Here I will comment on the difficulties linked to the Chinese culture, starting with those concerning the legal system (Urio 2004). This is, according to the overwhelming majority of Western scholars, one of the major weaknesses of the Chinese political and administrative system. I refer here to one of the most complex problems of the mastering of market economy in China, as it is deeply imbedded into some of the features of the Chinese culture.

It is necessary to point out that the Chinese tradition in this domain is quite different from the Western one, where behaviour based upon inter-personal relationships prevails over behaviour oriented by formal rules (laws and regulations). Since the political liberal revolution of the end of the XVIII Century and throughout the first part of the XIX Century, the idea of a legal structure to which all the people, including those in power, are subordinated, has been widely accepted in the West. It leaves to be seen to what extent this is being effectively implemented in the West.

The major features of the Chinese culture that make it difficult to set up a legal system based upon the rule of law, can be summarized as follows: weak attitude in favour of written documents, imprecision of legal texts (when they exist), in judicial procedures people are constrained by an excessive respect and/or fear of authority, and a widely diffused belief that laws and a too strict legal system may have the consequence of producing and exacerbating conflicts. If we add to this the weak separation of powers and the underlying tendency of the CPC to interfere with the judicial procedures you end up with a considerable uncertainty regarding the implementation of legal norms, and we may forecast that the recourse to interpersonal

2.5 The Cultural Difficulties on the Road to Market Economy

relations will make it difficult to effectively resolve the conflicts that inevitably arise in a market economy.

It is true that under pressure from the policy of opening up to the outside world, and even more after the entrance into the WTO, China has embarked upon a process of completely redesigning its legal system, either by amending the existing legislation or by passing an impressive amount of new laws and regulations (Peerenboom 2007, 2006, 2007). But the road which leads from the 'rule by law' to the 'rule of law' is still a long one. The result is that the legal norms are too often undetermined, and subject to interpretation, most of the time by political interferences. This may be one of the sources of difficulties for giving impetus to the private sector, as one of the major imperatives of market economy is that law, government and administrative behaviour, should be as predictable as possible. The difficulties arising from the uncertainties of the legal system are further strengthened by the cult of secrecy, which combined with the practice of retaining information, has the consequence of making the functioning of the whole system rather opaque, i.e. contrary to one of the requirements of a sound market economy: transparency and foreseeability.

Another cultural trait is the preference for practice and techniques as opposed to theoretical thinking. More precisely, the Chinese are not interested in theories that cannot be implemented in practice and obtain political meaningful results, as we have seen above (Zufferey 2008, pp. 22, 49–68). This may have the consequence of implementing theories without previously evaluating their theoretical validity. This seems to be the case in the domain of economics and social sciences, where there has been an import of foreign ideas (or more precisely of foreign ideologies) and that the practical arrangements (laws, regulations, administrative decisions) deriving from those ideas have been implemented without thorough scientific scrutiny. It is necessary here to refer to the adoption of a soviet-type command economy; to the Great Leap Forward, and to the strategy of economic development adopted at the end of the 1970's, that is clearly based upon an interpretation of parts of classical liberal market economy. At that time, the negative consequences of market economy were well known in Western literature, especially in the mainstream of welfare economics, and in the writings of those favourable to the establishment and development of the welfare state. It is surprising that it is only 15 to 20 years after the beginning of the reform process that these negative consequences have been publicly recognised by the Chinese leadership, alerted, it must be remembered, by some of the most skilful and imaginative Chinese scholars, as I explained elsewhere (Urio 2010a, pp. 103–119). But the facts are here: as we will see in Chap. 3, there have been several important negative consequences of the development of the economic system based upon market economy and opening up to the world economy.

To overcome these problems, the Chinese leadership seems to count on another cultural feature: the sense of cultural superiority, based upon a very long history, and the faith in the political genius of the Chinese People. However, this combined with the obsession for unity (also a cultural trait coming from that long history) leads to an obsession with political and social stability, and this in turn leads to little tolerance for the formation of autonomous social organisations, as they are interpreted as a menace to the leadership of the CPC. Moreover, as we have seen with Jiang, the CPC seems to want to control all kinds of organisations (e.g. Trade Unions, and Women's Organisations), and I have already pointed to the will of the CPC to interfere with all the stages of the legislative process.

In this context it is interesting to note that in the West scholars comparing public management between China and the West, consider that the West's superiority resides in the existence of different sources of power, and the tolerance of the expression of different opinions in the open (for or against the actions of those in power) has submitted the leadership to a type of control that most of the time has permitted to avoid making mistakes, or at least to be able to correct them in time. Contrary to this opinion, one can mention the management by Western countries of the 2008 financial and economic crisis. Many people lost their jobs and/or home, experienced a decrease of their income and have been deprived of any sort of expectations for the future, especially young people among whom long term unemployment has reached levels never seen before, after WW 2. Unfortunately, in order to overcome the consequence of the crisis, Western countries have implemented the same policies that were at the origins of the crisis. The consequence is that contrary to resolving these negative outcomes, they have been exacerbated, notably, unemployment, income inequality, and the poor quality of the jobs that have nevertheless been created (short term, part-time and low paid).[26] Nevertheless, the history of capitalism has shown that liberal democracy has been capable to overcome its crisis and to re-emerge with renewed strength and faith in its superiority.[27]

Another cultural feature further reinforces the above-mentioned ones, namely the obsession for power and prestige, both domestically and internationally. This seems to be linked to the preference for grandiose projects that may rapidly produce spectacular results: again the Great Leap Forward, but also the establishment of the Special Economic Zones, the will to accelerate the economic development, and the desire to rapidly restore China as one of the major world powers. We will see in Chaps. 3, 4 and Sect. 6.2, the consequences (positive and negative) of this strategy. Moreover, Deng's strategy in favour of rapid economic development giving priority to the coastal provinces, where factors capable of boosting economic development were significantly more favourable than in the inner and western regions, seems to be in line with the liberal motto: 'You must first create wealth before you can distribute it.' Quite clearly, as the Western experience has shown before China, creating wealth for some does not necessarily mean that the wealth so created will be equitably distributed within the whole of society. Huge disparities have developed in the West in spite of an extraordinary increase of wealth (measured by GDP). As I have mentioned above, China is now experiencing the same type of problems.

In summary, the main obstacles to the improvement of the market (or of the market mechanisms) based upon the traditional Chinese political culture can be summarized as follows. The various interferences by the Party within the political process (that can be characterized as being politically excessive, and technically insufficient) reinforce

---

[26]See the works of Joseph Stiglitz in the References to this chapter: Stiglitz (2002, 2006, 2009, 2010, 2012, 2013, 2015, 2016, 2017a, b).

[27]See again the quotation of Fernand Braudel on the nature of capitalism, Sect. 2.2.

2.5 The Cultural Difficulties on the Road to Market Economy 55

and are reinforced by some of the traditional features of the way of organizing society and polity, such as the imprecision and insufficiency of the legal norm, the propensity for secrecy, the lack of transparency and the retention of information. The other traditional elements of Chinese culture, namely the preference for grandiose undertakings producing rapidly spectacular results that may divert resources in favour of inefficient programmes, the obsession with unity and the resulting intolerance of the formation of autonomous social and political organizations, may divert the Party-State from its main role of developing the economy as a means to improve the standard of living of the population, to establish a relatively prosper society in which wealth is equitably distributed, and to restore China as a world power. Of course, this does not mean that remarkable achievements have not been obtained, nor that China will necessarily organise its economy, society and polity according to the Western model.

2.6 Conclusion

At the end of this chapter, we can conclude that during the transition from the Imperial, the first Republic, and the Maoist eras to the Deng, Jiang, Hu and Xi Jinping eras, the Chinese leadership has constantly adapted its ideology and development strategy not only to the Chinese situation and the Chinese characteristics, but also to the international situation, as well as to the consequences of the impact of policies implemented in the previous eras. For doing so, it has adopted a pragmatic approach, according to Deng's principle of 'seeking truth through facts', in spite of the problematic cultural features mentioned above. At the end of Chap 4, where we will deal with the rebalancing policies set up to overcome the negative consequences of the Deng-Jiang's development strategy, we will see that these difficulties have been largely overcome by a strategy that puts 'people first', i.e. shifting the axes of public policies away from the strategy of 'economic development at all costs'.

At the same time, we should not forget that the fundamental goal of the various Chinese leaderships has constantly been to restore China as a world power. As we will see in the following chapters, the successive Chinese leaderships have taken the measures they thought necessary for attaining this final goal (and very likely as soon as possible) and have adopted the corrective measures as soon as the impact of the previously implemented policies ran the risk of jeopardizing the realization of this fundamental goal. From the point of view of many Western scholars and observers of Chinese society, the strategy of the Party in constantly redefining its ideological base is interpreted as a device for maintaining power. This is of course an interesting question, but for me not the most important one. Apart from the fact that I do not know of any political system in which parties and politicians in power do not want to retain power, I am convinced that the most important question is to determine to what extent a party or a coalition of parties (no matter how they gained power) contribute to the improvement of the wellbeing of the people. In the following chapters we will evaluate to what extent China has been able to realize its objectives in spite of the limits and problems we have analyzed in this chapter.

References

Almond, G. A., & Powell, G. B. (1966). *Comparative politics: A developmental approach*. Boston: Little, Brown & Co.

Almond, G. A., & Verba, S. (1963). *The civic culture*. Boston: Little, Brown & Co.

Amable, Bruno. (2005). *Les cinq capitalismes: Diversité des systèmes économiques et sociaux dans la mondialisation*. Paris: Seuil.

Armitag, D., & Guldi, J. (2014). The return of the longue durée: An Anglo-American perspective', published in French. *Annales. Histoire, Sciences Sociales*, 69.

Aron, Raymond. (1967). *Les étapes de la pensée sociologique*. Paris: Gallimard.

Aron, Raymond. (2002). *Le Marxisme de Marx*. Paris: Editions de Fallois.

Bell, D. (1996). *The cultural contradictions of capitalism*. New York: Basic Books (Perseus Books, Twentieth Anniversary Edition with a new afterword by the author).

Bell, D. (2006). *Beyond liberal democracy. Political thinking for an east Asian context*. Princeton: Princeton University Press.

Bell, D. (Ed.). (2008). *Confucian political ethics*. Princeton: Princeton University Press.

Bell, D. (2015). *The china model. Political meritocracy and the limits of democracy*. Princeton: Princeton University Press, paperback edition with a new Preface by the author.

Bell, D., & Chaibong, H. (Eds.). (2003). *Confucianism for the modern world*. Cambridge: Cambridge University Press.

Bergère, M. C. (1986). *L'âge d'or de la bourgeoisie chinoise*. Paris: Flammarion.

Bergère, M. C. (2007). *Capitalismes et capitalistes en Chine. Des origines à nos jours*. Paris: Perrin.

Billeter, François. (2006). *Contre François Jullien*. Paris: Allia.

Braudel, F. (1958). La longue durée, *Annales. Histoire, Sciences Sociales*, 13e Année, (4, Oct.-Dec), 725–753.

Braudel, F. (1969). *Ecrits sur l'histoire*. Paris: Flammarion, 1969 (English translation: *On History*, Chicago, Univ. of Chicago Press, 1992).

Braudel, F. (1972). Fernand Braudel et les différents temps de l'histoire, interview published by *Jalons*, ORTF, (Collection: Signes des temps) 30 October 1972.

Braudel, F. (1979a). *Civilisation matérielle, économie et capitalisme (XVe–XVIIIe siècle)*, Paris: A. Colin, *vol. 1: Les structures du quotidien; vol. 2: Les jeux de l'échange; vol. 3: Le temps du monde* (English translation: *Civilization and Capitalism: 15th–18th Century, vol. 1: The Structure of Everyday Life; vol. 2: The Wheels of Commerce; vol. 3: The Perspective of the World*. Berkeley: University of California Press, 1992).

Braudel, F. (1979b). *Afterthoughts on material civilization and capitalism* (The Johns Hopkins Symposia in Comparative History), Baltimore, MD: Johns Hopkins University Press (French edition: La dynamique du capitalisme, Paris, Flammarion, 1985).

Chang, G. (2001). The Coming Collapse of China, New York: Random House.

Cheng, Anne. (1997). *Histoire de la pensée chinoise*. Paris: Seuil.

Chieng, André. (2006). *La pratique de la Chine, en compagnie de François Jullien*. Paris: Grasset.

Cui, Z. (1997). Privatization and consolidation of democratic regimes: An analysis and an alternative. *Journal of International Affairs, 50*(2, Winter), 675–692.

Cui, Z. (2005). Liberal socialism and the future of China: A petty bourgeois manifesto. In T. Y. Cao (Ed.), *The Chinese model of modern development*. London: Routledge.

Cui, Z. (2006). How to comprehend today's China. *Contemporary Chinese Thought, 37*(4), x–xx (translated from the Chinese original published in *Dushu* [Reading], no. 3, March 2004, pp. 3–9).

Dickson, B. J. (2003). *Red capitalists in China. The party, private entrepreneurs, and prospects for political change*. Cambridge: Cambridge University Press.

Dickson, B. J. (2008). *Wealth into power. The communist party's embrace of China's private sector*. New York: Cambridge University Press.

Domenach, J. L. (2002). *Où va la Chine?* Paris: Fayard.

Esping-Andersen, G. (1990). *The three worlds of welfare capitalism*. Princeton, NJ: Princeton University Press.

References

Frenkiel, E. (2011). From scholar to official. Cui Zheyuan and Chongqing City's local experimental policy. *La vie des idées (Books & Ideas)*, 25 January 2011, 3. Retrieved May 15, 2011 from http://www.booksandideas.net.

Goody, J. (2006). The theft of 'capitalism': Braudel and global comparison, chapter 7 of *The Theft if History* (pp. 180–211). Cambridge: Cambridge University Press.

Hall, P., & Soskice, D. (Eds.). (2001). *Varieties of capitalism: The institutional foundations of comparative advantage.* Oxford: Oxford University Press.

Hu, A. (2007). *Economic and social transformation in China.* London: Routledge.

Hu, A. (2011a). *Roadmap of China's rise.* London: Routledge.

Hu, A. (2011b). *China by 2030: A changing world towards common prosperity* (in Chinese). Beijing: Renmin University Press.

Hu A., & Men, H. (2004). The rising of modern China: Comprehensive national power and grand strategy, paper presented at the international conference on Rising China and the East Asian Economy, Seoul, 19–20, March 2004.

Hammer, Michel. (1998). *Au coeur de la politique chinoise: les débuts de l'ère Deng Xiaoping.* Genève: Institut Universitaire de Hautes Etudes Internationales.

Chen, J., & Dickson, B. J. (2008). Allies of the state: Democratic support and regime support among China's private entrepreneurs, *China Quarterly*, December 2008, 780–804.

Jullien, F. (1989). *Procès ou création: Une introduction à la pensée chinoise.* Paris: Seuil.

Jullien, F. (1995). *The propensity of things. Towards a history of efficacy in China.* New York: Zone Books.

Jullien, F. (2004). *A Treatise on efficacy. Between western and Chinese thinking.* Honolulu: University of Hawai'i Press.

Jullien, F. (2005). *Conférence sur l'efficacité.* Paris: Presses Universitaires de France.

Jullien, F. (2006). Postface, in André Chieng. *La pratique de la Chine, en compagnie de François Jullien* (2006, pp. 301–313). Paris: Grasset.

Jullien, F. (2008). *In Praise of Blandness. Proceedings from Chinese Thought and Aesthetics.* New York: Zone Books.

Jullien, F. (2011). *The Silent Transformations.* London: Seagull.

Jullien, F. (2015). *De l'être au vivre. Lexique euro-chinois de la pensée.* Paris: Gallimard.

Keith, R. C. (1991). Chinese politics and the new theory of rule of law. *The China Quarterly, 125*(March), 109–118.

Kynge, J. (2009). West miscasts Tiananmen protesters. *Financial Times, 3* (June).

Landes, David S. (1993). The fable of the dead horse; or, the industrial revolution revisited. In Joel Mokyr (Ed.), *The British industrial revolution: An economic perspective.* Boulder, CO: Westview Press.

Lee, C. P. (2015). Training the party. Party adaptation and elite training in reform-era China. Cambridge: Oxford University Press.

Losurdo, D. (2009). Tiananmen vingt ans après. L'échec de la première révolution colorée. Réseau Voltaire, 9 June.

Marx, Karl. (2000). *Manifest des Kommunistischen Partei.* Kückenshagen: Scheunen-Verlag.

McKinsey. (2009). *China's Green Revolution.* McKinsey Company, February 2009, available on the company's website: www.mckinsey.com.

Naughton, B. (2009). The turning point: First steps toward a post-crisis economy. *China Leadership Monitor, 31*(Winter), 2009–2010.

Naughton, B. (2010) Reading the NPC: Post-crisis economic dilemmas of the Chinese leadership. *China Leadership Monitor, 32* (Spring).

Peerenboom, R. (2002). *China's long March toward rule of law.* Cambridge: Cambridge University Press.

Preerenboom, R. (2006). A government of laws. Democracy, rule of law, and administrative law reform in China, in Zhao 2006, pp. 58–78.

Preerenboom, R. (2007). *China modernizes. Threat to the west or model for the rest?* Oxford: Oxford University Press.

Pillsbury, M. (2015). *The hundred-year marathon. China's secret strategy to replace America as the global superpower.* New York: Henry Holt & Co.

Pye, L. W. (1968). *Aspects of political development.* Boston: Little, Brown & Co.

Schram, S. R. (1984). Economics in command?—ideology and policy since the third plenum 1978–1984. *China Quarterly, 99*(September), 417–461.

Sorman, G. (2008) *The empire of lies. The truth about China in the XXI century.* New York: Encounter Books.

Stiglitz, J. E. (2002). *Globalization and its discontents.* New York: W.W. Norton, 2002.

Stiglitz, J. E. (2006). *Making globalization work. The next steps to global justice.* London: Penguin, 2006.

Stiglitz, J. E. (2009) *Around the world with Joseph Stiglitz: Perils and promises of globalization,* a documentary film realized by the author.

Stiglitz, J. E. (2010). *Freefall: America, free markets, and the sinking of the world economy.* New York: Norton.

Stiglitz, J. E. (2012). *The price of inequality: How today's divided society endangers our future.* New York: Penguin, 2012.

Stiglitz, J. E. (2013). The free-trade charade. *Project Syndicate,* 14 July 2013.

Stiglitz, J. E. (2015). The secret corporate takeover. *Project Syndicate,* 13 May 2015.

Stiglitz, J. E. (2016). Monopoly New Era. *Project Syndicate,* 13 May 2016.

Stiglitz, J. E. (2017a). Trumpian Uncertainty. *Project Syndicate,* 9 January 2017. Retrieved January 15, 2017, from www.project-syndicate.org.

Stiglitz, J. E. (2017b). Why Tax Cuts for the Rich Resolve Nothing. *Project Syndicate,* 27 July 2017.

Tomic, D. (2008). The *Longue Durée* and World-Sytems Analysis, Colloquium to Commemorate the 50th Anniversary of Fernand Braudel, 'Histoire et sciences sociales: La longue durée', *Annales E.S.C.* 13ᵉ Année, No. 4. 1958, October 24–25, Fernand Braudel Center, Binghamton University, Binghamton, NY.

Urio, P. (1984). *Le Rôle politique de l'administration publique.* LEP: Lausanne.

Urio, P. (2004). The provision of public services in the PRC in the age of reform: Reconciling state, market and civil society, paper presented at *the International Symposium on Public Service and Government Reform,* Haikou, China, October 30 31.

Urio, P. (2010a). *Reconciling state, market, and society in China. The long March towards prosperity.* London and New York: Routledge.

Urio, P. (2010b). De Genève à Pékin: entre le hasard et la nécessité. *Mélanges à l'occasion du 40ème anniversaire du Département de science politique* (pp. 73–86). Genève: Université de Genève, Département de science politique.

Urio. P. (2012). *China, the west, and the myth of new public management. Neoliberalism and its discontents.* London and New York: Routledge, 2012.

Urio, P. (2018). *China reclaims world power status. Putting an end to the world America made.* London and New York: Routledge, 2018.

Vine, D. (2015). *Base nation. How U.S. military bases abroad harm America and the world.* New York: Metropolitan Books.

Wallerstein, I. (1974 and 1980). *The modern world system. Vol. I. Capitalist agriculture and the origins of the European world-system in the sixteenth century.* New York: Academic Press, 1974; Vol. *II. Mercantilism and the consolidation of the European world-economy, 1600–1750.* New York: Academic Press, 1980.

Wallerstein, I. (1991). Braudel on capitalism, or everything upside down. *Journal of Modern History,* (June), 354–361.

Wallerstein, I. (2004). *World systems analysis. An introduction.* Durham and London: Duke University Press.

Wang, H. (1998). Contemporary Chinese thought and the question of modernity. In *Social text* (no. 55), Intellectual Politics in Post-Tiananmen China, Summer.

Wang, H. (2003). *China's New Order.* Cambridge, MA: Harvard University Press.

References

Weber, M. (1978). *Economy and society* (Vol. 1 and 2). Berkeley: University of California.

Xi, J. (2017). Secure a Decisive Victory in Building a Moderately Prosperous Society in All Respects and Strive for the Great Success of Socialism with Chinese Characteristics for a New Era, Xi Jinping speech at the 2017 Party congress, official translation available on *China Daily* website.

Zhang, W. (1996). *Ideology and economic reform under Deng Xiaoping*. Kegan Paul International: London and New York.

Zufferey, Nicolas. (2008). *Introduction à la pensée chinoise, Pour mieux comprendre la Chine du XXIe siècle*. Paris: Hachette.

Chapter 3
The New Public Management Comes to China

After one century of humiliations, the recovery of China started already during the Mao era. However, it is especially thanks to Deng that China's long march towards prosperity and world power gained momentum. The content of Deng's reforms, based upon the introduction of market mechanisms taking place alongside with a revised and limited form of the old planned economy of the Mao era, gives an idea of the scope of Deng's strategy. Inevitably, this epochal change was to pose many challenges, linked to one another, that needed a skilful leadership, capable of mastering the contradictions that inevitably would arise: economic development vs. environmental protection, rural development vs. urban development, economic efficiency vs. equitable distribution of wealth, to name just a few. The results obtained would inevitably be a mixture of success and failure, that the leadership would have to deal with after the end of Deng's era, should it wish to continue the long march toward prosperity (to be dealt with in Chap. 4).

3.1 Introduction: From Empire to the People's Republic of China

Already during the last decades of the XIX century China was quick to take advantage of the lessons learned from the failure of the Empire. Nevertheless, it is with the PRC that China recovered its full sovereignty and, in spite of Mao mistakes, paved the way for Deng to define China's development strategy, later further developed by Jiang Zemin, Hu Jintao and Xi Jinping.

This Chapter is based on several parts of Urio (2010, 2012, 2018), with many updates and comments.

The original version of this chapter was revised. The correct figure in page 105 is updated. The correction to this chapter is available at 10.1007/978-981-13-8879-8_7

© Springer Nature Singapore Pte Ltd. 2019
P. Urio, *China 1949–2019*, https://doi.org/10.1007/978-981-13-8879-8_3

3.1.1 The Lessons from the Fall of the Empire

China is generally recognized as one of the greatest civilizations, not only for the arts, but also for the organization of government. According to Max Weber, China was, together with ancient Egypt, the first country to develop a quasi-modern public administration, i.e. a public bureaucracy (Weber 1978, for Egypt, pp. 964, 971–973 and 1401–1402; for China, pp. 431, 477, 964 and 1401; and Balazs 1968). This great civilization suffered its most devastating humiliation between the XIX and the XX centuries when Western powers reduced it to semi-colonial status. Of course, this was not the first time China was defeated. The Mongols and the Manchus defeated China and ruled over it for several centuries. But they were almost completely assimilated into Chinese culture and governed it according to the traditional Confucian way, so that there is not discontinuity in China's history, which is structured according to the sequence of the Chinese dynasties until the fall of the last dynasty in 1911. But Western countries did not even dream of being assimilated into the Chinese culture. The reason why is very simple: they only wanted to do business in China, and quite naturally on their own terms. The humiliation was rendered even more deep when China was defeated by its 'small cousin of the rising sun', Japan, in 1894–1895, and lasted until 1949 when Mao proclaimed the founding of the People's Republic of China. The one-century long humiliation has not been forgotten.

Although most Western commentators recognize that the Chinese have some good reasons for remembering the 'humiliation', many of them are surprised that they still remember that sad period of their history. For example, Gordon Chang: 'Any matter can become emotional in China once it has been linked with the devil of history. (…) Yes, the British burned the Summer Palace and the Chinese have a right to be angry. Yet the British also burned the American capital, but when was the last time you heard anyone complaining of the War of 1812?' (Chang 2001, pp. 190–191). Chang forgets that after all, the American won that war, and it lasted only a few years (like the Nazi occupation of France during World War II), whereas the 'humiliation' inflicted on China by the Western powers (including the US) lasted over 100 years, between 1839 and 1949, and even after. Compare this with what emotion Americans remember the criminal attack of September-11, that launched the 'long war' against terrorism (see e.g. Zhang 2014).

How did China manage to become again not only a great civilization, but also a great power, capable of dissuading potential enemies from repeating the aggression of the XIX century? Through what strategies di China manage to realize this goal? Already after the defeat in the Opium Wars (1839–1860), China set up factories and dockyards to manufacture Western-style weapons and war-ships. Unfortunately, it takes a long time before a country can build warships capable of confronting a technologically more advanced foreign navy. Inevitably, in 1884–1885, it took only one hour for the French, in a conflict over Vietnam, to destroy the warships built by China, and a decade later (1894–1895) China lost the first Sino-Japanese War that was decided at sea (Buckley Ebrey 1999, pp. 245 and 252–254). In spite of these defeats, it is interesting to acknowledge that China was already aware of the importance

3.1 Introduction: From Empire to the People's Republic of China 63

of building a modern navy capable of confronting potential enemies. Moreover, at the beginning of the twentieth century, ideas of constitutionalism and parliamentary government were discussed at the Qing court, and in 1909 consultative provincial assemblies met in each province. But these initiatives came too late: the empire of the Qing Dynasty, which had been weakened for decades by foreign interventions and internal contradictions, collapsed at the beginning of 1912.

During the time of the Republic of China led by the Nationalist Party of Sun Yat Sen and Chiang Kai-shek (1912–1949), the civil war between the Nationalists and the Communists, the Japanese aggression and the numerous foreign interferences (especially from the US supporting the Nationalists) left few opportunities to develop China's power. It is only when the civil war ended with the victory of the Communists that China was in a position to organize and implement a strategy for building the power resources that would realize the objective of becoming again a world power.

3.1.2 China's Strategies for Recovering Wealth and Power

Hu Angang has analyzed the strategies implemented by the Chinese leadership to develop the country since 1949. Hu considers that there have been four successive versions of the regional development strategy corresponding to different development stages. The first three were mainly addressed to the Chinese territory from the perspective of geography and economy.[1] The first strategy (1949–1978, Mao era) organized a balanced development thanks to the planned economy but it had serious negative consequences, such as poor economic performance, limitation of personal freedom, little incentives for innovations, environmental damages, as well as the catastrophic impact of the Great Leap Forward and the Cultural Revolution. The second strategy (1979–1998, Deng Xiao Ping and Jiang Zemin) prioritized rapid economic development focused on the coastal and western regions thanks to the introduction of market mechanisms and the progressive opening up to the global economy; nevertheless, while it developed the economy and reduced poverty, it also increased disparities between regions, provinces and people. The third strategy (1999–2013, initiated by Jiang Zemin and developed by Hu Jintao) was based upon a regional balanced development and the reduction of disparities, thanks to investments in the inner and western regions, and the beginning of the development of a modern social security system. The fourth strategy (2013–...., Xi Jinping) 'will not only continue to reduce regional disparity and promote collaborative development among different economic blocks [i.e. Northeast, Central, East, and West], but also contributes to reshape the world economic geography, innovate international development mode, and construct a new international political and economic order toward the future.' (Hu 2016, p. 16).

---

[1] For more detailed analysis of the first three strategies see Urio (2018), in this chapter, Sects. 2 and 3, and Urio (2010).

So, after three stages of development strategy addressed to the Chinese territory, with the aim of developing the economy (first and second strategies) and to reduce inter-regional disparities (third strategy), China's fourth development strategy aims at further reducing disparities and building a developmental bridge between the country and its global environment. The fourth development strategy, that establishes for the first time a clear link between internal regional development and its projection to the outside world, has been included in the 13th Five-year Plan (2016–2020). This overall strategy integrates three regional development strategies (the Beijing-Tianjin-Hebei, the Yangtze River Economic Zone, and the BRI (the Belt and Road Initiative) in combination with the four economic regional blocks mentioned above. The three strategies and the four economic regional blocks are inter-connected to form China's grand strategy, that should reshape China's economic geography. Therefore, the novelty and the force of the BRI reside not only in the projection of China's economic power abroad, but it is also a means to strengthen and coordinate the internal economic and social development of the different parts of China (blocks, provinces, and regions).

The analysis of China's four development strategies shows that the Chinese leadership does not rely upon theoretical models defined prior to action, thereby following the traditional Chinese way to understand and implement strategy (Sect. 2.3). On the contrary, action is evaluated upon results, and then, as results are not only positive, but inevitably present some important negative aspects (e.g. the increase of disparities of Deng Xiaoping's reforms) some new ways of proceeding are defined and implemented (i.e. institutions and policies). And so forth. There are no a priori ideological choices: institutions and policies do not possess an intrinsic value, but are evaluated on the basis of their capacity to realize the policy goal, i.e. the recovering of world power status, that is the only element of the strategy that does not change. Also, China intervenes where and when it has a reasonable chance to succeed. Moreover, as everything is bound to change over time, the Chinese leadership waits until the 'silent transformations' have changed the 'situation potential' to its advantage (Sect. 6.2).

Let me end this introduction by explaining why I use New Public Management for qualifying the second strategy, that of Deng Xiao Ping. In my book on NPM in China and in the West (Urio 2012) I had to identify the core characteristics of NPM, i.e. to define NPM as a Weberian ideal-type, different from other types of public management, irrespective of the variations in reality. This ideal-type constitutes the basis upon which neoliberals have in practice oriented the definition and the implementation of both strategic goals (e.g. privatizations) and operational devices (e.g. analytic accounting) in their attempt to reform public management.[2] That China's reforms can be considered as a variant of NPM is attested by several scholars, for example by Ma Jun and Zhang Zhibin: 'The years since 1980 have witnessed a remarkable movement worldwide to reform public administration. For many (…) there is a striking international convergence of ideas among these administrative

---

[2]For a definition of the Weberian ideal-type methodology see Weber (1988), pp. 146–214, English Translation: Weber (2011), pp. 49–112.

3.1 Introduction: From Empire to the People's Republic of China

reforms, while others disagree (…). Despite these different stances, the international debate on administrative reforms has been overly influenced by the so-called New Public Management (NPM). In this context, the administrative reforms in China were also conceptualized as a variation of NPM with non-western characteristics (…).' (Ma and Zhang 2009). This is also my opinion in spite of the fact that, as I will show below in Chap. 4, the Chinese leadership started to introduce, since the mid-1990s, several correcting policies to overcome the negative consequences of the Chinese NPM, and to sustain those who suffered from the process of marketization.[3]

3.1.3 Mao's Achievements

The establishment of the People's Republic in 1949 was successful in reclaiming sovereignty after a century of foreign aggressions that had reduced China to a semi-colonial status. The reclaimed sovereignty and the new policies announced by the new leadership (e.g. the land reform) improved the morale of the Chinese people by giving them a renewed faith in the greatness of their culture, history and destiny.

Before 1949 the health of the Chinese people was rather poor in international comparison. It is to the credit of the Mao era to have succeeded in almost totally eradicating serious infectious and parasitic diseases, thanks to a medical system for common workers and peasants, and especially for poor people. Mortality rates dropped significantly both for young and adult people; life expectancy at birth increased from about 37 in 1950 to almost 66 in 1980. Moreover, this system assured a fair access to health care to all Chinese people. Literacy improved from as low as 25.5 to more than 65%. Finally, the process of industrialization was accelerated and the real GDP growth was quite impressive, and in spite of Mao's mistakes it increased every year, except in 1961 (–27.3) and 1962 (–5.6%) as a consequence of the Great Leap Forward, and in 1968 (–4.1) and 1976 (–1.6%) as a consequence of the Cultural Revolution (IMF World Economic Outlook, April 2018).

Improvement of health and the increased literacy of the Chinese population were two important features that allowed the developing of the economy, and especially industrialization, which is another achievement of the Mao era, in spite of the environmental damages it produced. In fact, it is on this basis (sovereignty, health, education, and industrialization), that Mao's successor, Deng Xiao Ping, was able to further develop China's economy, as we shall see below. But Deng had to face some serious difficulties, which are generally considered as serious failures of the Mao era, The Great Leap Forward, and the Great Cultural Resolution. The State had shown its incapacity to peacefully regulate tensions and conflicts within polity and society. And despite Mao's goal to develop the economy and catch up with Western countries,

---

[3] In their conclusion Ma and Zhang (2009) consider that NPM 'at best provides an incomplete picture of the inherent logic of rebuilding the Chinese administrative state during the reform era', ibidem, p. 246. Granted. But, as they admit, the logic of Chinese reforms (especially the process of marketization, a typical NPM policy device) has been the dominant policy option followed by the Chinese leadership since 1978 and up to about the mid-1990s.

the standard of living of Chinese families had fallen behind the level attained before the Great Leap Forward. It looked as if state, the Party, economy and society (i.e. people) had been disconnected from each other, or worse, that they had been put into a kind of permanent contradiction of each other. This was an extremely dangerous situation that could have drawn the People's Republic of China toward further conflict and disorder, and eventually to a final collapse. To avoid this tragic outcome, it was necessary to reconstruct, and, as history never repeats itself, to reinvent Chinese society, state, and economy; in other words, to find means to reconcile state, market, and society (Urio 2010).

My interpretation of this important phase of post-1949 China, amongst other possible and plausible interpretations, is that Mao, by launching the Great leap Forward and the Cultural Revolution, sought to accelerate economic development and to fight against three bureaucracies that were in the process of gaining power and stealing power from him, and deviating from his ideological line: the Party, the Government and the intellectual bureaucracies. But Mao's strategy to govern in a permanent state of Revolution was clearly in contradiction with Mao's aim of restoring China's power by developing its economic structure. Mao's way of managing the state and Chinese society necessitated politicians and civil servants who shared his ideology (no matter how he defined it); in other words, they ought to be 'red'. As Max Weber has demonstrated in his writings on economy, polity and society, the development of the economy (be it in the form of market economy or command economy) will inevitably need the development of bureaucracies in all parts of society, i.e. a special type of organization based, amongst other characteristics, upon technical competencies. Therefore, bureaucrats would inevitably acquire power and, at the end of the process of bureaucratization, they would govern instead of the politicians.[4] And this is what happened under the leadership of Deng Xiao Ping.

3.2 Deng's New Public Management

In Chap. 2 (Sects. 2.4.1, 2.4.2 and 2.4.3), I have shown how Deng changed the ideology of the Party. In this section, I will first discuss the very complex and skilful strategy defined and implemented by Deng for overcoming the consequences of the Great leap Forward and for defeating those who remained faithful to Mao and to his political line within the Party hierarchy. Then I will define the content of Deng's strategy and the formidable challenges it was necessary to master to succeed. This is a necessary step because it helps us to understand that such a vast societal project would not have been possible to achieve during Deng's life, and that some failures (to be dealt with in following sections) would inevitably appear along with some remarkable achievements.

---

[4]That is, organizations based upon formal and technical rules, hierarchies, competence and the practice of secrecy. See on this important point based upon the works of Max Weber, Urio (1984), pp. 45–59 and 217–282.

3.2.1 Deng's Strategy

Two constraints were facing Deng at the end of the Cultural Revolution: on the one hand, he was confronted with the necessity to improve the performance of China's economy, and on the other hand he had to re-establish the legitimacy and leadership of the Communist Party. Deng considers that a strong economic performance, especially if sustained by technological progress, is essential for assuring national security on one side, and on the other side for restoring the legitimacy of the Party, as the Party will be evaluated on its capacity to put goods and services at the disposal of the population. So, Deng works simultaneously towards the realization of two goals: the consolidation of Party power and a better economic performance. What distinguishes Deng as a rational actor is his pragmatism. 'For Deng Xiaoping, Communism was more an organizational rather than an intellectual response to the problems that China faced in the second half of the twentieth century.' (Goodman 2000, p. 83). In other words, in spite of Marxist ideology that was dominating the Party, Deng's pragmatism drives him to introduce into the Chinese economy some market mechanisms (the cat that catches more mice).

It is clear that the emphasis put by Deng on the development of the economy has necessitated important changes of other elements of Chinese society, in addition to the change in the Party ideology as I discussed in Sect. 2.4. It was in particular necessary to transform public administrations into organizations based more upon technical and scientific competences than on conformity to the Marxist-Maoist ideological line of the Party. This is in fact the major aspect of Deng's rejection of the Cultural Revolution.

After the reform of the organization of agriculture, Deng starts with experimenting market mechanisms within a few special economic zones. Then he evaluates the results and finally exports the good practices to other regions and so forth, in the framework of a gradual, incremental strategy. By doing this, Deng puts the emphasis on facts, i.e. on verified means and results, and not on ideological a priori. Moreover, the poor performing planned economy is progressively, even if not totally, abandoned. In my opinion it would be correct to say that the scope of planning is progressively limited to the strategic (or core) functions of the state, i.e. to sustaining a strong economic development while maintaining social, political, and economic stability, and at the same time safeguarding the fundamental and instrumental goal of maintaining and reinforcing the leadership of the Party. Maintaining the leadership of the Party is an instrumental goal, in the sense that Deng, as well as his successors, consider that the Party is the sole organization capable to lead China on the road to reforms. The special economic zones constitute the example of the implementation of the strategy the Party will use in practically all the domains: test policies that have produced good results abroad in a limited Chinese context and verify whether they are suitable to China; in case of success, export these good policies to the rest of the country.

It is clear that this way of analyzing the development of reforms in China by proposing Deng as a single rational actor, determining alone the trend and pace

68

of reforms, is too radical a simplification of reality. In fact, one can also analyse the reforms in China like a process implying the cooperation of several individual actors, factions, groups, and central and provincial leaders, not to mention the support of the majority of the population (Hu 2014). Moreover, we cannot exclude the impact of structural forces independent of the will of political leaders. As suggested by Fernand Braudel and François Jullien (Sect. 2.1) long term-changes have been developing silently for a long time in China: contradictions within the Empire, a beginning of market economy during the foreign occupation of the coastal provinces, the emergence of a new bourgeois class in the same areas, and the spread of Marxism, especially after the Russian Revolution (Bergère 1986, 2007). Deng has been skilful enough to take advantage of these changes that became visible and audible during the Cultural Revolution. So to speak, he was able to surf on the wave of the silent transformations that became evident at the end of the Cultural Revolution in 1976.

By pursuing the consolidation of the power of the Party, Deng Xiaoping postulated in 1979 the four Cardinal Principles that are still valid today, as we have already seen in Chap. 2.4.1: (1) every public policy is to be in conformity with the Marxist, Leninist and Maoist thought, (2) with the Socialist way, (3) with the continuation of the democratic dictatorship of the people and (4) with the leadership of the CPC. While the first three principles may give way to various interpretations, the fourth principle was used to consolidate the power of the CPC, and thus that of Deng, by not allowing any political force to rise within civil society to contest the supremacy of the CPC. The consequences of this policy appear in particular in the fact that the media remain basically under the control of the Party and that the Party, in spite of the reforms, retains control over the State's administration thanks to its organization which is in fact parallel and hierarchically superior to the governmental one at all levels of government (Lieberthal 1995, p. 135).

To achieve the second goal, the improvement of the economic performance, Deng remains faithful to the four modernizations already defined by Mao and Zhou Enlai (Sect. 2.4.1): agriculture, industry, science and technology, and national defence. It is clear that in order to mobilize the country's forces within Chinese society for improving economic performance, Deng must give some freedom to the Chinese people, and this has often been interpreted in the West as a contradiction to the political goal of maintaining the supremacy of the CPC. Nevertheless, this interpretation is only valid if one assumes that the political goal is the principal one and economic development simply the means for achieving the former. But if we consider that the two goals are imbedded into a single system in which they are interdependent, this interpretation loses its force. No matter what the dominant goal is, pursuing economic development will inevitably give more freedom to the Chinese people in the economic structure. What will be the consequences of this economic freedom in the political arena is by no means clear, and cannot be forecast on the basis of the Western experience, which is (and this should not be forgotten) a unique historical experience. Once again, what matters is the situation of the Chinese people (which has certainly improved since the beginning of the reforms) and the consequences the Chinese people will draw from this experience. What is also certain is that the reform era represents a radical

3.2 Deng's New Public Management

break from the Maoist past, and the way used by Deng to lead the country out of the Maoist era is an additional proof of the pragmatic character of his strategy.

Now, let me remind the reader the main features of Deng's strategy I have already mentioned in Sect. 2.4.2. The strategic level is divided into two complementary levels, i.e. the ideology and the economy-military levels. At the ideological level Deng reaffirms four of the main features of Party's ideology by defining the four Cardinal Principles mentioned above. At the economic-military level, Deng defines the target of China's modernization by identifying four domains necessary for restoring China's strength both internally and internationally, i.e.: agriculture, industry, science and technology, and national defence. At the operational level the main goal is to improve economic performance and the standard of living of the Chinese people. The means for realizing this goal is the introduction of market mechanisms and opening up to global economy. The behaviours linking the strategic and the operational levels in the day-to-day implementation of this vast policy objective can be defined as follows: (1) maintain the leadership of the Party and restore its legitimacy, (2) introduce reforms on an experimental basis, (3) reform gradually (not like Russia), (4) privatize gradually and partially, by keeping the strategic economic sectors in the hands of the state, and reinforcing the macro-economic policies of the state,[5] (5) maintain economic, social and political stability, (6) in case of difficulties, slow down or stop, then re-start.

3.2.2 The Content of Deng's Strategy

The content of Deng's reforms may be subdivided into the following dimensions: (1) the introduction of market mechanisms in the economy; (2) the creation of a 'pool of talent' necessary for managing the reform process; (3) the management of the relationship between state and society taking account of the degree of freedom introduced in the economy; (4) the reform of agriculture first; (5) then the reform of the urban economy; (6) and finally, the integration into the international economy (Lieberthal 1995, pp. 123–153; Riedel et al. 2007, pp. 1–17; Bergère 2007, pp. 223–241)

The first dimension of Deng's reforms is the introduction of market mechanisms into China's economy, that determine and orient all the other dimensions aimed at sustaining the economic development. Secondly, further developing Mao's strategy for improving the competencies of the Chinese population, (literacy sustained by good health) necessary for contributing to the development of the economy, Deng launched at the end of the 1970s the rehabilitation of the intellectuals who were purged during the Cultural Revolution. Professional qualifications are no more considered as an elitist characteristic but as a patriotic one. Moreover, Deng favours the accession of young educated people to the public administration which should thus favour the rationalization of public management. We will see in Sects. 5. 2 and 6.2.4 that this strategy has been developed through the whole process of

---

[5]To be developed in Chap. 6, Sect. 6.2.4.

modernization. Nevertheless, already in 1978, freedom of the intellectuals should not be equated with freedom to attack the political leadership and the state.

Thirdly, Deng had come to the conclusion that economic development required a certain degree of freedom and initiative from civil society. It was therefore necessary to increase the freedom of social actors and to relax the constraints of state power. Thus, through Deng's reforms, consumerism (in particular fashion) was again made socially possible and even accepted, and, for example, television sets were distributed massively at the end the Seventies in order to encourage positive attitudes towards consumerism instead of exclusively diffusing discourse with ideological contents. We can say that, through the development of consumption, the role of the state in orienting the moral behaviour of the people has been reduced, and that the expectations of the population (especially regarding the improvement of the material living conditions) have considerably increased. Nevertheless, we should not forget that consumerism is also based upon some ideological values, and this is the reason why many Chinese officials and intellectuals are worried today about the lack of moral restraints of a large part of the Chinese population which frenetically rushes towards enrichment at all costs and by all means.

Fourthly, at the beginning of the 1980s, Deng's reforms led to the abolition of the agricultural communes that were replaced de facto by family farms, since each family leased land from the commune. One must not forget that in 1978, 80% of the Chinese population lived in the countryside and worked in the primary sector (70.5% of the total manpower, Table 3.2a). The introduction of family farms led to a surplus of manpower in the rural areas. Deng compensated this surplus of workforce by allowing the creation of small enterprises and light industry. By these measures, the process of urbanization could be partially diverted from large urban areas towards small cities, where a strong demand of consumer goods was developing which in turn supported the development of light industry. During these reforms, millions of people changed their work, and these small cities or 'townships' became an important political and economic factor. However, agricultural production did not increase after 1984 in spite of demographic growth, and the uncontrolled industrialization of the rural areas started to raise concerns about the environmental consequences of this policy.

The fifth dimension of reforms concerns the urban economy, where Deng's strategy also led to an increase of the freedom of social actors. Thus, several forms of property were legalized, and the state gave up the absolute monopoly of production and distribution of goods and services. This is also witnessed by the limitation of the importance of the economic plan: in 1978 the plan still contained 600 items, while at the end of the 1980s their number was reduced to only 25. This reduction of the importance of the economic plan is on the one hand the result of decentralization (i.e. delegation of duties to the subordinate local authorities) but also, on the other hand, of the disappearance of some domains formerly regulated by the plan. (Riedel et al., p. 11). Moreover, during the 1980s the state weakened the administrative price control, and this has given rise to the 'dual price system': this system allows that goods which are produced in supplement of the economic plan can be sold at a higher

3.2 Deng's New Public Management

price in the market. This system has nevertheless also shown negative consequences like corruption or illegal 'prices arbitrage'.[6]

The sixth dimension of the reforms of Deng Xiaoping concerns the opening of China to the world economy. When Deng seizes power and launches the reform process, the immediate international environment of China had undergone important transformations since the time of the Cultural Revolution. Neighbours like Japan, South Korea, Taiwan or Singapore had experienced technological development and considerable economic growth thanks to their integration into the world economy (Chang 2003a, b, 2008). Deng considered that the catching up of Chinese economy compared to its neighbours was essential for China's national security. For this reason, the Chinese government already in 1979 offered a special tax treatment to foreign companies to attract investments. This opening has nevertheless made necessary the establishment of a more transparent legal system, the legal structure and the economic structure being functionally interdependent. Before the reforms, the legal Chinese system was mainly based upon personal decisions and had not known codified norms. Thus, the first foreign companies which settled in China were obliged to accept all the relevant rules without knowing the contents of these rules. During the 1980s, Deng was actually able to impose some changes of the legal system which made it more transparent and started to develop a court system. The development of the legal system also resulted in a great need for lawyers (Peeremboom 2002).

During Deng's era, China also started to be interested in the accession to international organizations like the institutions of Bretton Woods or the Asian Development Bank for the purpose of obtaining loans at low interest rates and of gaining access to the competencies of these organizations (Sect. 5.2). The opening of China to the world economy also involved a change of mentality for the export enterprises, for example in textile. During Mao's era, these enterprises were accustomed to producing according to the quantities set by the plan, whereas under Deng it was necessary to produce according to the demand of customers. This change of mentality favoured the reforms of the companies by introducing a rational managerial system, but it also implied the danger of destroying the bond between the enterprises and the community. In fact, under the planned economy, enterprises had a double role: on one side they had the economic function of producing according to the figures set in the plan and to distribute salaries to their employees; on the other hand, they had the social role of providing schools, medical care, and old age pensions to their workforce. The reforms, while boosting economic development by introducing some principles of market economy (namely competition as a condition for economic efficiency, and therefore the necessity of reducing production costs), had the consequence of driving enterprises to give priority to their economic function at the expense of the social one, thus laying off their redundant workforce and leaving the remaining employees without the social security to which they were accustomed during the Mao era.

The analysis of the main contents of the economic reforms I have just presented shows the importance of the changes introduced by Deng, through his pragmatic

---

[6]The economic actors acquire goods at the low prices set by the plan, and then sell them at the market price when the quantity set by the plan has been sold.

strategy based upon factual considerations more than on ideological a priori. Moreover, the analysis of the contents of these reforms illustrates very well that reforms in the economic structure may involve the need for reforms in other parts of society, for example in the legal and the cultural structures, as the different sub-structures are imbedded in a system where they are linked by a structural inter-dependency (Sect. 2.4). Finally, I have put forward the hypothesis that in the process of changing other sub-structures after the changes introduced into the economy, China may not necessarily follow the Western way, and may be able to find some functional equivalents capable of sustaining market mechanisms. I will provide some answers to this important question in Sect. 5.2.

3.2.3   The Challenges of Deng's Strategy

In order to understand the formidable problems Deng had to master, I will use and develop a framework for analysis for the interpretation of China's reforms which I presented for the first time in 2004 and later used for my 2010 book (Urio 2004, 2010). Figure 3.1 summarizes the major dimensions of the new Chinese economy and society, the problems, difficulties, and obstacles, as well as the policies needed to overcome the difficulties, by indicating the main links between these sets of variables.[7]

In the middle of Fig. 3.1 is represented the starting choice made by Deng in favour of the partial introduction of market mechanisms alongside with a more limited and flexible use of the old economic planning of the Mao era. Its success and failures depend upon the knowledge necessary for designing, implementing and mastering this fundamental development strategy. In particularly, this depends upon the mastering or at least the coordination of the contributions provided by banks, SOEs, and financial markets. This, in turn, implies the implementation of some of the policies presented at the bottom of the figure, namely the restructuring and eventually the recapitalization of SOEs and banks (more particularly the elimination of non-performing loans, should they occur). Moreover, this change necessitates the adoption of a legal system capable of sustaining the development of economic activities in the new areas of the economy open to competition, namely the establishment of the principle of legal security without which no rational activity is possible within this new type of economic space. This strategy needs, together with some of the other policies to be mentioned hereafter, a rational management of public finance (taxation and expenditures).[8] As the appearances of negative consequences cannot

---

[7]It goes without saying that the causal links suggested are purely qualitative in most cases. To our knowledge there is today no quantitative model able to take into consideration the complexity of these links. There is nevertheless sufficient empirical evidence that the arrows connecting the sets of variables, represented in the figure by the rectangles, are reasonably based upon a causal relationship.

[8]I understand that taxation is more important, and in any case must precede expenditures. This has become a crucial point when the fiscal decentralization of the 1980s showed that the central government did not possess the financial means needed to finance the policies necessary not only

3.2 Deng's New Public Management

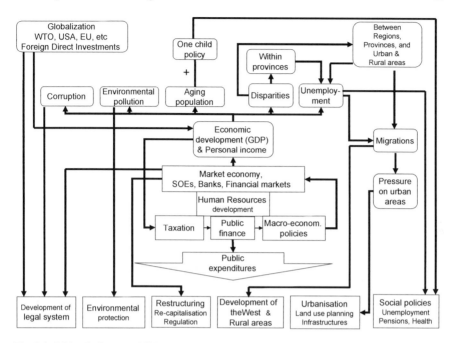

Fig. 3.1 Main challenges of China's reforms

be discarded in theory, and we shall see they occurred indeed simultaneously with the positive outcomes (this chapter and Chap. 4), the central government should be given the necessary means to finance the policies necessary for correcting the negative consequences of the introduction of market mechanisms. Depending upon the scope of the negative consequences, the central government will need huge financial means, that may require putting an end to the fiscal decentralization set up in the 1980s and to recentralizing the fiscal capacity in favour of the central government. This is exactly what happened from the middle of the 1990s onwards (Lou Jiwei 1997).

---

for sustaining the economic development, but also and above all in order to finance the policies needed to correct the unwanted consequences of the introduction of market mechanisms. Only an efficient economic system can provide the state with the financial basis from which it can draw the financial resources it needs.

74   3 The New Public Management Comes to China

Moreover, in order to make the transition from a command economy, where the government determines almost all the parameters of economic activity, to another economy in which market mechanisms play an increasing role, the state needs to develop and master the macro-economic policies typical of this type of economy. These new state functions entail the need to develop human resources, either by training the existing civil servants or by improving the competencies of the institutions of higher learning that will be entrusted with the task of training young people in those areas of management (e.g. modern statistical analysis, policy analysis, implementation and evaluation of public policies) necessary for university level students who may be tempted by a career in the Civil Service and in the SOEs. This strategy will create a reservoir of talents from which the state can in the future recruit the competencies it needs. Moreover, the Party schools at all levels could also play the role of training civil servants and cadres of the SOEs.[9] In Chap. 5 we will see how CPC has responded to the needs of training cadres, and in Sect. 6.2.4.2 how it has developed a strategy to attract talents form both China and abroad.

Coming now to the consideration of the results obtained by the development strategy adopted by China after 1978, we can again stress the spectacular improvements mentioned above. However, we must also refer to several negative consequences represented at the top of Fig. 3.1. Based upon the experience of Western countries, it was possible to forecast, as in fact happened, that the improvement of the economy, and the consequent increase of wealth (measured by GDP) would also increase all sorts of disparities within the country (to be developed hereafter in Sect. 3.4). First, economic development in conjunction with the one-child policy has accelerated the aging of the population, and this is the first factor demanding the setting up of a modern pension system. The other consequence of market mechanism has been the development of disparities within provinces and regions, as well as between provinces, regions and municipalities. The rift between rural and urban areas has also been considerably widened.

Moreover, the rapid introduction of market mechanisms and competition led state organizations (especially SOEs, but also state bureaucracies) to drastically reducing their staff and to laying off millions of employees and workers. This resulted in a huge rate of unemployment, as well as the emergence of new forms of poverty, that ran the risk of counterbalancing, at least in part, the impressive decrease of poverty achieved thanks to the reforms.

Third, the transition from a command economy to a new economic system, where market mechanisms (and hence competition among enterprises) were introduced quite rapidly, led the government to freeing the state-owned enterprises from the obligation of providing their workers and employees with the social services they were used to obtaining under the former command economy. This new way of organizing the production process, in conjunction with the one-child policy, was de-structuring

---

[9]Of course, another way of realizing this objective would be to hire talents from the private sector in China and abroad, both foreigners and (more likely) Chinese people who received university training abroad and have also been working in Western countries. It seems that, at least for the moment, this strategy is practiced more frequently by Chinese private companies and SOEs than by public bureaucracies.

3.2 Deng's New Public Management

both the traditional state's and intra-family solidarities, at least in the urban areas. But the reform process had also some negative consequences in the rural areas. Even the World Bank concedes that whereas one can consider that the dismantling of the Communes and the move to the Household Responsibility System have favoured the rapid decrease of rural poverty, 'a by-product of this institutional transformation was the increasing monetization and marketization of public service delivery in rural areas. In place of the communes, local governments were charged with administering and financing these services, which in poorer areas, they were unable to fully do because of a lack of fiscal resources. Schools and health facilities have therefore had to increasingly rely on charging user fees in order to cover their costs.' (World Bank 2009, p. viii).[10] The consequence has been that not only this new situation constituted an additional burden on rural families' budgets, but, for many of them, a serious obstacle to acceding to these services, and finally one of the causes of new forms of poverty. Therefore, the old solidarity system needed to be replaced in both urban and rural areas by a new safety net system in which, very likely, employers, employees and the state were to share the contribution to the various new social insurances. And this constitutes another challenge to the Chinese leadership, given the considerable cost implied by the new solidarity system.

Unemployment has also an impact on migrations. Unemployed and underemployed people in the most vulnerable zones (especially in the rural provinces and areas) try to seek working opportunities in the urban areas where the dynamism of the economy is creating new jobs. Of course, the majority of these new jobs are to be found at the lowest level of the salary hierarchy, especially in construction and services (Li Qiang 2002, 2003).[11] Working conditions of these people are most of the time minimum, to say the least. Nevertheless, as has happened in Europe and elsewhere for centuries, migrant people generally find in the hosting country (or in the case of China in the hosting provinces) better opportunities than they would have enjoyed, had they remained in their home town or village. Consequently, migrations

---

[10]The world Bank further explains that 'under the planned economy of the Mao era the communes were responsible not only for organizing production and distribution, but also for providing social services including health care. These services were financed by contributions from rural families (about 0.5 to 2% of their income), by the villages (from their income from agriculture and rural enterprises), and subsidies from higher-level government used mostly to pay for health workers' salaries and medical equipment.' (p. 125). The fundamental institutional change introduced by the reforms in the rural areas was 'the land reform characterized by the implementation of the household responsibility system in rural China, whereby farm households became residual claimants to output by receiving land use rights in return for delivery of a certain quota of grain to the village and meeting their tax obligations.' (p. 78).

[11]Li Qiang (2002) comments: 'According to my prestige and status surveys since 1996, peasant-workers are at the bottom of the social hierarchy. Peasants doing business in cities are ranked 92 in 100 occupations, while peasants finding employment in cities, 94. The last 10 in the list are typical occupations for peasant-workers, such as gatekeepers, carters, waste collectors, housemaids, porters and guards. Ironically, these peasant-workers are elites with apparently better personal qualities and abilities than those remaining in villages. They belong to a most active age group. They usually have a higher level of education, and are particularly capable in economic activities.' (p. 3 of the electronic version).

from rural villages may lead to significant increases in consumption per capita (De Brauw and Giles 2008, Tang and Yang 2008).[12]

Nevertheless, migrations are likely to exert a considerable pressure on the infrastructures of urban areas. This in turn necessitates the (re)definition of the land use planning policy (including urban infrastructures) and an additional pressure to set up a modern safety net also covering migrant workers. Moreover, in order to fix part of the population in the rural areas, and to reduce the gap between rural and urban areas, it may be necessary to set up a policy of investing in the infrastructures of the Western poor provinces and the rural areas in general. This is what China has done since the mid-1990s.[13]

Finally, the economic development, if not mastered, may pollute the environment and this requires the setting up of regulations supported by effective controls. The quasi-simultaneous aging of the population, the increase of disparities, unemployment, migrations, and environmental deterioration is likely to has a negative impact upon the health of the people both in the rural and urban areas. For the latter, an additional negative consequence of disparities may be the migration from rural to urban areas of competent people working in the health services, attracted as they are by better job and salary opportunities offered by the cities.

Last but not least, the opening up of the Chinese economy, especially after the entry of China into the World Trade Organization at the end of 2001, was likely to put additional pressure on the Government for the development of a legal system compatible with the international obligations China has subscribed to as a member of the international economic system. This pressure is complementary to the one exerted by the introduction of market mechanisms within the Chinese economy. They both require the establishment and implementation of legal rules compatible with the functioning of market mechanisms.

The number of problems and policies necessary to solve them is quite impressive. What is even more impressive is that the corresponding changes in Chinese society are happening practically simultaneously and over a relatively short span of time, contrary to their evolution in Western countries which had at least a century to adjust their policies to the consequences of the Industrial Revolution. In both cases, the consequences of economic development have been a radical change of the structure of Western and Chinese societies. Changes in social structure are per se neither positive nor negative. It all depends upon the balance between improvements and drawbacks, as well as upon the measures the governing elites take in order to help individuals to adjust to the transition.

---

[12]Tang and Yang comment: 'while migrant workers continue to occupy more blue-collar and service jobs than urban residents, their economic, social and political status has improved', p. 759. It is also interesting to note that the Chinese Trade Unions have admitted to the national congress of October 2008 47 representatives of migrant workers (China Daily, October 17, 2008) which shows that their status and needs are being recognized.

[13]Let us remark that at the same time the Government has publicly declared that it will take measures to accelerate the urbanization process in China. This is very likely because the urban areas are supposed to create more relatively well-paid jobs than the rural areas, and in any case the process of urbanization is the inevitable consequence of the development of a modern economy.

3.2 Deng's New Public Management   77

We will see below in Sects. 3.3 and 3.4, and in Chap. 4, to what extent China has been able to master these challenges. For doing so I will use several statistical data, ideally subdivided into three periods: the years of success, the years of negative consequences and imbalances, and the years of correcting the imbalances. It has been difficult to find a clear separation amongst these three periods. This did not come as a surprise as in the very complex historical process of China's reforms, positive, negative and rebalances have occurred often simultaneously. The solution has been to use the data as follows: the first period from 1978 to about 1995 shows that the results have been rather positive; difficulties appeared already between the end of the 1980s and the mid-1990s, and accelerated after the Party Congress of 1997 that led China to enter into the WTO at the end of 2001, but some important positive outcomes occurred even during this period. During the second period, between 1995 and about 2004–2005 the negative consequences become more important, and the Party starts to set policies to re-balance economy and society. During the third period, from 2004–2005, the rebalancing policies (already started in the mid-1990s with the policy of 'Open the West' and the centralization of fiscal policy) acquired momentum under the presidency of Hu Jintao (2002–2012). I will deal with periods 1 and 2 in this chapter, and I will examine the results of the rebalancing policies in Chap. 4.

3.3 The Impact of Marketization on China's Modernization

A few recent economic indicators give a first idea about the achievements realized thanks to the CPC's development strategy. Such a dramatic change had inevitably an impact on society's many dimensions: manpower distribution amongst agriculture, industry and services; demography; urban-rural characteristics; the appearance and development of the private sector and the new 'red capitalists'; the new structure of social classes; and the power elite. No less important has been the negative impact on the environment, due to the speed of economic development and the lack of environmental-friendly laws and regulations with huge environmental damages. These changes and the related difficulties explain the overall performance: a mix of achievements and problems.

3.3.1 The Major Economic Indicators and the Changing Structure of Employment

Maybe the best way to have a first insight of the impact of marketization on Chinese society is to consider the main indicators of China's economy between 2004 and 2016 (Table 3.1) and the changes in the distribution of manpower amongst agriculture, industry and services (Tables 3.2a). Overall, the picture shown in Table 3.1 is quite positive: GDP growth is quite high for all the period, except for 2016. This is mainly due to a real decrease of economic activity but also to the change of the development model from investments to domestic demand. The GDP increase is important measured by 'GDP (current $)', i.e. calculated at exchange rate, as well as by 'GDP PPP (2011 international dollar)'. The latter shows that China is above the EU (17,281 US$ bn, and even the US (19,390 US$ bn). Even more impressive is the increase of GDP per capita (in PPP) from $4,440 in 2004 to $15,470 in 2016, almost 3.5 times, which show that the cost of labour does not correspond any more to the idea of 'China the workshop of the world'. Current account balance and foreign exchange reserves witness the good health of China's economy. Moreover, the inflation rate is reasonable, and the exchange rate to the US$ has decreased from 8,277 in 2004 to 6,664 in 2016. The evolution of the exchange rate of the RMB has attracted criticism especially from the US, accusing China of exchange manipulation in order to boost its exports. However, on July 2018, Reuter reported that in its 24 July 2018 annual *External Sector Report* the IMF considered that the RMB, with an exchange rate of 6.8295 to the USD, was in line with fundamentals. Finally, the increase of the population was limited to 1.064% 2004 and 2016, which was the goal of the one-child policy set up during the 1980s. But this is probably the less positive indicator of Table 3.1 as it is likely to mask the aging of the population, which according to demographers will pose some important problems for the financing of public policies such as retirement pensions and health insurances.

This impressive picture reflects the impact of marketization on the relative importance of agriculture, industry and services: the contribution to labour by agriculture has decreased from 83.5% in 1952 to 27.7% in 2016, whereas during the same time the contribution of industry has increased from 7.4 to 28.8% and that of services from 9.1 to 43.5% (Table 3.2a). Even more spectacular has been the decline of the contribution of agriculture to GDP: during the same period, it has decreased from 50.5 to 8.6%, while the contribution of industry increased from 20.9 to 38.8%, and that of services from 28.6 to 51.6% (Table 3.2b). Moreover, the data suggests several changes in the structure of Chinese society, such as migrations, that we have already suggested in Sect. 3.2.3.

3.3.2 The Changing Structure of Chinese Society: Opportunities and Challenges

What is the new structure of Chinese society? This is not an easy question to answer, as data is not always either reliable or available. Nevertheless, this task is essential if we want to understand the challenges that are facing the Chinese leadership. First of all, there is a general agreement that the new social structure is considerably different from the old one, in spite of the persistence of some features of the old Maoist and even Imperial eras. The old 'class status system' of the Maoist era was mainly based upon political criteria, i.e. a mix of Marxist and political classifications. For example, in the rural areas: rural worker, poor peasant, middle-low peasants, middle-high

3.3 The Impact of Marketization on China's Modernization

Table 3.1 China's main economic indicators

	2004	2005	2006	2007	2008	2009	2010**	2016
Population million	1'296	1'304	1'311	1'318	1'325	1'331	1'338	1'379
Real GDP growth %	10,111	11,396	12,719	14,231	9,654	9,4	10,636	6,689
GDP (current $) US$ bn	1'955	2'286	2'752	3'552	4'598	5'110	6'101	11'199
GDP, PPP (constant 2011 international $) US$ bn	6'694	7'457	8'405	9'601	10'528	11'518	12'743	19'852
GDP per head US$ at PPP	4'440	5'060	5'870	6'880	7'680	8'360	9'290	15'470
Consumer inflation %	3,889	1,814	1,446	4,767	5,843	– 0,701	3,326	2,0
Current account balance US$ bn	68,941	132,378	231,843	353,183	420,569	243,257	237,81	196,38
Foreign exchange reserves US$ bn	614,5	821,5	1'068	1'530	1'949	2'416	2'862	3'030
Exchange rate RMB-US$	8,277	8,194	7,973	7,608	6,949	6,831	6,77	6,664

Source World Bank Data
Note I present 2 measures for GDP, the first 'GDP (current $)', i.e. calculated at exchange rate, and the second in 'GDP PPP (2011 international dollar)'

Table 3.2a Changes in employment of the three economic sectors (1952–2016)

	1952	1978	2003	2006	2008	2016
Agriculture	83.5%	70.5%	49.1%	48.2	38.1	27.7%
Industry	7.4	17.3	21.6	18.9	27.8	28.8%
Services	9.1	12.2	29.3	32.9	34.1	43.5%
Total	100	100	100	100	100	100

Source National Bureau of Statistics of China 2017

Table 3.2b Changes in GDP of the three economic sectors (1952–2016)

	1952	1978	2003	2006	2008	2016
Agriculture	50.5%	28.1%	14.6	12.5%	9.6	8.6
Industry	209	482	523	473	46.8	39.8
Services	8.6	23.7	33.1	40.2	43.6	51.6
Total	100	100	100	100	100	100

Source National Bureau of Statistics of China 2017

80   3 The New Public Management Comes to China

peasants, rich peasants, land owners; but also revolutionary soldiers and martyr-revolutionary families. This system made it possible to tell friends from enemies, the 'expropriables' from the beneficiaries. Moreover, the transition from a Marxist classification to a political classification based upon attitudes (the 'reds' vs. the 'bad categories') made it possible for Maoist power to isolate its enemies, and even to invent new categories according to the goals and strategies of Maoist power. Finally, since belonging to a category determined access to resources, (money, power, and prestige) this class system created new forms of inequalities. With reforms, the positioning of people within the social structure changed considerably, as a consequence of the changes of the economic structure, even if the political criteria did not completely disappear. But would inequalities disappear? Or would some new inequalities be the by-product of reforms? In the following paragraphs I propose to present the new demographic structure, the new uran-rural structure, the growing importance of the private sector and of the 'red capitalists', the power elite, the intellectuals, the middle class, and finally the social strata comprising workers, employees, peasants and migrant workers.

3.3.2.1 The New Demographic Structure

The changes in China's demography are closely related to the One-Child family planning policy started at the beginning of the 1970s, after two decades of very animated discussions within the Chinese leadership with some important inputs from the academy. This is contrary to the generally accepted opinion that Mao was against family planning. It is true that only in September 1980 the third session of the Fifth National People's Congress officially approved the State Council's policy of encouraging one couple to have one child, but family planning was progressively implemented already during Mao's era. The history of this policy is a good example of the Chinese way of discussing policy options, of adopting a solution, of implementing it progressively and with a certain amount of flexibility, taking into consideration the power relationships within the political elite, the objective characteristics of the Chinese situation, and the different situations of the people concerned, whether they live in urban or rural areas, or belong to ethnic minorities for example.[14] In order to control the dramatic increase of the size of the population, the central government decided to implement a number of regulations governing the size of Chinese families. This policy was in principle strictly enforced for urban residents and government employees.

Nevertheless, there were some exceptions that allowed having a second or even a third child. In urban areas it was possible to have a second child if the first child was disabled, or if both parents worked in high-risk occupations, or were themselves from one-child families. In rural areas, the implementation of this policy was more relaxed. For example, if the first child was a girl, a second child was generally allowed. For

---

[14]For a detailed history of the emergence and implementation of family planning in China see Hu Angang and Zou Ping 1991, pp. 67–109. The information mentioned above is on page 93.

3.3 The Impact of Marketization on China's Modernization

some ethnic minorities and for remote and under-populated areas, even a third child was allowed. Consequently, this policy, that existed from 1979 to 2015, allowed about half of all parents in China to have a second child. However, the first outcome of the family planning policy was that it played a very efficient role in restricting the size of the population. According to Chinese authorities, it prevented 250–300 million births. The total fertility rate, defined as the mean number of children per woman, decreased from 2.9 in 1979 to 1.7 in 2004, with a rate of 1.3 in urban areas and just fewer than 2.0 in rural areas (Wang 2003, pp. 1–15), and the birth rate also decreased rapidly from 29.77‰ in 1972 to 12.40‰ in 2005 (Lu Xueyi 2006). On the other side, thanks to the development of the health conditions and of the socio-economic situation, the life expectancy improved to attain 71 years for men and 74 for women in 2007 (World Health Organization 2007). Inevitably, the rapid decrease of the birth rate associated with the improved life expectancy makes the aging of the population a crucial issue as the dependency ratio is increasing. In China, the percentage of the population over 65 increased from 5% in 1982 to 7.5% in 2004, and was expected to rise to more than 15% by 2025 (Hesketh et al. 2005) To overcome these problems, the government started to relax this policy in November 2013, and because of disappointing results, it put it to an end in October 2015. However, the results of this decision are far from being positive, as the birth rate has not increased in a significant way. Therefore, this situation has today some negative consequences for the financing of retirement and health insurances.

The second outcome of the family planning policy has been the transition from the extended family to the nuclear family. This transition has resulted in the so-called "4-2-1" phenomenon, which is becoming predominant in Chinese society, i.e. an increasing number of couples will be responsible for the care of one child and four parents, and therefore the burdens borne by couples will become heavier and heavier. In international comparison, the speed with which China has entered into an aging society was much more rapid than that experienced in the past by Western countries. It took a transitional period of about 100 years for Western countries, but less than 20 years for China. Another important peculiarity of China's aging population is that it occurred while China was still in the phase of transition from an underdeveloped to a developed economy, while the aging of Western countries occurred after they had developed their economy. This means that the implementation of the policies needed for dealing with the problems of an aging society (especially old age pension, and health) have been financed more easily in the West, thanks to the financial means available in a relatively rich society. On the contrary, as China is still in the process of creating a well-developed economy, it is more difficult to raise the financial means needed for the implementation of these policies. Hence, the demographical structure of China has become a critical challenge for the Chinese leadership, and will necessitate, as we shall see in more detail in the next chapter, the design and implementation of a new social security system.

This policy appears to be even more urgent when we consider the changes in the employment structure. First, in Table 3.2a, we have already seen the huge and rapid transfer of manpower from agriculture to industry and services. Second, with the liberalization of the internal economy and the introduction of new forms of property, some new forms of companies started their economic activities within the new economic system. So, for example, foreign-invested companies and private companies became active along with the traditional state-owned enterprises (SOEs). The introduction of market mechanisms, and their corollary, competition, exerted a phenomenal pressure over SOEs that were forced to restructure, and to introduce modern managerial techniques that would enable them to reduce production costs. It was then inevitable that SOEs would lay-off huge numbers of redundant employees. Moreover, the traditional social security system, based upon the provision of social services by the SOEs's production units, was further damaging their competitiveness compared to the other companies. The consequence is that SOEs were no more in the position to fulfil their traditional social functions. It was then inevitable that they would be freed (at least partially) from their social obligations. And this situation further sustains the necessity to set up a modern social security system compatible with the new market-oriented dimensions introduced into the Chinese economic system.

3.3.2.2 The New Urban-Rural Structure

In order to speed up the pace of industrialization, the PRC adopted an imbalanced development strategy, giving priority to the development of urban and coastal areas. This resulted in disparities between rural and urban areas, which has become one of the typical and important characteristics of Chinese society. The consequence has been the difference in employment opportunities between rural and urban areas, so that from the mid-1980s the redundant peasants began to migrate to the cities, the townships and the villages where job opportunities were becoming more attractive in industry and services. Unfortunately, access to the local social security for migrant workers is related to their *Hukou* status. In the logic of the planned economy, this system restricted peasants from entering cities, which guaranteed the labour forces in rural areas but deprived them of many rights including social security benefits enjoyed by urban residents. When peasants started to migrate to the urban areas, attracted by better job opportunities after the beginning of reforms, the consequence of this system was that the migrants, who were still tied to their rural *Hukou*, could not enjoy the same benefits as the residents with the city *Hukou*.

This dual situation resulted in considerable differences of income and social welfare benefits between urban and rural areas, and it is generally admitted that the *Hukou* system has contributed, to a certain extent, to further increase this gap.[15] Nevertheless, very soon China started to implemented the *Hukou* in a flexible manner, mainly because economic development needed this type of cheap labour in the urban areas. Since the mid-2000s several provinces and municipalities started to transfer migrant workers to the urban areas, providing them with affordable and adequate lodgings and starting to integrate them into the new social security system (Sect. 4.4). Moreover, some pilot projects were implemented with the aim to permit the transfer of

---

[15]See however the results of the research by Keidel (2007), Sect. 3.4.3 below.

3.3 The Impact of Marketization on China's Modernization

the *Hukou* status, especially in some small and medium-size cities, but also in large administrative units such as the Chongqing municipality.[16]

Also, the integration of the social security system between urban and rural areas was put on the agenda. Nevertheless, the disparities between rural and urban areas, which in part correspond to the disparities between provinces, constitute one of the major negative consequences of the imbalanced economic strategy adopted by the PRC, especially after the beginning of reforms in 1978. These problems have been recognized by the Chinese leadership, as they constitute one of the more serious threats to social and political stability. Nevertheless, huge disparities still exist today, as we shall see below in Sects. 3.3.4, 3.4.2 and 3.4.3. In Chap. 4 we will see how the PRC has tried to correct these disparities.

3.3.2.3   The Importance of the Private Sector and the Emergence of 'Red Capitalists'

The explanations of the development of China's economy presented in the paragraphs above suggest that an important part of this development is to be attributed to the introduction of market mechanisms and therefore to the new economic forces that must have been developing in place of the old planned economy (at least in part) and within the new economy, i.e. a market economy. Therefore, one can expect that a great part of the economic development (in terms of both employment and contribution to GDP) has come from an increasing private sector managed by a new developing class of entrepreneurs, often called by Western pundits: 'red capitalists' (Dickson 2003, 2008). That the development of the private sector has greatly contributed to the development of the Chinese economy is generally admitted by the majority of scholars (e.g. Naugthon 2007; Nolan 2001, 2004). Amongst the many statistical data used to prove the increasing importance of the private sector let us take the data on the industrial output shared by different sorts of ownership, presented by Bennis So Wai Yip (Bennis 2006, p. 58). According to the data taken from the National Statistical Bureau of China, the contribution of SOEs declined from 77.63% in 1978 to 19.44 in 1998; during the same period, the contribution of Collective enterprises increased from 22.37 to 46.79% and that of others (i.e. private enterprises) increased from 0.5 to 33.77%. Comparable results can be obtained for employment and contribution to GDP. This seems to be a fair presentation of the situation as the collective enterprises are not included in the private sector. Unfortunately, sometimes collectives are included in the private sector with the consequence of overestimating the size of private enterprises and their contribution to China's development.

Most of the time collective enterprises are in fact (if not by law) the property of local (provincial or municipal) governments. Moreover, the imbrication between

---

[16]With a total population of about 32 million, distributed between about 6 million in the urban centre, and 26 million in the countryside, with many of them emigrating to the urban area in search of better employment opportunities, Chongqing is a good example. Chongqing initiated a pilot programme for poor people, including migrant workers and poor urban people in the late-1990s, providing them, in particular, with affordable and adequate lodgings. (Urio 2012, pp. 182–185).

private and public interests at the local Chinese level is well-known and widespread, as we shall see in Sect. 5.5 dealing with Public-Private Partnerships. Last but not least, one should not forget that the entire economic system is under the macro-economic (and political) control of the central government. This opinion is in part shared by Yasheng Huang who considers that the biggest difficulty in assessing the ownership structure of China's economy is that it is often unclear who controls a company (Huang 2003, 2008).

Moreover, contrary to a well-established Western opinion attributing the major contribution to innovation to the private sector, in many instances innovations have come from the state sector or with a substantial support from the government. For example, the very rapid development of the telecommunication infrastructure in China has been a market-oriented development, not allowing foreign participation, and with strong state initiatives: 'China's central planners played a pivotal role in introducing a variety of innovative measures to push the industry onto the takeoff track (...) Financial accountability of enterprises, prices and fees reflecting costs and scarcity, and government support with local initiatives, all have contributed to spectacular growth of telecommunications business.' (Lin Chun 2008)[17]. For the task leader of a World Bank research, 'the best solution, that is, the set of technologies that maximize both competitiveness and job creation capacity of Chinese enterprises, can only be found and installed by the collective action of the private sector and the market'. (Zhang Chunlin 2009)' It is certain that several of the World Bank suggestions make sense, such as the setting up of an institutional infrastructure and an incentives system capable to sustain private sector innovation. Nevertheless, considering that innovations are one of the major objectives of the Chinese leadership (as I showed at the end of the second chapter) it is more likely that for the time being the state will continue to play a central role in promoting and providing innovation. It is also interesting to note that the 23 Chinese firms that ranked in the top 500 in the *Fortune Magazine* in 2006 were all SOEs. We know, as is attested by many Western and Chinese scholars, that SOEs have made important progresses towards better management and efficiency to the point that some of them have started to invest abroad. In Sect. 6.2.4.2 I will show that the government plays a decisive role in R&D contributing to China's innovation in high-tech.

By these remarks I do not mean that in the future the private sector may not become within the Chinese economy a driving force more independent from the political leadership, as has been the case in the West since the industrial revolution. But for this to happen, several other changes in the organization of Chinese society will have to come to pass, and first of all the emergence of an independent new class of private entrepreneurs.

---

[17] And Lin Chun comments: This is one of the cases which prove that positive results can be attained through management and organizational reforms rather than property transfer, p. 24, note 42. Lin Chun further comments that 'the nation's largest SOEs turned around from struggling over losses to making $78.5 billion in profits in 2005 (...) In 2006, central SOEs earned $88 billion in the first 11 months, up 18.9% over the same period in 2005 (...) In fact large SOEs are rarely loss-makers; a large share of SOEs losses in China is concentrated in a small number of sectors, p. 24, note 43.

3.3 The Impact of Marketization on China's Modernization

I have already insisted upon the importance of the role of the state as a driving force deciding and orienting the development of market mechanisms alongside with a flexible planning. Moreover, as we have already seen in Sect. 2.4.4, the Party, under the leadership of Jiang Zemin and his Three Represents theory, called upon the entrepreneurs of the private sector to join the Party, and many have done so, in spite of the attitude of astonishment and scorn with which this proposal has been met with in the West. Again, this does not mean that in the future private entrepreneurs will not develop a set of values different from those of the political elite within the Party and government. Today, I have come to consider that this hypothesis is based upon the historical Western experience, and it is not at all certain that this experience can be duplicated within the Chinese cultural environment.

Nevertheless, some observers working within China have started to treat the emerging class of new entrepreneurs as a relatively independent group, that could in the future develop its own strategies regarding not only the development of the economy, but also the rest of the Chinese society. And is it not what happened in the West? In 2003, two academics from the Cheung Kong Graduate Business School in Beijing have proposed a typology of Chinese entrepreneurs (Xiang Bing and Teng Bingsheng 2008). They consider three generations of entrepreneurs. In 2008, the members of the first generation were more than 45 years old, were either college graduates or former military personnel, and most were employed by SOEs.[18] They benefited from the ideological change brought about by Deng Xiaoping, experienced the difficulties of the transition process, but were able to overcome these difficulties by using versatility and flexibility and, above all, they learned how to take advantage of experimentation. They were the first entrepreneurs that ran Chinese firms with the notion of market competition. Of course, their success can be attributed to the extraordinary growth opportunities offered by the Chinese economy at large during the first decades of the reforms, but they had to make decisions in order to take advantage of that situation as well as of the low cost of Chinese labour. The two authors consider that weaknesses remain within this first group of entrepreneurs, but they admit that some of them have improved to the point that they jumped to the third group.

In 2008, the entrepreneurs of the second generation were in their 30s and early 40s, and whereas the first generation focused its activity on manufacturing, they were mainly active in the service sector and high technologies.[19] They emerged in the late 90s and are generally well-educated and have studied abroad. They enjoyed, more than the first generation, the acceleration of market liberalization, and were more ready to adopt modern management tools imported from abroad.[20] They were also more skilled in dealing with overseas capital market, and this was particularly

---

[18]For example: Liu Chuanzhi (Lenovo), Zhang Ruimin (Haier), Ren Zhengfei (Huawei), and Li Dongsheng (TCL).

[19]For example; Neil Shen (Ctrip), Chen Tianqiao (Shenda), Jason Jiang (Focus Media), Jack Ma (Alibaba.com), and Robin Li (Baidu.com). Remark the Americanization of their names.

[20]Nevertheless, I should like to point out the Haier University I visited in 2005 that, at that time, combined modern management tools with traditional Chinese strategies and wisdom.

important as they lacked state support. Nevertheless, the two authors, while stressing the importance of this group for developing the service sector as an indispensable part of an advanced economy, consider that they lagged well behind their non-Chinese competitors, and moreover, their businesses remained largely confined to China.

Finally, the third generation has been capable of adopting a new approach to global competition. It is nevertheless a bit surprising that the two authors do not take a Chinese example for illustrating the third generation, but quote the Indian entrepreneur Lakshmi Mittal (head of Mittal Steel) who after acquiring its largest competitor, Arcelor of Luxemburg, became the world's number one steel company. The two authors conclude that this is the proof that companies in developing countries do not have to dominate the domestic market first, before investing global markets. Finally, they quote several examples of Chinese entrepreneurs of the first generations that moved into the third, such as Lenovo, TLC, Huawei and Haier. While it is certain that China needs this type of entrepreneur for sustaining the development of its economy, it is not at all clear yet whether these new entrepreneurs, evolving in the global markets, will develop a set of specific values of their own that may contradict the values of the political leadership. As I suggested in Sect. 2.4, it could very well be that there will be a convergence of the political leadership with the values of the new economic elite, or vice versa or, more likely, a mutual adjustment. In any case, this may be the logical outcome of the reform process that seems, still today, to be oriented by the Chinese traditional values of unity and harmony. For the time being, this outcome is confirmed by the authors of a research published in 2008: the majority of private entrepreneurs supports the Chinese leadership and is in favour of the *statu quo*. The reason for this attitude is explained thus: first, private entrepreneurs are the main beneficiaries of economic reforms and therefore are not likely to ask for fundamental political changes; second, they are satisfied with both their improved social and economic status and the performance of the government (Chen and Dickson 2008). Finally, one should not forget that in the logic of China's reforms, the form of the economy and polity is not an end in itself, but a means for reclaiming for China the statute of a world-power, and the attainment of this goal will be necessarily linked to the improvement of the performance of the economic system, that in turn will improve the standard of living of the population, and thus assure political and social stability.

It is widely recognized that China has made important and astonishing progresses towards the realization of this end. But it is also well-known that the positive outcomes of the reform process have generated some negative consequences that may constitute some obstacles to the completion of the process of modernization and constitute several formidable challenges to the Chinese leadership. I will examine them in the last part of this chapter (Sect. 3.4).

3.3.2.4 The Power Elite

This class is subdivided into two groups.[21] First, the political elite composed of the top cadres of the Party, within which they made their career, following a very strict evaluation and promotion path. This corresponds to Daniel Bell's meritocracy dimension of his China Model (see Sect. 6.2.1). Second, the economic elite composed of state's technocrats of state-owned banks and big SOEs, top cadres of big and medium-size private and semi-private enterprises (often former cadres of the Party), owners of big and medium-size private enterprises, often linked to the Party's cadres within the well-known exchange power-for-money. An increasing number of these people sit within official organizations such as the National Congress and the Consultative Conference.

3.3.2.5 The Intellectuals

Intellectuals are active in universities, public and private think tanks, and within state bureaucracies. Some of them, depending on the strength of their reputation and influence, may be considered as members of the power elite. Intellectuals may play very different roles regarding the Party State: political support, scientific knowledge it needs for its decisions, critique of the PRC from inside (i.e. without frontally attacking the Party-State), or even attacking frontally the Party-State by promoting radical changes in the organization of the polity, economy and society.

This is maybe the most difficult category to characterize. As it is generally admitted for other countries, Chinese intellectuals may not share the same political culture, but on the contrary may possess different ideals, and have different types of relations with the Party and the state. In fact, I came across several cases where an intellectual is classified by some observers as a conservative, and by some others as a reformist, or even as a member of the 'New Left'. A young Chinese intellectual has recently drawn my attention to the fact that the classification of intellectuals I will propose hereafter is strictly linked to the domain of economics and politics, and this runs the risk of neglecting other types of intellectuals. Moreover, according to this source, and also linked to the domains of economics and politics, Guan Zhixiong has classified Chinese intellectuals into four group: (1) Reform School, such as Zhang Wuchang, Yang Xiaokai, who insist not only on the market-oriented reform, but also on political democracy and constitutionalism; (2) Mainstream School, such as Wu Jinglian, Lin Yifu, Fan Gang, etc., who insist on the market-oriented reform. However, their attitude to the political reform is much more prudent than that of the reform school. (3) Non-mainstream School, such as He Qinglian, who pay more attention to social fairness and justice and hope to develop the democracy to combat corruption. (4)

---

[21]The distinction between these two components of the power elite (political and economic) is rather artificial, as there is a considerable overlapping between them. Nevertheless, I use here the accepted distinction based upon the main role played by members of these two groups (politicians or managers/owners of companies). The same phenomenon of overlapping exists in the West, even if with different modalities.

The New Left, such as Hu Angang, Wang Hui and Cui Zhiyuan, who focus on harmonization of economic development with social equity under the leadership of the Party.

Without being in the position of proposing a fully satisfactory classification of intellectuals, I nevertheless consider that the following classification gives an idea of the great variety of ideological positions of Chinese intellectuals, and may constitute a reasonable starting point for a research in view of a better classification (Urio 2012, pp. 26–47).

The liberal or neo-liberal supporters of economic and eventually also of political reforms have been very influential between 1978 and 1989. It is amongst these intellectuals that one can find the most radical liberal and neo-liberal reformers. Some of them even favoured more radical reforms, including democratization along Western lines, but they mainly favour the liberalization of the economy. They lost some of their power after the Tian An Men events of 1989, as the Party then adopted a more careful strategy towards reforms giving more influence to the second, group, often labelled the 'statists'. The 'statists' criticize the negative consequences of reforms, but for them the state should continue to lead the reforms, and they do not favour radical reforms towards democratization according to the Western model, but progressive democratization faithful to China's characteristics. Moreover, they do not challenge the leadership of the Party. They are active within the governmental think tanks (for ex. the National Reform and Development Commission—NDRC), within the universities (faculties, university research centres and think tanks). They constitute a highly competent, effective, and politically reliable support to Party and government, by providing both 'academic-scientific research' and policy advice in all domains of state activity.

Towards the end of the Hu Jintao era, the liberals again acquired a potentially strong position that reached its zenith when they worked with Western economists in a team within the World Bank, writing a report on the future of China (World Bank 2013). This report was signed by Robert B. Zoellick, WB President (2007–2012) and LI Wei, President of the Development Research Centre of the State Council, P.R.C. Dated 2013, it was in fact already available on the WB website at the beginning of 2012, a few months before the Party Congress of November. The dates are important. In fact, the report urged China to speed up reforms both internally and internationally, including the opening up of the capital account, very clearly along lines that neo-liberal experts could easily subscribe. The publication of such a report before the Party Congress could have been interpreted as a sign, or even a pressure, upon the new leadership that was to be appointed at the Congress. I was myself in Beijing at that time, and I submitted this idea to some people well acquainted with the competition that was going on within the Party. Their answer was very clear: Xi Jinping was going to follow the line adopted by the Party since the beginning of reforms and followed without fail since then: reforms should be good for China and therefore should not jeopardize stability, harmony, unity and national independence. This is in fact what happened since the beginning of the Xi Jinping era, and became clear when only one year after taking office, he announced the China grand strategy: the Belt and Road

3.3 The Impact of Marketization on China's Modernization

initiative, to be dealt with in Sect. 6.2.3. A clear sign that the neo-liberals had lost their favourable moment to the advantage of the 'statists'.

Some members of these 2 groups support the power elite, depending on whether they can influence the Party-State, and a minority of them belongs to the elite. They also have connections with the managers of the mass media controlled by the Party, as well as with the managers of SOEs or even private enterprises.

The members of the third group, often labelled, especially in the West, 'the New Left' are more radical than the 'statists', and are keen in safeguarding social equity. Some of them may still refer to Marxian analysis, but others are more generally open to critical analysis not necessarily of Marxian origin, and some of them try to find a Chinese way to modernity, which sometimes makes reference to genuine Confucian ideals. Some of them publish regularly in the *'New Left Review'*, and are active mainly within universities, sometimes in the same units as the 'Statists'.

Note that many of the Chinese intellectuals (especially those who graduated after the Cultural Revolution) have spent several months or even years abroad studying and/or teaching; and this has given them the competencies and knowledge that are useful for the Party and state in order to conceive strategies and policies for managing the problems Chinese society is facing today.

3.3.2.6 The Middle Class

It is difficult to have a precise idea of the size of the middle class, as there is no clear agreement about the criteria to be used to define it. Generally, a certain level of disposable income is used for this purpose. In a 2006 article, McKinsey made the hypothesis that China's middle class would develop in two waves: 'the first wave, in 2010, will concern the lower middle class, defined as households with annual incomes of 25,001 to 40,000 RMB. A decade later the upper middle class, with annual household incomes of 40,001 to 100,000 RMB, will follow.' (Gersch and Stephenson 2006). Using 2005 data from the National Bureau of Statistics of China on urban households (number of households and their disposable income) for the year 2005 McKinsey estimated the size of the middle class at 22% of China's population, composed of 12.6% for the 'Lower middle class' of urban households, earning between 25.001 and 40.000 RMB per year, and holding together 15.4% of the total urban disposable income; plus 9.4% for the 'Upper Middle class', earning between 40.001 and 100.000 RMB a year, and holding together 24.2% of total urban households disposable income, whereas the poor (earning less than 25,000 RMB) represents 77.3% of the total population.

Then McKinsey makes two projections. The first, for 2011, estimates that 'the lower middle class will number some 290 million people, representing the largest segment in urban China and accounting for about 44% of the urban population, according to our model. Growth in this group should peak around 2015, with a total spending power of 4.8 trillion RMB. A second transition is projected to occur in the following decade, when hundreds of millions will join the upper middle class. By 2025 this segment will comprise a staggering 520 million people—more than half of the expected urban population of China—with a combined total disposable income of 13.3 trillion RMB.' Overall, in 2015, the middle class will represent about 80% of the total urban population.

In a more recent study of 2013, McKinsey uses more than 70,000 interviews with Chinese consumers in 60 cities, representing 74% of China's GDP and 47% of its total population (Barton et al. 2013). Their results are quite interesting as they show a considerable increase of the middle class and its purchasing power. The middle class is defined by an income between 60,000 and 229,000 RMB a year, the upper middle class earning between 106,000 and 229,000 RMB. Whereas in 2012 the latter represented 14% of the urban households, it is forecasted that by 2022 it will account for 54%, while the lower middle class will have only 22%.

Based on these premises, McKinsey forecasts that this upper middle class will change its purchasing habits by buying more expensive goods such as laptops, digital cameras, specialized households such as laundry softeners, and luxury goods. The total middle class in 2012 was 256 million, and it will increase to 357 in 2022, less that the 520 million forecasted in the 2008 study for 2025, even if it is likely to increase between 2022 and 2025. The other interesting finding concern the behaviour of what the authors call 'Generation 2', i.e. typically teen-agers and people in their early 20s, born after the mid-1980s and brought up in a period of relative abundance. They represented only 15% of the urban consumers in 2012, but will surge to 35% in 2022. McKinsey says that this generation is the most Westernized to date: 'prone to regard expensive products as intrinsically better than less expensive ones, they are happy to try new things (…) seek emotional satisfaction through better taste or higher status (…), [however they] share with their grandparents a bias for savings, an aversion to borrowing, a determination to work hard, and a definition of success in terms of money, power, and social status. In spite of the continuity with traditional behaviour (i.e. savings) the research forecast that when they age, and eventually retire, they will have a 'younger' consumption mind-set than today's elderly do' (see also Farrel et al. 2006). A more recent research by the *China Power Project* of the CSIS, using a slightly different methodology, confirms McKinsey's findings, especially the spending habits of the middle class (China Power Report 2017, updates December 2018).

These results seem to suggest that this new middle class will be an asset for the new development strategy redirecting the development drivers away from investment and export towards domestic consumption. This is certainly good news for the perspective of the development of a market economy. Nevertheless, as the research of *China Power Project* quite rightly points out, this new trend may also exacerbate the tendency towards consumerism and individualism (especially in the forms of selfishness) that may further deteriorate (through consumption and production) the already heavy burden on the environment, as well as the traditional collectively cooperative attitude of Chinese people, not to speak of the further increase of income inequalities. This is what the neoliberal revolution of the West, may teach to China.

3.3.2.7 Workers, Employees, Peasants and Migrant Workers

Assuming that the size of the middle class is today around 450 million, the rest of the population is about 900 million, comprising three groups: farmers, workers and a special category of workers, i.e. migrant workers, with an income less than 60,000 RMB per year, and often considerably less than that sum. Here we find workers and employees with little or no qualifications working in SOEs, collective enterprises, joint ventures, and private enterprises, and peasants working in small farms or employed in bigger farms. Taking official data about employment in the three sectors (Table 3.2a) I calculate that workers have a population of around 260 million plus 140 million of migrant workers, i.e. a total of 400 people; the services 390 million plus 140 migrant workers, i.e. a total of 531 people.

It is interesting to remark that the changes in the structure of Chinese society are also recognized by the Chinese leadership. For example, according to the report to the 16th National Congress of the CPC, the new situation of social classes in China was described as follows: 'With the deepening of reform and opening up and economic and cultural development, the working class in China has expanded steadily and its quality improved. The working class, with the intellectuals as part of it, and the farmers are always the basic forces for promoting the development of the advanced productive forces and all-round social progress in our country. Emerging in the process of social changes, entrepreneurs and technical personnel employed by non-public scientific and technological enterprises, managerial and technical staff employed by overseas-funded enterprises, the self-employed, private entrepreneurs, employees in intermediaries, free-lance professionals and members of other social strata are all builders of socialism with Chinese characteristics.' (Xinhua Agency, http://news.xinhuanet.com/misc/2008-03/08/content_7746540.htm). This statement, while it recognizes the new and complex structure of Chinese society, is also a clear tribute to the theory of the Three Represents defined by President Jiang Zemin, as it translates the desire of the Chinese leadership to reconstruct the unity of the Chinese people in spite of the societal fragmentation produced by the development process.

I can conclude once again, that the changes driven by economic development must be evaluated by taking into consideration on one side the overall impact on the people concerned and, on the other side, the effectiveness of the measures taken by the state in order to make the transition as smooth as possible.

3.3.3 The Impact of Economic Development upon the Environment[22]

Let us remind the reader that China is a country where natural catastrophes are very frequent making the environment a naturally hostile force: from 200 B.C. to 1990, China suffered from 1029 floods, 1056 drought, some 800 earthquakes (Hu and Zou 1991, p. 62). At the beginning of the Mao era (see Table 3.2a), agriculture represented 83.5% of manpower and 50.5% of GDP. At that time the government gave priority to industrial development, so that already at the end of Mao's era the industrial sector became more important than the agricultural sector in terms of contribution to GDP (see Table 3.2b). The reduction of the rate of poverty became the top priority. To achieve this goal Mao developed industry, especially heavy industry, that needed huge quantities of raw materials and energy, thus relegating environmental concern to second place. Besides the emission of harmful substances, industrial production required large amounts of water.[23] Moreover, the idea of waste treatment was of secondary importance; development was the first priority.

Consequently, China's economic development had a very grave negative environmental impact, thus aggravating a worrying situation, existing already during the Empire. The rapid industrialization and urbanization processes are the main factors responsible for this difficult situation facing the Chinese leadership. Moreover, the impact on the physical environment (i.e. on soil, air, and water) has a dramatic collateral impact on human environment aggravating the health of large numbers of the Chinese people, whose health has been further worsened, at least until recently, by the weakness of the health insurance system, and more generally of the overall social security system (see in this chapter Sects. 3.3.4 and 4.3 and 4.4).

In China, the deterioration of the environment is mainly linked to two major factors: growing population and economic development, and the consequent urbanization affecting both urban and rural areas. These problems had already been addressed in the late 1980s by researches conducted by teams of young Chinese scholars who forecasted that the conjunction of these two factors would increase pressure on natural resources in the decades to come (Hu et al. 1992; Hu and Zou 1991). The Mao era is marked by an unprecedented population growth. While in 1954, the Chinese census counted about 600 million people, the population has reached 937 million at the time of Mao's death (1976) and has attained 1.379 billion today (Table 3.1).[24] This population explosion is due to socio-economic as well as to political factors. First of all, it is due to the Chinese tradition of early marriage and multiple offspring,

---

[22]In addition to many updates, this section is mainly based upon Joan Bastide and Alexandre Sonnay, *Le role de la Chine dans le protocole de Kyoto*, unpublished Master dissertation for the *Master degree in Asian Studies*, University of Geneva, 2005, under the supervision of Prof. Paolo Urio.

[23]To produce one ton of steel requires up to one hundred tons of water, an average factory of electronic chips consumes 18 million tons of water per day, equal to the annual consumption of a city of 60,000 inhabitants.

[24]For a historical analysis of the development and problems of the Chinese population see Hu Angang and Zou Ping (1991), pp. 14–15 for statistical data.

3.3 The Impact of Marketization on China's Modernization

and hence the maintenance of a high birth rate, and to a sharp reduction in mortality. Second, the political leaders were slow to recognize the problems engendered by the rapid and large increase of the population. Any reference to population problems were considered by the Chinese authorities of that time as an expression of rightist propaganda.[25] For Mao, a large population was synonymous 'with power: with a large population, power is great.'

During the Mao era, even the Party admitted that this policy choice was a mistake (Hu Sheng 1994, pp. 532–588). Indeed, the pressure exerted by the growing size of the population increases both the quantity of water used in productive processes, and the amount of polluting emissions. Moreover, it reduces the space available per capita (Vallée 2003, p. 19). The availability of land per capita was only half the world average around 1996 (World Bank 1997, p. 6). As a consequence, deforestation, pollution and famine have been the bitter consequences of these pro-natalist policies. Nevertheless, I would like to mention, that the case of the Chinese family policies is a good example of the difficulties in evaluating the validity of policy decisions. If from the environmental point of view the pro-natalist policies of the Mao era have been a mistake, from the point of view of China's position within the world economy that emerged during the 1990s, the fact of having a large workforce (half of which is still in agriculture, but can be transferred to industry and service at a relatively low labour cost), is certainly one of the factors that explains the comparative advantage of China over its international competitors.

Since the breakdown of the relationship between humankind and nature at the time of the Industrial Revolution, the links between economic growth and the environment have become more and more visible. Based on consumption, economic growth implies that we produce and consume more and more, and logically, that we use increasing quantities of natural resources, while rejecting more and more waste into the biosphere (Vallée 2003, p. 20). Therefore, economic growth implies in its very essence an impact on the environment. It is then up to the political agenda to determine what proportion of this impact is acceptable. However, if economic growth basically implies some pressure on the environment, it is important to consider that growth can be managed in a more or less friendly way for the environment.

Since the beginning of reforms, the spectacular economic development, the substantial improvement of the standard of living of almost the entire population, and the emergence of a middle class with a high propensity to increasing consumption, had the consequence that the production process has been further developed. Thereby, there has been some serious additional pressure that has resulted in an increased use of electricity and water, an expansion of the number of motor vehicles, and an increased consumption of goods that are no longer limited to those of first necessity. All this has led to an increased use of natural resources.

---

[25] Scientists who dared sustain Malthus's argument are disqualified and targeted as 'rightists'. Thus, Ma Yinchu, a prominent Chinese scholar and president of Peking University has suffered from a two-decade propaganda campaign, and was dismissed from his academic post after the publication in 1957 of a report entitled 'New demography', the product of years of in-depth research, which concluded that a too large population is detrimental to the development of China. See Hu and Zou 1991, especially Chaps 2 and 3.

This impressive industrial development has been accompanied by an increase in the emission of pollutants, characteristic of the early stages of industrialization. The modernization of production has created a demand for significant quantities of energy, especially coal, which is by far the most polluting source of energy. In addition, China's industry has shown low efficiency, i.e. in terms of the amount of energy required to produce one unit.

Not only industrialization has been the source of environmental damages, but also the agriculture can be a factor of global warming, as the culture of irrigated rice (which is very important in China) emits considerable masses of methane (CH_4, a greenhouse gas with a global warming potential 21 times higher than CO_2), because of the decomposition of vegetables. During the process of economic development, methods of intensive agriculture have been widely introduced in China. Therefore, the cultivation of land needs important irrigation devices, which have changed the hydrological balance. In China, the use of fertilizers and pesticides was introduced quite late, but it has grown rapidly making the country the first world producer and consumer already at the end of the 2000s (Lesbre 2004, p. 19 and Sect. 5.4). The resulting reduction of space available per capita, and therefore the increasing pressure on food have prompted authorities to launch campaigns for increasing agricultural production by reducing the size of forests for the benefit of agriculture.

Given these premises, China's major environmental problems are: water quality (i.e. pollution), shortage and access; air and soil pollution; deforestation, desertification and soil erosion; and deterioration of health. Consequently, the government has to allocate huge quantities of money to invest in policies aimed at eliminating these problems. Given the seriousness of the damages, this needs a long-term strategy. A few indicators will suffice to give an idea of China's situation compared to the world's: around 2006, China's per capita carbon emissions were 3.9 tons against 4.3 for the world; China's total carbon emissions in 2005 started to bypass the US's and was already much higher than the EU's; China's energy use (kg of oil equivalent) per $1000 GDP (constant 2011 PPP) in 2005 was much higher than the world's, i.e. 243.7 against 146.7. Moreover, at the same time, solar and wind energy use were practically non-existent.[26] In Sect. 4.2 we will see whether China has improved the relation between economic development and protection of the environment.

3.3.4 The Impact of Economic Development: Achievements and Problems

We can start to say that both Western and Chinese researchers consider that the reforms allowed an astonishing economic growth and a significant improvement of the living conditions of the Chinese people, even if there are substantial disparities between provinces, within provinces and between individuals. Should the govern-

---

[26]Data kindly provided by Hu Angang, Tsinghua University, based upon the World Bank database and the European Union.

3.3 The Impact of Marketization on China's Modernization

ment fail to eliminate or at least reduce these disparities, this would jeopardize the unity, harmony and stability of the reform process. In fact, during the reform process several widespread demonstrations by students, peasants and workmen inside the country have taken place, the events of Tian An Men Square of June 1989 being the most publicized in the West. Nevertheless, since the beginning of the 1980s, the economic annual growth rate has been between 8 and 10% for three consecutive decades. Thanks to cheap labour, globalization made China the workshop of the world. During the 1990s it became the second receiver of direct foreign investments of the world. Several researchers started to talk about the twenty-first century as the Chinese century.

The extraordinary speed of economic development has been recognized. In its 1997 report the World Bank compared the time needed for doubling the GDP by several countries: the United Kingdom needed 58 years (from 1780 to 1838), the USA 47 (from 1839 to 1886), Japan 34 years (from 1885 to 1919), South Korea 11 (from 1966 to 1977), and China only 9 years (from 1978 to 1987). Even though this type of comparison must be made with care (the overall situation at different historical periods of time is quite different and can, at least in part, explain the difference in speed), the achievements, when measured by GDP, are quite impressive. Even the 2008 crisis has not stopped China's GDP rise: 9.0% in 2008, 8.7 in 2009 and 10% in 2010.[27] In its 2009 report the World Bank considered that most of the Millennium Development Goals of the United Nations have either already been achieved or China is well on the way to achieving them (World Bank 2009).

The development of China's economy has gone hand in hand with the recovery of its place in the global economy. First of all, let us look at China's share in the world GDP since 1820 as shown in Table 3.3. Whereas China GDP (in PPP) was just under one third of world GDP in 1820 (i.e. before its decline during the Qing dynasty), it dropped dramatically to 17.05% a decade after the Second Opium War (1870) and continued to drop until 1973, during the Cultural Revolution and about seven years before the beginning of the reform era, to reach 4.62%. But 20 years after the beginning of reforms, i.e. by the year 2000, its share was already 11.23%; and it reached 17.50% in 2008, at the beginning of the 2008 financial crisis, when it surpassed Germany and Japan to become the world's second-biggest economy after the US. In 2015 China's share (in PPP) was more than four times what it was in 1950. Its ratio to American GDP decreased from 6.07 in 1950 to 1.03 in 2015. Hu Angang forecasts that in 2030 the share of China's GDP in the world total will reach 23.1% and its ratio to the US would be 0.75 (Table 3.3).

Let us take a further step by using Hu Angang's procedure for determining China's economic strength in the world compared to the members of the G20. This is done first by taking separately China's proportion of GDP (Table 3.4) and of import-export in the world (Table 3.5) compared to the G20 countries. Then, in Table 3.6 China's economic strength is calculated by integrating in a single indicator the GDP and the import-export percentages, giving a 2/3 weight to GDP and 1/3 to import-export (Hu

---

[27] According to IMF Data Bank 2009 for 2008, National Bureau of Statistic of China (NBSC) for 2009 and World Bank's Quarterly Update, November 2010 for the forecast for 2010.

Table 3.3 The Proportion of GDP (PPP) in the Total of the World (1820–2030)

	1820	1870	1913	1929	1950	1973	2000	2008	2015	2030
China	32.88	17.05	8.83	7.37	4.50	4.62	11.23	17.50	18.51	23.10
U.S.	1.80	8.84	18.94	22.70	27.32	22.07	20.96	18.60	19.06	17.30
US/China	0.05	0.52	2.14	3.08	6.07	4.78	1.87	1.06	1.03	0.75
Japan	2.98	2.28	2.62	3.45	3.02	7.76	6.87	5.70	5.05	3.60
U.K.	5.21	9.00	8.22	6.76	6.53	4.22	3.40	2.80	2.80	?
Germany	3.86	6.48	8.69	7.06	4.98	5.90	4.33	3.40	5.92	?
Russia	5.42	7.52	8.50	6.42	9.57	9.44	4.77	2.50	2.17	3.40
India	16.02	12.12	7.48	6.52	4.17	3.09	4.76	6.70	7.34	10.40

Note Calculated by PPP and 1990 International dollar by Prof. Hu Angang, Tsinghua University. Sources: Angus Maddison: The World Economy: A Millennial Perspective, Chinese edition, translated by Wu Xiaoying, Beijing University Press, 2003 edition, pp. 178, 208. Estimations for 2015 and 2030. Table kindly provided by Prof. Hu Angang

2016). We see in Table 3.4 that in 1990, ten years after the beginning of reforms, China's proportion of world GDP was only 3.89% of the world total against 25.09% for the EU, 20.92% for the US and 8.31% for Japan. These three countries, that are the members of the Trilateral commission, accounted for more than half of the world total, i.e. 54.32%.[28] At that time, China had a GDP smaller than Germany (5.30%), but not very different from other members of the G20, such as France (3.59%), Italy (3.63%), United Kingdom (3.60%), India (3.49%), and Brazil (3.50%). In 2014, 34 years after the beginning of reforms, China's part of total world GDP had surged to 16.59%, surpassing the US (16.04%), second only to the EU (17%); all the other members of the G20 have a considerably smaller share of world GDP.

Table 3.5 shows a similar pattern. China's position has dramatically increased in the global economy, if we take its share of exports and imports in the world. In 1990 China had only 1.63% of the world's share of exports and exports, i.e. ten years after the beginning of reforms, when the EU, the US and Germany dominated international trade with 45.60%, 12.29 and 11% respectively. The three countries of the Trilateral Commission represented 65.89% of total world trade. But in 2010,

---

[28] It is interesting to take the Trilateral commission into consideration, because it was set up by David Rockefeller and Zbigniew Brzezinski in July 1973, to develop cooperation between North America, Western Europe and Japan. The Commission has attracted criticism from both the right and the left. From the right, Republican Senator Barry Goldwater criticized the Commission for being a skilful, coordinated effort to seize control and consolidate the four centres of power: political, monetary, intellectual and ecclesiastical, and to promote the creation of a worldwide economic power superior to the political governments of the nation-states involved. People of the left have been even more critical: Noam Chomsky has described the Trilateral Commission as being the liberal wing of the intellectual elite, i.e. liberal internationalists from Europe, Japan and the United States. [...] [The Trilateral Commission] was concerned with trying to induce what they called 'more moderation in democracy'—turn people back to passivity and obedience so they don't put so many constraints on state power and so on. (https://en.wikipedia.org/wiki/Trilateral_Commission (accessed 12 February 2017).

3.3 The Impact of Marketization on China's Modernization

Table 3.4 G20's GDP (PPP) proportion in the world (1990–2014)

Unit: %

Country	1990	1995	2000	2005	2010	2014
Argentina	NA	NA	NA	NA	NA	NA
Australia	1.04	1.04	1.05	1.02	0.97	0.95
Brazil	3.50	3.58	3.29	3.14	3.17	3.01
Canada	1.95	1.87	1.86	1.78	1.54	1.44
China	3.89	6.13	7.65	10.08	13.98	16.59
France	3.59	3.37	3.29	2.94	2.64	2.37
Germany	5.30	5.16	4.55	4.06	3.66	3.41
India	3.49	3.94	4.37	5.01	6.08	6.80
Indonesia	1.84	2.36	2.02	2.11	2.27	2.46
Italy	3.63	3.41	3.15	2.63	2.33	1.96
Japan	8.31	7.86	6.83	5.95	4.89	4.26
South Korea	1.29	1.66	1.77	1.78	1.70	1.60
Mexico	1.80	2.06	2.20	2.03	1.96	1.98
Russia	4.16	2.28	2.08	2.60	3.31	3.45
Saudi Arabia	1.31	1.33	1.24	1.31	1.38	1.48
South Africa	0.82	0.76	0.72	0.72	0.68	0.65
Turkey	0.84	0.87	1.22	1.20	1.32	1.34
UK	3.60	3.35	3.36	3.20	2.55	2.36
US	20.92	20.95	21.37	20.04	16.93	16.04
EU	25.09	23.75	22.87	21.06	18.96	17.00
Total	80.25	80.44	80.54	79.83	79.14	79.05

Note The data for UK, Germany, France and Italy has been deducted from the total as they belong to EU

Source Data are calculated according to constant dollar price of 2011 and GDP(PPP) provided by World Bank database

30 years after the beginning of reforms and 9 years after its accession to the WTO, China's share surged to 9.62% surpassing all the other major G20 players, except the US (10.51%) and the EU (with an astonishing 34.1%) and remained the major economic block for import and exports whereas the three countries of the Trilateral Commission represent still a little less than 50% of the world total. Four years later with 11.30% China surpassed the US (10.59%), second only to the EU (31.98%), whereas the Trilateral Commission for the first time accounted for less than half of the world total with 46.5%.

By combining the share in the world GDP and in the export-import total of the world, we obtain the Economic strength (or power) of the members of the G20. In 1990, China's share of economic power was only 2.39%, far behind the EU (38.76%) and the US (15.57%), whereas the three Trilateral Commission countries accounted

Table 3.5 G20's imports and export volume proportion in the world (1990–2014)

Unit: %

Country	1990	1995	2000	2005	2010	2014
Argentina	0.23	0.39	0.39	0.32	0.40	0.36
Australia	1.16	1.09	1.03	1.08	1.34	1.26
Brazil	0.76	0.96	0.86	0.92	1.27	1.22
Canada	3.55	3.45	3.95	3.19	2.56	2.49
China	1.63	2.69	3.59	6.64	9.62	11.30
France	6.38	5.65	5.05	4.52	3.67	3.32
Germany	11.00	9.44	7.95	8.16	7.49	7.17
India	0.59	0.62	0.71	1.13	1.87	2.04
Indonesia	0.67	0.82	0.83	0.76	0.95	0.93
Italy	4.99	4.20	3.63	3.54	3.02	2.63
Japan	7.40	7.45	6.51	5.19	4.74	3.96
South Korea	1.91	2.49	2.52	2.55	2.89	2.88
Mexico	1.19	1.47	2.62	2.07	1.97	2.13
Russia	0.00	1.36	1.14	1.72	2.10	2.11
Saudi Arabia	0.97	0.75	0.82	1.12	1.16	1.36
South Africa	0.59	0.56	0.45	0.53	0.61	0.56
Turkey	0.50	0.55	0.62	0.89	0.97	1.05
UK	5.78	4.83	4.80	4.25	3.26	3.13
US	12.89	12.96	15.47	12.30	10.51	10.59
EU	45.60	41.26	37.73	38.49	34.01	31.98
Total	79.64	78.87	79.24	78.9	76.97	76.22

Note The data for UK, Germany, France and Italy has been deducted from the total as they belong to EU

for 62.04%, and the BRICS only 7.68%. In the framework of this book, it is important to take into consideration the BRICS organization because it comprises, in addition to the two Asian fast developing giants (China and India), one of the two major nuclear powers (Russia,) and two potentially promising developing countries, South Africa and Brazil, totalling in 2014 30.05% of the World GDP (Table 3.4), and 21.66 of economic strength. Moreover, one has also to take into consideration that Russia and China have become closer and closer, as we shall see in Chap. 6, thanks to their geographical position, and more particularly because of the US foreign policy that tries to keep its dominant position in the world by developing an aggressive policy of containment towards Russia and China. In 2014, China's share soared to 13.07%, second only to the US (12.41%9) and the EU (26.99%), whereas the countries of the Trilateral Commission lost 18.58% down to 43.56%.

Commenting upon these tables, we can agree with Hu Angang, who rightly concludes that they show the dramatic change that occurred in just a quarter of a century:

3.3 The Impact of Marketization on China's Modernization

Table 3.6 G20's economic strength proportion in the world (1990–2014)

Unit: %

Country	1990	1995	2000	2005	2010	2014	2010–2014 variance
Argentina	NA	NA	NA	NA	NA	NA	NA
Australia	1.12	1.07	1.03	1.06	1.22	1.15	−0.07
Brazil	1.67	1.84	1.67	1.66	1.91	1.81	−0.1
Canada	3.02	2.92	3.25	2.72	2.22	2.14	−0.08
China	2.39	3.83	4.95	7.79	11.08	13.07	1.99
France	5.45	4.89	4.46	3.99	3.33	3.00	−0.33
Germany	9.10	8.01	6.82	6.79	6.21	5.92	−0.29
India	1.56	1.73	1.93	2.42	3.27	3.63	0.36
Indonesia	1.06	1.34	1.22	1.21	1.39	1.44	0.05
Italy	4.53	3.94	3.47	3.24	2.79	2.41	−0.38
Japan	7.71	7.58	6.62	5.44	4.79	4.06	−0.73
South Korea	1.70	2.21	2.27	2.29	2.49	2.45	−0.04
Mexico	1.40	1.67	2.48	2.05	1.97	2.08	0.11
Russia	1.39	1.66	1.45	2.01	2.50	2.56	0.06
Saudi Arabia	1.08	0.94	0.96	1.18	1.23	1.40	0.17
South Africa	0.67	0.63	0.54	0.59	0.63	0.59	−0.04
Turkey	0.61	0.65	0.82	0.99	1.09	1.15	0.06
UK	5.05	4.34	4.32	3.90	3.02	2.87	−0.15
US	15.57	15.62	17.43	14.88	12.65	12.41	−0.24
EU	38.76	35.42	32.78	32.68	28.99	26.99	−2.00
Total	79.71	79.11	79.4	78.97	77.43	76.93	−0.5

Note The data for UK, Germany, France and Italy has been deducted from the total as they belong to EU

Source World Bank Database

the decline of developed countries and the surge of developing countries belonging to the G20, and to point to the decisive contribution of China to this outcome. Moreover, China is rising, whereas the US and the EU are declining, even if they retain with China the rank of the greatest economic powers. We will see in Chap. 6 how China has taken advantage of this situation.

So far, we have seen the overall performance of China's economic development measured by GDP and China's share in the world GDP, exports and industrial output, and we have combined them to obtain an index of economic power. How does this development translate into the lives of Chinese people? Table 3.7 provides some answers. For urban areas, the annual disposable income has increased from a very low 343 RMB per year in 1978, at the beginning of reforms, to a fairly high 36,396 RMB in 2017, i.e. 106 times more. The improvement in the rural areas has been also impressive: for net per capita income, it increased from a very low 133 RMB per year in 1978 to 13'432 RMB in 2017, i.e. 101 times more. Of course, the data provided in Table 3.7 also inform us of the income disparities between rural and urban areas. I will come back to this important aspect of China's development, in Sects. 3.4.2 and 3.4.3. What is interesting to note for the moment is that, in spite of significant disparities between urban and rural personal incomes, both have increased since the beginning of reforms (Keidel 2007).

Nevertheless, by international comparison, the improvement of the situation of the Chinese people is by far less spectacular than what appears from the overall economic indicators. Indeed, China's situation is much less favourable if we take into consideration GNI per capita (2011 PPP $). In 2017 when China was ranked 86 for the UNDP Human Development Index (to be discussed hereafter), China's GNI per capita was 15.270$ (UNDP 2018 Statistical Update). Comparatively, this was 4.45 times less than Norway (with GNI ranked 1), 3.77 less than Switzerland, 3.59 times less than the US, and 3.02 less than Germany. Amongst the Western European countries, only Greece had a GNI per capita only 1.58 times more than China, and amongst the Western European countries only Albania had a GNI lower than China (11.896 $), whereas Serbia had a GNI of 19.179 $, Hungary 25.393$ and Poland 26.150$.

Notwithstanding the above, there is no doubt that per capita revenue has been sustained by the growth of GDP, even if the newly created wealth has been very unevenly distributed amongst Chinese people, as I will consider in more detail later in this chapter. It is also plausible that in the future the evolution of per capita income will be more than proportionally linked to GDP growth, as the Chinese leadership has fully understood the danger of the inequalities that have dramatically increased since the 1990s, and is taking serious measures to rebalance the economy, especially after the adoption of the 11th Plan in 2005 and the decisions announced by President Hu Jintao at the November 2007 Party Congress, more particularly in the domain of social policies.

It is of course possible to sustain that monetary income is important for people living in a country where the main source of personal income is determined by one's position in the labour market. In fact, it is thanks to salaries earned in the labour market that one is able to purchase the goods and services he/she needs. Nevertheless, monetary income does tell only part of the story. This gap is filled, at least partially, by the Human Development Index (HDI) developed by UNDP, which combines life expectancy at birth, education (measured by literacy), and GNI per capita. Data from the UNDP annual reports shows that in 1980 China's HDI index was the same as Sudan's in 2007, and in 2007 China had the same HDI as the Dominican Republic in the same year. Taking the UNDP data for 1975, when China's HDI was 0.527, between 1975 and 1980 (i.e. during the Mao era) there was only a very small improvement (+ 0.033), whereas in the reform era, from 1980 on, the improvement is constant and impressive. According to UNDP calculations, between 1980 and 2006 China has improved its HDI by 0.226, second only to Egypt (+ 0.233) and before Nepal (+ 0.222), Iran (+ 0.218) and Indonesia (+ 0.205), while all the other countries in the UNDP statistics have increased their HDI by less than 0.200. It must

3.3 The Impact of Marketization on China's Modernization

Table 3.7 China's Urban Per Capita Annual Disposable Income and Rural Per Capita Net Income (1978–2017)

	Ratio [1]/[2]	Urban per capita annual disposable income (Yuan) [1]	Rural per capita net income (Yuan) [2]
1978	2.57	343	133
1979	2.53	405	160
1980	2.50	477	191
1981	2.24	500	223
1982	1.98	535	270
1983	1.82	564	309
1984	1.84	652	355
1985	1.86	739	397
1986	2.13	900	423
1987	2.17	1002	462
1988	2.17	1180	544
1989	2.28	1373	601
1990	2.20	1510	686
1991	2.40	1700	708
1992	2.58	2026	784
1993	2.80	2577	921
1994	2.86	3496	1221
1995	2.71	4283	1577
1996	2.51	4838	1926
1997	2.47	5160	2090
1998	2.51	5425	2162
1999	2.65	5854	2210
2000	2.79	6280	2253
2001	2.90	6859	2366
2002	3.11	7702	2475
2003	3.23	8472	2622
2004	3.21	9421	2936
2005	3.22	10493	3254
2006	3.27	11759	3587
2007	3.33	13785	4140
2008	3.31	15780	4760
2009	3.33	17174	5153
2010	3.23	19109	5919
2011	3.13	21810	6977
2012	3.10	24565	7916

(continued)

Table 3.7 (continued)

	Ratio [1]/[2]	Urban per capita annual disposable income (Yuan) [1]	Rural per capita net income (Yuan) [2]
2013	2.98	26467	8896
2014	2.92	28844	9892
2015	2.90	31195	10772
2016	2.72	33616	12363
2017	2.71	36396	13432

Source The data of 1978–2008 are from: *China Compendium of Statistics 1949–2008*, Compiled by Department of Comprehensive Statistics of National Bureau Statistics, Page 25. China Statistics Press, Beijing China, 2010. The data of 2009–2016 are from the National Bureau of Statistics of China

be said however, that whereas the HDI allows a comparison of countries using an overall indicator of their performance, it nevertheless masks differences within these same countries. I will come back to this important aspect of China's development (Sects. 3.4.1 and 4.7)

Since the 2009 Report the UNDP countries are classified into four categories: Very high (ranks 1–58), High (ranks 60–112), Medium (ranks 113–151) and Low development (ranks 152–189). All the Western countries are in the first group, except Serbia, Albania, Bosnia Herzegovina, and Ukraine. Between 1990 and 2017, China improved its HDI from 0.502 to 0.752, having progressed by 7 ranks to reach rank 86. This places China in the middle of the second category, i.e. in the High Human Development group, at about the same level as Thailand (83), Algeria (85), Ecuador (86), Ukraine (88) and Peru (89), after countries such as Iran (rank 60), Turkey (64), Serbia (67), Cuba (73), Mexico (74), Sri Lanka (76), and (Brazil 79), but before countries such as Colombia (90), and Tunisia (95).

As China is a very diverse country, it would be interesting to take the HDI per provinces, and see if some provinces have an HDI at the same level of some Western countries. Unfortunately, data at the provincial level are available only from 2008 on. Therefore, we will examine China HDI per provinces in Sects. 4.6, 4.7 and 4.8 where we will evaluate, as already said, whether China has succeeded in rebalancing its society.

3.4 The Imbalances of Deng's New Public Management

In Sects. 3.3 and 3.4, we have seen the spectacular improvement of the economy and also some negative consequences. Here we will develop this point in more detail. There are many researches on the imbalances introduced in China as a consequence of the reform process. They illustrate the complexity of the modernization strategy implemented by Deng and his successors and the formidable challenges facing

3.4 The Imbalances of Deng's New Public Management   103

China's leadership (see above, Sect. 3.2.3). Should the Party fail to correct these imbalances, it may jeopardize the realization of the stated goal of creating a prosperous society, while safeguarding the values of harmony, unity and stability. The major imbalances concern disparities between provinces, between rural and urban areas, between rural areas belonging to different provinces, and between individuals. Moreover, as has happened in the West, modernization has not completely eradicated poverty. This was due to two factors: first the failure to master the impact of all kinds of pollution of the environment due to the industrialization process, and second because people had to pay for part of the health services, which in fact excluded from health people who could not afford to pay.

3.4.1 Disparities Between Provinces

The coastal province and three of the four municipalities under the supervision of the central government (i.e. Shanghai, Beijing and Tianjin), that were already more developed before the creation of the PRC, have benefited from reforms more than the inner and western provinces, especially Tibet, Guizhou, Qinghai, Gansu, and Ningxia practically on every dimension (see map on p. 105 to locate China's provinces), the other provinces being placed in between: e.g. for economic development, regional development, productivity and R&D, human development, education, social equity, public services, social security, infrastructure, environmental protection, and natural resources and geographical location (Wang Xiaolu 2007). Moreover, using different indicators of development combined into an overall index, Wang Xiaolu shows that the level of economic development is the strongest factor explaining the gap between provinces, the other factors being infrastructure, education and institutional development.[29]

Using the UNDP well-known HDI indicators (life expectancy, education, and per capita income) Yang Yongheng and Hu Angang (2008) classify provinces in four tiers. The four tiers distribute in a hierarchy, which indicates that China's economic development is seriously polarized. Yang and Hu proceed to a historical analysis that shows the evolution of the Chinese provinces from one tier to another, by again using HDI data for 1982, 1995, 1999, and 2003. Since the beginning of reforms, the distribution of provinces within the four tiers has changed. Between 1982 and 1995 all four tiers made remarkable progress in economy and education, and three provinces jumped from the third to the second tier (Fujian, Shandong and Hainan) forming a group of coastal provinces, i.e. those provinces that benefited most from reforms and opening-up to the world economy. Nevertheless, some of the provinces that in the past constituted the industrial basis of China (Jilin, Heilongjiang and Shanxi)

---

[29] Wang uses the following indicators (that are in fact obtained by combining several sub-indicators): (1) productivity and research and development; (2) education; (3) public services; (4) infrastructure; (5) institutional development; (6) human development; (7) social equity; (8) social security; (9) environmental protection; and (10) natural resources and geographical location.

suffered by the restructuring due to the reforms and dropped from the second to the third tier. The overall result was that the disparities between the first two tiers and the other two have further increased. By 1999 there have been improvements in all four tiers for health and education, but the economic disparities have become even greater. Finally, by 2003 the third and fourth tier diminished the gap with the upper tiers in education, but due to the remarkable economic development of the first tier the gap in economic development with the other tiers has been further widened.

At the end of the process, in 2003, China's provinces were distributed in the four tiers as follows: the first tier (Shanghai, Beijing, Tianjin) realizes a comprehensive and coordinated development in economy, education, and health, and reaches a high level of human development as defined by UNDP; the second tier (Zhejiang, Liaoning, Guangdong, Jiangsu, Fujian, Heilongjiang, and Shandong, i.e. provinces in the coastal region) exceeds the national average in all the aspects, particularly in economic development; the third tier (comprising 16 provinces)[30] equals the national average in education and health, but lags behind in economic development; finally, the fourth tier (Qinghai, Gansu, Yunnan, Guizhou, and Tibet, i.e. several western or central provinces) falls behind the national average in all three development aspects, among which the gap in education is the most striking.

Commenting on the results of their research, Yang and Hu arrive at several conclusions. First, the reform strategy giving priority to economic development has brought a more rapid development in economy than in education and health. Second, a 'coordinated development of education, health, and economy is prerequisite to a more balanced development'. Third, all the four tiers are now heading towards a *Coordinated Human Development* as defined by UNDP. Fourth, the reforms 'have brought about increasingly serious regional economic disparities, and have made economic disparities the most predominant cross-regional gap'. Finally, they draw our attention to the fact that they use the provinces as the basic unit for their analysis, whereas 'the disparities within provinces, especially between urban and rural areas, can be extremely huge'.[31] This statement confirms one of the main findings of Hu Angang about the disparities in Chinese society as they have been developing since the 1980s: more particularly farmers have been left far behind the urban regions (especially in the coastal provinces). This segregation exacerbates income disparity between the rural and urban populations and is responsible for the decline in public services for the poor (Hu 2004). This is what we are going to analyse in the following sections and in Sect. 4.8.

---

[30] This tier comprises the majority of the Chinese provinces: Chongqing, Henan, Inner Mongolia, Jiangxi, Guangxi, Shaanxi, Sichuan, Anhui, Ningxia, Hebei, Xinjiang, Hubei, Shanxi, Hunan, Jilin, and Hainan.

[31] And Yang and Hu comment: 'taking in the first tier the city Shanghai as an example: in 2005, per capita disposable income of an urban household (18,645 yuan) was nearly 2.5 times that of a rural household (8,247 yuan).'.

3.4 The Imbalances of Deng's New Public Management 105

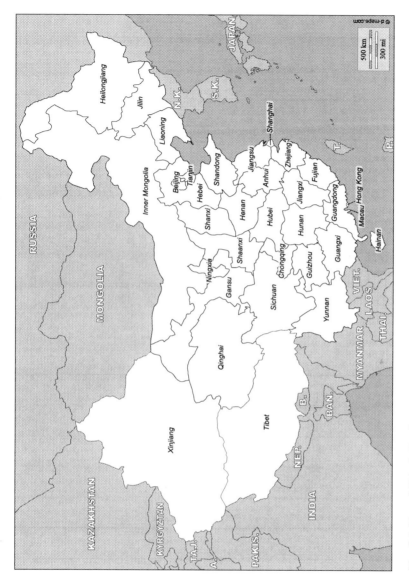

Map 5.1 Map of China's Provinces.
Source: d-maps, URL: http://d-maps.com/m/asia/china/chine/chine29.pdf

3.4.2 Disparities Between Rural and Urban Areas Within Provinces

We have already seen the data provided in Table 3.7, that show the increase of per capita income for both rural and urban areas. But this table also informs us of the income disparities between rural and urban areas. The ratio has varied from a low 1.82 in 1983, at the beginning of reforms, to a maximum of 3.33 in 2009, i.e. 12 years after the Party Congress of 1997 that accelerated reforms and led China into the WTO in 2001. It is interesting to note that the ratio, that had some ups and downs between 1978 and 1997, increased almost constantly from 1998 to 2009, when it started to decline, as a likely outcome of the rebalancing policies of the Hu Jintao era (to be presented in Chap. 4).

Table 3.8 presents the data on income disparities between urban and rural areas per provinces for 2006, i.e. four years after the beginning of Hu Jintao's 'policies that puts people first' These data confirm the statement of Yang and Hu mentioned above, suggesting the existence of huge disparities between rural and urban areas within provinces. Moreover, these disparities are generally higher within the less developed provinces situated in the interior and in the West. Taking disposable income in urban areas and net income in rural areas, the lowest ratios (between 2.26 and 2.49), are found in Tianjin, Shanghai, Beijing, Jiangsu, and Zhejiang. Disparity ratios between 2.5 and 3 are found in Hebei, Liaoning, Jilin, Heilongjiang, Fujian, Jiangxi, Shandong, Hubei, and Hainan. Ratios between 3 and 3.5 are found in Hunan, Shanxi, Inner Mongolia, Anhui, Henan, Guandong, Sichuan, Guangxi, Ningxia, and Xingjian. Ratios between 3.5 and 4 are found in Tibet and Qinghai. Finally, the highest ratio (over 4) exists in Chongqing, Gansu, Guizhou, Yunnan, and Shaanxi. In Chap. 4 we will use data for 2015–2017 and see whether the rebalancing policies introduced by Hu Jintao (2002–2012) and further developed by Xi Jinping after 2012, have decreased the gap between rural and urban areas within provinces.

3.4.3 Disparities Between the Rural Areas Belonging to Different Provinces

We have seen in Sect. 3.4.2, that there are disparities between rural and urban areas within provinces. But this does not mean that the situation of rural areas is basically the same in all the provinces. On the contrary, Albert Keidel has shown that there are considerable differences between rural areas belonging to provinces with a different level of urbanization (Keidel 2007). Keidel has aggregated some municipalities and provinces in order to construct four 'aggregated greater provinces' with both important urban and rural areas.[32] These are: Greater Hebei (comprising Hebei, Tianjin and Beijing), Greater Jiangsu (comprising Jiangsu and Shanghai), Greater Sichuan

---

[32]Keiled explains: 'Meaningful analysis of China's regional disparities requires a degree of aggregation over provincial-level entities. China has 31 provincial-level administrative units (hereafter

3.4 The Imbalances of Deng's New Public Management

Table 3.8 Per Capita Annual Income of Urban and Rural Households in China's provinces (2006)

Ratio (3)/(2)[a]	Region	Urban Areas		Region	Rural Areas
		Disposable Income (3)	Total Income (1)		Net Income (2)
3.27	National Average	11759.45	12719.19	National Average	3587.04
2.41	Beijing	19977.52	22417.16	Beijing	8275.47
2.29	Tianjin	14283.09	15476.04	Tianjin	6227.94
2.71	Hebei	10304.56	10887.19	Hebei	3801.82
3.15	Shanxi	10027.7	10793.89	Shanxi	3180.92
3.1	Inner Mongolia	10357.99	10811.87	Inner Mongolia	3341.88
2.53	Liaoning	10369.61	11230.03	Liaoning	4090.4
2.68	Jilin	9775.07	10245.28	Jilin	3641.13
2.58	Heilongjiang	9182.31	9721.9	Heilongjiang	3552.43
2.26	Shanghai	20667.91	22808.57	Shanghai	9138.65
2.42	Jiangsu	14084.26	15248.66	Jiangsu	5813.23
2.49	Zhejiang	18265.1	19954.03	Zhejiang	7334.81
3.29	Anhui	9771.05	10574.51	Anhui	2969.08
2.84	Fujian	13753.28	15102.39	Fujian	4834.75
2.76	Jiangxi	9551.12	10014.61	Jiangxi	3459.53
2.79	Shandong	12192.24	13222.85	Shandong	4368.33
3.01	Henan	9810.26	10339.2	Henan	3261.03
2.86	Hubei	9802.65	10533.34	Hubei	3419.35
3.09	Hunan	10504.67	11146.07	Hunan	3389.62
3.15	Guangdong	16015.58	17725.56	Guangdong	5079.78
3.1	Guangxi	9898.75	10624.3	Guangxi	2770.48
2.88	Hainan	9395.13	10081.7	Hainan	3255.53
4.02	Chongqing	11569.74	12548.91	Chongqing	2873.83
3.11	Sichuan	9350.11	10117	Sichuan	3002.38
4.59	Guizhou	9116.61	9439.31	Guizhou	1984.62
4.47	Yunnan	10069.89	10848.1	Yunnan	2250.46
3.67	Tibet	8941.08	9540.86	Tibet	2435.02
4.1	Shaanxi	9267.7	9938.19	Shaanxi	2260.19
4.18	Gansu	8920.59	9586.46	Gansu	2134.05
3.81	Qinghai	9000.35	9803.13	Qinghai	2358.37
3.32	Ningxia	9177.26	10002.03	Ningxia	2760.14
3.24	Xinjiang	8871.27	9689.07	Xinjiang	2737.28

[a] Author's calculation

Data Sources 2007 China Statistical Yearbook

108   3 The New Public Management Comes to China

(comprising Sichuan and Chongqing), and Greater Guangdong (comprising Guangdong and Hainan). The 26 'provinces' so obtained, are then regrouped into seven regions.[33] The 26 provinces and the seven regions constitute the two units of analysis of Keidel's research. In order to avoid measurement difficulties arising from the phenomenon of migration, Keidel proposes to use household survey data for rural households. which provides some very useful insights within rural China.

The first interesting result obtained by this method is that rural household disparities between China's regions are large, especially between the coastal and the interior areas. Using a historical approach (considering data every 5 years between 1985 and 2005) Keidel shows that rural per capita income has grown in all regions, but more in the coastal regions (between 7.4 and 8.5%) than in the interior (between 6 and 6.7%). Second, taking into consideration consumption expenses, the divergence is confirmed, and the ranking of regions is the same, even if the size of the divergence is weaker than for income. Moreover, the gap in terms of per capita income and consumption between Chinese rural areas is widening all the time. Third, Keidel proposes a sophisticated analysis to evaluate differences between rural areas in terms of the rate of poverty that is not possible to present here in detail.[34] It suffices to say that, by taking two coastal provinces and three inner ones, Keidel shows that the rate of rural poverty is much lower in the coastal provinces, using any of the available poverty measures.[35]

Fourth, these results suggested that divergence between coastal and inner rural areas were going to widen in the future in terms of income, consumption, and very likely also in terms of poverty rate. This constituted a formidable challenge for the Chinese leadership. Nevertheless, Keidel proposes an interesting and more encouraging interpretation, by putting these results in perspective with the overall development strategy of China. First, the rate of growth (in terms of both per capita

---

"provinces"), four of which are "municipalities." Three of these municipalities (Beijing, Tianjin, and Shanghai) have limited rural economies, making meaningful comparison with other entities especially difficult. Conversely, a province like Hebei, out of which both Beijing and Tianjin have been carved, has no real major urban area comparable to those of other provinces, undermining meaningful relevant comparisons.

[33] The seven regions are: (1) Far West (comprising Xingjiang, Tibet, Qinghai, Gansu, and Ningxia), (2) North Hinterland (Heilongjiang, Jilin, Inner Mongolia, Shanxi, and Shaanxi, (3) South Hinterland (Sichuan, Chongqing, Guizhou, Yunnan, and Guangxi), (4) Central Core (Henan, Anhui, Jiangxi, Hubei, and Hunan), North Coast (Liaoning, Hebei, Beijing, Tianjin, and Shandong), (6) East Coast (Jiangsu, Shanghai, and Zhejiang), and (7) South Coast (Fujian, Guangdong, and Hainan), in Keidel, ibidem, pp. 2–3.

[34] Keidel 2007, pp. 12–13, uses the revised World Bank's one-dollar-a-day standard to measure poverty by a consumption measure. China has not made consumption size distribution data available. 'China, however, has allowed the World Bank to post on its web site a statistical query facility called PovCal.ner, to allow approximation of China's consumption distribution for the national rural population'. Keidel limits the analysis to data about five provinces, two coastal regions, i.e. Jiangsu (representing Central Core), and Liaoning (representing North Coast), and three inner regions, i.e. Hunan (for Central Core), Sichuan (for South Hinterland), and Shaanxi (for North Hinterland). Moreover, Keidel considers that one should take into account the changes in savings habits.

[35] These are: in order of magnifying poverty rate: the Chinese Poverty line, the Old World Bank PPP $1/day Line, the New World Bank PPP $1/day Line, and the New World Bank PPP $2/day Line.

income and consumption) is so high in all the regions, that issues of convergence or divergence become less important. In other words, in spite of the widening gap between rural areas belonging to different provinces, the overall outcome of China's economic development is so important, that in every rural area there is a substantial improvement in terms of both per capita income and consumption.[36] Of course Keidel implicitly applies here the logic of economic development followed by Western countries since the beginning of the Industrial Revolution that led to an overall improvement of per capita income, in spite of an increasing divergence between different categories of people.[37] Moreover, Keidel suggests that whether inequalities will constitute a negative consequence of economic development or on the contrary 'useful incentives for voluntary labour force movement to more productive locations and vocations' will depend on the capacity of the market to create large numbers of better-paid jobs in the urban areas, and on the ability of the Government to favour the development of infrastructure in all domains (transport, communication, energy, but also education, health and social security) that will contribute to a more balanced development of the economy (Keidel 2007, pp. 16–17).

3.4.4 New Public Management, Income Distribution, and Inequality

We can have a first idea about income inequality in China, measured by the Gini index, thanks to a working paper published by the World Bank in August 2008, in which Xubei Luo and Nong Zhu calculated that China's 'Gini coefficient increased from around 30 to 45 over the past 35 years (Luo and Zhu 2008, p. 3). Moreover, in its report on China's anti-poverty strategy, published in 2009, the World Bank estimates China's Gini index for the year 2003 at 45.3 (for income inequality) and at 47.4 (for consumption inequality) (World Bank 2009, pp. 32–34). Finally, comparing China's income inequalities with a choice of Western countries, we find that around 2005 China had the highest Gini index (41.5) just above the US (40.8) (Table 3.9, based upon UNDP Human Development Report 2009).

Moreover, by taking the ratio between the 10% richest and the 10% poorest China, with a 13.2 ratio, takes its place within the group with the highest ratio, i.e. between New Zealand (12.5), the UK (13.8), Portugal (15.0) and US (15.9) and far from the countries of the lowest group with a ratio between 5.6 (Norway) and Denmark (8.1).

---

[36] I have already mentioned the results of a research by De Brauw and John Giles (2008) that revealed that migrations from rural villages led to significant increases in consumption per capita, and this effect is stronger for poorer households within villages.

[37] Clark (2007) shows that during the first phase of the Industrial revolution the standard of living of the large majority of the population increased considerably, compared to the previous centuries, and that disparities between the upper class and the lowest ones diminished. Nevertheless, after the initial stage divergences between these classes developed again. This process has been further amplified after the introduction of neo-liberal policies in the 1980s and the 1990s (Urio 1999).

Table 3.9 Gini index and ratio of richest 10% to poorest 10% in 20 Western countries and China, ca. 2005

Countries	Gini UNDP 2009	Rank	Richest 10% to poorest 10%	Rank	Countries	Gini UNDP 2009	Rank	Richest 10% to poorest 10%	Rank
Finland	26.9	4	5.6	1	Ireland	34.3	12	9.4	12
Norway	25.8	3	6.1	2	Greece	34.3	13	10.2	13
Sweden	25.0	2	6.2	3	Spain	34.7	14	10.3	14
Denmark	25.7	1	8.1	6	Australia	35.2	15	12.5	16
Germany	28.3	5	6.9	4	Italy	36.0	18	11.6	15
Austria	29.1	6	6.9	4					
					New Zealand	36.2	17	12.5	16
Belgium	33.0	10	8.2	7	UK	36.0	16	13.8	18
Netherlands	30.9	7	9.2	10	Portugal	38.5	19	15.0	19
France	32.7	9	9.1	9	US	40.8	20	15.9	20
Switzerland	33.7	11	9.0	8					
Canada	32.6	8	9.4	11	China	41.5	21	13.2	17

Source UNDP Human Development Report, 2009, pp. 195–196. Data ca. mid-2000s

3.4 The Imbalances of Deng's New Public Management   111

So, we can conclude that around 2005 China's situation concerning income inequality as a consequence of Deng's strategy was worse than in the majority of Western countries. But we must go into more depth within the world of inequalities in China, as the Gini coefficient tells only part of the story. Moreover, China is a very diverse country, with huge disparities between provinces, as we have seen above. Taking again data from the UNDP 2009 Report, we confirm that there are considerable disparities between provinces: the coastal provinces have a per capita GDP index significantly higher than those of the other provinces. The situation is more varied and balanced when taking into consideration the other two components of HDI (life expectancy and education), but the comprehensive HDI puts the coastal provinces and three of the four Municipalities under the direct supervision of the Central government (Beijing, Shanghai, and Tianjin) on top of the ranking, i.e. above 0.800, joined only by Inner Mongolia (0.803), whereas all the other provinces are below the national average (0.793), with the exception of Shanxi (0.800).[38] Here again, we shall see in Chap. 4 using UNDP data for 2015–2017 whether the situation has improved.

3.4.5 New Public Management and Poverty

The number of poor people has declined in China since the beginning of reforms, and this has been recognized by international organizations such as the UNDP, the OECD and the World Bank. Evaluations vary according to the authors, organizations and data base, but the general picture is basically the same. Let us take the assessment by the OECD around 2004 that is a good summary of the various evaluations: 'No matter which definition is adopted, be it the Chinese or the World Bank one, the trend is clear. According to the World Bank definition (income USD 1 per person per day at PPP), the number of people living in poverty in China fell from around 530 million (both in rural and urban areas) in 1981 to 129 million in 2004 and poverty incidence from 53% to 9.9%, respectively. The vast majority of those below the poverty line live in rural areas as indicated by a poverty incidence at 12.5% for rural China compared to 0.5% for urban China in 2001. Nevertheless, despite the progress made so far, a large part of the Chinese population still lives just above the absolute poverty line as shown by the share at 34.9% of those who lived below USD 2 per person per day in 2004' (OECD 2009).

The World Bank in its 2009 report says that between 1981 and 2004 the fraction of the population consuming less than a dollar-per-day fell from 65 to 10%, and more than half a billion people were lifted out of poverty. Even if the rate of poverty is higher when measured by the new international poverty standard of $1.25 per-person-per-day (using 2005 Purchasing Power Parity), the decrease since 1981 is no less impressive: from 85% in 1981 to 27% in 2004 (World Bank 2009, p. iii; Dollar 2009). Moreover, the World Bank considers that 'measured by the new international

---

[38]For more details see Table 6.8 in Urio (2012), pp. 156–157.

poverty standard of $1.25 per person per day (using 2005 Purchasing Power Parity for China), the levels of poverty are higher, but the decline since 1981 is no less impressive (from 85 in 1981 to 27% in 2004). In its 2018 overview, the World Bank considered that China has lifted more than 800 million people out of poverty, and that China reached all the Millennium Development Goals (MDGs) by 2015 and made a major contribution to the achievement of the MDGs globally (World Bank site 26 September 2018, https://www.worldbank.org/en/country/china/overview).

Nevertheless, Chinese scholars often consider that since the mid-1990s poverty has also arisen in urban areas, especially under the forms of new poverty, due to the weakness of the social security system, the very strong competition in the labour market, the policy of reducing cost of both enterprises (public and private) and public administrations by laying-off employees and workers, and the requirements for citizens to pay out of their pocket for education and health.

Let us take the data presented by the Oxford Poverty and Human Initiative's (OPHI) multidimensional poverty index (MPI), based upon a survey of 2003. This index is composed of three dimensions that are made up of ten indicators: health (child mortality, nutrition), education (years of school education, child enrolment) and living standards (electricity, drinking water, sanitation, flooring, cooking fuel, assets).[39]

First, the OPHI compares different measures of poverty: the OPHI's MPI index puts Chinese poverty at 12%, whereas the World Bank indicators put poverty at 16% (for the US$ 1.25 a day line) and 36% (for the US$ 2 a day line). Moreover, the OPHI compares these measures with the official national poverty line that puts poverty in China at only 3%. These different criteria for measuring poverty very clearly correspond to different appreciations of what are to be considered as 'poor living conditions'. Very clearly, by putting the poverty line well below the World Bank and OPHI criteria, the Chinese government takes into consideration the very low living conditions that existed in China at the beginning of reforms. Its more urgent goal was to lift out of extreme poverty as many people as possible as fast as possible. And this is what it succeeded in accomplishing.

Second, by taking the components of the MPI as indicators of deprivation, the OPHI shows the average proportion of indicators for which Chinese people are deprived as follows: schooling 10%, enrolment 0.0, nutrition 3.2, child mortality 0.0, electricity 0.0, sanitation 7.7, drinking water 3, flooring 3.2, cooking fuel 9.1, and assets 2.4%, from which it appears that the indicator that contributes most to the overall MPI is schooling, followed by cooking fuel, nutrition and sanitation. Third, the OPHI confirms the differences that exist between urban and rural areas. Finally, the OPHI provides comparative data between the 104 developing countries: China has a relative low percentage of poor, measured both by the MPI (12%) and the US$

---

[39]The MPI reflects both the incidence of poverty—the proportion of the population that is multidimensionally poor—and the average intensity of their deprivation—the average proportion of indicators in which they are deprived. The MPI is calculated by multiplying the incidence of poverty by the average intensity across the poor. A person is identified as poor if he or she is deprived in at least 30% of the weighted indicators (OPHI 2011).

3.4 The Imbalances of Deng's New Public Management 113

1.25 (16%) criteria, compared to other developing countries, of which 41 have an MPI over 40%, 34 over 50, and 26 over 60%.

3.4.6 New Public Management and Health

As we have already seen, health is the domain in which China has experienced the most difficult choices since the beginning of reforms and the demise of planned economy. Experts are unanimous in criticizing the introduction of measures that, by making people pay for part of health services, have brought the commodification of Chinese society to a point that large numbers of people were excluded from health care. Moreover, the dismantling of the health system (that during the Mao era had allowed rural China to escape from traditional infectious and parasitic diseases), the migration of medical personnel from the rural areas to the cities in search of better living and financial conditions, have left large sectors of Chinese rural society without proper health services. Hence, the deterioration, instead of the improvement of Chinese public health, as testified by many health indicators, such as life expectancy, as mentioned in one of the World Bank's influential annual reports (World Bank 2008, p. 83). In addition to this, the changing habits of the increasingly well-off urban population have fuelled the emergence and the development of diseases typical of a well-off society, such as cardio-vascular diseases, cancers, obesity and diabetes.[40] Finally, an insufficient regulation in favour of environmental protection has resulted in serious pollutions of water, air and land that have not only devastated huge areas of Chinese territory, but have also contributed to the deterioration of China's public health.

3.5 Conclusion

At the end of this chapter we can conclude that the reform process initiated by Deng Xiaoping has certainly allowed China to realize astonishing results both in terms of overall wealth creation (GDP) and in terms of per capita income and consumption improvement for the great majority of the Chinese people. Also, economic indicators have shown that the economy may constitute an asset for China's strategy to reclaim world power status. Unfortunately, several negative consequences have also emerged from this long process, that concern both the human and the physical environments.

---

[40]Information about these problems can be found in the leading journals on medicine such as the *New England Journal of Medicine,* and *The Lancet* and its *The Lancet series on health system reform in China.* For an overall presentation of China's health and poverty problems: Hu (2007), with chapters on 'China's economic growth and poverty reduction (1978–2002)', pp. 97–132; 'China's macro-economy and health', pp. 133–151; and 'Health insecurity: The biggest challenge to human security in China', pp. 152–166; and Chap. 44 in Hu 2011: 'A Healthy China: Progress and Problem', pp. 65–81.

At the beginning of the XXI Century inequalities and disparities in the distribution of the wealth are considerable. The gaps between rural and urban areas are the most striking, not only in economic terms but also (as there is a nexus between economy and other dimensions of the reform process) in terms of education, public services and infrastructure availability and access, including health care. The emergence of under-paid and under-protected rural migrants, and new forms of poverty touching both urban and rural areas, have put into light the losers of the economic development.

This situation is not very different from that which we experienced in the West during the first decades of the Industrial Revolution. Several generations of Western workers have been sacrificed on the altar of economic development. And nothing can be done today to redress the harm done to these people. The same situation is also basically valid for China. Nevertheless, it has been aggravated in China by the failure of replacing in time the old solidarities of the Mao era with a modern set of social policies. The difference is that in the West since the 1930s, and even more so after the Second World War, a welfare state has been implemented in every country, even if with different scopes. When the wave of neoliberalism arrived at the beginning of the 1980s, the attack on the welfare state had difficulties in succeeding to dismantle what had been realized before, even if several serious regressions were realized following the implementation of neoliberal dogmas (Urio 2012, Chap. 5; Suleiman 2003). On the contrary, in China the demise of the social functions of the SOEs of the Mao era created a vacuum that has no comparison with the reduction of the welfare state in the West. So, when people are, from one day to the next, immersed in a severely competitive labour market, and left there without proper social insurances (especially unemployment, health and age insurances), the road is wide open to the emergence of important disparities and, considerably worse, of new forms of poverty that put millions of people under the poverty line as defined by international norms. Moreover, the priority given to economic development had negative impacts on the environment, with damaging consequences for the health of people.

It is a pity the Chinese leadership has been rather slow in taking advantage of research already available at the end of the 1980s pointing out the negative consequences of the development strategy adopted in 1978 (Hu et al. 1992; Hu and Zou 1991). We will see in Chap. 4 whether the Party has been able to correct the inequalities and the damages of the environment due to a development strategy that has given priority to economic development. At the beginning of the 2000s we could forecast that should the Party fail to respond to these challenges, the Chinese people would lose faith in the capacity of the Chinese leadership to provide a fair distribution of wealth, and then the old demons of people's revolt, very frequent throughout Chinese history, may again emerge and put an end to China's stability and harmony and jeopardize its newly-found (relative) prosperity.

References

Balazs, E. (1968). *La bureaucratie céleste. Recherches sur l'économie et la société de la Chine traditionnelle*. Paris: Gallimard.

Barton, D., Chen, & Jin. (2013). Generational change and the rising prosperity of inland cities will power consumption for years to come, McKinsey, June.

So, B. W. Y. (2008). Privatisation. In C. Tubilewicz (Ed.), *Critical issues in contemporary China* (pp. 49–78). London: Routledge, 2006.

Bergère, M. C. (1986). *L'âge d'or de la bourgeoisie chinoise*. Paris: Flammarion.

Bergère, M. C. (2007). *Capitalismes et capitalistes en Chine. Des origines à nos jours*. Paris: Perrin.

Buckley Ebrey, P. (Ed.). (1999). *The Cambridge illustrated history of China*. Cambridge: Cambridge University Press.

Chang, G. G. (2001). *The coming collapse of China*. New York: Random House.

Chang, H. J. (2003a). *Globalization, Economic Development and the Role of the State*. New York: Zed Books.

Chang, H. J. (2003b). *Kicking away the ladder: Development strategy in historical perspective*. London: Anthem Press.

Chang, H. J. (2008). *Bad samaritans: The myth of free trade and the secret history of capitalism*. New York: Bloomsbury.

Chen, J., & Dickson, B. (2008). Allies of the state: Democratic support and regime support among China's private entrepreneurs. *The China Quarterly* (December, pp. 780–804).

China Power Project. (2017). Defining China's Middle Class, CSIS, 24 April, updated 3 December 2018. Retrieved March 14, 2019, from https://chinapower.csis.org/china-middle-class/.

Clark, G. (2007). *A Farewell to Alms. A Brief Economic History of the World*. Princeton: Princeton University Press.

De Brauw, A., & Giles. (2008). Migrant Labor Markets and the Welfare of Rural Households in the Developing World: Evidence from China, World Bank, February 10.

Dickson, B. J. (2003). *Red capitalists in China: The party, private entrepreneurs, and prospects for political change*. Cambridge: Cambridge University Press.

Dickson, B. J. (2008). *Wealth into power: The communist party's embrace of China's private sector*. New York: Cambridge University Press.

Dollar, D. (2009). Remarkable progress, remaining vulnerability among China's poor, World Bank site. Retrieved May 18, 2009, from http://web.worldbank.org.

Farrell, D., Gersch U. A., & Stephenson, E. (2006). The value of China's emerging middle class. *The McKinsey Quarterly*, 2006 Special Edition, pp. 62–69.

Farrell et al. (2006). *From 'Made in China' to 'Sold in China': The rise of the Chinese urban consume*. McKinsey Global Institute, November.

Goodman, D. (2000). Deng Xiaoping. In C. Mackerras, D. H. McMillen, & A. Watson (Eds.), *Dictionary of the politics of the people's republic of China*. Taylor & Francis, London: Routledge.

Hesketh, T., Lu, L., & Xing, Z. W. (2005). The effect of China's one-child family policy after 25 Years. *The New England Journal of Medicine, 353*(11, September), 1171–1176.

Hu, A. (2004). *China's New Development Strategy*, Zhejiang, People Publishing House of Zhejiang (3rd ed., in Chinese).

Hu, A. (2007). *Economic and social transformation in China*. London: Routledge.

Hu, A. (2014). *China's collective presidency*. Heidelberg: Springer.

Hu, A. (2016). Economic power evolution of G20 members (1990 − 2020), Beijing. *Institute for contemporary China Studies of Tsinghua University*, National Reports, Issue 8, 22 April.

Hu, A., Yi, W., et al. (1992). *Survival and development. A study of China's long-term development*. Beijing and New York: Science Press.

Hu, A., & Zou, P. (1991). *China's* population development. Beijing: China's Science and Technology Press.

Hu, S. (Ed.). (1994). *A concise history of the communist party of China*. Beijing: Foreign Languages Press.

116   3 The New Public Management Comes to China

Huang, Y. (2003). *Selling China*. Cambridge: Cambridge University Press.

Huang, Y. (2008). *Capitalism with Chinese characteristics*. New York: Cambridge University, Press.

Keidel, A. (2007). *The causes and impact of Chinese regional inequalities in income and well-being*. Carnegie Endowment for International Peace, December.

IMF. (2018). World economic outlook, April.

Lesbre, E. (2004). *Développement durable et environnement en Chine*, Article de la mission économique française en Chine, June.

Li, Q. (2002). Stratification in China's resident registration and peasant workers' social status, Social *Sciences in China*, Spring, 2002 (electronic copy provided by author).

Li, Q. (2003). An analysis of push and pull factors in the migration of rural workers in China. *Social Sciences in China*, January 2003 (electronic copy provided by author).

Lieberthal, K. (1995). *Governing China: From cultural revolution through reform*. New York: Norton.

Lin, C. (2008). Against privatization in China: A historical and empirical argument. *Journal of Chinese Political Science*, *13*(1).

Lou, J. (Ed.). (1997). *Macroeconomic reform in China*. Washington, DC: The World Bank.

Lu, X. (2006). On the changes and developments of the social structure of China. *Journal of Yunnan Nationalities University*, *23*(5, 2006), 28–35.

Luo, X., & Zhu, N. (2008). Rising income inequality in China: A race to the top. *World Bank, East Asia and Pacific Region, Poverty Reduction and Economic Management Department*, Policy Research Paper, No 4700, August.

Ma, J., & Zhang, Z. (2009). Remaking the Chinese administrative state since 1978: The double-movements perspective. *The Korean Journal of Policy Studies, 23*(2), 225–226.

Naughton, B. J. (2007). *The Chinese economy: Transition and growth*. Cambridge: The MIT Press.

Nolan, P. (2001). *China and the global economy*. Palgrave: Houndsmill, UK.

Nolan, P. (2004). *Transforming China: Globalization, transition and development*. London: Anthem Press.

OECD (2009), *OECD Rural Policy Reviews: China*, Paris, 2009.

OPHI.(2011). Country briefing: China. *Oxford Poverty and Human Initiative*. Retrieved April 3, 2011, from www.ophi.org.uk.

Peerenboom, R. (2002). *China's long March toward rule of law*. Cambridge: Cambridge University Press.

Riedel, J., et al. (2007). *How China grows*. Princeton: Princeton University Press.

Tang, W., & Yang. (2008). The Chinese urban caste system in transformation. *The China Quarterly*, December, 759–779.

Urio, P. (1984). *Le rôle politique de l'administration publique*. LEP: Lausanne.

Urio, P. (1999). *La gestion publique au service du marché*, in Marc Hufty (sous la direction de), *La pensée comptable. Etat, néolibéralisme, nouvelle gestion publique* (pp. 91–124). Paris: Presses Universitaires de France, 1999.

Urio, P. (2004). The Provision of Public Services in the PRC in the Age of Reform: Reconciling State, Market and Civil Society. Paper presented at the International Symposium on Public Service and Government Reform, Haikou, China, 30–31 October 2004.

Urio, P. (2010). *Reconciling State, Market, and Society in China. The Long March towards Prosperity*. London and New York: Routledge.

Urio, P. (2012). *China, the west, and the myth of new public management. Neoliberalism and its discontents*. London and New York: Routledge, 2012.

Urio, P. (2018). *China reclaims world power status. Putting an end to the world America made*. London and New York: Routledge, 2018.

Vallée, A. (2003). *Economie de l'environnement*. Paris: Editions du Seuil.

Wang, X. (2007). Who's in first? A regional development index for the PRC'. Asian Development Bank Institute, *Discussion Paper no. 66*, May.

References

Wang J. Y. (2003). *Evaluation of the fertility of Chinese women during 1990–2000.* Theses collection of 2001, National Family Planning and Reproductive Health Survey, Beijing, China Population Publishing House.

Weber, M. (1978). *Economy and society.* Berkeley: University of California Press.

Weber, M. (1988). Die 'Objektivität' sozialwissenschaftlicher und sozialpolitischer Erkenntnis. *Gesammelte Aufsätze zur Wissenschaftslehre.* Tübingen; J.C.B. Mohr.

Weber, M. (2011). 'Objectivity' in social science and social policy. In *Methodology of social sciences.* New Brunswick (USA): Transactions Publishers.

World Bank. (1997). *Clear water, blue sky. China's environment in the new century.* World Bank: Washington, DC.

World Bank. (2008). *The world bank report 2008: The challenges of a changing world.* Washington DC.

World Bank. (2009). *From poor areas to poor people: China's evolving poverty reduction agenda. An assessment of poverty and inequality in China,* March, Washington DC.

World Bank. (2013). *China 2030. Building a modern, harmonious, and creative society,* World Bank and Development Research Center of the State Council of the People's Republic of China.

Xiang, B., & Teng, B. (2008). China's start-ups grow up. *Far Eastern Economic Review,* September, 53–55.

Yang, Y., & Hu, A. (2008). Investigating regional disparities of China's human development with cluster analysis: A historical perspective. *Social Indicators Research,* Springer Science & Business Media, 86, 2008, pp. 417–432.

Zhang, C., et al. (2009). *Promoting Enterprise-Led Innovation in China.* Washington, DC: World Bank.

Zhang, W. (2014). *Never forget national humiliation: Historical memory in Chinese politics and foreign relations.* New York: Columbia University Press.

Chapter 4
The Rebalancing of Chinese Society

At the end of the third chapter I concluded that the reform process initiated by Deng Xiaoping had certainly allowed China to realize astonishing results both in terms of overall wealth creation (GDP) and in terms of per capita income and consumption for the great majority of the Chinese people. Unfortunately, at the same time, several negative consequences had also emerged from this long process. First, the development strategy had resulted in all kinds of disparities and inequalities between provinces, between urban and rural areas, and between individuals, that needed to be corrected in order to safeguard unity, stability and harmony. Second, the negative impact of Deng's policy of 'economic development first' had deteriorated the environment with negative impacts not only on the ecological equilibria but also on people's health, via the development of all kinds of pollutions, thus jeopardizing another of China's traditional values: the harmony between humankind and nature. This chapter examines how China changed its development strategy in order to overcome these challenges.

4.1 The New Development Strategy: Putting 'People First'

In Chap. 3 I have summarized the development strategies implemented by China since 1949. The first two strategies gave priorities to economic development with the negative outcomes I have just mentioned and summarized in Chap. 3. In order to correct these negative consequences the Chinese leadership started to move towards

---

This Chapter is based upon Urio 2010 (Chap. 3), Urio 2012 (Chap. 6) with many updates and new comments.

The original version of this chapter was revised. The author given name is corrected in reference list and the reference citation. The correction to this chapter is available at 10.1007/978-981-13-8879-8_7

© Springer Nature Singapore Pte Ltd. 2019
P. Urio, *China 1949–2019*, https://doi.org/10.1007/978-981-13-8879-8_4

120   4   The Rebalancing of Chinese Society

a third approach to development in the mid-1990s that clearly changed the focus of development from a purely economic perspective to a socio-economic one.[1] The ground for this fundamental change in the development strategy was prepared thanks to an important research work conducted by a group of young scholars within the China Academy of Sciences in the 1980s, i.e. already during the first decade of reforms.[2] Two researches are worth mentioning here: one on 'population and development' and another on 'survival and development' (Hu and Zou 1991; Hu, Wang et al. 1992).

One of the main conclusions of the research on 'population and development' is that both theoretical and empirical models, especially Western models, cannot be transposed mechanically and directly into China, but should be evaluated taking into consideration the characteristics of the Chinese situation. A population theory that would not conform to the actual conditions of China is bound to lead to errors, and become dogmatic. This leads the authors to reject both traditional Marxist development theory and the Soviet model of development, and to adopt a model based upon the contradictions existing within Chinese society between the rapidly increasing population and the shortage of economic resources that would have made it difficult to improve the living standards of the Chinese people (Hu and Zou 1991, pp. 79 and 84–85).[3] This change of paradigm led to the adoption of birth control with the aim of reducing the fertility rate and hence to resolve, at least partially, the contradictions mentioned above.

The book on 'survival and development' identifies the fundamental problems China must face on the road to development, starting from the conditions of Chinese population and territory: 'excessive large population; a very poor economic foundation; backward education, culture, science and technology; a relative shortage of natural resources and a very low per capita GNP by world standards. These characteristics have remained basically unchanged [since the beginning of reforms] and have become even worse in certain fields, although China has made great progress in the past decade of reform [i.e. the first decade].' (Hu and Wang 1992, p. xi).

It is even more interesting to note that, already at the end of 1988 (i.e. before the events on Tian An Men Square of June 1989) this report points to the major challenges resulting from the negative consequences of economic development, that the authors do not hesitate to name 'China's unprecedented multiple crises': (1) in spite of the birth control set up by the government, the population continues to grow, and its literacy level is still too low; moreover, population growth results in chronic unemployment and underemployment, especially in the rural areas; (2) agricultural resources are declining and approaching the limits of their carrying capacity; (3) the rapid expansion of environmental pollution and the ongoing degradation of the

---

[1] We will see in Sect. 6.2 that China adopted a fourth development strategy under the leadership of Xi Jinping.

[2] In Sect. 2.4 I have dealt with the Party's revision of the foundations of its ideology that made it possible to redefine its development strategy.

[3] They refer to the population theory of the famous Chinese demographer Ma Yinchu.

4.1 The New Development Strategy: Putting 'People First'

ecosystem, which will become a major crisis affecting the survival and development of China in the first half of the next century (Hu and Wang 1992, pp. xii–xiii).

The report also very strongly confirms that China should follow its own 'non-traditional' path to modernization, based upon (1) low consumption of resources in the production process; (2) moderate private consumption; (3) sustainable development with constant improvement of economic efficiency while controlling pollution, maintaining ecological balance, and a reasonable use of natural resources (ecological efficiency); (4) but also a social system that ensures social efficiency and justice; (5) an appropriate technological system that encourages innovations in all domains, including technological innovation; and (6) integration in the international economic system.

It is interesting to note that practically all the major problems that broke out in China at the end of the 1990s are identified and analyzed in the report and that all the major leitmotivs of the new development strategy defined by Hu Jintao that 'put people first' are already clearly broached in the report: economic efficiency, but also social equity and efficiency, ecological efficiency, and innovation in all domains.

In 1992, starting from these premises, two Chinese scholars further develop the analysis of China's development strategy and come to the conclusion that the policies mentioned above needed to be supported by state's interventions requiring some additional financial means. Quite rationally in a report entitled 'Strengthen the role of the Central Government during the transition towards a market economy' they suggest the centralization of Chinese policies, especially fiscal policy (Wang and Hu 1993). This report is circulated in China and is at the origin of the centralization of fiscal policy decided by Jiang Zemin in 1995, and which gave to the central government more fiscal revenues.

Following the change in fiscal policy, the government started in 1995 to re-define the development strategy at the 5th Plenum of the 14th CCP Central Committee comprising three dimensions: the development of the western provinces (2001); the rejuvenation of the old industrial bases in northern China (2004); and the development of the central provinces (2006). This new strategy (that looks like a correction of Deng's motto 'let some people get rich first') has given the incentive to a vast programme of investments in infrastructure in the northern, inner and western provinces. Even if one can regret, as I do, that at the beginning this programme gave priority to hard infrastructures and has neglected soft infrastructure (and we have already mentioned the negative consequences for public health) one must recognize that these investments have improved the physical assets of the less developed provinces and has prepared them, with the new policies that 'put people first', to start another long March, that will eventually lift these provinces close to the development level of the coastal ones in terms not only of economic but also of human development.

In February 2004, Zhu Rongji's successor, Premier Wen Jiabao recognized that China's fast economic development had resulted in the accumulation of issues and conflicts, such as enlarging gaps in income between urban and rural areas; enlarging regional gaps; increasing inequality in family income, mounting pressure of employment and social security; lags in the development of education, health, and culture; intensifying contradictions between the growing population, economic development, environment damages and the excessive use of natural resources; low quality of the economic system and lack of competitiveness. Based upon this appreciation of the situation of Chinese society, Premier Wen Jiabao concluded that China must solve these problems in good time. This strategy strongly suggests that the biggest challenge to China in the twenty-first century is not how to further speed up economic growth, but how to maintain a sustainable and equitable growth to reduce poverty and promote human development by focusing on the purpose of development, instead of on development for the sake of development. These policy options were introduced in the 11th Five-year plan (2006–2010) and confirmed at the Party Congress of November 2007. In the framework of the third development strategy, hundreds of billions of Yuan have been invested in the poor provinces and regions.

The investments in physical infrastructure needed to be complemented with some parallel investments in human capital (Wang 2008). This has been done first by abolishing some of the most irrational decisions taken in the past, and first of all by eliminating, between 2003 and 2006, the taxes and fees that peasants were obliged to pay and that constituted a heavy burden on their already meagre income; second, by abolishing the fees for elementary and junior high school, for rural areas in 2006 for western provinces, and in 2007 for inner and eastern provinces, and in 2008 for urban areas (PRC, State Council 2005 and 2008).[4] Then, at the Party Congress of November 2007 President Hu Jintao announced the adoption of China's new health system that should provide universal coverage by the year 2020. Of course, the major domain in which the new policy trend manifests itself is the one of social security (see below Sects. 4.3 and 4.4). Social welfare is necessary not only if one's attitude is oriented by considerations of equity, but also because a well-educated population protected by decent health, unemployment and old age insurances is better armed for contributing to the development of society and for assuring the stability it needs. Finally, in 2008 the new Labour Law improving the protection of employees and workers was adopted and implemented. The new Contract law improves the protection of employees in case of redundancy and of abuse of short-term contracts (for example, after 10 years within the same company short-term contracts become illegal). Moreover, the Chinese government has established the principle of minimum wages, the provinces being able to fix them taking into consideration the conditions of the local labour market. Even if the minima, as we shall see, are very low, this policy shows that the interests of the working people are being taken into consideration more seriously than in the past.[5]

---

[4]For an authentic account of the difficulties this neoliberal policy caused to poor peasants, one can read the diary of a young schoolgirl of Ningxia province, that describes the situation of peasants' families around the years 2000–2001 (Ma and Haski 2009).

[5]The highest minimum wage was first established on 1 July 2009 by the Shenzen government at 1,000 yuan, an increase of 20%. See below Sect. 4.3.4 for an update.

4.2 The Rebalancing Between Human and Physical Environments

Since the beginning of economic development, the Chinese leadership has been confronted with the dilemma opposing economic development to environmental protection. Between 1949 and the late 1990s, economic development was given priority over environmental considerations. Two reasons explain this choice: first, the CPC considered that it was necessary to develop the economy for improving the living conditions of the Chinese people; second, the CPC also considered a strong economy was one of the major means for recovering international power status and thus avoiding the return of 'the hundred years humiliations.' I have sustained in Sect. 2.4 and in Sect. 3.1 above, that these two goals were interdependent for both Mao and Deng, only the circumstances were different. Only when it became dramatically evident that the impact of the 'economy first' strategy was jeopardizing both the living conditions of the Chinese people and the strength of the country, the leadership decided to change strategy and to put 'people first', as we have seen above. This is not to say that economic development was going to take second place after environmental protection and a more equitable distribution of wealth. It means that the CPC has decided to find a better equilibrium between economic development on the one hand, and environmental protection and social equity on the other hand. Some pundits consider that the preference for economic development has gone too far and for too long. This is certainly true from the point of view of the environment: the damages have been so important that it will take a lot of time and money to reverse the trend. But on the other hand, it is also indisputable that the economy has been developed to a point that it constitutes today the major pillar of China's power, with its collateral consequences on technological advancement, including defence, as I will explain in Sect. 6.2. Moreover, China has attained a level of economic development that allowed it to acquire the financial means needed for correcting the negative impact of the 'economy first' strategy, thanks also to the centralization of fiscal policy.

Nevertheless, it is in the domain of environmental protection that improvements have been generally considered less impressive, especially by Western observers, worried as they are by the increasing use of natural resources by the Chinese economy that are in fact contributing to the world environmental damage. Moreover, not all the experts consider that the official Chinese statistics about the environment are reliable. However, one cannot say that the government has not taken and implemented several measures in order to put a halt to environmental degradation. And we have already seen, pollution is not only damageable for the physical environment, but also to the people, as it has affected their health. First, a number of non-performing and polluting SOEs have been shut down. Second, the use of coal for heating has been reduced in the cities. Third, an important effort of re-forestation has been carried out: for example, between 1998 and 2001, the central government invested over 42 billion yuan in reforestation, management and restoration of state forests in 25 regions. China plans to bring the forest coverage up to 28% of the territory by 2050.

124   4 The Rebalancing of Chinese Society

Fourth, since the beginning of the reform process, many laws and regulations have been adopted and implemented: after the first law on the protection of maritime environment of 1982, many other laws were passed in the domain of water, prairies, fishing, land, wild animals, agriculture, air, etc. Moreover, several research institutes provide expertise to the authorities that will be useful for designing better laws and regulations, such as the Chinese Academy of Sciences, the Chinese Academy for Environmental Sciences, as well as a number of research centres at the local level.

Last but not least, several efforts for educating the Chinese population in the domain of environmental protection have been undertaken by both governmental agencies and non-governmental organizations (Ran 2005). Education, if successful, will avoid the implementation of sanctions in case of violation of laws and regulations. Of course, education is a long-term endeavour, especially when it is bound to change well-entrenched everyday habits. The first experimental education programmes were introduced in Liaoning, Guangdong, Beijing, and Shanghai already in 1979. They were followed by a decision of the central government in 1987 (confirmed in 1991 and 1992) stipulating that environmental education be compulsory in the schools' curricula, at elementary and secondary levels. Non-governmental organizations are active in China, such as Friends of Nature, Global Village of Beijing, WWF, and The Trust for Environment, which promotes The Environmental Education Television Project for China. Moreover, several enterprises also have introduced programmes in the domain of environmental protection, such as Bell, Exxon-Mobil, and others.

It is in this context that Tsinghua professor Hu Angang has suggested to replace what he calls the 'black cat development' of the Deng era with the 'new green cat development' of the Hu Jintao era (Hu 2009; Hu and Guan 2017). Hu starts by reminding us of one of the major goals of the 11th Five-year plan (2006 to 2010) i.e. to reduce energy consumption per unit of GDP by 20%. Hu comments: 'the target is not simply economic; it is a political commitment by the government to its citizens. It indicates China's political will and its commitment to reducing emissions. (…) This target is the first step on the road to a low-carbon economy, and is of greater political and economic significance.' Moreover, Hu stresses that 'the Chinese leadership faces two pressing questions: how to transform China's economy into a low-carbon economy; and how to participate in global governance, moving from national to regional and worldwide governance.' (Hu 2009). This last goal is very important as it is the final step of the policies implemented from the beginning of the People's Republic of China: by taking the lead in the long March towards a global green economy, China has the great opportunity to restore itself as a world power.

According to Hu Angang, China should bind itself to international goals to slash greenhouse gas pollution: 'It is in China's own interest to accept greenhouse gas emissions goals, not just in the international interest. (…) China is a developing country, but is a special one, with the biggest population, high energy use and sooner or later, if not now, the biggest total greenhouse gas emissions. So, this is a common battlefront we must join.' (quoted by Buckley 2008). Moreover, Hu reminds us that 'like joining the WTO, this [strategy] should be used as international pressure to spur our own transformation.' (Hu 2009). Nevertheless, Hu Angang was not unaware of

4.2 The Rebalancing Between Human and Physical Environments

the difficulties that may arise on this road. It may be true that at that time the Chinese government was not yet ready to make concessions according to the line defined by the Tsinghua professor. But in an interview given to a Reuters journalist who made this remark, Hu replied not without some pride and a keen sense of humour: 'I've always started out in the minority but ended up as the mainstream.' (Buckley 2008, Wong 2008).

Already towards the end of the 2000s, this cautious optimism has been confirmed by several publications by influential organizations. First, the World Bank, in spite of considering that progress on the environmental objectives during the first two years of the 11th five-year plan, (i.e. between 2006 and 2008) has been mixed (especially insufficient progress in reducing energy intensity), it recognizes that improvements were seen in reducing air and water pollution, treating industrial solid waste, increasing the efficiency of water use, and expanding forest coverage (World Bank 2009). Second, McKinsey estimated in 2009 that 'China's current efforts and recently enacted policies could reduce the country's energy intensity by 17% during every five-year interval from 2005 to 2030.' (McKinsey 2009). Third, a 2010 report by the World Watch Institute recognizes that China has become the major producer and implementer of clean energy equipment such as light bulbs, solar water heaters, solar photovoltaic cells, and wind turbines which reflect 'a strong and growing commitment by the government to diversify its energy economy; reduce environmental problems, and stave off massive increases in energy imports. Around the world, governments and industries now find themselves struggling to keep pace with the new pacesetter in global clean energy development. (World Watch Institute 2010). Furthermore, the report explains that positive results have been achieved thanks to the implementation of a host of new policies and regulations that have resulted, during the first three years of the 11th Five-year plan (2006–2008), in a reduction of energy consumption per unit of GDP (the so-called energy intensity) 'by just over 10%, saving 290 million tons of coal equivalent and reducing the country's greenhouse gas emissions by 750 million tons of carbon dioxide-equivalent. This pace of energy conservation has rarely been achieved by the rest of the world.'[6] In spite of the persistence of problems for energy savings, especially in the industrial sector, the report is rather positive in recognizing that 'China's rapid rise to global leadership in clean energy is rooted in an unusual level of cooperation between government and industry (...) with the aim of making the country an innovator as well as a low-cost manufacturer of cutting-edge technologies.' Moreover, a 2011 publication by the World Watch Institute considers that thanks to the policies mentioned above, 'one of the greatest promises of China's green transition is the potential for expanded employment in industries and economic sectors that can help slow and possibly reduce the country's environmental impact'. (Pan et al. 2011).

---

[6]The report mentions the National Renewable Energy Law, the National Medium and Long-Term Development Plan for Renewable Energy, the Medium and Long-Term Energy Conservation Plan as well as the infrastructure-intensive government stimulus programme launched in late 2008 and the measures included in the 11th Five-year Plan.

126   4 The Rebalancing of Chinese Society

Parallel to these improvements, China has invested in the development of renewable energy equipment. Already in 2011 the World Bank recognized that 'over the last five years, China has increased its renewable energy generation to 8.8% of total primary energy consumption, making it one of the world's leading producers.' (World Bank 2011). And for wind power, Pinsent Mason recognized that 'at the end of 2010, China's became the world's largest wind power developer, having overtaken the US in installed capacity.' (Pinsent Mason 2011).

The environmental strategy followed since the adoption of the 11th Five-year Plan integrates a number of initiatives that have been summarized in a book published by Springer (Hu 2017). Hu is very clear in reaffirming a fundamental principle of the CPC strategic management that is implemented also within the environmental strategy, i.e. the complementarity between state and market, instead of their opposition: 'China's successful development has involved taking full advantage of using "two hands"—the mechanisms and advantages that come with using a market hand and a government hand.[7] The government's hand refers to national strategic decision-making, national development guidance, and national policy support. The state provides guidance through its development plans in addition to its views and notices, and national policy includes fiscal, financial, industrial policy, and human capital support. Green development depends on government guidance and national planning. However, it also needs to respond to the dynamic role of the market.' (pp. 183–184). The improvements in this domain have been realized thanks to this cooperation, which has been defined in the Five-year plans from the 6th to the 12th (pp. 108–126).

In order to prove the validity of this strategy, Hu has analysed several sectorial domains at the local level in which improvements have been made: the improvement of Beijing's environment; the reforestation of the rural area of Chongqing municipality; the transformation of Qinghai from an industrial to an ecological province (pp. 131–160). These findings are particularly welcome as improvements of the environment occur, if ever they do, at the local level, even if the policies are defined at the centre. To this we may add the development of eco-cities, of which the most acclaimed example is the Sino-Singapore Tianjin Eco-city with the support of the Singapore government and the World Bank (World Bank 2010; Koh 2018), and the development of innovative projects for improving air pollution supported by the World Bank (Han Shaoqing 2018). Of course, as is the case for other domains of China's development, not all the observers, especially in the West, recognize the progress made by China's environmental policies. The CPC is very well aware that air and water pollution are the major concerns for the Chinese citizens, just after corruption of officials, and thus improving the government performance on these topics is indispensable for maintaining citizens' support (Wike 2015).

At the end of this section, this is what we can say with a sufficient level of confidence, based upon data available from reliable sources.[8] First, between 2000

---

[7]We will see in Sect. 6.2.4.2 that this is also the opinion of Lee Kai-fu regarding the strategic domain of Artificial Intelligence (AI). Lee is an expert in AI.

[8]The following data come from the World Bank, the European Union and British petroleum. Kindly assembled and provided by Prof. Hu Angang, Tsinghua University.

4.2 The Rebalancing Between Human and Physical Environments 127

and 2017, China's total carbon emissions index (measured per 100 million tons) has increased from 33.50 to 92.33, with an increase of its share in the world from 14.18 to 27.61%. Comparatively, the US index decreased from 57.27 to 50.88, a decrease of its share in the world from 24.24 to 15.21%. Similarly, the EU index decreased from 40.78 to 35.42, its share in the world dropping from 17.26 to 10.59%. Nevertheless, since 2011 China's total carbon emissions have not increased, which means that China's environmental policies have started to produce good results. However, the level is still too high and should be reduced.

Second, taking the energy use (measured by kg of oil equivalent per $1000, at constant 2011 PPP) we see that it has decreased from 243.7 in 2005 to 175.3 kg in 2014, a decrease higher than the world. The same pattern is seen for CO_2 emissions (kg per PPP $ of GDP): they have decreased from 0.91 in 2004 to 0.56 kg in 2014, again a higher decrease than the world.

Even more positive results can be seen taking the use of wind and solar energy. In 2000 China's share for wind energy in the world was as low as 1.88%, compared to 17.98% for the US and 71.23% for the EU, which was at that time leading in this domain. In 2017, China's share increased to 25.48%, compared to 32.27% for the EU and 23.16 for the US. A similar pattern can be seen for solar energy. In 2005 China's share in the world was only 1.89%, compared to 34.32% for the EU and 17.62% for the US.[9] In 2017, China's share jumped to 24.44%, compared to 27.05% for the EU and 17.59 for the US. It seems that China is on the good road to become a green country, according to the will of the Party-State.

4.3 The Development of Social Security in Urban China

The development of a modern social security system, that would replace the social services enterprises and public bureaucracies provided during the Mao era, is certainly one of the most important tasks China had to set up for protecting its citizens from the risks deriving from the new economy based upon market mechanisms: unemployment, old age, and illness. These insurances have also the goal to reduce inequalities between poor people and the lower middle class on the one hand, and those who have been able to realize Deng's motto 'becoming rich is glorious' on the other. The latter, taking advantage of the opportunities offered by the new economy based upon competition, do not necessarily need the support of the state. As the development of social insurances in China has shown, rich people are able to cover those risks by subscribing private insurances or, in the case of illness, by paying out of their pocket for health care. In this section I will update the information given in my books on China's reforms (Urio 2010, 2012), starting from the insurances set up in the urban areas. I will provide many data concerning the numbers of people covered by insurances as well as the money the PRC is investing in China's new safety net. I will not do this for the pleasure of aligning tables and data, but in order to show the

---

[9]Data for 2000 were missing for China.

Table 4.1 People insured by the major social insurances in urban areas (millions) 2001–2016

Year	Old-age insurance	Medical insurance		Work-related injury insurance	Maternity insurance	Unemployment insurance
		For employed	For unemployed residents[a]			
2001	141.83	76.3	–	43.45	34.55	103.55
2002	147.36	94	–	44.06	34.88	101.82
2003	155.06	109.02	–	45.75	36.55	103.73
2004	163.53	124.04	–	68.45	43.84	105.84
2005	174.87	137.83	–	84.78	54.08	106.48
2006	187.66	157.32	–	102.68	64.59	111.87
2007	201.37	180.20	42.91	121.73	77.75	116.45
2008	218.91	199.96	118.26	137.87	92.54	124.00
2009	235.50	219.37	182.10	148.96	108.76	127.15
2010	257.07	237.35	195.28	161.61	123.36	133.76
2011	283.91	252.27	221.16	176.96	138.92	143.17
2012	304.27	264.86	271.56	190.10	154.29	152.25
2013	322.18	274.43	296.29	199.17	163.92	164.17
2014	341.24	282.96	314.51	206.39	170.39	170.43
2015	353.61	288.93	376.89	214.33	177.71	173.26
2016	379.30	295.32	448.60	218.89	184.51	180.89

[a]The medical insurance system for urban residents was introduced in 2007
Source Official Website of National Bureau of Statistics of China, *China Statistical Yearbook (2017)*

reader the impressive endeavour the PRC has undertaken in order to serve its people, especially those who have not been able, so far, to fully benefit from the economic development. A funny way of 'suppressing its own people', as Vice-President Mike Pence, among many others, has said 4 October 2018 in a speech given at the *Hudson Institute*. I will come back to this speech in the conclusion of Sect. 6.2.

Table 4.1 summarizes some data on the main social insurances in urban areas of China. From 2001 to 2016 the increase of the number of people covered by these insurances has been:

1. 2.67 times for old-age insurance,
2. 5.03 times for work-related injuries,
3. 5.34 times for maternity insurance, and
4. 1.74 times for unemployment insurance.
5. 3.87 times for medical insurance for employed people.
6. Medical insurance for unemployed residents started only in 2007, but by 2016 it had increased 10.45 times.
7. Combined, medical insurance for employed and unemployed people increased 9.75 times.

4.3 The Development of Social Security in Urban China

Table 4.2 Fund Revenues of the old-age insurance, basic medical insurance, unemployment insurance, work-related injury insurance, maternity insurance in urban areas 2001–2016 (billion yuan)

Fund revenues Year	Old-age insurance	Basic medical insurance	Unemployment insurance	Work-related injury insurance	Maternity insurance
2001	248.9	38.4	18.7	2.8	1.4
2002	317.2	60.8	21.3	3.2	2.2
2003	368.0	89.0	25.0	3.8	2.6
2004	425.8	114.1	29.1	5.8	3.2
2005	509.3	140.5	34.0	9.3	4.4
2006	631.0	174.7	40.2	12.2	6.2
2007	783.4	225.7	47.2	16.6	8.4
2008	974.0	304.0	58.5	21.7	11.4
2009	1149.1	367.2	58.0	24.0	13.2
2010	1387.3	430.9	65.0	28.5	16.0
2011	1800.5	553.9	92.3	46.6	22.0
2012	2183.0	693.9	113.9	52.7	30.4
2013	2473.3	824.8	128.9	61.5	36.8
2014	2762.0	968.7	138.0	69.5	44.6
2015	3219.6	1119.3	136.8	75.4	50.2
2016	3799.1	1308.4	122.9	73.7	52.2

Source Official Website of National Bureau of Statistics of China. *China Statistical Yearbook (2017)*

Even more impressive is the increase of expenditures for these insurances (Table 4.2). I suggest subdividing the 2001–2017 period into two parts. The first, 2001–2005, corresponds to the beginning of the implementation of the policies 'that put people first. The second, 2006–2016, corresponds to the full implementation of such policies. Let us see the development of expenditures for these insurances:

1. for unemployment, expenditures increased by 1.8 times in the first period, 3 in the second, for a total increase (2001–2016) of 6.6 times;
2. for old-age insurance, the increase was 2 times in the first period, 6 in the second, for a total of 15.2 times;
3. for maternity leave, expenditures increased 3.1 times in the first period, 8.4 in the second, for a total of 37.3 times;
4. for work-related injuries, the increase was 3.3 times in the first period, 6 in the second, for a total increase of 26.3 times;
5. for medical care, the increase was 3.6 times in the first period, 7.5 in the second, for a total increase of 34.4 times.

This clearly means that the CPC has understood the importance of setting up progressively, but as soon as possible, a comprehensive safety net that would assure harmony, security and stability. Ofcourse, up to today the coverage of these insurances is not very high, compared to the coverage in the West. Nevertheless, I should stress that this is only a first step covering the whole of the population, and within it, more particularly the poor and the lower middle classes, should the Party-State remain faithful to one of its mottos: build a relatively well-off society where wealth is equitably distributed. As happens in the West, well-to-do and rich people either subscribe to a private insurance or pay out of their own pocket. Developing, and then maintaining a satisfactory level of universal coverage of China's safety net, and assuring its sustainability in the long term, will not be an easy task, especially in the case of old age and health. In fact, the financing of these insurances is under stress because of the changing structure of the population (Sect. 3.3.2 above). First, the reduction of the fertility rate due to the one-child policy and to living styles typical of a well-off society, has reduced the number of young people and increased the number of people over the age of 65 to 11.4% of the total population (equal to 157.2 million of people) and those aged over 60 to 15.7% (equal to 241 million, 2016 (data by China Statistical Yearbook 2017). Second, whereas China has succeeded in eradicating transmissible diseases typical of an agrarian society, it is now experiencing a dramatic increase in chronic diseases, such as cardiovascular diseases, cancer, obesity and diabetes, all typical of a relatively well-off society. Now, these illnesses become more frequent and costly with the aging of the population. Therefore, one can expect that financing social insurances will become more and more costly in the future. Having pointed out the difficulties ahead, let us now add a few comments to complete the framework of the various insurances.

4.3.1 Old Age Insurance

By the end of 2016, the number of people participating in the basic old-age insurance scheme in urban China reached 379.3 million in 2016 from 141.83 in 2001 (Table 4.1). The revenues (Table 4.2, column 1) of the old-age insurance grew 15.2 times from 248.9 billion yuan in 2001 to 3,799.1 in 2016. One must be aware of the fact that the pension system is much more sophisticated in the urban areas than in the rural areas. Just as in the case of health insurance (to be dealt with hereafter), there are numbers of different kinds of pension systems in urban areas. Generally speaking, for urban people an estimated average amount of pension could be expected to be more or less the same as the salaries when they retire, and it will definitely be higher than the local low-income level. In addition to participating in the compulsory basic old-age insurance, enterprises with sufficient financial capacity are encouraged to set up enterprise annuities for their employees.

4.3 The Development of Social Security in Urban China

4.3.2 Health Insurance

As the reform of the economic system and the development of Chinese society were under way during the 1980s, the Chinese government began to undertake the reform of medical insurance. Several pilot experiments were carried out, the most significant, in my opinion, was the decision to require patients to pay for part of health services. This decision was concomitant with the requirement that hospitals (the main source of health care in China) cover their cost (after deduction of the subsidy paid by government) through the selling of services (both pharmaceuticals and treatments).

This system, of a clear neoliberal inspiration, had the catastrophic consequence of excluding from health care a huge percentage of the Chinese population in urban areas. In 2008, I took part in a research conducted in November-December by a team of Chinese scholars from Renmin University and their Swiss colleagues from Lugano University, who compared access to medical care in Guangzhou region and in the UK. These are the main findings:

1. 49% of Guangzhou residents rated their health status very good or good (versus 77% in the UK).
2. while 36% declared they had never been to a doctor during the previous year (versus 21% in the UK).
3. Compared to British residents, people living in Guangzhou consumed daily less medicines prescribed by a physician, and about 71% did not consume any kinds of drugs (versus 53% in the UK).
4. Regarding access to care, 30% of Guangzhou residents were not covered by any kind of medical insurance, while all British had universal access to their National Health Service; 54% of Chinese respondents had fully paid out-of-pocket for at least one access in their lives (versus 20% for UK residents) and about 30% for more than five accesses (versus 4% for the UK).
5. Considering only the years 2007–2008, 46% of Guangzhou residents (versus 10% for the UK) had fully paid out of pocket for at least one access.
6. While in China the cost of drugs is not, contrary to in United Kingdom, covered by any kind of health insurance, in Guangzhou area, private payment for medicines prescribed by a physician rated at the top (31.3%), followed by diagnostic tests (17 versus 3% in the UK), medical examination by a specialist (15 versus 5%), and gynaecological examination (5 versus 1%) (Domenighetti et al. 2010).

Based upon information given by Chinese colleagues, we were confident to assume that other urban areas were experiencing the same situation. It was therefore not surprising to see that China had already started several pilot programmes at the local level for health care. The results were analysed in a report by the NDRC that concluded that the existing system had failed due to a considerable increase in cost, inefficiency, and the exclusion of a large part of the population. The Party-State then set up a coordination group under the responsibility of the Ministry of Health and the NDRC. This group coordinated the works of several organizations: 12 agencies representing several ministries; the Universities of Peking, Fudan, Renmin, Tsinghua (in cooperation with Harvard) and the Normal University of Beijing; the World Health Organization; and the private consulting company McKinsey. Several reports were presented by these organizations, and a final report was presented to the Chinese leadership for evaluation and final decision. At the Party Congress of November 2007 President Hu Jintao announced the imminent publication of the new Chinese Public Health System. Of course, the implementation of this new health system would necessitate several years' work; nevertheless, the completion was planned for the year 2020.

We have seen above that the situation has improved since the time of that research, and that the number of people covered, and the revenues spent in this important insurance, have increased substantially. At the time of the research (end 2008) there were about 200 million employed people insured in urban areas (against almost 300 in 2016) and the health programme for unemployed people had just started in 2007, with only 43 million people covered, against almost 450 million in 2016. The total number of people covered by a health insurance in the urban areas was therefore equal to 744 million, very likely close to 100%. Nevertheless, improvements are still necessary as the coverage for hospitalization and for outpatient care are not very high, in international comparison, and different according to the local health policies.

4.3.3 Unemployment Insurance

The Chinese government has taken several measures for improving the unemployment insurance system and, thanks to the increase of the accumulated assets, the basic livelihood guarantee system for *xiagang* workers has been progressively integrated within the unemployment insurance programme since 2001. This task was completed by the end of 2005, and the concept of '*xiagang*' was cancelled.[10] Today, the Government pays more attention to re-employment and regards it as the foundation of people's livelihood. The increase in number of people covered and in revenue spent is quite impressive, but it is less spectacular than for the other social insurances: the number of people covered between 2001 and 2016 increased only 1.74 times, whereas revenues increased 6.6 times far below the other insurances that increased between 15.2 times (old-age) and 37.3 times (maternity). Finally, as for the health insurance, the exact unemployment insurance benefits also vary in different provinces.

---

[10]Let me remind the reader that *xiagang* people were still on the payroll of enterprises and bureaucracies and were benefiting from very small allowances, even if they were not working any more for their employer.

4.3.4 Other Insurances

The other social insurance worth mentioning are the Work-related injury insurance, the Maternity insurance and the Social relief. Work-related injury insurance is very important in every country, especially where several production processes are not organized to prevent injuries, as e.g. in coal mines, pharmaceutical and chemical plants, which, in spite of improvements made in recent years, is certainly the case in China. We have seen that this insurance covered in 2016 almost 220 million people, up from just 43.45 million in 2001, an increase of 5.03 times (Table 4.1). Even if the revenues spent on this insurance increased 26.3 times between 2001 and 2016, it is certain that it should be further developed to cover all the workers and employees in urban areas (Table 4.2).

The Maternity insurance is very important for a country that claims to have done a lot for families and women. We have seen that it has been extended to an increasing number of women, form 34.55 million in 2001 to 184.51 million in 2016, an increase of 5.34 times (see Table 4.1). This insurance deserves the same comment as the previous one: even if the revenues spent on it increased 37.3 times between 2001 and 2016, it should be extended to cover all the women in urban areas.

Finally, Social relief is a particularly important insurance as it concerns the poor people living in the towns mentioned in Table 4.3. In 1999, the Chinese government promulgated the 'Regulations on Guaranteeing Urban Residents' Minimum Standard of Living.' It stipulates that urban residents with non-agricultural permanent residence permits whose family's per capita income is lower than the local urban residents' minimum standard of living can receive basic subsistence assistance from the local government; those with neither source of income nor working capability, nor legal guardian, supporter or fosterer, can receive in full the minimum living allowance according to the minimum living standard of local urban residents. In 2017, there were 12.61 million urban residents nationwide drawing the minimum living allowance. Moreover, medical relief was carried out actively in urban areas. In 2012, the total expense for medical relief in urban areas was 7.09 billion yuan, an increase of 4.9% compared to the previous year (6.76 billion yuan in 2011). Chinese public authorities have progressively increased the minimum living standard line, as shown in Table 4.3.

By the end of 2018, the minimum living allowance, had increased substantially for all the towns mentioned in Table 4.3: between 3 and 3.9 times for 9 cities, between 2.5 and 2.9 times for 14 cities, and between 2 and 2.4 times for 7 cities. The major big cities such as Beijing, Tianjin, Shanghai and Nanjing having an increase of about 3.2 times, and Lhasa 3.9 times compared to 2005. This looks impressive but must be evaluated considering that the cost of living, especially in big cities, has also experienced an important increase.

Table 4.3 The minimum living standard line, 2005–2018

City	Standard line 2005 2018	City	Standard line 2005 2018	City	Standard line 2005 2018
Beijing	300 1000	Guangzhou	330 679	Haikou	221 485
Tianjin	265 860	Nanning	210 518	Chengdu	195 487
Fuzhou	210–230 602	Urumqi	161 414	Chongqing	210 500
Nanchang	190 573	Dalian	240 NA	Kunming	210 517
Jinan	230 515	Qingdao	260 NA	Guiyang	170 570
Zhengzhou	200 473	Ningbo	300 NA	Lhasa	200 783
Wuhan	220 570	Shenzhen	344 NA	Xian	200 534
Changsha	200 449	Xiamen	265–315 NA	Lanzhou	190 473
Shijiazhuang	220 590	Huhehaote	190 613	Xining	165 451
Taiyuan	183 474	Shenyang	220 566	Yinchuan	180 537
Changchun	169 483	Shanghai	300 970	Hangzhou	280–320 730
Haerbin	200 552	Nanjing	200–260 648	Hefei	230 535

Source China's Ministry of Civil Affairs

4.4 The Development of Social Security in Rural China

The most important social security policies in the rural areas are the old-age insurance and the new rural cooperative system.

4.4.1 Old-Age Insurance

As the process of modernization developed from the beginning of the 1980s, social structure underwent important changes also in the rural areas and a huge migratory movement developed from the rural to the urban areas. Consequently, the reliability on family security and solidarity decreased. Taking stock of these changes, the Chinese government began to experiment in the 1990s with a socialized old-

4.4 The Development of Social Security in Rural China

Table 4.4 Number of people covered by old age insurance in rural China 2010–2016

Number of People covered by old age insurance in rural areas (million) Year	Number of People million
2010	102.77
2011	331.82
2012	483.70
2013	497.50
2014	501.10
2015	504.72
2016	508.47

Data source *China Statistical Yearbook 2017*, 24–29, basic information of social insurance

age insurance system in accordance with the actual level of local socio-economic development in the rural areas. However, as the participation in the scheme was not compulsory, this resulted, by the end of 2007, in selective coverage in favour of the better-off rural households, and in a very low coverage ratio of 16.4%, corresponding to 51.71 million people. In 2007 there were 37 million peasants receiving old-age pension benefits, with a total expense of four billion yuan. According to the Ministry of Human Resource and Social Security Statistical Communiqué for Social Security 2009 and Statistical Yearbook 2010, by the end of 2009, 86.91 million people were covered by the old age insurance corresponding to a coverage of 12.19%. Since 2010 the number of people covered by old age insurance increased every year to reach 508.47 million in 2016, almost 5 times more than in 2010 (Table 4.4).

4.4.2 The New Rural Cooperative Medical System

By the end of 2013, 2489 counties had implemented this insurance up from 1451 in 2006 (Table 4.5), covering 802 million rural residents up from 410 million in 2006, with a participation rate of 98.8%. In 2014, 1652 million participants (or times) received compensation from this system. Similarly to what we said for the urban health insurance concerning the amount that is actually paid to the patients by the insurance, also in the rural areas there are differences in the coverage of the patients' costs for hospitalization and for outpatient care. The coverage may vary slightly with local policies, one's insurance fees, or the hierarchical level for governmental health insurances.

As to the hospitalization costs, the reimbursement cap is much higher. However, in rural areas, the differences are less important than in urban areas, because the health insurance system for rural people is a uniform system valid all over the country, i.e. the so-called 'New Rural Cooperative Medical System', which is implemented

Table 4.5 The new rural cooperative medical system 2006–2014

	2006	2007	2008	2009	2010	2011	2012	2013	2014
Number of counties carried out the system	1451	2451	2729	2716	2678	2637	2566	2489	–
Number of people insured (million)	410	726	815	833	836	832	805	802	736
Participation Rate (%)	80.7	86.2	91.5	94.2	96.0	97.5	98.3	99.0	98.9
Times of participants received compensation (million)	272	453	585	759	1087	1315	1745	1942	1652

Source China Statistical Yearbook 2015, health and social service

4.5 The Special Case of Migrant Workers

compulsorily by the Central government; consequently, local policies vary little in different rural areas.

4.5 The Special Case of Migrant Workers

In Sects. 3.2 and 3.3.2 of Chap. 3, I have discussed the changes in the demographic and in the urban-rural structures, both linked to the appearance and development of a huge number of migrant workers attracted to the job opportunities in the urban areas. For a long time, migrant workers did not have access to social services and insurances when they migrated to urban areas. This was because they had their residence permit (the *Hukou*) in their home villages, where they could have access to social service. But when they migrate to the urban areas, they are forbidden to have access to the same services as the urban residents. This is one of the most important problems China had to deal with. Some pundits calculated that migrant workers contributed to 16% of China's GDP increase during the 1980s and the 1990s. They represent about 35% of the work force of China (ILO 2016), equal to about 245 million in 2016. It was inevitable that a Party committed to create a harmonious society would take measures for alleviating the poor condition of migrant workers. Without entering into too much detail, China started to tackle this situation seriously in 2010 with the passing of the social security law that requires rural migrant workers to affiliate under the social insurance for urban workers (SIW), and 'the introduction of health and pension schemes for urban and rural residents (SIR) (…) migrant workers and their families are better integrated into urban life with higher levels of consumption and improved health status, all of which are essential for achieving a harmonious society, which is a national strategic objective.' (ILO 2016). China's safety net has been further improved by the 2008 Labour Contract Law (LCL): 'we find that the implementation of the LCL helped boost migrant workers' chance of social insurance participation consistently and significantly, especially for those who gained a long-term contract. These findings suggest that the LCL at least partly reached its intended policy goal of improving social protection for migrant workers, a disadvantaged group in the Chinese labour market.' (Gao et al. 2017).

However, the SIW has a better coverage than the SIR, and SIR does not provide any protection for work injury, unemployment and maternity. Moreover, most migrants are still covered by SIR, even if, as said above, they should be registered under SIW by their employers. At the end of 2015 around 80% of migrants were covered by an old-age insurance, over 95% by health insurance, and moreover, poor rural residents were entitled to a minimum living standard (see Table 4.3). Although the ILO recognizes that improvements have been made, substantial progresses are needed in the near future. In fact, the overall coverage is still rather low. The coverage rate of those working outside their rural town is less than 20% for pensions and health, about 10% for unemployment, and less than 10% for maternity, and about 30% for those who are insured by SIW. ILO warns that the achievement of basic and universal coverage is only the first step (ILO 2016; China Labour Bulletin 2019).

4.6 The Rebalancing Between Individuals

Let us start with the Gini index in international comparison (Table 4.6). The first evidence is that all the 20 Western countries do better than China with Gini indexes between 25.9 and 36.7, and Palma Ratio between 0.9 and 1.3, except for the US that, with Gini of 41.1 and Palma Ratio of 2, comes close to that of China, with Gini 42.2 and Palma Ratio of 2.1. It is interesting to note that the Western countries are subdivided into four groups. The first group, with Gini between 25.9 and 29.1 and Palma Ratio between 0.9 and 1, comprises Northern European countries, joined by Belgium and the Netherlands. The second group comprises Central European countries joined by the UK and Ireland, with Gini between 30.1 and 32.6, and Palma Ratio between 1.1 and 1.3. The countries of these two groups, especially the first, have a strong or fairly performing Welfare State and a relatively equitable distribution of income. Within the third groups we have countries with higher income inequalities and a weaker Welfare State. In the last group we have two Southern countries with a less developed economy, which can explain a higher income inequality. Finally, the US, a very rich country, is nevertheless behind the other Western countries on the two indexes: 41.1 for Gini and 2 for Palma Ratio.

What can China learn from this situation? First, the fact that China is closer to two European less developed countries, Portugal and Greece (and Spain and Italy are not much better), should not come as a surprise because China, in spite of its spectacular economic development, is still considered a developing country, with progresses to be made for reducing income inequalities and improving the Welfare State, one of the more effective policies for reducing disparities between households. It would perhaps be interesting for China to study the evolution of the Welfare State in these countries, as mistakes have been made recently, especially by reducing the coverage of social insurances, with negative impact on the stability and social cohesion of the population concerned. The case of the US may also be a source of inspiration: its Welfare State is less developed than that of Europe and its distribution of income is definitely more unequal, in part due to a fiscal policy that favours the highest revenues (i.e. the top 1% denounced by Joseph Stieglitz), with the consequences we have seen with the election of Donald Trump.

Gini index and Palma ratio allow to have a first idea about the inequalities in terms of revenue, but they do not tell the whole story. This is why the UNDP programme has developed the HDI index, that integrates income, health (measured by life expectancy), and education (measured by years of schooling). Countries are distributed within four groups: very high development, high development, medium development and low development. Table 4.7 shows the ranking with the HDI for 2015 for a choice of the Western countries we have taken into consideration above in Table 4.6 and in Sect. 3.4.4; China has been added in the last row.[11] We can see that in spite of the considerable progress realized since the beginning of reforms, China is still far away from the Western countries. Nevertheless, when we take the Gen-

---

[11]I take data for 2015 because hereafter I will comment on the HDI per provinces, for which only 2015 data are available.

4.6 The Rebalancing Between Individuals

Table 4.6 UNDP Gini index and Palma Ratio for 20 Western countries and China, ca. 2015

Countries	Gini UNDP 2015	Rank	Palma Ratio	Rank	Countries	Gini UNDP 2015	Rank	Palma Ratio	Rank
Norway	25.9	1	0.9	1	France	33.1	12	1.3	10
Finland	27.1	2	1	3	Canada	33.7	13	1.3	10
Sweden	27.3	3	0.9	1	Australia	34.9	14	1.4	14
Belgium	27.6	4	1	3	Italy	35.2	15	1.4	14
Netherlands	28	5	1	3	Spain	35.9	16	1.5	16
Denmark	29.1	6	1	3	Portugal	36	17	1.5	16
Germany	30.1	7	1.1	7	Greece	36.7	18	1.6	18
Austria	30.5	8	1.1	7	US	41.1	19	2	19
Switzerland	31.6	9	1.2	9					
Ireland	32.5	10	1.3	10					
UK	32.6	11	1.3	10	China	42.2	20	2.1	20

Source UNDP Human Development Report, 2016, pp. 208–209

der inequality index China does better: with rank 37, although behind the Western countries, China is well before the US (rank 43), even if this achievement must be qualified as the US is by far the worst Western country on this count.[12] Moreover, taking life expectancy (UNDP Report 2016, pp. 198–199) China, placed within the group of 'High Human development' at rank 90 in 2015, does even better: with life expectancy of 76 years, it does about the same as 16 countries (out of a total of 51) in the 'Very high Human Development', such as Poland, Portugal, Hungary, Croatia, and Rumania.[13] In the next section, by taking HDI for China's provinces, we will see that Chinese people are better off on many counts in some provinces. Moreover, these data will allow us to evaluate whether the rebalancing policies have reduced the gap between provinces.

4.7   The Rebalancing Between Provinces

As I have pointed out already, China is a very diverse country. Therefore, it is interesting to take into consideration data about the HDI of provinces and see whether some provinces are already at the level of some Western countries classified within the 'Very high human development' group. Let us start with the HDI referred to the Chinese provinces as presented in Table 4.8. I am going to limit the analysis to the 6th column with data of 2015. Pease refer to China's map, p. 105, to locate the Chinese provinces.

What can be said from the data of Table 4.8? First, the data confirm the unequal level of development of the Chinese provinces, already pointed out in Sects. 3.3.4 and 3.4.1. Second, the data of Table 4.8 allow us to place China's provinces within the ranking of the UNDP countries provided by the 2016 UNDP Report, with data of 2015. I remind the reader that countries are distributed within four groups: very high development, high development, medium development and low development. Six Chinese provinces take place within the 'Very High development Group' that comprises countries between the 51st rank (Kuweit) and the 1st rank (Norway), and with HDI scores between 0.800 and 1.

The UNDP reports cover 188 countries in 2015 listed by rank. Beijing occupies the 27th rank (equal to Spain), Shanghai the 28th rank (equal to the Czech Republic),

---

[12] *The Gender Inequality Index* measures achievements using the same indicators as the HDI but captures inequalities in achievement between women and men. It is simply the HDI adjusted downward for gender inequality. It takes into consideration: (1) health (maternal mortality ratio, adolescent fertility rate; (2) empowerment (female and male population with at least secondary education, female and male shares of parliamentary seats); (3) labour market (female and male labour force participation rates). The greater the gender disparity in basic human development, the lower is the adjusted HDI for gender inequality. *The Inequality adjusted HDI* takes into consideration: (1) long and healthy life, (2) knowledge (mean years of schooling, expected years of schooling); (3) a decent standard of living (GNI per capita in PPP US$).

[13] In 2017 China has further improved from rank 90 in 2015 to rank 86 for the HDI, as well as for its three components.

4.7 The Rebalancing Between Provinces 141

Table 4.7 HDI and ranking in 20 Western countries and China, ca. 2015

Countries	HDI 2015	HDI Rank	Inequality Adjusted HDI	Inequality Adjusted HDI rank[a]	Gender Inequality Index	Gender Inequality rank
Norway	0.949	1	0.898	1	0.053	6
Australia	0.939	2	0.861	3	0.120	24
New Zealand	0.915	13	NA	NA	0.158	34
US	0.920	10	0.796	20	0.203	43
Ireland	0.923	8	0.850	10	0.127	26
Netherlands	0.924	7	0.861	5	0.044	3
Canada	0.920	10	0.839	12	0.098	18
Sweden	0.913	14	0.851	11	0.048	4
Germany	0.926	4	0.859	5	0.066	9
Switzerland	0.939	3	0.859	6	0.040	1
France	0.897	21	0.813	22	0.102	19
Finland	0.895	23	0.843	14	0.056	8
Belgium	0.896	22	0.821	20	0.073	12
Denmark	0.925	5	0.858	7	0.041	2
Spain	0.894	27	0.791	26	0.081	15
Greece	0.866	29	0.758	35	0.119	23
Italy	0.887	26	0.784	29	0.085	16
Austria	0.893	24	0.815	21	0.078	14
United Kingdom	0.909	16	0.836	17	0.131	28
Portugal	0.843	41	0.755	42	0.091	17
China	0.738	90	NA	NA	0.164	37

[a]Calculated by author

Source UNDP Human development reports 2016

Tianjin rank 36th (equal to Poland), Jiangsu the 48th rank (equal to Montenegro), Liaoning the 49th rank (equal to Russia) and Zhejiang the 50th rank (equal to Romania). It is not surprising that these provinces (except Liaoning) have also the highest Gross National (i.e. provincial) Income, well above the national average. Two other provinces are not very far from the 'Very High Development Group', and are placed in the upper part of the 'High Development Group': Guangdong, with HDI 0.795, takes rank 54 (equal to Uruguay) and Shandong, with HDI 790, is placed at the rank 59 (equal to Malaysia). In addition to Guangdong and Shandong 18 other provinces are placed in the 'High development Group', requiring HDI between 0.701 and 0.799. Nevertheless, 12 amongst the latter have an HDI higher than the national average (HDI 0.762), with one, Chongqing, having the same HDI, 0.762. Finally,

Table 4.8 Human Development Indexes of Various Regions in China (1982–2030)

Region	1982	1990	2000	2010	2015	2020	2030
Whole China	0.344	0.499	0.603	0.718	0.762	0.794	0.861
Beijing	0.506	0.641	0.727	0.844	0.884	0.910	0.948
Tianjin	0.477	0.597	0.711	0.815	0.855	0.878	0.911
Hebei	0.339	0.495	0.619	0.716	0.747	0.772	0.810
Shanxi	0.335	0.486	0.584	0.715	0.743	0.770	0.815
Inner Mongolia	0.326	0.489	0.578	0.743	0.781	0.804	0.844
Liaoning	0.427	0.566	0.649	0.759	0.805	0.834	0.871
Jilin	0.349	0.515	0.627	0.736	0.775	0.803	0.839
Heilongjiang	0.333	0.492	0.617	0.724	0.761	0.792	0.833
Shanghai	0.542	0.653	0.739	0.833	0.872	0.894	0.926
Jiangsu	0.355	0.516	0.643	0.768	0.814	0.855	0.899
Zhejiang	0.366	0.527	0.655	0.764	0.802	0.829	0.871
Anhui	0.286	0.458	0.564	0.685	0.736	0.771	0.817
Fujian	0.307	0.493	0.627	0.739	0.782	0.815	0.859
Jiangxi	0.295	0.453	0.553	0.689	0.737	0.769	0.811
Shandong	0.343	0.515	0.625	0.748	0.790	0.822	0.864
Henan	0.288	0.470	0.580	0.705	0.744	0.776	0.817
Hubei	0.256	0.451	0.583	0.721	0.777	0.820	0.872
Hunan	0.297	0.459	0.574	0.706	0.754	0.787	0.832
Guangdong	0.362	0.549	0.647	0.758	0.795	0.825	0.870
Guangxi	0.286	0.457	0.563	0.683	0.728	0.759	0.802
Hainan	–	0.503	0.600	0.707	0.750	0.782	0.834
Chongqing	–	–	0.596	0.713	0.762	0.798	0.846
Sichuan	0.284	0.453	0.558	0.682	0.730	0.762	0.807
Guizhou	0.218	0.392	0.483	0.618	0.681	0.722	0.775
Yunnan	0.245	0.425	0.531	0.628	0.678	0.715	0.765
Tibet	0.206	0.329	0.466	0.590	0.626	0.666	0.720
Shaanxi	0.298	0.473	0.571	0.720	0.770	0.807	0.857
Gansu	0.296	0.444	0.525	0.651	0.695	0.728	0.776
Qinghai	0.288	0.438	0.515	0.658	0.698	0.731	0.780
Ningxia	0.317	0.473	0.561	0.698	0.739	0.773	0.824
Xinjiang	0.317	0.483	0.591	0.691	0.724	0.753	0.798
Diversity factor (%)	22.85	13.22	10.42	8.26	7.59	6.98	6.22

Note The HDI in this table is calculated according to the new method announced by the United Nations Development Programme in 2010, whereby 1990–2015 national data are derived from the United Nations Development Programme: Table 2 in the *Human Development Report 2016*; 2020, 2025, and 2030 data are estimated by Hu Angang. Data source: relevant data from the third, fourth, fifth, and sixth nationwide censuses, *China Statistical Yearbook* and the *Educational Statistics Yearbook of China*

4.7 The Rebalancing Between Provinces

five provinces are placed in the 'Medium Development Group', that requires HDI scores between 0.701 and 0.799: Qinghai (HDI 0.699) is placed at rank 107, Gansu (HDI 0.695) at rank 110, Guizhou (HDI 0.681) rank 118, and Tibet (HDI 0.638) at rank 127. This ranking corresponds to the level of economic development.

The same analysis can be made by taking separately the three components of the HDI. We will take health (measured by life expectancy) and per capita income. For health, measured by life expectancy. China's provinces do even better than for the HDI index. As for the HDI index, Shanghai (82.8 years), Beijing (82), Tianjin (81.3) are placed at the top of China's provinces for life expectancy, at the same level as the countries ranked at the first 26 places of the HDI 'Very High Development Group', such as Norway, Denmark, Netherlands, New Zealand, France, Germany, etc. With HDI between 75 and 79 years, 20 other provinces also take place in the 'Very High Development Group', above its last three countries (ranked 49 Russia, 50 Romania and 51 Kuwait); whereas 7 provinces have scores under 75 years (i.e. Shanxi, Guizhou, Gansu, Ningxia, Yunnan, Qinghai, and Xinjiang, and one, Tibet, is under 70. As for the HDI index, life expectancy seems to be linked to the level of economic development, even though the distance between the more performing provinces and the others is less important.

As already said in Sect. 3.4.4, GNI per capita is the weakest point of China's development. Before we come to the GNI of the provinces, let me say that in 2017 China's GNI was 4.45 times less than that of Norway (with GNI ranked 1), 3.77 less than Switzerland, 3.59 times less than the US, and 3.02 less than Germany. However, the 2017 data shows an improvement as in 2015 China's GNI was 5.06 times less than Norway (with GNI ranked 1), 4.22 less than Switzerland, 3.98 times less than the US, and 3.37 less than Germany. And when we come to the GNI of the provinces, we find that a few provinces do quite well, and some do fairly well.[14]

Based upon data in China's Statistic Year Book, it is interesting to distribute provinces into groups labelled according to their level of GNI:

1. Group 1, with provinces in the 'Very High Development Group' with GNI higher than 13,000 RMB comprises: Beijing (GNI per capita 16,070 USD) and Shanghai (15,450 USD), above the national average (13.345). All the other provinces wold be placed much lower in the UNDP ranking. Only Jiangsu, with 13,098 USD, is not too far from Beijing and Shanghai.
2. Group 2, with 4 provinces with a GNI between 10,048 and 10,866 USD: Zhejiang, Shanxi, Fujian and Guangdong).
3. Group 3, with 2 provinces with a GNI between 9,430 and 9,551 USD: Shandong and Inner Mongolia.
4. Group 4, with 4 provinces with a GNI between 7.089 and 7.788: Chongqing, Jilin, Hubei and Shaanxi.
5. Group 5, with 4 provinces with a GNI between 6,075 and 6,530 USD: Ningxia, Hunan, Qinghai, Hainan.

---

[14]Data on the GNI per capita of China's provinces are from the China Statistic Year Book, converted into USD.

6. Group 6, with 9 provinces with a GNI between 5,198 and 5,992: Tianjin, Xinjiang, Heilongjiang, Henan, Sichuan, Jiangxi, Anhui, Guangxi and Hebei.
7. Group 7, with 3 provinces with a GNI between 4,287 and 4,763 USD: Tibet, Guizhou and Yunnan.
8. Group 8, with just one province, Gansu, with a GNI of only 3,894 USD.

These findings confirm the consensus among experts of China's development: in terms of revenue per capita there are huge differences between provinces. With a few exceptions, the coastal provinces do much better. Beijing's and Shanghai's GNIs are approximately 4.27 and 3.97 times higher than Gansu, respectively; approximately 3.6 higher than the three provinces within Group 7 (4,000 USD); approximately 3 times more than the nine provinces within Group 6 (5,000 USD); approximately 2.6 times higher than the four countries within Group 5 (6,000 USD); 2.1 times higher than the four provinces within Group 4 (7,000 USD); 1.7 higher than the two provinces belonging to Group 3 (9.000 USD); and 1,5 times higher than the four countries within Group 2 (10,000 USD).

This difference is explained first by the inheritance from the Imperial era and the troubled times between the fall of the Empire (1912) and the beginning of the PRC (1949). Second, by Mao's Choice to invest not only in education and health, but also (and very heavily) in economic development starting from the provinces where the social conditions for development were more favourable, i.e. the coastal provinces. Third, Deng followed basically the same strategy, by betting on the coastal provinces, according to the mottos 'let some people become rich first', and 'to become rich is glorious.' Luckily, Deng did not commit the tragic mistakes of the Mao era. Nevertheless, by setting the goal to rapidly catch up with the West he also contributed to the development of inequalities in China. We have seen so far to what extent the Party has been able to correct these imbalances, the gap in personal revenue being certainly the one that needs much more attention. We are going to see below, that at least as far as the gap between personal income in the rural and urban areas, China seems to be doing much better.

But let us now conclude this section by examining how the HDIs of China's provinces have developed between the beginning of reforms and 2015. This will allow us to be more optimistic about the gap between provinces, than we have been by examining the GNI. In fact, we will see that there is a process of convergence from Low HDI to the High and even to the Very High HDI. We use here the same data we referred to above from the *China Statistic Year Books*, and we place the provinces in the four HDI levels and at five historical moments (1980, 1990, 2000, 2010 and 2015). This will allow us to see what changes have occurred in the distribution of provinces within the four HDI levels.[15] We consider the four levels of HDI as defined by the UNDP: Low HDI, less than 0.55; Medium HDI, between 0.55 and 0.7; High HDI, between 0.7 and 0.8; Very High HDI, higher than 0.8.

In 1982, i.e. a few years after the beginning of reforms, all the provinces are in the Low HDI group. This convergence is clearly the result of the Mao era development

---

[15]The analysis is based upon a table provided by Hu Angang, based upon the same HDI data presented above.

4.7 The Rebalancing Between Provinces

strategy: provinces, had basically the same level of development measured by the HDI index, in spite of differences already evident between the coastal and the inner provinces. So, convergence is obtained at the level of the Low HDI. Nevertheless, we should not forget that the Mao era had also its positive outcomes, namely the improvement of life expectancy and literacy, and the beginning of industrialization. From 1982 on, a divergence movement started to develop. By1990, four coastal provinces have jumped to the Medium HDI: Shanghai, Beijing, Tianjin and Liaoning, that may be considered the pioneers of HDI development (i.e. a combination of revenue per capita, health and education). This means that one of the consequences of the strategy focused on economic development of the coastal provinces, is that it started to produce a divergence movement, as the provinces are now distributed into two HDI categories.

Ten years later, in 2000, the divergence movement accelerates. Provinces are now distributed into three development groups: Low HDI, Medium HDI and High HDI. Only five provinces remain in the Low HDI group: Yunnan, Gansu, Qinghai, Guizhou and Tibet, i.e. Western and North-Western provinces. Three provinces left the Medium HDI group and joined the High HDI group; not surprisingly they are three of the four Municipalities depending on the central government (with a status equivalent to the provinces) Shanghai, Beijing and Tianjin. They are all placed in the coastal area. But at the same time a convergence movement towards the higher HDI groups appears: all the other 23 provinces jumped from the Low HDI to the Medium HDI group.

Ten years later, in 2010, the divergence movement towards the higher HDI groups seems to be confirmed as provinces are distributed, as in 2000, in three HDI groups, although at higher level, i.e. in the Medium, High and Very High groups, instead of the Low, Medium and High in 2000. In fact, not a single province has remained in the Low HDI group. The five provinces that were in the Low HDI in 1990 jumped into the Medium HDI group now comprising 11 provinces: Ningxia, Xinjiang, Jiangxi, Anhui, Guangxi, Sichuan, Qinghai, Gansu, Yunnan, Guizhou and Tibet. Beijing, Shanghai and Tianjin joined the Very High HDI. All the other 17 provinces were within the High HDI group. However, the convergence movement that appeared in 2000 is confirmed, as 25 provinces are now concentrated in the Medium HDI (11 provinces) and the High HDI (14 provinces).

Five years later, in 2015, Liaoning, Zhejiang and Jiangsu joined Beijing, Shanghai and Tianjin in the Very High HDI group. Only Qinghai, Gansu, Guizhou, Yunnan and Tibet remain in the Medium HDI group. All the other 20 provinces are placed within the High HDI group, up from 17 in 2010, thereby confirming an upward convergence movement toward the High HDI group, even if in 2015 provinces are distributed in three HDI groups as in 2010.

Starting from this encouraging evolution, Hu Angang forecasts (Table 4.8 two last columns) that by 2020 only Tibet will remain in the Medium HDI group, and by 2030 only 6 provinces will remain in the High HDI group (Xinjiang, Qinghai, Gansu, Guizhou, Yunnan and Tibet), all the other 25 provinces will be in the Very High HDI group. This would clearly confirm the convergence trend started in 2000 to a convergence of the 31 provinces towards the High HDI. Even if by 2030 many

146   4 The Rebalancing of Chinese Society

things can happen that may contradict this optimistic forecast, China's trajectory from 1978 on does point in this direction. Even if some mistakes have been made, the most important mistakes have been corrected and others are being addressed, and the analyses provided already in Chap. 3 and those presented in this chapter suggest that Hu's optimistic forecast in not at all without good reasons.

4.8 The Rebalancing Between Rural and Urban Areas

Let us see first how China's urban and rural areas compare taking data at the national level. Table 3.7 in Chap. 3 shows that the ratio between urban per capita annual disposable income has always been, since the beginning of the reform era in 1978, 1.82 to 3.33 times higher than the rural per capita net income. The ratio has first decreased from 2.57 in 1978 to 1.82 in 1983, very likely thanks to the reforms introduced in the rural areas that boosted rural incomes. But then, the ratio has almost constantly increased to reach 2.86 in 1994. Then, there has been a short period (1994–1999), during the implementation of the first policies to 'open the west', when the ratio decreased to reach 2.65 in 1999. It is also interesting to note that the ratio started to increase again after the September 1997 Party Congress decided to accelerate market reforms with the goal to bring China within the WTO. I remind one that at that time peasants were subject to heavy taxes that were abolished only between 2003 and 2006, and had to pay fees for elementary and junior high school, that were abolished only between 2006 and 2007. After the decisions of the 1997 Party Congress produced their impact, the ratio rose from 2.47 in 1997 to 3.33 in 2008 and stayed at about the same level until 2012. Then it started to decrease to reach 2.71 in 2017, very likely thanks to the positive impact of the social policies discussed above.

Let us see now how the provinces compare in terms of ther ratio between urban and rural personal income. In my 2010 book (Urio 2010, pp. 87–91), taking data for 2006, I already found that there were important differences between provinces. In my 2012 book (Urio 2012, pp. 164–168), based upon the finding on the changes in the development strategy, and taking data for 2006 and 2009, I found that there were differences between provinces between these two dates. The result was interesting, but the span of time was too short to forecast whether we were at the beginning of a downward trend. Here, I will take data for 2006 and 2017, a sufficient span of time to arrive at some reliable conclusions.

In the first column of Table 4.9 you will find the ratios between urban and rural areas personal incomes within the Chinese provinces for 2006 and 2017. The ratios for 2006 are taken from a table presented in Urio (2010) pp. 88–89, where you can find the data for rural and urban personal income.[16] The data for 2017 are presented in the other columns of Table 4.9.

---

[16]In order to avoid having a too complicated table, the data of 2006 are not presented in Table 4.9.

4.8 The Rebalancing Between Rural and Urban Areas

Table 4.9 Per Capita Annual Income of Urban and Rural Households in China's provinces (2006–2017)

Ratio (2)/(1)[a]		Urban areas		Rural areas	
		Regions	Disposable income (2) 2017	Regions	Net income (1) 2017
2006[a]	2017	National average	36396.2	National Average	13432.4
3.27	2.71				
2.41	2.57	Beijing	62406.3	Beijing	24240.5
2.29	1.85	Tianjin	40277.5	Tianjin	21753.7
2.71	2.37	Hebei	30547.8	Hebei	12880.9
3.15	2.7	Shanxi	29131.8	Shanxi	10787.5
3.1	2.83	Inner Mongolia	35670	Inner Mongolia	12584.3
2.53	2.55	Liaoning	34993.4	Liaoning	13746.8
2.68	2.19	Jilin	28318.7	Jilin	12950.4
2.58	2.17	Heilongjiang	27446	Heilongjiang	12664.8
2.26	2.25	Shanghai	62595.7	Shanghai	27825
2.42	2.28	Jiangsu	43621.8	Jiangsu	19158
2.49	2.05	Zhejiang	51260.7	Zhejiang	24955.8
3.29	2.48	Anhui	31640.3	Anhui	12758.2
2.84	2.39	Fujian	39001.4	Fujian	16334.8
2.76	2.36	Jiangxi	31198.1	Jiangxi	13241.8
2.79	2.43	Shandong	36789.4	Shandong	15117.5
3.01	2.32	Henan	29557.9	Henan	12719.2
2.86	2.31	Hubei	31889.4	Hubei	13812.1
3.09	2.62	Hunan	33947.9	Hunan	12935.8
3.15	2.6	Guangdong	40975.1	Guangdong	15779.7
3.1	2.88	Guangxi	30502.1	Guangxi	11325.5
2.88	2.39	Hainan	30817.4	Hainan	12901.8
4.02	2.55	Chongqing	32193.2	Chongqing	12637.9
3.11	2.51	Sichuan	30726.9	Sichuan	12226.9
4.59	3.28	Guizhou	29079.8	Guizhou	8869.1
4.47	3.14	Yunnan	30995.9	Yunnan	9862.2
3.67	2.97	Tibet	30671.1	Tibet	10330.2
4.1	3	Shaanxi	30810.3	Shaanxi	10264.5
4.18	3.44	Gansu	27763.4	Gansu	8076.1
3.81	3.08	Qinghai	29168.9	Qinghai	9462.3
3.32	2.74	Ningxia	29472.3	Ningxia	10737.9
3.24	2.79	Xinjiang	30774.8	Xinjiang	11045.3

[a]Author's calculation; for 2006 data from the 2007 China statistical Yearbook, see Urio 2010, pp. 88–89

Data Sources 2018 China Statistical Yearbook 2007 and 2018

148 4 The Rebalancing of Chinese Society

Taking disposable income in urban areas and net income in rural areas within China's provinces, we can compare the situations in 2006 and in 2017. I subdivide the provinces into 6 groups, according to the level of the urban-rural ratio (Table 4.10). In 2006 there was no single province in the first group with a ratio less than 2 between urban and rural personal incomes. Only five provinces were in the second group with ratios 2 to 2.5. Not surprisingly, they were: Tianjin, Shanghai, Beijing, Jiangsu and Zhejiang, i.e. all coastal provinces. In the second group, with ratios 2.5 to 3, we find 9 coastal provinces, except Jiangxi and Hubei; but the latter are very close to the coastal provinces. In the third group, with ratios 3 to 3.5, we have 10 provinces, a mix of coastal provinces (Guangdong and Guangxi), one inner province close to the coastal ones (Anhui), and 8 inner or northern provinces (Hunan, Shanxi, Henan, Ningxia, Inner Mongolia, Sichuan, and Xinjiang). Two north-western provinces were in the fourth group with ratios 3.5 to 4 (Tibet and Qinghai); finally, five provinces were in the sixth group (with ratio higher than 4), two central (Chongqing and Shaanxi), one southern with no sea access (Guizhou), one northern (Gansu) and one southern (Yunnan). This distribution is not surprising as it reflects the different level of development, and confirms the hypothesis, many times put forward, that the smallest difference between urban and rural areas is to be found in the most developed provinces.

Between 2006 and 2017 many interesting changes have occurred (Table 4.9). First, at the national level, the gap has been reduced from 3.27 in 2006 to 2.71 in 2017. Second, comparing the provinces, the difference between the highest and the lowest scores has been reduced: 2.33 in 2006 (Guizhou 4.59 divided by Shanghai 2.26); 1.59 in 2017 (Gansu 3.44 divided by Tianjin 1.85). More generally, all the provinces have reduced the gap, except Beijing, but only by very little, with an increase from 2.41 to 2.57. The most spectacular change occurred in Chongqing that passed from 4.02 to 2.55, and from the sixth group to the third, reflecting the impact of the policies implemented since the mid-2000s in favour of peasants and migrant workers. Third, leaving aside the exceptional case of Tianjin, that constitutes a group on its own, there is a clear convergence movement. First, within the provinces the gap between urban and rural personal income has decreased. Second, there is a convergence between provinces: in 2006 provinces were distributed into 5 groups, in 2017 into only three, with ratios between 2 and 3.44, whereas no provinces are to be found in groups 5 and 6, defined by the highest inequality between urban and rural personal incomes. Finally, whereas in 2006 groups 2 and 3 comprised 14 provinces, in 2017 they comprise 27 provinces, and only four provinces are in the less favourable group 4. We can conclude that there is a remarkable convergence of provinces towards a smaller ratio between personal income of their urban and rural areas.

The reasons for these positive changes are to be found first in the new fiscal policy that since the mid-1990s gave more financial means to the central government for investing in the development of the inner and northern provinces; second, to the new regional integration and coordinated development strategy adopted in 1995 at the 5th Plenum of the 14th CCP Central Committee, mentioned above, which includes the *Development of the West Regions Strategy* (2001), *Rejuvenation of Old Industrial*

4.8 The Rebalancing Between Rural and Urban Areas

Table 4.10 Five groups of Provinces with different urban-rural personal income ratios (2006 and 2017)

2006					
Group 1 Less than 2	Group 2 2.2–2.5	Group 3 2.5–3	Group 4 3–3.5	Group 5 3.5–4	Group 6 More than 4
None	Tianjin, Shanghai Beijing Jiangsu Zhejiang N = 5	Hebei Liaoning Jilin Heilongjiang Fujian Jiangxi Shandong Hubei Hainan N = 9	Hunan, Shanxi Inner Mongolia Anhui Henan Guangdong Sichuan Guangxi, Ningxia Xinjiang N = 10	Tibet, Qinghai N = 2	Chongqing Gansu Guizhou Yunnan Shaanxi N = 5
2017					
Tianjin N = 1	Shanghai, Jiangsu Zhejiang, Hainan Jilin, Heilongjiang Jiangsu, Anhui Fujian, Jiangxi Shandong, Henan Hubei, Hebei N = 14	Beijing, Chongqing Shanxi, Sichuan Hunan, Guangxi Inner Mongolia Liaoning, Guangdong Tibet, Shaanxi Ningxia, Xinjiang N = 13	Guizhou, Yunnan Qinghai, Gansu N = 4	none	none

Source Table 4.9

Bases in Northeastern China (2004) and *Rise of Central China Strategy* (2006); third, to the social policies implemented and developed especially since 2002 (Sect. 4.4 above); fourth, to the massive migration of workers from the poor inland rural areas to the rich urban coastal areas which contributes to reducing inter-regional disparities.[17]

---

[17] This conclusion was also partially confirmed by a research conducted by Albert Keidel already in the mid-2000s that proved that migrant workers, by sending back money to their families in the rural areas, contributed to the improvement of their standard of living for both income and consumption: Keidel (2007), presented above in Sect. 3.4.3.

4.9 Conclusion

In this chapter I have evaluated to what extent the new development policy that 'puts people first' has succeeded in eliminating, or at least in reducing the imbalances and the contradictions of the 'economy first strategy' of Deng Xiaoping. We have seen that this new policy was based upon some serious academic research already available in the 1980s, and the political will of the Party-State whose goal was to reconcile economic development (based on economic efficiency) on the one hand, and social equity, people livelihood and environmental protection on the other. The ultimate interrelated goals were to improve the living conditions of all the Chinese people and to strengthen the country in order to avoid the repetition of the 'one hundred years of humiliations.' This choice was made after it was recognized that the consequences of the economic development of the Deng era were damaging both these goals.

The setting up of a system of social security covering the main risks of life, such as unemployment, old-age and illness, was therefore a must. We have seen that a quasi-universal safety net has been implemented both in the urban and the rural areas by the end of the 2010s. The Party-State has invested huge amounts of money for this purpose. Nevertheless, progresses are needed, especially for increasing the coverage of all insurances. In particular, the health insurance should improve the level of coverage and should increase the number of medical acts covered, including consultations and drugs. The effort should be focused on establishing universal insurances that should cover the needs of the poor and the lower middle classes, as the upper middle class can afford, as is the case in the West, to subscribe private insurances. Improvements are also necessary for migrant workers, even if important progresses have been made compared to the situation existing at the beginning of reforms, so that migrant workers living in urban areas will enjoy the same insurance benefits as the urban residents.

The rebalancing between individuals has also witnessed important improvements. Nevertheless, China's improvements measured by the Gini index, the Palma ratio and HDI index at the national level, shows that China is still today well behind Western countries. With a Gini index of 42.2 and a Palma ratio of 2.1 China does much worse than all the European countries; only the US, with a Gini of 41.1 and a Palma ratio of 2 does almost as badly as China. Not a very encouraging consolation, knowing the traditional US fiscal bias in favour of rich taxpayers and the limited welfare state that leaves millions of people under the level of poverty with little help from the state. The same is true for the HDI index, that, so far, places China at rank 86, far away from Western countries, in spite of continuous improvements since the 1980s. But China does better if we take the HDI of the provinces. Six Chinese provinces are placed today within the 'Very High Development Group', at the same level as Western countries such as Spain and Poland. Nevertheless, the gap between provinces remains rather high, especially when measured by the per capita GNI. Furthermore, we observed not only a convergence between provinces, but also an upward movement towards a better living standard. This is the case not only for the

4.9 Conclusion

HDI of the provinces (Sect. 4.7), but also for the ratio between personal incomes of the urban and rural areas within provinces (Sect. 4.8).

These improvements have been obtained thanks to a restructuring of the political system, especially of its decision-making process, that has transformed the Party-State from an ideological entity into a learning organization. This has been obtained through the opening up to both national and international sources of information, that improved the Party-State capacity to adopt and implement decisions in tune with the declared objectives, thereby avoiding the irrational decisions that led to the Great leap Forward and to the Cultural Revolution in the Mao era. These changes are dealt with in the following chapter.

References

Buckley, C. (2008). China government adviser urges greenhouse gas cuts. *Financial Times*, September 8.

China Labour Bulletin. (2019). China's social security system. *China Labour Bulletin*, First published 2012, last upadated (in part) March 2019. Retrieved April 3, 2019, from https://clb.org.hk/content/china%E2%80%99s-social-security-system.

Domenighetti, G., et al. (2010). Health status, medical consumption and access to care in Guangzhou (China) and the United Kingdom, Beijing and Lugano. *Renmin University (Beijing) and University of Italian Speaking Switzerland (Lugano)*, unpublished research report.

Gao, Q., Yang, S., & Li, S. (2017). Social insurance for migrant workers in China: Impact of the 2008 labour contract law. *Economic and Political Studies, 5*(3), 285–304.

Hu, A. (2009). A new approach at Copenhagen, *China Dialogue*, April 6. Retrieved September 15, 2009, from www.chinadialogue.net.

Hu, A. (2017). *China: Innovative green development* (2nd ed.). Berlin: Springer.

Hu, A., & Guan Q. (2017). *China: Tackle the challenge of global change*. London & New York: Routledge.

Hu, A., & Wang, Y., et al. (1992). *Survival and development. A study of China's long-term development*. Beijing and New York: Science Press.

Hu, A., & Zou, P. (1991). *China's population development*. Beijing: China's Science and Technology Press.

ILO. (2016). Extending social protection to rural migrants. People's Republic of China, September. Retrieved June 20, 2017, from http://www.social-protection.org/gimi/RessourcePDF.action?ressource.ressourceId=53859.

Keidel, A. (2007). *The causes and impact of Chinese regional inequalities in income and well-being*. Carnegie Endowment for International Peace.

Koh, C. (2018). Eco-cities: China's next leap forward. *Journal of International and Public Affairs, 1*(1). Retrieved February 10, 2019, from https://www.jipasg.org/posts/2018/9/6/eco-cities-chinas-next-leap-forward.

Ma, Y., & Haski, P. (2009). *The diary of Ma Yan. The struggle and hopes of a Chinese schoolgirl*. New York: Harper Collins.

McKinsey. (2009). China's green opportunity, McKinsey Quarterly, May, available on its website: www.mckinseyquarterly.com.

Pan, J., Ma, H., & Zhang, Y. (2011). *Green economy and green jobs in China: Current status and potentials for 2020*. Washington, DC: Worldwatch Institute, Worldwatch Report 185.

Pinsent Mason. (2011). Update, March 2011, received through the author's e-mail subscription.

PRC, The State Council. (2005). Circular of the State Council Concerning promoting the reform in Rural compulsory education's funding insurance system [Guowuyuan Guanyu Shenhua Nongcun

Yiwujiaoyu Jingfei Baozhang Jizhi Gaige De Tongzhi], 24 December. http://www.gov.cn/zwgk/2006-02/07/content_181267.htm.

PRC, The State Council. (2008). Circular of the State Council Concerning remitting the Urban compulsory education's tuition and miscellaneous fees [Guowuyuan Guanyu Zuohao Mianchu Chengshi Yiwujiaoyu Jieduan Xuesheng Xuezafei Gongzuo De Tongzhi]. August 12. http://www.gov.cn/zwgk/2008-08/15/content_1072915.htm.

Ran, Y. (2005). L'éducation à l'environnement en Chine, Master dissertation for the Master in Asian Studies. University of Geneva.

Urio, P. (2010). Reconciling State, Market and Society in China. The long march toward prosperity: London & New York: Routledge.

Urio, P. (2012). China, the West and the Myth of New Public Management. Neoliberalism and its disontent. London & New York: Routledge.

Wang, S. (2008). Great social transformation afoot in China. *China Economist*, July, pp. 55–69.

Wang, S., & Hu, A. (1993). Report on China's state capacities. Shenyang: Liaoning People Press.

Wike, R. (2015). Corruption, pollution, inequality are top concerns in China. *Pew Research Center*, 24 September. Retrieved October 15, 2016, from https://www.pewglobal.org/2015/09/24/corruption-pollution-inequality-are-top-concerns-in-china/.

Wong, J. (2008). Voices that carry-advocating for carbon caps in China. An influential voice from within calls for hard carbon emission targets. *The Green Leap Forward Website,* 9 September. Retrieved June 6, 2009, from https://greenleapforward.com/2008/09/09/voices-that-carry-advocating-for-carbon-caps-in-china/.

World Bank. (2009). *Mid-Term Evaluation of China's 11th 5 Year Plan.* Washington, DC.

World Bank. (2010). Chinese eco-city project gets boost from global environment facility, Press Release, 22 July. Retrieved August 12, 2010, from www-worldbank.org/en/news/2010/07/22/Chinese-eco-city-project-gets-boost-global-environment-facility.

World Bank. (2011). Empowering China's green growth, World Bank website 31 May. Retrieved June 8, 2011, from www.wolrdbank.org/en/news/2011/05/31/empowering-chinas-green-growth. print.

World Watch Institute. (2010). *Renewable energy and energy efficiency in China: Current status and prospects for 2020.* Washington, DC: World Watch Institute, Worldwatch Report 182, 2010.

Chapter 5
The Opening of China's Economy and the Changing Role of the Party-State

We have seen in Chap. 3 that since 1978, the introduction of market mechanisms has degenerated into a surge in inequalities and aggravated the environmental damages already existing during the Maoïst period. In fact, the liberalization introduced through market mechanisms is quite limited. It is not about leaving the economy free to develop in any direction or in the interest of a minority group. Certainly, by doing so, the Party-State had to make concessions and compromises. It had to accept the emergence of new socio-economic categories, which could attempt to make the most of this limited new freedom to pursue purely personal interests. This may be the result of the emergence of what some called a new class of 'Red Capitalists.' Admittedly, they exist in China, but for the time being the Party-State keeps them under control and maintains its control of the economic development strategy. Moreover, under Jiang Zemin, the Party-State had the brilliant idea of calling the 'Red Capitalists' to join the Party. According to a serious investigation carried out by American researchers, a significant number of those new capitalists joined the Party and most of them are satisfied with what the Party-State enables them to achieve. Thus, they do not pose a threat or an opposition force to the Party (Chen and Dickson 2008; Dickson 2008; Li 2012, 2014).

The Party also had to accept, at least until the Xi Jinping era, that some of its senior cadres engage in practices, clearly of corruption, for their own personal benefit. We may consider that this had the consequence of boosting economic development, by bypassing the rigidity of bureaucratic norms (Lin 2001). However, reforms resulted in a spectacular and rapid increase in inequality between regions, provinces, households and between urban and rural areas, as well as in serious damages to the environment (Sects. 3.3.4 and 3.4). When one knows that the different types of pollution in soil, water and air have harmful effects on human health, we assess the breadth of the

---

This chapter is based upon parts of Urio (2010a, b), Urio and Yuan (2014), with many updates and new comments.

The original version of this chapter was revised. The author given name is corrected in reference list. The correction to this chapter is available at 10.1007/978-981-13-8879-8_7

© Springer Nature Singapore Pte Ltd. 2019
P. Urio, *China 1949–2019*, https://doi.org/10.1007/978-981-13-8879-8_5

154   5 The Opening of China's Economy and the Changing Role of the Party-State

distance separating China and a harmonious society at the moment of Deng's death on February 19, 1997. In addition, the inevitable implementation of the concept of economic efficiency led to the adoption of organizational techniques imported from the Western public sector, which has had an impact on human resources management not only in private enterprises, but also in SOEs and state bureaucracies.

The consequence was that within a very limited time frame, the companies and the state bureaucracies laid off a considerable number of people. Moreover, the collapse of old solidarities organized by companies and state bureaucracies during the Mao era, left millions of people without the social services to which they had been accustomed before the reforms. As a result, the causes of the new forms of poverty can easily be imagined: unemployment or underemployment, illness, accident, and old age. While in the Maoist period the Gini index was barely above 20, after reforms the dramatic increase of the country's wealth (measured by GDP) has not prevented the Gini index from climbing up to more than 40. Finally, we can imagine the consequences that this type of rapid development can have on populations both in rural areas and in the cities, following a partial but very real retreat of the State from the social domain.

Further to the policies that 'put people first' discussed in Chap. 4, in order to analyse the strategy implemented by the Party to overcome these negative consequences, we will first analyse the changes in China's power structure. Then we will discuss the opening of the political system, taking more particularly into consideration the development of NGOs, the import of Western technologies, such as shale gas fracking, and the import of Public Private Partnerships, as an example of Western management arrangements.

5.1 Analyzing Power in China and in the West

When analyzing the opening of China's economy, one cannot avoid dealing with the question of the nature of Chinese power. In the West, the dominant opinion qualifies China's power at best as an authoritarian regime, at worst as a dictatorship. But what is the real nature of Chinese power today? In order to answer this question, I will first present, as briefly as possible, the model of power I use for this purpose (Urio 1984, Chap 6; Urio 2010a, pp. 156–171; Urio 2018, Chap. 2). I will then apply this model to the case of Western liberal democracies, before I use it for China. This sequence is necessary for several reasons. First, as modernization has been historically first experimented by Western countries, and is now followed in other parts of the world, very often by their imitating the West, it is necessary to first understand the institutional responses the West has given to the challenges of modernization. Second, many scholars and more generally many observers of non-Western countries, consider that the latter must adopt the Western model if they want to succeed in their journey towards modernization. We may call this the 'westernization thesis' more often called 'the convergence thesis'. The realization of this hypothesis is by no means certain. Third, and linked to the previous reasons, the case of China is an interesting one for testing the Westernization thesis, as the Chinese leadership has always sustained the idea that China must modernize according to its own characteristics. In other words, modernization may be supported in China by institutional arrangements different from the Western ones.

I analyze power within a country by referring to its principal constitutive elements, i.e. three power levels: power structure, interactive processes and resources. I have suggested that this approach can be used to understand power in any society (Urio 2010a, pp. 156–171). On the structural level, we find the characteristics of the power structure endowed with a certain amount of stability over time and limiting the actors' freedom. This structure defines the rules of the game (or the rationality) inside which, on the second level, the actors behave within interactive processes. The latter produce and distribute resources among the social actors. This distribution may change or confirm the power structure and/or endow or deprive the actors of their resources, that will be used in the subsequent interactive processes.[1] From an analytical point of view, one can subdivide the power structure into sub-structures, each one having its own rules of the game. One should analyse the interactions that may occur between the sub-structures and find a global logic accounting for the overall power structure, thus taking into consideration the unitary reality of power (Urio 2018, pp. 36–43).

I suggest isolating the following five sub-structures without which society could not exist: the socio-biological structure, the economic structure, the legal structure, the cultural structure and the communication structure.[2] First, the socio-biological structure assures the reproduction of humankind. Second, the economic structure assures the production of goods and services necessary to the survival of humankind, eventually (but not necessarily) to its economic development. Third, the legal structure that produces formal norms. Fourth, the cultural structure producing social norms, including values, beliefs, norms of behaviour, representation of reality, intellectual means for understanding and eventually supporting the form of the society in which one lives. It is within this structure that one will be able to situate the political culture or the ideology. Finally, the communication structure assures the circulation of the values, etc. produced by the cultural structure, thanks to the technical support of vehicles such as education institutions, mass media, newspapers, radio, TV, and more recently internet and social media. The rationality of each of these sub-structures constitutes the framework within which the interactive processes take place (second level) the essential result of which is the production and the distribution of resources (third level). The result of these processes has an impact on the overall power structure by confirming or modifying its rationality.

The features of these sub-structures are relatively stable in time, and this is why their identification is important in order to understand the scope of freedom the actors enjoy within each of them and what are their positive and negative characteristics that favour or limit their power. However, in spite of their relative stability, the five sub-

---

[1] Within the power structure of a country, resources may be grouped into two categories: (a) simple resources, such as information, knowledge, competencies, biological characteristics, formal norms, social norms (e.g. values, beliefs) and economic resources; (b) complex resources: manipulation, rewards, sanctions, force, charism, tradition and legality.

[2] I am indebted to Jean-William Lapierre for this approach: Lapierre (1973). For a different, but similar perspective (see Urio 1984, pp. 254–282; Urio 2010a, pp. 157–164) for a state's system; and for power in the international system Urio (2018, Chap. 2, pp. 35–82).

structures 'silently change', as suggested by François Jullien and Fernand Braudel (Jullien 2011; Braudel 1958, and Sect. 2.1 above). It is therefore important to identify the changes that occur 'silently' in the 'long time', because on this depends the ability of the skilful strategist to discover the changes in the power structure that may evolve to its advantage, as well as the elements of the structure on which he can intervene with a reasonable chance of success, whereby contributing to the change of the overall power structure that will turn in favour of its policy goals (Sect. 2.3 above). I have suggested to call 'the dominant group' the entity that exerts power by mastering all of the five sub-structures. The composition of the dominant group may vary from one country to another. Generally, it is made up of the most influential representatives of economic organizations, a political party or several political parties, some managers of leading private or public mass media, and some intellectuals, eventually also the upper levels of the armed forces and of the intelligence agencies.

The considerations developed in the preceding paragraph suggest the necessity of a certain level of coherence between the rationality of the five sub-structures, or else, in the opposite case, the emergence of contradictions and ruptures risk to put in danger the existence of this type of societal organisation, and as a consequence the position of the dominant group. Thus, the necessity for the latter to control the five above-mentioned sub-structures, as well as the interactive processes occurring within them, as it is within these processes that the social actors intervene, eventually to change the distribution of resources to their advantage. Whatever the situation may be, I suggest considering two types of systemic coherence: on the one hand, a material coherence that must assure, e.g. in the framework of a liberal democracy with a market economy, the non-contradiction of state functions with the rationality of the economic structure. On the other hand, I suggest considering a cognitive coherence (rational and/or affective) between the economic structure and the legal structure (i.e. the production of formal norms by the state), guaranteed by political culture or ideology. In other words, it is not enough to avoid material contradictions between law production of the state on the one hand, and the principles of the market economy on the other; it is also necessary that the social actors regard that type of society as a fundamental coherent entity, sufficiently adapted to everybody's needs.

One can then conclude that the rules of the rationality of the structure as well as the degree of material and cognitive coherence of the power system constitute the operational code of the corresponding society. In such a way, the operational code of a society constitutes the framework in which interactive processes take place. To the extent that these processes are not zero-sum games, i.e. if the distribution of economic, legal and ideological resources does not completely proceed to the benefit of the dominant group, one can forecast that a social actor benefiting from a sufficient amount of economic, legal and ideological resources may be in a position to escape the control of the dominant group and consolidate its power resources. Eventually, thanks to these resources it may be able to conceive a strategy through which it will erode step by step the power position of the dominant group or knock it down by a revolutionary short-term movement.

The foregoing paragraphs suggest that the dominating group must act so that (1) the interactive processes do not result in a redistribution of resources that may endanger its strategic position, even if this redistribution does not affect fundamentally the

5.1 Analyzing Power in China and in the West

overall power structure (tactical level); and (2) the same interactive processes do not directly result in a fundamental change of the rationality of the overall power structure (strategic level).

5.1.1 Power in Western Countries

The first remark that is necessary to put forward is that the liberal theory of democracy considers that market economy and liberal democracy are strictly linked together in what I may call a necessary and indispensable interdependence.[3] It is therefore necessary to briefly explain the origins of the Western model as it stands today in reality and not as it is presented in theory. Moreover, this is also necessary because China has decided to introduce into its society some elements that are clearly adopted from the Western experience, even if they are implemented with great care so as not to be contradictory with Chinese characteristics. As we have seen in Chap. 2. (Sects. 2.4.1 to 2.4.3), since the end of the 1970s the Chinese leadership has opted in favour of market economy (or at least of market mechanisms) with the clear aim of increasing the performance of the economic system, because the Western experience had proved that market mechanisms were more efficient than planned economy. Can China benefit from the analysis of the historical process through which the West has adopted a market economy?[4]

The market can be viewed as a set of laws (based upon economic theory) and technical tools and arrangements (based upon theory and practical experience). It is my opinion that this view of the market is not sufficient for understanding its very special and demanding way of organizing the production process. A historical analysis is necessary, starting from the Greco-Roman world to the three major revolutions (scientific, industrial and liberal) for understanding how it has been possible to impose this type of economic system as the best means of producing and distributing wealth. In short, it has been a long transformation process involving all the dimensions of society (Braudel 1979a, b; Landes 1999; Wallerstein 1974, 1980).

In the framework of this chapter, I have to restrain myself to the consequences of the Industrial Revolution that made the provision of social services a political issue put forward by socialist movements since the second half of the nineteenth Century, and was finally adopted by all the Western countries. The problems experienced by these countries in the process of developing a market economy have disrupted the traditional social structure, and in spite of the spectacular gain of productivity, they have put large numbers of workers at the mercy of unscrupulous owners and managers. The reaction to this situation, aimed at helping the workers to face the risks of this

---

[3]One of the best statements is provided by Nobel prize-winner Milton Friedman (1962), Chap. 1: 'The relation between economic freedom and political freedom', pp. 7–21, and Chap. 2 'The role of government in a free society', pp. 22–36.

[4]Let me warn the reader that in this section for the sake of simplicity I use 'market economy' (or simply 'market') as a synonym of 'capitalism', whereas in Chap. 2 (Sect. 2.2), I have made a clear distinction between 'market economy' and 'capitalism'. Moreover, I use 'market mechanisms' to refer to the very partial introduction of market within China's economy.

158   5 The Opening of China's Economy and the Changing Role of the Party-State

new type of life (above all, unemployment, low pay, illness, accidents, unhealthy and dangerous working conditions, poor lodging and unhealthy living conditions, and old age) has taken more than a century to enable the setting up of a complete system (the 'Welfare State') aimed at satisfying these needs. Starting with the first state's interventions adopted during the late nineteenth century and the Great Depression of the 1930's and ending with those leading to the establishment of a complete Welfare State during the twentieth century, Western states have responded to the needs of the masses by a huge legislative and financial intervention into the social system. At the same time, states have built all kinds of infrastructures necessary to the development of the market economy, as well as an important set of regulations aimed at (1) limiting some unwanted consequences of the market (e.g. pollution), (2) sustaining the development of market economy (e.g. counter cyclical policies), (3) protecting the citizens, workers, and consumers (e.g. against false information about the goods sold in the market), and (4) at limiting (or even forbidding) some commercial practices, contrary to the classical orthodoxy of market economy (e.g. anti-trust legislation). Of course, all these policies had to be financed by a substantial increase of all sorts of taxations. It is at the end of this historical process that liberal democracies organized their power structure that could have become a stable institutional arrangement distributing societal functions between state and market. This happened towards the end of the 1970s, more or less at the time of the end of the Chinese Cultural Revolution.

While on the one hand it was possible, towards the end of the 1970s, to take stock of the impressive increase of wealth created thanks to this mix of market and state activities, on the other hand, huge structural annual deficits appeared and contributed to a massive increase of public debt. The dominant opinion was that the expenses necessary for financing the state's interventions could no longer be balanced by an additional increase of taxation without hampering the good functioning of market economy.

Indeed, it is at this time that neoliberal economists and political scientists were able to come out in the open, proposing their cure to the state's illnesses, known as the New Public Management (NPM). After the Second World War, the generally agreed policy among Western policy makers was to reconstruct Europe. This necessity became even more compelling when, at the end of the 1940's, Europe became divided into Western and Eastern Europe. People in favour of a limited role of the state in society (and especially in the economy) had no chance of being heard.[5] Nevertheless, with the support of several rich foundations (financed by the private sector, especially in the USA) they prepared themselves for the time when their expertise would seem, to many policy-makers, inescapable. This has been the case, for example, for Prime Minister Margaret Thatcher and President Ronald Reagan (elected in 1979, 1980, respectively). From that time on, the neoliberal revolution was on its way, benefiting from a formidable alliance between business leaders, politicians, mass media, and think tanks, that used all the devices of the communication structure to diffuse their ideology and policy options. It was thus possible to assure both the material and

---

[5]Milton Friedman complains about this kind of blackout in the preface to the second edition of his (now) famous book: Friedman 1982 (first edition 1962).

5.1 Analyzing Power in China and in the West

cognitive coherence of the power structure. It is at this time that the 'New Public Management—NPM' became the armed wing of neoliberalism for the developed countries, whereas the other armed wing, the 'Washington Consensus', had been imposed by the West upon developing or in-transition countries for a long time.

In short, NPM proposes to reduce the state's size, by privatizing and/or contracting out state's activities, with the consequence of reducing the state's burden, and thereby reducing the level of taxation. This in turn would free the economy, by using the money not taken by the state to stimulate economic growth. Finally, it is said that this new impetus would benefit the entire society. Other measures were the deregulation of the markets, the adoption by the state of management techniques imported from the private sector, and consequently the 'flexibilization' and deregulation of human resource management not only in the private but also in the public sector. The general principle, upon which NPM is based, is that of economic efficiency (David and Ted 1992; Osborne and Plastrik 1997; Barzeley 1992, 2001; Urio 1999).

As a consequence, practically all the OECD states have adopted a strategy that, with different scopes and impetus, is based upon the prescriptions of NPM. During this period, and in fact up to the 2008 financial and economic crisis, it was the turn of the defenders of the Welfare State, and more generally of state's intervention in the economy and the society, to be on the defensive, and with practically little hope of being heard. It is only after the 2008 crisis that several scholars have pointed out the negative consequences of the implementation of NPM prescriptions (Stiglitz 2008a, 2009, 2010; Urio 1999, 2012; Suleiman 2003). This might be of some interest to Chinese decision makers, as a careful examination of some of the trends launched by the reform process in China shows that they have some similarities with the NPM prescriptions.

It is undeniable that by succeeding in combining market economy and liberal democracy during their long historical process, Western countries have developed an unshakeable faith in the virtues of the free market, in spite of numerous economic and political crises. This is not to say that a market economy implemented in another part of the world and in another era will necessarily need to be sustained by the same type of state, and the same types of relationships connecting state, legal system, and economy, as has been the case for the West. But, I just want to suggest that it would be foolish not to take advantage of learning something useful from the success, but also from some of the dramatic failures, that have characterized the long history of market economy in the West, not only the 2008 crisis but also the development of anti-system political movements that manifested themselves in the election of Donald Trump, the British citizens' vote in favour of Brexit, and the so-called populist and sovereignist movements critical of the EU and globalization.

In this respect, it is important to remember that NPM was introduced in the West at a time when its society was being organised in a fundamentally different way compared to China, and when the general standard of living of Western people was considerably higher than in China. It is therefore necessary to examine with great care the possibility of transposing to China the same NPM-type reforms (Schick 1998). Moreover, it is necessary to take into consideration the long history of Chinese reforms (started at the end of the 1970's) and to evaluate the actual consequences

160   5   The Opening of China's Economy and the Changing Role of the Party-State

of these reforms on Chinese society. I have done this in Chaps. 3 and 4, where I presented the positive consequences of China's reform process, mainly driven by economic considerations based upon the increase of wealth measured by GDP, and the negative consequences that led to and the adoption of re-balancing policies putting 'people first'.

5.1.2   Power in the People's Republic of China

Applying the framework of analysis presented in the above section for the understanding of the Chinese political system and society is not an easy task. Nevertheless, this is what I will try to do in the following sections of this chapter. Here it suffices to briefly develop four preliminary considerations. I will use the same structure of the power model used for analysing in power in the West, as I have made the assumption that the five sub-structures hold for any type of society.

It is easy, and trivial, to confirm that the CPC constitutes the dominant group within the Chinese society throughout the life of the PCR from Mao to the present. In short, the Party still controls the socio-biological, the economic, legal, cultural and communication structures of the power system. This is true in spite of the numerous changes that have occurred within Chinese society and its power structure. In addition to the analysis of Western scholars that point to the strong (and for many to the authoritarian or even totalitarian) power of the CPC, the Party itself, and its most prominent leaders, publicly confirm this statement (Chap. 2, especially Sect. 2.4). I am not interested in evaluating China's power by using the standard of Western liberal democracy. I find it more interesting to analyze how the Party has managed reforms and the related changes in the five sub-structures, while safeguarding the Chinese fundamental values of unity, stability and harmony. This is not different from what the West has done since the Industrial Revolution, by adapting the relations between market and state according to the circumstances, as we have seen above. By doing this we will see how China's power is very different from the dictatorship or even the strong authoritarian state often presented by Western scholars and mainstream media.

Let us start with the economic structure. In Chap. 2 (Sect. 2.5) I have analyzed the cultural difficulties on the road to market economy. In summary, weak attitude in favour of written documents; imprecision of legal texts (when they exist); in judicial procedures people are constrained by an excessive respect and/or fear of authority, and a widely diffused belief that laws and a too strict legal system may have the consequence of producing and exacerbating conflicts; tendency to secrecy and intolerance at the appearance of social groups that may constitute a threat to the PCP power; attraction for grandiose undertakings not necessarily based upon a cost-benefit analysis. If we add to this the weak separation of powers and the underlying tendency of the CPC to interfere with the judicial procedures we end up with a considerable uncertainty regarding the implementation of legal norms, and the behaviour of economic actors. Some of these characteristics are also an obstacle

5.1 Analyzing Power in China and in the West

to establishing a liberal democracy which in the West goes hand in hand with market economy. But does China need a liberal democracy to sustain market economy? The answer is, so far, clearly not, if we examine China's experience since 1978.

In the process of introducing market mechanism, the Party has taken, implemented, and monitored all the decisions. But, as in the case of Western liberal democracies, the relationship between the Party-State and the people is by no means a one-way one, in which the Party-State gives orders and the citizen obeys. Already since the Mao era, the goal of the Party-State has been to restore China's power and to provide the Chinese People with better living conditions, the two objectives being strictly linked to each other in a two-way causal relationship. That has been obtained already during the Mao era, although with limited economic results that, moreover, have been overshadowed by the mistakes of the Great Leap Forward and of the Cultural Revolution. In this perspective, Deng's choice in favour of market mechanisms is strictly in line with the objectives of Mao's strategy. Only the means change (Chap. 2, Sect. 2.4.1).

Of course, by introducing market mechanisms within its economy, China has automatically given more freedom to the people in this domain. The consequences have been the emergence of professional associations, which are not really a novelty for China as similar organizations already existed under the Imperial regime and during the first half of the twentieth century (Bergère 1986, 2007). Moreover, mass organizations such as the Trade Unions and the All-China Women's Federation have developed many activities that are linked to the changes in Chinese society after the introduction of market mechanisms, even if they are in fact organizations of the Party. For example, following the increasing number of divorces that are, at least financially, more harmful to women, and following the emergence of unemployment (that touches more women than men) the Women's Federation (which has branches all over China) has implemented a variety of activities aimed at helping women that suffer from the consequence of divorce and/or unemployment. The activities of this type of association can bring to the attention of the Chinese leadership problems and solutions that it has not thought of by itself. Similarly, the partial retreat of the State from the social domain has given way to an increasing number of Non-Governmental and Non-profit organizations, although the government keep them under control for reasons that will be explained in Sect. 5.3 below (Urio and Yuan 2014).

Changes have also been introduced into the socio-biological and the legal structures. By relaxing and then deleting the one-child policy, freedom has been given to couples to decide how they want to manage their relation towards parenthood. Moreover, the legal structure has progressively introduced important novelties such as private property, linked to the introduction of market mechanisms in the economic structure (Peerenboom 2002, 2007).

Even more interesting are the changes that occurred within the cultural and the communication structures. As happens in the West, the dominant group (the Party) wants to have control over the production of ideas, values, intellectual means for understanding and eventually supporting the way society is organized. On the one hand, the Party sees that the instances that produce and diffuse representations of reality (such as publications, film broadcasting, think tanks, mass media, internet, the NGOs, and teaching institutions at all levels) are not contradictory to the power structure and the public policies of the state. The control is explained by the fact that China is aware that these channels may diffuse ideas with subversive potential, or may even be used in order to obtain regime changes, such as the West has unfortunately had the habit to use them for quite often (see Sect. 6.1). The US interventions in Tibet in 1959 and in Hong Kong in 2014 have not been forgotten. Additional control means have been introduced by Xi Jinping, namely by video camera surveillance and the 'social credit system'. These are not dissimilar from the means used in the West, and more particularly by the US.[6] Ample proofs available today allow me not to comment that any power, even the more democratic, uses all the means (legal and illegal) at its disposal to fight against real or perceived threats to its sovereignty.

The only reasons that may justify Western criticisms are that the Western power system is better (whatever the criteria used) than the Chinese one. A simple historical analysis should advise Western pundits to be a bit more modest. The other justification would be the Fukuyama's end of history according to which all countries are inevitably driven, at the end of history, to adopt liberal democracy and market economy (see my critique below, Sect. 6.1.2). It is also important to acknowledge, with Western pundits, that China is now at a difficult stage of its economic and social development. At present, the problem is that China society is more open than when Deng started its reforms. Therefore, a further relaxation of societal control will open the door to internal and external forces critical of the present power structure. It is significant that the Party has cracked down on both neo-maoïst and neo-liberal movements.[7] Moreover, China is still today aware of the negative consequences Russia experienced at the time of its opening up thanks to the shock therapy suggested by self-proclaimed Western experts. Today, Western experts warn China: it was easy to master the introduction of market mechanisms at the beginning of the reform process, but today, the Chinese economy has become so complex (just as the Western one has) that it needs additional and more in-depth reforms, or the system will collapse. Clearly this necessitates a freer market economy, its further opening to the global economy, especially the financial system, strongly recommended by the World Bank (World Bank 2012), and all this sustained by liberal democracy.

Now, the important questions are: first, what are the benefits of the reforms for the Chinese people, and second, does the Party meet the approval and support of the majority of the Chinese people? In Chaps. 3 and 4 I have provided some evidence that remarkable improvements in the standard of living of the Chinese people have been realized, especially after the reform started in the 1980s, and accelerated after the 1997 Party Congress. What are then the reactions of the Chinese population? Official records show an increasing number of protest movements throughout the country. But these are mainly due to the difficulties the Chinese leadership had, at least until the Xi Jinping era, to combat illegal and immoral behaviour on the part of those, especially

---

[6]Two articles published by the *Monde Diplomatique* on these practices show very clearly the similarity between the West and China: Zuboff (2019), Raphaël and Ling Xi (2019).

[7]It is interesting to note that the former have not been condemned by Western media, whereas the latter have.

5.1 Analyzing Power in China and in the West

but not only at the local level, who ruthlessly profit from the opportunities (i.e. from more freedom) offered by the reforms. Corruption, illegal sale of land to real estate promoters and consequent destruction of old habitations and the displacement of the tenants, non-payment of wages to migrant workers, etc. In spite of these problems, which the Party-State is taking very seriously today, especially under the leadership of Xi Jinping, the majority of the Chinese people seem to support the development strategy set up by the Party-State. The support that the Party enjoys from the Chinese citizen cannot be denied. It seems that the rebalancing policies have achieved the intended goal (Saich 2016; Forsythe 2015).

Clearly, there are not throughout the country the vast protest movements against the regime that many naïve Western observers have predicted during the whole life of the PRC, basing their forecast mainly on the conception of the freedom that is dominant in the West.[8] It seems that the Chinese idea of freedom and human rights places first economic development as a means of giving the people the opportunity of becoming free from poverty, hunger, and ignorance. This choice has consistently been followed by the Chinese leadership.

5.2 The Opening up of the Political System

The opening up of the Chinese political system was inevitable if the process of modernization was to succeed.[9] As I have pointed out in Chap. 3, the process of modernization implies the availability and use of technical competencies that by far exceed ideological values. Mao managed Chinese society and polity through a revolutionary public management. This led him to organize several political campaigns that culminated in the Cultural Revolution which I have interpreted as a move to retain and reclaim the power that was in the process of being seized by the bureaucracies that were emerging within the Party, the government and the universities. This bureaucratization process was necessary during Mao's initiation of the modernization of China. Figure 5.1 summarizes the transition from Mao's public management to Xi Jinping's.

Let me point out that this transition inevitably drove Chinese management towards the well-established rational logic of modern public management based upon, as far as possible, scientific evidence. This logic was confirmed by Hu Jintao (Chap. 2, Sect. 2.4.5). Furthermore, this corresponds to one of Deng's slogans 'seeking truth from facts', as one of its most important outcomes is to improve the predictability of actors' behaviour, especially the predictability of public authorities. This is in

---

[8]The *South China Morning Post* has published several articles about this type of social protest movements, as well as on the more invasive control the Party is today exerting on social dissent.

[9]This section is based upon the idea that the political system is a very large system comprising within it an extremely important sub-system, the 'decision-making system process', upon which depends the capacity of the political system to make 'good' decisions, whatever the criteria may be (Urio 1984, pp. 254–282). Therefore, the opening up of a political system must also be evaluated by considering the 'decision-making system'.

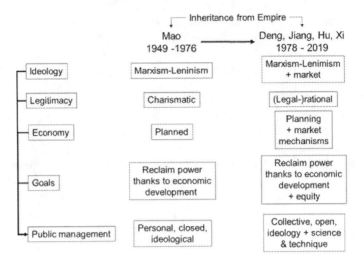

Fig. 5.1 Public management from Mao to Xi Jinping

fact a characteristic modern societies need in order to support the rational behaviour within the market economy where actors, in order to make rational calculations, need to count upon the predictability of state's behaviour (Weber 1985).

In order to acquire the competencies necessary to manage modernization thanks to the introduction of market mechanisms, the Party has implemented a set of measures that in fact opened the Party-State to the sources of competence it needed. These sources are both internal to China: universities, intellectuals, and businessmen; and external: developed countries (both Western and Eastern) and international organizations. Amongst the numerous examples, let me quote the following. First of all, three reports prepared under the auspices of the World Bank with teams of Western and Chinese experts: *China: Deepening Public Service Unit Reform to Improve Service Delivery* (World Bank 2005b); *Mid-Term Evaluation of China's 11th 5 Year Plan* (World Bank 2008); *From poor areas to poor people: China's evolving poverty reduction agenda. An assessment of poverty and inequality in China*, (World Bank 2009). This last example is quite exceptional as it has been prepared at the request of the Development Planning Department of China's National Development and Reform Commission (NDRC) under the responsibility of the Prime minister. I do not know any other country that has submitted to the scrutiny of an international organization the major planning instrument of its societal development. The other document worth mentioning is McKinsey's *China's Green Revolution* (McKinsey 2009), to which many scholars from several Chinese universities have contributed together with a team from the Energy Research Institute of the NDRC.

The importance of acquiring technical competencies both in the domains of public management and in enterprises (especially SOEs) has been strongly emphasised by Chinese leaders, for example at the Party Congresses of 2002, 2007, 2012 and 2017 (Sect. 2.4). In Sect. 6.2.4.2 you will find an analysis of the extraordinary develop-

5.2 The Opening up of the Political System

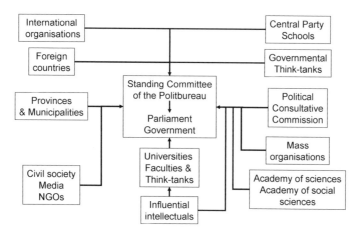

Fig. 5.2 The new structure of the decision-making process "where do correct ideas come from?"

ment of China's technology. Moreover, the Party has opened the decision-making process thanks to four types of measures: association, cooperation, consultation, and appointment. First, it associated with the decision-making process researchers and think tanks of some universities where one can find researchers studying the negative consequences of development, as well as the development of law and civil society. Second, it started to cooperate with international economic organizations such as the World Bank and the Asian Development Bank. These organizations are mainly interested in the improvement of economic efficiency, but from the last few years also with equity (World Bank 2005a, 2008, 2009; McKinsey 2009). Third, the Party-State started to consult non-communist experts either within the above-mentioned organizations or through bilateral cooperation projects. Finally, several non-communists top level experts have been appointed within the administration, and more recently even at the top political level; I can quote the appointments of the Minister of Science and Technology, Wan Gang, appointed in April 2007, and the Minister of Health, Chen Zhu, appointed in May 2007, who are not members of the CPC.

As a consequence, the structure of the decision-making process has become more open and this allows the Chinese leadership to acquire the scientific knowledge it needs to choose the policy options that best fit its overall development strategy, not only for sustaining economic development, but also for adopting the policies necessary for re-balancing the Chinese society, as we have seen in Chap. 4. Figure 5.2 summarizes this new decision-making structure.

Of course, this structure does not correspond to the Western idea of a democratic process, where political parties, pressure groups, and all sorts of organizations are either invited to take part in the decision-making process or have the possibility of expressing their ideas in case they are not consulted. Nevertheless, liberal democracy has to cope with the difficult question posed by the opposition between the law of numbers (i.e. the fact that in a liberal democracy, decisions are taken generally by majority vote) and the problem of choosing the best possible option, which cannot be based on a majority vote but on the best possible solution supported by scientific evidence. Indeed, we must admit that since the end of Mao's era the Chinese choices of public policies have been increasingly determined by the latter. And this explains the opening up of the Chinese decision-making process to all sorts of sources of knowledge.

The search for the knowledge useful for the decision-making process is further strengthened by the development of the Central Party Schools (Shambaugh 2008; Lee 2015; Pieke 2016). Four Party schools have been set up in the 2000s by the CPC to complete the training organised traditionally within the Beijing Central Party School: in Dalian for the top SOEs' managers, who study the improvement of the management of SOEs in the modern economy, in Yanan and Jinggangshan for the training in revolutionary traditions and conditions of the country, and in Shanghai (Pudong) for the training in international affairs. In these schools, modern management techniques as well methodology for analyzing policy options are offered to the top cadres of the Party. For example, the Party School of Shanghai-Pudong (China Executive Leadership Academy Pudong—CELAP) organises training in different technical and strategic domains.

Training abroad is also organized for cadres of all levels, especially for top leaders. I was personally involved in one of these training programmes organized between 1998 and 2003 for top leaders of the public administration and the Party at the central and local level. The topics chosen after in-depth discussion with our Chinese partner (a training centre reporting directly to the Organisation Department of the Politburo) are quite instructive of the seriousness with which these cadres have envisaged their training, that covered practically all the most important domains of public management, as well as the interface between government and economy, including privatization and contracting out.

Since the 2000s, the Chinese leadership has sustained the development of first class think tanks that should provide policy analyses suggesting ways of avoiding policy-making errors and correcting them promptly when they occur.[10] On 27 October 2014, the 6th meeting of the Central Leading Group for Comprehensively Deepening Reforms, defined the functions of new think tanks with Chinese characteristics: 'policy consultation and suggestions, theoretical innovation, public opinion guidance, social services, public diplomacy and other important functions. It also clearly stated that high priority should be paid to the establishment of 25 first class domestic think tanks by the year 2020.' In December 2015, the first group of first-class-think-thanks was approved by the Chinese authorities and their goal was defined as 'serving the decision-making of the central committee of CPC and the development of the country and providing knowledge support.'

Within this context, the case of the Institute for Contemporary China Studies directed by Prof. Hu Angang of Tsinghua University is an interesting example show-

---

[10]Information on the Centre's activities described hereafter are based upon discussions with Hu Angang and a non-published paper by Hu Angang, Jiang Jiaying and Yan Yilong, 'The influence of Think Tanks in China's Medium and Long-term Strategic Plan: A Case Study of Institute of Contemporary China Studies of Tsinghua University', kindly provided by the main author. For more detail on the role of think-tanks see Hayward (2018), Li (2009, 2017).

5.2 The Opening up of the Political System

ing the kind of contribution think-tanks can provide to the Chinese leadership. The Institute was included in the first group of first class think tanks approved by the Party-State. The quality of the Institute's research and advocacy work was thus recognized by the Chinese leadership. It is in this context that the Institute has become, since it first started its activities in 2000, one of the most influential Chinese think tanks. Not only it directly participates in the practice of China reform and opening up, but also actively participates in the major policy-making consultation process about China's medium and long-term development planning. Thanks to its policy reports (called 'China Study Reports') the Institute has influenced Chinese policy-makers by providing information about the national conditions and advice on national policies with a number of policy reports. Its director, Hu Angang, has provided relevant information since the 9th 5-year Plan (1999–2000) and, as a member of the National Development Planning Expert Committee since 2005, he has been entrusted with the independent evaluation of the 11th (2006–2010), 12th (2011–2015) and 13th (2016–2020) five-year programmes.[11] These researches allow Hu Angang to explain the functioning of the Chinese political system as a performing collective presidency (Hu 2014).

The development of first-class think tanks may have the consequence of integrating Chinese experts into the category of experts of the global capitalist system. Based upon an in-depth analysis of contemporary Chinese think tanks, Jane Hayward concludes that China's leaders 'seek to produce a community of highly-trained, internationally oriented, globally competitive experts and technocrats capable of providing timely and sophisticated analysis and advice to relevant government bureaus, and of manoeuvring between the state and international institutions to impact policy making at the transnational level. They seek a more powerful voice in deliberations about how this global capitalist system is organized, with a view to shaping the global ideological consensus and, indeed, a new global order. Yet, at the same time, they endeavour to transform China's institutions and social structure to become compatible with the requirements of global capital—thus to *internationalize* the Chinese state'. (Hayward 2018, pp. 45–46). It remains to be seen, as Hayward suggests, whether China will be able to influence the establishment of the new global order compatible with its national interests (i.e. of its people) or will its new elite (of which think tanks are a new important component) join the international capitalist elite more oriented to the maximization of its parochial interests or to continue to improve the living conditions of the majority of Chinese citizens, at which has been able to do so far.

During the last decade particular importance has been conferred on the contributions to the decision-making process from the major universities. These fulfil three major roles: first the training of young scholars who could later become civil servants or Party cadres, as well as adult education programmes addressed to civil servants and Party cadres. The government has invested a lot of money to improve both university infrastructure and the salaries of academic personnel. Moreover, the government has

---

[11] The National Development Planning Expert Committee was instituted by the State Council in 2005 and comprises more than 40 Chinese best scholars, including Hu Angang.

financed study abroad of many professors and young advanced students, and has conferred on the best universities the organization of Master programmes in public administration. The second task of universities, which has been much developed, is the provision of expertise to the government. Third, the universities constitute an intellectual open space where discussions about the policy options are freely discussed amongst academics of all levels. Within the best universities a great deal of research has been developed dealing with several very delicate topics, such as corruption, disparities, the role of NGOs, foreign policy, the relationship with the US, the best way towards further economic development, social security reform, etc. These academic activities testify to the vibrant development that is taking place within Chinese universities, and more widely within the Chinese intelligentsia, in spite of the new measures taken under Xi Jinping to better control that it will not openly produce ideas contrary to the Party line.

By draining information, expertise and scientific analyses from these various sources, the Chinese leadership has considerably improved its capacity to design, implement and monitor public policies aimed at sustaining economic development and rebalancing the Chinese society. We may consider that the Chinese Communist Party has become a learning organization. A good example is the case of the preparation of the new Chinese health system. After years of experimentation at the provincial level, a report of the NDRC concluded to the failure of the existing system, due to a considerable increase in cost, inefficiency and exclusion of a large part of the population. The Party-State then set up a Coordination group under the responsibility of the Ministry of Health and the NDRC. This group coordinated the works of several organisations: twelve agencies representing several Ministries; the Universities of Peking, Fudan, Renmin, Tsinghua (in cooperation with Harvard) and the Normal University of Beijing; the World Health Organisation; and the private consulting company McKinsey. Several reports were presented by these organizations, and a final report was presented to the Chinese leadership for evaluation and final decision. At the Party Congress of November 2007 President Hu Jintao announced the imminent publication of the new Chinese Public Health system.

It is at the end of this long process that the Chinese leadership has confirmed the development strategy that puts 'people first': while reaffirming the dominant role of the Party as well as its historic mission of leading the Chinese people towards a restored power and prosperity; it has also confirmed that the contradictions created within Chinese society by economic development must be resolved, namely the contradictions between rural and urban areas, economy and society, development of economic capital and human capital, economy and environment (Xi Jinping speech at the 2017 Party Congress, Xi Jinping 2017). In order to do so it is recognized that it will be necessary to: (1) rebalance the economy by reducing the inequalities; (2) develop the economy, science and technology, and urbanization; (3) reduce unemployment, the contradictions between capital development and human capital development; (4) coordinate the development between rural and urban areas, economy and people, economy and the use of non-renewable resources, and between economy and the respect of the environment; (5) improve the social security system, housing, transportation and health; (6) safeguard the interest of migrant workers;

5.2 The Opening up of the Political System 169

(7) the role of the CPC in international relations reclaiming world power status as a means to realize the China dream (Sect. 6.2).

The conclusion that can now be drawn from the strategy of opening up the decision-making process to all kinds of sources, national, international, public, and private, is the sign of a formidable will to collect information favouring the adoption and implementation of policies aimed at improving the two interrelated goals already defined by Mao: the improvement of the condition and the strength of the Chinese population and the reclaiming of world power status. The signal given to the world is thus very clear: never in the future China will be subject to aggression, nor will tolerate policies aiming at imposing the adoption of policies and international agreements that may be interpreted as a unilateral will of foreign parochial interests. In the last chapter I will explain through what long-term strategy China has been able to achieve this result.

5.3 The Development of NGOs in China

It is against the background presented above that we need to understand the development of Chinese NGOs, characterized on the one hand by the freedom offered by the relative withdrawal of the Party-State, but on the other hand, by the limits it imposes upon them. What are the reasons explaining this seemingly contradictory strategy? On one side, the NGOs are essential to fill the vacuum left by the State in certain areas, especially in the social domain, but on the other side, they can represent a threat to the Party's power (Urio and Yuan 2014). Since the beginning, all sorts of means have been used to keep the NGOs under control: registration procedure, obligation of getting a public 'sponsor', being placed under a double control (during registration and during the daily activities), establishment of a Party's committee in NGOs which includes at least three employees, who are members of the Party.

Recently, China has adopted two new laws: the Charity Law and the Foreign NGO Management Law (Backer 2017, China Development Brief, NGOs in China). The former clearly constitutes an important improvement, as it gives a broad definition of charity, it encourages fund-rising with some tax preferences, it simplifies the registration and control procedures, and it establishes more precise regulations to avoid corruption and to assure accountability. The foreign NGOs' law clarifies the way China intends to manage its relations with foreign NGOs, and has attracted much criticism (Shi-Kupfer and Lang 2017). In fact, whereas charity organizations are subject, as before, to the civil affairs departments, foreign NGOs are placed under the public security organs of the State. At least, the new law has the merit of giving clear and strong signals to foreign NGOs wanting to develop their activities in China. With the old NGOs' law, foreign NGOs were in a kind of limbo, the legislation having avoided clearly distinguishing between Chinese and foreign NGOs nor did it not set up any clear norms regarding this type of NGOs. Nevertheless, today's objective is not dissimilar to that existing before the new laws were adopted. As I have analysed elsewhere (Urio and Yuan 2014) the goal was the same as it is today: to give to the state's organs sufficient latitude and means to keep foreign NGOs under control. I will explain hereafter the reasons of this different treatment between charity organizations and NGOs. For the moment, it suffices to say that China is open to both charity and NGOs provided that they contribute to the realization of the Party-State objectives, without developing activities that may be considered as contrary to the Party-State's authority and/or to its development strategy.

Let us note that the Western criticism toward the treatment of foreign NGOs by the Party-State is not fundamentally dissimilar from that addressed by multinational companies (especially in the financial sector) to what they consider to be the insufficient opening of China to the global economy. These enterprises eagerly hope, and wait, for a wider opening, that ideally should be total, in order to further developing their profits by doing business in China. But as China wishes to keep control over the development of its economy, and fears that an excessive opening may give to foreign multinational the means to limit China's autonomy, it would be rather naïve to believe that China will further open up in the near future. At least until its economy (especially in the financial sector) is strong enough to compete with foreign companies doing business on its territory.

The Party-State attitude regarding the NGOs is actually a special case within the much larger context of the management strategy of Chinese society adopted by the Party. In fact, the Party reserves the right to be able to intervene at any time in economic and social spheres; NGOs are not, and by far, the only field where the Party-State claims this right (Urio and Yuan 2014, pp. 78–199).

Despite the change, there is still continuity between the Maoist period and the era of Deng's reforms (see Sects. 2.4, 3.1 and 3.2). Sovereignty was the first main achievement of Mao, and the main objective was, as it is today, to restore China's status as a great power while leading the Chinese people towards a better quality of life; those two objectives are interdependent. The reforms are not about denying the past but about adopting another method: namely changing economic planning, and partly replacing it with the introduction of market mechanisms, under the Party's leadership. Indeed, the Party considers itself as the only authority being able to achieve those objectives while safeguarding the integrity and the stability of the country. Thus, to return to NGOs, the Party is not about to allow them too much freedom, especially if this risks putting into question its leadership or jeopardizing the structure of the political system, which safeguards its staying in power. But this is to ensure realizing the goal of prosperity and world power status.

5.3.1 The Party's Strategy for Foreign NGOs

One understands therefore, the particular attention the Party devotes, not only to Chinese NGOs, but also and especially to foreign NGOs and to foreign-funded Chinese NGOs. From a Western point of view, that may be intolerable, as long as we are committed to the principles of freedom of speech and association, and to the spread and confrontation of ideas all over the world. Even if recent events (especially

5.3 The Development of NGOs in China

the election of Donald Trump, Sect. 6.1.6) seem to have put an end, or at least a halt, to the neoliberal globalization, criticism of China's protectionist policies is continuing to orient the relation between China and the West, as the ongoing trade war between China and the US shows very well.

In our research on NGOs in China, Yuan Ying and I were able to ascertain that the foreign NGOs do not hesitate to disseminate ideas such as liberal democracy and human rights, usually by focusing on civil and political rights (Urio and Yuan 2014, pp. 78–87, 109 and 163–199). In fact, this is not something new or limited in China. China has actually experienced the interference of foreign powers since the 19th century which continued during the 20th century and until the establishment of the People's Republic of China in 1949, if not beyond. It is sufficient to mention here the almost unconditional support that the United States have always given to Taiwan, which is still today considered by the PRC as one of its provinces. It is also especially worth mentioning the policy of encirclement of China implemented by the United States since 1949 (as part of the fight against communism that led to the Korean and Vietnam wars), a policy that was confirmed and even reinforced under the presidency of Obama, who declared his decision to shift the pivot of American international policy to the Far East, affirming furthermore that the United States have a national interest in the region. This was confirmed by the Trump administration as we shall see in Sect. 6.1.6. Moreover, the role still played today by foreign NGOs in the US addiction to regime change is not going to convince China that foreign NGOs will develop on China's territory activities in tune with the Party-State's strategy.

In fact, China viewed with apprehension the multiple interferences of the West after the fall of the Soviet empire. Investors, speculators, multinationals, economic advisers, and NGOs rushed to the Eastern European countries and even Russia to exploit Russia's weakness to their own advantage (Mettan 2017). On the one hand the result was the seizure of a significant portion of the wealth of those countries, often with the support of new local oligarchs, and on the other, the accession to NATO of several Eastern European countries representing the culminating point of the strategy of encirclement of Russia. Until Putin put an end to this process. Yet, even with Putin at the head of Russia, this strategy has not stopped. In fact, China also witnessed the most recent western interventions in Eastern Europe, in Georgia and in Ukraine, where the United States organized a 'coup d'état', one out of the long list starting in 1949 and still going on in Venezuela at the time of writing. (Blum 2004, 2014 and 2018; Weisbrode 2014). Coming back to China, the 'Umbrella protest' that exploded in Hong Kong in 2014 with the active support of US politicians and pseudo NGOs, such as the National Endowment for Democracy, in fact financed by the US federal budget, not the right strategy to favour a peaceful settlement of the divergences between China and the West.

5.3.2 The Strategy of Western NGOs in the International System

In order to better understand China's attitude towards foreign NGOs, it is necessary to look at the strategy of those NGOs on the international scene. In this regard, the analysis of the role and the strategy of large American NGOs is particularly enlightening. Most of them were introduced at the beginning of the XX Century into Latin America, the Far East and Europe, and have developed considerably since the end of the Second World War in the context of the Cold War (Tournès 2010). These organizations (e.g. foundations such as Carnegie, Rockefeller, Ford, Soros, etc.) share 'a common Universalist project aiming at building a global system strongly based upon American values (…) that we can summarize in three words: peace, democracy and market economy.' (Tournès 2010, p. 5, all Tournès quotations are my translations from the French).

Firstly, the strategy of these NGOs consists 'to rely on the elites of knowledge', seen as the main driving force of change and progress, both in the United States and anywhere else in the world. This explains why 'the research and higher education institutions or think tanks are privileged vehicles,' to which we can add NGOs (Tournès 2010, p. 9). Some think tanks are also a form of NGO and this term is used very broadly in English. Regarding the research and higher education institutions, this resulted in a strong commitment to this type of institution in China since the early 20th century. For example, for Tsinghua University in Beijing, which still maintains important cooperation with American think tanks, with a formal presence in its School of Public Policy and Management: *The Bookings Institution* based in Washington, one of the most influential American think tanks. According to the Financial Times of October 9, 2016, 'it will be funded by John Thornton, former chairman of Goldman Sachs who quit the investment bank in 2003 to teach at Tsinghua University in Beijing. He has committed $2,5 million a year for the next five years. (…) Mr. Thornton said the approach of Hank Paulson, the [then] US secretary and former colleague of his at Goldman Sachs, who visited China last month [November 2006], set a benchmark for how US officials should interact with their Chinese counterparts.'

In our research on NGOs, we have also seen that those foundations often fund foreign students studying in the United States, where they are exposed to western ideas, especially in the departments of economics. On their return to their countries, they are expected to disseminate the ideas and the practices learned during their studies. Many of them held positions in universities, academic and state think tanks. For example, the Centre for Economic Research at Beijing University counted in 2005, among its 24 professors, 21 who had obtained a university degree in the United States, one in England, one in Belgium, and one in Japan (Li 2009, 2017).

Secondly, those NGOs create numerous networks in the host country: not only academic networks, but also networks of policymakers covering economic and government circles. They also build collaborations with international organizations. After 1945, those foundations 'finance projects launched by UN as well as by satellite organizations as FAO or even WHO.' (Tournès 2010, p. 17). For example, thanks to these

5.3 The Development of NGOs in China

networks the Ford Foundation was able to obtain the Chinese Academy of Social Sciences, one of the most prestigious institutions in China, as its host institution.

Thirdly, from those networks, the foundations have been working on 'promoting the creation of a set of operation bases in key locations of the planet and on placing themselves in a central position so as to act as coordinators.' (Tournès 2010, p. 10).[12] The liaison with the American government is established through recruiting personalities who held or had held government posts at the highest level. Indeed, it is recognized that those foundations enjoy a certain degree of autonomy from the government of the United States. The foundation of former President Carter is a good example, which monitors with obvious sympathy the progress achieved by China regarding open elections at local level (The website of the Carter Foundation: http://www.cartercenter.org/). Nevertheless, there is a set of values that those foundations share with the American government, even though they do not manifest an attitude as critical, and often quite aggressive, towards China.

Our research led us to conclude that the US government and the US foundations are working on transforming China into a liberal democratic country integrated in the global capitalist system. When we know, as mentioned above, that one of the key aspects of globalization is the deregulation of financial of markets, we can easily understand the concern that this strategy may raise in the eyes of Chinese authorities. That this has been the goal of US foreign policy is attested by numerous statements by politicians, journalists and think tanks researches as well as the visit of President Richard Nixon to China in February 1972. It is only recently that influential American analysts of China policy, have acknowledged that this policy has been a failure (Chap. 2, pp. 31–32; 6, pp. 216 and 301–303). In short China has not behaved as the US wanted it to behave, i.e. to be integrated into the world America made. Indeed, China's integration within this world would open China to foreign investments and to foreign bank activities on Chinese territory, which is not necessarily in line with the control that the CCP wants to keep over the economic development.[13] Moreover, the expertise that foreign NGOs may provide to the Party-State is not necessarily what China needs for its social policies. China has tried for more than a decade to establish a set of social policies to address the negative consequences of economic development based on the recourse to market mechanisms (Chap. 4). When one knows that the existing social policies in the United States are not particularly generous, and that American and Europeans have implemented since the 1980s neoliberal policies that led (1) to the crisis of 2008, (2) to the explosion in inequalities, (3) to the austerity policies, which reduced among other things, the funding for social policies, and (4) to the implementation of the same policies which have precipitated the crisis with the aim of resolving it, one cannot see how the Western countries could set themselves as an example to China in its attempt to create a prosperous and harmonious society.

---

[12]The quotation attributes this role to the Rockefeller Foundation; but it is clear that it has been mentioned as an example; this role can be attributed to other American foundations of the same type.

[13]The deregulation of financial markets is considered by a number of serious economists as one of the main causes of the crisis of 2008, as well as the Asian crisis of 1997. See for example Joseph E. Stiglitz's works in the References below.

Of course, in China there are not only large foundations as mentioned above. Other NGOs, of more modest size, do not necessarily have the same strategies and work honestly and selflessly to help China to tackle its concrete problems without pushing it to adopt the western way of economic, political and social organization (Urio and Yuan 2014, Chap. 7). Thus, I would like to propose the following reasonable conclusion: if the ideas and the practices spread by foreign NGOs contribute to provide the Chinese population with the social services that the Party-State is not able to or does not want to provide, without disseminating ideas that are contrary to the political line of the Party, and if the foreign funding of Chinese NGOs contributes to improve their effectiveness and efficiency in politically less sensitive areas, Chinese government will certainly have no objection to formulate. After all, China is a sovereign country. We Westerners are also very sensitive to threats to our sovereignty. Why should it be any different for China?

5.3.3 Foreign NGOs and the New Generation of Mega Free Trade and Investment Treaties

To complete the analysis of the role of foreign NGOs in China we have to transpose it to the international level. Despite the warnings against the excesses of neoliberalism and of free-trade fundamentalism that became frequent after the 2008 crisis (Rachman 2008; Stiglitz 2013) two international treaties, negotiated with the utmost secrecy, deserve our attention and certainly also that of Chinese authorities: The Transatlantic Partnership Agreement (TTIP) and the Trans-Pacific Partnership Agreement (TPP), which implements the same type of provisions in Asia (Wallach 2013, pp. 4–5; Kelsey 2011; Lafer 2014; Porcher and Farah 2014; Vaudano 2015). Even if President Trump has withdrawn from the TPP and has put a halt to the negotiations for the TTIP, it is not impossible that he, or his successors may review his decisions. It is therefore important to understand the meaning of these treaties, and I will develop this understanding in more detail in Sect. 6.1.5. Here it is sufficient to remind that these treaties would allow the multinationals to sue the states before a private court (with no possibility of appeal) if their public policies had to reduce not only the profits achieved, but also the expected profits. So, these treaties represent a threat to states' sovereignty, as well as to the policies that those states have defined autonomously in sensitive areas such as health, environment, labour and finance. Furthermore, from the geopolitical perspective, these treaties are the spearhead of the United States' strategy for containing and isolating China and Russia. Moreover, these treaties may be supported by foreign NGOs, especially those that favour the globalization of the world economy and the consequent loss of state's power and independence. So, foreign NGOs working in China are to be evaluated also for their impact on the policies that China has developed (both nationally and internationally) aimed at safeguarding its independence, that converged and merged in 2013 into its grand strategy, the Belt and Road Initiative (BRI), to be dealt with in Sect. 6.2.

5.4 The Import of Western Technologies

Since the beginning of reforms, China has imported all kinds of technologies as well as managerial tools from the West. It is my opinion that most of the time China has based its choice on the famous Deng Xiaoping motto about the white and the black cat. As the Western (especially the American) cat had caught more mice than the planned economy, Deng started to introduce market mechanisms within the Chinese economy. The reason, as I explained on many occasions, was that a strong economy would be an essential means for China's recovering world power status. With the same purpose in mind, China has imported some Western technologies, especially from America, that unfortunately may constitute a danger to China's strength, as they may damage health and environment, two important dimensions that contribute to a country' power: namely shale gas fracking, GMO (Genetically Modified Organisms, i.e. seeds, e.g. rice, soya, corn), pesticides (whose sale is most of the time linked to the sale of GMO), western fast food, western medical drugs, western vaccines, and nuclear power. Many of these technologies have given way in the West to controversies amongst experts, but today there is sufficient evidence for encouraging public authorities to ban some of these technologies, or at least to implement the principle of precaution and decide for moratoriums, waiting for more conclusive scientific evidence. On the contrary, it seems that China has imported and implemented them without hesitation.

The strongest case against several of these technologies has been made in a controversial book published in 2014, significantly entitled '*Target China. How Washington and Wall Street Plan to Cage the Asian Dragon*' (Engdahl 2014). Space does not allow me to provide an in-depth account of the scientific evidence available today. Nevertheless, I will briefly discuss the problems related to shale gas fracking, one of the most controversial technologies implemented on a large scale both in the US and in China.

It is undisputable that the decision taken by the US in favour of shale fracking, was to make the US not only self-sufficient, but also an exporter, thus adding this resource to the already vast repertoire of US power resources (see Sect. 6.1).[14] In fact, the US, already under the Obama administration very strongly 'suggested' to European allies to buy shale gas from the US instead of importing gas and oil from Russia. Recently, the US has threatened Germany and its companies with heavy sanctions, should it not discontinue the building of the *North Stream 2* pipeline between Russia and Germany. Now, shale gas in the US has a number of problems.[15] Already in 2010, the US think tank 'Food & Water Watch' has pointed to the dangers of fracking, as it can deplete local water, contaminate local water, cause house and well explosions, produce toxic wastewater, have wide-ranging health and environmental effects, and cause not only water but also air pollution. It recommended a moratorium on issuing new permits for hydraulic fracturing until the results of research on the effects of fracking on water

---

[14]In this very short analysis of fracking, I will not make a distinction between oil and gas fracking.

[15]For a brief analysis of the pros and cons of fracking see the Yale Climate Connection's article: 'Pros and cons of fracking: 5 key issues', 27 May 2015, https://www.yaleclimateconnections.org/. Let me remind one that in Europe many protest movements are opposed to oil fracking.

quality, human health and environment would be available (Food&Water Watch 2010). Two years later, Marianna Lavelle pointed to links between fracking and earthquakes (Lavelle 2012). Moreover, in 2015 the Bloomberg School of Public Health of Johns Hopkins University referred to a research suggesting that 'expectant mothers who live near active natural gas wells operated by the fracking industry in Pennsylvania are at an increased risk of giving birth prematurely and for having high-risk pregnancies' (Johns Hopkins Bloomberg School of Public Health 2015).

In spite of these warnings, the US fracking industry developed at an exponential rate, with heavy Wall Street financing (Hauter 2016, pp. 219–225). Already in 2017, but more particularly during 2018, several reliable sources pointed out the serious problems this industry was facing, not only for its impact on the environment, but also because of its flawed business plan. Let me just quote the Wall Street Journal (7 July 2017), and Forbes (26 January 2018). Moreover, the Financial Times (13 December 2018) quite rightly pointed out the quality problem of shale gas: 'Crude extracted from shale rock is generally far lighter than conventional oil and is not the type wanted by the world's oil refiners as demand for heavier products such as diesel increases and demand for petrol decreases.' Even more critical articles can be found in the DESMOG's website, especially the 4 May 2018 article significantly entitled 'How Wall Street Enabled the Fracking "Revolution" That's Losing Billions' (Mikulka 2018).[16] The article makes a comparison with the investors' behaviour that led to the 2008 crisis: making bets without caring about the final outcome, waiting for the government to bail out the losses. This may be true, if, as I said before, the US strategic goal is to become number one in shale gas export, thereby maintaining the US position in the international oil industry.

Coming now to China, it is in 2009 that Presidents Obama and Hu Jintao agreed to develop China's shale gas resources. A few years before, the US Energy Information Administration (EIA) estimated that China had the largest reserve of shale gas in the world. In 2015 it estimated the shale gas reserve to be 1,115 trillion cubic feet. No wonder that China, the largest importer of oil and gas, would envisage to develop this industry. But China will have to face the same problems as the Western countries, i.e. soil and water pollution and hence health problems. Moreover, China has an additional problem: its gas reserves are deeply located inside the earth, up to 3,5 km deep, in areas prone to earthquakes because of the proximity with the geological fault lines between Tibet and the Sichuan basin, where the technology developed in the US cannot work. For some observers (such as Business Insider) this is the main reason why, in addition to lack of competition between companies, China will not have a shale boom, similar to the US, (Slav 2018). Nevertheless, the author recognizes that 'Beijing has been proving repeatedly that its brands of planned economy surprisingly works for the most part. Where it doesn't seem to work is in making realistic plans about supply and demand in a way that would ensure there is enough of the former to satisfy the latter.' Moreover, China has cut tax of shale gas by 30% and is stimulating production with subsidies. Chen Aizhu, reporting for Reuters, recognizes that shale output is rising, in spite of technical difficulties, that forced Western companies such

---

[16]Desmog, founded in January 2006, is a blog that focuses on topics related to global warming.

as Exxon Mobile, Royal Dutch Shell, Total, ConocoPhillips, and Chevron to abandon 'China's shale scene after disappointing initial results'. (Aizhu 2018).

And here comes what might be China's answer to the difficulty of extracting gas at a depth of 3.5 km. Chen Stephen, writing for *The South China Morning Post* (SCMP) reports that in order to have access to this gas reserve, equal to 80% of the total, China has to develop a new technology, as the classical US hydraulic fraction does not work at this depth. The idea developed by a professor at Xian Jiaotong University is to use a powerful electric current to generate concentrated, precisely controlled shock waves to achieve the same result, in other words 'to use a nuclear bomb detonator to release shale gas'. As this is forecasted to be implemented in the 'earthquake-prone Sichuan', SCMP asks the big question: crazy or brilliant? (Chen 2019). Leaving the answer to the Chinese experts, it is nevertheless important to mention again that the largest part of China's shale gas reserves is located in Sichuan, probably the province most susceptible to earthquakes. If we take into consideration the other negative consequences of fracking, the next question is to find out what the reactions of the Chinese people are, above all of those living in the local communities where fracking has been operated for some time. This is even more important for comparing China with Western countries, where numerous protest movements against fracking are operating today, both in the US and the EU. Unfortunately, there is still today very limited serious research on this important domain.[17] Recently the *SCMP* has published a series of articles on fracking in China, especially an article entitled 'Chinese protesters blame fracking for earthquakes that killed two people in Sichuan.' (Chen 2019). The author reports that protesters targeted local government headquarters in southwest China after earthquakes, blamed on shale gas fracking, killed two people and injured 12 others, and that three earthquakes struck Sichuan's Rong county ranging from 4.3 to 4.9 magnitude, affecting more than 13,000 residents and damaging more than 10,000 buildings. It would be surprising if more in-depth research would not find other protest movements in those areas.

Finally, one of the major problems with the development of fracking is that it is diverting investments from renewable energy technologies to fossil resources, which goes contrary to the stated governmental policy to give priority to clean energy resources.

5.5   The Import of Management Tools: The Case of Public Private Partnerships

Since the beginning of reforms China has introduced some market mechanisms, thereby privatizing some sectors of its economy that developed alongside the SOEs. It is therefore not surprising that the idea of establishing some forms of cooperation between the public and the private sectors appeared already at the end of the 1980s (Yang and Zhang 2010). Nevertheless, it is only at the beginning of the Xi Jinping era

---

[17]Nevertheless, see the research by Sher and Wu (2018).

that PPPs, a clear import from the West, became an important tool for the provision of public services, in spite of the serious caveats that have emerged in the literature over the last 20 years or so. It is interesting to note that this decision was taken at a time when international organisations, favouring the private sector over the public sector, such as the World Bank and the United Nations Economic Commission for Europe, developed a world-wide strategy for sustaining the adoption of PPPs in practically all domains and in all parts of the world.[18] It remains that China's decision in favour of PPPs was taken to curb the debt that provinces and municipalities had accumulated during the development phase dominated by public investments. PPPs was then seen as a means to resort to private investments for the provision of public services, thus alleviating the burden from the public local authorities.

At first sight, associating private and public actors seems to be a good idea. But the Western experience shows that PPPs are not necessarily a good option, or more exactly, they may deliver positive outcomes only under certain conditions and in certain sectors. Moreover, experience shows that it is not easy to transpose institutional arrangements such as PPPs from the Western political environment, where they took form, to a country with very different polity, economy and cultural values. It is therefore necessary to evaluate under what conditions PPPs may produce the expected positive outcomes (Urio 2010c).

5.5.1 Definition of PPPs

Let us start with the definition of PPPs. For the sake of simplicity, let me take the general definition suggested by the Fiscal Affairs Department of the IMF: 'Public-Private partnerships (PPPs) refer to arrangements where private sector supplies infrastructure assets and services that traditionally have been provided by the government' (IMF 2004, pp. 4 and 7). The IMF further develops this definition by considering that 'a typical PPP takes the form of a design-build-finance-operate (DBFO) scheme. Under such scheme, the government specifies the services it wants the private sector to deliver, and then the private partner designs and builds a dedicated asset for that purpose, finances its construction, and subsequently operates the asset and provides the services deriving from it. This contrasts with traditional public investment where the government contracts with the private sector to build an asset, but the design and financing is provided by the government. In most cases, the government then operates the asset once it is built. The difference between the two approaches reflects a belief that giving the private sector combined responsibilities for designing, building, financing, and operating an asset is a source of the increased efficiency in service delivery that justifies PPPs'.

---

[18] World Bank: https://ppiaf.org/about-us; UNECE: https://www.unece.org/unece/search?q=PPP&op=Search; for a critical approach: Public Services International Research Unit—SPIRU: http://www.psiru.org/.

5.5 The Import of Management Tools: The Case of Public Private Partnerships 179

I propose the following 'reasonable' definition: under the term PPP I will take into consideration all arrangements between the public and the private sectors (both domestic and foreign) based upon a contract that may improve all or some of the four basic operations: design, construction, finance and operation of public services, no matter the mix of them. I further consider PPP for both physical capital infrastructure (like power plants, roads, etc.) and human capital infrastructure (like health and education); and I will include within the private sector both private-for-profit and private-not-for-profit organisations, including all kinds of stakeholders (including community organisations). The inclusion of non-for-profit organizations is today generally accepted, as they may contribute to the realization of public goals (Skelcher 2005, p. 347). I will further consider that PPPs may have an impact on 3 fundamental values, that are at stake in the public domain, and that the contribution of PPPs should be evaluated against these values: efficiency, equity, and sustainability (i.e. sustainable development), whose definitions are well understood in the literature.

5.5.2 PPPs, Contracting Out, New Public Management, and the 'Washington Consensus'

Two remarks: first, PPP appears to be another expression for referring to the policy of contracting out State activities. In this sense PPP corresponds to one of the major dimensions of New Public Management (NPM). Seen in historical perspective, contracting out is not, and by far, something new. Examples of contracting out can be found in the XVIII and XIX Century. 'Contracting was commonplace (…) in eighteenth- and nineteenth-century England. Services provided by the private sector under contract included prison management, road maintenance, the collection of public revenue, and refuse collection. (…) Similarly, in nineteenth-century France, the rights to build and operate railways and water storage and distribution facilities were auctioned by competitive tender.' (Domberger 1998, pp. 8–9). It is nevertheless true that, following the huge development of State intervention in economy and society (approximately between the end of the XIX century and the late 1970s) contracting out has become, since the beginning of the 1980s, part of the vast NPM programme and of its major explicit goal, i.e. the reform of the State and the improvement of its efficiency.

In the first phase of NPM priority has been put on privatising State's activities; but since the second part of the '90s contracting out has become the preferred device, either because in some countries there was not much left to be privatised or because privatisations had lost their initial appeal to decision-makers. The Implementation of NPM would in turn improve the efficiency of market economy, thanks to the elimination of part of the State regulations, the privatisation or the contracting out of State activities, the decrease of the level of taxation, and the adoption by the State bureaucracy of the managerial tools of the private sector (Urio 1999, 2012). Although NPM is generally meant for reforming the States in developed countries, there is no doubt that it is part of a broader policy programme in which the so-called 'Washington Consensus' constitutes its counterpart for developing and in transition countries (Williamson 1990, 1993; Stiglitz 2008b; Hayami 2003). Or, if you prefer, the general set of coherent policies aimed at improving the efficiency of the State has two ideological, theoretical and methodological similar components: one addressed to developed States (the NPM) and another meant for developing and in-transition countries (the 'Washington Consensus'). In this framework the State is conceived as an institution whose main goal is to serve the market (World Bank 1997, Vol. 1, p. ix). According to this view, and in the perspective of NPM and the 'Washington Consensus', economic development will necessarily improve the well-being of the populations concerned, eliminate extreme poverty, substantially reduce poverty, and drive the countries towards liberal democracy.

Second, and more interesting, I believe that contracting out, and the larger set of reforms under NPM, should be evaluated taking into consideration not only their advantages in strict economic terms (like saving on the public budget, sustaining the development of the market economy, increasing the GDP, etc.) but also in terms of its impact on society as a whole, and on the physical environment. In other words, any institutional arrangement (including PPPs) aimed at improving the provision of resources and services to the population concerned should be evaluated taking into consideration three sets of interrelated phenomena linked to 3 basic structures: economy, society and environment (Bürgenmeier 2005; OECD 1996; World Bank 2003, 2005a). Moreover, I believe that PPPs should also be part of a general development strategy defined by the countries that benefit from PPPs. I will develop this last point below.

The three structures (Economy, Society, and Environment) are based upon some fundamental values that are not necessarily in harmony. Both theory and experience show that the underlying values cannot be maximized simultaneously (Stone 1997). Therefore, it is plausible that the implementation of PPPs will necessitate several trade-offs between the values of these three structures: efficiency, equity, and sustainability. In doing this, one may encounter some difficulties.

The experience of NPM in developed countries is quite interesting in this respect. NPM proposals have been based upon the empirical evidence that Western States who had intervened 'too much' in economy and society, have considerably reduced the fundamental value of a market economy, i.e. efficiency both for market and State. The general pattern is the following: generous welfare policies, too numerous regulations of all kinds (including those protecting the environment), relatively non-efficient heavy state investments in hard and soft infrastructure, and consequently heavy taxation, and high compulsory contributions by the private sector to the safety nets set up by governments.

In the NPM era that started around 1980, the implementation of the NPM policies, while it has improved efficiency of both enterprises and governments, has considerably reduced equity, i.e. a "fair" distribution of wealth. Not only income distribution has become more unequal, but, at its lower end the number of poor people has increased, not to mention the appearance of the social category of the working poor. Needless to mention the negative consequences of the development of the Western economy on the environment that nowadays is being addressed with considerable difficulty by the international community, especially after the withdrawal of the US from the Paris 2016 agreement decided by President Trump. Hence, the development of the concept of sustainable development, i.e. a strategy of economic development that preserves nature (especially non-renewable resources) and safeguard the interests of future generations. Another interesting consequence is that this situation has created a significant level of social unrest, or at least of opposition to the official policies of some of the Governments concerned, both nationally and internationally. It is enough to mention the negative 2005 vote of the French and Dutch citizens on the European Constitution (clearly of neoliberal inspiration), the opposition to the WTO negotiations, the more recent anti-establishment protest movements in the US and the EU, as well as the protest movements against the two mega-treaties (TTIP and TPP) which, should they have been approved, may have constituted the apotheosis of New Public Management and its underlying neo-liberal ideology,

In this respect China presents an interesting experience, that points in the same direction (Chap. 3 and 4). Whereas during the Mao era, the planned economy maximised equity (the Gini index being just above. 22) efficiency was very low, with huge numbers of poor people. The development strategy that followed that era (based upon the introduction of some market mechanisms) eliminated almost completely extreme poverty, produced spectacular results with an astonishing increase of GDP for 3 consecutive decades, but resulted in a huge increase of inequality (Gini higher than. 45), in new forms of poverty (as the traditional forms of solidarity were not replaced in time by a modern safety net) and in considerable damages to the environment and to the health of millions of people.

The Western and the Chinese experiences briefly presented above confirm that society, economy and environment are closely interrelated, and that the management of the problems related to them necessitates the implementation of policies that will have to manage a complex set of interrelated trade-offs between efficiency, equity, and environmental protection. An important effort of coordination will be necessary and, as resources are limited even in the event of private (foreign and domestic) investment, priorities will have to be established. It is my opinion that coordination will have to take place within the framework of a development strategy, in which the introduction of PPPs should take place, and within which PPPs should be evaluated. Of course, the relevant decisions will have a heavy political (and even ideological) character, in particular the policies towards capital liberalisation, property rights, and privatisation.

5.5.3 Conditions for the Viability of PPPs

My approach to the viability of PPPs is based upon two fundamental hypotheses. The first one is that PPPs may contribute to the economic development of the countries concerned by attracting actors from the private sector to finance, or at least to provide their expertise to some activities considered to be of 'public' importance. Second, if the partnership between public and private actors is to deliver interesting results, PPPs should maximize the respective strengths of public and private sectors and minimize their weaknesses. In the literature on PPPs it is further said that an effective and efficient PPP should be based upon some common goals, and that the private partner should acquire a sense of 'social responsibility' and the public actor a sense of 'managerial culture'. This sounds quite reasonable, and I agree that these questions are at the heart of the design of PPPs. The problem is that the two partners (especially if the partner on the private side is a private company) have quite specific and different operating strategies, philosophies, and institutional environments that monitor and control their activities, and give them the necessary legitimacy: the public actor will be more oriented by equity and effectiveness, the private partner by efficiency (Wang 2000, pp. 5–6).

Very often the rationale in favour of PPPs is based upon postulates, i.e. on self-evident truths not to be submitted to empirical tests. But this is not a scientific approach, that should discover the conditions under which PPPs can deliver results that enhance at least one of the 3 values (equity, efficiency, sustainability), without at the same time worsening the 2 others.

Given the difficulties mentioned above, a more realistic approach could be that an efficient and equitable PPP, favourable to sustainable economic development, should be based not on common goals, but on fundamentally non-contradicting interests, bounded in a legal document that should contain the following necessary and minimal elements: specify the characteristics of the service or goods to be delivered in terms of quantity and quality, and the time framework; clearly identify the beneficiaries, and the condition of access; define the organisational setting, including the respective responsibilities and roles of both partners (financial, decisional), and the procedures for settling disputes and for assuring transparency, monitoring, and accountability for both partners; and, last but not least, specify who will pay.

This last point is particularly important as it is at the heart of the choice in favour or against PPPs. Those who favour PPP instead of State provision of public services frequently take advantage of the difficulty the State is experiencing to lift additional money for financing public services. This may be the case when there is a political will against an increase of taxation and/or when the State is experiencing the persistence of an increasing annual deficit and consequently a considerable increase of public debt. The argument goes on to say that the private sector is ready 'to put in the money needed' and moreover it has better technical competencies and managerial skills than the State. The expected outcome is better service at lower cost. This correspond to a well-known slogan of NPM: 'value for money'.

Nevertheless, this option in favour of PPPs is by no means evident, nor supported by clear theoretical analysis and empirical evidence. In fact, when it is a question of building efficient and universal public service, the fundamental question is that there is no free lunch. The money must come from somewhere, and the private sector 'does not put the money on the table'; it simply invests and expects to count upon conditions that will safeguard the capital invested, and the realization of a profit on top of that. So, in principle, either the State (i.e. the taxpayers) pay for the service, or the citizens pay (or, better the customers, according to a well-established NPM

5.5 The Import of Management Tools: The Case of Public Private Partnerships 183

terminology). Of course, one can envisage a mix of financing, part from the State (the taxpayers) and part from the users (citizens or customers). But one cannot avoid giving a clear answer to this question, that will inevitably pose the question of finding a trade-off between economic efficiency and social equity. The importance of this point will become more evident when I shall deal hereafter with the question of the soft infrastructures.

The difficulties I have just mentioned have already been recognized by the academic literature (Rosenau 2000; Zammit 2003), and even the IMF recognizes that 'Much of the case for PPPs rests on the relative efficiency of the private sector. While there is an extensive literature on this subject, the theory is ambiguous, and the empirical evidence is mixed.' It further recognizes that 'the case for PPPs is weaker where the government cannot write complete contracts because service quality is non-contractible' (IMF 2004, pp. 11 and 14). Moreover, independently of the cases in which service quality is non-contractible, it has been widely recognized that PPP contracts are by nature incomplete (Williamson 1985; Hart 2003). So, the most important task when deciding in favour of PPPs is to define what conditions the implementation of PPPs must comply with, in order to sustain economic development, equitable access to the services provided, and the preservation of the environment.

5.5.4 The Distinction Between Hard and Soft Infrastructure

When evaluating the possibility to set up PPPs, it is important to bear in mind the distinction between soft and hard infrastructure, the two vast domains where PPPs may provide an alternative to services entirely produced and distributed by the State. Of course, the distinction between hard and soft infrastructures is not absolutely clear-cut, as some 'soft infrastructures' need some 'hard structures' to function, like hospitals, schools, etc.[19] But the distinction is better than that between core and non-core services, as it is based upon the target of the infrastructure, i.e. the distinction between human capital and physical capital. Clearly hospitals, schools, etc. are directed towards the improvement of the human capital. Roads and railways, also, of course, but not so directly. It is access to human capital infrastructure (mainly education and health) that allows people to have access to the labour market, and through this to hard infrastructures; and in case they are excluded from the labour market, 'safety nets', as a special case of soft infrastructure, can provide these people with the resources necessary to buy essential goods and services.

'Hard infrastructure' refers to physical resources and services (like roads, railways, energy, housing, etc.). Although hard infrastructure is not aimed at directly developing the human capital, it contributes nevertheless in a decisive manner to its improvement, provided people are in a position to have an equitable access to

---

[19]The World Bank has recognised the importance of soft infrastructure in its 2004 World Development Report, significantly entitled *Making Services Work for Poor People*, (World Bank 2003).

184   5 The Opening of China's Economy and the Changing Role of the Party-State

these resources. In order to enable people to take advantage of physical infrastructure it is necessary to develop the second type of infrastructure: "soft infrastructure", whose aim is not to develop anything physical, but to directly improve human capital, namely attitudes, knowledge, skills, as well as physical and mental health. It is the domain of education, science and technology, health, and more generally, the development of safety nets. Safety nets are necessary for helping people experiencing financial difficulties, that would otherwise exclude them from the social and economic systems: during childhood, when living in poor families, for acquiring the knowledge and skills necessary for entering the economic system; during adult active life for helping them to recover from illness or unemployment and for re-entering the economy; when retired, for helping them to have a decent life when not working any more in the economy. If people are excluded from the market for one reason or another, or if work does not provide sufficient financial means (as is the case for the working poor) some sort of redistributive policies will be necessary to enable these people to have access to resources, either by subsidizing the production of these services, or by directly subsidizing the people concerned. In this perspective, safety nets are to be considered as soft infrastructure insofar as they are in fact a substitute for human capacities allowing people excluded from the market (because of illness, accidents, unemployment, or old age) to have access to resources, thanks to the insurances covering these situations. The policies of water provision, housing, education, health and safety nets are the domains that should be examined with great care from the point of view of equitable access, as they are vital to the individual, bearing in mind the possibility (even if highly debatable) of making these services accessible to people at a different price, depending on their financial situation.

5.5.5 PPPs and the Development Strategy

The considerations developed so far are clearly in favour of a comprehensive approach in which PPPs is part of the strategy governments have to set up for managing the development process.[20] The importance of the role of the State for the development of in-transition countries has been recognised (Stiglitz and Charlton 2005; Chang 2003). The main purpose of the government's strategy is twofold. First, it must coordinate, both synchronically and diachronically, the various policies driving the development process. Second, as resources are limited, it also must set up priorities. We certainly cannot ignore that the implementation of PPPs may not deliver the expected results, or may even produce an inefficient allocation of resources, unless they are part of a comprehensive strategy of development, integrating investment in hard and soft infrastructures.

The final, strategic decision in favour of PPPs needs to be preceded by 4 prior decisions: the 'time decision', the 'efficiency decision', the 'management decision', and the 'who will pay? decision'. The 'time decision' refers to the fact that providing

---

[20]For a general discussion of the development strategy, see above Sects. 1.7 and 3.2.

5.5 The Import of Management Tools: The Case of Public Private Partnerships

a new service (or improving an existing one) will depend on the urgency of the matter. If there is no urgency, the government could first implement a set of policies aimed at improving the economy, which will eventually enhance its fiscal capacity. It will then be able to finance the provision of the service concerned by the State. The urgency will depend on several domestic factors, such as the demand from the citizens. But one external factor will play a determinant role, and this is globalization. Not the globalization of the economy, but globalization of information, and above all the access, even for population living in remote areas, to the image, through TV programmes and commercial advertisements, of the living conditions of developed countries, or the more developed regions of a country, as it is today the case for China. This is very likely the most powerful factor determining the urgency of financing services permitting the population to adopt the way of life of developed countries, and, if public money is not sufficient, to resort to private money, either domestic or foreign, invested either in fully foreign-funded companies or in PPPs. Nevertheless, it should be noted that the choice in favour of PPPs based upon the urgency, is valid only if the government suffers a lack of liquidities. If this is not the case, the government should turn to the other prior decisions, and first of all to efficiency.

The second prior decision is the efficiency one. If the government comes to the conclusion that private provision of services is more efficient than State provision (and/or if quality is better) then it would favour private investment.[21] But we have already seen that the evidence in favour of private efficiency is mixed. Moreover, financing through the market is generally costlier than through government borrowing, and management of important infrastructures like hospitals, prisons, and schools by private bodies may be more expensive (Pollock 2004; Flynn 2007). Consequently, decision in favour of private provision might be heavily oriented by ideological considerations.

Here, we find one of the fundamental difficulties of PPPs. One of the advantages put forward by promoters of PPPs is that by introducing private capital, we simultaneously introduce competition, and this will lead the bidders to reduce cost as much as possible, to the advantage of the public partners and the people it is supposed to serve. Tow difficulties. First, there is competition only in the bidding phase; once the contract has been signed, competition disappears, and as many contracts are signed for long periods of time (generally around 25–30 years) it means that the incentive that operates when enterprises are in a real market situation, will lose its appeal. Moreover, during the bidding phase some bidders may underestimate the cost in order to win the contract, especially if the orientation of the public partner is toward reducing the cost thus giving the contract to the bidder that presents the lowest cost. Generally, this is justified by saying that the public authority has also taken into consideration the quality of the service. But this is clearly a bet that should come true during the whole duration of the contract. Second, some bidders (especially multinational working all over the world), may be willing to artificially lower the cost (i.e. not covering the actual cost) to obtain the contract, knowing that thereby they

---

[21] The case in favour of PPP has been made by international organizations. I have discussed the OECD case in favour of PPPs in Urio (2010b), pp. 337–347.

186   5 The Opening of China's Economy and the Changing Role of the Party-State

will be affirming their competence and get more contracts in the future. So, from the point of view of economic efficiency, the contract may be based more on ideological considerations than on a scientific evaluation of the bidders' capacity to deliver the service for the quality and cost agreed (OECD 2008; Conclusion in Urio 2010b).

The 'management decision' concerns some of the advantages of public management put forward by proponents of PPPs, deriving from sharing tasks between the public and private partners. In particular, the government must evaluate what the benefits are of transferring to the private partner the construction and the management of the infrastructure or service concerned, as well as the advantages of postponing the payment to the future. Finally, the last question is: do PPPs permit to transfer the risk to the private partner, or at least to sharing it? These decisions are not simple as the evidence in favour of PPP is at best ambiguous (Flynn 2007, pp. 252–269).[22]

Dealing with the fourth prior decision, the government must choose who in the end will pay the service provided. The previous discussion suggests a truism that is perhaps worth mentioning again: money must come from somewhere. If private companies are the only investor in a PPP, money will have to come from consumers, and as this will have to cover production costs (including profits) this may pose some problems for equitable access. If on the contrary, the money comes from the government this may pose problems of high taxation (that may be supported by companies and/or tax-payers), increasing public debt, reduced efficiency and quality of the service provided.

The final decision in favour of private provision will be based upon a delicate balance between the evaluations of the dilemmas posed by the 4 prior decisions, to which the government will certainly add some strategic considerations, which may exclude from private provision sectors considered of political and economic strategic importance in particular those analyzed in Sect. 6.2.4.2. These considerations will certainly orient the government decisions in this domain. In the case where the government decides in favour of private capital, it must be able to attract private investors. In this context, a reasonable hypothesis is that investors, both local and foreigners, will be willing to enter PPPs in sectors where return is attractive and safe. It is not certain that all the countries concerned are able to provide a sufficient level of security. Nevertheless, the international organizations supporting PPPs tends to envisage PPPs in practically all domains of State activity. For example, this was the case of the international Conference organized in Israel at the beginning of June 2007 by the UN Economic Commission for Europe (UNECE). The objectives and scope of the conference were defined as follows: 'PPPs refer to contractual agreement formed between a public-sector agency and a private sector entity that allows for greater private sector participation in the delivery of public services. PPPs are becoming increasingly commonplace for building new and upgrading existing facilities such as schools, hospitals, roads, waste and water treatment, as well as power plants and

---

[22] For the argument in favour of postponing payment, Flynn says that: 'The advantage to the Treasury was that they would not have to borrow the money and that the capital spending would not appear as public expenditure, thus keeping borrowing and spending low in the year in which the deal was done. (…) What PFI does to the public accounts is to accumulate future liabilities: once long-term contracts are entered, there is no cheap way of exiting.' (Flynn 2007, pp. 252 and 254).

5.5 The Import of Management Tools: The Case of Public Private Partnerships 187

telecommunication networks. They can be a useful tool as part of regional policy, for urban regeneration and sustainable development. (…) … the conference provides an opportunity for government and business to meet and discuss project ideas in sectors as: transport, water, energy, and social services.' (UNECE 2007, p. 2). Practically all the public services are targeted, with the possible exceptions of police and army. The parenthood with one of the more radical versions of NPM is therefore evident (Friedman 1962, Chap. 1).[23]

In conclusion, the important question to be answered is the following: is the choice in favour of PPP based upon scientific evidence or is it oriented *mainly* by ideological considerations? Even the very pro-business *Financial Times* has recognised the importance of avoiding ideological biases (Cohen 2017). The analysis of the pros and cons for PPPs I presented above has been the basis for my conferences I have given in China between 2005 and 2016, e.g. at Tsinghua and Renmin Universities, the China Executive Leadership Academy Pudong (CELAB), and the National Development and Reform Commission.

5.5.6   The Special Case of PPPs in China

How does the Party deal with PPPs today? There are today so many researches on the implementation of PPPs in China, that it is not possible to summarize them within this chapter. Nevertheless, I will briefly provide some comments based upon articles by the *Financial Times* and information obtained in China.[24] China has introduced a phenomenal number of PPPs. According to the database developed by the Ministry of Finance within its PPP Center, PPPs have been developing rapidly in China, and have been favoured by many local governments: there has been a total of about 14,000 PPP projects with an investment of almost 20 trillion Yuan. Recently the government has limited the use of PPPs by local government, because this has in many cases increased the local debt, contrary to the initial argument in favour of PPPs. Nevertheless, in 2018 by the third quarter, there were more than 4000 projects financed by approximately 6.3 trillion Yuan. PPPs projects for municipal authorities, transportation, and environmental protection, account for 62.3% of the total number recorded by the PPP Centre of the Ministry of Finance, corresponding to 72.2% of the total investment. Municipal projects include in particular sewage, water supply, garbage disposal, and municipal roads.

At the beginning of 2018, the Ministry of Finance removed from the database of its PPP centre about 7,000 projects, corresponding to a total investment of about 10 trillion yuan. Official data shows that there is a considerable number of PPPs

---

[23]The 'PPP knowledge Lab' of Asian Development Bank lists under 'Sectors': health, education, power, water and sanitation, and agrobusiness (https://library.pppknowledgelab.org/documents/5706?ref_site=kl).

[24]I should like to thank Ms Wang Yingying of Tsinghua University for providing data and information about the implementation of PPPs in China.

projects where the 'private partner' is, in fact, a state enterprise owned by local authorities. According to the statistical information from the PPP Centre of the Ministry of Finance, SOEs constitute about 35.3% of the total number of PPPs, which accounts for 34.0% of the total investment. Indeed, several other problems have been acknowledged by both international and official Chinese sources. Interestingly, the poor quality of some projects has been recognized, resulting from the fast development of PPPs, from the non-standardized operation of the projects, from the sharp increase of hidden debt, and the insufficient participation of private enterprises. The 'very pro-business' *Financial Times*, citing official Chinese sources, comments that in China public-private partnerships for infrastructure investment have become a vehicle for 'disguised borrowing' by local governments, with the consequence of increasing local public debt. Local officials have continued to exploit loopholes in local borrowing rules to keep infrastructure projects cashed up, in spite of the government measures taken to limit this behaviour' (Wildau 2017).

The reason for this problem is to be found in the fact that investment in infrastructure (as I pointed out above) is often unattractive to private business in China. Moreover, as it happens in the West, some private investors prefer a totally private project, independent from governmental supervision, rather than to run a PPP with local authorities. Quoting a Fitch rating report, the *Financial Times* comments that public-private partnerships will serve as the main financing model for China's local-government infrastructure projects in the coming years—but for now, at least, state-owned enterprises (SOEs) have emerged as the main partners for local governments because of the low returns of around 5 to 8% that usually make these projects unattractive to private firms (Lockett 2017).

Although the debt risk must be seriously taken into consideration, it remains, as I pointed out above, that the most serious problem for PPPs is to harmonize the opposite interests of the private partner (return on investment) and the public partner (equitable access to services). Unless the government comes in by guaranteeing, one way or the other, the private partner, which could be costly, the partnership between two public partners could be the best solution. In fact, it will be easier to harmonize the interest of two public partners, eventually under the control of the central government, than to harmonize the inevitably contradictory interests of the public and the private partners which is the norm for PPP (see for example Hall et al. 2009).

It remains to be seen if PPPs will turn out to be beneficial to all categories of Chinese citizen or whether the possible gains in economic efficiency will have been obtained at the expense of an equitable distribution of wealth and of the value of equitable access to the public goods produced by PPPs.

5.6 Conclusion

This chapter permits us to arrive at the conclusion that China is certainly not the dictatorship that 'oppresses its own people', as several Western observers have been

5.6 Conclusion

in the habit of bombasting, such as Vice-President Pence in his 2018 speech at the Hudson Institute (see Sect. 6.2.7 Conclusion). Another example shows how China is viewed at by some influential American think tanks and how they praise their own political system: 'the United States, while an imperfect democracy, is an inspiration to people everywhere who yearn for the freedom and dignity that come from having a representative government, independent legal system, and market economy. In contrast, all power in the PRC is monopolized by the Chinese Communist Party, a political organization whose legitimacy is called into question by its troubled history. Read the State Department annual report on human rights and it quickly becomes apparent that this is a deeply authoritarian regime, and one that continues to oppress the Chinese people' (Easton 2016).

Certainly, China is not a liberal democracy, but since the beginning of the reforms it has relaxed its control on economy and society in the many ways I described in this chapter. Viewed form the point of view of Western liberal democracy, China has a long way to go before it can be praised not only for its economic performances but also for the respect of human rights. I will come back this important question in the general conclusion of this book. For the moment it is important to mention some of the major dimensions that should be taken into consideration when evaluating China's historical experience. Can Western democracy and the values it represents be considered as the universal model every country should imitate in order to be considered as belonging to the civilized world? What is the value of the Western liberal democracy model when compared to what it is in practice? Or do we have enough evidence proving that the Western liberal model has shown its limits and can no longer be used as a standard with which to evaluate countries belonging to other cultures? What shall we understand by 'human rights'? How long did it take for the West to build its civilization from the time the first ideas of democracy that appeared in Greece 2.5 millennia ago? When can we say that the West has realized liberal democracy? What has the West done in the meantime? Has the West the right to interfere within the internal affairs of other countries? Does it have the right to intervene even in order to 'defending the weak' at the cost of killing innocent people whereby meriting Bartolomé de Las Casas's 'eternal damnation'? (see the beginning of Chap. 6). Is it legitimate for a country like China to resist the opening of its culture, economy, and polity to the West, when Western forces are primarily interested in realizing their own interests within China's territory? Hopefully, the following and last chapter, examining the relations between the US and China will provide some answers to these questions.

References

Aizhu, C. (2018). Stepping on the gas: Home-built fracking boom, *Reuters*, 21 June. Retrieved September 28, 2018, from https://www.reuters.com/article/us-china-shale-analysis/stepping-on-the-gas-chinas-home-built-fracking-boom-idUSKBN1JH0M5.

Backer, L. (2017). Commentary on the new charity undertakings law: Socialist modernization through collective organizations. *The China Nonprofit Review, 9*(2), 273–309.

Barzeley, M. (1992). *Breaking through Bureaucracy. A new vision for managing in government.* Berkeley: University of California Press.

Barzeley, M. (2001). *The new public management, improving research and policy dialogue.* Berkeley: University of California Press.

Bergère, M. C. (1986). *L'âge d'or de la bourgeosie chinoise.* Paris: Flammarion.

Bergère, M. C. (2007). *Capitalisme et capitalistes en Chine.* Paris: Perrin.

Blum, W. (2004). *Hope. U.S. Military and C.I.A. interventions since world war II.* Monroe (ME): Common Courage Press.

Blum, W. (2014). *Rogue state. A guide to the world's only superpower.* London: Zed Books.

Blum, W. (2018). *Overthrowing other people's governments: The Master List*, no date. Retrieved April 5, 2018, from https://williamblum.org/essays/read/overthrowing-other-peoples-governments-the-master-list.

Braudel, F. (1958). 'La longue durée', *Annales. Histoire, Sciences Sociales, 13e Année* (4, October–December), 725–753.

Braudel, F. (1979a). *Civilisation matérielle, économie et capitalisme (XVe–XVIIIe siècle)*, Paris: A. Colin, *vol. 1: Les structures du quotidien; vol. 2: Les jeux de l'échange; vol. 3: Le temps du monde* (English translation: *Civilization and Capitalism: 15th–18th Century, vol. 1: The Structure of Everyday Life; vol. 2: The Wheels of Commerce; vol. 3: The Perspective of the World*, Berkeley: University of California Press, 1992).

Braudel, F. (1979b). *Afterthoughts on material civilization and capitalism* (The Johns Hopkins Symposia in Comparative History). Baltimore, MD: Johns Hopkins University Press (French edition: La dynamique du capitalisme, Paris, Flammarion, 1985).

Bürgenmeier, B. (2005). *Economie du développement durable.* Louvain-la-Neuve: De Boeck.

Chang, H. (2003). *Globalization, economic development and the role of the state.* New York: Zed Books.

Chen, L. (2019). Chinese protesters blame fracking for earthquakes that killed two people in Sichuan. *South China Morning Post,* 26 February. Retrieved March 1, 2019, from https://www.scmp.com/news/china/society/article/2187718/chinese-demonstrators-rage-sichuan-government-and-blame-fracking.

Chen, S. (2019). Is China's plan to use a nuclear bomb detonator to release shale gas in earthquake-prone Sichuan crazy or brilliant? *South China Morning Post*, 27 January. Retrieved February 12, 2019, from https://www.scmp.com/news/china/science/article/2183466/chinas-plan-use-nuclear-bomb-detonator-release-shale-gas.

Chen, J., & Dickson, B. J. (2008). Allies of the state: Democratic support and regime support among China's private entrepreneurs. *The China Quarterly*, December 2008, 780–804.

Cohen, G. (2017). Public-private partnerships need to bypass ideology. *Financial Times,* October 11. Retrieved November 25, 2017, from https://www.ft.com/content/823c1e22-a829-11e7-ab55-27219df83c97.

David, O., & Ted, G. (1992). *Reinventing government: How the entrepreneurial spirit is transforming the public sector.* New York: Plume Book.

Dickson, B. J. (2008). *Wealth into power. He communist party's embrace of China's private sector.* New York: Cambridge University Press.

Domberger, S. (1998). *The contracting organization. A strategic guide to outsourcing.* Oxford: Oxford University Press.

Easton, I. (2016). *Strategic standoff. The U.S.–China Rivalry and Taiwan.* Arlington, VA: Project 2049 Institute, March.

References 191

Engdahl, W. F. (2014). *Target China. How Washington and wall street plan to cage the Asian dragon.* San Diego: Progressive Press.

Flynn, N. (2007). *Public sector management.* London: Sage.

Food&Water Watch. (2010). *Not so fast natural gas. Why accelerating risky drilling threatens American water.* Washington, DC, 2010.

Forsythe, M. (2015). Q. and A.: Tony Saich on what Chinese want from their leaders. *Sinosphere,* 11 September. Retrieved October 18, 2015, from https://sinosphere.blogs.nytimes.com/2015/09/11/anthony-saich-china-communist-party/.

Friedman, M. (1962). *Capitalism and Freedom.* Chicago: University of Chicago Press, 1982 edition with a new Preface by the author.

Hall, D. et al. (2009). *Public-public partnerships (PUPs) in water,* March, PSIRU. Retrieved February 15, 2010, from http://www.psiru.org/reports/public-public-partnerships-pups-water.html.

Hart, O. (2003). Incomplete contracts and public ownership: Remarks and an application to Public-Private Partnerships. *The Economic Journal, 113*(2003), 69–76.

Hauter, W. (2016). *Frackopoly. The battle for the future of energy and environment.* New York: Free Press.

Hayami, Y. (2003). From the Washington consensus to the post-Washington consensus: Retrospect and prospect. *Asian Development Review, 20*(2), 40–65.

Hayward, J. (2018). The rise of China's new-type think tanks and the internationalization of the state. *Pacific Affairs, 91*(1, March), 27–47.

Hu, A. (2014). *China's collective presidency.* Berlin: Springer.

IMF. (2004). *Public-Private Partnerships,* prepared by the Fiscal Affairs Department (in consultation with other departments, the World Bank, and the Inter-American Development Bank), March 12.

Johns Hopkins Bloomberg School of Public Health. (2015). *Study: Fracking industry wells associated with premature birth,* 8 October, Retrieved November 25, 2015, from https://www.jhsph.edu/news/news-releases/2015/study-fracking-industry-wells-associated-with-premature-birth.html.

Jullien, F. (2011). The Silent Transformations. London: Seagull.

Kelsey, J. (2011). *International civil society demands end to secrecy in TPPA talks, media release,* February 16, 2011. http://tppwatch.org.

Lafer, G. (2014). Partnership or Putsch? *Project Syndicate,* January 14, 2014. Retrieved January 15, 2014, from www.projectsyndicate.org.

Landes, D. S. (1999). *The wealth and poverty of nations. Why some are so rich and some so poor.* New York: Norton.

Lapierre, W. (1973). *L'analyse des systèmes politiques.* Paris: Presses Universitaires de France.

Lavelle, M. (2012). Tracing links between fracking and earthquakes. *National Geographic,* 4 January.

Lee, C. P. (2015). *Training the party. Party adaptation and elite training in reform-era China.* Cambridge: Cambridge University Press.

Li, C. (2009a). China's new think tanks: where officials, entrepreneurs, and scholars interact. *China Leadership Monitor,* no. 29. Retrieved October 20, 2009, from http://www.hoover.org/publications/china-leadershipmonitor.

Li, E. X. (2012). Why China's political model is superior. *The New York Times,* 16 February.

Li, E. X. (2014). The post-democratic future begins in China. *Foreign Affairs,* January–February, pp. 34–46.

Li, C. (2017). *The power of ideas. The rising influence of thinkers and think tanks in China.* Singapore: World Scientific, 2017.

Lin, Y. (2001). *Between politics and markets.* Cambridge University Press.

Lockett, H. (2017). China's state firms lead on public-private infrastructure projects: Fitch. *Financial Times,* 20 February. Retrieved September 27, 2017, from https://www.ft.com/content/14a44049-22bf-3062-b5b2-79ebe77b0d95.

McKinsey, China's Green Revolution. (2009). *McKinsey Company*, 2009, available on the company's website: www.mckinsey.com, to which many scholars from several Chinese universities have contributed together with a team from the Energy Research Institute of the NDRC.

Mettan, G. (2017). *Creating russophobia. From the great religious schism to anti-putin hys-teria* (p. 2017). Atlanta, GA: Clarity Press.

Mikulka, J. (2018). *How wall street enabled the fracking 'Revolution' That's Losing Billions DESMOG*, Friday, May 4. Retrieved October 27, 2018, from https://www.desmogblog.com/2018/05/04/wall-street-shale-oil-fracking-revolution-losing-billions-continental-resources. NGOs in China—http://ngochina.blogspot.ch/.

OECD. (1996). *Réconcilier l'économique et le social. Vers une économie plurielle.* Paris: OECD.

OECD. (2008). *Public-private partnerships. In pursuit of risk sharing and value for money.* Paris: OECD.

Osborne, D., & Plastrik, P. (1997). *Banishing bureaucracy. The five strategies for reinventing government.* New York: Penguin.

Peerenboom, R. (2002). *China's long March toward rule of law.* Cambridge: Cambridge University Press.

Peerenboom, R. (2007). *China modernizes. Threat to the west or model for the rest?* Cambridge: Cambridge University Press.

Pieke, F. N. (2016). *The good communist. Elite training and state building in today's China.* Cambridge: Cambridge University Press.

Pollock, A. (2004). *NHS plc. The privatisation of our health care.* London: Verso.

Porcher, T., & Farah, F. (2014). *TAFTA. L'accord du plus fort.* Paris: Milo.

Rachman, G. (2008). Conservatism overshoots its limits, *Financial Times*, October 6.

Raphaël, R., & Xi, L. (2019). Bons et mauvais chinois. Quand l'Etat organise la notation de ses citoyens. *Le Monde Diplomatique*, Janvier.

Rosenau, P. V. (Ed.). (2000). *Public-private policy partnership.* Cambridge, Mass: The MIT Press.

Saich, T. (2016). How China's citizens view the quality of governance under Xi Jinping. *Journal of Chinese Governance, 1*(1), 1–20.

Schick, A. (1998). Why most developing countries should not try New Zealand reforms. *The World Bank Research Observer, 13*(1), 123–131.

Shambaug, D. (2008). Training China's political elite: The party school system. *China Quarterly*, December 2008, pp. 827–844.

Sher, C., & Wu, C. (2018). Fracking in China: Community impacts and public support of shel gas development. *Journal of Contemporary China, 27*(112), 626–641.

Shi-Kupfer, K., & Lang B. (2017). Overseas NGOs in China: Left in Legal Limbo, *The Diplomat*, 4 March.

Skelcher, C. (2005). Public-private partnerships and hybridity. In E. Ferlie et al. (Ed.), *The Oxford handbook of public management.* Oxford: Oxford University Press.

Slav, I. (2018). Here's why China won't have a shale boom, *Business Insider*. 23 April. Retrieved September 27, from https://www.businessinsider.com/heres-why-china-wont-have-a-shale-boom-2018-4?IR=T.

Stiglitz, J. E. (2008a). The triumphant return of John Maynard Keynes, *Economists' Voice*, Project Syndicate, December.

Stiglitz, J. E. (2008b). Is there a Post-Washington consensus consensus? In N. Serra & J. Stiglitz (Eds.), *The Washington consensus reconsidered* (pp. 41–56). Oxford: Oxford University Press.

Stiglitz, J. E. (2009). *Around the World with Joseph Stiglitz: Perils and promises of globalization*, documentary film by the author.

Stiglitz, J. E. (2010). *Freefall: America, free markets, and the sinking of the world economy.* New York: Norton.

Stiglitz, J. E. (2013). The free-trade charade. *Project Syndicate*, 14 July.

Stiglitz, J. E., & Charlton, A. (2005). *Fair trade for all. How trade can promote development.* Oxford: Oxford University Press, 2005.

Stone, D. (1997). *Policy paradox. The art of political decision making.* New York: Norton.

References

193

Suleiman, E. (2003). *Dismantling Democratic States*. Princeton: Princeton University Press.

Tournès, L. (2010). *L'argent de l'influence. Les fondations américaines et leurs réseaux européens* [Money of Influence. American Foundations and Their European Networks]. Paris: Editions Autrement.

UNECE. (2007). *International Conference "knowledge sharing and capacity building on promoting successful public-private partnerships in the UNECE region"*, UNECE document ECE/CECI/PPP/2007/INF.1, 19 March.

Urio, P. (1984). *Le role politique de l'administration publique*. Lausanne: LEP.

Urio, P. (1999). La gestion publique au service du marché. In M. Hufty (Ed.), *La pensée comptable. Etat, néolibéralisme, nouvelle gestion publique* (pp. 91–124). Paris: Presses Universi-taires de France.

Urio, P. (2010a). *Reconciling state, market, and society in China. The long March towards prosperity*. London & New York: Routledge.

Urio, P. (Ed.). (2010b). *Public private partnerships. Success and failure factors for in-transition countries*. Lanham, MD: University Press of America.

Urio, P. (2010c). Under What Conditions Can Public-Private Partnerships Improve Efficiency, Equity, Security and Sustainable Development, in Urio (2010b), pp. 25–69.

Urio, P. (2012). *China, the West and the myth of new public management. Neoliberalism and its discontents*. London & New York: Routledge.

Urio, P. (2018). *China reclaims world power status. Putting an end to the world America made*. London & New York: Routledge.

Urio, P., & Yuan, Y. (2014). *L'émergence des ONG en Chine. Le changement du rôle de l'Etat-Parti*. Bern: Peter Lang.

Vaudano, M. (2015). *Docteur TTIP et Mister TAFTA. Que nous réserve vraiment le traité Translatlantique Euroope/Etat-Unis?* Paris : Les Petits Matins.

Wallach, L. M. (2013) Le traite transatlantique, un typhon qui menace les Europeens [The Transatlantic Agreement, a typhoon threatening Europeans], *Le Monde Diplomatique*, November.

Wallerstein, I. (1974 and 1980). *The modern world system* (Vol. 2). New York: Academic Press.

Wang, Y. (Ed.). (2000). *Public-Private Partnerships in the Social Sector. Issues and Country Experiences in Asia and the Pacific,* Asian Development Bank Institute, 2000.

Weber, M. (1985). *Wirtschaft und gesellschaft*. Tübingen: J.C.B. Mohr (first edition by Marianne Weber, 1922).

Weisbrode, K. (2014). Twilight of the proconsuls. On victoria Nuland's gaffe and the cold war echoes of American diplomacy abroad. *Foreign Policy*, 10 February 2014. Retrieved February 12, 2014, from http://www.foreignpolicy.com/articles/2014/02/10/twilight_of_the_proconsuls_victoria_nuland_american_diplomacy.

Wildau, G. (2017). China admits to disguised fiscal borrowing risk, *Financial Times*, 2 August. Retrieved September 28, 2017, from https://www.ft.com/content/5fe8b3c2-7754-11e7-90c0-90a9d1bc9691.

Williamson, O. (1985). *The economic institutions of capitalism*. New York: The Free Press.

Williamson, J. (1990). *Latin American adjustment: How much has happened*. Washington, DC: Institute for International Economics, 1990.

Williamson, J. (1993). Democracy and the Washington consensus. *World Development, 21*(8).

China Development Brief—http://www.chinadevelopmentbrief.cn/.

World Bank. (1997). *China 2020: Development challenges in the new century*, Report no. 17027-CHA.

World Bank. (2003). *Making services work for poor people*. World Bank and Oxford University Press.

World Bank. (2005a). *Equity and development*. The World Bank and Oxford University Press.

World Bank. (2005b). *China: Deepening public service unit reform to improve service delivery*. Beijing: Citic Publishing House, published for the World Bank.

World Bank. (2008). *Mid-term evaluation of China's 11th 5 Year Plan*.

World Bank. (2009). *From poor areas to poor people: China's evolving poverty reduction agenda. An assessment of poverty and inequality in China.*

World Bank. (2012). *China 2030. Building a modern, harmonious and creative society*, officially dated 2013, but already available on line Spring 2012.

Yang, Y., & Zhang, W. (2010). The future of PPPs in China: A preliminary assessment, in Urio 2010b, pp. 280–311.

Zammit, A. (2003). *Rethinking UN-Business Partnerships*, Geneva, South Centre & UNRISD (United Nations Research Institute for Social Research).

Zuboff, S. (2019). Un capitalisme de surveillance, *Le Monde Diplomatique,* No. 778, 66e années, Janvier.

Chapter 6
China and the New World Order. Why and How China's Foreign Policy Has Put an End to the World America Made

In order to understand China's foreign policy, one has to understand the foreign policy of the countries that have been China's most serious competitors, first European powers in the XIX Century, then the US in the XX and XXI centuries. Both have implemented, at least since the discovery of the Americas, a global foreign policy aimed at dominating the rest of the world. For dealing with both of China's competitors it would have been necessary first to fully analyse the foreign policy of European powers, especially England and France. In my previous books (Urio 2010, 2012, 2018) I have already dealt, even if very briefly, with the aggression of European powers starting from the first Opium War (1839–1842). I have explained how this defeat had been an unbearable national humiliation that lasted more than one century, until Mao proclaimed the People's Republic of China, proudly stating that 'ours will no longer be a nation subject to insult and humiliation. We have stood up' (Mao 1949). In this chapter I will therefore start directly with the origins of US foreign policy.

Before we go any further it is necessary to warn the reader that by identifying the main features of American ideology and its implementation (more particularly in foreign affairs), I do not consider by any means that all its dimensions are specifically and exclusively American. Several aspects of American ideology are also present in other cultures, and above all in the European culture. After all, Americans and Europeans belong to the same cultural matrix. For example, the sense of superiority, racism and expansionism in the forms of colonialism and imperialism, have been some of the major dimensions of European ideology that has taken its modern form after the Renaissance and the discovery of the Americas. From the time of the Renaissance, Europe has developed the ideological foundations of its relationships with the other cultures, that can be briefly defined as follows: (1) the sense of superiority and the belief in the exceptional character of European culture, (2) the belief in the values of Christian religion and in the values and laws of capitalism, (3) the definition of European values as universal, (4) the right to diffuse these values and therefore to civilize

---

The original version of this chapter was revised. The correct figure in page 294 is updated and the reference citation corrected. The correction to this chapter is available at 10.1007/978-981-13-8879-8_7

© Springer Nature Singapore Pte Ltd. 2019
P. Urio, *China 1949–2019*, https://doi.org/10.1007/978-981-13-8879-8_6

the *barbarians* and the *savages*, (5) the belief in economic growth and progress based upon European values, (6) the right to take possession of the land of the barbarians as it is not protected by legally binding property rights, (7) the right of the 'civilized world' to intervene into the 'non-civilized' world to end practices that violate 'European' universal values'; (8) the belief that the diffusion (and expansion) of European values is beneficial to mankind and historically inevitable. This ideology was operating since the beginning of the European conquest of the rest of the world, starting with South America. 'The expansion has involved, in most regions of the world, military conquest, economic exploitation, and massive injustices (…) justified on the grounds of the greater good that such expansion has had for the world's population' (Wallerstein 2006, p. 1). Immanuel Wallerstein summarizes the debate in favour and against the brutal conquest of South America by Spain at the beginning of the XVI century, between Juan Ginès de Sepúlveda justifying the conquest, and the Catholic priest Bartolomé de Las Casas, criticizing it (Wallerstein 2006 pp. 1–29). In particular, it is interesting to note that already in the XVI Century, 'Las Casas was implacable against what we would call collateral damage: "it is a sin meriting eternal damnation to harm and kill innocents in order to punish the guilty, for it is contrary to justice"' (quoted by Wallerstein 2006, p. 9; for more detail see Las Casas 1974, 1992).

6.1 The Development of the Imperial US Foreign Policy[1]

Analyzing US Foreign policy is not an easy task. Several reasons explain this difficulty. But one is enough: there are many contradictory interpretations (even amongst American scholars) between those who criticise the imperial posture of the US foreign policy and those who on the contrary praise its devotion to diffusing democracy, equality, human rights and free markets. Amongst those who recognize the imperial character of this policy, some analyse its beginning and/or development during the transition from the XIX to the XX century (e.g. Karp 1979; McCormick 1995, Chap. 2) or after World War II, or even after the collapse of the Soviet Union (e.g. Scott 2007; Bacevich 2008, 2012). These writers are certainly interesting for understanding the US foreign policy after these dramatic events. Personally, I have been convinced by the writing of those who consider that the US imperial posture appeared right at the beginning of the US Republic (e.g. La Faber 1994; Zinn 1999; Griffin 2018; Green 2018; Losurdo 2007, 2011). I will briefly explain my preference for this interpretation. By doing so, I will show that whereas the partition between the imperial US Republic and the rest of the world is of primary importance for understanding the US foreign policy, there are also partitions within US society that should be taken into consideration.

---

[1] Part 6.1 of this chapter is a summary of Urio (2018), Chap. 4, with many updates and new comments. I should like to make it clear from the beginning, in the hope of avoiding being described as an 'Anti-American fundamentalist', that I will not deal with the American people but only with the US establishment's foreign policy. For a history of the American people, covering both domestic and foreign policies, I recommend Zinn (1999).

6.1 The Development of the Imperial US Foreign Policy

First, the partition between the US and the rest of the world and the clearest case in favour of the appearance of the imperial posture of the US foreign policy since the beginning has been put forward by one of the most influential neo-conservatives, Robert Kagan: 'America did not change on September 11. It only became more itself. Nor should be any mystery about the course America is on, and has been on, not only over the past year or over the past decade, but for the better part of the past six decades, and, one might even say, for the better part of the past four centuries. It is an objective fact that Americans have been expanding their power and influence in ever-widening arcs since even before they founded their own independent nation. The hegemony that America established within the Western hemisphere in the nineteenth century has been a permanent feature of international policy ever since. The expansion of America strategic reach into Europe and East Asia that came with the Second World War has never been retracted ...' And he concludes: the US 'remains, and clearly intend to remain, the dominant strategic force in both Asia and Europe' (Kagan 2003, pp. 85–86).[2]

The second partition is between the US oligarchy (today we would say: the establishment) and the rest of American society. Analysing the transformations that occurred in the US between 1890 and 1920, when the US fought two wars, one against Spain and the other against Germany, Walter Karp considers that 'the triumph of [President] Wilson and the war party struck the American Republic a blow from which it has never recovered. If the mainspring of a republican commonwealth (...) is the perpetual struggle against oligarchy and privilege, against private monopoly and arbitrary power, then that mainspring was snapped and deliberately snapped by the victors in the civil war over war.[3] (...) [After the First World War] the nation's Republican rulers governed with impudence and impunity. A major administration scandal scarcely cost them a vote. They not only served the interests of trusts, they boasted openly of doing so, for the "captains of industry" were now restored to their former glory as if the pre-war reform movement had never existed. The Republican rulers set about creating multicorporate cartels to enable the monopolists to govern themselves and the American people as well' (Karp, pp. xiii, 324, 341). Quite true. But the dominance of the economy (and of its major representatives) was there since the Declaration of Independence. The signatories of this document, considered as the founding milestone of the US Republic, were lawyers, rich merchants, land (plantation) owners, and several were slaves-owners. During the XIX century, espe-

---

[2]It is interesting to remind the reader that in this book, entitled: *On Paradise and Power* (2003), Kagan describes the US and Europe as Mars and Venus, respectively (p. 3). This is certainly not a new statement about the 'warrior character of the US'. Amongst the numerous quotes one may mention, the following one is quite revealing: in his crusade to convince Americans to support the government's will to enter the First World War, Theodore Roosevelt in April 1917 gave a speech to the Harvard Club referring to 'Socialists (...) and others who wanted peace as "a whole raft of sexless creatures"'; clearly for Roosevelt the best way for men to prove their sexual performance was to make war instead of love, which is clearly a contradiction in terms; quoted by Zinn 1999, p. 369 in Chap. 14, with the title: 'War Is the Health of The State'.

[3]By 'civil war' Karp refers to the struggle that developed in the US between those who wanted to join England in the First World War (the establishment) and those who were opposed to it.

cially after the Civil War, when the US started its industrial revolution, businessmen engaged in unethical and monopolistic practices (the Robber Barons), utilized corrupt political influence, faced almost no business regulation, and amassed enormous wealth. Examples include Cornelius Vanderbilt, owner of steamship lines and railroads; Andrew Carnegie, steel manufacturer; J.P. Morgan, financier and banker; John D. Rockefeller, founder of Standard Oil; Jay Gould, Wall Street trader; Jim Fisk, Wall Street trader; Russell Sage, financier.[4] The analysis of today's situation shows that in the American Republic this partition has not changed since then. Joseph Stiglitz in his article 'American Democracy on the Brink' (2018a) has significantly introduced this subtitle: 'Of, By, and For the Corporations'. This was and still is the situation inside the US Republic.

Third, since the beginning the US Republic was based upon another type of partition: the distinction within American society between the 'white people, chosen by God' and the rest. Since the time of the Declaration of independence this partition existed between three ethnic groups: Whites, Negros and Indians.[5] In fact, these ethnic groups lived on the same territory as three castes: the dominant ethnic group, i.e. the free Whites (divided between the oligarchy and the rest, as mention above), the Negros working as slaves in the plantations, and the savage Indians who had to be 'naturally' dispossessed of their territory (and in fact culturally destroyed) to make place for the expansion of the free Whites resulting from their 'multiplication', i.e. the rapid development of their population (see hereafter the second quotation of Thomas Jefferson).[6] From the second part of the XIX Century on, this partition became less evident. The Indians ceased to exist as an ethnic group after the conquest of the West was completed, officially in 1890 after the massacre of Wounded Knee. After the end of the Civil War (1865), the Negros were liberated, but remained in a subordinate position compared to the Whites. They obtained officially the parity in formal rights with the Whites only in the middle of the 1960s. Nevertheless, even today they constitute an ethnic group which suffers from unofficial (or even official) discriminations, as well as frequent manifestations of racism. Moreover, compared to the Whites, they present a higher percentage of poor, under-educated, and unemployed people, with poor access to public services, i.e. health, education and housing.

---

[4]For the complete list of those who are generally considered 'robber barons' see Wikipedia, *Robber Baron (industrialist)*, (https://en.wikipedia.org/wiki/Robber_baron_(industrialist), accessed 15 December 2018; see also Zinn (1999), Chap. 11: Robber Barons and Rebels).

[5]I use here the term 'Negros' instead of the today politically correct 'Afro-Americans', to replace the reader within the atmosphere of that time.

[6]See for example the statement by President Andrew Jackson in his fifth annual message, 3 December 1833: 'My original convictions upon this subject have been confirmed by the course of events for several years, and experience is every day adding to their strength. That those tribes cannot exist surrounded by our settlements and in continual contact with our citizens is certain. They have neither the intelligence, the industry, the moral habits, nor the desire of improvement which are essential to any favourable change in their condition. Established in the midst of another and a superior race, and without appreciating the causes of their inferiority or seeking to control them, they must necessarily yield to the force of circumstances and ere long disappear.' *Native News Online* (2017), and https://newsmaven.io/indiancountrytoday/archive/nice-day-for-a-genocide-shocking-quotes-on-indians-by-u-s-leaders-pt-2-itTXslul5EKc694gf4DLfA/.

6.1 The Development of the Imperial US Foreign Policy

A final remark about ideology versus practice. Some critics of the US foreign policy regret the time when the US was implementing the values that have inspired the Founding Fathers (e.g. Karp, Chap. 14: 'The Old America That Was Free and Is Now Dead', Stiglitz 2018b). But has that time ever existed? As I sustained above, right from the beginning the US establishment has implemented both domestic and foreign policies that are at odds with the proclaimed values of democracy, equality, human rights and freedoms. Since the beginning, expansion has been justified by the need of acquiring new territories for the 'multiplication' of the American people and the needs of the US economy, as well as by the establishment's will to develop power at home (brutal crash of the working class's protest movements against inhuman treatment by owners of land and capital) and to project power abroad: wars against the native Indians; southern expansion at the expense of Spain; expansion in the Pacific especially after the economic crises of the 1890s; Far Eastern and European expansion after World War II; and world-wide expansion after the fall of the Soviet Union. No matter how one justifies this expansion, it is impossible not to see the impressive gap between the stated ideology of US foreign policy and its implementation: right from the beginning, the US has developed an imperial foreign policy.

Having clarified the several aspects of the partition within American society and between the US and the rest of the world, I will start with the analysis of the original American ideology, that will be completed with an overview of its contemporary developments. I will show that, in spite of changes in the international system, that have emerged during the XX century, today's US ideological foundations present some remarkable similarities, *mutatis mutandis*, with those that appeared right at the beginning of the US Republic and remained remarkably faithful to the conquering ideology of the Founding Fathers. Second, I will show that this ideology has been the basis orienting US expansion in the world that I will present hereafter (for more details see Urio 2018, pp. 108–129). Finally, I will discuss the US foreign policy towards China that started already towards the end of the XVIII century, right at the beginning of the US republic, and that has become one of its central dimensions during the XX Century, and its major concern for the safeguard of the dominant role of the US in the international system. This will allow us to better understand China's foreign policy of today, which will be the last part of this chapter.

6.1.1 The Historical Origins of US Ideology: 'Chosenness', God, the 'Manifest Destiny' and the 'End of History'

In spite of the cultural similarities between Europe and America, the US has developed an ideology that, considered in its totality, is quite different from the ideology of other cultures and other countries, including Europe. A territory protected by two wide oceans which spared the country from wars of invasion, the presence of native inhabitants badly equipped for resisting foreign colonizers, a declining colonial power at the southern border (Spain) not prepared to sustain war with the US, and in the North an ideologically compatible neighbour (Canada), these were the ideal pre-conditions for developing a peculiar ideology for a country, separated geographically and also culturally from the original homeland of the Pilgrim Fathers. The first immigrants who came to North America were Europeans who took with them the European ideology structured according to a mix of religious and secular beliefs (Christianism and capitalism), even if, as we will see hereafter, Americans have developed a variant with some specific features. Indeed, these features were already embedded into a variant of Protestantism, that is to say Puritanism, that the first immigrants took with them to the New World.

The ideology that took form in the 13 British colonies and then in the United States of America since the XVII Century, a variant of the European one, is rather complex, but if one has to choose one feature upon which all its other dimensions depend, I would take the one that Stephanson has called 'chosenness', i.e. the profound belief shared by the Founding Fathers that the American people had been chosen by God (or the Providence) to create a new republic, away from 'corrupt Europe', free from the European wars, persecutions, etc., and to organize it as a 'pure' and exceptional example that the rest of the world should imitate.[7] It is important to understand the meaning of this first element of US ideology: it establishes a partition between the US and the rest of the world, between 'we and they'. The US is exceptional, meaning that having been chosen by God (whereas the other countries have not) America is, thanks to this choice, exceptional, i.e. different from the corrupt European countries that the English Pilgrims had left behind. This vision of the world persisted until the present day, where the clearest formulation has been that of President Bush (son) establishing a clear partition between 'WE, being equated with the Good, and THEY, being qualified as the Evil'.

The consequence of exceptionalism is that America should stay away from Europe, or it will be contaminated and the dream of establishing a pure republic will vanish for ever. So, isolationism is the consequence of exceptionalism and it constitutes the first dimension of US foreign policy. The additional meaning of exceptionalism is that the US should be a model other countries should imitate. In 1816 Thomas Jefferson put it very clearly:

> We are destined to be a barrier against the return of ignorance and barbarism. Old Europe will have to lean on our shoulders, and to hobble along by our side (quoted by Stephanson 1995, p. 24).[8]

This attitude towards Europe was later strengthened by the Monroe doctrine of 1823 that forbade European states to interfere within the Americas. Moreover, isolationism towards Europe persisted until WW2. True, the US entered WW1 in 1917 and President Wilson imagined and promoted a new organisation of the world (the League of Nations) that would have rendered impossible the resurgence of European

---

[7]Stephanson (1995). See also, Griffin (2018): 'Since its formation, US politicians have referred to America in divine terms', and 'America as Divinely Founded and Guided', p. 9, with quotations of Presidents George Washington, Andrew Jackson, Ronald Reagan and George W. Bush, pp. 9–18.

[8]It is interesting to note that 'old Europe' has been used by Secretary of Defence Donald Rumsfeld, two centuries after Jefferson used it (i.e. 22 January 2003).

6.1 The Development of the Imperial US Foreign Policy

wars. Unfortunately for the President, the American Senate did not ratify the treaty of the League of Nations, thereby forbidding the US to become part of that organization. In the interwar period, the US did not interfere with the establishment of Fascism in Italy in the 1920s, of Nazism in the 1930s, nor did they interfere when Germany attacked the Soviet Union in 1941. Only when the US was attacked by Japan at Pearl harbour, it entered WWII at the end of 1941, and later in Sicily (July 1943) and Normandy (June 1944).

But being chosen by God has a second consequence in addition to isolationism. In the words of Stephanson: 'the nation had been allowed to see the light and was bound to show the way for the historically retrograde. This vision has been the constant throughout American history, but historically it has led to two quite different ways of being toward the outside world. The first [as we have seen above] was to unfold into an exemplary state *separate* from the corrupt and failed world, leaving others to emulate it as best they can. The second [based upon universalism] (...) was to push the world along by means of regenerative *intervention* (Stephanson 1995, p. xii, emphasis in original).' Having been chosen by God, as God is universal, the chosen people has been entrusted with universal values. But these will be universal only when they are implemented all over the world. Hence the right, and even the duty, for the chosen people to intervene abroad to make those values universal indeed.

It is clear that there is a contradiction between the two dimensions of US foreign policy: isolationism versus interventionism. But they have coexisted in fact and are at the origin of numerous debates within the US elite when confronted with international events that may or may not require the US to intervene abroad (Kinzer 2017, p. 3). Stephanson is of the idea that isolationism has prevailed. I am not so sure. In fact, right from the beginning of the US republic, interventionism has been a dominant dimension of US foreign policy. Putting aside the war of independence with England, which in fact was a civil war, the first important act of US foreign policy was the war against the Indians (the so-called Indian Wars) that lasted until the end of the XIX century, and officially ended with the Wounded Knee massacre in 1890. Then followed the wars against Spain, Mexico, etc. Moreover, since the Monroe Doctrine of 1823, the US kept its grip over Latin America, continued its expansion in the Caribbean and the Pacific, and in the interwar period kept economic relations with Europe, including Fascist Italy and especially Nazi Germany, that became useful for sustaining the US policy of Europe's reconstruction (especially Germany) after World War II (Lacroix-Riz 2014, pp. 31–46; Migone 2015, pp. 141–149, 165–170). Needless to mention the numerous and persistent US interventions abroad since 1945.

More about US foreign policy below. For the moment it is interesting to quote President Thomas Jefferson, from a letter to James Monroe (when he was governor of Virginia) that summarizes the essence of US ideology and in fact set the dream that subsequent Presidents (and more generally the American elite) have tried to realize: Jefferson to Monroe in 1801:

> However our present interests may restrain us within our limits, it is impossible not to look forward to distant times when our multiplication will expand it beyond those limits, and cover

the whole northern, if not the southern continent, with people speaking the same language, governed in similar forms, and by similar laws (quoted by Anderson 2015, p. 4).[9]

In 1845, the ideology described above was completed by the invention of a new expression, 'Manifest Destiny', that gives a formidable strength to the exemplary status and to the right of intervention of the People chosen by God: clearly, having been chosen by God, the US people is evidently blessed by a manifest destiny. In the words of John O'Sullivan, an advocate of Andrew Jackson who invented this expression: 'the right of our manifest destiny to overspread and possess the whole continent that providence has given us for great experiment of liberty and federated self-government.' (Anderson 2015, p. 4; see also Stephanson 1995, pp. 38–48). Moreover, as it has been already true for Europeans, 'land not occupied by recognized members of Christendom was theoretically land free to be taken.' So, manifest destiny 'became a catchword for the idea of a providentially or historically sanctioned right to continental expansionism.' (Stephanson 1995, p. xii).[10] Surely, at the beginning this mission was limited to the conquest of the American West, but in fact, the only long-term limit to the 'expansion' of this model to the rest of the world was the capacity to do so. As I mentioned above, that capacity manifested itself first in the Americas, then in the Asia-Pacific, and in the rest of the world after World War II. It culminated with the apotheosis that followed the collapse of the Soviet Union (Todd 1979). The manifest destiny had reached its end. And here we find another belief of the US ideology emerging in the 1980s, that further strengthens all the others: the idea that the chosen people, entrusted with a divine manifest destiny to serve as a model and having the right and the duty to intervene abroad to diffuse the universal values that it is the only one to possess, is indisputably the 'Indispensable Nation'.

Also, it is necessary to insist upon the religious sources and foundation of this ideology. In fact, the British immigrants that first colonized New England were a 'particularly fierce and uncompromising phalanx within the Reformation—the Puritans. (...) English Protestantism, early on, had developed a notion of England as not only spatially but also spiritually separate from the European continent, as the bastion of true religion and chief source of its expansion: a place divinely singled out for higher missions. The Separatists who crossed the Atlantic were part of this tradition, only more radical.' It is upon this religious basis that the idea of exceptionalism and separateness took form. Within this vision, the New World could quite easily be conceived, contrary to the vision of the Spanish and the Portuguese, as the Promised Land, a sacred territory. In this framework, the manifest destiny was embedded in 'the biblical notions, recharged through the Reformation, of a predestined, redemptive destiny revealed. The world as God's "manifestation" and history as predetermined "destiny" had been ideological staples of the strongly providentialist period of Eng-

---

[9]The complete text of the letter can be found at: https://founders.archives.gov/documents/Jefferson/01-35-02-0550.

[10]Stephanson further comments that this attitude 'was anything but new. Already in 1616, an agent of colonization had ended a prospectus of fabulous green vistas in North America to an English audience with this rhetorical flourish: "What need wee then feare, but to *goes up at once as peculiar people* marked and chosen by the finger of God to possess it?"' (emphasis in original).

6.1 The Development of the Imperial US Foreign Policy

land between 1620 and 1660, during which, of course, the initial migration to New England took place' (Stephanson 1995, p. 5). Moreover, this religious way of conceiving the manifest destiny is clearly tainted with a kind of messianic belief, and the consequent messianic activism necessary for the realization of this project.

Within this religious vision, manifest destiny is not only a possible outcome of separation (exceptionalism) or intervention (universalism) but it also defines the duty of the Puritan Christian: 'to be a Protestant and especially a Puritan was to master the Bible as an epistemic code of revelation, to understand the always causally effective providential hand in the world. Current events were fulfilments or re-enactments of the Scriptures. By mastering prophecy, one would be able to understand the course of history and "cooperate" with it. To be free was precisely to *understand this destiny* and conform to the direction of divine will, to "make our destiny our choice", as it was said at that time. (…) Once destiny was known with reasonable certainty, there remained the personal responsibility of choosing to follow it or to turn away.' The missionary aspect of this endeavour was therefore well-established since the beginning. And Stephanson comments: 'obscure but enormously suggestive [this thinking] offered the fullest vision of the end of history and the aftermath. It is a story of deadly struggle between the forces of good and evil, ending after many phases in final victory for the good and the Messiah's reappearance.' (Stephanson 1995, pp. 5–9, emphasis in the original).

It must be noted, that the Puritans' way of interpreting Christianity, is based upon the belief that there is a division of mankind between the believers and the others: WE apart from THEM (isolationism), or against THEM (regenerative interventionism). This interpretation clearly goes contrary to the real message of Christ: a practice of communion which is the contradiction of separation, and even more so than of regenerative intervention. This is shown by Christ's 'welcome of the sinners, the prostitutes, the tax collectors, the adulterous woman, i.e. of people considered [at that time] as morally impure or contaminated because of their contact with the pagans'. The Puritans had in fact a defensive conception of purity, quite the opposite of Christ's teaching: there is nothing exterior to man that can make him impure, but only what comes out of man. This conception displaces the origin of impurity: the words and deeds of man are the origins of purity or impurity, not what exists in his environment. The relation to the other is no longer a danger, but an opportunity, not a potential risk of contamination and impurity, but a domain where the believer is invited to put into concrete action his purity (Marguerat and Junod, pp. 32–33, my free translation from the French).[11] What is even more interesting is that this posture of Puritanism persists still today in a variety of American churches that trace their origins to Protestantism and consider the Book as an epistemic code of revelations.[12]

---

[11] Not being an expert in religion, I base this comment on the work of a world-famous specialist of the New Testament, Marguerat, author of the first part of the book.

[12] It is out of the question in this book to deal with the spread all over the world, e.g. in Latin America, Eastern Europe, Russia, and Africa, of a variety of Protestant Churches that still today share this posture with the Puritans. Needless to say that, insofar as these Churches tend to cooperate with conservative political forces, it should be necessary to take into consideration their activities and

One of the most interesting features of this ideology is the mix of religious and secular values. The duty to behave in order to fulfil the prophecies of the Book is clearly a religious imperative. But the English colons who came to the New World, took with them not only Puritanism, but also the ideas that had emerged in Europe at that time about new ways of managing the State, i.e. republicanism later translated into liberal democracy, and of managing the economy, i.e. market economy/capitalism. Similarly, to the religious values, these secular values were also considered as universal. The consequence is similar: the believer in democracy and capitalism has the duty (and the right) to do whatever is in his power to diffuse these values all over the world. What is remarkable of American ideology is the mix of religious and secular values that have been combined through history: the predestined, redemptive role of God's chosen people in the Promised Land; Christianity (in the Protestant form); redemption; a new world order; freedom; liberal individualism; democracy; free trade; and capitalism (Stephanson 1995, p. 16; Anderson 2015, p. 5).

Another element of the US ideology is worth mentioning here. Although the belief that the US were destined to lead the rest of the world was not explicitly affirmed until the messianic activisms of President Wilson (Karp 1979, Part I; Stephanson 1995, pp. 112–121) and systematically asserted since the time of World War II, it was certainly imbedded in the American ideology since the beginning. Indeed, we have seen above the references to the duty of Europe 'to hobble along by the US side', the second variant of US foreign policy (i.e. regenerative interventionism), the messianic activism, and the duty of the believer to understand the course of history, 'cooperate' with it and diffuse the content of the ideology to the rest of the world.

The ideology I have reconstructed above, constitutes a formidable and coherent set of interrelated beliefs. It has become a way of thinking, that when it is imbedded into the human mind, it is practically impossible not to follow for analyzing the world and giving meaning to one's position and action inside that world. This ideology has been used through history as the guide and a permanent justification of US foreign policy that in fact has operated since the foundation of the American republic, and still operates today. If one looks at the implementation of this ideology since the foundation of the US republic, one cannot but help considering that this ideology has become a formidable Weapon of Mass Destruction.

First of all, it has destructed the capacity of the American elite to conceive any other world in which the US could play another role (Porter 2018b). This capacity would have been necessary for taking into consideration the formidable changes that have occurred since the end of World War II in the distribution of power resources within the international system, that no longer correspond to those existing at that time. On the contrary, as I will show hereafter, the American elite still today tries desperately to maintain the international order America made after 1945, especially after the fall of the Soviet Union. Look at the hysteria that developed within the US establishment over the alleged interference of Russia in the 2016 presidential election with the purpose of favouring the 'outsider candidate' (Trump) and harming

---

influence in the perspective of an overall analysis of the restructuring of the power within both the national and the international systems.

6.1 The Development of the Imperial US Foreign Policy

the 'establishment candidate' (Hillary Clinton). This hysteria reached a climax when Trump made public the idea of discussing with Russia, in my opinion the most brilliant policy option put forward by a US President since the end of the Cold War.[13]

Second, by implementing that ideology, the US has thought it to be its duty and its right (in practice of God's imperative) to embark on a long series of mass destructions all over the world, many of which could hardly be justified by the necessity to defeat a mortal enemy ready to defeat the 'people chosen by God' and with it the values it claimed to defend (Ganser 2016; Blum 2013–2014).[14] On the contrary, by doing so the US has invariably ended by justifying its own operation of mass destruction (and those of its allies) combining the implementation of economic and military resources and condemning the same type of mass destructions perpetrated by its enemies.[15] This corresponds to the well-known use of double standards, by both the US and the EU.

Finally, the frequent use of economic, and especially military means contradicts another fundamental belief of the American elite: that the US has been able to exercise its power mainly thanks to the 'attraction' of all dimensions of its culture (Nye 2004, 2011). By so conceiving its relations with the rest of the world, the American elite has not been able to understand that it is mainly thanks to economic and military power that this has been possible. Nevertheless, several members of the establishment have very clearly understood that military means are the most important element of US power, when the other means have failed to obtain compliance with the US national interests (Kagan 2004, 2017a).

This is not to say that this ideology has not been contested within America right from the beginning. Many American 'voices denounced the megalomania of Manifest Destiny, the plunder of Mexico, the seizure of Hawaii, the slaughter of the Philippines, attacking every kind of racisms and imperialism as a betrayal of the anti-colonial birth right of the republic' (Anderson 2015, p. 5). Indeed, even today several voices denounce the same megalomania and the devastating consequences of its implementation in many parts of the world, especially since the end of World War II.[16]

---

[13]It is reasonable to consider that this option may be used to attract Russia to the West (US plus EU) and avoid the de facto alliance between Russia and China.

[14]For example, the napalm bombing of 67 Japanese towns (spring of 1945), followed by the atomic bombing of Hiroshima and Nagasaki (August 1945), which according to former Secretary of State McNamara would have ended by the condemnation of the US for war crimes, should the US have been defeated in World War II (McNamara 2009). Then followed a long series of attempted and very often succeeded mass destructions: Korea, Vietnam, Iraq, Afghanistan, Syria, Libya, Iran, to quote just a few.

[15]These resources are equated by Joseph Nye (2004 and 2011) with 'hard power' (comprising economic and military resources) and 'soft power' (comprising cultural resources). I have criticized elsewhere this absurd typology, that in fact constitutes an intellectual fraud (Urio 2018, pp. 36–43).

[16]See amongst many others: Stephanson (1995), to be completed with Anderson 2015; Stephanson 2010; Vidal 2003; La Faber 1994, 1998, and his magisterial article 2012; Griffin 2018; Scott 2007; Pfaff 2010; Bacevich 2008, 2012; Bradley 2009, 2015; Andersen 2017).

206   6 China and the New World Order. Why and How China's Foreign Policy …

Nevertheless, history shows that in spite of these voices, the tendency has been constantly and consistently to intervene everywhere, whenever possible, by any means, to diffuse the good news of the new world order.

6.1.2 The Actualization of American Ideology

Since the time of the establishment of the US many changes have occurred within the country as well as in the international system. One may think that the ideology described above may have lost some of its most important features. It is my opinion that the essential components of the initial ideology are still operating today, even if the drive to expansion seems to have come to a halt (Stephanson 1995, pp. 112–129; Porter 2018a, b).[17] Not only the space for further expansion has considerably diminished, but several territories seem to be developing towards more independence, whereas yet others correspond to the emergence of new powers (such as China) or to re-emerging powers such as Russia, and still some others are reclaiming an independent role in their area, such as Turkey, Iran and, hopefully, Europe. Daniel Bell has brilliantly summarized the persistence of US ideology through time: 'This blind faith in the universal potential of liberal democracy would not be so worrisome if it had not taken the form of US government policy to promote human rights and democracy abroad, regardless of local habits, needs, and traditions. Notwithstanding the rather huge gap between liberal democratic ideas and the reality at home, the repeated history of misadventures abroad due (at least partly) to ignorance of local conditions (…), nothing seems to shake the faith in the universal potential of Western democracy in [US] official circles.' (Bell 2006, pp. 4–5).

Let us now analyse how the fundamental features of the original US ideology are still operating today. Space permitting, it would be easy to sustain this statement by referring the reader to a very long series of quotations from the speeches of eminent American politicians (Urio 2018). Here a few quotations will be enough. They show a remarkable consistency in the foreign policy discourse, no matter if the speaker is Democrat or Republican.

We will begin with the reference to God. First, all the US Presidents have mentioned God in their inaugural speeches (Newcombe 2017). Second, since 1937 all the 13 Presidents have invited at least one representative of Christian churches and/or of Jewish faith to give prayers at their inaugural ceremony. Moreover, according to *Christian Headline,* at least 8 Presidents looked to God for guidance 'in times of personal and national crisis' (Neffinger 2017).[18] This is not to say that all the Presidents or the US political leaders are religious believers. On the contrary, it seems that many may be considered as atheist, and there have been several attempts to

---

[17]Let us remark that Porter focuses his analysis on the post-World War 2 period, and especially after the fall of the Soviet Union.

[18]The presidents are: George Washington, John Adams, Abraham Lincoln, James Madison, Grover Cleveland, Jimmy Carter, Ronald Reagan, and George W. Bush.

6.1 The Development of the Imperial US Foreign Policy

forbid the reference to God in public ceremonies. Moreover, reference to God by the elected Presidents is not necessarily the manifestation of their profound faith in God; on the contrary it may be a rhetorical tribute to the overwhelming attitude of the American people. And the reference is certainly the manifestation of the profound belief of the American people in a God who has chosen America and continues to bless it. Finally, and more interestingly, the participation of religion at the inaugural presidential ceremonies, one of the most important American public events, is a clear proof of the mix of religious and secular dimensions of US politics: the beliefs in the Book and the belief in democracy and capitalism combined in one of the most important (or the most important?) national public ceremonies.

Second, this leads me to the two dimensions of US foreign policy: exceptionalism/isolationism and universalism/interventionism, strengthened by the belief in the 'indispensable nation' and in the 'natural or divine' role of the US to lead the world. As I mentioned before, interventionism has prevailed throughout history. The switch in favour of interventionism occurred already during the XIX Century, and should have become evident, if necessary, even to the most fervent defenders of the narration of the 'benevolent American Republic', during the 2016 presidential campaign. During this campaign the theme of the 'indispensable nation' was one of the major issues discussed both by the candidates and the press.[19] Trump said that he dislikes the term 'American exceptionalism' and described it as insulting to other nations. Immediately Hillary Clinton criticized Trump by saying that he 'missed something important' and made a link between exceptionalism (which normally should lead to isolationism) the 'indispensable nation' and the leading role of the US in the world, i.e. the opposite of isolationism. She said that 'part of what makes America an exceptional nation is that we are also [the] indispensable nation. (…) People all over the world look to us and follow our lead.' (Kaplan 2016). Clinton further explained: 'when America fails to lead, we leave a vacuum that either causes chaos or other countries or networks rush into fill the void. So, no matter we lead. What kind of ideas, strategies, and tactics we bring to our leadership. American leadership means standing with our allies because our network of allies is part of what makes us exceptional.' (Clinton 2016).[20] The causal link between exceptionalism (in the new variant of interventionism) and the right to lead the world could have not been asserted with more clarity.

President Obama also established a clear link between the 'indispensable nation', and the leading role of the US, e.g. in his commencement speech at the U.S. Air Force

---

[19]It seems that the 'indispensable nation' was used for the first time by former Secretary of State Madeleine Albright 19 February 1998 on NBC's *Today Show*, speaking about US intervention against Iraq: 'It is the threat of the use of force [against Iraq] and our line-up there that is going to put force behind the diplomacy. But if we have to use force, it is because we are America; we are the indispensable nation. We stand tall and we see further than other countries into the future, and we see the danger here to all of us' (Albright 1998). Nevertheless, President Bill Clinton used this expression in his inaugural address of January 1997 (Clinton 1997). The same expression has been used by one of the most influential American geo-strategists, Zbigniev Brzezinski (1997).

[20]On the theme of the indispensable nation see for some contradictory opinions: Pfaff (2010), Wicket (2015), Lee (2016), Zenko (2014).

Academy: the United States is exceptional, and will always be 'the one indispensable nation in world affairs. (…) I see an American century because no other nation seeks the role that we play in global affairs, and no other nation can play the role that we play in global affairs. That includes shaping the global institutions of the XX century to meet the challenges of the XXI century' (Klein 2012).

Moreover, Obama referred to surveys confirming the acceptance of the leading role of the US: 'Surveys show our standing around the world is higher than when I was elected to this office, and when it comes to every important international issue, people of the world do not look to Beijing or Moscow to lead—they call us.' More specifically, in this same speech, speaking about one of the major components of his international strategy for maintaining the US as the world hegemon (the Transpacific Partnership), President Obama made it clear that the US has the responsibility, and very likely the right, to set the rules governing international trade and investments: 'With TPP, China does not set the rules in that region; we do. You want to show our strength in this new century? Approve this agreement. Give us the tools to enforce it. It's the right thing to do. (Applause)" (Obama 2016a).[21]

The next question is to find out through what means the US will lead the world. Of course, the most favourable answer, and the one which is generally given by the American elite, is by attraction of the American culture and its components: freedom, democracy, free market economy, human rights, arts, films, and even cuisine, the implementation of these values at home and their defence abroad. Nevertheless, reference to the paramount importance of economic and especially of military means is frequently mentioned by politicians and experts. For example, President Obama has frequently referred to the overwhelming superiority of the US military. Moreover, recently both Presidents Obama and Trump announced the investment of several billions of US dollars to improve the nuclear arsenal of its armed forces (Bandow 2016; McPhilips 2016; Wittner 2016; O'Hanlon 2017).

On several occasions, President Obama reassured the country that the US would not refrain from using military means, whenever necessary. In his 2016 'State of the Union Address' President Obama made it clear that military power is an essential part of US power: 'I told you earlier all the talk of America's economic decline is political hot air. Well, so is all the rhetoric you hear about our enemies getting stronger and America getting weaker. Let me tell you something. The United States of America is the most powerful nation on Earth. Period. (Applause.) It's not even close. It's not even close. (Applause.) It's not even close. We spend more on our military than the next eight nations combined. Our troops are the finest fighting force in the history of the world. (Applause.) No nation attacks us directly, or our allies, because they know that's the path to ruin' (Obama 2016a).

And speaking at the American University in Washington about the 'Iran Deal', President Obama did not hesitate to speak as the Commander in Chief: 'As Commander-in-Chief, I have not shied from using force when necessary. I have

---

[21] See Solis (2016), Director—Center for East Asia Policy Studies, Senior Fellow—Foreign Policy, Center for East Asia Policy Studies, Philip Knight Chair in Japan Studies, published by the *Brookings Institution*, that supports this partnership for maintaining the US leadership in Asia.

6.1 The Development of the Imperial US Foreign Policy

ordered tens of thousands of young Americans into combat. I have sat by their bedside sometimes when they come home. I've ordered military action in seven countries. There are times when force is necessary, and if Iran does not abide by this deal, it's possible that we don't have an alternative' (Obama 2015). And this of course contradicts Nye's concept of soft and hard power (Nye 2004, 2008, my critique: Urio 2018, pp. 36–43). Let us note that the theme of the commander in chief has been one of the major attacks on Trump by Hillary Clinton: 'Trump is not suited to be the next Commander in Chief, I am'. No doubt about that, when we know the aggressive policies implemented by the then-Secretary of State towards Russia, China, and her role in the launching of the war against Libya and more generally in the Middle East.[22]

A similar praise for military power is sustained by the neo-conservative Robert Kagan (2017a). After he concedes 'that Russia can thrive in the international economic order upheld by the democratic system, even if it is not itself democratic', he strongly considers that 'military and strategic competition is different. The security situation undergirds everything else. It remains true today as it has since World War II that only the United States has the capacity and the unique geographical advantages to provide global security and relative stability. There is no stable balance of power in Europe or Asia without the United States.' And Kagan adds, not without reason, that 'soft power' and 'smart power' will always be of limited value when confronting raw military power.

Quite logically the next step is to affirm the duty and the right of the US to lead the world toward the end of history, especially after the collapse of the Soviet Union, as Francis Fukuyama has strongly asserted in 1989 (Fukuyama 1989, 1992). Later, Fukuyama claimed that he changed his mind (Fukuyama 2008, pp. 224–225, 2012). Nevertheless, in spite of some departure from the messianic character of the end of history Fukuyama remains faithful to his first approach. And indeed, in 2016, the end of history is still there, although under the wording of a 'softer' kind. In an interview given to the German *Die Zeit,* Fukuyama answers the last question of the journalist 'do we have to adjourn the end of history?' by saying: 'By the end of the story I meant that I see no alternative that would be better than democracy. This end of history is not adjourned, but certainly it is not a reality for many people. We are currently going in the wrong direction.' (Thumann and Assheuer 2017).[23] So, the 'new end of history' is here to stay and, taking into consideration the events that have occurred since the 2016 Fukuyama interview, in particular the election of Donald Trump, it is likely that the US will continue to manage its foreign policy hesitating between 'universalism and intervention' and 'exceptionalism and separation', more likely a combination of both.[24] But what will remain, is the 'ideal liberal democratic republic with capitalist

---

[22] See the video on Hillary Clinton commenting the death (in fact the murder) of Gaddafi, available on You Tube, https://www.youtube.com/watch?v=Fgcd1ghag5Y, accessed 26 September 2018.

[23] My free translation from the German: 'Mit dem Ende der Geschichte meinte ich, dass ich keine Alternative sehe, die besser wäre als die Democratie. Dieses Ende der Geschichte ist nicht aufgeschoben, aber sicherlich ist es nicht die Realität für viele Menschen. Wir gehen derzeit in die falsche Richtung'.

[24] Against Fukuyama's thesis see: Kagan (2008), Kupchan (2005, 2012), Haas (2014, 2016, 2019).

economy' towards which every country should converge, either by imitating the 'exceptional republic' or by being led to it by US intervention.[25]

We have seen above that the leading role of the US was based upon the belief that the US has been entrusted with a 'manifest destiny'. To my knowledge this term is less frequently used than 'exceptionalism', 'indispensable nation' and the right to lead the world. It is nevertheless interesting to remark that it has been mentioned twice in the history of the Department of State prepared by the Historian of the Department (US 2017):

1830–1860: Diplomacy and Westward Expansion:

During this crucial period, the US pursued a policy of expansion based on *'manifest destiny'* (emphasis added), the ideology that Americans were in fact destined to extend their nation across the continent. The United States even proved to be willing to go to war to secure new territories. While it managed to negotiate an agreement with Great Britain to secure the Oregon territory [1846], acquiring the valuable territory south of it—including California and its important Pacific harbours—required the use of force, and, in 1845, the United States embarked on its first offensive war by invading Mexico [in fact, the second, after the Indian Wars].

1853: The United States and the Opening to Japan:

The same combination of economic considerations and belief in *'Manifest Destiny'* (emphasis added) that motivated the U.S. expansion across the North American continent also drove American merchants and missionaries to journey across the Pacific. At the time, many Americans believed that they had a special responsibility to modernize and civilize the Chinese and Japanese [another clear reference to the leading role of the US].

Probably the best case in favour of 'manifest destiny' has been presented by one of the most influential neo-conservatives, Robert Kagan. Kagan is the co-founder of the neoconservative *Project for the New American Century*. My analysis of US foreign policy led me to the conclusion that Kagan's analysis is generally shared by all the components of the establishment. Robert Kagan is a senior fellow at the influential think-tank *Brookings Institution* and a member of the not less influential *Council on Foreign Relations*.[26] In February 2017, i.e. after the Donald Trump election, Robert Kagan summarized his views in a long article published simultaneously by the

---

[25]The indispensable link between liberal democracy and capitalism does not need to be explained here. It suffices to mention the work of Nobel prize-winner Friedman (1982), Zakaria (1997).

[26]'The Project for the New American Century (PNAC) was a neo-conservative think tank (1997 to 2006) that had strong ties to the American Enterprise Institute. PNAC's web site said it was 'established in the spring of 1997 as "a non-profit, educational organization whose goal is to promote American global leadership.' and founded by William Kristol and Robert Kagan. (…) PNAC's stated goal was "to promote American global leadership." The organization stated that "American leadership is good both for America and for the world," and sought to build support for "a Reaganite policy of military strength and moral clarity." Of the twenty-five people who signed PNAC's founding statement of principles, ten went on to serve in the administration of U.S. President George W. Bush, including Dick Cheney, Donald Rumsfeld, and Paul Wolfowitz.' See Wikipedia: https://en.wiin1996kipedia.org/wiki/Project for_the_New_American_Century, accessed 28 March 2017. The following article, published by the influential *Foreign Affairs*, can be considered as the founding text of the neoconservative movement (Kristol and Kagan 1996).

6.1 The Development of the Imperial US Foreign Policy

influential magazine *Foreign Policy* and the not less influential *Brookings Institution* think-tank's website (Kagan 2017b).[27] The article can be considered as the most complete and coherent version of the 'New Manifest Destiny', even if this term does not appear explicitly in the text.

First of all, Kagan says that it is absolutely necessary to maintain the 'dominant position the US has held in the international system since 1945', referred to also as 'the US-led post-war global order, the US supported world order, or the world they [i.e. Americans] created after World War II, a clear reference to his book *The World America Made* (Kagan 2012a). The reason is that otherwise 'the existing order collapses and the world descends into a phase of brutal anarchy'. The values that this event is likely to damage are free market capitalism, democracy and political freedom(s), associated with American national interests. Moreover, 'the liberal enlightenment project elevated universal principles of individual rights and common humanity over ethnic, racial, religious, national, or tribal differences.' (Kagan 2017b).

The danger comes from the new enemies, i.e. 'two great revisionist powers, Russia and China (...) [who] are dissatisfied with the current global configuration of power. Both seek to restore the hegemonic dominance they once enjoyed in their respective regions. (...) Both Beijing and Moscow seek to redress what they regard as an unfair distribution of power, influence, and honour in the US-led post-war global order. As autocracies, both feel threatened by the dominant democratic powers in the international system and by the democracies on their borders. Both regard the United States as the principal obstacle to their ambitions, and therefore both seek to weaken the American-led international security order that stands in the way of their achieving what they regard as their rightful destinies. (...) It is a myth, prevalent among liberal democracies, that revisionist powers can be pacified by acquiescence to their demands' (Kagan 2017b).

Consequently, and quite logically, Kagan rejects the idea of the emergence of a multi-polar world, that would be governed by a joint leadership shared between US, Russia and China, because 'revisionist great powers are not easy to satisfy short of complete capitulation. Their sphere of influence is never quite large enough to satisfy their pride or their expanding need for security.' Moreover, 'revisionist great powers with growing military capabilities invariably make use of those capabilities when they believe the possible gains outweigh the risks and costs.'[28] And this poses a threat not only to the US but also to its allies and partners. The consequence is that the US must remain the 'indispensable nation' and continue to lead the liberal world it made.

Very generously Kagan concedes that 'within the liberal order, China can compete economically and successfully with the United States; Russia can thrive in the international economic order upheld by the democratic system, even if it is not itself democratic. But military and strategic competition is different. The security situation

---

[27]See also Kagan (2008, 2014).

[28]The subtitles of the last section of the article is quite revealing: 'Give 'em an inch, they'll take a mile'.

undergirds everything else. It remains true today as it has since World War II that only the United States has the capacity and the unique geographical advantages to provide global security and relative stability. There is no stable balance of power in Europe or Asia without the United States.' And Kagan adds, not without reason, that 'soft power' and 'smart power' will always be of limited value when confronting raw military power.

To sustain his demonstration Kagan uses a few historical examples that, according to him, make it clear that revisionist powers are very aggressive towards the US-led liberal order. On the one hand, Kagan considers that Russia has been far more aggressive: it invaded two neighbouring states, Georgia in 2008 and Ukraine in 2014, is implementing 'repressive policies toward his own people', sent 'substantial forces into Syria' where its role 'increased the refugee flow into Europe', 'funds right-wing populist parties across Europe', and uses its media outlets to support favoured candidates and attack others'.

Here we have another example of the pattern described by Diana Johnstone (2016, pp. 98–101) for creating the 'enemy' before attacking it, to be developed below. This way of presenting the Georgian and the Ukrainian conflicts shows how neoconservatives (but this could be said more generally of the US establishment and the majority of Western governments) consider the 'invasion' of one country by another. Clearly for them the only way to invade a country is to occupy it by military means, all other means such as NGOs, economic advisers and investors being excluded from the category of 'invasion'. A rather restrictive way to define 'invasion'. Or should one explain this by reference to the will to simply 'expand' all over the world anticipated by Jefferson since the beginning of the XIX century (see above) where 'expansion' very clearly is not considered as an 'invasion' but as a liberation of the ignorant and oppressed people? On the other hand, Kagan considers that 'Beijing, until recently has succeeded mostly in driving American allies closer to the US out of concern for growing Chinese power—but could change quickly.'

Clearly Kagan has some serious problems with history. First, he forgets (or does he really?) that the West has not ceased to provoke Russia since the end of the Cold War by breaking the promise made to Gorbachev (in exchange for the approval of the reunification of Germany) not to expand the NATO military alliance and the European Union into Eastern Europe (Sakwa 2017; Mettan 2017).[29] Several commentators deny that this promise has ever been made as they argue that the US did not confirm that promise in writing. It is thus easy to deny that the promise was ever made, or to refuse to accept an oral promise as legally, or at least morally binding.[30] Even so, one

---

[29]Sakwa has provided the best analysis of the motives and reasons of the progressive ideological and policy gap between the West (especially the US) and Russia. Read at least the Introduction (pp. 1–10), a magisterial summary of the dynamic of the relations between the West and Russia, analysed in depth in the book. The Mettan (2017) book is an ideal companion to Sakwa as it presents a historical analysis of the development of the Russo-phobia that has developed in the West since the Great Eastern Schism.

[30]This promise has been the source of a controversy between the defenders of the West and those who try to have a more balanced and objective view of this event. From the latter see Shifrinson (2016). Those who sustain that there has been no promise argue on the basis of the absence of a

6.1 The Development of the Imperial US Foreign Policy

can hardly deny that NATO and EU have expanded in Eastern Europe to the border of Russia; this policy can be qualified at best as a series of provocations, at worst as a number of aggressive moves toward Russia. It has never been a wise policy to humiliate the defeated adversary and to ignore its legitimate needs to assure security at its borders.

Second, Kagan also forgets that the main reasons for the catastrophe in Syria (and elsewhere) have been provoked by the US by encouraging, training, and funding fundamentalist Islamist organizations.[31] Moreover, it is the US massive military presence in the Far East that is at the origin of the development and modernization of the Chinese military resources.

Finally, whereas he maintains, as we have seen above, that the sphere of influence of Russia and China 'is never quite large enough to satisfy their pride or their expanding need for security', he does not see that this is just what the US has done already with the Monroe Doctrine, and, especially, after the end of World War II. The only reason that can explain this patent contradiction is that for Kagan the US are on the side of the 'good', whereas Russia and China are on the side of the 'evil'.[32]

The similarity is therefore evident with the 'old' Puritan Manifest Destiny, where God (or the Providence) had given to the chosen people the Promised Land and the right, and even the duty, to realize the prophecy of the Book, i.e. to expand their republic beyond the limits existing at the beginning of the XIX century. The prophecy of Thomas Jefferson quoted above will then be realized: 'However our present interests may restrain us within our limits, it is impossible not to look forward to distant times when our multiplication will expand it beyond those limits, and cover the whole northern, if not the southern continent [and today the whole world], with people speaking the same language, governed in similar forms, and by similar laws'.

In analysing the US foreign policy to face the declining power of the US, Kagan is very critical of the Bush administration for its failures in Iraq and Afghanistan, and more particularly of the Obama administration for 'not restoring American power and influence but by further reducing them (...) Obama, in fact, publicly acknowledged Russia's privileged position in Ukraine even as the United States and Europe sought to protect that country's sovereignty. In Syria, the administration practically invited Russian intervention through Washington's passivity, and certainly did nothing to discourage it, thus reinforcing the growing impression of an America in retreat across the Middle East.' Finally, regarding the Obama policy toward China, Kagan considers that 'despite the Obama administration's insistence that American strategy should be geared toward Asia, U.S. allies have been left wondering how reliable the U.S. commitment might be when facing the challenge posed by China.'

---

formal (i.e. written) document; see in this sense: Sarotte (2014). Nevertheless, newly-declassified documents show that the promise was made: Smith Yves (2017). The most recent article dealing with the West's promise is Richard (2018) with numerous references.

[31] For the reasons for the American intervention in Syria: Kennedy (2016).

[32] For the Russo-phobia and the Ukrainian crisis, I suggest Guy Mettan (2017, pp. 72–99), and Lendman (2014).

Even the competing candidates in the 2016 presidential election, Donald Trump and Hillary Clinton, take their dose of criticism. Hillary Clinton, because she declared that she was no longer supporting the Trans-Pacific Partnership, one of the pillars of US foreign policy to contain China. On the contrary, for Kagan, what is needed is a more affirmative strategy towards the revisionist powers, otherwise the US will lose its leading dominant role in the world. More interesting is the critique of the newly elected President. For Kagan, Donald Trump's foreign policy is too weak because it redefines American interests in a too narrow way, meaning that by criticizing NATO and the European Union, and suggesting that the US would not necessarily defend its allies in all circumstances, his foreign policy is a dangerous departure from the neoconservative foreign policy according to which the US should be present all over the world in order to defend its national interests. And this is what the founding document of the neo-conservative movement very well sustained (Kristol and Kagan 1996).

One may think that this analysis of the role of the US in the world is typical of the neoconservatives. This is not the case. If we analyse the US foreign policy from at least the end of World War II, the main features of the US foreign policy we have described above and summarized thanks to the (2017b) Kagan article, are basically the same. Differences, when they exist, are marginal, limited to different forms of rhetoric, a different mix of means, and/or different priorities. But the main goal remains the same: maintain the US as the sole superpower (Porter 2018a, b). During the Cold War, the 'indispensable nation' concept had its good historical, economic, cultural and military *raisons d'être*, given the menace that the Soviet Union represented for the US and the West. At the end of the Cold War the US had the opportunity, unique in world history, to become the world benevolent hegemon they claimed to be. This is the period that Bacevich describes as the 'age of great expectations' (in French one would say: *'l'âge de la folie des grandeurs'*), when the US leadership thought that, after the collapse of the Soviet Union, there were no limits to the fulfilment of the promises of the 'Manifest Destiny': the world was wide open to the diffusion of the good news of global capitalism and liberal democracy ... by all means (Bacevich 2017, 2008). A new version of the megalomania criticized already in the XIX Century, as we have mentioned above. Indeed, the US engaged in a series of wars, proxy-wars, regime change, and all sorts of interferences within other countries. If there is a reason why the US lost their reputation, it is not, as Kagan suggests, because of loss of military power and assertiveness in managing its foreign policy, but because of the mistakes made by using that military power in a variety of unnecessary ways. As Chalmers Johnson would say: today the consequence of these mistakes has been a 'blowback' (Johnson 2000, 2004, 2006, 2010).

We can now summarize the US ideology as it is today: America has been chosen by God—therefore it has a manifest destiny—and the indispensable nation has the right and the duty, through exceptionalism-universalism (with a switch from isolationism to interventionism) to lead the rest of the world toward the end of history—i.e. the victory of the Good over the Evil—i.e. a rule-based American-led liberal international order, i.e. democracy and capitalism and their values.

6.1 The Development of the Imperial US Foreign Policy

The consequence of this sequence is the necessity to identify, combat, contain and finally defeat the enemy. Let us start by saying that the most important feature is not compliance with democracy and human rights, but the threat that the country can represent for US interests. Otherwise one cannot understand why the US is supporting today non-democratic countries and has supported similar countries in the past. Only when the competitor is not any more a threat to US interests it ceases to be considered as a potential enemy. This appeared since the beginning of the American foreign policy. As long as the Indians were an obstacle to the expansion to the West they were considered as the enemy; and once they had been defeated (and the defeat was final in 1890 after the last massacre of Indians at Wounded Knee) the US started to consider them as people worth being considered with sympathy.[33]

The fight against the enemy is implemented through a variety of means that can be used in sequence and/or simultaneously (Johnstone 2016, pp. 98–101).[34] First, it is a question of disqualifying the enemy by focusing on its leader, by qualifying him as a savage (e.g. the Indians), a dictator (e.g. Saddam Hussein), a new 'Hitler' (e.g. Vladimir Putin), or a non-human, e.g. an animal (e.g. Assad).[35] This necessitates 'a propaganda war, waged by mainstream media and think tanks' whose goal is to obtain the support of the majority of citizens and of the 'international community'. This propaganda makes it clear that the dictator must go, one way or the other, and is operating through the whole process. The second measure (or stage) concerns the implementation of economic sanctions that serve to destabilize the country by deteriorating its economy, so that the enemy loses the support of its people, i.e. by 'making the economy scream', as happened in Chile in 1973 (watch today's ongoing sanctions against Iran, Venezuela, and Cuba).[36] The next measure concerns the mobilization of local clients, of which numerous examples may be quoted, e.g. present-day meddling in Iran, Venezuela and Syria. The fourth stage, that can be concomitant with the third one, is the use of NGOs, especially Human Rights NGOs, but in fact any kind of NGOs, especially those specialized in the diffusion of the ideal of market economy (in fact, capitalism), liberal democracy and human rights, such as those financed directly by the US government, e.g. the National Endowment for Democracy and its subsidiaries (numerous examples in Eastern Europe and Russia after the collapse of the Soviet Union). The goal is to create a climate of protest and

---

[33] The US Declaration of Independence qualifies the native Indians as 'the merciless Indian Savages, whose known rule of warfare, is an undistinguished destruction of all ages, sexes and conditions' (US 1776). See also situation of Indians in today's America: Chomsky Aviva (2018).

[34] Johnstone analysis the US interventions in Kosovo and in Ukraine.

[35] The first three qualifications are well-known and do not need references. The last (Assad is an animal) is from Donald Trump commenting on the alleged chemical attack by Syria of April 2018: 'Many dead, including women and children, in mindless chemical attack in Syria,' Trump tweeted. 'Area of atrocity is in lockdown and encircled by Syrian Army, making it completely inaccessible to outside world. President Putin, Russia and Iran are responsible for backing Animal Assad. Big price...', reported by *CNN*: Watkins (2018).

[36] This expression was used in 1970 when President Nixon ordered the CIA to 'make the economy scream' in Chile to 'prevent Allende from coming to power or to unseat him.' (Democracy Now 2013).

disorder in the name of democracy that, should it become violent, will inevitably lead the local police and/or army to violently intervene. This may lead to a regime change (as in Ukraine in 2014), or it may force the enemy to negotiate (as is the case today with the US sanctions on Iran). If the outcome of these actions is not satisfactory, the next move is to submit to the enemy a solution that he cannot accept. For example, in the case of Kosovo, Secretary of State Madeleine Albright organized false negotiations between the Yugoslav government and the Albanian Nationalists and introduced 'an ultimatum (total military occupation of Serbia by NATO) that obliged the Serbs to refuse and thus take the blame for refusing to negotiate'. During these actions, it is possible (and necessary) to continue the criminalization of the enemy, especially if his intervention to control the protest is sufficiently violent to qualify it as 'genocide', or at least that he is killing his own people. Finally, 'the sword of Damocles [i.e. the menace to resort to military means] that is hanging over every dispute' during the whole process (Urio 2018, pp. 37–42) may finally be implemented, should the 'evil enemy' fail to comply to the dictate of the 'good'.

This is not to say that the 'new believers' have not identified the major changes in the US domestic and international system that constitute a threat to the leading role of the US. But they fail to draw the conclusion that US foreign policy needs to be reformed. On the contrary, they persist in suggesting policies the aims of which is to maintain the structure of the international system America made and that strengthen the dominant role of the US. The analysis developed by the new believers' manifest destiny can be summarized in four main specific themes, that show the extent to which they are worried by the trends that have emerged during the last decades within the international system, and that risk putting an end to the realization of the 'manifest destiny'.[37]

The first theme concerns the recognition that there is a China threat. But even more, China is *the real threat* and must be distrusted as it has duped the US since the Mao era (Pillsbury 2015; Getz 2015; Scissors 2017b; Campbell and Ratner 2018). In his 2016 annual 'State of the Union Address' President Obama (2016a) has clearly identified China as a formidable rival to the global influence of the US. And he has warned members of Congress that failure to support the Trans-Pacific Partnership agreement could be paramount to ceding America's leadership to China. Voices have arisen to beware of China's Grand Strategy. Fears that China is planning to destroy the US have been put forward by serious American sources. And therefore, the worrying question remains: can China be contained? (Browne 2015; Christensen 2015; Smith Jeff 2015; Freeman 2016).

The second theme the 'new believers' are worrying about concerns the crisis of liberal democracy. Not only at the end of the Cold War and the collapse of the Soviet Union there has been a considerable surge of illiberal democracies, but today a crisis is even developing within liberal democracy itself. This leads strong believers in the 'manifest destiny' to ask the question: is there an American political decay and if so, is its renewal at all possible? And even worse, the debates during the

---

[37]For a good idea of the persistence of the belief in the 'manifest destiny' one can read the excellent book review by Meaney (2016), see also Porter (2018a, b).

6.1 The Development of the Imperial US Foreign Policy

2016 presidential campaign, that ended with the election of Donald Trump, have unmasked to the American citizens, and to the world, the very serious contradictions that have developed within American society after several decades of neoliberalism: unemployment, poverty, crime, racism and lies (Zakaria 1997, 2013; Fukuyama 2016; Ranciman 2016).[38] So, the question is: is this how democracy ends? The only possible way to explain this attitude, is to refer to the division of the world between 'good' and 'evil', already present at the beginning of the building of the American Republic, as we have seen above (a good example of the use of 'double standards'). Clearly, this division is still operating today: the US, the paramount representative of 'good', is 'entitled' to intervene all over the world to fight against 'evil', even if by doing so it is necessary to violate international laws that the US proudly claims to have contributed to establishing under its leadership (Ganser 2016; Marty 2018).[39]

The third theme concerns the crisis of the US-led liberal international order: the election of President Trump imperils the international liberal order that America has championed since World War II. As Robert Kagan, one of the most influential 'new believers', has put it: 'The world America made'. Trump has questioned long-standing US alliances like NATO and has promised to abandon or renegotiate major international trade agreements, such as the Trans-Pacific Partnership and the NAFTA. Some even consider that the Trump administration will 'become complicit in dismantling' the very world that America made, i.e. the expansion of liberal democracy all over the world and the integration of the world economy into the capitalist order (Kagan 2017a).

Fourth, given the themes and trends recognized above, the next worrying question the 'new believers' are compelled to ask is: what can we do to preserve US primacy? Even more than the other themes mentioned above, this fourth dimension takes the form of a mix of worries and assertive statements. Preserving primacy first of all means to fight against those who are seeking to overturn the rule-based international order under the leadership of the US, above all China, Russia and the Islamic State (Thornberry and Krepinevich 2016; Haas 2014, 2016; Mazarr 2016).

Having analysed the origins of US ideology, its developments since the XVIII century to the beginning the XXI century, and having introduced the reaction of the 'new believers' to the election of Donald Trump, we can now turn to the implementation of this ideology. First, we will analyse the general strategy that led the US leadership to consider that the end of history had come and that the rest of the world could be re-built, under the US leadership, according to the image of the US (liberal democracy and capitalism). Second, we will analyse how this strategy has been implemented with regard to China.

---

[38] For the origins and the resurgence of racism in today's US (see Whitman 2018). Introducing this book, whose title is quite revealing (Hitler's American Model), the author writes: 'This book turned out to be more timely than I expected. I received the proofs on the eve of the Election Day, 2016. (…) Over the subsequent year and half, American racism has climbed back up out the gutter and into national politics (p. xi).

[39] For the justification of the use of military force see Kagan 2004.

6.1.3 The Implementation of the US Ideology to International Relations

It is out of the question to describe in detail the US expansion since the founding of the American republic. A summary will be enough, subdivided within the most meaningful period of the US expansion.

For the period 1750–1904, I will summarize the major events by referring to the development of US foreign policy as described by the Office of the Historian of the Department of State, that refers to the different means of this expansion, i.e. wars, invasions, annexations, purchases, acquisitions, treaties, embargo, openings of countries, disputes, and interventionism (US 2017). One is stunned and astonished, by the scope, rapidity and consistency of the US expansion: conquest of the West, integration (most of the time at the expense of Spain) of Florida, Texas, California, Nevada, New Mexico, Arizona, Utah, Washington, Oregon; as well as a portion of what would become later Oklahoma, Colorado, Kansas, Wyoming and Montana; acquisitions of Louisiana from France and Alaska from Russia, thus excluding these powers from the Americas; annexation of Guam, Porto Rico and the Philippines. To this one can add the Monroe Doctrine (1823): the US forewarned the imperial European powers against interfering in the affairs of the newly independent Latin American States or potential United States territories. Finally, the Theodore Roosevelt Corollary to the Monroe Doctrine (1904) stated that the United States would intervene as a last resort to ensure that other nations in the Western Hemisphere fulfilled their obligations to international creditors, and did not violate the rights of the United States or invite 'foreign aggression to the detriment of the entire body of American nations. As the corollary worked out in practice, the United States increasingly used military force to restore internal stability to nations in the region' (US 2017). During this period the US developed its military resources (especially the Navy), and accelerated the development of its economy, under the screen of protectionist laws. The US was then ready to make the new century the 'American century'.

The US entered World War I in 1917. In spite of the strong support from President Woodrow, the US Senate voted against the participation of the US in the League of Nations, one of the most important outcomes of the peace conference. The US entered a period of relative isolation, but maintained its dominance over the Americas, followed the events of the interwar period in Europe,[40] maintained its presence in the Pacific (especially in the Philippines and China), and continued to develop its economy under the protection of a very strong protectionist trade policy. After the Japanese aggression on Pearl Harbour (7 December 1941) the US entered World War II, defeated Japan and installed in Japan its military forces (later transformed into military bases) and promoted the development of a liberal democratic Japan favourable to US national interests in the region. On the other hand, by intervening in Europe, the US put a term to the policy of exceptionalism-isolationism of the inter-

---

[40] In fact, political and economic relationships between Europe and the US were quite intense during the inter-war period; for a short summary see Lacroix-Riz (2014), Chap. 2: Le facteur américain. De la reintegration 'européenne' du Reich, pp. 31–46.

6.1 The Development of the Imperial US Foreign Policy

war period. They came back to the land of the Pilgrim Fathers as the liberators and established themselves on the Western European countries with a massive presence of military means (also later transformed into numerous military bases) with the purpose of containing Soviet Russia. At the end of the war, the US was ready to reclaim a leading role in international affairs, by implementing a formidable mix of power resources. Moreover, the US offered the Marshall Plan for the reconstruction of Europe to both Westerns and Eastern European countries (a clear violation of the Yalta Agreements)[41] and, after the inevitable refusal of the latter under pressure from Moscow, and after the Soviet Union set up communist regimes in Eastern Europe (also a clear violation of the Yalta agreements), the US concluded a military alliance (NATO) with Canada and Western European countries and favoured the integration of Europe.[42] It was the beginning of the Cold War.

Having become the most powerful state in the world, in spite of the competition with the Soviet Union (the other major winner of World War II), the fundamental guiding principle of US strategy since 1945 has certainly been the containment of potential competitors. Clearly, expansion since the end of World War II could not be envisaged as it was in the XIX century when US power expanded in the Americas, as we have seen above. At the end of World War II, further expansion could only have been possible by implementing a different strategy combining a variety of different means. It is here that containment becomes a fundamental principle to orient US foreign policy (Kennan 1947; Menand 2011; Rojansky 2016).

6.1.4 The Development of the US Power Resources Since WW2

In order to understand today's China foreign policy, we have to evaluate the means at the disposal of its major competitor, the US. The US foreign policy, as we have seen above, is a global policy whose aim is to establish and maintain the supremacy of the US in the world. Let us note that these resources have in fact been implemented since the beginning of US foreign policy, i.e. during the Indian Wars (1975–1890): economic and military resources, the imposition of international treaties favourable

---

[41] 'The Americans and the British generally agreed that future governments of the Eastern European nations bordering the Soviet Union should be "friendly" to the Soviet regime while the Soviets pledged to allow free elections in all territories liberated from Nazi Germany', US (2017), Department of State, Office of the Historian, The Yalta Conference, 1945, https://history.state.gov/milestones, last accessed 18 April 2017.

[42] Of course, the US had a complex set of motives for supporting Western Europe, especially the policy of containment of Soviet Russia, and not only the unselfish generosity of financing the reconstruction of the devasted European continent. For a critical analysis of the establishment of the Marshall Plan see La Faber (1994), Chap. 14: 'The Cold War, or the Renewal of US-Russian Rivalry (1945–1949)'; Griffin (2018), Chap. 8 'Creating the Cold War'; Green (2017), Part Three: The Rise of the Soviets; Lacroix-Riz (1985), Chap. 4 'La mise en place du plan Marshall: les mécanismes de la dépendance européenne (mai–décembre 1947)' and Chap. 5 'Le poids de Washington sur la politique française au début du plan Marshall'; Lacroix-Riz (2014).

to US interest (quite often violated)[43], military bases (Vine 2015, pp. 19–22), intelligence, interferences into other countries (starting with the Indian territories and then extended to Latin America). In other words, the imperial character of US foreign policy was there since the beginning. As China has started to go abroad, and in fact all over the world, as we will see in the last part of this chapter, China needs a global foreign policy that inevitably risks being a menace to the supremacy of the US.

The impressive number and types of power resources implemented within the US foreign policy is well known and has been dealt with in a great number of publications by the US government, think tanks, university researchers, and investigative journalists. The US foreign policy combine (1) military resources supported by a budget more than three times that of China, including both conventional and nuclear weapons, that can be deployed all over the world thanks to several hundreds of military bases with the support of the most powerful Navy and Air Forces, whereas China has only one military basis, but may build several in the near future; (2) the control of maritime routes; (3) a dozen of intelligence agencies, in addition to the world famous CIA; (4) the possession of the unique reserve currency (at least until recently, but still today the major reserve currency); (5) a network of political and military alliances and partnerships such as NATO, Japan, South Korea, Philippines, Australia, New Zealand; (6) the use of a number of devices for diffusing American values; (7) investments of American companies abroad, including China; and (8) two mega-treaties on trade and investment proposed by the Obama administration to the European Union and eleven countries of the Pacific region, whose goals were evidently to contain Russia and China (to be discussed below). Hereafter, I will insist on some problems resulting from the use of these resources that are more particularly interesting for the understanding of China's strategy to safeguard its own interests.[44]

The main problems with the US power are linked to the way it has implemented throughout history these resources to become the dominant state in the world, especially after the collapse of the Soviet Union at the beginning of the 1990s. Little by little, since at least the end of World War II, the US managed to set up the rules that govern the international system that in fact, if maintained, will assure the safeguard of its own national interests: the so-called 'liberal US-led international order', based upon the World Bank, the International Monetary Fund and the General Agreement on Tariffs and Trade (the predecessor of the World Trade Organization) and the dom-

---

[43] 'Through a combination of coerced treaties and the contravention of treaties and judicial determination, the United States Government succeeded in paving the way for the westward expansion and the incorporation of new territories as part of the United States', US (2017), Chapter: 'Indian Treaties and the Removal Act of 1830'. 'For centuries, treaties have defined the relationship between many Native American nations and the U.S. More than 370 ratified treaties have helped the U.S. expand its territory and led to many broken promises made to American Indians': Wang Hansi Lo 2017. The Historian of the Department of State (US 2017) in its 'Indian Treaties and the Removal Act of 1830' milestone concede that 'the U.S. Government used treaties as one means to displace Indians from their tribal lands, a mechanism that was strengthened with the Removal Act of 1830. In cases where this failed, the government sometimes violated both treaties and Supreme Court rulings to facilitate the spread of European Americans westward across the continent'.

[44] For more details and references about US power resources see Urio (2018), pp. 160–171.

6.1 The Development of the Imperial US Foreign Policy

inant role of the US dollar.[45] This is why the US establishment is doing whatever it can to maintain this order.

The first problem with this strategy is that the CIA (founded in 1947) has been from the beginning involved not only in intelligence activities, but also in activities that have nothing to do with intelligence.[46] The number of such activities increased up to the end of the Cold War. Although subsequently it has decreased, it remained quite high after the end of the Cold War. They include: meddling in other countries' elections (Shane 2018; Levin 2016), attempts at regime change (Blum 2013–2014, 2014a, b, c; Valentine 2017), setting up of secret armies in European countries (Ganser 2005), launching illegal wars (Ganser 2016; Jones 2017) and setting up illegal prisons where torture of US enemies could be secretly practiced (Marty 2018, pp. 153–193).[47] It should be noted that these interventions have been against not only authoritarian countries, but also against democratic governments whose mistake was to be an obstacle to US economic and geopolitical interests, such as the regime change in Iran (1953) and Chile (1973) or meddling into the elections in countries favourable to US interests but at risk of losing an election to leftist parties, such as the meddling in the Russian presidential election of 1996 for the purpose of succeeding in the re-elections of the US-friendly Boris Yeltsin against his communist opponent, or the support of the non-democratic Saudi Arabia regime (Beinart 2018; Kramer 2001). These numerous interventions show very clearly that the US foreign policy is more determined by the US national interest (especially of the US economy) than for a genuine defence of democracy and human rights. In the forefront of these illegal activities, it is not possible to forget that the US has been at war 93% of the time (222 out of 239 years between 1776, year of the Declaration of Independence, and 2015 (Washington Blog 2015, that gives the complete list of wars during this period).[48]

---

[45]To my knowledge, the best analysis of the US strategy for establishing world domination since at least the Second World War, are developed by Michael Hudson's books, significantly entitled: *Super Imperialism. The Origins and Fundamentals of US World Dominance* (Hudson 2003) and *Global Fracture. The New International Economic Order* (Hudson 2005).

[46]On the transition from the CIA to the National Endowment for Democracy see Blum (2014a), Chap. 19: Trojan Horse. The National Endowment for Democracy, pp. 238–243.

[47]Levin (2016) has identified 81 cases of electoral meddling between 1945 and 2000, of which 19 after the end of the Cold War, the most instructive classical example being the re-election of Boris Yeltsin in 1996 (Kramer 2001), Blum (2013) has identified 59 cases of attempted regime change (1949–2014), of which 14 after the end of the Cold war, 37 have been successful, of which 14 after the end of the Cold War; Ganser (2016) has identified and documented no less than 13 illegal wars between 1953 and 2015, of which seven after the end of the Cold War; illegal armies were set up during the Cold War (Ganser 2005).

[48]See also the report of the Senior Research Librarian of the US Congress (Salazar Torreon 2017) that covers 1798–2017, with the following comment: 'This report lists hundreds of instances in which the United States has used its Armed Forces abroad in situations of military conflict or potential conflict or for other than normal peacetime purposes. (...) (...) Covert operations, disaster relief, and routine alliance stationing and training exercises are not included here, nor are the Civil and Revolutionary Wars and the continual use of U.S. military units in the exploration, settlement, and pacification of the western part of the United States. (...) [only] eleven times in its history, the United States has formally declared war against foreign nations'.

The second problem is linked to the limits of the use of military power and the consequences for US strategy. Notwithstanding the massive contribution of the Soviet Union, of the United Kingdom and of the European national liberation movements, the US emerged from World War II with the reputation as the major (or even the sole) defender of freedom and democracy. Nevertheless, despite the considerable accumulation of military resources, the Cold War and the diffusion of communism during the Cold War in Europe, Asia, Africa and Latin America inevitably led the US to develop a more complex strategy to defend its interests and those of the West. So, the diffusion of American values become a must to the US, should it choose to restrain from primarily using its economic and military resources to obtain acceptance of its international policy. For this purpose, in addition to the statements by politicians, journalists and think tanks, the US establishment has set up a whole set of instruments to diffuse the values of democracy, human rights and free trade: radio and TV broadcasting companies such as the Voice of America, Radio Free Asia and CNN, mainstream media, governmental agencies such as the US Agency for International Development (USAID), the 'American Cultural Centres', think tanks such as the Council on Foreign relations and the Brookings Institution, not-for-profit foundations dedicated to the growth and strengthening of democratic institutions around the world, NGOs, some of them in fact government-funded organizations such as the National Endowment for Democracy and its subsidiaries.[49] To this we can add the financing of foreign students (including Chinese) to attend American Universities with the aim to open their minds to American values, such as liberal democracy and free market economy.

Unfortunately, as I mentioned above, these means have been used all over the world, quite often to destabilize countries by supporting, financing and training opposition groups and organizations. Moreover, with the help of governmental agencies such as the CIA and the National Endowment for Democracy (NED) and its subsidiaries, there have been many cases where these activities have favoured regime changes with the aim of putting into power a new government more likely to support American interests. The most recent case is that of Ukraine in 2014, another is still going on today under our very eyes in Syria, and another example is also underway today in Venezuela, and it is not impossible that another one may also be ongoing in the Philippines. These interventions are often prepared and/or accompanied by the training and financing of local police and armed forces, or even covert war interventions by special operation forces such as the Green Berets and the Navy SEALs. So, in these cases there is an overlapping between quasi-military and economic power resources on the one hand, and cultural resources on the other. If US cultural power is so strong, one does not understand why it has been very often necessary to resort to military power (under the form of both overt and covert warfare) to obtain compli-

---

[49]For example, 'each year, NED makes more than 1,200 grants to support the projects of non-governmental groups abroad who are working for democratic goals in more than 90 countries. Since its founding in 1983, the Endowment has remained on the leading edge of democratic struggles everywhere, while evolving into a multifaceted institution that is a hub of activity, resources and intellectual exchange for activists, practitioners and scholars of democracy the world over.', website of the NED, http://www.ned.org/about/, accessed 17 May 2017.

6.1 The Development of the Imperial US Foreign Policy

ance with US interests.[50] This seems to be one of the important reasons that explains the loss of power of the US since the end of the Cold war, in addition to the emergence of new powers, such as China, and the re-emergence of old powers such as Russia, as well as the awakening of Europe that seems to be on its way to developing a new defence and foreign policy more independent from the US. And the latter may represent an additional reason for the loss of US power.

The third problem is related to the collapse of the Soviet Union at the beginning of the 1990s.[51] A I have already mentioned above, the road was then wide open in front of the US to become the sole superpower. Then follows the years of 'great expectations' or of the '*folie des grandeurs*': the US and its European allies started an aggressive policy toward Russia by expanding NATO to Eastern Europe and admitting several Eastern European countries into the European Union. Moreover, military interventions in Yugoslavia allowed the US to establish a huge military base in Kosovo (Camp Bondsteel), in addition to the many other military bases established by the US after World War II in Europe and everywhere else.[52] This aggressive policy had the result (desired or undesired) of humiliating the defeated enemy, and rejecting its understandable needs to assure security at its borders, in spite of the many moves by Russian leaders (and especially Vladimir Putin) to associate Russia with the management of European security. Russia's only international policy choice would have been to accept the dominance of the West and to integrate the international world that the US made. This shortsighted US policy was based upon the belief that the world that emerged after the collapse of the Soviet Union was there to stay forever thus realizing Fukuyama's end of history (Fukuyama 1992). For some observers of international politics this was the beginning of Cold War II targeting Russia and later China with the aim of establishing a unipolar world dominated by the US and its allies: the 'expansion' of US power would by then have realized Thomas Jefferson's dream above any optimistic expectations. But this type of behaviour, as well as the two problems mentioned above, did not remain unnoticed by the Chinese leadership.

---

[50]On the transition of American warfare from overt (Bush) to covert warfare (Obama) see Turse (2012a, b, 2015, 2018). For a short presentation Urio (2018), pp. 161, 165–166. According to Turse during the Bush administration the US special operation forces intervened in 60 countries, under the Obama administration they operated in 133 countries and in 2017 under Trump they were operating in '149 countries—about 75% of the nations on the planet. At the halfway mark of this year [2018], according to figures provided to TomDispatch by U.S. Special Operations Command (USSOCOM or SOCOM), America's most elite troops have already carried out missions in 133 countries. That's nearly as many deployments as occurred during the last year of the Obama administration and more than double those of the final days of George W. Bush's White House' (Turse 2018).

[51]Among the vast literature on the reasons explaining the collapse of the Soviet Union, see the interesting and unusual interpretation of the French historian and demographer Emmanuel Todd (1979).

[52]The illegal war against Serbia (1999), as well as the Iraqi war (2003) were started by the US without the approval of the UN (Ganser 2016, Chaps. 11 and 13); they have been justified by Robert Kagan in his 2004 book, on the basis of 'the humanitarian duty the civilized world has to intervene where and when the tyrant massacres his own people', the presence of weapons of mass destruction and the support of terrorist organizations. This is a good example of the euphoria that oriented US foreign policy after the collapse of the Soviet Union. See the statement by Las Casas about this type of justification, at the beginning of this chapter.

224

In fact, several major changes have been underway since at least the end of the Cold War. The unipolar world that emerged after the collapse of the Soviet Union did not last long. Powerful long-term forces (the 'silent transformations'—above Sects. 2.1 and 2.3) had been at work for a long time and prepared the emergence of a multi-polar world, with China the most serious competitor of the US, and Russia coming back to the international scene under the presidency of Vladimir Putin. I shall now examine with what strategy the US has tried to maintain its global leadership in order to 'contain' the rise of China.

6.1.5 *US Strategy Toward China in the XXI Century*

We have seen above that the interest of the US in the Far East started between the end of the XVIII Century and the first half of the XIX Century. But at that time, the goal was mainly to safeguard American economic interests by joining the European powers to sign unequal treaties with China, whereby obtaining the same economic advantages, thanks to the application of the most favoured nation principle. In fact, we have here the first manifestation of the 'China Mirage' or the 'China Dream' (Bradley 2009, 2015) that would become the dominant drive of the US expansion in the Far East, and is still working today.[53] The Historian of the Department of State under the title 'United States Maritime Expansion across the Pacific during the XIX Century' very well explains the motivation of the US expansion in the Pacific and the importance of China (emphases added):

> The westward expansion of the United States during the XIX century was not limited to North America, but rather included an ongoing push to establish a stronger U.S. presence in and across the Pacific Ocean. This maritime expansion, *driven mostly by commerce*, had important implications for U.S. foreign policy. *The appeal of profits* to be earned from the China trade served as the initial impetus to motivate U.S. citizens and officials to enter into the Pacific region.[54] China was the source of some of the world's most sought-after commodities—tea, porcelain, and silk—and Western merchants had sought access to this highly lucrative trade since at least the XVII century. Following U.S. independence, U.S.-based merchants continued to seek opportunity in China. In February 1784 the 'Empress of China' became the first [commercial] ship to sail from the United States to China, and in its wake came a steady flow of merchants *in search of wealth*. During the first decades of the

---

[53] According to an article published by the influential *American Enterprise Institute (AEI)*, since the last quarter of the XVIII Century, 'from the American perspective, there was the potentially vast Chinese market to tap into, millions of Chinese to preach the Cristian Gospel to, and cheap Chinese labour to help build the American West', Schmitt (2019). Founded in 1938, AEI is closely associated with conservatism and neoconservatism, although it is officially non-partisan.

[54] It is interesting to remark that the British expansion in Asia, especially in India, was also motivated by the will of private investors to enrich themselves, well before the government took over the policy from the British East India Company: Ferguson (2004). For the role of the British merchants in the making of America: Butman and Targett (2018).

6.1 The Development of the Imperial US Foreign Policy

XIX century, U.S. merchants amassed *sizeable fortunes* that they subsequently invested in the development of their homeland.[55]

As this trade grew, U.S. traders built a small outpost in China and their interactions with Chinese subjects became more complex and occasionally contentious. The U.S. Government realized that it had to establish formal diplomatic ties *in order to protect the interests of its citizens*. In the wake of war between Britain and China, and the subsequent opening of diplomatic relations between those two countries, the United States moved to negotiate its own treaty with the Chinese Government. The resulting agreement, the Treaty of Wangxia, was ratified in 1844, and soon thereafter U.S. ministers and consuls took up residence in China's capital and port cities.

Making the journey to China and maintaining the U.S. presence there also required *a network of ports* extending across the Pacific Ocean, and as such, the China trade soon drove the United States to expand its presence throughout the Pacific region. U.S. *expansion* across the Pacific fundamentally changed the global position of the United States (US 2017).

Nobody better than Indiana Senator Albert J. Beveridge has sustained, in a 1900 speech to the US Congress, the idea that China was the final goal of the US expansion in the Pacific:

> Mr. President, the times call for candor. The Philippines are ours forever, "territory belonging to the United States," as the Constitution calls them. And just beyond the Philippines are China's illimitable markets. We will not retreat from either. We will not repudiate our duty in the archipelago. We will not abandon our opportunity in the Orient. We will not renounce our part in the mission of our race, trustee, under God, of the civilization of the world. And we will move forward to our work, not howling out regrets like slaves whipped to their burdens but with gratitude for a task worthy of our strength and thanksgiving to Almighty God that He has marked us as His chosen people, henceforth to lead in the regeneration of the world (Beveridge 1900).[56]

Nevertheless, only recently, when it became clear that the development of China's economy occurred not only in low-value-added goods, but also in high-tech products, and, more worrying, in the military domain, the threat from the Soviet Union, which vanished (or should have vanished) at the beginning of the 1990s, was soon replaced by the 'China threat' exorcised by the forecast of the 'coming collapse of China' ... which did not come. While it could be possible to sustain this by quoting the numerous articles and reports published by the most influential American think tanks, here it suffices to quote a passage of a report from the very influential *Council on Foreign Relations*:

---

[55] It is necessary, and only fair, to mention that many of these merchants enriched themselves by being very active in the opium trade (Bradley 2015, pp. 17–19, 47–49).

[56] In more popular mood, an Emil Flohri's cartoon, published by *Judge* (a weekly satirical magazine published in the United States from 1881 to 1947) illustrates a scene where Uncle Sam is seen stepping across the ocean into the Philippines loaded down with symbols of modern civilization, including books labeled 'Education' and 'Religion', bridges, railroad trains, sewing machines, farm machinery. A short distance beyond the Philippines a small figure representing China stands with a happy expression and open arms, surrounded by signs saying large quantities of modern goods are wanted, https://commons.wikimedia.org/wiki/File:Flohri_cartoon_about_the_Philippines_as_a_bridge_to_China.jpg, accessed 15 December 2018.

To deal with Xi's more assertive foreign and defence policies, the United States should devise a grand strategy for Asia at least as coherent and coordinated as the one that has been formulated in Beijing, which appears designed to maximize China's power while challenging the long-standing role of the United States in the region. (…) the United States should use a variety of instruments of statecraft to incentivize China to commit to a rule-based order but impose costs that are in excess of the gains Beijing would reap if it fails to do so. This American grand strategy should account for the fact that the decades-long endeavour to integrate China into the global order has not significantly tempered China's strategic objective to become the most powerful and influential country in Asia. This being the case, the United States needs a long-term approach that demonstrates U.S. internal strength, external resolve, and steadiness of policy (Blackwill and Campbell 2016; see also from the RAND think tank: Gompert 2016).

The reason is clear: China is challenging 'the long-standing role of the United States in the region' and, we have to add, elsewhere in the world.[57] These assertive policy analyses and proposals are not only the opinion of influential think tanks but also that of eminent US officials. See for example the speeches of President Obama (Obama 2016a, b).

In fact, it appears that the main theme that summarizes American reactions to China's rise is the fear of losing the capacity to lead the world, to lose the status of sole world super-power that sets the rules of the international system, i.e. of the 'world America made', according to Robert Kagan's famous statement (Kagan 2012a). Even Brzezinski, while he recognizes that the US 'is no longer the globally imperial power', affirms that the US 'needs to take the lead in realigning the global architectures' (Brzezinski 2016). Given these fundamental policy goals, shared by all the components of the US establishment, it is understandable that the election of Donald Trump has provoked an unbelievable hysteria which cannot be explained only (or, more likely, mainly) by the domestic policies announced by candidate Trump and implemented by President Trump, nor by his being a womanizer, a racist and an inexperienced politician. It seems to me that what worries more the US establishment are the international policies changes announced by Trump. Otherwise one cannot understand the establishment's hysteria about the alleged contacts Trump and his associates may have had with Russia and the alleged meddling of Russia into the 2016 presidential election. The hysteria came to its apex at the moment of the meeting between Trump and Putin in Helsinki 16 July 2018. The irrational excitement led some observers to accuse Trump of treason. Given that the war between Trump and the establishment has been going on for more than two years (in fact it started well before the day of the election), the establishment is likely to go on with this strategy together with its political ally, the Democratic Party. The latter should instead proceed to an in-depth and dispassionate analysis of the mistakes it has been making for a very long time. It should eventually define a more efficient strategy, instead of its present one which does not take into consideration the needs of large portions of the American people which it has neglected by giving priority to the greed of the financial actors. But is it able to do it?

---

[57]See also from the influential Brookings Institution's the report written by ten authors (among them Robert Kagan) within the *Order from Chaos Programme*: Chollet et al. 2017.

6.1 The Development of the Imperial US Foreign Policy

The hysteria against Putin is irrational if one takes into consideration the interests of the American people. In fact, the idea of finding an agreement with Russia is certainly the most brilliant move announced by a US president since the end of the Cold War. The US establishment should not forget that Russia and China may further develop their cooperation and contest the leading role of the US. An agreement with Russia may be the only way to break the de facto alliance, or partnership, between Russia and China, which could become the dominant actor in Asia and beyond, thanks to regional partners such as Iran (Esfandiary and Tabatabai 2018).

So, while Russia remains still today a serious competitor, the US has to face an even more formidable competitor: China. These are not new ideas, as the experts in geopolitics have already put forward for a long time. Let us take the analysis of Zbigniew Brzezinski. Already in 1997 Brzezinski develops an in-depth analysis of the strategy the US should implement in order to maintain its leading role in the world: the future of US leadership will be decided in Asia (Brzezinski 1997a, b). In summary:

'Eurasia is the world's axial supercontinent. A power that dominated Eurasia would exercise decisive influence over two of the world's three most economically productive regions, Western Europe and East Asia. A glance at the map also suggests that a country dominant in Eurasia would almost automatically control the Middle East and Africa.' Moreover, 'what happens with the distribution of power on the Eurasian landmass will be of decisive importance to America's global primacy and historical legacy. (...) In the short run, United States should consolidate and perpetuate the prevailing geopolitical pluralism on the map of Eurasia. This strategy will put a premium on political manoeuvring and diplomatic manipulation, preventing the emergence of a hostile coalition that could challenge America's primacy ...' Finally, by the medium term, 'the foregoing lead to the emergence of strategically compatible partners which, prompted by American leadership, might shape a more cooperative trans-Eurasian security system. In the long run, the foregoing could become the global core of genuinely shared political responsibility (Brzezinski 1997a).

Brzezinski is very clear in considering that Russia should be integrated into a larger network of European cooperation, which the US has failed to do, as I said above. As for China, he considers that much will depend on its relationships with the US: 'More specifically, the medium-term goal requires fostering genuine partnerships with a more united and politically defined Europe, a regionally preeminent China, a post-imperial and Europe-oriented Russia, and a democratic India. But it will be success or failure in forging broader strategic relationships with Europe and China that shapes Russia's future role and determin Eurasia's central power equation.' (Brzezinski 1997a). This may be an alternative, and for me a very complicated one, to Trump's strategy (as we will see below) to attract Russia to the West in order to isolate and contain China. But given the hostility the US establishment persists in manifesting towards Russia, this policy is not likely to be implemented in the near future.

Whatever the strategy the US will be willing and able to implement, for Brzezinski, as well for Kagan, the fundamental goal of US foreign policy remains the same: to keep US dominance and, under the leadership of the US, integrate the other countries into the liberal and capitalistic order 'that America made'. This must be achieved by implementing the fundamental principle guiding the US foreign policy since the end of the Cold War, i.e. a strategy of containment of potential competitors all over the world. The distribution and development of power resources at the turn of the millennium, especially in Asia, should have led the US to define a new strategy. However, even the majority of books published recently by mainstream think tanks and university professors, just before or after the beginning of the Trump presidency, remains faithful to the idea that the international liberal order America made should be preserved by containing potential competitors, especially China, whose goal is perceived as a will to change the rules of the international system and to challenge the leadership of the US. Therefore, the US should maneuver so that China will not dominate the XXI Century. The only policy option left to China and other potential competitors is to integrate the liberal world by adopting its major characteristics, i.e. liberal democracy and capitalism. Or, should they prefer to keep some of their non-liberal features at home, they will have to integrate the liberal international order and behave according to the rules America made.[58] And this seems to be the conclusion the majority of American observers arrive at.

The reader who is interested in more radical criticisms of the US foreign policy should consult alternative websites, such as *Tom Dispatch*, that defines itself as 'a regular antidote to mainstream media', with contributions from reliable scholars and serious investigative journalists such as Noam Chomski, Tom Engelhardt, David Vine, Nick Turse, Alfred McCoy, Dilip Hiro, Nomi Prims and many others.[59] The 'mainstream reader' may be horrified by these references, but I trust the attentive reader to be critical towards alternative websites, as well as towards mainstream media and authors. Professor emeritus John W. Dower in the Preface of his 2017 books pays a tribute to 'the many investigative reporters who have written perceptively on the multiple tragic faces of violence of our post-World War II world', and quotes 'the invaluable website *TomDispatch*' (Dower 2017, p. xiv).

Before we turn to the analysis of Trump's foreign policy, it is important to mention that in addition to the resources mentioned above, one of the most important elements of the US containment strategy has been developed by President Obama through two mega treaties: the Transatlantic Trade and Investment Partnership (TTIP) and the Transpacific Partnership (TPP), the latter being an important part of his 'pivot to Asia' strategy.[60] The aim of the TTIP was to strengthen the containment of Russia by further integrating Europe into an Atlantic area dominated by the US and by the Western multinational companies, in addition to the NATO military alliance (Le

---

[58] See for example the book by one of the most renowned American sinologists, Shambaugh (2016). But rest assured China will not dominate the XXI Century. If you follow the demonstration by Fenby (2014), the answer is given in the last chapter entitled: 'China will not dominate the XXI century', pp. 117–131.

[59] Tom Dispatch website: http://www.tomdispatch.com/. Other alternative websites worth consulting: *FAIR* (https://fair.org/) and *Naked Capitalism* (https://www.nakedcapitalism.com/), among many others.

[60] 'President Obama's Asia strategy represents a significant shift in American foreign policy from a Middle Eastern/European focus to an East/South Asian one, but the US had already deployed additional naval and air forces in the Far East under the presidency of Bill Clinton and George Bush (son). For the US pivot to Asia (see Lieberthal 2011; Clinton Hillary 2011).

6.1 The Development of the Imperial US Foreign Policy

Corre and Pollack 2016). The aim of the TPP was to strengthen the containment of China by integrating the economies of 12 countries of the Pacific region into an economic area dominated by the US. These two treaties, if approved, would constitute two formidable tools for containing the rise of the two major competitors of the US.[61] The project of the Transatlantic Agreement has long been supported by the Trans-Atlantic Business Council (TABC), created in 1995 under the sponsorship of the European Commission and the US Department of Commerce. Similarly, the Trans-Pacific Agreement is supported by multinationals, especially American, for example those in the pharmaceutical and tobacco industries. The objective of these treaties is to eliminate practically all the obstacles to trade and investment other than tariffs and quota, that had already been reduced to a very low level. For this purpose, these treaties would allow the multinationals to sue the States before a private court if their public policies had reduced, or could reduce in the future, the profits the investors would have achieved in the absence of these policies. Moreover, the decisions taken by these private courts would be final, i.e. not subject to appeal.[62] If those two treaties were approved, they would legitimize the domination of multinationals (especially those of the finance sector) over the States in a vast area, and would be able to dictate these treaties' conditions beyond its borders.[63]

It must be said that these treaties have been very seriously criticized by civil society organizations, ad hoc associations of citizen and academic researchers. The criticism of these treaties has been based upon research made on the consequences of the implementation of the North American Free Trade Agreement (NAFTA), a similar treaty between the US, Canada and Mexico, in force from 1994 and 2018, showing that the implementation of this treaty has destroyed millions of jobs in the US.[64] What is feared with TPP and TTIP is that these treaties will open to the multinational companies the possibility to invest abroad and transfer national industrial activities to countries where the cost of production is lower, due to lower labour costs and to less stringent health and environmental regulations (when they exist) and thus export these goods to developed countries with a massive profit. And this is the reason why the multinationals supported these treaties. This was also a recurrent theme of Donald Trump during the 2016 presidential campaign. In January, President Trump withdrew the US from the TPP, re-negotiated and obtained a new version of NAFTA, and postponed the decision on TTIP to an unknown date. This is one of the major reasons explaining the ferocious opposition from representatives of the US establishment to Donald Trump, especially from the multinationals, including investors, big banks and the mainstream media and think tanks.

---

[61]The 12 countries of the TPP: Australia, Brunei, Canada, Chile, Japan, Malaysia, Mexico, New Zealand, Peru, Singapore, the United States (until 23 January 2017) and Vietnam. On the strategy for containing China see McCoy (2015).

[62]For a critique of the procedure called 'Investor-state dispute settlement (ISDS)' see Eberhardt (2016).

[63]For a critical analysis see Stiglitz 2016; Wallach 1998, 2013, 2014, 2017; Kelsey 2011; Jäcklein 2014.

In favour of these treaties see Rashish 2014; Montanino and Wayne 2016.

[64]Against NAFTA (see Public Citizen 2014, 2018). For a different opinion see Bahar (2017).

230   6 China and the New World Order. Why and How China's Foreign Policy …

Nevertheless, even if the TPP has been abandoned by the US and the TTIP negotiations have been suspended by Trump's administration, the power resources that may be used to contain Russia and China will remain in the hands of the new president (and/or of his successor) as a framework within which to re-orient the US strategy of containment.

However, before this may possibly happen, it is not impossible that Trump may be forced by the establishment to finalize both the TPP and the TTIP, eventually in a different form, as he has obtained for the NAFTA, to be commented below.

6.1.6   US Foreign Policy of President Donald Trump

The election of Donald Trump has put the US establishment in a terrible situation. Divided about what is today necessary to do for safeguarding the US national interests, obsessed by the Russian 'enemy', fearful of the emerging Chinese giant, doubtful of the capacity of its enormous military resources, unsure whether its culture (i.e. liberal democracy, human rights and free market economy) is still capable to attract leaders and citizens of other countries, incapable to figure out in what direction the new president will lead the 'chosen people', fearful that the end of history may be quite different from that envisaged by the Founding Fathers (as other powers seem to be able to drive the world toward 'another end of history'), aware of the contradictions that have weakened and fractured the 'melting pot' after 40 years of neoliberalism, the US establishment seems to be unable to find an agreement to redefine its role at home and in the world.[65] At the end of August 2017, at the moment of concluding the writing of my 2018 book (Urio 2018, p. 134) I said that whereas it was difficult less than one year after the election to forecast what policies the new president would implement, it was nevertheless possible (as it is today) to suggest some possible outcomes, by taking simultaneously into consideration the career and the personality of the new president, his statements during the presidential campaign, and the decisions taken since January 2017. This should be done also by taking stock of the 'silent transformations' (Sects. 2.1 and 2.3 above) that have been shaping the new multi-polar world, and the gap between presidential candidate Trump's foreign policy proposals and the policies actually implemented after election. Moreover, one should also compare the latter with the traditional imperial foreign policy the US establishment has consistently implemented since the end of World War II.

In my 2018 book I also wrote: 'In fact, Trump's slogan "America First" does not preclude the use of force, should the president consider that US' national interests are at stake. Nor that he will be able to refrain from military interventions abroad, should the establishment put such a pressure on him that he will be compelled to satisfy its interests. This could be done by a combination of pressures coming from both Repub-

---

[65]The title of the March 2017 issue of *Foreign affairs* is quite revealing: 'What Was the Liberal Order? The World We May Be Losing', *Foreign Affairs,* March 2017, a collection of articles written between World War II and 2017. See also Allison 2018a, b; Porter 2018a, b.

6.1 The Development of the Imperial US Foreign Policy

lican and Democrat members of the US Congress, the industrial-military complex, the so-called "intelligence community" (more than a dozen agencies, including the CIA), university scholars, and mainstream think tanks, media.[66] The latter can play an important role in 'informing' the US citizens about the situation that, according to them, requires a military intervention' (Urio 2018, p. 139). If we accept the Perry Anderson statement about 'the provincialism of an electorate with minimal knowledge of the outside world' (Anderson 2015, pp. 1–2), this possibility is far from being unthinkable, when we know the ability of mainstream media to manipulate information.[67]

Here it is interesting to suggest that the capacity to manipulate information may be better understood thanks to the concept of propaganda. In his introduction to the work of Edward Bernays (Bernays 1928, pp. 9–33), Mark Crispin Miller, professor of media studies at New York University, considers that propaganda has been practiced by governments for centuries, but 'it was not until 1915 [during the First World War] that governments first systematically deployed the entire range of modern media to rouse their population to fanatical assent (…) The Anglo-American drive to demonize "the Huns" and to cast the war as a transcendent clash between Atlantic "civilization" and Prussian "barbarism", made so powerful an impression that the worlds of government and business were forever changed' (Miller 2004, pp. 11–12).[68] In fact, this campaign was so successful that after the war the propagandists put their competencies at the service of entities such as General Motors, Procter & Gamble, John D. Rockefeller, General Electric with the success we know. For the political domain, it is interesting that Miller quotes *'How we Advertised America'* by George Creel (2012, p. 3, first edition 1920), director of the US Office of War Information: 'Our effort was educational and informative throughout, for we had such confidence in our case as to feel that no other argument was needed than the simple, straightforward presentation of facts'. And Miller comments: 'the passage itself, of course, is a stunning bit of propaganda, as it bluntly reconfirms the Manichaean plot that Creel & Co. had hammered home throughout the war: Germans always lie, Americans always tell the truth' (p. 14). Just replace 'Germans' with 'Russians', 'Chinese', or 'Iranians', and you will have an idea about how and why propaganda may be used nowadays for selling a political party, a candidate, a form of economy, a type of democracy, the expansion of a country (or a coalition of countries) abroad, the dismembering

---

[66]These are the generally admitted components of the 'establishment'. Space does not allow me to discuss in detail the composition and meaning of the 'establishment', versus the 'blob', the 'deep state', the 'shadow government', and the 'foreign policy establishment'. See e.g. Lofgren (2016, Scott (2017), Engelhardt (2014).

[67]This has been the case for Iran (1953), Chile (1973), Irak (2003), and Ukraine (2014) to quote just a few.

[68]For the propaganda during the First World War (see Ponsonby 1928), and for the origins of propaganda and the psychology of masses (or groups) see Freud (2016, original German edition 1921), Le Bon (1905) (a book that has been read by several public opinion manipulators, e.g. Benito Mussolini), and Bernays (1928). For a recent update of the literature (see Bakir et al. 2018), who propose a new conceptual framework that theorizes precisely manipulative forms of persuasion, as well as demarcating what might count as non-manipulative or consensual forms of persuasion.

232   6 China and the New World Order. Why and How China's Foreign Policy …

of a country, all this in the name of the fight against dictatorship, i.e. against todays 'Huns', in an endless fight between the 'evil' and the 'good'.

A first conclusion, two years after the Trump election, is that the establishment has not yet 'eaten the spinach' of the failure of its candidate, Hillary Clinton, to conquer, again, the White House.[69] If one has followed the presidential campaign and knows enough about the power structure of the US, one can easily understand that several of Trump's foreign policy proposals were at odds with some of the most important interests of the establishment. Let us see what Trump has said, that can help us to understand in what direction he wanted to lead US foreign policy.[70]

In spite of all the criticisms addressed to Trump, there is one thing that we should recognize: as a former businessman, Trump understands the basics of accounting, even if the management of public finances is by no means the same as that of a private company. He was certainly aware that the US had been living for a long time above its means and that it could not go on implementing its traditional policies to intervene militarily (overtly or covertly) wherever and whenever some countries constitute an obstacle to its national interests:

> Our country is a debtor nation, we're a debtor nation. I mean, we owe trillions of dollars to people that are buying our bonds, in the form of other countries. You look at China, where we owe them $1.7 trillion, you have Japan, $1.5 trillion. We're a debtor nation. We can't be a debtor nation. I don't want to be a debtor nation. I want it to be the other way. One of the reasons we're a debtor nation, we spend so much on the military, but the military isn't for us. The military is to be policeman for other countries. And to watch over other countries. And there comes a point that, and many of these countries are tremendously rich countries. Not powerful countries, but—in some cases they are powerful—but rich countries (Trump 2016b).

What are then the major policy proposals Trump has put forward during the presidential campaign and the first months of his administration?

First, Trump declared that it is better to negotiate with Russia. A very wise attitude indeed, when we know that Russia is a nuclear power, second only to the US, and that by keeping on bullying this great power, as the West has done since the end of the Cold War, there is a serious risk of starting World War III, something that the mainstream media and think tanks have been (and still are) envisaging with unbelievable

---

[69]This expression is taken from the colourful language of Victoria Nuland. When she was chief of staff to Deputy Secretary of State Strobe Talbott, she encouraged the US to 'get the Russians to eat their spinach' in the circumstances described by Tony Wood: 'Already on Washington's agenda even before the fall of the USSR, the expansion of NATO was treated as a given from 1994 onward, the only question being how to make the Kremlin swallow it—to get the Russian to eat their spinach', Wood (2017).

[70]An extraordinary number of articles critical of Trump's foreign policy have been published and have been largely diffused by mainstream media and think tanks. See for example the articles of Robert Kagan (2017a, b) mentioned above. For a different point of view (see Bandow 2016; Blum 2016). To complete the picture, it would also be necessary to consult the writings of some 'Traditional Rightists' supporting Trump, that give some interesting insights (often well-documented) about the actions taken by the 'Deep State', see: Horowitz (2017), Corsi (2018), Malloch (2018), Roberts (2018), an American economist who was the United States Assistant Secretary of the Treasury for Economic Policy under President Reagan in 1981. Sere also an article quoting a retired Berkeley Professor (George Lakoff) with the warning 'to not underestimate Trump': White (2017).

6.1 The Development of the Imperial US Foreign Policy

nonchalance. But if Russia joins the US and the EU within an organization entrusted with guaranteeing security in Eurasia (as Putin has requested on many occasions) there is a chance that the 'Russia threat' will vanish from the articles published by mainstream media and think tanks. Or maybe, this is the real problem for mainstream media and think tanks?

In my 2018 book (p. 139), I also pointed out that it was possible that Trump was envisaging to attract Russia to the West so that it ceases its cooperation with China. Given the old rivalry between China and Russia, this is not at all impossible. This may correct the mistake made by all the US Presidents since the end of the Cold War to attack Russia in Eastern Europe, thus jeopardizing its understandable need to secure its border. This strategy has favoured the establishment and the development of the Russia-China partnership that risks weakening, and in fact has already considerably weakened, the US strategy to contain Russia and China. If one adds to this the non-ratification of the Trans-Pacific Partnership by the US, the disaster of the Obama strategy is even more evident.

Second, linked to the first proposal, Trump criticized the NATO alliance as being 'obsolete', with some very good reasons. NATO was established 4 April 1949 to face the perceived threat of the Soviet Union. But after the collapse of the latter at the beginning of the 1990s, the enemy had been defeated and it was no longer able to represent a real threat to the US and Europe. Moreover, after the devastating 'shock therapy' promoted by self-proclaimed Western experts in Eastern Europe and in Russia (with the help, it is fair to mention, of former nomenklatura's members re-cycled as crooked businessmen) the Eastern European leaders and especially the Russians, could do nothing but witness the cultural, social, economic and political decadence of their countries. The Soviet Regime was certainly a brutal one, but helping the Russians to replace it with a fair and viable economic and political system capable to lead towards a more open society would have been a better bet than the 'shock therapy'. Instead, the US considered that part of the world as a space where they could 'expand' to take advantage of the national resources these countries were no longer able to keep under the control of their national government and economy. Offers by Russia (especially by Vladimir Putin since 2000) to set up a common security organization were ignored with arrogance.[71] Instead, the West expanded the NATO military alliance and the European Union to Eastern Europe as far as the border of Russia. In fact, the alliance has implemented a strategy of global expansion, well outside the periphery of its original enemy, Soviet Russia, that justified its creation in 1949: the reach of the alliance has been extended to Afghanistan, the Persian Gulf, Lebanon, Syria, Iraq, Africa, Eurasia, and the Far

---

[71] 'In 2000–2002, Putin was publicly hinting at, and privately seeking, NATO membership for Russia. (…) The principal supposed change was that, from now on, Russia would be a co-equal member of the group, no longer confronted by a unified NATO "side". This did not work out as hoped.' (Trenin 2011, p. 106). See also the interviews with Vladimir Putin made by the German journalist Seipel (2015). Among the numerous accounts on the relationship between the US and Putin's Russia, I suggest Mettan (2017), Legvold (2016), Trenin (2016), Conradi (2016), Sakwa (2017), Ganser (2016), Chap. 15: 'La guerre illegal contre l'Ukraine en 2014', pp. 291–317. For an excellent update: Richard (2018).

East (Nazemroaya 2012). After the end of the Cold War US foreign policy looked as if the US considered that the time had come to fulfil Jefferson's dream and the Puritans' end of history. The 'end of history' was there to come soon (Fukuyama 1989, 1992).

Third, Trump criticized US allies (especially the EU) for not investing enough to fulfil common defence commitments. Quite true. If these countries consider that there is a threat to their security in Europe, Middle East and the Far East, why do they rely mainly on the US, whereas their economy is strong enough to finance military equipment and personnel? In fact, this is what Europe has started to do (under the leadership of Germany and France) by discussing the possibility to set up a European army, that may develop a strategy independent from the US. But will the US establishment accept this outcome? Moreover, the criticism of NATO and the pressing demand to allies to invest more in their own defence, has been interpreted as a signal that the US would not necessarily defend its allies and partners in all circumstances. This has been further reinforced by the following statement.

Fourth, Trump also announced that he is going to reduce US military commitments all over the world, i.e. spending American money on military bases, military equipment, military personnel. This potential change in US foreign policy would have the consequence of reducing the US military budget, and therefore may reduce US procurements to the military-industrial complex.

Fifth, in a remarkable interview of March 2016, Trump spoke about how he saw the situation in the Middle East (Trump 2016a). He compared the engagement of the US in Syria, and more generally in the Middle East with the Soviet Union intervention in Afghanistan, between 1979 and 1989, and said: because of that war 'they went bankrupt'. Of course, there have been other reasons explaining the collapse of the Soviet Union. But overspending on the military is certainly one of the reasons. This interview also seems to have suggested that the US should get out of Syria and maybe also from the Middle East and Afghanistan. Moreover, Trump said that he was very much aware of the fact that the US had financed 'rebels' without knowing who they were. Maybe he was wrong. The US Defence and State Departments and the CIA very likely knew who they were supporting and financing. But it remains that Trump considered that it was unwise to support that type of people, in fact terrorists.[72] In 2018 I wrote that 'this suggests that Trump may be much less prone to intervene

---

[72]It is interesting to note that Trump met Democratic Congresswoman Tulsi Gabbard, a member of the left wing of the Democratic Party, who cannot be suspected of supporting neoconservative views on foreign policy. In January 2019 Gabbard announced that she was going to run run for the 2020 Democratic presidential nomination. She is one of the most severe critics of US foreign policy especially on Syria. Gabbard supports abortion rights, opposed the Trans-Pacific Partnership, has called for a restoration of the Glass–Steagall Act, and has been in favour of same-sex marriage since 2012. She opposes US-led regime-change wars like those in Iraq, Libya, and Syria, and has opposed removal of Bashar al-Assad from power, arguing that US regime-change intervention in Syria's civil war is a source of the Syrian refugee crisis.', *Wikipedia*, https://en.wikipedia.org/wiki/Tulsi_Gabbard, accessed 31 March 2017. Several interviews of Tulsi Gabbard are available on Youtube. Gabbard was violently criticized by the establishment. See the articles by Amber Phillips, January 26, 2017, and Josh Rogin, 17 January 2017, in *The Washington Post*.

6.1 The Development of the Imperial US Foreign Policy

militarily abroad and to organize regime change, than the previous administrations who have done so on a large scale' (Urio 2018, p. 137).

Sixth, Trump also criticized international trade and investment treaties. As we have seen above, these treaties, conceived by the Obama administration to contain Russia and China, are the last tools the trade fundamentalists have invented to further expand the liberalization trend that started at the end of World War II, and further expanded by adding the deregulation of financial markets and services after the beginning of the 1980s. Moreover, by allowing foreign companies to sue in a private court a state whose policies are reducing (or may reduce in the future) their profits, multinationals may dictate their will to national governments in a large number of very sensitive domains for the populations concerned, such as health, environmental protection, education, and energy.

Trump had very well understood that these treaties, in addition to causing massive transfers of jobs to developing countries (Stiglitz 2002, 2009; Stiglitz and Charlton 2005), could be used against the US. In fact, this type of treaty is generally in favour of the most developed countries and their multinationals (American, European and Japanese). But today, multinationals based in other countries and investing in the US, such as China, may sue the US government. My guess is that Trump has very well understood that the time when the US could impose its own way to organize the global economy is coming to an end with the emergence of China and the re-emergence of Russia, but also of other countries with regional ambitions, such as Iran.[73]

Seventh, in spite of a longstanding aggressive US policy toward North Korea, that goes back to the end of World War II, on 1 May 2017 Trump told Bloomberg News: 'If it would be appropriate for me to meet with [Kim Jong-un], I would absolutely; I would be honoured to do it. There is no telling whether this was serious, or just another Trump attempt to grab headlines. But whatever else he might be, he is unquestionably a maverick, the first president since 1945 not beholden to the Beltway. Maybe he can sit down with Mr Kim and save the planet' (reported by Cumings 2017).[74]

Finally, Trump has clearly identified China as the US major competitor and threat. If we consider this statement together with his will to negotiate with Russia, we have here an additional proof that the new president was not totally without a clear vision (as too many of his opponents tend to think) of the international situation and the developments it is likely to undergo. As we have already seen in Chaps. 3 and 4, and which I will further develop in Sect. 6.2, China is rapidly catching up with the US in every domain, and given its size in terms of population and GDP, it is clearly the only country which can catch up and even surpass the US in a not too distant future.

---

[73] See for example the declaration of General Joseph Votel, Commander of the U.S. Central Command, reported by Daniels (2017). See also Cheng (2017) referring to a declaration of, 'Bernard-Henri Levy, a prolific [French] writer and widely followed philosopher, told CNBC in an interview Thursday: (…) those five empires are, according to Levy: Russia, Iran, Turkey, Islamic extremism and the commercial power of China'.

[74] For those not familiar with US political terminology: Beltway means the political and social world of Washington, D.C., viewed especially as insular and exclusive. Cumings' article is an excellent short history of US policy towards North Korea.

In summary, these are the possible changes in US foreign policy suggested by Donald Trump during the presidential campaign: negotiate with Russia and North Korea, reform NATO, not necessarily defend allies in all circumstances, reducing defence commitments abroad (as well as expenditure on conventional armaments), asking allies (especially the EU, Japan and South Korea) to increase their spending in common defence, getting out of Syria and very likely also out f of the Middle East and Afghanistan, abandon or re-negotiate multilateral trade and investment agreements, face China as the major US competitor. Apart from the last point, all the others are contrary to the traditional US foreign policy implemented since 1945 by Democratic and Republican Presidents and supported by the establishment and, to a large extent, by the neoconservatives, despite Kagan's criticism explained above.

Two years after the presidential election, the extraordinary pressure that the establishment has already put on Trump, has led him to satisfy at least some of the interests of the establishment. This pressure has come from both Republican and Democrat members of the US Congress, from the so-called 'intelligence community', the industrial-military complex, the judicial sector, as well as from mainstream intellectuals, think tanks and media. One should not forget that mainstream media generally support the foreign policy favoured by the establishment, and can easily influence the people, given 'the provincialism of an electorate with minimal knowledge of the outside world' I mentioned above with Anderson (2015, pp. 1–2).[75] Space does not allow me to present even a short analysis of the unbelievable coalition of large sectors of the establishment that has used, and is still using today a great variety of means to destabilize the new President. It succeeded in defeating him in the November 2018 mid-term elections, when he lost the majority in the House of Representatives; and it seems that it is envisaging seriously to launch the impeachment procedure.

Let me just mention one of the most remarkable examples of the strategy for influencing the new President that occurred already on 20 July 2017 when a meeting was organized by the Pentagon 'largely billed as a briefing [of the President] on the Afghanistan conflict and the fight against the Islamic State group (…) In the weeks since the briefing (…) Trump has split with top adviser Steve Bannon, the engine of many of his nationalist, isolationist policies. He threatened war with North Korea and agreed to send more troops to Afghanistan, abandoning his promise to withdraw quickly. (…) Armed with charts, maps and diagrams, those briefers spent the next roughly 90 min explaining to Trump the critical importance of forward worldwide deployments of U.S. military, intelligence and diplomatic assets, according to two current officials and one former official familiar with the meeting. While the war in Afghanistan and against the Islamic State group in Syria and Iraq were major topics, the stationing of U.S. personnel in Asia, Africa, Europe and Latin America were also covered, said the officials who were not authorized to discuss details of the highly classified briefing and spoke on condition of anonymity'. After the meeting, Trump

---

[75] As it is the case for other Western countries (Noam 2016), also in the US there is a very high degree of concentration of mainstream media, many of which are the propriety of rich billionaires, such as Michael Bloomberg (Bloomberg LP and Bloomberg Media), Rupert Murdoch (News Corp.), Jeff Bezos (Washington Post), Vinton (2016).

6.1 The Development of the Imperial US Foreign Policy

explained: 'My original instinct was to pull out—and, historically, I like following my instincts, but all my life I've heard that decisions are much different when you sit behind the desk in the Oval Office; in other words, when you're president of the United States. So, I studied Afghanistan in great detail and from every conceivable angle' (Associated Press 2017).[76]

Another episode shows that Democrats and Republicans do not differ on important policy issues that belong to the US traditional imperial way of implementing foreign policy, i.e. aggressive actions toward US enemies. On 19 July 2017, the day before the Pentagon's briefing mentioned above, *The Washington Post* was first to report Trump's decision to discontinue the CIA programme in support of the 'Syrian moderate rebels.' Immediately, the mainstream media interpreted this as a 'gift to Putin'. This happened in the midst of investigations going on about possible collusion between Russia and Trump's team. It is therefore not surprising that a few days later a large majority, comprising both Democrats and Republicans, passed a law that in fact not only denies the president the possibility to eventually reduce or even discontinue sanctions on Russia, Iran and North Korea without Congress approval, but may as well impose upon him to take new sanctions on these countries. This was clearly a quasi-unanimous decision (Senate 92–8, House 419–3) taken by the US parliament with no consultation with US allies within NATO, that shows once again with what arrogance the US congressmen consider the European members of the NATO as vassals and not as allies. This decision also shows that the establishment's opposition to Trump is not determined by his unusual personality, nor by its destructive social and environmental policies, nor by his ostensibly pro-business fiscal policy, but by some of the policies that are at odds with the interest of the establishment, represented, in this episode, by a large majority of congressmen of both parties.

But, let us see first what Trump has actually been able to do. Trump has nevertheless taken some initiatives that are at odds with the interests of the establishment. First, he met both Russia and North Korea presidents. In spite of the hysteria that these initiatives have caused to in the mainstream US media (including accusation of treason), I still persist in considering that these moves go in the right direction and may, in the long term, lead to a pacific solution of the conflicts between the US, the EU, Russia, North Korea, South Korea, Japan, China and other countries. In particular, these moves may contribute to a pacific solution of the disputes between China and its neighbours. But as long as the US establishment maintains its fundamental hostility towards China and Russia, that are considered as the major threat to US dominance, it is clear that Trump will have difficulties to finalize these policies.

Second, today Trump seems to be able to finalize part of one of his major proposals: the many initiatives he has taken to put an end to the 'globalization as we have known it' for a very long time. At last, the damages made by the 'market fundamentalists' are dealt with by one of the major or even, for the time being, the major power. As I have already mentioned, Trump pulled the US out from the TPP (Trans-Pacific

---

[76]I was not aware of this meeting when, end of August 2017, I finished writing my 2018 book. The Associate Press article was published 18 September 2017.

Partnership) and suspended the negotiations of the TTIP (Trans-Atlantic Trade and Investment Partnership).

Consequently Trump has been accused of abandoning free trade in favour of protectionism, because free trade is considered by 'free trade fundamentalists' to be the main drive for the improvement of the wealth of all countries, developed and developing, both in terms of GDP and per capita income.[77] As we have seen above, these treaties give the multinationals the possibility of transferring abroad production and jobs of many industrial sectors and give them the right to sue a government should its public policies harm their profits, especially in sensitive domains such as health, environment and social policies. It is possible that Trump may try to re-negotiate these treaties. A first step in this direction has been taken by Trump by obtaining a revised version of NAFTA (North Atlantic Free Trade Area, now called USMCA, i.e. the US-Mexico-Canada Agreement). It seems that this strategy is obtaining the support of think tanks that have been very critical of the neo-liberal globalization. For example, *Public Citizen* after having read the 900 pages of the new NAFTA treaty, declares that 'the NAFTA renegotiation includes some important improvements for which we have long advocated and some new terms we oppose'. Consequently, *Public Citizen* consider that 'more work is required to stop NAFTA's ongoing job outsourcing, downward pressure on our wages and environment damage', which is exactly one of the objectives Trump has put forward during the presidential campaign.[78]

Nevertheless, Trump has implemented several policies that are in favour of the interests of the establishment, and that altogether are the source of concern and conflicts all over the world. First, he did not reduce the military budget. On the contrary, the 2019 budget is planned to exceed for the first time 700 billion, and he announced a substantial investment in military technology and nuclear power.[79] Moreover, he has increased the overt US military presence in Afghanistan and, in spite of the December 2018 decision to withdraw the 2000 US soldiers from Syria (to which the establishment has reacted violently as it considers that this may benefit Russia) it is not at all sure that Trump will not keep a covert and/or a by proxy presence there, as has been US' practice in many parts of the world, as we have seen above.

However, on 3 December 2018 Trump 'shocked the defence establishment with a tweet describing the current level of U.S. military spending as "crazy," and endorsing a "meaningful halt to what has become a major and uncontrollable Arms Race." The President predicted that he and the leaders of Russia and China would one day

---

[77]On 'free-trade fundamentalists' see Stiglitz 2013.

[78]Received 5 October 2018 by author's subscription to *Public Citizen's* news. Nevertheless, *Public Citizen* continue to be very critical of NAFTA and the USMCA: see its more recent report: *Public Citizen* 2018.

[79]Note that the same decision concerning the modernization of nuclear armaments was decided by President Obama in 2016, before he left the White House. Hartung (2017), has calculated that the total spending on national security for the next fiscal year (2018) amounts to almost 1.1 trillion USD, well above the Pentagon budget. This includes the Pentagon, the war budget, nuclear warheads, other defence, homeland security, military aid, intelligence, supporting veterans, military retirement, and defence share of interest on the debt, the latter an impressive $100 billion per year.

6.1 The Development of the Imperial US Foreign Policy

begin discussing how to bring about such a halt' (Thompson 2018).[80] According to Thompson, 'Trump's tweet adds to mounting evidence he plans to do precisely that— trim the defence budget back to $700 billion'.[81] Moreover, Thompson considers that 'Trump now realizes in a way few average citizens do that there really is an arms race under way. China and Russia are modernizing their nuclear arsenals; moving to deny America's military use of the electromagnetic spectrum in wartime; undermining U.S. capabilities in space; launching daily cyber attacks to compromise Western networks; and developing new tools of war such as hypersonic weapons against which Washington has few defenses. Faced with such developments, it will cost the Pentagon trillions of dollars to stay ahead in the military competition. Having established what he considers good working relationships with Presidents Xi and Putin, Trump is probably thinking he can do a deal to avoid some of the costs of responding'. This takes us back to what businessman and candidate Trump said during the presidential campaign in 2016, already mentioned above: 'Our country is a debtor nation, we're a debtor nation. I mean, we owe trillions of dollars to people that are buying our bonds, in the form of other countries. You look at China, where we owe them $1.7 trillion, you have Japan, $1.5 trillion. We're a debtor nation. We can't be a debtor nation. I don't want to be a debtor nation.' (Trump 2016b). Moreover, during a Briefing at Al Asad Air Base (Irak), that came ten days after having announced the withdrawal from Syria, Trump again very heavily complained about the billions of dollars the US is spending for the security of its allies, strongly suggesting that they should spend more and the US less, thus confirming what he had declared during the presidential campaign (Trump 2018).

Second, coming back to what Trump did in line with the interests of the establishment, he has launched several massive military attacks (mainly by air raids) on Syria. For example, the attack of March 2017 on a huge dam located in the small town of Tabqa, some 40 km east of the ISIS stronghold in Syria, Raqqa. Another attack was launched 4 April 2017 on a Syrian military base as a retribution to the alleged bombing by chemical gas by the Syrian government on the town of Khan Sheikhun, in the southern province of Idlib. Finally, in April 2018 Trump decided to launch another attack on Syria reacting to an alleged use of chemical weapons by the Syrian army. Announcing this military action in a television-broadcasted speech, he violently attacked the Syrian president (an ally of Russia), thus following the mainstream media. These military actions have further deteriorated the relations between the US and Russia, already quite tense due to the sanctions imposed on Russia by the US and the EU after the US-orchestrated 2014 regime change in Ukraine. The US

---

[80]Loren Thompson focuses on the strategic, economic and business implications of defence spending as the Chief Operating Officer of the non-profit Lexington Institute and Chief Executive Officer of Source Associates.

[81]Thompson comments: 'From a fiscal perspective the $700 billion spent each year on defense is money unavailable to the government for other purposes such as rebuilding infrastructure. With the Trump Administration facing the prospect of needing to borrow $1.3 trillion this year to finance a rapidly growing national debt, the president has little room for new spending initiatives. That presumably puts Pentagon spending increases in a different perspective for the president' (Thompson 2018).

establishment, far away from Europe, can easily consider the relations with Russia as a kind of strategic video-game. But for Europe, sanctions against a neighbour such as Russia cannot go on forever, a diplomatic solution must be found.

Third, Trump unilaterally withdrew the US from two important agreements which the Obama administration had signed: the Paris agreement on climate change and the nuclear agreement with Iran. Moreover, he is imposing a very heavy economic embargo (especially on oil) on Iran, with the purpose of obtaining the re-negotiation of the agreement in more favourable terms for the US. More important, by doing so, the US also targets any country who will continue to trade with Iran.[82] The consequence has been that many countries, especially those belonging to the EU, China and Russia have started to consider strategies to avoid US sanctions should they want to continue to do business with Iran. This move against Iran is part of a more general trade-war Trump has launched on countries that are accused of being the cause of the US balance of trade deficit by subsidizing their exports to the US and by manipulating the exchange rate of their currencies. Here China is the main target, to which we can add Venezuela, another oil rich country. By doing so, while he is satisfying some of the interests of the establishment, he is also contributing to further deteriorate the conflictual climate that many of his foreign policy initiatives have produced since the beginning of its presidency. Moreover, it is not at all sure that the trade-war against China will end up to the advantage of the US.

Fourth, it is also important to mention that the official documents published about the US foreign policy strategy under the responsibility of President Trump, do not suggest any radical change compared to the policy implemented by his predecessors.[83] For example, the *National Defence Strategy* still considers that: 'The central challenge to U.S. prosperity and security is the re-emergence of long-term, strategic competition by what the National Security Strategy classifies as revisionist powers. It is increasingly clear that China and Russia want to shape a world consistent with their authoritarian model, gaining veto authority over other nations' economic, diplomatic, and security decisions. China is leveraging military modernization, influence operations, and predatory economics to coerce neighbouring countries to reorder the Indo-Pacific region to their advantage. As China continues its economic and military ascendance, asserting power through an all-of-nation long-term strategy, it will continue to pursue a military modernization program that seeks Indo-Pacific regional hegemony in the near-term and displacement of the United States to achieve global pre-eminence in the future'. This means that it is necessary 'to build a more lethal force' (title of the first paragraph of the chapter on the strategic approach): 'the surest way to prevent war is to be prepared to win one. Doing so requires a

---

[82] By doing so, Trump follows a very well-established US strategy to impose economic embargoes on countries whose policies are an obstacle to US national interests. This may also be interpreted as the continuation of the traditional US strategy to control the oil rich countries of the Middle East.

[83] See the official documents: National Security Strategy (Trump 2017), Summary of National Defence Strategy (US 2018a), Military and Security Developments Involving the People's Republic of China 2018 (US 2018c), as well as documents by influential think tanks, e.g. for the *Brookings Institution* Chollet et al. (2017), and Dollar et al. (2018); and for the *Project 2049 Institute*: Easton (2017).

6.1 The Development of the Imperial US Foreign Policy

competitive approach to force development and a consistent, multiyear investment to restore warfighting readiness and field a lethal force. The size of our force matters. The Nation must field sufficient, capable forces to defeat enemies and achieve sustainable outcomes that protect the American people and our vital interests. Our aim is a Joint Force that possesses decisive advantages for any likely conflict, while remaining proficient across the entire spectrum of conflict.' (US 2018a, pp. 2 and 5). This is a statement that neo-conservative Robert Kagan could have written himself (see above, pp. 210–213).[84]

However, for a moment Trump has given the impression of abandoning the long-term US foreign policy of intervening within other countries all over the world, as I pointed out already in my 2018 book (p. 137). In the *National Security Strategy*, Trump has declared that 'we are also realistic and understand that 'the American way of life cannot be imposed upon others, nor is it the inevitable culmination of progress' (Trump 2017, p. 4), confirming what he had declared in 2015 when he was a Republican frontrunner for the US Presidency (Jacobs 2015). This change, which is not totally incompatible with the slogan 'America first', is another proof that Trump is at least aware of the limits of the attractiveness of the US culture and of its economic and military power, so much praised by all the presidents and the establishment for a very long time. A clear proof of the decline of the American imperial Republic. Moreover, this corresponds clearly to the long-term changes in the balance of power and to Trump's understanding that these changes necessitate a revision of the US foreign policy. Is this the sign that Trump's 'end of history' will be substantially different for the one the US presidents and the establishment have implemented for a very long time? The answer has come with the Venezuela Crisis, that proves that the long-trend imperial US policy is still there, supported by the establishment which has been profiting from this policy for a very long time. It is according to this long-term imperial policy that Trump (following his predecessors) has continued to meddle with a variety of means within the internal affairs of Venezuela, imposing a devastating embargo, and finally recognizing the self-proclaimed and non-elected interim President in place of the elected president (Zayas 2019a, b). Immediately, mainstream media applauded the President's statement. This is valid for the other contradictions of Trump's foreign policy mentioned above. Indeed, we have also seen above the formidable alliance between the major components of the establishment and its strategies to retain control over US foreign policy, e.g. the briefing organized by the Pentagon on 20 July 2017, and Trump's reaction to this meeting (above, pp. 236–237). As Braudel would say: 'if the profound movements are in your favour, you will be served, independently of your intelligence, your merits, your thoughts', but if they are not …

Finally, an overall evaluation of Trump's administration is not possible without a brief evaluation of the initiatives he has taken in domestic policies. If the picture here is quite negative, it nevertheless confirms the traditional support that the US

---

[84]The speech given by Vice-President Mike Spence 4 October 2018 (to be analysed hereafter in the conclusion of this chapter) confirms, if necessary, that the traditional imperial foreign policy (in the form of neo-conservatism) is still alive in the US (Pence 2018).

administration (both Democratic and Republican) have given to US capitalism and the elites that benefit most from it. As we have seen at the beginning of Sect. 6.1, for a very long time America has been developing an ideological pro-business stance that constitutes a threat to democracy and a massive imbalance between employers and workers (Stiglitz 2018a, b).[85] Add to this an ideological pro-military stance, and you will understand the increase of expenditures for the military-industrial complex and the intelligence community, thus subtracting resources from other sectors, such as infrastructures, education, environment, social security and health. Add to this a fiscal policy that favours multinationals over employees, increasing inequalities, discriminations, racism, and unemployment (masked by inadequate statistics), the deterioration of public health (especially in terms of the decrease of life expectancy and the spectacular increase of deaths by overdose), and the pernicious influence of religious fundamentalism, and you will understand why many US traditional voters of the Democratic Party have voted for the candidate (Bernie Sanders) who constituted a threat for the candidate of the establishment, and many traditional voters of the Republican Party have preferred to vote for an unusual candidate. Serious problems at home have often redirected foreign policies towards a more aggressive posture against the rest of the world, which seems to be a fair qualification of Trump's foreign policy.

Will a new generation of politicians be able to redirect American politics towards the realization of the democratic ideals of the Founding Fathers? For the moment, in spite of the innovations mentioned above, Trump seems to be a prisoner of the American way of conceiving relationships with the rest of the world that has oriented the foreign policy of practically all the US presidents. This confirms Fernand Braudel's statement: 'the individual actor is imbedded into a history, which can be a very old one (…) So, one may have the illusion of having some kind of responsibilities, and therefore of freedoms, and to be able to choose among several possibilities. But in fact, one's freedom is much more limited, and one is not completely the master of one's destiny, because, in reality, he is submerged by the flow of history through the slow time ('*la marche lente*'). If the profound movements [Julien's silent transformations] are in your favour, you will be served, independently of your intelligence, your merits, your thoughts' (Braudel 1972). This way of understanding history and Trump's place in this history, may help us to understand the contradictions of Trump's policies. History is not a simple nor linear process. Several long-term contradictory processes are developing simultaneously. For example, I have shown with overwhelming evidence the long-trend imperial characteristic of the US imperial policy. But I have also shown that during the same time, long-term, silent transformations, have been changing the balance of power within the international system to the disadvantage of the US. To paraphrase Braudel's statement, Trump 'is submerged by the

---

[85] The example of anti-competitive work contracts is a good illustration of this imbalance: these contracts prohibit employees, not only managers, from leaving their job for a competitor. Starr, Prescot and Bishara (2018) have found that 'Nearly 1 in 5 labour force participants were bound by noncompetes in 2014, and nearly 40% had signed at least one noncompete in the past.'

6.1 The Development of the Imperial US Foreign Policy 243

flow of history through the slow time', where contradictory long-term phenomena are developing.

6.1.7 Conclusion

So, this is the dilemma of Trump's foreign policy: 'follow his instincts' (as he said in July 2017) and re-direct the US foreign policy, or follow the long-term implementation of the establishment's imperial foreign policy? What is certain, is that Trump will probably become the first American President who will have the difficult task to lead his country through the labyrinths of the new multi-polar world. It is always difficult to adapt to a changing environment, especially when one has been used to acting within the post-World War II relatively stable power structure (the world America made) within which one thinks he has found the best way to act for safeguarding the interests of his country. What is astonishing about the way the American establishment has reacted to the foreign policy statements of the new president, is that it has not realized that the world has changed, not since the beginning of the third millennium, but well before. The uncritical way with which the establishment has supported its candidate, Hillary Clinton, who implemented, when she was Secretary of State, the traditional imperial US foreign policy, and the hysterical way with which it has reacted, and is reacting still today, to the election of the candidate it did not want, show that it is not ready yet to accept the necessary reorientation of US foreign policy within the new international context.

The acceptance of US leadership by all the major powers after World War II had given the illusion that it was because of its cultural attractiveness that the US has been able to make other people and countries accept, almost naturally, to comply with its national interests. Moreover, the US establishment came to consider the latter as an 'indispensable' component of the interests of the whole international system, namely stability, security and peace (Kagan 2012b). Unfortunately, the US establishment behaved as if the faith it had in its culture (liberal democracy and capitalism in the form of market fundamentalisms) was not strong enough to avoid the use (more often than necessary) of its economic and military resources whenever it has failed to impose its will by persuasion, diplomacy and by cultural means. Paradoxically, the faith in the superiority of its ideology has led the US establishment to implement some unfriendly and/or violent activities, such as spying on both enemies and allies, financing opposition movements in other countries, organizing numerous regime changes, intervening militarily, overtly or covertly, in many countries, and using double standards to support friends and criticise enemies for the same type of reprehensible behaviour.

The implementation of this foreign policy has not only devastated large areas of the world (with the death of thousands of civilians and massive movements of refugees) but has also damaged the image and reputation (attractiveness) of some of the most positive features of the Western ideology. The case of the US shows that powerful people and countries have often the desire to be loved and feared at the same time, and how difficult it is to achieve simultaneously these two objectives. Unfortunately, it seems that Trump, *volens nolens,* is going back to the megalomania of the 'manifest destiny', the arrogance and unilateralism of the 'indispensable nation' and the illusion of the 'American end of history'. Nevertheless, by his reaffirming his will to cooperate with Russia and to discuss with North Korea, at least he gives the impression that he has understood a couple of important things about the new world: the US can no longer act as if it were the sole superpower, and behave as if its values and national interests coincided perfectly with the values and interests of the rest of the world.

Power implies the implementation of a mix of military, economic and cultural resources (Urio 2018, pp. 35–82). The US foreign policy shows that the problem is that a mix may have negative consequences. First, the constant increase in spending on military weaponry, wars, bases and special operations forces has considerably increased the US budget, thus subtracting resources that may (and according to some, should) be spent in other domains, such as the maintenance and upgrade of infrastructure, social security, health and education. These domains are also important because they significantly contribute to the strength of a country. Second, the domestic problems that derives in part from the shortcomings mentioned above, as well as from decades of neoliberal policies at home and abroad, have contributed to the increase of disparities and unemployment, as well as to the failure of the integration of Afro-Americans, to quote just a few. Third, the excessive importance of private money into politics (especially into the electoral and legislative processes) and the extraordinary development of pressure groups' influence on parliament and government, the sad spectacle of the unbelievable conflict between Trump and large segments of the establishment, accusing external evil forces (Russia, and recently also China) to undermine 'our democracy' instead of taking stock of the mistakes made for a very long time by the establishment and 'its presidents', deteriorate the image of the US democracy abroad: one important component of a country's comprehensive power. Finally, the excessive use of military power (both for overt and covert warfare, worsened by the inefficiency of overt warfare), the frequent use of media, NGOs, and special operation forces for sustaining and provoking regime change have the consequence of reducing not only military power, but also considerably the cultural power as a means of 'attraction and acquiescence' to US foreign policy, and hence to the overall capacity of the US to impose its will upon others.

My interpretation of the US foreign policy echoes the more general analysis of François Jullien. Dealing with the transition from strength to weakness, from growth to decline Jullien writes: 'Growth (…) does not give way at the approach of the Decline but, precisely as its development increases, it is itself already yielding towards decline. (…) As I have been extending my strength with success during the time of the Growth, I have in fact already started to wear myself out, because the more I display my capabilities, the more fragile they become, the more ground I occupy, the more I must toil to conserve it (…) (Jullien 2011, pp. 82–83).

The world still needs the US, but not as an exceptional and indispensable nation, nor as a hegemon that considers the rest of the world as a territory to be conquered, entrusted with the right and even the duty to lead humankind toward an end of history based upon a parochial and provincial 'manifest destiny'. I have suggested above that

6.2 China's Strategy for Reclaiming World Power Status[86]

On 21 September 1949 Mao proudly announced to the Chinese people and to the world: 'Ours will no longer be a nation subject to insult and humiliation. We have stood up' (Mao 1949). Surely that was a statement justified by the victory over the nationalists of Chiang Kai-shek supported by the US. Mao expelled the foreigners and started building the New China, a backward country devastated by a century of foreign occupation and a decades-long civil war. It was the beginning of a long March that would make China a new world power at the beginning of the XXI Century. When in 2012 Xi Jinping succeeds to Ju Jintao as the core leader of China, he is in the position to give to Mao's 1949 statement its full meaning.

Since ancient times, China has established relationships with other countries. Whereas in some cases this has meant conquest by force at the periphery of what is generally accepted to be 'the Chinese space', most of the time these contacts have been motivated by the interest in other cultures and by the will to develop commercial exchanges without territorial conquest. The famous Chinese historian Sima Qian has reported the exploration of Central Asia (and beyond) by the imperial envoy Zhang Qian between the second and first centuries BC. After translating Sima Qian, the French sinologist Jacques Pimpaneau synthesizes Zhang's life as follows: 'He lived and took wife amongst these people of the West [of Asia] [...] and defended the idea, not of armed conquest but of cul-tural and commercial exchanges on an equal footing?' (Pimpaneau 2011). It is significant to acknowledge that in 2013, President Xi Jinping, announcing the launch of the new 'One Belt One Road', came back to Zhang Qian's travels:

> Over 2100 years ago during China's Han Dynasty, a Chinese envoy, Zhang Qian, was sent to Central Asia with a mission of peace and friendship. His journey opened the door to friendly contacts between China and Central Asian countries, as well as the Silk Road linking East and West, Asia and Europe (Xi Jinping 2013a).

The purpose of the second part of this chapter is to explain why and how China has implemented the strategy that would lead to modernity and world power. It started to take form during the last decades of the empire, and underwent an increasingly spectacular development with Deng Xiaoping's reforms, and even more so from the beginning of the twenty-first century when China established commercial and financial exchanges with foreign countries all over the world. The 'One Belt One Road' initiative is the last and comprehensive development of this strategy that will be analysed in the last part of this chapter.

---

[86]This section is a new expanded version of Chap. 5 of Urio (2018), with several updates and new comments.

6.2.1 The Improbable 'China Model' and the Origins of Contemporary China's Foreign Policy

For a long time, the US has had some unrealistic expectations that China would cease to be at worst a dictatorship, at best an authoritarian regime, and by doing so, it would become a liberal democracy imbedded into the global capitalist world order America made. But reality is not so simple. I have had several occasions to contradict these views, as they are based upon an incomplete analysis of contemporary China, biased by Western ethnocentric perspectives. Now the question is: what is the very nature of the China political and economic system and in what direction may it evolve? (Sect. 5.2 above) Dealing with the 'China model', in the conclusion of my book on NPM in China and in the West, I wrote that 'based on the findings presented in this book, as well as on my evaluation of China's reforms, (…) for the time being, (…) there is no China model; or more precisely, and maybe also paradoxically, the China model is that there is no model, but a continuous transformation of the ways of thinking and managing the modernization process of this great country.' (Urio 2012, pp. 209–210; Urio 2010, pp. 193–204). The French philosopher and sinologist François Jullien qualifies the Chinese way as 'an unmodelled model of becoming' (Jullien 2011, p. 70).[87] This means that the 'China model' is moving, it changes according to the changes in the internal and international situation, only the goal remains constant, i.e. the development of the country to finally attain world power status, thus fully realizing Mao's statement: 'Ours will no longer be a nation subject to insult and humiliation. We have stood up' (Mao 1949).

Nevertheless, should somebody want to find a synthetical definition of the 'China model', he may refer to the definition given by one of the most knowledgeable Western scholars of contemporary China, Daniel Bell (2016). Bell defines the China model as a three-layer construction: democracy at the bottom (referring to the organization of fairly open electoral processes at the lowest level of the State's organization), experimentation at the middle (referring to the practice of experimenting policies at the province level before eventually transposing them at the national level), and meritocracy at the top (referring to the very strict policy of choosing and promoting administrative and political senior officials, based much more on expertise than on compliance with ideology). Nevertheless, the 'model' is defined by Bell as 'an evolving three-pronged approach to political governance that cannot be accurately captured by labelling China a "bad" authoritarian regime similar in nature to, say, dictatorships in North Korea and the Middle East.' Thus, Bell suggests that the 'model' is not fixed, but changes permanently, which does not comply with the accepted Western definition of a 'model' (Bell 2016, p. 180). Moreover, the whole book is in fact an analysis of the 'China model' as both an ideal and a reality, thus showing the shortcomings of the actual implementation of the 'model', and suggesting improve-

---

[87]The full sentence is: 'Are we looking for an unmodeled model of becoming, a matrix which integrates its renewal at the very heart of transformation and serves to grasp this "change of change" that Aristotle, refusing to think *between forms,* tells us is impossible?'

6.2 China's Strategy for Reclaiming World Power Status

ments from 'within' Chinese history and culture. So, I persist in sticking to my idea that there is not a China model.

Coming now to the origins of China's foreign policy, one can go back in history as I have done for the US. Here we find a major difficulty: Western scholars and journalists try to find events in the history of China that contradict the official history accepted by Chinese authorities and the majority of Chinese scholars, according to which China is a peaceful country as is shown by the analysis of its long history. In fact, China has developed through the centuries a whole set of weaponry, most of the time well before the West, (Temple 1998, pp. 215–298) and it has used them both internally (i.e. in several 'civil wars') and externally. There have been events in which China has attacked foreign countries (Kyle Crossley et al. 2017).[88] Under the Qing Dynasty, instituted by the Manchus (1636–1912), China intervened in Tibet (1718 and 1720) to repeal a tentative invasion by the Dzungar Mongols; 'Tibet was made a protectorate and a permanent Manchu garrison was established there.' Similarly, the Manchus acquired the region of today's Xinjiang 'in the 1750s when their armies defeated the Dzungar Mongols and Uighurs in a series of campaigns. (…) Still, the Qing interfered relatively little in Tibetan affairs, allowing local leaders to do most of the actual governing. (…) [Similarly, in the Uighurs region] like for Tibet, these largely Muslim areas were ruled rather lightly. The local population was allowed to keep their own religious leaders, follow their own dietary rules, and not wear the queue [which was required for the Han majority in sign of submission to the ruling Manchu dynasty].' (Buckley Ebrey 1999, pp. 220–258, quotation p. 227). Moreover, these excursions of China outside its border, have never gone beyond Asia, Eastern Africa, and the Middle East, and in any case, they were motivated more by the hope of developing trade and cultural exchanges, than by the will to conquer foreign countries.[89] We can see this since the XXI Century when China started to invest abroad: no political conditions such as reform of the political system (i.e. introducing liberal democracy), or privatizations of public assets. In fact, China never wanted to shape other countries according to its own social, political and economic systems.

Of course, the Chinese are proud of their country, and 'believe in China's exceptionalism, based on its different history and culture that is perhaps seen as superior to the West.' (Harris 2014, p. 5). But this is not a significant information. I do not know any people who think that their country is not exceptional: the French, the British, the Germans, the Italians, even the citizens of small Switzerland share the same feeling. The difference between the US and China is that China has never, so far, tried to conquer (especially militarily) the rest of the world nor to change it to its own image. Exceptionalism, yes, but no 'manifest destiny' giving the right and the duty to 'expand' and to impose its rules on the rest of the world. Now the question

---

[88] The authors write: 'This exceptionalist narrative ignores the fraught history by which the former frontiers of empire became the borders and boundaries of a nation. This month, my students, undergraduates from several different U.S. colleges and universities who are studying in Beijing, are looking at the legacy of Qing imperial expansion in the 17th and 18th centuries during which the Qing Empire fought wars in both Burma and Vietnam on the pretext of enforcing regional order.'

[89] Nevertheless, for excursion to Europe and America, see Levathes and Louise (1994), Menzies (2003, 2008).

248

is: why did China start, towards the end of the XX century, to 'go abroad' (and, as we shall see, all over the world), why and how?

Let's take the logical sequence of steps that lead to the implementation of strategies. We have, starting from the top: fundamental values, ideology, choice of institutions for realizing values and the associated goals, adoption and then implementation of policies within those institutions, evaluation of policies, and feed-back. If we compare the US (and more generally the West) with China, we see that the US has made its choices for values, ideology and institutions between the end of the XVIII century and the first half of the XIX century. Which means that since then, feedback from successes and failures (and there have been many) concerned only policies and their implementation. Fundamental values, ideology and institutions (i.e. liberal democracy and capitalism) were not questioned. On the contrary, China has put into discussion all the levels, except part of the upper level (traditional values) and has integrated them with the new values imported from the West (e.g. economic efficiency, Sect. 2.4). It is true that after the collapse of the Empire, Confucianism was practically banned from Chinese political discourse by both Nationalists and Communists as they considered that Confucianism was at the origin (together with foreign aggression) of China's decline. But Confucian ideas were not eradicated from China's collective conscience and came back in the open after the tragedy of the Cultural Revolution. This is the clear manifestation of the Chinese capacity to take into consideration the 'real' situation and not to act on the basis of an ideal plan or model. Values, institutions, and policies are chosen, implemented, and eventually changed on the basis of their capacity to realize the fundamental goal of reclaiming world power status,[90] after a continuous in-depth analysis of the 'situation potential' (Sects. 2.1 and 2.3). If we look at China's strategy since the last decades of the XIX century, we can see that it looks like a quasi-perfect implementation of the Chinese traditional way of conceiving and implementing strategy.

When the West aggressed China in the XIX century, China was sure of the superiority of its culture whose fundamental values were based on an interpretation of Confucius: harmony (meaning absence of contradictions and conflicts, i.e. peace), stability, and unity. The quasi-isolation from the rest of the world, in terms of military and economic relations, allowed China to avoid being entangled into major international conflicts and to preserve its fundamental traditional values. But when China is forced to open to the West and to integrate, *volens nolens*, into the conflictual international order (that the West made), the illusion of benefiting from a harmonious and peaceful international environment China enjoyed until then is torn to pieces. The only way to reconstruct a peaceful international environment where each country's values are preserved and respected, is first to reconquer the status of great power capable to resist foreign aggression, and second to work for the (re)establishment of a peaceful international environment. Since the second half of the XIX century China had no plan and I add, no model either, as I explained in Sect. 2.4, but a continuous search for means to realize the goal to become strong and respected again. It

---

[90]The explanation why the goal of 'reclaiming world power status' can be considered as the fundamental goal of China's foreign policy since the Opium Wars, can be found in Urio (2012, pp. 92–96).

6.2 China's Strategy for Reclaiming World Power Status

is the fundamental change of China's international environment that has inevitably oriented its foreign policy and the choice of means to become powerful again and to re-establish a peaceful international environment, at least near its borders.

6.2.2 The Construction of China's Strategy: Building Power Resources

We can limit ourselves to focusing our attention on the XIX century because at that time China presented basically the same characteristics it had developed through the centuries since the Qin Dynasty. This is not to say that China had not changed since the establishment of the Qin Dynasty two centuries B.C. (Zufferey 2008). But it is true that the ideology that supported the Empire had been established for a very long time, based upon an interpretation of Confucius, despite its numerous revisions and development. (Urio 2010, pp. 2–44).

Let's start with fundamental values and ideology. In Confucian ideology, human relations are conceived on the basis of family relations, and then they are transposed to the rest of society. This society is hierarchical, and its management is paternalistic: the civil servants, ministers and the ordinary people must submit themselves to the Emperor, the son to his father, the wife to her husband, the junior to the elder. The goal of this construction is to create a society which is harmonious, united and stable. Moreover, harmony must also exist in the relation between humankind and nature. One may think that this ideology is incompatible with democracy as we conceive it in the West, where one cannot accept the idea that an entire society may be structured according to several types of submissions, that leave little space for the development of individual potentials and aspirations for everybody, not to mention human rights. This was certainly true under the Empire, and this explains why the Chinese Empire lasted more than two millennia. Nevertheless, one must not forget that the goals are harmony, stability and unity, and the hierarchical organization of society is just the means to achieve these goals. So, one can imagine different means (i.e. a different societal organization) that may guarantee harmony, stability and unity, while safeguarding other values, e.g., those imported from the West. This is what happened after the fall of the Empire, with many hesitations, experimentations, and changes (Chaps. 2, 3 and 4).

Already during the last decades of the Empire China imported ideas, values and principles from the West. As mentioned above, one may consider that these new values imported from the West may be incompatible with the traditional values of harmony, stability and unity.[91] Nevertheless, within the Confucian ideology there are several values that may be used as 'bridge values' to make the traditional Chinese values compatible with the new ones imported form the West: *ren* (humanity, or love of humanity) corresponds to the Christian 'love thy neighbour'; *lǐ* (rites) corresponds

---

[91] For an in-depth analysis of the compatibility of liberal democracy and Confucianism (see Bell 2006).

to the Western 'good manners'; *xìnyòng* (trust), *yì* (justice) and *zhì* (intelligence, wisdom) have their corresponding values in the West. It is possible to show that since the end of the XIX century China tried to integrate into its ideology several Western values such as economic efficiency, market, social equity, justice, and law, without abandoning the traditional Chinese values of stability, unity and harmony, as I showed by examining the discourse of Jiang Zemin, Hu Jintao and Xi Jinping in Chap. 2. The dominant Western opinion is that this integration is not entirely satisfactory and/or successful and will remain unfinished (and, for some, with the likely outcome of the final collapse of the Party-State) until China abandons its authoritarian form of the state within which it is difficult (or even impossible) to integrate traditional Chinese and Western values. For avoiding to collapse, China should adopt liberal democracy, and complete the transition from command economy to free market economy. In short, China should 'become like us'. I have shown in Chaps. 3 and 4 that, so far, the results obtained by China are impressive for the development of the economy and the standard of living of the great majority of its people. Moreover, significant improvements have been achieved for freedom and human rights, even if the Party-State maintains all the components of society under its control (Sects. 5.2 and 5.3).

Based upon this mix of Chinese and Western values, China has been very skilful in choosing the institutional arrangements that allowed it to build year after year, in the 'long time', after a careful analysis of the 'situation potential', the resources that constitute today its Comprehensive National Power—CNP (Hu and Men 2004; Urio 2018, Chap. 3). Already after the defeat in the Opium Wars, China set up factories and dockyards to manufacture Western-style weapons and warships. Unfortunately, it takes a long time before a country can build warships capable to confront a technologically more advanced foreign navy. Inevitably, in 1884–1885, it took only one hour for the French, in a conflict over Vietnam, to destroy the warships built by China, and a decade later (1894–1895) China lost the first Sino-Japanese war that was decided on the sea (Buckley Ebrey 1999, pp. 245 and 252–254). In spite of these defeats, it is interesting to acknowledge that China was already aware of the importance of building a modern navy capable to confront potential enemies. This power resource was to be developed from the last quarter of the XX century when China fully understood that for safeguarding its national interests, it had to develop a modern navy capable to confront the US navy in the China Sea. Moreover, at the beginning of the XX century, ideas of constitutionalism and parliamentary government were discussed at the Qing Court, and in 1909 consultative provincial assemblies met in each province (Buckley Ebrey, pp. 262–264). But these initiatives came too late: the Empire of the Qing Dynasty, that had been weakened for decades by foreign interventions and internal contradictions, collapsed at the beginning of 1912.

During the time of the Republic of China led by the Nationalist Party of Sun Yat Sen and Chiang Kai-shek (1912–1949) the civil war between the Nationalists and the Communists, the Japanese aggression, and the numerous foreign interferences (especially from the US supporting the Nationalists) left little opportunities to develop China's Comprehensive National Power. It is only when the civil war ended with the

6.2 China's Strategy for Reclaiming World Power Status 251

victory of the Communists that China was in a position to organise and implement a strategy for building the power resources that would realize the objective of becoming again a world power.

The first resource that the People's Republic of China recovered was full sovereignty.[92] After one century of foreign interventions that reduced China to a semi-colonial status, this is a fundamental achievement.[93] In spite of the cooperation that developed with Soviet Russia, Mao was able to keep its 'ally' at a distance and finally to sever the cooperation. In this sense, it is reasonable to sustain that Mao chose to close the country to foreign influence in order to autonomously intervene within the elements of the internal situation it was reasonably possible to improve: first of all, education and health, then industrialization of the economy in the framework of a command economy. Certainly, this strategy had its negative consequences: poor economic performance, limitation of personal freedom, little incentives for innovations, environmental damages, as well as the catastrophic impact of the Great Leap Forward and the Cultural Revolution. Nevertheless, it is certain that Mao set the bases that allowed Deng Xiaoping to further develop Chinese society. Moreover, Deng took stock of the negative consequences of Mao's personal leadership, changed the economy, by progressively introducing market mechanisms and opening China to the global economy, and re-instituted the collective leadership, that Mao had abandoned after 1958 (Hu 2014). It is only with Xi Jinping that many pundits, both in China and in the West, have come to consider that the grip of the Party-State over society has been strengthened (Sect. 5.1.2). Moreover, Deng further improved Mao's strategy by clearly identifying the four domains in which China should invest in order to reclaim world power status: agriculture, industry, science and technology, and national defence. During this period, Chinese leaders abstained from implementing assertive foreign policies that may have caused hostility from other countries. A peaceful international environment was necessary, they thought, to allow China to focus on the improvement of its national power resources such as health, literacy, and heavy industry.

Whereas Deng's reforms produced an impressive improvement of China's economy, nevertheless, as I sustained in Chap. 4, the scope and speed of Deng's reforms resulted in several negative consequences: disparities between regions and provinces, as well as between people within regions, provinces and municipalities. The absence of regulations aiming at protecting the environment resulted in considerable deteriorations of the already precarious conditions of the Chinese environment. The rapid introduction of market mechanisms and competition led State organizations (especially SOEs, but also State bureaucracies) to drastically reduce their staff and to lay off millions of employees and workers. This resulted in a huge rate of unemployment, as well as the emergence of new forms of poverty, that run the risk of counterbal-

---

[92] Here I summarize, what I have analyzed in Chap. 3, Sects. 3.1 and 3.2. And I will add some new comments related to China's strategy.

[93] This is the opinion shared by practically every Chinese intellectual. See for example Wang Hui (2009, pp. xii–xxxiii). See also on the important question of China's transition from Empire to State: Wang Hui (2014).

ancing, at least in part, the impressive decrease of poverty achieved thanks to the reforms. This trend, and especially the appearance of new forms of poverty, also had an impact on the increase of crime, especially petty crimes. Finally, the transition from a command economy to a new economic system, where market mechanisms (and hence competition among enterprises) were introduced quite rapidly, led the government to freeing the SOEs from the obligation of providing their workers and employees with the social services they were used to obtaining under the former command economy. This new way of organizing the production process, in conjunction with the one-child policy, was de-structuring both the traditional State's and intra-family solidarities. Finally, the imbalances of society and economy had a negative impact on the realization of the traditional values of harmony, stability and unity.

It became therefore necessary to introduce several changes at different levels of the strategy, and first of all the introduction of new values in the ideology of the Party, such as social equity, law, ruling by law or according to law, and innovation (Sect. 2.4). Second, at the institutional level, part of the implementation of market ideology, led China to make all citizens (even the poor ones) pay for part of public services such as health and schooling. Moreover, the labour market was introduced with very limited protection for employees against non-justified lay-offs, working hours, and safety working conditions. Under Hu Jintao these problems were addressed to give space to the beginning of the development of a modern safety net system covering health, unemployment and old age, more protection for the employees, as well as a new strategy for environmental protection (Chap. 4).

The result of these innovations in the definition and implementation of China's strategy is that at the beginning of the XXI century China became one of the three major world economies (with the EU and the US) with an annual increase of GDP of about 10% for three consecutive decades, a significant increase in personal income for almost every Chinese social strata, as well as a relatively harmonious and stable society (Urio 2010, pp. 87–90; Keidel 2007, Chaps. 3 and 4 above). It is during the two mandates of Hu Jintao (2002–2012) that China started to 'go abroad' (or to 'go out') encouraged by its accession to the WTO in December 2001.[94] As we have seen, for about half a century (between 1949 and 2012) China intervened mainly on its internal 'situation potential' by counting on the silent transformations that had been operating since at least the end of the Empire and on the persistence of some features of China's traditional culture. First, its population, which was already very large (about 300 million) at the beginning of the XIX century before Western aggression, has never stopped increasing 'silently', in spite of the one-child policy introduced by Deng in the 1980s. This is certainly due to the agrarian origins of China, where having a large family has been viewed, at least until recently, as a sign of wealth. Second, Chinese families have been traditionally prone, at least in the urban areas, to favour the literacy and education of their children. Third, the Confucian values (harmony, stability, and unity) that shaped the Empire did not disappear in 1912, but continued to operate 'silently' as they were permanently imbedded into the Chinese

---

[94]This expression is used to qualify China's strategy to encourage its enterprises to invest overseas.

mind, ready to become 'audible' after Mao's era.[95] In particular, as Deng's reforms provided the Chinese people with new opportunities to improve their standard of living, families were ready to heavily invest in the education of their children, which was the condition for having access to the better and more qualified jobs required by the modernization process. Moreover, harmony, unity and stability would continue to sustain a new form of authoritarian government, namely the Party-State led by the Communist Party. Of course, an educated population in good health, ready to accept an authoritarian leadership, is not a sufficient condition for becoming a power resource. The leadership must provide better living conditions for everyone and a new faith in a bright future for the Chinese nation. This is where the choice of policies become of great importance. If you are able to implement the four modernizations mentioned above (agriculture, industry, science and technology and national defence) you have a good opportunity to satisfy your citizens and to become a world power again.

The West has witnessed the implementation of these policies with some sense of superiority: granted, China had become the workshop of the world, but only for low value-added goods. In the West the declarations of Chinese leaders to improve economy and society have been taken for a long time as the manifestations of propaganda and the necessity to maintain the grip of the Party upon society (Edelman 1985). In particular, the West, convinced that China was only good at imitating Western technologies, has not taken seriously the declarations of Chinese leaders who insisted, among other things, on the necessity for China to undertake the road of 'independent innovation' (declaration of Hu Jintao at the Party Congresses of October 2007). Today China has caught up with practically all the technology domains, including military equipment (Hu Angang and Ren Hao 2016; Wübbeke et al. 2016). I will develop this point hereafter in Sect. 6.2.4.2.

So, by analysing China's development since 1949, we see very clearly that decisions taken (i.e. events) are the audible manifestation of silent transformations of which Chinese leadership has taken advantage to further develop internal power resources. These policies, especially the development of national defence, were clearly a reaction to the events such as the Opium wars, China's exclusion from the Peace treaty negotiations of 1919 (in spite of its contribution to the victory against Germany), the numerous interferences of the US in the Far East, and the massive presence of US military forces in the vicinity of China's borders.

Having consolidated its internal power resources, China was ready to 'go out' during the leadership of Hu Jintao. This became a necessity. As China became more and more imbedded into the global economy, restoring national power by isolating itself as it had done in the past was no longer possible. Inevitably, China had to cope with the 'transformations' at work since the XIX century in the international system. Under pressure from the traditional colonial European countries, then from the US, the economy had become more and more open. If China was to benefit from the global market, it had to comply with the international rules established by the West. The

---

[95]For the concepts of 'silent' and 'audible' referred to the 'silent transformations' and the 'audible' events as presented in the news see Sect. 2.1.

process of economic globalization that started in the XIX century was brought to a halt in the 1930s, but this did not last long. After the end of World War 2, the liberalization process restarted more vigorously than ever, under the leadership of the US, and even accelerated from the beginning of the 1980s under pressure from neo-liberalism. Hence the accession of China to the WTO. As the Chinese economy did not cease to grow, it became important to assure access to the global market not only for selling goods, but also for importing the raw material and energy resources necessary for sustaining China's growing economy. Moreover, China had accumulated enough funds to start to invest abroad, in particular buying shares of high-tech enterprises, real estate, ports, etc. This trend finally led China to become more active in international organizations, to establish commercial agreements with other countries, to contribute to instituting regional organizations, such as the Shanghai group, and to improve its national defence both quantitively and qualitatively. As relations with the US become more and more tense, in spite of the rhetoric of 'strategic partnership', and because the US dollar becomes a source of instability, China started to develop a strategy to become progressively independent from the US dollar, and eventually to transform the RMB into a new international currency. As we shall see, this is a long term strategy, progressing step by step, taking advantage not only of the growing strength of the Chinese economy, but also by taking advantage of the declining power of the US, and the favourable opportunities afforded by the strategy of other countries, such as Russia and Iran, eager to escape from the dominant role of the US based upon the US dollar as the major reserve and payment currency in the international economic system.

Given the massive military presence of the US in the Far East, its pretence to unilaterally assure freedom of navigation in the China Sea, its aggressive attitudes (together with those of its European allies) in Europe and in the Middle East led China to develop a grand strategy to confront the US and to assure its political and economic security. This strategy is generally known as the Belt and Road Initiative (BRI) that has been labelled by a leading Western newspaper, *The Financial Times*: 'China encircles the world with One Belt, One Road strategy' (Hancock 2017). In fact, BRI may be interpreted as China's response to US strategy to retain the status of sole world super-power, by encircling Russia and China, intervening massively in the Middle East, keeping Latin America under its control, increasing its interventions in Africa, and maintaining the USD as the major international currency. As I have shown in Sect. 6.1, it is the US global reach that constitutes its power, and it is upon each of its dimensions that China must contest US supremacy if it wants to become again a world power. In fact, I suggest to analyse the various activities developed by China to reclaim world power status in relation to the BRI grand strategy, as each of them contributes to the overall aim of the BRI.

6.2.3 The Belt and Road Strategy: Encircling the World

It is not surprising that President Xi Jinping used the sentence quoted at the beginning of Sect. 6.2 of this chapter when in 2013 he announced for the first time China's project to build an 'economic belt along the Silk Road' (speech in Astana, 7 September 2013). Referring to the already ongoing cooperation with Russia, Xi Jinping clearly stated the objectives of the initiative: expand the regional cooperation, improve policy communication, promote unimpeded trade, enhance monetary circulation, and increase understanding between peoples (Xi 2013a). This announcement came less than one year after Xi Jinping had been voted by the Party Congress to be the next Secretary General of the CPC. Less than a month later, Xi Jinping proposed to add a New Maritime Road in a speech given in Jakarta, 2 October 2013 (Xi 2013b). These new roads were later referred to as the 'Belt and Road Initiative (BRI)'. Clearly, such a vast project must have been in preparation for a long time, and in any case, it is the logical consequence, integration and rationalization of the previous moves made by China to recover world power status (see Chaps. 3 and 4).

A lot of factual information is now available on the BRI thanks to several serious sources (e.g. Swaine 2015; Leverett et al. 2015).[96] Therefore, I will focus my analysis on the core of the BRI, and I will show to what extent it represents a serious challenge to US leadership not only in Asia, but also all over the world. First, I take stock of the various dimensions of China's strategy implemented prior to the BRI that contributed to its appearance, and that persist today after its official announcement in 2013, thereby contributing to its success. Amongst the major initiatives China developed before announcing the BRI initiative I will deal with the most important ones: the development of China's economy and its place in international trade; the transition of China's economy to the 4th industrial revolution. i.e. the transition to high-tech products and services; the challenge to the international role of the US dollar; the development of bilateral alliances and partnerships and the implication in international organizations; the diffusion of Chinese culture abroad; and finally the development of military resources. Second, I will analyse the strategic importance of the BRI for China's reclaiming its world power status, as well as the problems and obstacles it will have to face.

---

[96]Information about BRI from the Western point of view can be found in the *Financial Times*; in the publications of the *Centre for strategic and International Studies;* the *China Leadership Monitor* of the *Hoover Institution* at Stanford University; the *American Enterprise Institute;* the *Council of Foreign Affairs* (its journal *Foreign Affairs*); *Mercator Institute for China Studies* (MERICS); and Picquart (2018). For Chinese sources, in addition to those quoted below, see the official Chinese news agency, *Xinhua* (http://www.news.cn/english/); the *South China Morning Post* (https://www.scmp.com/frontpage/international); the *Caixin* magazine (http://www.caixinglobal.com/); a book by a professor at Renmin University: Wang Yiwei (2016); and a collective of Chinese scholars and officials: Wei Liu (2018).

6.2.4 The Way Toward the Belt and Road Strategy

As we have seen above (Sect. 2.3) China's strategy takes advantage of the 'situation potential'. At times this may give the impression of being chaotic. However, the goal still orients actions, and actions are implemented when and where the 'situation potential' suggests that the chances to succeed are reasonably favourable. Moreover, if the situation potential is not favourable, or in case of failure, China does not act or retreat, but waits for the long-term 'silent transformations' to change the 'situation potential' to its advantage. Then, it is important to act with no hesitation, otherwise the favourable moment may vanish. This is what China has done for instance in order to arrive at the implementation of its Grand Strategy, the Belt ad Road Initiative (BRI). As André Chieng has very well explained: the essence of strategy is on the one hand to gradually trap the competitor into a fixed position upon which the strategist can act, and on the other hand to constantly change one's position in order to make its own strategy incomprehensible for the competitor (Chieng 2006, p. 210; Jullien 1995, Chap. 1). The analysis that follows shows that China is working to this end. This is what we analyse in the following paragraphs. Some of the actions I will analyse were implemented simultaneously, others in sequence. But the ultimate strategic goal remains to reclaim world power status. I will present these several actions in a way that, hopefully, will make sense to the reader, even if sometimes I will depart from the chronological sequence of events. What is important is to understand that together these actions lead to the realization of the strategy goal within the One Belt One Road.

In summary, the starting point has been the development of the domestic economy, thanks to the introduction of market mechanisms, and also to the opening of the economy to the rest of the world, that allowed China to export its goods and to benefit from foreign investment in Chinese economy. This allowed on one hand to improve the living conditions of the Chinese people, and on the other hand to develop an increasingly positive balance of trade, and the acquisition of monies by both private and SOEs that could be used for investing in the global market. This also allowed the government to acquire an astonishing amount of foreign currencies that could also be invested in the global market, either directly or through new financial institutions promoted by China. Moreover, this strategy allowed acquisition of technology, through joint ventures with foreign companies. The consequence has been the development of China's investment in many countries on all the continents, including in the US. China started this development first by making low-added values products, hence the myth of the China factory of the world, that has been regarded with some condescendence by the West: the Chinese are good at producing low value-added products, eventually by stealing Western technologies, they are not able to invent by themselves. Then in 2007 came the announcement made by the General Secretary of the CPC (Hu Jintao) that China would develop autonomous innovation in many strategic sectors (Sect. 2.4.5 above). The following year, China published the 'Thousand talents' project, whose goal was to attract to China top-level scientists from abroad, and to repatriate Chinese scientists educated abroad. These announce-

6.2 China's Strategy for Reclaiming World Power Status

ments were confirmed twice in 2006 and 2011 by the State Assets Supervision and Administration Commission (SASAC).

In 2013, the newly appointed Party Secretary, Xi Jinping, announced the launching of a vast project, the Belt and Road initiative, that would link China's economy to the rest of the world, this time in a leading position. The same year, in October 2013, China announced the creation of the Asian Infrastructure Investment Bank (AIIB), immediately seen by the US as a competitor of the financial institution it dominates (IMF and WB). Consequently, the US and its allies have turned down China's proposals to reform the international financial organisations, dominated by the US, EU and Japan. China considered that the architecture of these institutions did not reflect the economic weight of China. The Chinese proposals had also the goal to diminish China's dependence upon the US dollar that dominates the international finance. Confronted with the hostility of the US, China has implemented a strategy to progressively become less dependent on the US dollar. These measures, that together constitute what is often called the 'de-dollarization' of the global economy, include the signing of bilateral swap agreements, that allow the contracting countries to pay trade in their currencies instead of the US dollar; the launch in March 2018 of a yuan-denominated crude oil based in Shanghai; initiatives to create, alone or with some other countries, a new society for enabling financial institutions worldwide to send and receive information about financial transactions in a secure, standardized and reliable environment, instead of the US-dominated SWIFT, the *Society for Worldwide Interbank Financial Telecommunication*.

Less than two years after the announcement of the AIIB, in May 2015, the Prime Minister made public the 'Made in China 2015' project, thereby making it clear that this time the projection of China abroad was going to be based upon its first-class high-tech competencies. At the same time, China started to buy enormous quantities of gold, giving the impression that it was preparing for a change of the international financial system that could be based upon gold. China also started to develop its military resources, thus making it clear to the US that it was prepared to face the massive military presence of US and its allies in the vicinity of its borders. Simultaneously to these initiatives, China has increased its presence within international organizations, both global and regional, and established cooperation with countries who are also eager to diminish their dependency on the US dollar. This cooperation has also the purpose of assuring the security of the countries concerned in their region. Finally, China started to develop instruments not only for diffusing its culture all over the world, but also, and maybe mainly, for making accessible to people outside China its position on the many problems that are at stake in the international system. Let me start with the development of China's economy.

6.2.4.1 The Development of China's Economy and Its Place in the International Trade

Whereas China remained isolated from the global economy until the end of the Mao Era, the development of its economy, based upon Deng's reforms (competition and opening to the world) inevitably led China to increase its exports and imports to and from the rest of the world. We have already seen in Chap. 3 how China's development has been very rapid since the beginning of Deng's reform. Let me briefly summarize this achievement. In 2000, one year before China accessed to the WTO, China's part in the world import-export total was only 3.59%, against 15.47% for the US, and 37.73% for the EU. In 2014, one year after the announcement of the BRI and one year before the announcement of 'Made in China 2025', China's part had sprung to 11.30%, against 10.59% for the US and 31.98% for the EU. The part of China in the world GDP (in PPP) in 2000 was only 7.65%, against 21.37% for the US and 22.87% for the EU. In 2014 China's GDP (in PPP) percentage of the world was up to 16.59%, and the US's was down to 16.04% and the EU's down to 17.00%.

Coming now to China's investments abroad, it was towards the beginning of the third millennia that China started seriously to invest abroad, thus confirming the analysis of Fernand Braudel: '… capital and credit have always been the surest way of capturing and controlling a foreign market. Long before the twentieth century the exportation of capital was a fact of daily life, for Florence as early as the thirteenth century.' (Braudel 1979, pp. 113–114). This quotation may be embarrassing for the Chinese leadership as Braudel refers explicitly to the behaviour of capitalist investors. Shall we consequently consider that investments abroad by China are the indicator of China's evolving towards a capitalist economy and that she will use investments to 'conquer the world' as Western countries have done so for a long time. I will come back to this question in the Conclusion of this book.

For the moment I will refer to the extraordinary development of China's investments abroad. Between 2000 and 2009 Chinese investment abroad increased very slowly, but then accelerated dramatically (Business Insider 2017). Even more impressive is the announcement made by Xi Jinping in May 2017 during the September 2017 BRI Forum, when he pledged a massive funding boost to the BRI, including: 'an extra 100 billion yuan ($14.50 billion) into the existing Silk Road Fund, 250 billion yuan in loans from the China Development Bank, 130 billion yuan in loans from the Export-Import Bank of China, 60 billion yuan in aid of developing countries and international institutions in new Silk Road countries, encouraging financial institutions to expand their overseas yuan fund businesses to the tune of 300 billion yuan, 2 billion yuan in emergency food aid, $1 billion to a South–South Cooperation fund, $1 billion for cooperation projects in countries on the new Silk Road. (Goh and Chen 2017; Wu Gang 2017). Outbound investments diminished after the Chinese government halted overseas investments in 2016 to control non-performing and/or speculative investments abroad (Weinland 2016). But after then it is forecasted that the increase will resume in the framework of the implementation of the BRI initiative, to be dealt with below.

An in-depth analysis by Derek Scissor (writing for the *American Enterprise Institute*—AEI) gives a synthetic idea of the scope of China's investments abroad (Scissors 2017a, 2019). These documents starts by warning the reader that China's 'construction activity is often treated by host countries and foreign observers as investment. 'This is an error—construction is valuable but does not involve ownership. While construction contracts are smaller on average, there are more $100 million con-

6.2 China's Strategy for Reclaiming World Power Status

struction contracts than $100 million investments since 2005.' Granted, but China's construction activities cannot be considered only from a strict economic point of view. They are also a political instrument to establish a cooperative relationship between China and receiving countries, especially the less developed ones. Moreover, the construction contracts do not force the receiving countries to accept politically and ideologically oriented counterparts, such as privatizations, regime change and human rights, to comply with liberal democracy and market economy standards. China's way of organizing its relationship with these countries (especially in Africa and Latin America) offers the choice between Chinese and Western construction contracts.[97]

Figure 3 in the 2019 AEI document allows us to see China's worldwide reach. From 2005 to 2018 the combined value of China's investment and construction exceeded $1.9 trillion globally with a significant increase from the $1.6 trillion in 2017. This amount is distributed among the following areas as follows: $385.1 billion to Europe (291.9 in 2017), 299.1 to Sub-Saharan Africa (272.1 in 2017), 275.1 to West Asia (240.4 in 2017), 266.4 to East Asia (214 in 2017), 182.6 to the US (172.4 in 2017), 182.2 to Arab Middle East and North Africa (149.8 in 2017), 169.4 to South America (144.7 in 2017), 111.6 to Australia (100.8 in 2017), and 69.8 to North America, excluding US (66.7 in 2017). Table 2, concerning construction and investment by sector allocation, shows the great variety of China's construction and investment abroad, energy and power being the most important, followed by transport, metals, real estate, finance, agriculture, technology, tourism, entertainment, logistics, and health.[98] Finally, Table 3 shows the relative importance of the share of private investment (as opposed to SOEs): from 2010 to 2018 the share of private investment rose from 9.5% to 47.4% in 2016, decreased sharply to 31.5% in 2017, but increased again to 44.3% in 2018. Whereas the decrease in 2017 may be explained by the decision taken by China in 2016 to control non-performing and/or speculative investments abroad, it is difficult to explain the increase of 2018. Even if private investments may again increase after 2019, it is very probable that China will not diminish SOEs investments in the strategic sectors, as they are easier to orient and control than private investments. This is part of the general CPC strategy to keep in its hands the management of China's development strategy.

The West has always considered the intrusion of other countries into its 'exclusive influence zones', as an unacceptable threat to its interests, especially in Africa and in Latin America. This was in particular the case during the Cold War regarding the interferences of Soviet Russia and China. When dealing hereafter with the West's reaction to the 'Made in China 2015' programme, which in fact, among other features, projects China's investments abroad in the domain of high-tech, we will see that today's critique of the Chinese investment abroad is dealt with in conjunction with practically all the dimensions of the relationship between China with the West. For the

---

[97]Moreover, the AEI documents allow us to see that there is only a small difference between the AEI estimates and the official data of the Chinese Ministry of Commerce. For the total investment between 2005 and 2018 the total for AEI is $ 1,137.9 billion and for the Chinese Ministry $1,153.8 billion.

[98]Note that in the 2018 documents 'chemicals' have disappeared from the AEI list.

moment it suffices to mention two critiques limited to the commercial and economic aspects of the Chinese investments abroad.

First, today the West criticizes the fact that China's investments often come under the form of long-term loans, and this may plunge the recipient countries into the so-called 'debt trap'. Of course, Western critics, who know the history of the relations between the West and these countries, are rather hypocritical in formulating these fears, as they should remember that the West has implemented exactly the same policy by investing in these countries to its own advantage, most of the time in the form of long-term loans under the cover of the so-called 'Washington Consensus'.[99] When these countries were not able to pay the interest on the loans so obtained, Western countries (with the support of the US treasury, the World Bank and the International Monetary Fund) have imposed radical changes in the political and economy systems of the beneficiary countries, including privatizations of whole pieces of state sectors (especially social policies, education and health) should these countries be wanting to obtain additional loans. This policy has devastated the countries in question. This is not to say that the local elites have not made mistakes. But the well-documented rapacious policy of the West cannot be forgotten. On the contrary, China does not require changes in the political and economic systems of these countries. And this is why African countries most of the time prefer to borrow from China rather than from the West. Moreover, China contributes to investments in the infrastructures, according to the success of its own development experience, that shows that economic development is impossible without first improving a country's infrastructure with the support and guidance of the state. However, this does not mean that these countries should not be careful in managing their own public finances. Therefore, they should remember what happened during the 'Washington consensus' years. Much will depend upon the impact of these Chinese investments on the development of these countries. A positive outcome will strengthen their economy and will make them able to pay the interests and repay the capital. Also, much will depend upon the willingness of China to re-arrange the loans, should the recipient countries experience difficulties. In this respect, China should not forget that it is the ruthless behaviour of the West towards the countries in question that explains their resentment toward the West, one of the reasons that explains why they prefer to negotiate investments with China.

Second, the West criticizes Chinese companies because they bring to the recipient countries their own manpower, thus not transferring their know-how to the local

---

[99]Let me remind the reader that the policies imposed upon the developing countries by the 'Washington Consensus' were based upon the neo-liberal ideology, according to which the state cannot be considered as one of the main means to solve the problems of development. On the contrary it is itself an obstacle to development. The dysfunctions of the governments of the developing countries are due to the corruption of civil servants, militarism, and the protection of non-competitive national industries. Consequently, liberalization (in fact de-regulation) of the market, as well privatization and decentralization. The market is the main means to sustain economic development, thanks to its driving force, as competition assures the optimal allocation of resources as well as the optimization of their use, and should imbalances occur, the market will resolve them thanks to its capacity to regulate itself without state intervention. For a critique see Stiglitz (1998), Urio (1999).

6.2 China's Strategy for Reclaiming World Power Status

workers, employees, managers and engineers. Here again, this critique ignore the fact that this was exactly the practice of the West at the time of the colonial empires and also after these countries had recovered their political independences, at least in theory. A research conducted by McKinsey shows exactly the reverse for the Chinese companies investing in Africa (Jayaram et al. 2017). Let me remind the reader that by 2015 China had become the biggest economic partner in Africa for goods trade, with $188bn, well over India ($59bn), France ($57bn), US ($53bn) and Germany ($46bn). Also, in 2015, China's infrastructure financing reached $21bn, well above France, Japan, Germany and US (with 3, 2, 1, and 1 $bn, respectively). McKinsey estimates that around 2017 there were more than 10,000 Chinese firms in Africa, with around 905 of these firms privately owned, 'calling into question the notion of a monolithic, state-coordinated investment drive by "China, Inc". Although state-owned enterprises tend to be bigger, particularly in specific sectors such as energy and infrastructure, the sheer number of private Chinese firms working toward their own profit motives suggest that Chinese investment in Africa is a more market-driven phenomenon than is commonly understood.'[100] The report considers that there are areas for significant improvement, namely the percentage of local managers (44% as an average, but 54% for manufacturing and 49% for services). It also reports instances of labour and environmental violation, such as inhuman working conditions as well as illegal extraction of natural resources including timber and fish. Nevertheless, the high percentage of local employees contradicts the general idea that is presented by Western media: 81% for SOEs and 92% for private enterprises. Moreover, Chinese enterprises run apprentice or professional programmes (62% for SOEs and 64% for private).

Before we turn to the ambitious 'Made in China 2015' programme, let me remark that China by 'going out' to the global economy, is following in some respects the same trajectory as the West has implemented at least since the beginning of the industrial revolution. An economy whose development leads to the production of goods and capital that cannot be absorbed by the national demand, inevitably leads to a search for external markets to whom one can sell in-excess goods and invest in-excess capital. This is what the development of China's foreign investment is all about. And this is the source of worries of Western countries who see China 'invading' the economy of countries where they have been used to selling goods and investing money for a very long time. Should China start to move from the production of low-value goods to goods with a high technological content, one can understand that the concerns of the West (especially the US but also the EU) would inevitably reach a climax. And this is exactly what happened at the beginning of the XXI Century. I will come back to these concerns when dealing with the reactions of the West to China's Grand Strategy (the Belt and Road Initiative) in the last part of this chapter, as the developments with which I shell be dealing in this section are to be seen as a prelude to, and the strengthening of the BRI and its major dimensions, as it is also the case for the 'Made in China 2015' plan to be dealt with hereafter.

---

[100]The study is based upon 8 African countries: Angola, Côte d'Ivoire, Ethiopia, Kenya, Nigeria, South Africa, Tanzania, and Zambia.

6.2.4.2 The Development of the Chinese Economy and Its Transition to the 4th Industrial Revolution

Already in his speech at the Party Congress of 2007, President Hu Jintao insisted upon the necessity for China to improve its economy by developing innovations independently from the West in many crucial domains, such as: re-balancing between regions, general management, banks, enterprises and their modernization, army, science and technology, Chinese investments abroad, and use of Foreign Direct Investments (FDI) in China. (Chap. 2 above, Sect. 2.4.5). The year before, 2006, the State Assets Supervision and Administration Commission (SASAC) had already published a list of seven sectors critical to the national economy and in which public ownership was considered essential: armaments, electrical power and distribution, oil and chemicals, telecommunications, coal, aviation, and shipping. (According to Xinhua, updated: 18 December 2006). In 2011 the SASAC government announced 7 strategic industries that will receive new support from the government: energy saving and environmental protection (clean energy technology); next generation IT (modernization of the country's telecommunications' infrastructure); bio-technology (pharma and vaccine manufacturers); high-tech equipment (airplanes, satellites, manufacturing technology); new energy (nuclear, wind, solar); new materials (rare earths); and new energy cars, i.e. electric and hybrid cars, and batteries.

The Chinese leadership knew very well that the mastering of these developments needed substantial improvement of the skills in science and technology essential to the development of these sectors, thus following the ideas already put in practice by Mao, Chu Enlai and Deng.[101] For this purpose, China launched the 'Thousand Talents Programme' in 2008, with the declared purpose of strengthening innovation and international competitiveness, by attracting to China scientists, academics and entrepreneurs, both foreigners and Chinese nationals living abroad. This ambitious programme targets top level academics with a well-established international reputation, except for its Junior sub-programme for which requirements are less stringent. Working conditions for senior successful applicants seem quite interesting: they can expect a 1 million yuan (US$151,000) starting bonus, and the opportunity to apply for a research fund of 3–5 million yuan. Under the senior Thousand Talent Plan, foreign scientists receive additional incentives, such as accommodation subsidies, meal allowances, relocation compensation, paid-for visits home and subsidized education costs. Employers are also obliged to find jobs for foreign spouses, or provide an equivalent local salary. During the first decade of existence the programme has attracted between 7,000 and 10,000 people. China is becoming attractive to global talent on an unprecedented level because of the nation's economic size and vibrancy, according to a report released in October 2017 by US business magazine *Forbes*, *The 2018 Global Talent Mobility and Wealth Management Report* that predicts the

---

[101] Information I give on this programme is based upon its official site http://www.1000plan.org/en/, an article published by Nature (https://www.nature.com/articles/d41586-018-00538-z), The China Daily (http://www.chinadaily.com.cn/china/2017-10/23/content_33596566.htm), Wikipedia, and an FBI note (FBI 2015).

6.2 China's Strategy for Reclaiming World Power Status

country will be a major exchange hub for global talent flow by 2022: 'By that time, China will be not only the largest export country of students studying abroad, but also a major destination for global talent to settle down. China's role as a hub in global talent mobility will further consolidate, and it will help the country to integrate its educational resources globally. Meanwhile, it will provide more competitive job opportunities for overseas talent,' said Russell Flannery, Shanghai bureau chief of *Forbes China*'.[102]

The recruitment of scholars and scientists trained in the US, and employed in China in sensitive high-tech domains, has raised some serious concerns in the US, to the point that the FBI has devoted a special attention to the Chinese 'talent programmes' within its *Counterintelligence Division*. It is interesting to note that in September 2015, only 5 months after the announcement of the 'Made in China 2015' programme (to be dealt with hereafter), the FBI issued a note entitled 'Chinese Talent Programs'.[103] The FBI, that also refers on the previous talent programmes (the first one already set up in 1994), identifies what is the interest for a foreign country to set up a programme such as the 'Thousand Talents Programme', and the problems that may arise: 'Chinese Talent Programs' are a vital part of Chinese industry. Talent programs recruit experts to fill technical jobs that drive innovation and growth in China's economy. National, provincial, and municipal talent recruitment programmes provide opportunities for experts to work in industry and academic organizations supporting key areas deemed critical to China's development.

The FBI acknowledges that the talent programmes recruit experts globally from businesses, industry, and universities with multiple incentives to work in China. Associating with these talent programmes is legal and breaks no laws. However, individuals who agree to the Chinese terms must understand what is and is not legal under US law when sharing information. A simple download of intellectual property or proprietary information has the potential to become criminal activity. Moreover, the large number of foreign students, researchers, scientists, and professionals in the United States, combined with current technological capabilities, allows foreign governments to contact and recruit individuals with the hopes to acquire advanced technology without research costs. While the majority of the population are law-abiding individuals, anyone has the capability to acquire information. The theft of information can come from current or former employees, business partners, consultants, contractors, temporary hires, foreign agents, suppliers, or even vendors who have access to proprietary information.

The FBI further considers that recruiting these individuals allows China to: (1) gain access to research and expertise for cutting edge technology; (2) benefit from years of scientific research conducted in the United States supported by US Government grants and private funding; (3) severely impact the US economy.

Even more interesting, the FBI note provides an overview of the reason why this programme poses a variety of potential threats to the US. More particularly, the FBI

---

[102] According to the *Straits Times* (Singapore), 24 October 2017 (https://www.straitstimes.com/asia/east-asia/china-a-strong-magnet-for-global-talent-forbes-report), accessed 20 December 2018.

[103] Hereafter I have reproduced several passages of this FBI note, with only a few editorial changes.

insists upon a special programme within the general programme, i.e. the 'Recruitment of Global Experts', which focuses on identifying key national level organizations and associated personnel involved in implementation and management. Its goal is to recruit ethnic Chinese experts from Western universities, research centres, and private companies to boost China's national capabilities in the science and technology fields and to move China forward as an innovative nation. The programme has also implemented sub-programmes for both young and foreign (non-ethnic Chinese) experts of age below 40 years of age.

The FBI further explains that in order to be eligible as a candidate for the Thousand Talents Programme concerning people aged 55 and over, an individual must be in a field of study that the Chinese Academy of Science (CAS) deems critical or meet the following criteria: (1) expert or scholar with full professorship in a prestigious foreign university or research and development institutes; (2) technical managerial professional in a senior position at an internationally known company or financial institution; (3) entrepreneur holding IP rights or key technologies and possesses overseas experience.

Moreover, the FBI note considers that the Chinese Talent Programmes pose some serious threat to US businesses and universities through economic espionage and theft of Intellectual Property (IP). The different programmes focus on specific fields deemed critical to China, to boost China's national capability in science and technology fields. These experts are often not required to sign non-disclosure agreements with US entities, which could result in loss of unprotected information that jeopardizes contracts or research funding. One of the greatest threats toward these experts is transferring or transporting proprietary, classified, or export-controlled information, or intellectual property (IP), which can lead to criminal charges. This threat not only targets businesses or universities but potentially targets the researchers or scientists themselves. The technology researched or developed not only costs millions of dollars but costs years, if not decades to develop. Additionally, the theft of information or IP creates a risk that someone else could take credit for the researcher's efforts. The information stolen can be recreated, resold or claimed by others, which in turn will cost the originator creditability and potential funding for future endeavours. Theft of intellectual property is an increasing threat to organizations and can go unnoticed for months or even years. In today's society, technology affords easier access to every aspect of academia and business. Some of these tools have become effective for recruiting, such as social media. Social media websites often display large amounts of personal data, such as who an individual works for, phone numbers, known associates, previous jobs, and locations. Additionally, websites like LinkedIn have full resumés, detailing with the history of an individual's achievements and accomplishments. The FBI claims that each year the United States loses billions of dollars due to technology transfer.

Finally, while the FBI concedes that it is important to conduct collaborative research, it is vital for the survival of US businesses and universities that they protect their information and mitigate lost or stolen information. In the last part of its note, the FBI explains how businesses and universities can protect themselves. The consequence of this situation, worsened by the US-China trade war, is that it has become

6.2 China's Strategy for Reclaiming World Power Status   265

more difficult for Chinese scholars to obtain a visa, and 'fewer US Universities are willing to accept Chinese visiting scholars, and US professors are reluctant to invite Chinese since it may trigger an investigation (Huang and Lo 2019).

The US worries about what it considers to be the Chinese habit of acquiring top-level experts in strategic sectors, have been further confirmed in May 2015 when China published a strategy for transforming China into a modern economy, based upon technological innovation. This has been defined in a document called 'Made in China 2015'.[104] This project, that was made public only 19 months after the announcement of the BRI, is a ten-year comprehensive blueprint aimed at transforming China into an advanced manufacturing leader (PRC 2015c). This plan defines several key-domains in which China has decided to develop first-class technologies. It consists of eight broad domains, subdivided into 22 sectors:

1. Biotechnology, comprising: (1) Target identification technology; (2) Plant-animal varieties and drug molecular design technology; (3) Gene manipulation and protein engineering technology; (4) Stem cell based human tissue engineering technology (5) Next-generation industrial biotechnology
2. Information Technology comprising: (6) Intelligent sensing technology; (7) Ad hoc network technology; (8) Virtual reality technology
3. Advanced Materials Technology comprising: (9) Intelligent materials and structural technology; (10) High-temperature superconducting technology; (11) Efficient energy material technology
4. Advanced Manufacturing Technology comprising: (12) Extreme manufacturing technology; (13) Intelligent service robotics; (14) Service life prediction technology for major products and facilities
5. Advanced Energy Technology comprising: (15) Hydrogen and fuel cell technology; (16) Distributive energy supply technology; (17) Fast neutron reactor technology; (18) Magnetic contained fusion technology
6. Marine Technology comprising: (19) 3-D marine environment monitoring technology; (20) Ocean floor based multi-parameter fast sounding technology; (21) Natural gas hydrate exploitation technology; (22) Deep-sea operation technology
7. Lasers Technology, and
8. Aerospace technology

By reading this list, one can understand the importance the Chinese government attributes to this vast programme, and the challenge it constitutes to the West, especially to the US, should it wish to maintain its dominant role in the world, as is indeed the case (Sect. 6.1 above). The impact that this project has made on the West, on governments, think tanks, media, and scholars is testified by numerous reactions, statements, analyses, and even bombastic declarations, as this project is much more that a project limited to technology improvements. In fact, if and when fully realized,

---

[104] Information on this project can be found in the *Financial Times*; the *American Enterprise Institute;* the *Council of Foreign Affairs* (its journal *Foreign Affairs)*; Mercator Institute for China Studies (MERICS), the *South China Morning Post*, the *Caixin magazine,* and the official Chinese news agency, *Xinhua.*

this project will have an impact on practically all the dimensions that determine the power of a country and therefore its relations with other countries. This is especially true for the US that for a long time has considered itself as the 'indispensable' dominating power, that tries to maintain the perennial character of the world it made.[105]

Even if many pundits in the West have put forward several doubts about the capacity of China to realize this project, especially after the US has declared a trade war on China more particularly in sectors mentioned in 'Made in China 2015', the worries that were already evident in the 2015 FBI note presented above, have not vanished today, as the speech given by Vice-President Mike Pence 4 October 2018 at the *Hudson Institute* very well demonstrates. I will come back to this speech at the end of this chapter as it is the latest formulation of US foreign policy toward China.[106] This speech shows, if necessary, that the trade war between the US and China is much more than a trade war. In fact, this speech is a foreign policy statement addressed to the Chinese leadership to force it to comply with the requirements of the US; a condition for avoiding being submitted to the heavy pressure that the US is willing to resort to, with both means already available today and those the US is in the process of developing in the near future. This speech can be considered as a neo-conservative document confirming the imperial policy the US has been implementing for a very long time, as I have sustained in the first part of this chapter. It very well corresponds, in particular, to the strategy defined by Robert Kagan, I have analyzed above (pp. 210–213).

In fact, what worries the West is that there is today enough information showing that China has already made several improvements in the mastering of high technology in several sectors mentioned in the project. Already in 2016 two specialists of strategic innovation have warned: 'today every senior executive of a Western corporation needs to understand the tidal wave of innovation flowing from China that is about to engulf Western markets (…) We believe this challenge is unprecedented in the global economy and more substantial and longer lasting than the Japanese challenge of the 1970 s'. (Yip and Mickern 2016, p. 3).

The advance of China's high-tech technology has been recognized by the 2018 Annual Report to Congress on *US-China Economic and Security Review Commission,* (US 2018b), that has introduced for the first time a new chapter entitled *China High-Tech Development,* with sections dealing with 'China's Industrial policy blueprints, the internet of things, and the fifth-generation wireless technology'. This Report has very well understood that there is a clear link between 'Made in

---

[105]European Chamber (2017), US Chamber of Commerce (2017), Wübbeke (2016), PRC (2015c), Hu Angang and Ren Hao (2016).

[106]The *Hudson Institute* is a politically conservative, non-profit American think tank based in Washington, D.C. It was founded in 1961 in Croton-on-Hudson, New York, by futurist, military strategist, and systems theorist Herman Kahn and his colleagues at the RAND Corporation. According to its website, the Institute is committed to innovative research and analysis that promotes "global security, prosperity and freedom." It promotes public policy change in accordance with its stated belief that "America's unique and central role in the global system offers the best foundation for security, the defense of liberty, and assuring economic growth.', https://en.wikipedia.org/wiki/Hudson_Institute, accessed 15 January 2019.

6.2 China's Strategy for Reclaiming World Power Status

China 2015' not only with trade, but also with the capacity of China to develop high-tech military resources. Moreover, this Report has also understood that China's high-tech project is meant to strengthen the BRI (to be dealt with hereafter), the global Chinese strategy that will connect China with the rest of the world, where China will be able to sustain competition from any country, including from the US. It would take too much space to deal with all the domains in which China has already caught up with the West or in which it is not far from achieving this goal.[107] Here, it suffices to mention a few examples.

First, in the framework of China's industrial policy, the *Yunfu Park* in Northern China, has been set up to use generous state subsidies to develop and dominate emerging industries critical to the 'Made in China 2015' shift to high-tech manufacturing. 'Beijing has spent an estimated $58.8 bn subsidising its electric car industry over the past decades (…) creating the world's largest market for electric cars as well as a dominant position in batteries, surpassing Japan and South Korea. Subsidies also helped propel Chinese solar makers into the ranks of the world's largest producer, overtaking competitors in the US and Europe' (Sanderson 2019).

Second, according to an article published by the influential *Foreign Affairs,* 'Beijing is striving to become a world leader in quantum technology through large-scale state-guided investments, which may total tens of billions of dollars in the years to come. Under its 13th five-year plan, introduced in 2016, China has launched a "megaproject" for quantum communications and computing, which aims to achieve major breakthroughs in these technologies by 2030, including the expansion of China's national quantum communications infrastructure, the development of a general quantum computer prototype, and the construction of a practical quantum simulator. China is also building the *National Laboratory for Quantum Information Sciences*, which, with over $1 billion in initial funding, could emerge as a key centre of gravity for future research and development' (Kania 2018).

Third, China is developing its ambitious space exploration programme. In this context, China's robotic Chang'e 4 mission touched down on the floor of the 115-mile-wide (186 kilometres) Von Kármán Crater 2 January 2019, pulling off the first-ever soft landing on the mysterious lunar far side. To realise this performance, China launched a relay satellite called Queqiao in May 2018, after having launched the Chang'e 1 and Chang'e 2 orbiters in 2007 and 2010, respectively, and pulled off a near-side landing with the Chang'e 3 mission in December 2013. China also launched a return capsule on an eight-day trip around the moon in October 2014, a mission known as Chang'e 5T. That was a test run for the Chang'e 5 sample-return effort, which could launch as early as this year. China also has ambitions for crewed lunar missions, but its human-spaceflight programme is focused more on Earth orbit

---

[107]I will not deal with the question to know whether China has already surpassed the US in all the domains which constitute a country's Comprehensive National Power, as what is certain is that China is likely to develop an economy as powerful as that of the US, unless China makes some serious mistakes. Considering how China has, so far, avoided to make such mistakes, it is more interesting to evaluate how it is organizing the development of its power resources. This is exactly what I try to do in this chapter.

in the short term. The nation aims to have a space station up and running there by the early 2020s (Wall 2019).

Fourth, since its foundation, the *China's Renewable Energy Institute* has worked to establish the *Asia Super Grid* across Eurasia and beyond, to support investments thanks to the exchange of abundant natural renewable energy resources, such as wind, solar and hydropower. This project must be seen in the framework of the Belt and Road Initiative, to be dealt with hereafter, that needs energy infrastructure investments. For the moment it suffices to say that this is an ambitious outbound investment strategy which links at least 65 countries along terrestrial and maritime trade routes. Chinese state-owned banks and companies dominate investments in oil, gas and hydropower along BRI. The China Development Bank has already granted $160bn in loans to countries involved in the BRI, and has identified a further $350bn worth of projects. Given these projects, an interconnection of energy across borders is needed for securing these investments, water supply and long-term regional stability. Moreover, these projects will be implemented by taking into consideration the *Asian Development Bank* project, the $1bn Tutap project aimed to link the power grids of Turkmenistan, Uzbekistan, Tajikistan, Afghanistan and Pakistan into a unified grid system from existing hydropower and coal and gas-fired plants, as well as the World Bank-led $1bn Casa-1000 project will enable Tajikistan and Kyrgyzstan to deliver excess hydropower in the summer season to Afghanistan and Pakistan. By securing better government policies on renewables, BRI can create a step-change in renewable energy investment. China's bold vision is to create a global renewable energy grid that connects renewable energy generation across hemispheres. This would create a continuous source of clean power across national borders. The Beijing-based *Global Energy Interconnection Development and Cooperation Organisation* (Geidco) and *China's State Grid Corporation* have proposed a layout for such a system in Asia. This would develop six ultra-high voltage grids across China, North-East Asia, South-East Asia, South Asia, Central Asia and West Asia to cement a clean power system in the region. With the Paris Agreement serving as an initiative towards transitioning to carbon-free societies in the latter half of the 21st century, as well as the growing demand for realizing 100% renewable energy, development of global energy interconnections have become an even more important challenge to address (Litovsky 2017, and Renewable Energy Institute—no date).

Fifth, recently the *Chinese Institute for High Energy Physics* (IHEP, within the Chinese Academy of Sciences) has announced in November 2018 plans to build its own particle accelerator, the CEPC (Circular Electron Positron Collider), five times more powerful than the LHC situated at the CERN (European Organization for Nuclear Research). Two documents describing the project have been published in December 2018, after six years of preliminary research (IHEP 2018). Construction will be preceded by a five-year 'research and development' phase (2018–2022) during which prototypes of key technical components will be built. Construction is expected to start in 2022 and be completed in 2030. Moreover, the document comments that 'the CEPC is an important part of the global plan for high-energy physics research. It will support a comprehensive research programme by scientists around the world. Physicists from many countries will work together to explore the frontiers of science

6.2 China's Strategy for Reclaiming World Power Status

and technology, thus taking our understanding of the fundamental nature of matter, energy and the universe to a new level.' (IHEP 2018).

It is interesting to acknowledge that the last two projects show that China is ready to cooperate with the WB, the ADB and international scientists all over the world, and that all the above-mentioned projects show that China is on its way to becoming a world leader in high-tech. But it is the Artificial Intelligence (AI) domain that is certainly the most promising sector for China, because it may lead to potential applications in many sectors, including military equipment. Here it is interesting to quote one of the most renowned experts in this domain, Kai-Fu Lee.[108] Commenting upon China's decision to develop an ambitious plan to build artificial intelligence (AI) capabilities, Lee says. 'when Chinese investors, entrepreneurs, and government officials all focus on one industry, they can truly shake the world. Indeed, China is ramping up AI investments, research, and entrepreneurship on a historic scale. Money for AI start-ups pouring from venture capitalists, tech juggernauts, and Chinese government'. Referring to the decades needed to arrive at today's situation, and linking AI with deep learning and big data, Lee considers 'that revolution has finally arrived. It will usher an era of massive productivity increases but also widespread disruptions in labour markets, and profound sociopsychological effects on people, as AI takes over human jobs across all sorts of industries' (Lee 2018, p. 5).

Having said that, Lee believes that 'the skilful application of AI will be China's greatest opportunity to catch up with, and possibly surpass, the United States.' (Lee 2018, pp. 3 and 5–6). In fact, Lee believes that China will be the biggest beneficiary of AI and this will lead to a balance of power in the AI world order between China and the US. Why is Lee so confident of China's success in developing AI and its applications to a variety of domains? First, compared to Silicon Valley's entrepreneurs, who have a reputation to be the hardest working in the US, their Chinese competitors have to work even harder as they 'have risen to where they are by conquering the most cutthroat competitive environment on the planet.' (p. 15). In the context, quite surprisingly for a Western audience, Lee praises the Chinese 'copycat': contrary to Silicon Valley companies where copying is stigmatized. This attitude had the consequence of a lack of competition and consequently of complacency, 'with entrepreneurs failing to explore all the possible iterations of their first innovation. The messy markets and dirty tricks of China "copycat" era produces some questionable companies, but they also incubated a generation of the world's most nimble, savvy, and nose-to-the-grindstone entrepreneurs. These entrepreneurs will be the secret sauce that helps China become the first country to cash in on Age of implementation [of AI]'. China's second advantage is to have an over-abundance of data (i.e. big data), needed to take advantage of AI. 'China has already surpassed the US in terms of sheer volumes as the number one producer of data'. Third, for Lee the government has, and is still playing today, a determinant role favouring the

---

[108] Kai-Fu Lee is chairman and CEO of Sinovation Ventures, a leading technology-savvy investment firm focusing on developing the next generation of Chinese high-tech companies. Before founding Sinovation in 2009, Lee was the president of Google China. Previously he held executive positions at Microsoft, SGI, and Apple.

270   6   China and the New World Order. Why and How China's Foreign Policy …

development of AI: 'the Chinese government's sweeping plan for becoming an AI superpower pledged widespread support for AI research, but most of all it acted as a beacon to local governments throughout the country to follow suit,' (p. 17). In summary: 'putting all these pieces together (…) China's world-class entrepreneurs and proactive government, I believe that China will soon match or even overtake the US in developing and deploying Artificial intelligence. This new AI world order will be particularly jolting to Americans who have grown accustomed to a near-total dominance of the technological sphere.' (p. 18).

6.2.4.3   The Challenge to the International Role of the US Dollar

We have seen under Sect. 6.1 above that the two most important power resources of the US are the military and the international status of the US dollar. Whereas improving the military resources is a relatively independent endeavour (provided one has the technology and the money), contesting the supremacy of the US dollar necessitates a complex strategy, as it is almost impossible to proceed immediately to a frontal attack. So, China has progressively explored several ways to diminish, and at the limit to escape, from the dependence on the US dollar for its economic development both internally and internationally, by initiating and supporting what is generally called: a strategy of 'de-dollarization' of the global economy. These measures include the creation of international banks as competitors to the international financial institutions dominated by the US and its allies; obtaining a better position within international financial organization more conform to the economic weight of China; set up bilateral agreements allowing the contracting countries to pay for their trade in their local currencies instead of the US dollar; developing an alternative to the petro-dollars, i.e. the petro-yuan; setting up new institutions enabling to send and receive worldwide information about financial transactions in a secure, standardized and reliable environment, independent from the SWIFT, dominated by the US; setting up international trade and investment partnerships excluding the US as a response to the partnerships planned by the US to exclude, isolate and contain China, such as the TPP; and prepare for a possible return to a new gold-standard totally or partially independent from the US dollar, by buying important quantities of gold.[109]

The Chinese leadership has been dissatisfied for a long time with the way the governance of the international financial system is organized, i.e. within the IMF, the World Bank and Asian Development Bank which are dominated by the US, the EU and Japan. China's criticism became more pressing when the 2008 financial and economic crisis revealed the instability of the US currency and its negative impact on the world economy. Already on 23 March 2009, a clear warning came from the Governor of the People's Bank of China, Zhou Xiaochuan: 'The crisis called again for creative reform of the existing international monetary system toward an international

---

[109] In addition to Hudson (2003) that explains the US strategy for establishing world dominance since the end of the Second World War, see for the recent development of this strategy the brilliant articles by Michael Hudson (Hudson 2019a, b).

6.2 China's Strategy for Reclaiming World Power Status

reserve currency with a stable value, rule-based insurance and manageable supply, so as to achieve the objective of safeguarding global economic and financial stability' (Zou 2009).

The creation of the AIIB, an international bank initiated by China, is the first clear response to the obstruction by the US to the reform advocated by China of the above-mentioned financial institutions. This is directly connected with China's investment strategy, as we have seen above, and is also an important support for the Belt and Road initiative, to be dealt with below. It is in the context of these initiatives that the proposal for the creation of an *Asian Infrastructure Investment Bank* (AIIB) was first made by the Vice Chairman of the *China Centre for International Economic Exchanges*, a Chinese think-tank, at the Bo'ao Forum in April 2009, only a month after the warning of the Governor of the People's Bank of China. In spite of these warnings, the US and its European and Japanese allies did not envisage to negotiate a reform of the global financial governance. So, President Xi Jinping's official proposal to create the AIIB, during a visit to Indonesia, 2 October 2013, should not have come as a surprise. Also, it is interesting to note that this announcement was made at the same time as the announcement of the second part of the BRI (the maritime road), the first part (the silk continental road) having been announced a month before, 7 September 2013. Immediately, the AIIB attracted many countries, including the closest US allies, in spite of very strong opposition from the latter, as well as the BRICS countries (Russia, India, Brazil and South Africa).[110] The strong criticism from the US and some of its allies, the doubts about the governance of the bank and the fear that China may be use it for political purposes, could not avoid the outcome that today, the AIIB has 67 members and 24 prospective members around the world.

The importance of establishing the AIIB became evident for China, not only for geo-strategic purposes, but also considering the economic imperatives for sustaining economic development throughout the Asian continent, when the Asian Development Bank (ADB) estimated in 2010 that Asia required 8 trillion US dollars to be invested in infrastructure from 2010 to 2020, should the Asian countries wish to improve their economies. China was certainly willing to contribute to this endeavour. Unfortunately, as the ADB is dominated by the US and Japan, the latter would be in fact the decision-makers determining the activities of this bank for investments in Asia. Moreover, the slow process towards the goal of reforming the international financial system, that China has been asking for, for a long time, convinced China to take the initiative to launch its own investment bank. The US, considering this move as an attack on its dominant position, decided not only not to join, but tried very hard, and also very awkwardly, to dissuade, unsuccessfully, its allies from joining,

---

[110]Here is a non-exhaustive list. Western countries: Australia, Canada, Denmark, Finland, France, Georgia, Germany, Italy, Netherlands, New Zealand, Norway, Poland, Portugal, Russia, Spain, Sweden, Switzerland, United Kingdom); Asian: Azerbaijan, Bangladesh, Brunei, Cambodia, India, Indonesia, Kazakhstan, Laos, Malaysia, Mongolia, Myanmar, Nepal, Pakistan, Philippines, Singapore, Sri Lanka, Tajikistan, Thailand, Uzbekistan, and Vietnam), as well as other countries from other continents, in particular the other BRICS countries (Brazil and South Africa, in addition to China, Russia and India), and Egypt, Ethiopia, Iran, Israel, Jordan, South Korea, Kuwait, Oman, Qatar, Saudi Arabia, Turkey, and United Arab Emirates.

as mentioned above. This was certainly the first move that showed to the US that China was on its way to become an international player that it would be difficult to control. This Chinese success was the prelude to the RMB admission into the IFM Special Drawing Right Basket.

It is interesting to note that the 'Made in China 2025' (the logical consequence of the 'Thousand talents' project mentioned above), the development of research and development in high-tech, the One Belt and One Road and the Asian Infrastructure Investment Bank projects, have been announced, and started to take form during a very short period of time, i.e. between 2013 and 2015. The following year, in 2016, the RMB was admitted into the FMI Special Drawing Rights Basket. Today, its share is 10.92%, alongside the US, that nevertheless keeps the largest share: US 41.73%, the EU 30.93%, Japan 8.33%, and the UK 8.09% (IMF website). At the same time, the voting power of China within the Board of Governors of the IMF was increased from 3.8 to 6.09%, still much lower than the 16.52 of the US, and about the same as that of Japan (6.15) and not much higher than that of the major European countries.[111] Moreover, the use of the USD as an international payment currency has declined from 43.89% in 2015 to 40.47% in November 2018, compared to EUR 34.13%, GDP 7.27%, JPY 3.55%, and RMB 2.09%, up from 0.5% in 2014 (SWIFT 2018).[112] Although the increase in percentage is quite spectacular, the actual use of the Yuan in international trade payments is still quite modest, especially compared to the US (40.47%) and the EU (34.13%) (SWIFT 2018).

In face of this situation, China has started to use different means for avoiding using the US dollar and for increasing the use of the RMB. The first means is the use of bilateral swap agreements that China has passed with several countries and economic organizations, e.g. Russia, Brazil, and South Africa (i.e. the BRICS countries, but not India), Pakistan, Australia, Brazil, UK, Canada, the EU and even Switzerland. Bilateral Swap agreements allow the contracting countries to pay for their trade exchanges in their own currency instead of in USD. These agreements and the success of the BRI initiative (to be discussed below) show the growing attractiveness of China's economy, today the only large country that is increasing its GDP at an annual rate of just below 7% (Prasad 2017).

Recently, the trend to use national currencies instead of the US dollar has been growing. This is due essentially to the aggressive policy of the US against countries that do not comply with its national interests. It is necessary here to remind the reader that many countries have been attacked by the US through economic embargo and/or military interventions, because they manifested the will to sell their petrol in another

---

[111] Compare China's voting power to the power of a choice of other countries: Germany 5.32%, UK and France 4.03%, Italy 3.02%, Spain 1.92%, Switzerland 1.18%; according to the IMF site: IMF Members' Quotas and Voting Power, and IMF Board of Governors, February 13, 2019.

[112] This document considers RMB's share as a domestic and international payments currency Customer initiated and institutional payments. Messages exchanged on SWIFT based on value. The attentive reader has certainly remarked upon the high percentage of transactions made in Euro; which lead some economists to consider that before China's rise, it was then Eurozone and its 'unique currency', that the US considered as their more serious competitor (Zaki 2011).

6.2 China's Strategy for Reclaiming World Power Status

currency, namely the Euro instead of the USD. This has been the case of Libya, Iraq, Iran and Venezuela.

The recent crisis between the US and Iran was caused by the US President's decision to withdraw from the Iran nuclear deal (The Joint Comprehensive Plan of Action—JCPOA) and by the subsequent decision to impose a very strict embargo on Iran, especially on its export of petrol. By doing so, the US in fact forbids non-American enterprises to develop economic exchanges and investments in Iran. These countries (mainly European, China and Russia) are not ready to accept the US diktat. Whereas the EU countries may not be in a position to avoid the US sanctions, and thereby to continue their economic exchanges with Iran, in spite of having set up a SPV (Special Purpose Vehicle) for this purpose (to be explained hereafter), China and Russia seem to be more able to do so. In fact, these two countries had already signed in 2014 an agreement of 400 billion equivalent of US dollars to use their own currencies to finance the exchange of their goods, especially petrol. China claims to have already signed several dozen of such agreements. Moreover, China reportedly has been in the process of negotiating with Saudi Arabia to sell its petrol in Yuan instead of US dollars.[113] Should the Saudi agree, this would be a strategic loss for the US, as since the beginning of the 1970s the value of the US dollar has been based upon the agreement the US obtained from Saudi Arabia and the members of the petrol club to sell their petrol in USD (Hudson 2003).

An additional move to avoid US dominance in the international financial domain is today under way. Indeed, China, as well as other countries such as Russia, Iran, Venezuela and the member-states of the EU have today additional good geo-political reasons for avoiding using the US-dominated SWIFT for their international payments and to resort to alternative institutions. SWIFT was created in 1973 in order to facilitate financial transactions through a secure means. Since the attack on the Twin Towers on 11 September 2001, using as a pretext the fight against terrorism, the US has set up a strategy to force SWIFT (including by sanctions) to gain access to information allowing to determine the origin and the destination of financial transactions. Several US public bodies were implicated in this strategy, such as the Treasury, the CIA and the National Security Agency (NSA). Information about these moves were made known by the Danish newspaper *Berlingske* and the German *Der Spiegel*, as well as by the documents leaked by Edward Snowden, that revealed that the NSA spied on SWIFT using a variety of methods, including reading SWIFT printer traffic from numerous banks.[114] Thanks to the information thus acquired, the US can block the transactions, seize money being transferred to countries under US sanctions, threaten to exclude the companies concerned from the US market, and eventually

---

[113]Cooperation between the two countries has been going on for several years. Already in March 2017, Bloomberg reported that 'Saudi Arabian Oil Co. may deepen investment in China's oil industry as part of $65 billion worth of potential deals signed between the two countries in everything from energy to manufacturing and theme park'. (Bloomberg 16 March 2017).

[114]For more details, see the article 'Society for Worldwide Interbank Financial Telecommunication', i.e. SWIFT, by Wikipedia and the refences quoted therein, https://en.wikipedia.org/wiki/Society_for_Worldwide_Interbank_Financial_Telecommunication, accessed 10 February 2019; and the SWIFT official site: https://www.swift.com/

charge them with very severe fines, as the US has done habitually in the past. Based on past experience, it is clear that this US policy is particularly dissuasive. For example, the French Total multinational had planned in 2017 to conduct a $4.8 billion Iranian gas field project, after the signing of the 'Iran Nuclear Deal'. But it was forced to backtrack after the US threatened to impose penalties on any companies that persisted with doing business with Iran.

This of course is not new in US foreign policy. Countries such as Russia, Germany, France and China have been envisaging for several years to take measures in order to put an end to this US strategy. Recently this movement has been accelerated by the US policy of economic sanctions on Iran and also those on Venezuela, in addition to those imposed upon Russia since the Ukrainian crisis of 2014. The latter harm more particularly European businessmen who consider Russia as a natural economic partner. The last straw came on 13 January 2018 in the form of a bombastic declaration by the US Ambassador to Germany threatening this country and its companies with heavy sanctions, should it not discontinue the building of the *North Stream 2* pipeline between Russia and Germany. The reason is that the US, already under the Obama administration at the time of the Ukraine crisis, had strongly suggested that the EU should import shale gas from the US instead of oil from Russia.[115] Very strong reactions to this type of behaviour came from several top-level politicians in several European countries, especially from the 'three big founders' of the European integration movement, France, Germany and Italy. This type of reaction would have been unthinkable only few years ago. This habit of the US to give orders not only to competitors but also to allies is probably coming to an end. Even the influential *Bloomberg* entitled an article published on 14 February 2019: 'Europeans Grow Tired of the U.S.-Led Alliance. Trump is downgrading America's pre-eminent role in the liberal world order. Second-tier powers are trying to figure out what comes next'.

It is in this context that the UK, Germany and France have announced at the end of January 2019 their decision to set up the instrument (called *INSTEX, Instrument In Support of Trade Exchanges*) that they will use instead of SWIFT, thus avoiding US sanctions. This Special Purpose Vehicle is headquartered in Paris and is headed by Per Fischer of Germany, who formerly served as Head of Financial Institutions at *Commerzbank*, between 2003 and 2014. Although it is not clear, at the time of writing, if INSTEX will actually work, it is nevertheless a strong sign that these EU members, that the US claims to be its privileged allies within the NATO military alliance, are no longer prepared to accept of being treated as vassals by the US (Irish 2019).

It is interesting to note that not only European states are dissatisfied with SWIFT, but also Russia and China, who have also been seriously envisaging setting up alternatives to SWIFT. At the beginning of December 2018, the US attacked Huawei,

---

[115]The US has been investing massive amounts of money in this technique for becoming the 'number one' in oil production, thus not only assuring independence from abroad, but also becoming a petrol exporter. Clearly a move to add another resource to its already impressive arsenal of power resources. It is clear that within this strategy the EU is a 'natural' customer, even if buying patrol from Russia is cheaper.

6.2 China's Strategy for Reclaiming World Power Status

a strong competitor of US companies, by asking Canada to arrest its technology's chief financial officer, Ms Sabrina Meng Wanhzhou, with an extradition warrant to the US. She is accused with charges of misleading banks about the company's business and violating US sanctions. In particular, she is accused of using an unofficial subsidiary to skirt US and EU sanctions to conduct business in Iran. The company is also charged in a separate case with stealing trade secrets from T-Mobile, according to federal prosecutors. Here we have a case illustrating the US fears that Chinese companies may steal technology from its companies, as we mentioned above. But what is interesting is that this case has highlighted 'how the US's dominance of international financial markets bolsters its geopolitical clout and allows it to police the world. As the trade war rages on and China grows more frustrated with the US dollar hegemony which gives the US such authority on the world stage, it may step up efforts to create an alternative payments system to rival the American currency, experts have said' (Karen 2018). This episode came after 'the US-China competition over technology reached a peak in recent months. In August this year [2018], the Trump administration signed a bill banning government use of Huawei and ZTE technology as part of the broader *Defense Authorization Act*. This was the latest salvo by Washington after a 2012 House of Representatives report that labelled both Chinese firms as national security threats, with the heads of U.S. national security agencies recommending against using either companies' products' (Tham 2018).

An additional move to contest the supremacy of the US dollar came in 2018 when after 25-years' wait, China, the biggest oil buyer, announced the opening, on March 27, of its crude-futures contract in the Shanghai International Energy Exchange (SIEE), that will allow trading petrol in yuan. This has given birth to a new expression, the 'petro-yuan' that may constitute a challenge to the petro-dollar, i.e. the dollar-denominated oil benchmarks Brent and West Texas Intermediate (Bloomberg 2018; Park 2018). The SIEE had an impressive start with over 10 billion Yuan notional trade within the hour, and in spite of the alarms expressed by the Western media, six months later (beginning of October 2018) the oil markets continue to function, and China's futures have established themselves and overtaken in volume the dollar-denominated oil futures traded in Singapore and Dubai. Nevertheless, this constitutes a small fraction of the amount traded in US dollars. However, according to the *South China Morning* Post, the SIEE 'is being taken seriously by multinational commodity traders (like Glencore) and it prices in a manner comparable to the Brent and West Texas Intermediate indices. All this suggests that China's oil futures could bring the RMB to the core of global commodity markers (Mathews and Selden 2018).

Nevertheless, influential Western media still today have doubts about the future of the SIEE. Already at the end of March 2018, *The Economist* admits that 'countries under US sanctions, such as Iran, Russia and Venezuela, may be tempted to trade oil in Yuan as this would wean them off dollar-based earnings and help them to steer clear of US banks', but it warns that 'so long as China excludes its financial system from the rest of the world, talk of petroyuan replacing the petrodollar will be premature' (Economist 2018). A more precise statement came towards the end of 2018 by the influential *Forbes*: while admitting that 'oil exporters such as Iran, Iraq, Indonesia, Angola, Nigeria and Russia declared they were amenable to purchase in yuan', *Forbes* remarks that the 15.4 million barrels traded through the SIEE corresponds to what China imports in two days, and that this is a small fraction of the annual trade value of around $14 trillion (2017), about the equivalent to China's gross domestic product in 2017' (Sharma 2018; Katada 2018). *The Economist* and *Forbes* have here a good point, but this move toward the petroyuan must be evaluated within the number of initiatives China is taking to weaken the international position of the US dollar, as well as in the general framework of China's moves to recover world power status. Moreover, their remarks are valid in the very short run. However, one should not ignore that China's moves must be considered in the framework of its long-term, strategy. Finally, as mentioned several times, China's strategy is implemented within the changing structure of the international system, that very clearly shows that the West, and especially the US, are losing their dominant position thanks to which they have been accustomed to benefit from, since at least the Renaissance. This is not to say that the RMB will replace the US dollar. It simply means that the changing structure of the international power balance is changing in favour of China, and this means that the US dollar will not remain the unique international currency through which the US has dominated the world since WW2 and more so since the end of the Cold War. Another governance of the international economic and financial system is coming sooner than several influential pundits have today foreseen, or fear.

The time of the end of the domination of the US dollar in international finance is also suggested by the phenomenal amount of gold bought recently by several countries, such as China and Russia. This seems to suggest that even if today there is no other currency to replace the US dollar, it is likely that we may evolve towards the establishment of regional payment systems, based upon a regional basket of currencies, possibly sustained by gold, pending an international agreement between the major economic blocs on the establishment of a new international currency, that would replace the unstable US dollar. This is exactly what China has asked for in 2009 (as mentioned above) after the outbreak of the international financial crisis of 2008. By reading the comments by US mainstream pundits on this possible development, it is clear that this has resulted in a nightmare, as not only this will *ipso facto* considerably reduce the scope of the US dollar, but because it may also put additional pressure on the US, as it is not at all sure that it still today retains the amount of gold it used to have in the past. In this respect it is interesting to note that Germany (similar to many other countries), who had deposited its gold in the US during the Cold War, has experienced many serious difficulties in recuperating its gold. Some observers use this situation to consider that it is possible that the US has used a large part of the gold it had at the beginning of the Cold War for financing its foreign policy, especially a long series of overt and covert military interventions. With the dollar having lost its rank as the major international currency and the coffers of Fort Knox being almost empty, the place of the US in the new international order would be reduced to the real strength of its economy. Many have doubts that the US would then be able to play the role that it plays still today.

To conclude this section on the role China may play in the future in the international financial system, it remains that the internationalization of the RMB may represent a danger for the independence of China's development strategy. This is likely to

6.2 China's Strategy for Reclaiming World Power Status

happen if China opens its capital account, considered by experts in these matters, to be a necessity should China want to play a leading role in international finance. This means freeing the flow of capital to and from China, thus allowing international investors (American, but also European and Japanese) to operate within the China market, putting a huge pressure on China's central bank and its State-owned banks. I should like to remind the reader that China has been able to overcome the Asian financial crisis of 1997 and the global crisis of 2008, thanks to the closeness of its capital account. There is no secret that the West, and especially the US and its major banks and multi-national companies, are pressing the Chinese government to open its capital account. For the time being, China is very keen on safeguarding its control over the movements of capitals and thereby on its development strategy.

6.2.4.4 Bilateral Alliances and Implication in Global and Regional Organizations

Several Western pundits claim that one of China's weaknesses compared to the US is that it does not possess by far the same number of allies both within international organizations such as the US-led NATO alliance or through bilateral cooperation. The inevitable conclusion is that China is isolated within the international system. The same evaluation is made about Russia. Nothing is farther from the real situation. China was certainly isolated during the Mao era. But this was due to an autonomous decision China took to isolate itself taken at the end of the Chinese civil war, that came after more than one century of foreign aggressions. China decided that it needed to reconstruct its polity, economy and society autonomously, without foreign interferences. International cooperation, for example with Russia, was established and eventually terminated according to an autonomous evaluation. Moreover, we have here another example of how Chinese culture differs, still today, from the West on many counts. Interpersonal relations are still important, and even if the signing of formal agreements is becoming the rule, this is preceded by taking time for establishing mutual respect and understanding. This is important because the rise of China has worried its neighbouring countries. But one must also understand that the rise of China constitutes a powerful attraction for its neighbouring countries. So, if China wants to play a leading role in Asia, thereby limiting, and in the end eventually excluding the US, it has to make it clear to its neighbours that it does not want to dominate them but wants to set up win-win cooperation, as it has claimed to do so for a long time. The US are aware of this trend and tries by any means to persuade China's neighbours that the US represents a more reliable and stable solution, that much better guarantees their security and independence. This is why the US is trying to attract intro its orbit countries like India, a serious competitor to China. Here again, it is up to China to persuade India that a win-win cooperation is possible. The US should understand that Asian countries have not forgotten the aggression the West, including the US, has perpetrated at their expense during more than three centuries.

Rivalries do not for ever exclude cooperation, and this is borne out by what happened in Europe after the end of WW 2.[116]

Given these premises, it is enough here to mention the numerous bilateral cooperations China has established with Eurasian countries, especially with Russia. The US committed a devastating strategic mistake at the end of the Cold War by continuing to implement toward Russia the containment strategy adopted at the end of WW 2 when Soviet Russia represented a serious competitor. At the beginning of the 1990s, this was clearly not the case. Being stuck within its ideology analyzed at the beginning of this chapter, incapable of changing strategy, the US has forgotten the teaching of some of its own strategists warning that the US should avoid the emergence of a world power in Eurasia, as this power will inevitably dominate the world given the weight and the centrality of this continent. By continuing to attack Russia after the end of the Cold war, by expanding NATO and the EU eastward, thereby betraying the promise made to Gorbachev, the US has practically pushed Russia into the arms of China. This is today a formidable coalition in terms of economic, technological and geo-political resources. As we have seen above, the US establishment has preferred to engage in a time-consuming war (one of the favourite words of American political vocabulary) against its unusual President, instead of taking advantage of several of his policy proposals, namely to negotiate with Russia, as I have sustained above, in Sect. 6.1.6.

In addition to the excellent cooperation with Russia, China has established good to excellent cooperation with a variety of countries in Asia, Africa, Latin America, the Middle East and even in Europe. In particular, cooperation with de facto or potential strategic importance include Turkey, Iran, Syria, the Philippines, and the countries situated along the One Belt One Road project, the 'Grand Chinese strategy', to be dealt with hereafter.

In addition to bilateral cooperation, China's strategy has developed an increasing implication in international, regional and global organisations through which it can acquire additional power resources. China has been a member of the Security Council of the UN since 1971, and its role has increased as a country using its veto power, generally with Russia to oppose US initiatives concerning, for example, Georgia, Ukraine and Syria. More recently China has increased its contribution to UN peacekeeping operations, of which it is one of the major contributors (Perlez 2015). Moreover, and maybe more interestingly, China has contributed to the creation of international regional organizations that are in fact an obstacle to the US leadership in some parts of the world, such as the BRICS and the Shanghai Cooperation Organization.

Probably, the most important is the Shanghai Cooperation Organisation (SCO).This is a political, economic, and security organisation, the creation of which

---

[116]Let me just give an example concerning India, that the majority of experts give as an example of the positive heritage left by the British colonization, thereby making India a 'natural' ally of the West. Shashi Tharoor, former Under-Secretary General of the UN and Congress MP in India and former Minister writes in his book significantly entitled *Inglorious Empire. What the British Did to India*: 'Indians can never forget the conditions in which they found our country after two centuries of colonialism' (Tharoor 2016, p. 216).

6.2 China's Strategy for Reclaiming World Power Status

was announced in 2001 in Shanghai by the leaders of China, Kazakhstan, Kyrgyzstan, Russia, Tajikistan, and Uzbekistan. The *Shanghai Cooperation Organisation Charter* was signed in June 2002 and entered into force on 19 September 2003. This organization is a development of the *Shanghai Five group*, founded on 26 April 1996 in Shanghai with the signing of the *Treaty on Deepening Military Trust in Border Regions* in Shanghai by the heads of states of China, Kazakhstan, Kyrgyzstan, Russia and Tajikistan. In 1997, the same countries signed the *Treaty on Reduction of Military Forces in Border Regions*. It is interesting to note that already in 1997 the President of Russia Boris Yeltsin and Prime Minister of China Jiang Zemin, signed a declaration on a 'multipolar world', and in 2000, the SCO members agreed to 'oppose intervention in other countries' internal affairs on the pretexts of "humanitarianism" and "protecting human rights"; and support the efforts of one another in safeguarding the five countries' national independence, sovereignty, territorial integrity, and social stability.'[117] A clear reference to the intervention in other states' territory by Western powers for 'humanitarian rescuing and human rights protection'. In 2017 India and Pakistan joined the organization. Over the years, the SCO has developed cooperation in many domains, and more particularly in security, resolving border issues, military cooperation, intelligence sharing, countering terrorism and countering American influence in Central Asia, where it plays the role of an eastern counter-balance to NATO.

With the admission of India (the other economic giant with China) and Pakistan, SCO is today the most populous organization in the world, with more than 3 billion of people. If we add the 125 millions of the four countries with an observer's status (Iran, Afghanistan, Mongolia and Belarus), the SCO has about 3.2 billion people, more than 42% of the world population. The SCO is also the biggest area in the world, with more than 60% of Eurasia. Its GDP (in PPP) is more than $37. 200 billion, almost as much as the US and the EU combined. The SCO has combined military forces of 5.6 million and a combined military budget of $370 billion, compared to the more than $900 billion of the NATO countries. But what is remarkable with the SCO is the combined quality of several of its members and observers covering not only Eurasia but also the Middle East: China, Russia, India, Iran, Afghanistan (plus the other 4 'Stan').

The 18th SCO annual meeting was held in Qingdao (China) 9–10 June 2018, with the presence of Nerendra Modi, Prime Minister of India, Xi Jinping, President of China, Vladimir Putin, President of Russia and the presidents of the other member-states. States with observers-status were also represented by their presidents: Iran, Afghanistan, Belarus, Mongolia. The meeting confirmed the support of the members to several policy options and initiatives: facilitating the emergence of international relations of a new type and the importance of improving global economic governance architecture (this being a clear sign to the US); an open world economy; the settlement of crises in Afghanistan, Syria, the Middle East and the Korean Peninsula; the opposition to terrorism, separatism and extremism; and the support to the UN Global

---

[117]The website of SCO, https://en.wikipedia.org/wiki/Shanghai_Cooperation_Organisation, accessed 24 July 2017.

Agenda for Sustainable Development. Moreover, what is of paramount importance, China, Russia, Kyrgyzstan, Pakistan, Tajikistan and Uzbekistan reaffirmed their support for China's BRI, including the coordination and development of the Russia-led Eurasia Economic Union and the BRI. The results seem rather encouraging, even if some problems remain, in particular the fact the India did not support the BRI. Here again, in contributing to the activities and increasing strength of the Shanghai Group (SCO) China acquires additional resources useful for the realization of its national and international interests.[118]

The BRICS is the other interesting organization of which China is one of the founding members. The BRICS was created between 2006 and 2009. It comprises five of the major countries in the world: Brazil, Russia, India, China and South Africa, all members of the G-20. Since 2009, the BRICS have been meeting annually at formal summits. In 2015, the five BRICS countries represented over 3.6 billion people, or about 40% of the world population and had a combined nominal GDP of US$16.6 trillion, equivalent to approximately 22% of the gross world product, and an estimated US$4 trillion in combined foreign reserves.

The BRICS deal with economic, financial and global governance issues. In 2013, the member countries agreed to create the New Development Bank (NDB) with the purpose of rivalling with the Western-dominated IMF and World Bank, with an initial capital of US$100 billion. In March 2014, the BRICS foreign ministers issued a communiqué that 'noted with concern, the recent media statement on the forthcoming G20 Summit to be held in Brisbane in November 2014 [and reminded those concerned that] the custodianship of the G20 belongs to all Member States equally and no one Member State can unilaterally determine its nature and character.' A clear reference to the habit of the US to determine the G20 agenda and the writing of the final communiqué. Moreover, referring to the Ukraine crisis, the BRICS ministers remarked that 'the escalation of hostile language, sanctions and counter-sanctions, and force does not contribute to a sustainable and peaceful solution, according to international law, including the principles and purposes of the United Nations Charter', a clear critique of the US regime change in that country, and beyond.[119]

Some observers warn that the development of the BRICS cooperation may be endangered by the economic difficulties experienced recently by Brazil and South Africa, as well as by disagreements between China and India (over territorial disputes) and between Russia and China (because of competition between the Russia-led Eurasian Economic Union and the China-led BRI). Moreover, the election of a far-rightist president of Brazil may pose some difficulties for harmonizing the interests of the member-states. However, it seems that it is in the interests of Brazil not to create a clash with China, should Brazil wish to continue benefiting from Chinese investments (Oliveira 2019). All things considered, it is clear that if the BRICS countries succeed in solving these difficulties they may continue to pose their orga-

---

[118]Other organizations with which China is cooperating include the Asia-Pacific Economic Cooperation (APEC), the Association of Southeast Asian Nations (ASEAN) and the Eurasian Economic Union.

[119]https://en.wikipedia.org/wiki/New_Development_Bank, accessed 24 July 2017.

6.2 China's Strategy for Reclaiming World Power Status

nization as a competitor, if not an alternative, to the US-led international order. Several countries have expressed strong interest in full membership of the BRICS, such as Afghanistan, Argentina, Indonesia, Mexico, Turkey, Egypt, Iran, Nigeria, Sudan, Syria, Bangladesh and Greece. The great variety of members and interested countries, explains why China is very keen to contribute to the development of inter-BRICS cooperation, as it has a clear link with the China-led One Belt One Road Initiative (BRI).

6.2.4.5 The Diffusion of Chinese Culture Abroad

The Fifth dimension of China's strategy is the development of diffusing its culture abroad. This is realized mainly thanks to two initiatives. First, by the creation abroad of many *Confucius Institutes*. Their main role is to make the Chinese language and culture accessible to foreign audiences, through the teaching of Chinese to young university students, but also through public conferences for larger audiences. In some cases, the Institutes may also support research activities between Chinese and local scholars. The Institutes have been criticized as being a propaganda tool in the hands of the CPC. If this is true, the same can be said of Western countries' similar institutions such as the German Goethe Institutes, the French 'Institut Français', the American Cultural Centres, and the British Councils. Nevertheless, these institutes are certainly a good means to improve the mutual understanding between different cultures. It is only when they are used to support ideas and protest movements inside the hosting country that their activity may be criticized. This does not appear to be the case of the *Confucius Institutes*.

The other means to diffuse language, culture and ways of thinking and of analysing problems and issues, is certainly the broadcasting of news and the analysis of political, economic and social issues. China is trying to reach other cultures by developing a worldwide broadcasting network, China Global Television Network (CGTN) available in English and in French, and in a near future in other languages. Since its beginning (as the CCTV—China Central Television) China's international channel has considerably improved its offer with a variety of cultural programmes and news covering all the continents. A choice of several excellent journalists allows the presentation of news in a more balanced way than some Western (mainly American) channels, including CNN and BBC. While in China in 2016 during the US presidential campaign I had the opportunity to compare CNN with CGTN and came to the conclusion that CGTN was more balanced. The same is true when comparing news about Syria, Russia or the Middle East, for example. Moreover, the debates organized by CGTN bring together debaters coming from different perspectives (generally one Chinese and one or two participants from other countries). CGTN is an invaluable source of information to understand how China sees and analyses national and international issues. Of course, the critical reader knows that in order to acquire a balanced view of an issue, it is necessary to have access to different sources of information, i.e. to several channels from different countries and, maybe more important to have access to written information, a mix of mainstream and alternative media.

6.2.4.6 The Development of Military Resources

We now come to the last dimension of China's strategy, before we turn to the BRI, i.e. the development of military resources.[120] As I explained when criticizing the concept of 'soft power' (Urio 2018, pp. 36–43) military resources are the most important asset for a country that aims at reclaiming world power status, especially when in order to do so it must confront the existing 'sole superpower'. Defence was one of the four modernizations defined by Deng Xiaoping but, as we have seen in this chapter (Sect. 6.2.2 above) China started to build its military power already towards the end of the XIX century. In fact, one cannot understand the development of China's military power without taking into consideration that its encounter with the West has led it to a continuous race to catch up with the Western military superiority. It is this gap that was used first by the West (mainly by European powers) in the mid-XIX century to force China to open itself to the global economy, and second, after the end of World War II, by the US to establish near the Chinese territory a set of military alliances and bases for safeguarding its national interests as well as those of its allies. This unequal relationship has put some serious limits on China's freedom for safeguarding its own national interests and on its will to contribute to the revision of the rules of the international system. China's limits have been very well affirmed and reaffirmed by the US since the end of World War II (Sect. 6.1.2 above) and, and for a very clear example, the declaration by President Obama quoted above, pp. 207–208): the US wants to maintain its role of sole superpower and define the rules of the international game.

Still today, military resources are the only domain where China clearly lags behind the US. Nevertheless, the gap is narrowing, as China has massively invested in science and technology, especially artificial intelligence as we have seen above, whose innovations have been transferred into the improvement of the quality of its weaponry (Feng 2017; Chan 2017). I will not discuss here the question as to whether China's military resources are offensive or defensive. Everyone who has a little knowledge about armaments knows that it is very difficult to qualify weapons as exclusively offensive or defensive, as everything depends on the strategy of the leadership and on circumstances. But it is evident that thanks to the build-up of military resources China has been able to develop a more assertive (for some aggressive) foreign policy, e.g. in the China Sea.

One way to evaluate China's military would consist in discovering how its major competitor assesses it. While the US leadership has an unfailing confidence in the US military (see Obama declaration, pp. 208–209), it also evaluates very seriously the 'China military threat'. Whereas it is difficult to tell whether this evaluation is based upon an objective analysis of the threat, or is exaggerated in order to obtaining more funds from the federal budget, it is nevertheless clear that the consequence

---

[120]This part is based upon the Reports to Congress on the *US-China Economic and Security Review Commission* (US 2016b, 2018b; PRC 2015a); the US-China Military scorecard: Heginbotham et al. (2015); an evaluation of the PLA Navy (US 2006a); Nuclear Threat Initiative (2015); an evaluation of China's military power (US 2019); and articles by the *South China Morning Post*, 2016–2019.

6.2 China's Strategy for Reclaiming World Power Status

has been the increasing US investments in the military, especially with the intention of improving the quality of air and sea weaponry, and nuclear arsenal (Sect. 6.1.4 above). So, the most important question for both China and the US is to determine whether their respective military resources constitute a deterrent powerful enough to discourage aggression, especially for the first nuclear strike.

The US-China Economic and Security Review Commission's 2016 and 2018 Reports to Congress present a remarkable analysis of the increasing power of China and the threats it poses to the supremacy of the US and to the 'world America made' (US 2016b, 2018b). These reports cover not only the military, but all aspects of China's growing power resources. However, the reports insist heavily on military resources, thus confirming my analysis of powers that consider military resources to be at the core of power, either as a menace or as an actual use, without which power could not exist (Urio 2018, Chap. 2). The comparison between the 2016 and the 2018 reports manifest a growing worry: the development of China's power resources is threatening the international order whereby the US has been able to realize its the national interests. The 2016 Report considers, and seems to regret, that 'China's actions in the economic, foreign policy, and military realms suggest China's leaders have decided the time has come for China to leave behind its long-held strategy, espoused by Deng Xiaoping, of "hide your strength, bide your time". China is showing itself to the world now, and the outcome is not what many had hoped for 15 years ago when the country was welcomed into the WTO and the global economic system. Our Report and recommendations reflect the China that is, not the China for which some have hoped.' (US 2006b, p. viii, quotations are from the Executive summary). What then went wrong? This statement comes after the Report very strongly criticizes China's behaviour in the international system: 'China continues to violate the spirit and the letter of its international obligations by pursuing import substitution policies, imposing forced technology transfers, engaging in cyber-enabled theft of intellectual property, and obstructing the free flow of information and commerce. China is also becoming a less welcoming market for foreign investors' (US 2016b, p. vii). More particularly, the Report complains that China does not comply with the rules of the free market economy: 'Despite repeated pledges to let the market play a "decisive role" in resource allocation, Beijing continues to use State-owned enterprises (SOEs) as a tool to pursue social, industrial, and foreign policy objectives, offering direct and indirect subsidies and other incentives to influence business decisions and achieve state goals' (US 2016b, p. 4).

It is in this context that the Report takes stock of the modernization (both for quantity and quality) of China's military, especially for the navy and air forces. Consequently, it considers: 'The military capabilities China is developing and will expand or improve the ability of the People's Liberation Army to conduct a range of externally focused operations (…) Improvements in these areas can also strengthen China's traditional warfighting capabilities against weaker neighbours. Given its enhanced strategic lift capability, strengthened employment of special operations forces, increasing capabilities of surface vessels and aircraft, and more frequent and sophisticated experience operating abroad, China may also be more inclined to use force to protect its interests.' (US 2016b, p. 12). Moreover, 'the PLA Navy's underway replenishment capability, which will improve its ability to sustain long-distance operations, will be augmented by China's first overseas military support facility in Djibouti. China's pursuit of expeditionary capabilities, coupled with the aggressive trends that have been displayed in both the East and South China seas, are compounding existing concerns about China's rise among U.S. allies and partners in the greater Asia.' (US 2016b, p. 12). Also, the Report takes stock that 'China operates an increasingly sophisticated and extensive array of intelligence, surveillance, and reconnaissance assets capable of monitoring U.S. forces deployed to the Western Pacific. (…) Chinese intelligence collection operations against the United States pose a large and increasing threat to U.S. national security. (…) China has targeted a wide range of U.S. national security organizations, (…) Given rising U.S.-China competition and China's increasing military might, China's extraction of U.S. national security information through these operations has significant implications for U.S. military superiority in the Western Pacific and the security of U.S. plans and decision-making processes related to potential conflicts with China' (US 2016b, p. 13).

Moreover, quite rightly the Report establishes a clear link between China's willingness to project its power abroad with the BRI initiative, to be dealt with below: 'China's willingness to reshape the economic, geopolitical, and security order to accommodate its interests are of great concern as China's global influence grows. This influence has been manifesting most recently with China's "One Belt, One Road" initiative aimed at connecting China with great portions of the rest of the world via a wide range of investments and infrastructure projects.' (US 2016b, p. vii). Nevertheless, the authors of the 2016 Report did not think it necessary to devote a full section to BRI, whereas the 2018 Report deals with BRI in a new section of more than 30 pages (pp. 259–291).[121] It is interesting to note that the 2018 Report, as we have seen above dealing with China's development of high-tech technologies, has also introduced a new Chapter entitled *China High-Tech Development*, with sections dealing with China's 'Industrial Policy Blueprints, The Internet of Things, and the Fifth-Generation Wireless Technology'. This shows that the analysis of China's power resources has become more sophisticated, taking stock of two of the most important dimensions of its power (military and technology) as well as their mutual strengthening impact.

The 2018 Report confirms and exacerbates the criticism of the 'Chinese approach' to solving problems. As in 2016, the 2018 Report regrets the good old time of Deng Xiaoping's motto: 'hide your capabilities and bide your time', that unfortunately 'faded into history'. In fact, in 2017, at the 19th National Congress of the CPC, 'Xi Jinping announced a "new era" that sees China "moving closer to the world's centre stage" and offering "a Chinese approach" to solving problems'. Inevitably then comes the existential question: is Xi Jinping's pursuit of structural changes in the global order to facilitate Chinese ambitions, compatible with the existing order

---

[121] The 2016 Report treated BRI within Chap. 3 (China and the World) on pp. 316–318, 332, 336, 340–341, 488, and 492–493 (pages in the complete report). Moreover, the 2016 Report mentions BRI only 27 times, compared to more than 300 times in the 2018 Report.

6.2 China's Strategy for Reclaiming World Power Status

or is it creating a new era of persistent competition? The answer comes immediately: 'China's attempt to seize leadership has undoubtedly put at risk the national security and economic interest of the US, its allies and partners'. Then the report builds upon one of the recurrent leitmotivs of the US official discourse on China: we helped China in the past in many ways, e.g. by facilitating its accessions to the WTO, hoping 'it would also deepen reforms and perhaps eventually spark political liberalization. The opposite has happened. The CCP has used economic growth—coupled more recently with its anticorruption campaign—to strengthen its own grasp on authority, advance its state-capitalist model, buttress authoritarian governments abroad, leverage its market against other nations, and fund a massive buildup of Chinese military power to intimidate and silence its neighbours' (US 2018, p. vii; all subsequent references are from the Executive summary). Then follows the long list of grievances: difficulties for foreign companies to have access to the Chinese market, plus forced transfer of technology and regulations in favour of national companies; trade-distorting policies; stolen intellectual property; dumped products flooding the US market (with the resulting US goods deficit of $374 billion in 2017). Moreover, China 'views a strong military as essential for supporting its global ambitions, with the ultimate goal of becoming a world-class force. In the Indo-Pacific China intensify preparation for combat and enhancing its capabilities to deter and defeat the US military should it be required to do so in a future conflict'.[122] The Report also criticizes China's behaviour within the BRI. China 'engages in predatory economic practices. Rather than providing development finance in line with established rules, China provides loans and investment in non-transparent ways on projects that do not always meet global governance standards and pass tests of commercial viability. Rather than respecting other countries' sovereign rights, China is altering the status quo in the Indo-Pacific and has publicly congratulated itself on its militarization of the South China Sea.'

The 2018 Report's general evaluation of China's foreign policy is rather negative: 'For several decades, U.S. policy toward China was rooted in hopes that economic, diplomatic, and security engagement would lay the foundation for *a more open, liberal, and responsible China*. Those hopes have, so far, proven futile. Members of Congress, the Administration, and the business community have already begun taking bipartisan steps to address *China's subversion of international order*. Washington now appears to be calling with a unified voice for *a firmer U.S. response to China's disruptive actions*. In many areas, the CPC will be quick to cast any pushback or legitimate criticism as fear, nationalism, protectionism, and racism against the Chinese people. As a new approach takes shape, U.S. policy makers have difficult decisions to make, but one choice is easy: *reality, not hope, should drive U.S. policy toward China* (p. viii, emphasis added).

---

[122]Let us note that 'the Commission's work this year led to a lively, yet unfinished, debate on China's status as a "peer" to the U.S. military. In the coming year we will explore the accuracy of such claims, the qualifications under which such a title is warranted, and the implications for U.S. national security of facing a "peer competitor" with self-described competing national security interests' (p. vii).

In spite of this alarmistic analysis, the US retains still today the most powerful army, at least on paper, if we take into consideration the numerous failures in overt warfare since the end of World War II. How does China fit in with this military and geopolitical environment?

First, in 2017 the US spent $610 billion (i.e. 3.1% GDP), almost three times more than China ($228, rank 2, equal to 1.9% GDP). The other countries are far behind, including Russia (rank 4, $66.3, 4.3% GDP) and Saudi Arabia (rank 3, $69.4, 10% GDP), India (63.9 rank 5, 2.5 GDP), France (57.8 rank 6, 2.3% GDP), United Kingdom (47.2 rank 7, 1.8 GDP, all WB data). But, by taking into consideration all the expenditures for national security, we arrive at an astonishing total of 1.1 trillion USD (Hartung 2017). No similar calculation has been made to my knowledge for China, but even if we add expenses for national security to the figures reflecting strictly official military expenses (that are today reliable) the total will certainly be very likely a small fraction of the US expenditures (CSIS 2015). Nevertheless, China is steadily increasing every year its defence budget.

Second, nuclear power is a special weaponry as it is the main resource capable to deter a potential aggressor. Here again, compared to the US that possesses 6,450 nuclear heads (of which 1750 deployed), with only 280 non-deployed heads China lags far behind the US. The same is true for other military weaponry, especially for the navy and air weaponry. Nevertheless, since the beginning of the 2000s China has realized several qualitative breakthroughs such as the new domestically-produced aircraft carrier, the new J-20 air fighter, and the new DF-21D 'carrier-killer' (Statista 2015; Nuclear Threat Initiative 2015).

Even if China is still below the US with only 250 nuclear heads, the analyses made by US federal departments and agencies, as well as by think tanks close to the establishment, shows that it is unlikely that the US will today dare to attack China on its territory. And this is good news, as no reasonable person would like to see the competition between China and the US end with an overt military conflict. The January 2019 evaluation of China military force by the US Defence Intelligence Agency confirms this statement (US 2019). It is interesting to start with the Preface written by the Director of the Defense Intelligence Agency, Robert P. Ashley, Jr. Lieutenant General, U.S. Army: 'China's double-digit economic growth has slowed recently, but it served to fund several successive defense modernization Five-Year Plans. As international concern over Beijing's human rights policies stymied the PLA's search for ever more sophisticated technologies, China shifted funds and efforts to acquiring technology by any means available. Domestic laws forced foreign partners of Chinese-based joint ventures to release their technology in exchange for entry into China's lucrative market, (…) The result of this multifaceted approach to technology acquisition is a PLA on the verge of fielding some of the most modern weapon systems in the world. In some areas, it already leads the world.'[123] And this will lead China to 'achieve great power status'. Indeed, China is building a robust, lethal force with capabilities spanning the air, maritime, space and information

---

[123]For example: China's technological advancement in naval design has begun to approach a level commensurate with, and in some cases exceeding, that of other modern navies (p.70)

6.2 China's Strategy for Reclaiming World Power Status

domains which will enable China to impose its will in the region. As it continues to grow in strength and confidence, our nation's leaders will face a China insistent on having a greater voice in global interactions, which at times may be antithetical to U.S. interests.' And he concludes: 'This report offers insights into the modernization of Chinese military power as it reforms from a defensive, inflexible ground-based force charged with domestic and peripheral security responsibilities to a joint, highly agile, expeditionary, and power-projecting arm of Chinese foreign policy that engages in military diplomacy and operations across the globe (p. v)'.

The Report refers to the last (2016) *China's Military Strategy Biennial Review*: 'What differentiated the document from its predecessors was that it, for the first time, publicly clarified the PLA's role in protecting China's evolving national security interests and shed light on policies, such as the PLA's commitment to nuclear deterrence.[124] The report affirmed many of China's longstanding defence policies but also signalled a shift toward emerging security domains, such as cyber and space, and also emphasized the need to focus on global maritime operations. The report outlined eight 'strategic tasks': 'safeguard the sovereignty of China's territory; safeguard national unification; safeguard China's interests in new domains, such as space and cyberspace; safeguard China's overseas interests; maintain strategic deterrence; participate in international security cooperation; maintain China's political security and social stability; and conduct emergency rescue, disaster relief, and "rights and interest protection" missions.' The Report concludes that 'Beijing almost certainly views these missions as necessary national security tasks for China to claim great-power status' (p. 13).

In order to understand the strategic meaning of these reforms, quite rightly the Report refers to the China's 13th Five-Year Plan (2016–2020), that 'includes the establishment of focus areas for research, development, and innovation. Several of these have defence implications: aerospace engines—including turbofan technology—and gas turbines; quantum communications and computing; innovative electronics and software; automation and robotics; special materials and applications; nanotechnology; neuroscience, neural research, and artificial intelligence; and deep-space exploration and on-orbit servicing and maintenance systems. Other areas where China is concentrating significant R&D resources include nuclear fusion, hypersonic technology, and the deployment and "hardening" of an expanding constellation of multipurpose satellites. China's drive to expand civil-military integration and international economic activity supports these goals' (p. 105).

Moreover, the Report focuses on the relations between civil and military dimensions of defence in China: 'the PLA initiated defence-industrial reforms in 2016 that aimed to (…) promote innovation, and institutionalize civil-military integration. Within an industrial context, the latter entails establishing a formal relationship between China's defence and civilian industrial bases to develop a technologically advanced, domestically reliant, and internationally relevant defense-industrial complex (…) These reforms are expected to be implemented by 2020'. Scien-

---

[124]China's nuclear missiles have a range between 1,500 and 13,000 km. The Report devotes an in-depth analysis of China's missiles capabilities.

tific and technological disciplines with military applications targeted for development include hypersonics; nanotechnology; high-performance computing; quantum communications; space systems; autonomous systems; artificial intelligence; robotics; high-performance turbofan engine design; new, more efficient and powerful forms of propulsion; advanced manufacturing processes (including additive manufac-turing/3-D printing); and advanced aerospace quality materials, just to name a few' (p. 49).

The last part of the Report deals with logistic capabilities, especially around the globe, by stressing the probable link between commercial and military capabilities: 'PLA's efforts to obtain access to commercial ports in Africa, the Middle East, and South Asia would align with its future overseas logistic needs and meet its evolving naval requirements. The PLA is likely to use commercial ports and civilian ships to support its international and domestic logistic operations, resupply, replenishment, and maintenance. China's territorial claims in the South China Sea are driving major logistic developments in the Spratly and Paracel Islands. China's reclaimed territory in the South China Sea is equipped with harbours and berthing areas that are capable of accommodating large naval ships (...) China is expanding its access to foreign ports, such as in Gwadar, Pakistan, to pre-position the logistic framework necessary to support the PLA's growing presence abroad, including normalizing and sustaining deployments into and beyond the Indian Ocean' (p. 103).

Finally, the Report quite righty establishes a clear link between military transportation and the BRI initiative: 'transportation is also at the heart of the Belt and Road Initiative (BRI), which consists of establishing roads, railways, and ports to connect to countries from Asia to Africa and Europe. Although the BRI is marketed as primarily an effort to increase trade and development, China's improved domestic transportation infrastructure and access to transportation infrastructure abroad also would benefit the PLA by enhancing PLA access to transportation hubs and road systems.' (p. 104). And this leads us to the last part of this chapter.

6.2.5 The Belt and Road Initiative, or China's Grand Strategy

China's strategy transition towards an internationalization of its development strategy integrating its national territory and the international territory could have been anticipated by analysing the changes at work in the global economy since at least the end of the XX Century. This has been done in 2011 by a study of the HSBC Bank: '...in twenty years' time, China's biggest trading partners might be India, Brazil and Russia, in combination, will likely be threatening to overtake the US as important destinations for Chinese exporters. (...) The scope for India, Brazil and Russia to trade with each other is big enough to eclipse trading relations with the US and Europe. And what's true of the BRICS is also true at the continental level: we believe linkages between Asia, Latin America and Africa are set to expand at an exponential rate. As South-South trade picks up, so should South-South capital flow,

6.2 China's Strategy for Reclaiming World Power Status

undermining the US dollar's reserve currency status and fostering the development of major new financial centres, notably in Asia (King 2011).

Of course, many changes have occurred since this study was published, namely the economic difficulties of several Latin American countries (e.g. Brazil and Venezuela) and relations between China and India have not always been without problems (Baru 2017).[125] But the trend described by HSBC persisted and even accelerated in 2014 when, during the Ukraine crisis, the US and its European allies put heavy economic sanctions on Russia, thus contributing to the already ongoing development of China-Russia cooperation. In May 2017, a HSBC briefing note takes stock that 'the One Belt One Road is an infrastructure initiative conceived and promoted by the Chinese Government to connect more than 65 countries and 4.4 billion people worldwide corresponding to 40% of world GDP' (…) Although potential investment opportunities are very heterogeneous by sector and geographic location, HSBC has highlighted how they tend to focus on areas of strong economic interest for Chinese companies, such as Thailand, Malaysia, Singapore and Indonesia, and sectors such as transport, energy, renewables and industrials through the creation of new and important railway networks, highways, pipelines and electricity networks. (…) the opportunities [for foreign investors] do not come only from the infrastructure side. By 2050 there will be 3 billion people joining the middle class in emerging markets entailing a huge explosion of service demand, including technology but also entertainment or healthcare. HSBC's analysis also points out that most of the projects are now at an early stage of planning and tendering and that is the reason why for European businesses and states this could be a perfect opportunity to join one of the largest economic initiatives in the world' (HSBC 2017, Rapoza 2017).

Despite the criticisms that appeared in the Western media immediately after the announcement of the BRI in September-October 2013, and that persist still today, pointing to the imprecisions, difficulties and uncertainties of the project, some attentive observers of the development of China's strategy have understood right from the beginning the importance of the initiative and the threat that it poses to US primacy in Asia. Some attentive observers of China's foreign policy at the beginning of the Xi Jinping era tried to anticipate China's 'pivot to the West' (Bao et al. 2013). The answer to the question came a few months later, on 13 September 2013, as we have seen above. And then, some other attentive observers were quick to understand the challenge of Xi Jinping's initiative to the US. For example, the *Washington Post* commented already on 24 October 2013: '[Xi Jinping] has eclipsed an American vision of a New Silk Road that was advanced with much fanfare by then-Secretary of State Hillary Rodham Clinton two years ago and was supposed to revitalize Afghanistan as the link between Central and South Asia. The contrast between the two visions—one with huge sums of money on the table, the other struggling to get off the ground—only underlines how China's ever-growing clout in Asia is challenging the influence of the Unites States' (Denyer 2013). It would be easy here to refer to the increasing number of acknowledgments by Western media of the success of the BRI

---

[125]This article points to the possible conflict between China and India over one of the dimensions of BRI: the $46 billion China-Pakistan Economic corridor 'that is still legally India's'.

290   6 China and the New World Order. Why and How China's Foreign Policy …

since its announcement in 2013. Let me just quote an article by *Forbes,* 9 September 2016: 'Unfortunately this bold plan [i.e. the Clinton's New Silk Road] appears to have flopped before it even got started. Now China is making good of this ambition by integrating Afghanistan in with their BRI initiative (…) As part of this endeavour, a pair of cargo trains departed from two Chinese cities at the end of August bound for Afghanistan' (Shepard 2016).

What is then the real meaning of the BRI initiative?[126] Let me start with some considerations about the terminology associated with BRI. Chinese officials, as well as some intellectuals, prefer to use terms such as 'economic geography' and admit that BRI is 're-shaping the world economic geography'. (Hu Angang 2016; Wong et al. 2017). But in the West, the concept most frequently associated with BRI is: geopolitics, meaning that through BRI China is developing its geopolitical strengths to achieve its national goals all over the world. (Donnan 2014; Smith 2015). Chinese officials reply that the BRI is not about politics but about economic cooperation based upon a 'win-win' strategy. Nevertheless, history shows that economic resources (i.e. 'geo-economics' or 'geo-economic power') have been very frequently used (together with military means, discussed above) to achieve geopolitical goals. An article by the influential *South China Morning Post* of June 2017 says: 'The initiative is supported by US3$ trillion of foreign currency reserves and state-owned enterprises. The new Silk Road also reflects geopolitical ambitions; it shows how the Chinese leadership wants to shape the order of an area that represents more than half the world' (Clauss 2017). We will see in the future whether China has been able to avoid this historically demonstrated causal link between economic and military resources and geopolitical ambitions. Finally, BRI can be considered as China's reaction to US presence in the Far East and more particularly to the Obama 'Pivot to Asia' and the Trans-Pacific Partnership.[127]

In order to understand the meaning and scope of the BRI, I will first rely upon Hu Angang's analysis of the strategies implemented by the Chinese leadership to develop the country since 1949, that we have already seen in Sect. 3.1.2. In fact, the progression from the first strategy to the fourth help us to understand that the first three strategies led inevitably to the fourth, which projects China abroad, in fact all over the world. These strategies take into consideration the diversity of the Chinese territory and the human activities developed on it during the XX century and first half of the XXI century. Hu considers that there have been four successive versions of the regional development strategy corresponding to different development stages. The first three were mainly addressed to the Chinese territory from the perspective of geography and economy. The first strategy (1949–1978) organized a balanced development thanks to the planned economy but it had serious negative consequences, such as poor economic performance, limitation of personal freedom,

---

[126] A detailed analysis of the many components of BRI can be found in PRC (2017).

[127] Two official Chinese documents are worth reading, even if they have been acknowledged with some sarcasm and criticisms by some Western observers: PRC (2015b), 'Vision and Actions on Jointly Building Silk Road Economic Belt and XXI century Maritime Road', and PRC (2017), *Building the Belt and Road: Concept, Practice and China's Contribution.*

6.2 China's Strategy for Reclaiming World Power Status

little incentives for innovations, environmental damages, as well as the catastrophic impact of the Great Leap Forward and the Cultural Revolution. The second (1979–1998) prioritized rapid economic development focused on the coastal and western regions thanks to the introduction of market mechanisms and the progressive opening to the global economy; nevertheless, while it developed the economy and reduced poverty, it also increased disparities between regions, provinces and people. The third strategy (1999–2013) was based upon a regional balanced development and the reduction of disparities, thanks to investments in the inner and western regions, and the beginning of the development of a modern social security system. The fourth strategy (2013–…) 'will not only continue to reduce regional disparity and promote collaborative development among different economic blocks [to be explained below], but also contributes to reshape the world economic geography, innovate international development models, and construct a new international political and economic order toward the future' Hu Angang (2016, p. 1).

So, after three stages of development strategy addressed to the Chinese territory, with the aim of developing the economy (first and second strategies) and to reduce inter-regional disparities (third strategy), China's fourth development strategy aims at further reducing disparities and building a developmental bridge between the country and its global environment. We now understand that the worries expressed by US politicians, academics and think tanks were, and are still today, quite understandable. In particular, I remind the reader that President Obama was very keen to keep the US in charge of defining the rules of the international system: 'with TPP, China does not set the rules in that region; we do. You want to show our strength in this new century? Approve this agreement. Give us the tools to enforce it. It's the right thing to do.'(Obama 2016a). But as I said on several occasions, the changes, i.e. the 'silent transformations', that have been at work since at least the end of the Cold War, little by little have weakened the dominant position of the US. The 2011 HSBC study quoted above is a good example of an in-depth analysis confirming some of the most important changes in the international system. Finally, the move from internal to external development, which is one of the main aspects of the BRI, is the logical consequence of these changes as well as of the development of China's economy. Through the selling of its products abroad China has accumulated a lot of money that can be invested in the global economy, has developed over-production in several sectors that may be sold overseas, and needs to import raw material and energy resources necessary to its economic development. Therefore, the acceleration and expansion of the trend to 'go out' appears to be the only rational, and hopefully reasonable and peaceful, move to sustain a steady, balanced economic development, thus guaranteeing the traditional values of stability, unity and harmony.

The fourth development strategy, that establishes for the first time a clear link between internal regional development and its projection to the outside world, has been included in the 13th Five-year Plan (2016–2020, adopted March 2016). This overall strategy integrates three regional development strategies (the Beijing-Tianjin-Hebei, the Yangtze River Economic Zone, and the BRI) in combination with four economic regional blocks, i.e. Northeast, Central, East, and West.[128] The three strategies and the four economic regional blocks are inter-connected to form China's grand strategy, that should reshape China's economic geography. In addition to this, China formulated a special planning for urbanization development for 2014–2020. Moreover, the fourth strategy aims at further improving the reduction of regional development gaps already started during the third stage (1999–2013) by realizing full coverage of social security in both urban and rural areas. It is interesting to note that the BRI strategy involves all four economic blocks, comprising 25 provincial-level administrative units out of a total of 31.[129] For the Belt road: Heilongjiang, Liaoning, Jilin, Henan, Jiangsu, Shaanxi, Gansu, Qinghai, Ningxia, Sinkiang, Chongqing, Sichuan, Yunnan, Guangxi, Tibet, and Inner Mongolia. For the Maritime Road: Zhejiang, Fujian, Guangdong, Shanghai, Hainan, Liaoning, Tianjin, Shandong, and Guangxi.

So, one can understand the importance China attributes to the BRI strategy not only for its projection abroad but also for the development of its provinces: the fourth Chinese development strategy, 'in particular the BRI, will extend domestic regional development to neighboring countries through strengthening the infrastructure construction with relevant countries and enhance the cooperation in investment, trade, and finance, therefore reshaping world economic geography (…) and more importantly emphasizes the coordinated development among different [Chinese] economic blocks.' (Hu 2016, p. 15). Therefore, the novelty and the force of the BRI reside not only in the projection of China's economic power abroad, but it is also a means to strengthen and coordinate the internal economic and social development of the different parts of China (blocks, provinces, and regions).

The analysis of China's four development strategies shows that the Chinese leadership does not rely upon theoretical models defined prior to action, thereby following the traditional Chinese way to understand and implement strategy. On the contrary, action is evaluated upon results, and then, as results are not only positive, but inevitably present some important negative aspects (e.g. the increase of disparities of Deng Xiaoping's reforms) some new ways of doing are defined and implemented (i.e. institutions and policies). And so forth. In Hu Angang's words: 'It needs to emphasize that no regional development strategy can accomplish its aims in one move. (…) each stage experiences the process of adjustments and upgrading, reflecting the feature of "learning by doing". By the same token, the fourth strategy will also experience the process from "strategy proposal" to "policy implementation", "policy adjustment", and "policy maturity" to cope with new opportunities and challenges

---

[128]The four blocks are: Northeast (comprising the provinces of Liaoning, Heilongjiang, and Jilin), Central (Shanxi, Henan, Hubei, Hunan, Jiangxi, Anhui), East (Beijing, Tianjin, Hebei, Jiangsu, Zhejiang, Shanghai, Fujian, Guangdong, Hainan, Shandong), West (Inner Mongolia, Sichuan, Chongqing, Yunnan, Guizhou, Shaanxi, Gansu, Qinghai, Ningxia, Sinkiang, Tibet, Guangxi). Source: Hu Angang (2016), p. 16.

[129]China has 33 provincial-level administrative units: 22 provinces, 4 municipalities (Beijing, Tianjin, Shanghai and Chongqing), 5 autonomous regions (Guangxi, Inner Mongolia, Tibet, Ningxia, and Xinjiang) and 2 special administrative regions (Hong Kong and Macau). The Hu Angang analysis does not include Hong Kong and Macau.

6.2 China's Strategy for Reclaiming World Power Status   293

[i.e. resulting from the evolution of the "situation potential", [Sects. 2.1 and 2.3] from domestic and external development.' (Hu 2016, p. 24). There are no a priori ideological choices: institutions and policies do not possess an intrinsic value, but are evaluated on the basis of their capacity to realize the policy goal, i.e. the recovering of world power status, that is the only element of the strategy that does not change. Also, China intervenes where and when it has a reasonable chance to succeed. Moreover, as everything is bound to change over time, the Chinese leadership waits until the 'silent transformations' have changed the 'situation potential' to its advantage, in this case the distribution of power resources in the international system. Then, it acts within the new situation, e.g. Trump's retreat from the Trans-Pacific Partnership. Finally, the way China manages its development strategies also shows that Chinese leaders do not make a clear distinction between theory and practice (Chap. **2**).

6.2.6 *The Belt and Road Initiative and the End to the 'World America Made'*

By going now into more detail inside the BRI, we are able to see more clearly why this strategy constitutes a serious threat to the 'world America made' not only in Asia but all over the world (here I rely more particularly on PRC 2017). China has defined five routes for the BRI: three routes for the Road Belt and two for the Maritime Road (see BRI map, p. 294). The first route of the Road Belt goes from Northwest China and Northeast China to Europe and the Baltic Sea via Central Asia and Russia; the second goes from North-west China to the Persian Gulf and the Mediterranean Sea, passing through Central Asia and West Asia; and the third from Southwest China through the Indochina Peninsula to the Indian Ocean. The first route of the Maritime Road starts at the coastal ports of China, crosses the South China Sea, passes through the Malacca Strait, and reaches the Indian Ocean, extending to Europe and the Mediterranean Sea; and the second starts at the coastal ports of China, crosses the South China Sea, and extends to the South Pacific.[130]

Within the framework of the five routes China has proposed 'six corridors, six means of communication, multiple countries, and multiple ports'. The 'six corridors are: the New Eurasian Land Bridge Economic Corridor, the Russia Economic Corridor, the China-Central Asia-West Asia Economic Corridor, the China-Indochina Peninsula Economic Corridor, the China-Pakistan Economic Corridor, and the Bangladesh-China-India-Myanmar Economic Corridor. The 'six means of communication' concern rail, highways, seagoing transport, aviation, pipelines, and aerospace integrated information network, which comprise the main targets of infrastructure connectivity. 'Multiple countries' refer to the countries along the BRI that first joined the initiative, with which China will cooperate to start with, but the leading Group' document forecasts that more countries will be attracted to participate in the initiative. 'Multiple ports' refer to a number of ports that ensure safe and smooth sea passages, to be built along the BRI.

---

[130]For the importance of BRI for Europe and the Mediterranean countries see: Putten et al. (2016), Fardella et al. (2016).

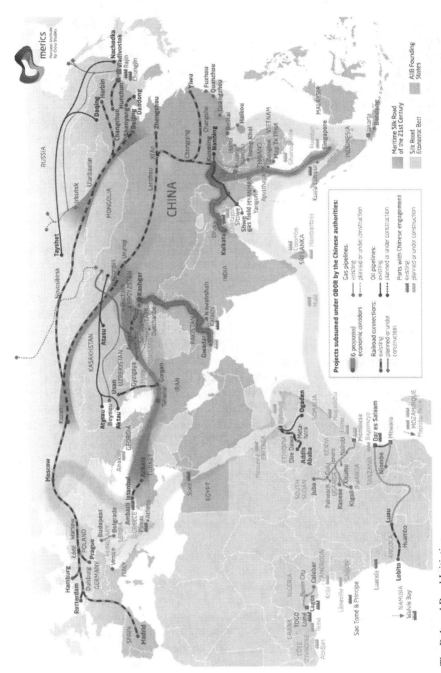

The Belt and Road Initiative.

6.2 China's Strategy for Reclaiming World Power Status

It is not necessary to summarize here the detailed description of the six corridors given by the Leading Group. In order to give an idea of the scope of the BRI, it suffices to see how the Group envisages the interactions between corridors, and therefore their strategic meaning. For example, the China-Pakistan corridor connects the Road Belt (from Kashgar -Xinjiang Autonomous region) to the Maritime Road in Gwadar, a port city on the southwestern coast of Balochistan, Pakistan, thus avoiding the Malacca strait.[131] The Leading Group insist on the intersections between corridors:

1. between the New Eurasian Land Bridge Economic Corridor and the China-Mongolia-Russia Economic Corridor;
2. between the China-Central Asia-West Asia Economic Corridor that 'runs through central and eastern Eurasia, connecting the economically-dynamic East Asian economic circle and the developed European economic circle, while also building a smooth cooperation channel from the Persian Gulf to the Mediterranean and the Baltic Sea. They make it possible for establishing an efficient and smooth Eurasian market, and create opportunities of development for countries in the hinterland of Eurasia and along the Belt and Road;
3. between the China-Indochina Peninsula Economic Corridor; the China-Pakistan Economic Corridor, and the Bangladesh-China-India-Myanmar Economic Corridor. The last three corridors 'run through eastern and southern parts of Asia, the world's most densely populated areas, connecting major cities and population and industrial clusters along the Belt and Road. The Lancang-Mekong River international sea-lane and regional railways, highways, and oil and gas networks link the Road Belt with the Maritime Silk Road, whose economic radiation effects cover South Asia, Southeast Asia, the Indian Ocean, the South Pacific and other regions.' (Navarro 2015, pp. 11–12).

Clearly, as it stands today, the BRI is not at the stage of a project. Already at the end of 2016, the Leading Group very proudly enumerates in its report an apparently non-exhaustive list of realizations. First, the Group quotes several features of the BRI that are in fact the development of moves that started before it was announced in 2013: the use of the resources of international organisations such as the Shanghai Cooperation Organization, the United Nations and its Development Programme (UNDP); Chinese investment abroad; the creation of the AIIB and the implications of the State-owned banks in financing BRI projects, such as the China Development bank, and the Export-Import Bank of China; the internationalization of the RMB through currency swap agreements with 22 BRI countries such as Russia, Kazakhstan Vietnam, Mongolia, Laos, Kyrgyzstan, Belarus and Nepal, as well as six RMB clearing banks in BRI countries out of a total of 23, and finally, the fact that the RMB can be traded directly

---

[131]The importance of the Malacca strait has been stressed by Peter Navarro: '… whoever controls the South China Sea's gateway to the Indian Ocean, through the narrow and perilous Malacca Strait, also controls South Asia—and perhaps East Asia too, given that much of the oil that lights lamps in Japan and South Korea must first pass through the South China Sea.' Navarro (2016), p. 14. See also Navarro (2015). Peter Navarro is an American economist who currently serves as the Assistant to President Trump, Director of Trade and Industrial Policy, and the Director of the White House National Trade Council.

with 21 currencies other than the USD, through China's interbank foreign exchange market (Prasad 2017; SWIFT 2017).

Second, the Leading group emphasizes more particularly several realizations, that correspond to the moves initiated by the BRI itself. These cover general support to BRI, connections between China and the rest of the world, and China's investments abroad. Among the long list it is interesting to note: the opening of 39 China-Europe rail routes, entailing the operation of some 3,000 trains to 14 cities in 9 European countries; the ongoing projects with Kazakhstan and the Port of Piraeus; the cooperation with Pakistan, in particular the construction of the Gwadar Free Zone has been accelerated; the launch of energy and power projects along the China-Pakistan Economic corridor; and the ongoing operation of the China-Russia Oil Pipeline, and the construction of the China-Russia Gas Pipeline.

Third, the Leading group establishes a clear link between the BRI and China's investments abroad, the Asian Infrastructure Investment Bank (AIIB), with a legal capital of US$100 billion, that by the end of 2016 had provided US$ 1.7 billion in loans to nine projects in fields such as energy, transport, and urban development in Indonesia, Tajikistan, Pakistan, and Bangladesh; the Silk Road Fund with US$40 billion in starting capital and 15 projects already signed with an estimated investment value of US$6 billion. Moreover, the China state-owned banks, the China Development Bank and the Export-Import Bank have signed more than 100 projects in the BRI countries, for more than US$ 140 billion, and more than US$110 billion in loans (PRC 2017, pp. 7–9, 13, 16, 22–23, 29–34).

The information given above by the Leading Group shows the global scope of the BRI: its routes, corridors, means of communication, multiple countries, and multiple ports cover the whole world with activities concerning (in addition to trade and financial cooperation), investments in a great variety of strategic domains, such as railways, high-speed trains, highways, oil and gas networks, ports, sea transport, aviation, pipelines, energy power, submarine and land cables, integrated information network, and water conservancy.

Several features of BRI are clearly meant to challenge the US power in Asia and in the rest of the world. For example, the China-Pakistan Corridor is meant to avoid the passage through the Malacca strait where the US Navy may forbid Chinese trade with its suppliers of raw material and energy resources, in case of serious disagreements with China (Navarro 2016, p. 14); similarly, the numerous railways from China to Europe permit China to trade with Europe by land, thus avoiding the shipment of goods by sea, where the US has so far a clear superiority that may be used to block trade between China and Europe; moreover, the corridors to Europe, as well as the investments in European ports, e.g. the Port of Piraeus, give China the possibility to compete with the US on the territory of its traditional European allies; the same is true for the roads to the Middle East; finally, the maritime road from China to the Pacific region may open the Americas to China, where it has already invested heavily.

Let us note that it is possible that China may develop, in a not too distant future, another route, i.e. an Arctic shipping channel. There are multiple strategic reasons for sustaining this project: avoiding the geopolitical risk deriving from the competition

6.2 China's Strategy for Reclaiming World Power Status

with the US when passing through the already existing maritime routes; avoiding passing through politically unstable regions (e.g. for the Road Belt); avoiding the difficulty of passing though regions with different religions and cultures; and avoiding energy security risks, that we have already mentioned regarding the competition with the US, as is the case for the BRI Maritime Road. This new route 'refers to the Arctic shipping channel which is the ocean shipping channel connecting the Pacific Ocean and the Atlantic Ocean via the Arctic Ocean, including the North-east channel (also known as the Northern channel) and the North-west channel. As the shortest sea route connecting North-east Asia and Western Europe, the North-east channel starts from the northern waters of north-west Europe in the west and reaches Vladivostok at the east, passing through Barents Sea, Kara Sea, Rapp Jeff Sea, Novosibirsk Sea and the Bering Strait. The North-east channel is currently navigable for 2–3 months, and the entire route reaches Sweden, Iceland, Finland, Russia and other countries.' (Hu Angang, Zhang Xin, and Zhang Wei 2017, see also PEN Charitable Trust 2017).

The BRI has attracted much criticism and fears from Western official public bodies, pundits and mainstream media.[132] However, many Western influential observers consider that the BRI is on its way to become the greatest economic and geo-political endeavour ever. For example, the first page of the HSBC site dealing with the BRI (dated 9 March 2018) says that 'China's Belt and Road is now gaining greater impetus with 67 countries partnered with China. (…) Trade between countries that link the officially named 'One Belt, One Road' project, already exceeded USD3 trillion between 2014 and 2016, with China's investment in these nations surpassing USD50 billion. (…) Already BRI is extending beyond China's immediate neighbours and into regions and countries not traditionally known for its economic links with Beijing. The Asian Infrastructure Investment Bank (AIIB), Silk Road Fund and the New Development Bank have also already committed roughly USD1.1 trillion to develop infrastructure under the banner of the BRI.'

The *South China Morning Post* (SCMP) has recently admitted that the BRI 'may have its flaws, but some critics are taking it too far'. The US Vice-President Mike Pence 'who launched a savage attack on Chinese "debt trap" tactic during the APEC summit last November [2018].' According to the SCMP quotes, Pence declared: 'we don't drown our partners in a sea of debt [and] we don't coerce or compromise your independence," he said.' And the SCMP could not resist pointing out Pence's ridiculous claim, commenting: 'this was a bit rich given the way that US banks lent billions of dollars to Latin America causing a huge debt crisis there in the 1980s. Ditto at the time of the Asian Debt Crisis [1997]' (SCMP, 20 January 2019). On its site devoted to the BRI, the SCMP informs its readers of the progress of five major projects within the BRI that have strong symbolic, economic and political impacts: the railways to London, the Gwadar Port in Pakistan (that allows China to avoid the

---

[132] In addition to the US official documents analyzed above (especially the US Intelligence Agency report), one can consult the reports by the European Union and of the Mercator Institute for China Studies (MERICS), the HSBC bank's site, the Belt and Road Portal of the Chinese government, and the analyses by influential media such as the *Financial Times*, the *Caixin*, and the *South China Morning Post*.

Malacca Strait), the railway to Iran, the Asian gas pipeline, and the Khorgos Gateway, that it qualifies as 'a new Dubai in China'.[133]

The BRI is a long-term project, extending over 25 to 30 years. Time will tell if it succeeds and how. The analysis of the foreign policies of China and the US in the changing world system presented in this book, does not allow us to forecast that China will replace the US as the sole superpower. Nevertheless, China is already becoming a world power, and if it does not commit major mistakes (and it has not made any since 1978) it will certainly become, in a not too distant future, a new world power on equal footing with the US. So far, China is achieving this objective without using its military power (that is not even mentioned in the official BRI documents), except as a means to deter the type of aggressions it suffered during the XIX century.

As described by the Leading Group, the BRI initiative looks like a grandiose project, many parts of which are still to be defined, accepted and implemented. Nevertheless, it has already achieved remarkable results, including the contribution (with some other emerging and re-emerging powers) of putting into the minds of American leaders the feeling (and maybe even the certitude) that the US is no more the sole superpower. Moreover, BRI should be considered as a contemporary example of the Chinese traditional way of defining and implementing strategy. The general framework is described in general, but in meaningful terms. It is during the 'practice' of its implementation that actual decisions, international agreements, and formal projects will be chosen, accepted by other countries, and implemented, depending upon the actual opportunities that the evolving 'situation potential' presents to the Chinese leadership. The difference with the first three development strategies (explained above), especially with the second one of Deng Xiaoping, is that the general objective is expressed more openly and transparently. China is today strong enough to publicly declare its objectives and ambitions. It suffices to add to this, taking into consideration the grandiose presentation of the project, that the BRI is not simply a new 'economic geography' of China, nor a simple 're-shaping of the world economic geography' (Hu et al. 2017). BRI is above all a geo-strategic project that, if fully realized, will allow China to reclaim its status as a world power, thereby putting an end to the uni-polar 'world America made'.

6.2.7 Conclusion

I have analyzed in this chapter the strategy implemented by China to confront the competition, and quite often the hostility, from Western powers, especially from the US. Many fears that this competition will lead China to try to become a hegemonic country. Will China be satisfied to have put an end to the world America made, or will it want to replace the US as the new hegemonic power?

---

[133]The US government has officially identified the ten largest BRI projects for a total of $US 90 billion, of which 4 under construction, 2 constructions expected 2019, 2 MOU signed, 1 feasibility study completed, and 1 under review (US 2019, p. 13).

6.2 China's Strategy for Reclaiming World Power Status 299

I see two difficulties, should China be willing to follow this road. First, Chinese history and culture seem to suggest that China never had an imperial strategy, in the sense of the Western powers, who had the dream to conquer the world and impose their rule. China Empire has always been limited to the periphery of the 'Chinese space'. Even when China had the technological capacity to conquer the world, it did not. Even when its vessels were much bigger and more performant than the feeble caravels Christopher Columbus used to discover the Americas, China limited its excursion abroad to establish cultural and trade relations.

Second, today's situation is quite different. After the discovery of the Americas Western powers had developed, especially since the Industrial Revolution, such a formidable economic and military strength that no other country has been able to resist them. Driven by economic interests, and by the missionary dream to diffuse its culture in all its dimensions (political, economic, social, and religious) the West has dominated the world for several centuries. But should China today try to impose its will on the rest of the world, it will face a formidable opposition first of all from the US and its allies, but also from regional powers, as no one wants to be the vassal of anybody else. Certainly, if China does succeed to put an end to the international system dominated by the US, it will weaken the US, but it will not be able to destroy its power resources, especially if the US should renounce to behave as if it were the master of the world because of the superiority of its culture, and to adopt a cooperative stance. Moreover, should the US develop at home a real democracy, not dominated by an almighty plutocracy, its culture will possibly appeal to many people and countries around the world. In this context, Europe, that seems to have forgotten the imperial features that oriented its relations with the rest of the world in the XIX century, may play the role of a broker between the Americas and the Eurasia continent.

Finally, we should not underestimate other areas, such as Africa, the Middle East and Latin America, or countries such as Russia, Iran, Turkey, and Brazil, that are already asserting their national interests in their areas. It would be a mistake for the two big powers not to take into consideration the legitimate interests of these countries. An even more serious mistake would be that one of the two great powers would consider these countries as potential allies to be put under its domination in order to compete aggressively against the other great power. We will be driven back to the power struggle we experienced in the XIX century that led the world to the disaster of two world wars.

Today, it seems that the US is not ready, to envisage its relations with the rest of the world, and more particularly with China, in a constructive cooperative way. First, we have already seen that the US *National Defence Strategy* (US 2018a) considers that 'the central challenge to U.S. prosperity and security is the re-emergence of long-term, strategic competition by what the National Security Strategy classifies as *revisionist powers*. It is increasingly clear that China and Russia want to shape a world consistent with *their authoritarian model*—gaining veto authority over other nations' economic, diplomatic, and security decisions. China is leveraging military modernization, influence operations, and predatory economics *to coerce neighbouring countries to reorder the Indo-Pacific region to their advantage*. As China continues its economic and military ascendance, asserting power through an all-of-nation long-term strategy, it will continue to pursue a military modernization program that seeks Indo-Pacific regional hegemony in the near-term and *displacement of the United States* to achieve global pre-eminence in the future' (p. 2). Given these premises, the document considers (under the sub-title 'Build a More Lethal Force') that 'the surest way to prevent war is to be prepared to win one. Doing so requires a competitive approach to force development and a consistent, multiyear investment to *restore warfighting readiness and field a lethal force*. The size of our force matters. The Nation must field sufficient, capable forces to defeat enemies and achieve sustainable outcomes that protect the American people and our vital interests. Our aim is a Joint Force that possesses decisive advantages for any likely conflict, while remaining proficient across the entire spectrum of conflict.' (p. 5). Moreover, 'The 2018 National Defense Strategy underpins our planned fiscal year 2019–2023 budgets, accelerating our modernization programs and devoting additional resources in a sustained effort *to solidify our competitive advantage*'. In particular, these include, among other measures, to 'modernize key capabilities: Nuclear forces; Space and cyberspace as warfighting domains; computers and intelligence, surveillance, and reconnaissance; Missile defence.' (pp. 6–7, emphasis added).

Second, President Trump announced the withdrawal from the Intermediate Range Nuclear Forces Treaty (INF), signed by Presidents Reagan and Gorbachev in 1987. Immediately Russia declared that it was also going to withdraw from the INF. This treaty had decided the removal of intermediate nuclear missiles (between 1500 and 5,500 km) from Europe and Western Russia. But today, the main target of the US withdrawal is more likely to be China. In fact, China not being part of the INF treaty, has been able to develop this type of missiles, which, according to experts, put China to an advantage towards the US in the China Seas. Should the US develop 'intermediate-range missile systems and cruise missiles [this] would considerably enrich U.S. capabilities in a potential clash over Taiwan or other contentious strategic issues. As the PLA has a variety of cruise missiles that can be launched from land, air, sea, and sub-surface platforms, returning to intermediate-range systems would equip American forces with the capability to strike targets that are highly difficult to penetrate for conventional weapons at present'. Nevertheless, 'any additional U.S. conventional military superiority gives China considerable incentive to increase reliance on an escalatory and possibly deterrence strategy'(Kuo 2018).

Third, the US military posture toward China has been confirmed by the speech given by Vice-President Mike Pence at the Hudson Institute 4 October 2018. As I mentioned above, this speech is a foreign policy statement addressed to the Chinese leadership to force it to comply with the requirements of the US. It is also a clear manifestation of how the US perceives China's power development as a threat to the US leadership. Moreover, in spite of its neo-conservative rhetoric, this speech is faithful to the way all the US administrations have interpreted China's development, since at least the end of the XX Century, and with what means the US will try to maintain it in the future. In spite of the innovations Trump has tried, and failed, to introduce in the US foreign policy, it seems that this analysis is here to stay for a long time, no matter who will win the Presidential elections of 2020. Therefore, I think

6.2 China's Strategy for Reclaiming World Power Status

that it is important to reproduce hereafter several passages of Pence's speech (Pence 2018).

Right from the beginning of his speech the Vice-President warns his compatriots that 'Beijing is employing a whole-of-government approach, using political, economic, and military tools, as well as propaganda, to advance its influence and benefit its interests in the United States'. It then refers to the US National Security Strategy that acknowledged that we are now entering *'a new era of "great power competition."* Foreign nations have begun to "reassert their influence regionally and globally," and they are *"contesting [America's] geopolitical advantages and trying to change the international order in their favour."* And this is clearly the problem: the US wants to maintain the present order that is in favour of its national interests' (emphasis added in all the quotations).

Pence clearly develops the rest of his speech according to the ideology I have analyzed at the beginning of this chapter, based, in short, on the partition between 'We, the US' and 'Them, China'; we the good, them the evil, even if these words are not explicitly used. Pence describes the idyllical relationship between the US and China between the end of the XVIII Century and the beginning of ther XIX. Clearly, Pence has some problems with history: he claims that 'When our young nation went searching in the wake of the Revolutionary War for new markets for our exports, the Chinese people welcomed Americans traders laden with ginseng and fur...' A Clear reference of the 'China Mirage', forgetting that the 'rush' to China was not as disinterested as Pence suggests it was. In fact, as the Historian of the US State Department writes: 'China was the source of some of the world's most sought-after commodities—tea, porcelain, and silk—and Western merchants had sought access to this highly lucrative trade since at least the XVII century. Following U.S. independence, U.S.-based merchants continued to seek opportunity in China. In February1784 the 'Empress of China' became the first [commercial] ship to sail from the United States to China, and in its wake came a steady flow of merchants *in search of wealth*. During the first decades of the XIX century, U.S. merchants amassed *sizeable fortunes* that they subsequently invested in the development of their homeland' (US 2017).[134]

Then, Pence goes on to say that: 'when China suffered through indignities and exploitation during her so-called "Century of Humiliation, [1839–1949]" America refused to join in, and advocated the "Open Door" policy, so that we could have freer trade with China, and preserve their sovereignty...' It is true that the US did not join England in the first Opium War (1839–1842) that ended with the signature between England and China of the first of a long series of the so-called 'unequal treaties'. But the US was very quick in profiting from the opening of China by the British to sign its 'unequal treaty' already in 1844. And from then on, the US did exactly the same as the other imperial powers. Pence is proud in saying that the 'American missionaries brought the good news to China's shores' and the US 'also founded some of China's first and finest universities ...'. Moreover, Pence reminds

---

[134]It is necessary, and only fair, to mention that many of these merchants enriched themselves by being very active in the opium trade (Bradley 2015, pp. 17–19, 47–49).

the audience and the Chinese leadership, that during the Second World war, 'we stood together as allies in the fight against imperialism (sic) ... And in that war's aftermath, America ensured that China became a Charter member of the United Nations, and a great shaper of the post-war world'. That sounds very liberal, and corresponds to the idea of US politicians, merchants and missionaries, that the poor Chinese needed to be benevolently civilized by the great civilized American nation. Forgetting that at the same time, in spite the 'self-evident truth that all men are created equal', the US was keeping in slavery a few millions of Afro-Americans (in today's politically correct denomination, in fact, at that time, negroes or niggers), and was at the same time murdering and destroying the whole nation of the Native Indians.[135]

Clearly for Pence, that was the 'good old time'. Then, in 1949, came the uncivilized communists and, 'soon after it took power in 1949, the Chinese Communist Party began to pursue authoritarian expansionism'. Here Pence forget that between 1949 and 1979 China isolated itself from the rest of the world for the purpose of starting to re-build its nation, avoiding foreign interferences that had lasted, as Pence recognizes, 'a century of humiliations'. After the fall of the Berlin wall, then came the time of great expectations and of the end of history: 'after the fall of the Soviet Union, we assumed that a free China was inevitable. Heady with optimism, at the turn of the 21st Century, America agreed to give Beijing open access to our economy, and bring China into the World Trade Organization'.

But the hopes of the previous US administrations have gone unfulfilled, i.e. the hopes that 'freedom in China would expand in all forms—not just economically, but politically, with a newfound respect for classical liberal principles, private property, religious freedom, and the entire family of human rights. (...). The dream of freedom remains distant for the Chinese people'.[136]

Pence also complains that China 'controls and oppresses its own people' through an 'unparalleled surveillance state', implementing 'an Orwellian system premised on controlling virtually every facet of human life—the so-called social credit score.' And then comes another intolerable sin: '*Within our own hemisphere*, Beijing has extended a lifeline to the corrupt and incompetent Maduro regime in Venezuela, pledging \$5 billion in questionable loans that can be repaid with oil.[137] And since last year, the Chinese Communist Party has convinced 3 Latin American nations to sever ties with Taipei and recognize Beijing. These actions threaten the stability of

---

[135]Declaration of Independence, 4 July 1976: 'We hold these truths to be self-evident, that all men are created equal, that they are endowed by their Creator with certain unalienable Rights, that among these are Life, Liberty and the pursuit of Happiness.' In the books of James Bradley, you will find the reproduction of a choice of original cartoons showing how American Indians, Japanese and Chinese people were represented in a choice of popular US media: Bradley (2009, pp. 65, 182, 279, 283), Bradley (2015, pp. 38, 43, 186, 233).

[136]Let me note that Pence refers to Michael Pillsbury, an expert at the Hudson Institute who developed a similar narrative in his book *The Hundred-Year Marathon. China's Secret Strategy to Replace America as the Global Superpower*, see Chap. 2, note 12 above.

[137]An implicit reference to the Monroe doctrine of 1823, to which John Bolton has referred to explicitly a few months later.

6.2 China's Strategy for Reclaiming World Power Status

the Taiwan Strait.' Finally, Pence also complains that China is meddling in America's democracy with a variety of means.

Moreover, 'the Chinese Communist Party has also used an arsenal of policies inconsistent with free and fair trade, including tariffs, quotas, currency manipulation, forced technology transfer, intellectual property theft, and industrial subsidies doled out like candy, to name a few. These policies have built Beijing's manufacturing base, *at the expense of its competitors—especially America'*.

What are according to Pence the strategies China has implemented to realize this objective? 'To win the commanding heights of the 21st Century economy, Beijing has directed its bureaucrats and businesses to obtain American intellectual property— *the foundation of our economic leadership*—by any means necessary. Beijing now requires many American businesses to hand over their trade secrets as the cost of doing business in China. It also coordinates and sponsors the acquisition of American firms to gain ownership of their creations. Worst of all, Chinese security agencies have masterminded the wholesale theft of American technology—including cutting-edge military blueprints. And using that stolen technology, *the Chinese Communist Party is turning plowshares into swords on a massive scale...*' Which means that China now spends as much on its military as the rest of Asia combined, and Beijing has prioritized capabilities to erode America's military advantages—on land, at sea, in the air, and in space. China wants nothing less than to push the United States of America from the Western Pacific [a Chinese Monroe Doctrine?] and attempt to prevent us from coming to the aid of our allies'.

Pence consider that he has not given a complete list of China's wrongdoings: 'These are only a few of the ways that China has sought to advance its strategic interests across the world, with growing intensity and sophistication. Yet previous administrations all but ignored China's actions—and in many cases, they abetted them' But here is the good news: 'those days are over'. How?

The answer is clear: use what some pundits call 'hard power', i.e. the use of economic sanctions and military resources to realize US national interests: *'We've been making the strongest military in the history of the world stronger still.* Earlier this year, the President signed into law the largest increase in our national defence since the days of Ronald Reagan—*$716 billion to extend our military dominance in every domain.* We're modernizing our nuclear arsenal, we're fielding and developing new cutting-edge fighters and bombers, we're building a new generation of aircraft carriers and warships, and *we're investing as never before in our Armed Forces*.[138] This includes initiating the process to establish the United States Space Force to ensure our continued dominance in space, and authorizing increased capability in the cyber world to build deterrence against our adversaries'. (...) As we rebuild our military, *we will continue to assert American interests across the Indo-Pacific'*.

---

[138]Mike Pence should read the article by former US Secretary of Defence Robert McNamara where he qualifies US nuclear policy as 'immoral, illegal, militarily unnecessary, and dreadfully dangerous'. The article was published in 2005. Clearly the US nuclear strategy has not changed since (McNamara 2005).

304   6 China and the New World Order. Why and How China's Foreign Policy …

All this clearly means that China has to comply with the US requirements, both domestically and internationally. This for China. If in addition to this we consider parts of Pence's speech at the Warsaw Conference of January 2019 asking Europe to keep side to the US against Russia, we can conclude by quoting one of the most famous Jefferson's statements (already mentioned above, Sect. 6.1.1, quoted by quoted by Stephanson 1995, p. 24): 'We are destined to be a barrier against the return of ignorance and barbarism. Old Europe will have to lean on our shoulders, and to hobble along by our side'.

Finally, if we add to this the other speeches of Pence (especially the one on Venezuela), those of Secretary of State Mike Pompeo, the ejaculations of John Bolton and Elliot Abrams, and the articles published by mainstream media, we can see that the US foreign policy is deeply stuck in the original ideology I have analyzed at the beginning of this chapter. Even the 'unusual' President has not succeeded so far (as we have seen above) to escape from the dictatorship of the dominant ideology. I have qualified this ideology as a 'weapon of mass destruction', as it has destructed the capacity of the American elite to conceive any other world in which the US could play another role. At the same time, it seems that China has been successful, thanks to a long series of actions, when it had a reasonable chance to succeed, and non-actions, waiting for the 'silent transformations' to change the 'situation potential' to its advantage. By doing so it succeeded in trapping the US in a fixed position, from which it seems unable to escape, i.e. continuing to implement a foreign policy based upon the menace, and eventually the actual use of economic and military resources. During the same period of time, China has given the impression of being all the time on the move, evolving from one move to the other: from the economy to the military, the technology, the investments abroad, the training of talents, the diffusion of Chinese culture; from copying the West to innovating autonomously; from opening up its economy to the world to protecting its national market from predatory capitalists; from bilateral agreements to new multilateral organizations; from asserting local interests (the China Seas, Taiwan) to developing global interests in Eurasia, Africa, Latin America, and the Arctic; from criticizing traditional enemies (e.g. Japan and India) to negotiating with them, etc. Thereby, China confirms the analysis of François Jullien and André Chieng (already quoted in Chap. 2): 'the essence of strategy is on the one hand to gradually trap the competitor into a fixed position [i.e. from which it cannot escape] upon which the strategist can act, and on the other hand to constantly change its position in order to make its own strategy incomprehensible to the competitor' (Chieng 2006, p. 210; Jullien 1995, Chap. 1) … and when it starts to understand it, it is too late. As the Chinese calligrapher Lei Pingyang says: 'foolishness is like bamboo, empty inside but unshakable (chǔn zhě ruòzhú: zhōngkōng ér bù dǎo).[139]

---

[139]In April 2019, when I was about to finalize the writing of this book, we learned that the investigation on the so-called 'Russia Gate' concluded that there had been no collusion or conspiracy between Trump and his entourage and Russia, as one would have forecasted right from the beginning. But not for the establishment and the Democrats that give the impression of counting on some new revelations, instead of trying to reconstruct their strategy for the 2020 presidential election. Clearly, they have not yet 'eaten the spinach' of the defeat of their champion in 2016. Well, clearly

References

Albright, M. K. (1998). Interview on NBC-TV 'The Today Show' with Matt Lauer, Columbus, Ohio, February 19, 1998. As released by the Office of the Spokesman U.S. Department of State. Retrieved September 18, 2018, from https://1997-2001.state.gov/statements/1998/980219a.html.

Allison, G. (2018a). The Myth of the Liberal Order. From Historical Accident to Conventional Wisdom, Foreign Affairs, July/August Issue. Retrieved September 25, 2018, from https://www.foreignaffairs.com/articles/2018-06-14/myth-liberal-order.

Allison, G. (2018b). The Truth About the Liberal Order. Why It Didn't Make the Modern World, *Foreign Affairs,* 28 August. Retrieved September 25, 2018, from https://www.foreignaffairs.com/articles/2018-08-28/truth-about-liberal-order.

Andersen, K. (2017). *Fantasy land. How America went haywire. A 500-year history.* London: Penguin.

Anderson, P. (2015). *American foreign policy and its thinkers.* London: Verso.

Associated Press. (2017). Trump's Advisers Schooled Him on Globalism, September 18. Retrieved October 20, from https://www.voanews.com/a/trump-advisers-globalism-session/4033541.html.

Bacevich, A. (2008). *The limits of power. The end of American exceptionalism.* New York: Henry Holt.

Bacevich, A. (Ed.). (2012). *The short American century. A postmortem.* Cambridge, Mass: Harvard University Press.

Bacevich, A. (2017). *The age of great expectations and the great void. History after "the End of History", TomDispatch.com,* 8 January. Retrieved March 28, 2017, from http://www.tomdispatch.com/blog/176228/.

Bahar, D. (2017). When renegotiating NAFTA, Trump should re-evaluate his premises on international trade. *Brookings,* 17 August 2017. Retrieved August 20, 2017, from https://www.brookings.edu/blog/up-front/2017/08/17/when-renegotiating-nafta-trump-should-re-evaluate-his-premises-on-international-trade/.

Bakir, V. et al (2018). Organized persuasive communication: A new conceptual framework for research on public relations, propaganda and promotional culture. *Critical Sociology*, 15 May, pp. 1–18.

Bandow, D. (2016). 'Ripped Off. What Donald Trump Gets Right About U.S. Alliances', *Foreign Affairs*, 12 September. Retrieved October 15, 2016, from https://www.foreignaffairs.com/articles/world/2016-09-12/ripped.

Bao, B., Eichacker, C., & Rosenthal M. J. (2013). 'Is China pivoting to the Middle East?' Chinese people have begun casting their gaze westward. But will the government follow suit? *The Atlantic*, 28 March. Retrieved February 29, 2016, from https://www.theatlantic.com/china/archive/2013/03/is-china-pivoting-to-the-middle-east/274444/.

Baru, S. (2017). For China's one belt one road initiative is not just about economics. *The Economic Times*, 25 April. Retrieved July 27, 2017, from http://blogs.economictimes.indiatimes.com/et-commentary/chinas-one-belt-one-road-initiative-is-not-just-about-economics/.

Beinart, P. (2018). The U.S. Needs to Face Up to Its Long History of Election Meddling. *The Atlantic,* 22 July. Retrieved August 25, 2018, from https://www.theatlantic.com/ideas/archive/2018/07/the-us-has-a-long-history-of-election-meddling/565538/.

Bell, D. (2006). *Beyond liberal democracy. Political thinking for an east Asian context.* Princeton: Princeton University Press.

Bell, D. (2016). *The China model: Political meritocracy and the limits of democracy.* Princeton: Princeton University Press.

Bernays, E. (1928). *Propaganda.* New York: Ig Publishing (reprinted 2005).

---

anti-Russian hysteria is going on, and stupidity seems to be there to stay for a long time with the Democrats and their allies.

306 6 China and the New World Order. Why and How China's Foreign Policy …

Beveridge, A. (1900). In Support of an American Empire. *Record, 56* Cong., I Sess., 1900, pp. 704–712. Retrieved December 15, 2018, from https://www.mtholyoke.edu/acad/intrel/ajb72.htm.

Blackwill, R. D., & Campbell, K. (2016). *Xi Jinping on the Global Stage. Chinese Foreign Policy Under a Powerful but Exposed Leader, Council on Foreign Relations,* Council Special Report No. 74, February.

Bloomberg. (2018). China Ends 25-Year Wait as Yuan Oil Futures to Start Trading, *Bloomberg News*, 9 February. Retrieved March 15, 2018, from https://www.bloomberg.com/news/articles/2018-02-09/china-ends-25-year-wait-as-yuan-oil-futures-set-to-start-trading.

Blum, W. (2013–2014). Overthrowing other people's governments: The Master List, Published February 2013 (updated 2014) by *William Blum org*. Retrieved March 29, 2015, from https://williamblum.org/essays/read/overthrowing-other-peoples-governments-the-master-list.

Blum, B. (2014a). *Rogue state. A guide to the world's only superpower*. London: Zed Books.

Blum, W. (2014b). *Killing hope.US military and CIA interventions since world war II*. Monroe, ME: Common Courage Press.

Blum, W. (2014c). Overthrowing other people's governments: The master list. Retrieved September 26, 2018, from https://williamblum.org/essays/read/overthrowing-other-peoples-governments-the-master-list.

Blum, W. (2016). What can go wrong? The brighter side of Trump's election. *Foreign policy Journal*, 2 December. Retrieved December 19, 2016, from https://www.foreignpolicyjournal.com/2016/12/02/what-can-go-wrong-the-brighter-side-of-trumps-election/.

Bradley, J. (2009). *The imperial cruise. A secret history of empire and war*. New York: Little, Brown & Co.

Bradley, J. (2015). *The China mirage. The hidden story of American disaster in Asia*. New York: Little, Brown & Co.

Braudel, F. (1972). Fernand Braudel et les différents temps de l'histoire', interview published by *Jalons*, ORTF (Collection: Signes des temps) 30 October.

Braudel, F. (1979). *Afterthoughts on material civilization and capitalism*. Baltimore: The Johns Hopkins University Press.

Browne, A. (2015). Can China be contained? *The Wall Street Journal* 12 June. Retrieved June 13, 2015, from https://www.wsj.com/articles/can-china-be-contained-1434118534.

Brzezinski, Z. (1997a). A geostrategy for Eurasia. *Foreign Affairs*, September 1. Retrieved December 6, 2016, from https://www.foreignaffairs.com/articles/asia/1997-09-01/geostrategy-eurasia.

Brzezinski, Z. (1997b). *The grand chessboard: American primacy and its geostrategic imperatives*. New York: Basic Books.

Brzezinski, Z. (2016). Toward a global realignment. As its era of global dominance ends, the United States to take the lead in realigning the global power architecture. *The American Interest*, 17 April 2016.

Buckley Ebrey, P. (1999). *The Cambridge illustrated history of China*. Cambridge: Cambridge University Press.

Business Insider. (2017). China's investments abroad, 15 April. Retrieved August 4, 2017, from http://www.businessinsider.com/states-that-get-the-most-china-investment-2017-4?IR=T. All data are cumulative investments 2000–2016.

Butman, J., & Targett, S. (2018). *New world Inc., The making of America by England's merchants adventurers*. New York: Little, Brown & Company.

Campbell, K. M., & Ratner, E. (2018). The China Reckoning. How Beijing Defied American Expectations. *Foreign Affairs*, 13 February. Retrieved February 15, 2018, from https://www.foreignaffairs.com/articles/united-states/2018-02-13/china-reckoning?cid=nlc-fa_fatoday-20180214.

Chan, M. (2017). Chinese military sets up hi-tech weapons research agency modelled on US body, 25 July. Retrieved July 31, 2017, from http://www.scmp.com/news/china/diplomacydefence/article/2104070/chinese-military-sets-hi-tech-weapons-research-agency, and then follow the additional links mentioned in this article.

References

Cheng, E. (2017). Five empires threaten to replace US and Europe on the global stage, writer says', *CNBC*, 30 March. Retrieved March 30, 2017, from http://www.cnbc.com/2017/03/30/five-empires-may-replace-the-united-states-on-global-stage.html.

Chieng, A. (2006). *La pratique de la Chine, en compagnie de François Jullien*. Paris: Grasset.

Chollet, D., et al. (2017). Building 'situations of strength. A national security strategy for the Unites States, *Brookings*, February.

Chomsky, A. (2018). The DNA Industry and the Disappearing Indian. *TomDispatch*, 29 November 2018. Retrieved November 30, 2018, from http://www.tomdispatch.com/blog/176501/tomgram%3A_aviva_chomsky%2C_making_native_americans_strangers_in_their_own_land/.

Christensen, T. J. (2015). Obama in Asia. Confronting the China challenge. *Foreign Affairs*, September/October issue. Retrieved November 24, 2015, from https://www.foreignaffairs.com/articles/asia/obama-and-asia.

Chollet, D. et al. (2017). Building Situations of Strength. A National Security Strategy for the United States, Order from Chaos Project, Foreign Policy in a Troubled World. *Foreign Policy at Brookings*, February.

Clauss, M. (2017). Why Europe and the US cannot afford to ignore China's belt and road. *South China Morning Post*, 16 June 2017. Retrieved August 8, 2017, from http://www.scmp.com/comment/insight-opinion/article/2098527/why-europe-and-us-cannot-afford-ignore-chinas-belt-and-road.

Clinton, H. (2011). America's Pacific Century. *Foreign Policy*, 11 October. Retrieved June 7, 2014, from http://foreignpolicy.com/2011/10/11/americas-pacific-century/.

Clinton, H. (2016). Speech given at the American Legion's national convention. *Time*, 31 August, full transcription available at, Retrieved March 5, 2017, from http://time.com/4474619/read-hillary-clinton-american-legion-speech/.

Clinton, W. (1997). Inaugural address, 20 January. *The American presidency project*. Santa Barbara: University of California. Retrieved March 5, 2017, from http://www.presidency.ucsb.edu/ws/?pid=54183.

Conradi, P. (2016). *Who lost Russia? How the world entered a new cold war*. London: Oneworld.

Corsi, J. R. (2018). *Killing the deep state. The fight to save president Trump*. West Palm Beach: Humanix Books.

Creel, G. (2012). *How We Advertised America: The First Telling of the Amazing Story of the Committee on Public Information That Carried the Gospel of Americanism to Every Corner of the Globe Corner*, Forgotten Books (Classic Reprint). Retrieved from https://www.forgottenbooks.com/en (first edition 1920).

CSIS. (2015). What does China really spend on its military?, Centre for Strategic and International Studies China Power Team, 28 December. Retrieved March 25, 2017, from https://chinapower.csis.org/military-spending/.

Cumings, B. (2017). A murderous history of Korea. *London Review of Books*, 18 May 2017. Retrieved May 20, 2017, from https://www.lrb.co.uk/v39/n10/bruce-cumings/a-murderous-history-of-korea.

Daniels, J. (2017). General calls Iran 'destabilizing' force, suggests US 'disrupt' regime by military means. *CNBC*, 29 Mar. Retrieved March 29, 2017 from http://www.cnbc.com/2017/03/29/general-calls-iran-destabilizing-force-suggests-us-disrupt-regime-by-military-means.html.

Democracy Now. (2013). 'Make the economy scream': Secret documents show Nixon, Kissinger Role Backing 1973 Chile Coup. *Democracy Now*, 10 September. Retrieved October 25, 2016, from https://www.democracynow.org/2013/9/10/40_years_after_chiles_9_11.

Denyer, S. (2013). China bypasses American New Silk Road with two of its own. *The Washington Post*, 14 October. Retrieved June 24, 2015, from https://www.washingtonpost.com/world/asia_pacific/china-bypasses-american-new-silk-road-with-two-if-its-own/2013/10/14/49f9f60c-3284-11e3-ad00-ec4c6b31cbed_story.html?utm_term=.058ccff83b09.

Dollar, D. et al. (2017). Avoiding containment, competition, and Cooperation in US-China Relations. *A Brookings Interview*, November.

Donnan, S. (2014). Geopolitics cast shadow over New Silk Road. *Financial Times*, 17 October, accessed 24 February 2015.

Dower, J. (2017). *The violent American century. War and terror since world war II*. Chicago: Haymarket Books.

Easton, Ian (2017), *The Chinese Invasion Threat: Taiwan's Defense and American Strategy in Asia*. Arlington, VA: Project 2019 Institute.

Eberhardt, P. (2016). The Zombie ISDS. Rebranded as ICS, rights for corporations to sue states refuse to die. *Corporate Europe Observatory*.

Economist. (2018). China wants to reshape the global oil market. *The Economist*, 28 March. Retrieved April 15, 2018, from https://www.economist.com/finance-and-economics/2018/03/28/china-wants-to-reshape-the-global-oil-market.

Edelman, M. (1985). *The symbolic uses of politics*. Chicago: University of Illinois Press.

Engelhardt, T. (2014). *Shadow government. Surveillance, secret wars, and global security state in a single-superpower world*. Chicago: Haymarket Books.

Esfandiary, D., & Tabatabai, A. (2018). *Triple axis. Iran's relations with Russia and China*. London: I.B. Tauris.

European Chamber. (2017). China Manufacturing 2015, Putting Industrial Policy Ahead of Market Forces. Retrieved from www.europeanchamber.com.cn.

Fardella, E. et al. (2016). La Belt and Road Initiative: la globalizzazione secondo Pechino. *Rivista bimestrale di politica, relazioni internazioneli e dinamiche socio-economiche della Cina contemporanea* (Vol. 7, No.6), December.

FBI. (2015). Chinese Talent Programs. *Federal Bureau of Investigation (FBI)*, Counterintelligence Strategic Partnership, Intelligence not (Spin), September. Retrieved January 25, 2019, from https://info.publicintelligence.net/FBI-ChineseTalentPrograms.pdf.

Fenby, J. (2014). *Will China dominate the XXI century?* Cambridge (UK): Polity Press.

Feng, E. (2017). China agency targets high-tech weapons development. *Financial Times*, 26 July. Retrieved July 31, 2017, from https://www.ft.com/content/2c9b4370-71c5-11e7-aca6-c6bd07df1a3c.

Ferguson, N. (2004). *Empire: How Britain made the modern world*. Eastbourne: Gardners Books.

Fleitz, F. (Ed.). (2016). *Warning order: China prepares for conflict and why we must do the same*. Washington: Center for Security Policy Press.

Foreign Affairs. (2017). What Was the Liberal Order? The World We May Be Losing. *Foreign Affairs*, March Issue, a collection of articles written between WWII and 2017.

Freeman, K. D. (2016). China, unrestricted warfare, and the challenge to America. In F. Fleitz (Ed.), *Warning order: China prepares for conflict and why we must do the same* (pp. 55–80). Washington: Center for Security Policy Press.

Freud, S. (2016). *Group psychology and the analysis of the ego*. CreateSpace (Amazon), Scotts Valley: California Originally published 1921.

Friedman, M. (1982). *Capitalism and freedom*. Chicago: University of Chicago Press, 1962 (1982 with a new Preface by the author).

Fukuyama, F. (1989). The end of history? *The national interest* (Summer, No. 16, pp. 3–18).

Fukuyama, F. (1992). *The end of history and the last man*. New York: Free Press.

Fukuyama, F. (2008). 'Soft talk, big stick'. In M. P. Leffler & G. W. Legro (Eds.), *To lead the world. American strategy after the Bush Doctrine* (pp. 204–225). Oxford: Oxford University Press.

Fukuyama, F. (2012). The future of history. Can liberal democracy survive the decline of the middle class? *Foreign Affairs*, 1 January. Retrieved May 15, 2014, from https://www.foreignaffairs.com/articles/2012-01-01/future-history.

Fukuyama, F. (2016). American political decay or renewal? *Foreign Affairs*, 13 June. Retrieved December 11, 2016, from https://www.foreignaffairs.com/articles/united-states/2016-06-13/american-political-decay-or-renewal.

Ganser, D. (2005). *NATO's secret armies. Operation gladio and terrorism in western Europe*. New York: Frank Cass.

References

Ganser, D. (2016). *Les guerres illégales de l'OTAN. Comment les pays membres de l'OTAN sapent l'ONU*. Plogastel Saint-Germain (France): Editions Demi-Lune.

Gertz, B. (2015). Top China analyst: Beijing has been duping the US since Mao. *Business Insider* (The Washington Free Beacon), 2 February. Retrieved February 24, 2015, from http://uk.businessinsider.com/?IR=C.

Goh, B., & Yawen, C. (2017). China pledges $124 billion for new Silk Road as champion of globalization. *Business Insider*, 13 May. Retrieved July 4, 2017, from http://www.businessinsider.com/r-china-pledges-124-billion-for-new-silk-road-says-open-to-everyone-2017-5?IR=T.

Gompert, D., et al. (2016). *War with China. Thinking the unthinkable*. Santa Monica, California: Rand Corporation.

Green, M. J. (2017). *By more than providence. Grand strategy and American power in the pacific since 1783*. New York: Columbia University Press.

Griffin, R. D. (2018). *The American trajectory. Divine or demonic?* Atlanta, GA: Clarity Press.

Haas, R. (2013). *Foreign policy begins at home. The case for putting America's house in order* (pp. 11–80). New York: Basic Books, especially Part I, 'The return of history'.

Haass, R. N. (2014). The unravelling. How to respond to a disordered World. *Foreign Affairs*, November/December issue. Retrieved April 22, 2016, from https://www.foreignaffairs.com/articles/united-states/2014-10-20/unraveling.

Haas, R. N. (2016). America and the world in transition. *Project Syndicate*, 23. Retrieved November 27, 2016, from https://www.project-syndicate.org/commentary/trump-america-world-in-transition-by-richard-n–haass-2016-11?barrier=accessreg.

Haas, R. N. (2019). How a World Order Ends. And What Comes in Its Wake. *Foreign Affairs*, January/February 2019 issue. Retrieved January 2, 2019, from https://www.foreignaffairs.com/articles/2018-12-11/how-world-order-ends.

Hancock, T. (2017). Silk Road. China encircles the world with One Belt, One Road strategy. *Financial Times*, 4 May. Retrieved July 22, 2017, from https://www.ft.com/content/0714074a-0334-11e7-aa5b-6bb07f5c8e12.

Harris, S. (2014). *China's foreign policy*. Cambridge (UK): Polity.

Hartung, W. (2017). The Hidden Cost of "National Security". Ten ways your tax dollar pays for war—past, present, and future, Retrieved July 29, 2017, from http://www.tomdispatch.com/blog/176213/tomgram%3A_william_hartung,_trump_r_the_defense/.

Heginbotham, E. et al. (2015). *The U.S.-China military scorecard. Forces, the evolving balance of power 1996–2017*. Santa Monica, California: The Corporation.

Horowitz, D. (2017). *Big agenda. President Trump's plan to save America*. West Palm Beach, FL: Humanix Books.

HSBC. (2017). One Belt One Road briefing note, 12 May. Retrieved May 20, 2017, from http://www.lmfinternational.com/index.php/news/560-trends/40553-hsbc-one-belt-one-road-briefing-note.

Hu, A. (2004a). *China's new development strategy*. Zhejiang: People Publishing House of Zhejiang, (3rd ed., in Chinese).

Hu, A. (2004b). China's economic growth, human resources development and poverty reduction (1978–2003), a contribution to the September 7–9, 2004 International Population and Development Forum, (Wuhan City, Hubei Province, China): Eliminating Poverty.

Hu, A. (2007). *Economic and social transformation in China*. London: Routledge.

Hu, A. (2014). *China's collective leadership*. Heidelberg and Beijing: Springer.

Hu, A. (2016). One belt one road: Reshaping Chinese economic geography, Beijing, April. *Institute of Contemporary China Studies*, Tsinghua University, paper kindly provided by author.

Hu, A., Wang Y. et al. (1992). *Survival and development. A study of China's long-term development*. Beijing & New York: Science Press.

Hu, A., & Zou, P. (1991). *China's population development*. Beijing: China's Science and Technology Press.

Hu, A., & Men, H. (2004). The Rising of Modern China: Comprehensive National Power and Grand Strategy, paper presented at the international conference on 'Rising China and the East Asian Economy', Seoul, 19–20 March, kindly provided by authors. The original Chinese version was published in *Strategy & Management*, No 3, 2002. This article is available on the website of Wikipedia, under 'Comprehensive National Power'.

Hu, A., & Hao, R. (2016). How can China's high-technology industry catch up with United States. *Strategy and Policy Decision Research* (Vol. 31, pp. 1355–1364), Proceedings of Chinese Academy of Sciences, 1355 Phase 12.

Hu, A., Zhang, X., & Zhang, W. (2017). Strategic connotation and conception of the development of the Belt, Road and Channel (Arctic Shipping Channel) Initiative. Beijing, School of Public Policy and Management, Tsinghua University, 12 April, kindly provided by main author.

Huang, K., & Lo, K. (2019). As China and US spar over tech, scientists would rather not talk about their talent awards. *South China Morning Post*, 14 January.

Hudson, M. (2003). *Super imperialism. The origin and fundamentals of US world dominance.* London: Pluto Press, Second edition with a new preface (first edition 1972).

Hudson, M. (2005). *Global fracture. The new international economic order.* London: Pluto Press, Second edition with a new introduction (first edition 1977).

Hudson, M. (2019a). Trump's brilliant strategy to dismenber US dollar hegemony, Hudson Website, 1 January. Retrieved January 2, 2019, from https://michael-hudson.com/2019/02/trumps-brilliant-strategy-to-dismember-u-s-dollar-hegemony/.

Hudson, M. (2019b). Venezuela as the pivot for New Internationalism? Michael Hudson Website, 6 January. Retrieved January 8, 2019, from https://michael-hudson.com/2019/02/venezuela-as-the-pivot-for-new-internationalism/.

IHEP. (2018). CEPC (Circular Electron Positron Collider) Design Report Released, Institute of High Energy Physics, Chinese Academy of Sciences, 11 November. Retrieved January 29, 2019, from http://english.ihep.cas.cn/doc/3229.html.

Irish, J. (2019). Skirting US sanctions, Europeans open new trade channel to Iran. *Reuters*, 31 January. Retrieved February 10, 2019, from https://www.reuters.com/article/us-iran-usa-sanctions-eu/skirting-u-s-sanctions-europeans-launch-trade-mechanism-for-iran-idUSKCN1PP0K3.

Jäcklein, W. (2014). Transatlantic Trade and Investment Partnership: Ten threats to Europeans. Le Monde Diplomatique, 14 2014. Retrieved May 23, 2017, from http://mondediplo.com/2014/06/11ttip.

Jacobs, B. (2015). The Donald Trump doctrine: 'Assad is bad' but US must stop 'nation-building'. *Guardian*, 13 October. Retrieved December 15, 2016, from https://www.theguardian.com/us-news/2015/oct/13/donald-trump-foreign-policy-doctrine-nation-building.

Jayaman, K. et al. (2017). The closet look yet at Chinese economic engagement in Africa, *McKinsey&Company*, Report, June.

Johnson, C. (2000). *Blowback. The costs and consequences of American empire.* New York: Henry Holt.

Johnson, C. (2004). *The sorrows of empire. Militarism, secrecy, and the end of the republic.* New York: Henry Holt.

Johnson, C. (2006). *Nemesis. The last days of the American republic.* New York: Henry Holt.

Johnson, C. (2010). *Dismantling the empire. America's last best hope.* New York: Henry Holt.

Johnstone, D. (2016). *Queen of chaos. The misadventures of Hillary Clinton.* Petrolia (California): Counterpunch.

Jones, O. (2017). Americans can spot elections meddling because they've been doing it for years. *The Guardian*, 5 January. Retrieved June 13, 2017, from https://www.theguardian.com/commentisfree/2017/jan/05/americans-spot-election-meddling-doing-years-vladimir-putin-donald-trump.

Jullien, F. (1995). *The propensity of things. Towards a history of efficacy in China.* New York: Zone Books.

Jullien, F. (2011). *The silent transformations.* London: Seagull.

Kagan, R. (2003). *Of paradise and power. America and Europe in the new world order.* New York: Vintage Books.

Kagan, R. (2008). *The return of history and the end of dreams.* London: Atlantic Books.

Kagan, R. (2012a). *The world America made.* New York: Alfred A. Knopf.

References

Kagan, R. (2012b). Not fade away: Against the myth of American decline. *Brookings Institution*, 17 January.

Kagan, R. (2014). Superpower don't get to retire. What our tired country still owes to the world, 27 May. *New Republic*. Retrieved March 20, 2017, from https://newrepublic.com/article/117859/superpowers-dont-get-retire.

Kagan, R. (2017a). The twilight of the liberal world order. *Brookings Report*, 24 January 2017. Retrieved January 27, 2017, from https://www.brookings.edu/research/the-twilight-of-the-liberal-world-order/.

Kagan, R. (2017b). Backing into World War III. *Brookings Institution*, 6 February. Retrieved February 14, 2017, from https://www.brookings.edu/research/backing-into-world-war-iii/.

Kania, E. B. (2018). China's Quantum Future. Xi's Quest to Build a High-Tech Superpower. *Foreign Affairs*, 26 September. Retrieved October 20, 2018, from https://www.foreignaffairs.com/articles/china/2018-09-26/chinas-quantum-future.

Kaplan, T. (2016). Jabbing at Trump, Clinton extols US as 'indispensable nation. *Seattle Times*, 31 August. Retrieved March 5, 2017, from http://www.seattletimes.com/nation-world/jabbing-at-trump-clinton-extols-us-as-indispensable-nation/.

Karen, Y. (2018). As trade war rages, China may step up efforts to create an alternative to US dollar hegemony. *South China Morning Post*, 18 December. Retrieved January 10, 2019, from https://www.scmp.com/print/economy/china-economy/article/2178037/trade-war-rages-china-may-step-efforts-create-alternative-us.

Karp, W. (1979). *The politics of war. The story of two wars which altered forever the political life of the American republic (1890–1920)*. New York: Harper Colophon Books.

Katada, S. N. (2018). Can China internationalize the RMB? Lessons From Japan. *Foreign Affairs*, 1 January. Retrieved September 10, 2018, from https://www.foreignaffairs.com/articles/china/2018-01-01/can-china-internationalize-rmb.

Keidel, A. (2007). *The causes and impact of Chinese regional inequalities in income well-being*. Carnegie Endowment for International Peace, December.

Kelsey, J. (2011). International civil society demands end to secrecy in TPPA talks, media release, February 16, 2011. Retrieved March 29, 2011, from http://tppwatch.org.

Kelsey, J. (2017). *TISA foul play*, Nyon, Switzerland, Uni Global Union. Retrieved from http://www.uniglobalunion.org/news/tisa-foul-play.

Kennan, G. (1947). The sources of soviet conduct. *Foreign Affairs*, July issue. Retrieved May 15, 2017, from https://www.foreignaffairs.com/articles/russian-federation/1947-07-01/sources-soviet-conduct.

Kennedy, R. F. Jr. (2016). Why the Arabs don't want us in Syria. They don't hate "our freedoms". They hate the fact that we've betrayed our ideals in their own countries. *Politico*, 16 September 2016. Retrieved December 18, 2016, from http://www.politico.eu/article/why-the-arabs-dont-want-us-in-syria-mideast-conflict-oil-intervention/.

Kinzer, S. (2017). *The true flag. Theodore Roosevelt, Mark Twain, and the birth of American empire*. New York: Henry Holt.

King, S. (2011). *The southern silk road. Turbocharging 'South-South' economic growth*. HSBC. Global Research, 6 June 2011, p. 6. Retrieved June 25, 2012, from https://www.hsbc.fr/1/PA_esf-ca-app-content/content/pws/corpo/main-page-campagne-marque/pdf/111013-the-southern-silk-road.pdf.

Klein, K. (2012). Obama: US the one indispensable nation in world affairs, Voice of America News, 28 May. Retrieved April 18, 2016, from http://www.voanews.com/content/obama.

Kramer, M. (2001). Rescuing Boris. *Time*, 24 June. Retrieved June 10, 2017, from http://content.time.com/time/printout/0,8816,136204,00.html.

Kristol, W., & Kagan, R. (1996). Toward a neo-reaganite foreign policy. *Foreign Affairs*, 1 July. Retrieved March 27, 2017, from https://www.foreignaffairs.com/print/1109929.

Kuo, M. A. (2018). US Withdrawal From INF Treaty: Impact on China. *The Diplomat*, 6 November. Retrieved December 15, 2018, from https://thediplomat.com/2018/11/us-withdrawal-from-inf-treaty-impact-on-china/.

Kupchan, C. (2005). *The end of the American Era. US foreign policy and the geopolitics of the twenty-first century*. New York: Vintage Books.

Kupchan, C. (2012). *No one's world. The west, the rising rest, and the coming global turn*. Oxford: Oxford University Press, 2012.

Kyle Crossley, P. et al. (2017). How does China today's imperial past shape its foreign policy today? *A ChinaFile Conversation*, 15 March. Retrieved March 19, 2017, from http://www.chinafile.com/conversation/how-does-chinas-imperial-past-shape-its-foreign-policy-today.

Lacroix-Riz, A. (1985). *Le choix de Marianne. Les relations franco-américaines 1944–1948,* Paris: Messidor/Editions sociales.

Lacroix-Riz, A. (2014). *Aux origines du carcan européen 1990–1960*. Paris: Delga.

La Faber, W. (1994). *American age. US foreign policy at home and abroad. 1750 to the present*. New York: W.W Norton (second edition).

La Faber, W. (1998). *The new empire. An interpretation of American expansion 1860–1898*. Ithaca and London: Cornell, Thirty-fifth Anniversary Edition.

La Faber, W. (2012). Illusions of an American century. In A. Bacevich (Ed.), *The short American century. A postmortem* (pp. 158–186). Cambridge, Mass: Harvard University Press.

Las Casas, B. (1974). *The devastation of the Indians: A brief account* (translated by Herman Briffault). Baltimore, MD: Johns Hopkins University Press, first published in Spanish 1552.

Las Casas, B. (1992). *In Defense of the Indians*. DeKalb, Illinois: Northern Illinois University Press, translated and edited by Stafford Poole, Foreword by Martin Marty.

Le Bon, G. (1905). *Psychologie des foules*. Paris: Felix Alcan.

Le Corre, Philippe and Jonathan Pollack (2016), China's Global Rise. Can the EU and US Pursue a Coordinated Strategy?, *Brookings Institution,* October.

Lee, Kai-fu (2018), *AI Superpowers. China, Silicon Valley, and the New World Order*, Boston, Houghton Mifflin Harcourt.

Lee, Peter (2016), 'America: the Indispensable Nation…Not!', *Counter Punch*, 5 September, http://www.counterpunch.org/2016/09/05/america-the-indispensable-nationnot/, accessed 5 March 2017.

Legvold, R. (2016). *Return to Cold War*. Cambridge: UK, Polity.

Lendman, Stephen, ed. (2014), *Flashpoint in Ukraine. How the Drive for Hegemony Risks World War III,* Atlanta, Clarity Press, 2014.

Levathes, Louise (1994), *When China Rules the Seas. The Treasure Fleet of the Dragon Throne, 1405–1433*, New York, Oxford Univ. Press.

Leverett, Flynt et al. (2015), China Looks West: What Is at Stake in Beijing's "New Silk Road" Project, *The World Financial Review*, 25 January, http://www.worldfinancialreview.com/?p=3388, accessed 15 June 2015.

Levin, Dov H. (2016), Sure, the US and Russia often meddle in foreign elections. Does it matter?, *The Washington Post,* 7 September 2016, https://www.washingtonpost.com/news/monkey-cage/wp/2016/09/07/sure-the-u-s-and-russia-often-meddle-in-foreign-elections-does-it-matter/?utm_term=.ca54b59ff042, accessed 13.06.2017.

Lieberthal, Kenneth (2011), The American Pivot to Asia, *Foreign Policy*, 21 December, http://foreignpolicy.com/2011/12,/21/the-american-pivot-to-asia/, accessed 7 June 2014.

Litovsky, Alejandro (2017), China plans super-grid for clean power in Asia, *Financial Times*, 5 December, https://www.ft.com/content/e808a542-d6c6-11e7-8c9a-d9c0a5c8d5c9, accessed 20 December 2018.

Lofgren, Mike (2016), *The Deep State. The Fall of the Constitution and the Rise of a Shadow Government*, New York, Penguin Books.

Losurdo, D. (2007). *Il linguaggio dell'Impero*. Bari, Laterza: Lessico dell'ideologia americana.

Losurdo, D. (2011). *Liberalism*. London, Verso: A Counter-History.

Malloch, Theodor Roosevelt (2018), *The Plot to Destroy Trump. How the Deep State Fabricated the Russian Dossier to Subvert the President,* New York, Skyhorse.

Mao ZeTong (1949), The Chinese People Have Stood Up! Opening address by Mao Zedong, Chairman of the Chinese Communist Party, at the First Plenary Session of the Chinese People's Political

References

313

Consultative Conference, September 21, 1949, https://china.usc.edu/Mao-declares-founding-of-peoples-republic-of-china-chinese-people-have-stood-up.

Marguerat, D., & Junod, E. (2010). *Qui a fondé le christianisme?*. Labor et Fides: Genève.

Marty, D. (2018). *Une certaine idée de la justice. Théchénie, Kosovo, CIA, Drogue*. Lausanne: Favre.

Mathews, J. A., & Selden, M. (2018). China's petroyuan is going global, and gumming the US dollar. *South China Morning Post*, 4 December. Retrieved December 10, 2018, from https://www.scmp.com/comment/article/2176256/chinas-petroyuan-going-global-and-gunning-us-dollar.

Mazarr, M. J. (2016). The once and future order. What comes after hegemony. *Foreign Affairs*, 12 December 2016. Retrieved December 20, from https://www.foreignaffairs.com/articles/2016-12-12/once-and-future-order.

McCormick, T. J. (1995). *America's half-century. United Stated foreign policy in the cold war and after*. Baltimore: The Johns Hopkins.

McCoy, A. W. (2015). Grandmaster of the great game. Obama's geopolitical strategy for containing China', 15 September. Retrieved September 18, 2015, from http://www.tomdispatch.com/post/176044/tomgram:_alfred_mccoy,_maintaining_american_supremacy_in_the_twenty-first_century/.

McNamara, R. (2005). Apocalypse Soon. *Foreign Policy*, May–June, reprinted 21 October 2009. Retrieved January 15, 2019, from https://foreignpolicy.com/2009/10/21/apocalypse-soon/.

McNamara, R. (2009). The fog of War, lesson 5. *Youtube*, July 26. Retrieved September 16, 2018, from https://www.youtube.com/watch?v=hOCYcgOnWUM.

McPhillips, D. (2016). U.S. A global leader in military spending. national defence budgets may affect global perceptions of power. *US News*, 11 November 2016. Retrieved December 15, 2016, from http://www.usnews.com/news/best-countries/articles/2016-11-11/10-countries-with-the-largest-military-budgets.

Meaney, T. (2016). So it must be for ever. *London Review of Books*, Vol. 38, No. 14, 14 July. Retrieved July 8, 2016, from https://www.lrb.co.uk/v38/n14/thomas-meaney/so-it-must-be-for-ever.

Menand, L. (2011). Getting Real: George F. Kennan's Cold War. *New Yorker*, November 14 Issue. Retrieved May 16, 2017, from http://www.newyorker.com/magazine/2011/11/14/getting-real#.

Menzies, Gavin (2003), *1421 The Year China Discovered America*, Harper Collins.

Menzies, G. (2008). *1434 the year a magnificent Chinese fleet sailed to Italy and Ignited the renaissance*. New York: Harper Collins.

Mettan, G. (2017). *Creating russophobia: From the great religious schism to anti-putin hysteria*. Atlanta: GA, Clarity Press.

Migone, G. G. (2015). *The United States and Italy. The rise of American finance in Europe*. New York: Cambridge University Press.

Miller, M. C. (2004). Introduction to Bernays (1928) *Propaganda*, pp. 9–33.

Montanino, A., & Wayne, E. A. *The Arguments for TTIP and the Concerns to Address*, Atlantic Council, Global Business and Economic Programme, April.

Native News Online. (2017). US presidents in their own words concerning American Indians. *Native News online.net*, 20 February. Retrieved March 6, 2017, from http://nativenewsonline.net/currents/us-presidents-words-concerning-american-indians/.

Navarro, P. (2015). *Crouching Tiger. What China's militarism means for the world*. New York: Prometheus Books.

Navarro, P. (2016). Introduction: Crouching Tiger—China acts, America dithers. In F. Fleitz (Ed.), *Warning order: China prepares for conflict and why we must do the same*. Washington: Center for Security Policy Press.

Nazemroaya, M. D. (2012). *The globalization of NATO*. Atlanta, GA: Clarity Press.

Neffinger, V. (2017). 8 Presidents who looked to god for guidance. *Christian Headline*, 10 February. Retrieved September 18, 2018, from https://www.christianheadlines.com/slideshows/8-presidents-who-looked-to-god-for-guidance.html.

Newcombe, J. (2017). Presidents have always kept god in inaugural address. *Newsmax,* 19 January. Retrieved October 18, 2018, from https://www.newsmax.com/jerrynewcombe/president-trump-inaugural-address-bible/2017/01/19/id/769369/.

Noam, E. M. (2016). *Who owns the world's media? Media concentration and ownership around the world.* Oxford: Oxford University Press.

Nuclear Threat Initiative. (2015). China Nuclear, April. Retrieved May 26, 2016, from http://www.nti.org/learn/countries/china/nuclear/.

Nye, J. (2004). *The soft power. The means to success in world politics.* New York: Public Affairs.

Nye, J. (2008). *The powers to lead.* Oxford: Oxford University Press.

Nye, J. (2011). *The future of power.* New York: Public Affairs.

Obama, B. (2015). Remarks by President Obama on the Iran Nuclear Deal, The White House Office of the Press Secretary, For Immediate Release, August 05, 2015, American University. Washington, DC. Retrieved March 7, 2016, from https://obamawhitehouse.archives.gov/the-press-office/2015/08/05/remarks-president-iran-nuclear-deal.

Obama, B. (2016a). Remarks of President Barack Obama. State of the Union Address as Delivered, 16 January 2016. Retrieved January 27, 2016, from https://www.whitehouse.gov/the-press-office/2016/01/12/remarks-president-barack-obama-%E2%80%93-prepared-delivery-state-union-address.

Obama, B. (2016b). Remarks by the President in Commencement Address to the United States Air Force Academy, The White House, Office of the Press Secretary, For Immediate Release, June 02. Retrieved January 20, 2017, from https://obamawhitehouse.archives.gov/the-press-office/2016/06/02/remarks-president-commencement-address-united-states-air-force-academy.

O'Hanlon, M. (2017). Trump's $54 billion rounding error. *Foreign Affairs,* 1 March. Retrieved May 6, 2017, from https://www.foreignaffairs.com/articles/2017-03-01/trumps-54-billion-rounding-error.

Oliveira, G. (2019). China needs a new strategy to deal with Brazil's new right-wing president. *South China Morning Post,* 13 January. Retrieved January 22, 2019, from https://www.scmp.com/news/china/diplomacy/article/2181854/china-needs-new-strategy-deal-brazils-new-right-wing-president.

Park, S. (2018). How China is about to shake up the oil futures market. *Bloomberg*, 8 March. Retrieved March 15, 2018, from https://www.bloomberg.com/news/articles/2018-03-08/how-china-is-about-to-shake-up-the-oil-futures-market-quicktake.

PEN Charitable Trust. (2017). The integrated arctic corridors framework. Planning for responsible shipping in Canada's arctic waters, a report of the *PEN Charitable Trusts*, April 2016. Retrieved June 10, 2017, from http://www.pewtrusts.org/en/research-and-analysis/reports/2016/04/the-integrated-arctic-corridors-framework.

Pence, M. (2018). Vice President Mike Pence's remarks on the administration's policy towards China. *Hudson Institute*, 4 October. Retrieved November 15, 2018, from https://www.hudson.org/events/1610-vice-president-mike-pence-s-remarks-on-the-administration-s-policy-towards-china102018m.

Perlez, J. (2015). China surprises U.N. with $100 million and thousands of troops for peacekeeping. *New York Times*, 28 September. Retrieved May 25, 2016, from https://www.nytimes.com/interactive/projects/cp/reporters-notebook/xi-jinping-visit/china-surprisesu-n-with-100-million-and-thousands-of-troops-for-peacekeeping?mcubz=3.

Pfaff, W. (2010). *The irony of manifest destiny.* New York: Walker & Co.

Picquart, P. (2018). *La renaissance de la route de la soie.* Favre: Lausanne.

Pillsbury, M. (2015). *The hundred-year marathon. China secret strategy to replace America as the global superpower.* New York: Henry Holt & Co.

Pimpaneau, J. (2011). *Les chevaux célestes. L'histoire du Chinois qui découvrit l'Occident.* Arles, France: Philippe Pic-quier.

Ponsonby, A. (1928). *Falsehood in war time. Containing an assortment of lies circulated throughout the nations during the great war.* New York: Dutton & Co.

References

Porter, P. (2018a). Why America's grand strategy has not changed. Power, habit, and the US foreign policy establishment. *International Security, 42*(4, Spring), 9–46.

Porter, P. (2018b). A world imagined: Nostalgia and liberal order. *Cato Institute,* Policy Analysis No. 843, June 5.

Prasad, E. S. (2017). *Gaining currency. The rise of the RMB.* New York: Oxford University Press.

PRC, Sate Council. (2005). The National Medium- and Long-Term Program for Science and Technology Development (2006–2020) An Outline.

PRC. (2015a). The Information Office of the State Council of PRC. 'China's Military Strategy', May, Beijing. Retrieved March 25, 2017, from http://www.chinadaily.com.cn/china/2015-05/26/content_20820628.htm.

PRC. (2015b). Vision and Actions on Jointly Building Silk Road Economic Belt and XXI century Maritime Road, 28 March, Issued by the National Development and Reform Commission. Retrieved July 15, 2015, from http://en.ndrc.gov.cn/newsrelease/201503/t20150330_669367.html.

PRC. (2015c). *The National Medium- and Long-Term Program for Science and Technology Development (2016–2020)* known as *'Made in China 2025'.* The State Council. Retrieved September 26, 2016, from http://english.gov.cn/2016special/madeinchina2025/.

PRC. (2017). Office of the Leading Group for the Belt and Road Initiative. *Building the Belt and Road: Concept, Practice and China's Contribution.* Beijing: Foreign Language Press, May.

Public Citizen. (2014). *NAFTA's 20-Year legacy and the fate of the trans-pacific partnership, public citizen.* February 2014. Retrieved April 4, 2015, from www.tradewatch.org.

Public Citizen. (2018). *Fracasso: NAFTA's disproportionate damage to US Latino and Mexican working people. Neither neoliberal business-as-usual trade policy nor Trump's economic nationalism is the way forward for NAFTA 2.0, Public Citizen,* December.

van der Putten, F. P. et al. (Eds.). (2016). *Europe and China's New Silk Roads.* The European Think-tank Network on China (ETNC), December Report.

Ranciman, D. (2016). Is this how democracy ends? *London Review of Books, 38*(23), 1 December. Retrieved November 25, 2016, from https://www.lrb.co.uk/v38/n23/david-runciman/is-this-how-democracy-ends.

Rapoza, K. (2017). Why HSBC loves China's silk road. *Forbes,* 17 May. Retrieved May 29, 2017, from https://www.forbes.com/sites/kenrapoza/2017/05/17/why-hsbc-loves-chinas-silk-road/#201c2faf697e.

Rashish, P. (2014). *Bridging the pacific: The Americas' new economic frontier?* Atlantic Council, Global Business and Economic Programme, July.

Renewable Energy Institute. (no date). About 'Asia Super Grid (ASG)'. Tokyo. Retrieved December 25, 2018, from https://www.renewable-ei.org/en/asg/about/.

Richard, H. (2018). Lonely Russia. No room for Moscow in 'common European home'. *Le Monde Diplomatique*, English edition, October.

Roberts, P. C. (2018). Will the Conspiracy Against Trump and American Democracy Go Unpunished? Paul C. Roberts website, 6 February. Retrieved March 15, 2018, from https://www.paulcraigroberts.org/2018/02/05/will-conspiracy-trump-american-democracy-go-unpunished/.

Rojansky, M. (2016). George Kennan is still the Russia expert America needs. *Foreign Policy*, 22 December. Retrieved May 16, 2017, from http://foreignpolicy.com/2016/12/22/why-george-kennan-is-still-americas-most-relevant-russia-expert-trump-putin-ussr/.

Sakwa, R. (2017). *Russia against the rest. The post-cold war crisis of world order.* Cambridge: Cambridge University Press.

Salazar Torreon, B. (2017). *Instances of Use of United States Armed Forces Abroad, 1798–2017.* US Congressional Research Service, 7–5700, R42738, 12 October.

Sanderson, H. (2019). Hydrogen power: China backs fuel cell technology. Producers are buying foreign tech but industry must build for future after subsidies. *Financial Times*. Retrieved January 15, 2019, from https://www.ft.com/content/27ccfc90-fa49-11e8-af46-2022a0b02a6c.

Sarotte, M. E. (2014). A Broken Promise? What the West Really Told Moscow About NATO Expansion. *Foreign Affairs*, 11 August. Retrieved May 20, 2017, from https://www.foreignaffairs.com/articles/russia-fsu/2014-08-11/broken-promise.

Schmitt, G. (2019). The China dream: America's, China's, and the resulting competition. *American Enterprise Institute,* January. Retrieved January 19, 2019, from http://www.aei.org/publication/the-china-dream-americas-chinas-and-the-resulting-competition/.

Scissors, D. (2017a). China Investment: Revenge of the State. *American Enterprise Institute,* July. Retrieved August 8, from http://www.aei.org/publication/chinese-investment-revenge-of-the-state/.

Scissor, D. (2017b). How China cheats. *American Economic Institute,* National Review, November 2.

Scissor, D. (2019). Chinese Investments: State-Owned Enterprises Stop Globalization, for the Moment, January. *American Economic Insitute.* Retrieved January 19, 2019, from http://www.aei.org/wp-content/uploads/2018/11/Updated-BRI-Report.pdf.

Scott, P. D. (2007). *The road to 9/11. Wealth, empire and the future of America.* Berkeley: University of California Press.

Scott, P. D. (2017). *The American deep state. Big money, big oil, and the struggle for US democracy.* New York: Rowman & Littlefield.

Seipel, H. (2015). *Putin: Innenansichten der Macht.* Hoffmann und Campe: Hamburg.

Shambaugh, D. (2016). *China's future.* Cambridge, UK: Polity Press.

Shane, S. (2018). Russia Isn't the Only One Meddling in Elections. We Do It, Too. *The New York Times*, 17 February. Retrieved March 25, 2018, from https://www.nytimes.com/2018/02/17/sunday-review/russia-isnt-the-only-one-meddling-in-elections-we-do-it-too.html.

Sharma, G. (2018). Market Chatter About Rise of 'Petro-Yuan' misses Mark Cy Trillion Dollars, *Forbes.*

Shepard, W. (2016). China's "New Silk Road" picks up where Hillary Clinton's flopped, *Forbes. Asia, Foreign Affairs,* 9 September 2016. Retrieved July 28, 2017, from https://www.forbes.com/sites/wadeshepard/2016/09/09/chinas-new-silk-road-picks-up-where-hillary-clintons-flopped-in-afghanistan/#61af395963f9.

Shifrinson, J. R. (2016). Deal or no deal? The end of the cold war and the U.S. offer to limit NATO expansion. *International Security, 40*(4, Spring 2016), 7–44.

Smith, J. M. (2015). Beware of China's Grand Strategy. *Foreign Affairs*, 20 May. Retrieved June 13, 2015, from https://www.foreignaffairs.com/articles/china/2015-05-20/beware-chinas-grand-strategy.

Smith, Y. (2015). How the China's New Silk Road is Shifting Geopolitics, 27 May, *Naked Capitalism*. Retrieved May 27, 2015, from https://www.nakedcapitalism.com/2015/05/how-the-chinas-new-silk-road-is-shifting-geopolitics.html.

Smith, Y. (2017). Newly-Declassified Documents Show Western Leaders Promised Gorbachev that NATO Would Not Move "One Inch Closer" to Russia. *Naked Capitalism,* 15 December. Retrieved January 3, 2018, from www.nakedcapitalism.com/2017/12/newly-declassified-documents-show-western-leaders-promised-gorbachev-nato-notmove-one-inch-closer-russia.html.

Solis, M. (2016). The Trans-pacific Partnership. The politics of openness and leadership in the Asia-Pacific. *Brookings Institution,* October. Retrieved September 15, 2017, from https://www.brookings.edu/research/the-trans-pacific-partnership-the-politics-of-openness-and-leadership-in-the-asia-pacific-2/.

Starr, E., Prescott, & Bishara. (2018). Noncompetes in the U.S. Labor Force. *University of Michigan Law & Econ Research Paper No. 18–013*, 74 Pages, Posted: 3 Jul 2015 Last revised: 13 September 2018. Retrieved December 16, from https://papers.ssrn.com/sol3/Papers.cfm?abstract_id=2625714.

Statista. (2015). The countries holding the world's nuclear arsenal. Retrieved June 20, 2017, from https://statista.com.

Stephanson, A. (1995). *Manifest destiny. American expansion and the empire of right.* New York: Hill & Wang.

References

Stephanson, A. (2010). The Toughness Crew. *New Left Review*, July-August 2013, pp. 145–152. Review of Peter Beinart, *The Icarus Syndrome. A History of American Hubris*. New York: Harper & Collins, 2010.

Stiglitz, J. E. (1998). More instruments and broader goal: Moving toward the Post-Washington consensus. *Wider Annual Lectures 2*, Helsinki: UN World Institute for Development Economics Research.

Stiglitz, J. E. (2002). *Globalization and its discontent*. New York: W.W. Norton.

Stiglitz, J. E. (2006). *Making globalization work: The next steps to global justice*. London: Penguin.

Stiglitz, J. E. (2009). *Around the world with Joseph Stiglitz: Perils and promises of globalization*. A documentary film realized by the author.

Stieglitz, J. E. (2013). The free-trade charade. *Project Syndicate*, July 14. Retrieved September 25, 2013, from www.projectsysndicate.org.

Stiglitz, J. E. (2016). Monopoly's new era. *Project* Syndicate, 13 May 2016. Retrieved May 16, from https://www.projectsyndicate.org.

Stiglitz, J. E. (2018a). American Democracy on the Brink. *Project Syndicate*, 29 June. Retrieved July 15, 2018, from https://www.project-syndicate.org/onpoint/american-democracy-on-the-brink-by-joseph-e–stiglitz-2018-06?barrier=accesspaylog.

Stiglitz, J. E. (2018b). Can American Democracy Come Back? *Project Syndicate,* 6 November. Retrieved November 11, 2018, from https://www.project-syndicate.org/commentary/american-democracy-under-attack-midterms-by-joseph-e-stiglitz-2018-11.

Stiglitz, J. E., & Charlton, A. (2005). *Fair trade for all: How trade can promote development* (p. 2005). Oxford: Oxford University Press.

Swaine, M. D. (2015). Chinese Views and Commentary on the "One Belt, One Road" Initiative. *China Leadership Monitor,* (47, Summer).

SWIFT. (2017). *Will the Belt and Road revitalise RMB internationalisation?* RMB Tracker Special Report, July. Retrieved July 31, 2017, from https://www.swift.com/news-events/press-releases/rmb-internationalisation_can-the-belt-and-road-revitalise-the-rmb_.

SWIFT (2018), RMB Tracker Monthly reporting and statistics on renminbi (RMB) progress towards becoming an international currency, December. Retrieved January 20, 2019, from https://www.swift.com/our-solutions/compliance-and-shared-services/business-intelligence/renminbi/rmb-tracker/document-centre.

Talbot, D. (2015). *The Devil's chessboard. Allen Dulles, The CIA, and the rise of America's secret government*. London: William Collins.

Temple, R. (1998). *The genius of China. 3,000 years of science, discovery and invention*. London: Prion, (introduced by Joseph Needham). Revised, full-colour, illustrated edition.

Tham, J. (2018). Why 5G Is the Next Front of US-China Competition. *The Diplomat*, 13 December. Retrieved December 20, 2018, from https://thediplomat.com/2018/12/why-5g-is-the-next-front-of-us-china-competition/.

Tharoor, S. (2016). *Inglorious empire: What the British did to India*. London: Penguin.

Thornberry, M., & Krepinevich Jr. A. F. (2016). Preserving Primacy. A defence strategy for the new administration. *Foreign Affairs*, 3 August, 2016. Retrieved August 26, 2016, from https://www.foreignaffairs.com/articles/north-america/2016-08-03/preserving-primacy.

Thompson, L. (2018). Trump Says U.S. Defense Spending Is 'Crazy'. It May Signal An Important Shift. *Forbes*, 4 December. Retrieved December 27, 2018, from https://www.forbes.com/sites/lorenthompson/2018/12/04/trump-says-u-s-defense-spending-is-crazy-does-that-signal-a-shift/#7c2e33345248.

Thumann, M., & Assheuer, T. (2017). Demokratie stiftet keine Identität. Ist das Modell des Westens am Ende? Ein Gespräch mit dem amerikanischen Politikwissenschaftler Francis Fukuyama, Interview. *Die Zeit*, 31 March. Retrieved May 25, 2017, from http://www.zeit.de/2016/13/francis-fukuyama-politikwissenschaftler-populismus-usa.

Todd, E. (1979). *The final fall: An essay on the decomposition of the soviet sphere*. New York: Karz Publishers.

318   6 China and the New World Order. Why and How China's Foreign Policy …

Trenin, D. (2011). *Post imperium. A Eurasian story*. Washington, DC: Carnegie Endowment for International Peace.

Trenin, D. (2016). *Should we fear Russia?*. Cambridge, UK: Polity.

Trump, D. (2016a). Donald Trump telling the truth about Syrian war. *Youtube,* 4 November. Retrieved March 29, 2017, from https://www.youtube.com/watch?v=bhDj1kEy5Go. not available any more, but from author Paolo Urio.

Trump, D. (2016b). Transcript: Donald Trump Expounds on His Foreign Policy Views. *New York Times*, 26 March. Retrieved April 20, 2016, from https://www.nytimes.com/2016/03/27/us/politics/donald-trump-transcript.html?r=0.

Trump, D. (2017). *National security strategy of the United States of America*. The White House: Washington DC.

Trump, D. (2018). Remarks by President Trump in Briefing at Al Asad Air Base Al Anbar Province, Iraq, 26 December. Washington D: The White House. Retrieved January 14, 2019, from https://www.whitehouse.gov/briefings-statements/remarks-president-trump-briefing-al-asad-air-base-al-anbar-province-iraq/.

Turse, N. (2012a). The new Obama doctrine: A six-point plan for global war—special ops, drones, spy games, civilian soldiers, proxy fighters, and cyber warfare. *Tom Dispatch*, 14 June. Retrieved June 10, 2016, from www.tomdispatch.com/blog/175557nick_turse_changing_face_of_empire.

Turse, N. (2012b). *The changing face of the empire. Special ops, drones, spies, proxy fighters, secret bases, and cyberwarfare*. Chicago, IL: Haymarket Books and Dispatch Books.

Turse, N. (2015). *Tomorrow's battlefields. US proxy wars and secret ops in Africa*. Chicago: Haymarket Books and Dispatch Books.

Turse, N. (2018). Commando sans frontières. *TomDispatch,* 17 July. Retrieved August 15, 2018, from http://www.tomdispatch.com/blog/176448/tomgram%3A_nick_turse%2C_special_ops%3A_133_countries_down%2C_17_to_go.

Urio, P. (1984). *Le Rôle politique de l'administration publique*. Lausanne: L.E.P.

Urio, P. (1999). La gestion publique au service du marché. In M. Hufty (Ed.), *La pensée comptable: Etat, néolibéralisme, nouvelle gestion publique* (pp. 91–123). Paris: Presses Universitaires de France, Collection Enjeux, Cahier de l'IUED, Genève.

Urio, P. (2010). *Reconciling state, market, and society in China. The long March towards prosperity*. London and New York: Routledge.

Urio, P. (2012). *China, the west, and the myth of new public management. Neoliberalism and its discontents*. London and New York: Routledge, 2012.

Urio, P. (2013). Reinventing Chinese Society, Economy and Polity: A Very Short History and Interpretation of China's Reforms. *Politics and Society, Special Issues of Journal of Central China Normal University*, Wuhan, *1*(2, September), 1–39.

Urio, P. (2018). China Reclaims World Power Status. Putting an End to the World America Made. London and New York: Routledge, 2018.

US. (1776). In Congress, July 4, 1776, The unanimous Declaration of the thirteen united States of America. Retrieved May 22, 2017, from http://www.ushistory.org/declaration/document/.

US. (2016a). Office of Naval Intelligence, The PLA Navy. New Capabilities and Missions for the 21st Century. Retrieved July 27, 2016, from, http://www.dtic.mil/docs/citations/ADA616040.

US. (2016b). *US-China Economic and Security Review Commission, 2016 Report to Congress*, November. Retrieved March 7, 2017, from https://www.uscc.gov/Annual_Reports/2016-annual-report-congress.

US. (2017). Department of State, Office of the Historian. *A short History of the Department of State, Milestones in the History of U.S. Foreign Relations, Key Milestones 1750–2000*. Retrieved April 18, 2017, from https://history.state.gov/milestones.

US. (2018a). *Summary of the National Defense Strategy of the United States of America. Sharpening the American Military's Competitive Edge*. Department of Defense.

US. (2018b). *US-China Economic and Security Review Commission, 2018 Report to Congress*. November. Retrieved January 12, 2019, from https://www.uscc.gov/Annual_Reports/2018-annual-report.

References

319

US. (2018c). *Military and Security Developments Involving the People's Republic of China 2018.* Office of the Secretary of Defense.

US. (2019). *China Military Power. Modernizing a Force to Fight and Win.* Defense Intelligence Agency. Retrieved January 15, 2019, from http://www.dia.mil/News/Articles/Article-View/Article/1732500/defense-intelligence-agency-releases-report-on-china-military-power/.

US Chamber of Commerce. (2017). Made in China 2015: Global Ambitions Built on Local Protections. Retrieved March 15, 2018, from https://www.uschamber.com/sites/default/files/final_made_in_china_2025_report_full.pdf.

Valentine, D. (2017). *The CIA ad organized crime. How illegal operations corrupt America and the world.* Atlanta, GA: Clarity Press.

Vidal, G. (2003). *Inventing a Nation. Washington, Adams, Jefferson.* New Haven: Yale University Press.

Vine, D. (2015). *Base nation. How U.S. military bases abroad harm America and the world.* New York: Metropolitan Books, 2015.

Vinton, K. (2016). These 15 Billionaires Own America's News Media Companies Forbes, 1 June. Retrieved September 22, 2016, from https://www.forbes.com/sites/katevinton/2016/06/01/these-15-billionaires-own-americas-news-media-companies/.

Wall, M. (2019). China Makes Historic 1st Landing on Mysterious Far Side of the Moon. *Scientific American,* 3 January 2019. Retrieved January 15, 2019, from https://www.scientificamerican.com/article/china-makes-historic-first-landing-on-mysterious-far-side-of-the-moon/.

Wallach, L. (1998). A dangerous new manifesto for global capitalism. *Le Monde Diplo-matique.* English edition, February 1998. Retrieved May 23, 2017, from http://mondediplo.com/1998/02/07mai.

Wallach, L. (2013). The corporation invasion. *Le Monde Diplomatique,* English edition, December. Retrieved May 22, 2017, from http://mondediplo.com/2013/12/02tafta.

Wallach, L. (2014). Transatlantic Trade and Investment Partnership: ten threats to Americans. *Le Monde Diplomatique,* June. Retrieved May 23, 2017, from https://mondediplo.com/2014/06/10ttip.

Wallach, L. (2017). The choice is not between TPP or no trade. *Huffington Post,* 25 March. Retrieved May 15, 2017, from http://www.huffingtonpost.com/lori-wallach/the-choice-is-not-between_b_9541300.html.

Wallerstein, I. (2006). *European universalism. The rhetoric of power.* New York: The New Press.

Wang, H. L. (2017). Broken Promises On Display At Native American Treaties Exhibit. *Code Switch,* 18 January 2015. Retrieved August 18, 2017, from https://www.npr.org/sections/codeswitch/2015/01/18/368559990/broken-promises-on-display-at-native-american-treaties-exhibit.

Wang, H. (2009). *The end of the revolution, China and the limits of modernity.* London: Verso.

Wang, H. (2014). *China from empire to nation-state.* Cambridge, Mass: Harvard University Press.

Wang, Y. (2016). *The belt and road initiative. What will China offer the world in its rise.* Beijing: New World Press.

Washington Blog. (2015). America Has Been At War 93% of the Time—222 Out of 239 Years—Since 1776, 20 February. Retrieved March 18, 2016, from https://washingtonsblog.com/2015/02/america-war-93-time-222-239-years-since-1776.html.

Watkins, E. (2018). Trump blames Putin, Obama for 'Animal Assad', tweets 'big price' after reports of Syrian chemical attack. *CNN,* 9 April. Retrieved September 20, 2018, from https://edition.cnn.com/2018/04/08/politics/donald-trump-syria-assad/index.html.

Liu, W. (Ed.). (2018). *China's belt and road initiatives. Economic geography reformation.* Springer: Singapore.

Weinland, D. (2016). China halts overseas investment schemes. *Financial Times,* 28 February. Retrieved February 29, https://www.ft.com/content/c64b3fc6-dc2e-11e5-a72f-1e7744c66818, accessed 29 February 2016.

White, D. (2017). Berkely Author George Lakoff says 'Don't understimate Trump. *Berkeleyside,* 2 May. Retrieved December 13, 2017, from https://www.berkeleyside.com/2017/05/02/berkeley-author-george-lakoff-says-dont-underestimate-trump.

Whitman, J. (2018). *Hitler's American model*. Princeton & Oxford: Princeton University Press.

Wicket, X. (2015). Why the United States Remains an Indispensable Nation, Chatham House, 30 June 2015. Retrieved March 5, 2017, from https://www.chathamhouse.org/expert/comment/why-united-states-remains-indispensable-nation.

Wittner, L. (2016). The Trillion Dollar Question. *The Huffington Post*, 17 March. Retrieved December 5, 2016, from http://www.huffingtonpost.com/lawrence-wittner/the-trillion-dollar-question_b_9481432.html.

Wong, E., Lau, K. C., Sit, T., & Wen, T. (2017). One Belt One Road. China's Strategy for a New Global Financial Order. *Monthly Review*, 1 January. Retrieved May 15, 2017, from https://monthlyreview.org/2017/01/01/one-belt-one-road/.

Wood, T. (2017). Eat Your Spinach. *London Review of Books, 39* (5), 2 March. Retrieved March 15, 2017, from https://www.lrb.co.uk/v39/n05/tony-wood/eat-your-spinach.

Wu, G. (2017). China touts more than 270 Belt and Road agreements. *Caixin*, 15 May. Retrieved May 25, 2017, from http://www.caixinglobal.com/2017-05-15/101090756.html.

Wübbeke, J. et al. (2016). *Made in China 2025. The making of a high-tech superpower and consequences for industrial countries*. Berlin: MERICS, Mercator Institute for China Studies, No. 23, December.

Xi, J. (2013a). Speech of 7 September, Astana. Retrieved June, 14, 2015, from www.fmprc.gov.cn/ce/cebel/eng/zxxx/t1078088.htm.

Xi, J. (2013b). Speech of 2 October, Jakarta. Retrieved July, 22, 2017, from http://www.asean-china-center.org/english/2013-10/03/c_133062675.htm.

Yip, G. S., & Mickern, B. (2016). *China's next strategic advantage. From imitation to innovation*. Cambridge: MIT Press.

Zakaria, F. (1997). The rise of illiberal democracy. *Foreign Affairs, 76*(6, November–December), 22–43.

Zakaria, F. (2013). Can America be fixed? The new crisis of democracy. *Foreign Affairs*, 1 January. Retrieved February 13, 2017, from https://www.foreignaffairs.com/articles/united-states/2012-12-03/can-america-be-fixed.

Zaki, M. (2011). *La fin du dollar. Comment le billet vert est devenu la plus grande bulle spéculative de l'histoire*. Lausanne: Favre.

de Zayas, A. (2019a). Un coup contre le droit international. Geneva: *Le Courrier*, 24 January.

de Zayas, A. (2019b). Interview by Amy Godman: There is nothing more undemocratic than a coup d'état, *Democracy Now*, 24 January, https://www.democracynow.org/2019/1/24/former_un_expert_the_us_is, accessed 25 January 2019.

Zenko, M. (2014). The myth of the indispensable nation. *Foreign Policy*, 6 November. Retrieved May 15, 2016, from http://foreignpolicy.com/2014/11/06/the-myth-of-the-indispensable-nation/.

Weiwei, Z. (1996). *Ideology and economic reform under Deng Xiaoping*. London and New York: Kegan Paul International.

Zhou, X. (2009). Reform the International Monetary System, Bank of China. Retrieved March 23, 2009, from www.pbc.gov.cn/english/detail.asp?col=6500&id=168.

Zinn, H. (1980). *A people's history of the United States*. New York: Harper Collins, first edition 1980.

Zufferey, N. (2008). *Introduction à la pensée chinoise, Pour mieux comprendre la Chine du XXIe siècle*. Paris: Hachette.

Correction to: China 1949–2019

Correction to:
J. Urio, *China 1949–2019*,
https://doi.org/10.1007/978-981-13-8879-8

In the original version of the book, the following corrections were carried out:
In Chapters 3 and 6, author-provided figures were included.
In Chapters 2, 4 and 5, authors' names in the reference list were corrected.
In Chapters 4 and 6, reference citations provided in the text were corrected.
The book and chapters have been updated with the changes.

The updated version of these chapters can be found at
https://doi.org/10.1007/978-981-13-8879-8_2
https://doi.org/10.1007/978-981-13-8879-8_3
https://doi.org/10.1007/978-981-13-8879-8_4
https://doi.org/10.1007/978-981-13-8879-8_5
https://doi.org/10.1007/978-981-13-8879-8_6
https://doi.org/10.1007/978-981-13-8879-8

© Springer Nature Singapore Pte Ltd. 2019
P. Urio, *China 1949–2019*, https://doi.org/10.1007/978-981-13-8879-8_7

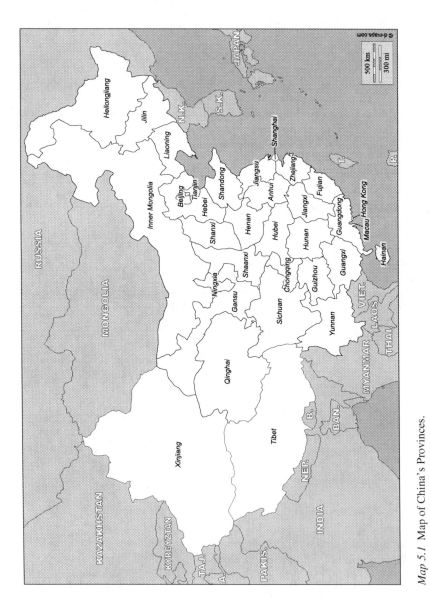

Map 5.1 Map of China's Provinces.

Source: d-maps, URL: http://d-maps.com/m/asia/china/chine/chine29.pdf

Correction to: China 1949–2019

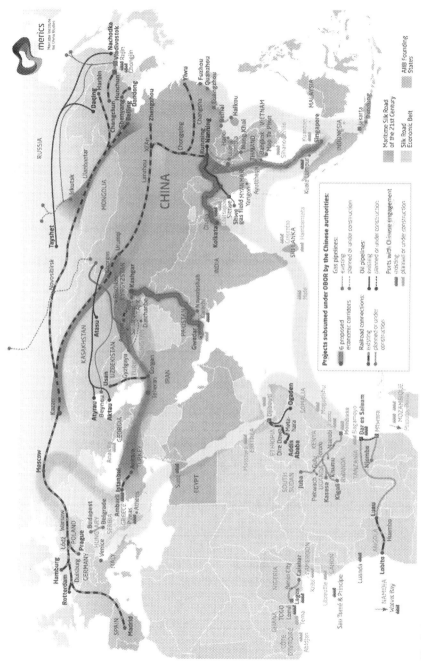

The Belt and Road Initiative.

Conclusion

In this book I have summarized and updated my writings on China published between 1999 and 2014 concerning China's development strategy (Urio 1999, 2010, 2012; Urio and Yuan 2014) and its will to recover world power status (Urio 2018). Overall, the findings presented in this new book confirm the trends already evident during the last decade of the XX Century. I will not reproduce here the conclusions I arrived at in my previous books, although I have no reasons for changing them, except for a few minor details. After a brief reminder of the sequence of public policies implemented by the West and China between 1980 and 2012, I will rather insist upon some aspects that this new book has made even more pertinent for understanding in what direction China will evolve in the future. More particularly, I will examine the question of democracy and human rights, the nature of China's economy, and the integration of China into the capitalist economy.

Since the beginning of the neoliberal revolution the West has implemented strategic public management decisions favouring privatization, deregulations and globalization, under pressure from multinational corporations, especially those of the financial sector, with the support of international economic organizations such as the WB the IMF, the WTO, and central banks such as the US Federal Reserve and the European Central Bank. This had two interrelated goals: first, to limit the power of the states within their own territories, and second to erase the states' boundaries, thereby making capital free to move all over the world in search of profits. The apotheosis of this movement could have been the adoption of two mega-trade and investment treaties, the Trans-Pacific Partnership and the Transatlantic Trade and Investment Partnership (TTIP) that President Trump decided to put to a halt at the beginning of his administration.

The consequences of neoliberalism were already evident in the mid-1990s. In 1999 I wrote: 'the future of those countries having adopted in a systematic way and over an extended period the precepts of the NPM [one of the armed wings of neoliberalism, the other one being the Washington Consensus], is not as bright as

© Springer Nature Singapore Pte Ltd. 2019

P. Urio, *China 1949–2019*, https://doi.org/10.1007/978-981-13-8879-8

claimed by university professors, consultants and practitioners (…) The demonstration of superiority of the NPM management in economic efficiency terms is yet to be made, whilst its incapacity to solve societal problems seems to be confirmed by existing data. (…) In this article, my concern was to highlight the logical and methodological shortcomings of NPM and to start providing some proofs in favour of a public management less oriented by economic rationality and the desire to serve the market, and more respectful of the democratic values that constitute the real foundations of a society of belonging and not of exclusion' (Urio 1999).

The 2008 crisis did not reverse the neoliberal policies, on the contrary, they were imposed with increased vigour upon the countries that tried to escape the dictatorship of capital markets, and moreover submitted their people to merciless austerity programmes. It was then forecasted that the persistence of this way of conceiving economic development and social progress was going to further deteriorate the living conditions of an increasing number of people. A few years later, it was possible to confirm this forecast (Urio 2012, Chaps. 5, 6 and Conclusion).

At the same time, China started to introduce some market mechanisms within its economy and to open it to the world. This has contributed to the improvement of the living conditions of the majority of Chinese citizens in spite of some important negative consequences, such as increasing disparities between regions, provinces, rural and urban areas, and individuals, and the deterioration of the environment (Urio 2010, Chaps. 2 and 3, and Conclusion).

The 2008 crisis, contrary to what happened in the West, was taken as an opportunity to further develop re-balancing policies under the slogan 'putting people first' instead of giving priority to economic development *per se*. The forecast for the years to come was that living conditions would improve and the disparities mentioned above would decrease, which is what I confirmed in my 2012 book (Chap. 6 and Conclusion).

Moreover, within the international system, since at least the end of World War 2, silent transformations were changing the relative political, economic and military weight of countries, thus pointing to a radical change from a uni-polar world, dominated by the US, to a multipolar world in which new powers, such as China, and re-emerging powers, such as Russia, would be able to challenge US domination, not to mention the emergence of regional powers whose behaviour would not necessarily comply with the imperial interests of the US in their region. My 2018 book confirmed the decline of the US power; and Chap. 6 of this book provides some additional proofs.

Chapters 3, 4 and 6 of this book confirm the accuracy of the forecasts related to the opposing trends of the West and China, the West increasing imbalances, China reducing them. In particular, neoliberal policies have been easily implemented, in spite of some resistance and social protest already emerging in the 1990s, until the poor and the lower middle classes represented less than 30% of the electorate. But when the electoral basis of these social groups approached 50%, many events, unimaginable until then, burst out in the face of the national and global elites: Brexit; Trump's election; so-called populist, anti-system, sovereigntist movements and parties; the Yellow jackets protest movement in France; the formation of the

Conclusion 323

new Italian government, an apparently impossible alliance between a clearly anti-system movement and a populist party.[1] These qualifications, with their intentional negative connotations, mean, in fact: 'anti-globalization', 'pro-protectionism', 'anti-financial market dictatorship', 'anti-neoliberal European Union', 'anti-technocracy' and, especially in the US, a clearly 'anti-establishment movement'.

Based upon these findings, the trajectory of the West and China since the beginning of the 1980s seems to be in favour of the latter. Moreover, the resilience of China's economy contradicts the thesis of the coming collapse of China (Lee 2017).[2] This is not the opinion of the majority of Western pundits and journalists, who point to the non-democratic features of China's political system, this being the main reason why authoritarian or dictatorial China would inevitably collapse. I have said in Chap. 5 that China is clearly an authoritarian state but certainly not a dictatorship, as its citizens enjoy a significant amount of freedom in the economy, can set up NGOs even if under strict control by the Party-State, and citizens and journalists are free to discuss controversial issues such as corruption, inequalities, and environmental damages, even if they cannot criticize frontally the Party-State and its leaders. Nevertheless, there is no substantial evidence to change my statement, in spite of measures taken by Xi Jinping to increase the Party-State's control over its citizens, something that is also implemented in a large scale by the US, not only nationally but also internationally. Moreover, after having recognized that China does not possess the features of the ideal model of liberal democracy, we have made no significant progress towards the understanding of how China's political system really functions and how it has been able to achieve such outstanding results for the benefit of its citizens, in spite of the absence of a Western liberal democracy. This is what I tried to discover in my research on China's strategic public management.

This is not to say that Western sinologists have not tried to understand China. To my knowledge the best analysis of China's political system has been provided by Jean-Pierre Cabestan, in a book significantly entitled 'Tomorrow China: democracy or dictatorship?' (Cabestan 2018). This is certainly a very balanced analysis, and the author is careful enough not to give a definite answer to his question. Nevertheless, when summarizing his findings, Cabestan cannot avoid the appearance of the cultural bias typical of so many Western sinologists: 'I think that at the end, Fukuyama analysis will be correct: good governance is important, but democracy is equally important' (p. 266). Quite. As somebody jokingly once said: democracy is a great idea; someone should start to implement it!

It is surprising that a European sinologist accepts the Fukuyama idea of the end of history without a comparative analysis of how democracy has been, and is still

---

[1]Italy is the first member of the G7 who has signed a formal agreement with China related to the Belt and Road Initiative, despite opposition from the US, Germany and France.
[2]To my knowledge this is the best analysis of the weaknesses and strengths of China and the US. For the resilience of China's economy see Chap. 3.

today implemented in the West, in particular in the US. Fukuyama's end of history, that I have deconstructed above in Sect. 6.1.2, is clearly based upon a peculiar knowledge of history, put forward by an intellectual who was, at the time of the publication of his 'end of history article', an active member of the 'neoconservative movement', representing an empire that at that moment in history (the fall of the Soviet Union) had the arrogance of considering that the rest of the world should (or quite naturally would inevitably) adopt the Western political model. It is interesting to observe that the Fukuyama statement combines the two dimensions of US foreign policy I have analyzed in Sects. 6.1.1 and 6.1.2: interventionism (suggested by 'should adopt') and isolationism (suggested by 'naturally would adopt'). What is striking in Cabestan's appreciation is that whereas his analysis of China's political system is a balanced discussion of positive and negative aspects, by a surprising contrast, his synthesis is an enumeration of negative features that leaves little place for any positive consideration: 'it is clear that this [i.e. China] is a decadent regime, that buried its communist and even socialist illusions, and replaced them with a nationalist dream of power without democracy, of greatness without freedom, of prosperity without equity'. We could slightly change this statement by referring it to the US: 'it is clear that this is a decadent regime, that buried its liberal illusions, and replaced them with a nationalist dream of power with little democracy, of greatness with little freedom, of prosperity without equity'. In fact, what irritates most Western sinologists and journalists is that China has succeeded in considerably improving the living condition of its people, of correcting the mistakes of a too rash implementation of market mechanisms (in fact based upon the mirages of neoliberal public policies, e.g. in education and health), thereby destroying the thesis, so many times proclaimed, of the coming collapse of China. This forecast, that has failed for forty years now, should advise Western pundits to revise their understanding of China's political system. Moreover, China's success to restore the power it enjoyed until the Western aggression of the XIX century, will help you to better understand the West's irritation.

Nevertheless, the thesis of China implementing, one day or the other, liberal democracy, cannot be discarded without a thorough examination. The question can be formulated as follows: why should China adopt liberal democracy? In order to answer this question, I will first examine to what extent the Universal Declaration of human rights may be used as an ideal model for orienting the development of democracy and human rights in China, and second I will examine whether the actual implementation of liberal democracy in the West may serve as a practical model for China.

Certainly, one could consider that universal rights and values exist as ideals that must be discovered during history by the various civilizations. One can formulate the hypothesis that even countries that today do not agree with some of the rights defined in the Universal Declaration may one day 'discover' and recognize them as universal, not imposed unilaterally by Western countries. But as civilizations have evolved at different paces and have developed different cultural frameworks, the core values of their cultures differ in important aspects that have resulted in different conceptions of the relationship between individuals and society, as well as between

Conclusion

individuals and polity, and consequently in different conceptions of human rights (Sect. 2.4 above, Peerenboom 2002, 2006, 2007). In this situation, how to manage the relations between civilizations when one of them considers that it has discovered universal human rights, and is moreover convinced that it is invested with a civilizing mission of imposing them on the rest of the world? This is clearly the answer the 'end of history' has given to this question.

Even so, one could still consider that the Universal Declaration constitutes a reasonable ideal model providing a set of standards against which different civilizations can be evaluated. By doing so, one is forced to admit that human rights as defined by the Universal Declaration are rarely fully implemented even by countries that explicitly consider that these rights constitute the foundations of their political system, and that moreover use them as standards for evaluating and criticizing other countries. Several problems make it difficult to use the Universal Declaration as a standard against which to assess China's compliance with human rights.

First, one cannot consider the implementation of human rights as something that can be realized simultaneously and in a short period of time. The very long history the West had to go through before it was able to claim it had adopted today's version of human rights very well demonstrates this claim. The Universal Declaration was adopted at the end of a long, incremental, non-linear process that the atrocities of the Second World War have brought dramatically to completion. It should thus come as no surprise that some countries, in their quest for a reasonable implementation of human rights, have chosen to start implementing some of them and not others, this choice being very clearly oriented by other fundamental values typical of the culture of the countries concerned. In Western countries the ideals of formal democracy, separation of powers, political freedom and equal formal political rights, and the right to own private property (art. 17 of the Universal Declaration) had acquired paramount importance for the functioning of liberal democracy and the capitalist economy towards the second part of the eighteenth century. It is not therefore surprising that they gave priority to these rights at the partial (or in some cases the total) expense of substantive rights, such as the right to work, to freely choose one's employment, the right of protection against unemployment, the right to a just and favourable remuneration ensuring for people and their families an existence worthy of human dignity (art. 23), the right to a standard of living adequate for the health and well-being of themselves and their families, including food, clothing, housing and medical care and necessary social services, and the right to security in the event of unemployment, sickness, disability, widowhood, old age or other hindrances to livelihood in circumstances beyond their control (art. 25). Many of these rights have been introduced in the West only after decades of political struggle between the defenders of a radical conception of capitalist economy giving priority to the freedoms and rights of capital, and those defending the rights and freedoms of workers and employees. This opposition is based upon some other fundamental values, namely the opposition between individual and collective responsibilities.

At the beginning of the twentieth century China's economy and society were in a state of backwardness, and hundreds of millions of Chinese people were living below the poverty line. Is it therefore impossible to accept that China has given priority to economic development with the aim of allowing its people to attain for themselves and their families 'an existence worthy of human dignity'? (art. 23 of the Universal Declaration), and to effectively 'enjoy freedom from fear and want', as stated in paragraph 2 of the Preamble of the Universal Declaration? This is a very long process, as we have seen in Chap. 4. Impressive improvements have been realized, but the level of personal income of the majority of Chinese citizens is still today far below that of the West, in spite of the fact that the personal income in a few provinces is already today at the same level as some European countries such as Poland and Portugal. Why should China today change its development strategy that has so far realized such improvements? By implementing the neoliberal policies that the West would like it to adopt as stated in the 2012 World Bank report, in particular the quasi-total opening up of its economy to Western predatory investments? (World Bank 2012).

China is well aware that it is only after the Great Depression and especially after the Second World War that workers' rights have been more fully recognized in Western countries, even if to a lesser degree than capital's rights. Unfortunately, since the 1980s, neo-liberal policies have deteriorated the situation of people in the labour market where the number of low-paid, short-term and part-time jobs have increased, whereas the amount of coverage by social security policies has been reduced; this resulted in a more unequal distribution of income, an increase of the rate of poverty and of the rates of crimes, and a deterioration of the health of people in an unstable labour market situation (Urio 2012, Chap. 5). There is therefore little to be proud of and little that deserves the teaching of lessons to the rest of the World.

These last considerations lead me to the question whether the actual implementation of liberal democracy in the West may serve as a practical model for China. Let me first say that democracy as it is practiced today in Western countries is characterized by an inextricable symbiosis between the political elite, the economic elite that dominates market economy, and the cultural elite. It is within a complex game between economic, political and intellectual elites, and in the case of the US the powerful military-industrial complex and the intelligence community, that policy options are examined, choices are made and then presented to the public. Citizens have little means to interfere within these processes. Furthermore, Western governments have abdicated in favour of the managers of multinationals and financial institutions, in particular by renouncing to better regulate financial markets. The consequence is that public policies are mainly evaluated and approved insofar as they satisfy the market. The crucial question is: 'what will the market say?'.

Of course, liberals claim that there exists a 'free press' that can monitor the work of the elites. Nevertheless, the majority of the media that have a large circulation nationally and internationally is under the control of powerful companies and billionaires that themselves belong to the economic elite, with which they share ideological values and economic interests. It is not likely that these media can exert an efficient and impartial control over the ruling elite. It would be easy to give

Conclusion 327

examples of this collusion, the last of a long series being the support given to the ongoing coup d'état attempted by the US in Venezuela by mainstream Western media and politicians representing powerful economic interests. This means that in the West economy dominates politics, thus making it difficult to implement policies that 'put people first'.

The abdication of politicians resulted in a change of the domain where political competition takes place. For several decades, political competition had developed on a horizontal axis opposing the Right and the Left. In the age of neoliberalism, left-wing parties started to converge towards the centre already since the beginning of the 1980s, so that, at the end of this process, there was no significant difference between the Right and the Left, the latter having accepted the major ideological and policy options of the former. The final result has been that poor and lower middle-class people had the feeling that they were not represented on the horizontal Right-Left axis. The foreseeable consequence was that the place of political competition would shift to a vertical axis opposing anti-establishment (or anti-system) movements to the traditional elite, as it finally happened.

Moreover, the techniques used for manipulating the minds of people, that have been developed since the seminal works of Gustav Le Bon (1905), Edward Bernays (1928) and critically updated in the brilliant synthesis by Shoshana Zuboff (2019), are used today for influencing the behaviour of citizens in the polity, and consumers in the market. The freedom often used in the rhetoric of both private and public defenders of the free market and of liberal democracy has been reduced in practice to the 'freedom to shop', as an American economist said a few years ago (Galbraith 2008, pp. 15–24).

Nevertheless, one cannot deny that there are some democratic features in Western countries. However, they have been marginalized in favour of the rule of money, of its owners and of their representatives (lobbyists and politicians) active within the 'democratic institutions' that have been emptied, to a large extent, of the democratic features existing in the formal instruments typical of a liberal democracy. If somebody still may have today the faith that democracy is still alive in the West, he should consider the behaviour of Western countries in the international arena. There can be no true democracy at home when in the international arena countries seek to impose their will by force, thus violating international norms and fundamental principles of democracy and human rights. In Chap. 6 I have enumerated the list of US behaviours that are not in harmony with the professed values of democracy and human rights: 81 cases of meddling in other countries' elections, 59 cases of attempted regime change, setting up of secret armies in European countries, 13 cases of illegal wars, and the setting up of illegal prisons where torture has been secretly practiced.[3] The great number these violations of international norms and of human rights cannot be considered as accidents occurring in particular circumstances. On the contrary, they are the trademark of an imperial foreign policy that does not hesitate to resort to illegal practices and the use of force to realize its

---

[3]References in Sect. 6.1.4.

328   Conclusion

own goals and interests. It is also the trademark of the nonchalance with which the US establishment envisages quite often to engage in criminal activities.[4] One could say that this does not concern the democratic allies of the US, especially European countries. It is true that European capitalism has traditionally been less aggressive than the American one. But apart from the fact that since the neoliberal revolution European capitalism has adopted some of the features of the American one, it remains that in the international system European members of the NATO alliance share with the US the responsibility for too many of the above-mentioned behaviours. So, why should China take liberal democracy as is practiced in the West as a model for reorganizing its own political system?

Let us now examine the question of the integration of China into the capitalist economy. Several scholars consider that China is already integrated into the capitalist economy (e.g. Li Minqi 2008). There is no doubt that since the beginning of reforms China integrated progressively into the capitalist economy. But does this mean that China behaves as a capitalist country within the capitalist economy? The fact of having introduced market mechanisms is not a sufficient proof. Several facts point to the opposite direction. First, Western countries complain that China distorts competition, both internally and internationally, by subsidizing its SOEs, by subsidizing its exports and by manipulating the exchange rate of the Yuan. These actions are clearly incompatible with the behaviour of a truly capitalist state, that should not interfere with the 'natural' laws of the market. This critique clearly underestimates the role states have played in the development of the economy and of technological innovation in many countries both Western, such as England and the US, and Eastern, such as Japan and South Korea, analyzed by many authors such as Chang (2008) and brilliantly updated by Mariana Mazzucato (2018, 2019).

Second, Western countries complain that China's economy is not as open to the Western countries' goods and capital, as the Western countries are to China. These claims are true to some extent. But why should China behave as a capitalist country in the capitalist economy? The only reason could be that market economy (i.e. capitalism) is, according to the West, the only, or the best economic system that every country should adopt. But, again, why? History shows that Western capitalist countries have very often violated the rules of market economy, starting from the colonial era and until today, by profiting from their 'comparative advantage' based upon their technological superiority and a dominating currency, artificially sustained by a whole set of national practices and international organizations. Is it reasonable to ask developing countries to compete in such a biased system? Or should we recognize that the goal of the West is to keep them in a subordinate position, a kind of periphery of the capitalist world? Chapter 6 has provided some proofs that this seems to be the case. Clearly, here I depart from a purely economic approach and I turn to using the analysis of power in international relations I developed elsewhere (Urio 2018, Chap. 2) and used for empirically analysing the

---

[4]This is the qualification used by the former Rapporteur of the Council of Europe on the illegal prisons set up by the US; interview by the Swiss television 11 May 2019 (see Report: Marty 2006).

Conclusion 329

relationships between the US and China (Chap. 6). From this point of view, there is no reason why China should not behave in accordance with its national interests. This does not mean that China should be free to use any means to this end, but it should work with other countries to set up new rules of the game respectful of the interests of all. Now, for the time being, the US and its allies do not seem ready to undertake such a complicated but necessary task. Until this is openly and honestly undertaken, it is naïve to expect that China will comply in all circumstances with the rules the West made, especially if its national interests at home and abroad would be in peril. I have explained in Sect. 6.2 why China has developed and projected abroad power resources to safeguard its national integrity and independence. But there are also some reasons related to its project to realize a well-off society at home, where wealth would be equitably distributed amongst its citizens. For this reason, China will be well advised to avoid being fully integrated into the capitalist economy, or its society will run the risk of resembling to the Western one, with the negative outcomes I have mentioned above.

If China wants to make its dream come true (Chap. 1 above), it would be well advised to mistrust not only the external pressures exerted by the West, but also, and perhaps especially, the internal forces, e.g. the new 'Red Capitalists'. Certainly, until now the Party keeps them under control, but leaves them sufficient freedom, for them to be satisfied with the activities they are allowed to develop. However, nothing can categorically exclude that one day those actors will develop interests that the Party will not be able to satisfy any more. In addition, they might find in China some allies among the executives of semi-private/semi-public enterprises and of large state enterprises, as well as liberal intellectuals active within universities and think tanks, both private and state-run.

Those actors can then try to force a regime change in China. But that is not all. The 'Red Capitalists' will be able to find allies not only among those actors, but also, and this is a Chinese paradox, even within the Party elite, or in the immediate entourage of its leaders. In fact, the significant enrichment of public figures of the Party or of their families has for a long time been known to the experts of contemporary China, and has been made public knowledge in recent years. It is likely that the behaviours leading to an enrichment of such scope, is the result of positions of power that make possible the appropriation of assets belonging to the State and thus to the people. Those behaviours concern a large part of the Party's elite and are well known to the Chinese people. The information published since 2012 by generally trustworthy investigative journalists has confirmed the extent of the enrichment of many Party leaders and their families, as well as the transfer of their assets abroad, especially to tax havens (Urio and Yuan 2014, p. 260, note 491). This is completely contradictory to the official statements of the Party about its commitment to create a harmonious society in which wealth will be equitably shared.

Indeed, the new leadership under the direction of Xi Jinping has undertaken a campaign on an extraordinary scale against this type of corruption. It is essential that the CPC should succeed in this endeavour, otherwise Fernand Braudel's statement about capitalism's ability to reinvent itself after each crisis, and Li Minqi's predictions about China's inevitable integration into global capitalism, will prove to be correct and China's dream of creating a harmonious and prosperous society, where wealth will be equitably distributed, will have vanished for a long time.

Nevertheless, we cannot exclude that China will one day be fully integrated into the global system based on the western model, including a set of liberal democratic regimes interconnected in the context of a capitalist economy. In this case, it is expected that the major actors of international finance and the multinationals will dominate the world. Certainly, amongst them, there will be many having registered offices in China. But will they really be Chinese? Or, as the Romans used to say *'ubi pecunia ibi patria'*, will they not become new international actors sharing the same interests with the western multinationals, that is to say the interests of the 'top 1%' denounced by Joseph Stieglitz? If this happens, another Roman motto will be confirmed: *'pecunia regina mundi'*. But then again: what will happen to the Chinese dream of a harmonious society where prosperity would be equitably shared?

Let me finish with a short remark at the conjunction of theory and empirical research. My research has shown the difficulties in understanding China by using the standards of capitalism and liberal democracy. The analysis of the US foreign policy (Sect. 6.1) has shown a considerable lack of democracy and expertise. I am convinced that the expertise we need should not be at the service of an ideology designed to favour a small number of people, but should be at the service of all the citizens. As it is practically impossible, even at the age of the communication revolution, to open up the decision-making process so that citizens may have a-quasi 'in real time control' over the elites, the problem is that of reconciling on the one hand the capacity of the people to monitor whether or not the government' policies are in favour of their rights, and on the other hand the expertise the elite should possess for the realization of those rights. In this respect, in spite of several serious violations of some of the human rights included in the Universal Declaration, my research shows that, for the time being, China is progressing towards this end more than Western countries. As a Chinese proverb says: a journey of a thousand miles begins with the first step' (Qiānlǐ zhī xíng, shǐ yú zúxià).

References

Bernays, E. (1928). *Propaganda*. New York: Ig Publishing (reprinted 2005).

Cabestan, J. (2018). *Demain la Chine: démocratie ou dictature?*. Paris: Gallimard.

Chang, H. (2008). *Bad samaritan. The myth of free trade and the secret history of capitalism*. New York: Bloomsbury.

Galbraith, J. (2008). *The predator state. How conservatives abandoned the free market and why liberals should too*. New York: Free Press.

Le Bon, G. (1905). *Psychologie des foules*. Paris: Felix Alcan.

Lee, A. (2017). *Will China's economy collapse?*. Cambridge, UK: Polity.

Li, M. (2008). *The rise of China and the demise of the capitalist world economy*. New York: Monthly Review Press.

Marty, D. (2006). Alleged secret detentions and unlawful inter-state transfers of detainees involving Council of Europe member states Report, Doc. 10957, 12 June.

Mazzucato, M. (2018). *The entrepreneurial state. Debunking public vs private sector myths*. London: Penguin. 2nd edition with a new Forward, 1st edition 2013.

Mazzucato, M. (2019). *The value of everything. Making and taking in the global economy*. London: Penguin.

Peerenboom, R. (2002). *China's long March toward rule of law*. Cambridge: Cambridge University Press.

Peerenboom, R. (2006). A government of laws: democracy, rule of law, and administrative law reform in China. In Z. Suisheng (Ed.), *Debating political reform in China: Rule of law vs. democratization* (pp. 58–78). New York: M.E. Sharpe, 2006.

Peerenboom, R. (2007). *China modernizes. Threat to the west or model for the rest?* Oxford: Oxford University Press.

Urio, P. (1999). La gestion publique au service du marché. In M. Hufty (Ed.), *La pensée comptable. Etat, néolibéralisme, nouvelle gestion publique* (pp. 91–124). Paris: Presses Universi-taires de France.

Urio, P. (2010). *Reconciling state, market, and society in China. The long March towards prosperity*. London and New York: Routledge.

Urio, P. (2012). *China, the west and the myth of new public management. Neoliberalism and its discontents*. London and New York: Routledge.

Urio, P. (2018). *China reclaims world power status. Putting an end to the world America made*. London & New York: Routledge.

© Springer Nature Singapore Pte Ltd. 2019
P. Urio, *China 1949–2019*, https://doi.org/10.1007/978-981-13-8879-8

Urio, P., & Yuan, Y. (2014). *L'émergence des ONG en Chine. Le changement du rôle de l'Etat-Parti*. Bern: Peter Lang.

World Bank. (2012). *China 2030. Building a modern, harmonious and creative society.* officially dated 2013, but already available on line Spring 2012.

Zuboff, S. (2019). *The age of surveillance capitalism. The fight for a human future at the new frontier of power*. London: Profile Books.